W9-BNZ-176

CONNECT FEATURES

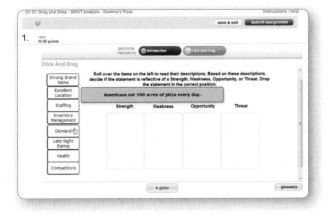

Interactive Applications

Interactive Applications offer a variety of automatically graded exercises that require students to **apply** key concepts. Whether the assignment includes a *click and drag*, *video case*, or *decision generator*, these applications provide instant feedback and progress tracking for students and detailed results for the instructor.

Case Exercises

The Connect platform also includes author-developed case exercises for all 12 cases in this edition that require students to work through answers to assignment questions for each case. These exercises have multiple components and can include: calculating assorted financial ratios to assess a company's financial performance and balance sheet strength, identifying a company's strategy, doing five-forces and driving-forces analysis, doing a SWOT analysis, and recommending actions to improve company performance. The content of these case exercises is tailored to match the circumstances presented in each case, calling upon students to do whatever strategic thinking and strategic analysis is called for to arrive at a pragmatic, analysis-based action recommendation for improving company performance.

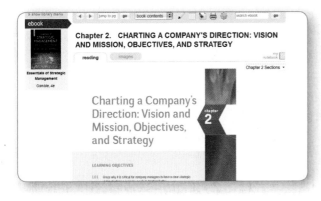

eBook

Connect Plus includes a media-rich eBook that allows you to share your notes with your students. Your students can insert and review their own notes, highlight the text, search for specific information, and interact with media resources. Using an eBook with Connect Plus gives your students a complete digital solution that allows them to access their materials from any computer.

Tegrity

Make your classes available anytime, anywhere. With simple, one-click recording, students can search for a word or phrase and be taken to the exact place in your lecture that they need to review.

EASY TO USE

Learning Management System Integration

McGraw-Hill Campus is a one-stop teaching and learning experience available to use with any learning management system. McGraw-Hill Campus provides single sign-on to faculty and students for all McGraw-Hill material and technology from within the school website. McGraw-Hill Campus also allows instructors instant access to all supplements and teaching materials for all McGraw-Hill products.

Blackboard users also benefit from McGraw-Hill's industry-leading integration, providing single sign-on to access all Connect assignments and automatic feeding of assignment results to the Blackboard grade book.

POWERFUL REPORTING

Connect generates comprehensive reports and graphs that provide instructors with an instant view of the performance of individual students, a specific section, or multiple sections. Since all content is mapped to learning objectives, Connect reporting is ideal for accreditation or other administrative documentation.

Essentials of
Strategic Management

4e

The Quest for Competitive Advantage

John E. Gamble
Texas A&M University–Corpus Christi

Margaret A. Peteraf
Dartmouth College

Arthur A. Thompson, Jr.
The University of Alabama

Mc
Graw
Hill
Education

ESSENTIALS OF STRATEGIC MANAGEMENT: THE QUEST FOR COMPETITIVE ADVANTAGE, FOURTH EDITION

Published by McGraw-Hill Education, 2 Penn Plaza, New York, NY 10121. Copyright © 2015 by McGraw-Hill Education. All rights reserved. Printed in the United States of America. Previous editions © 2013, 2011, and 2009. No part of this publication may be reproduced or distributed in any form or by any means, or stored in a database or retrieval system, without the prior written consent of McGraw-Hill Education, including, but not limited to, in any network or other electronic storage or transmission, or broadcast for distance learning.

Some ancillaries, including electronic and print components, may not be available to customers outside the United States.

This book is printed on acid-free paper.

1 2 3 4 5 6 7 8 9 0 DOW/DOW 1 0 9 8 7 6 5 4

ISBN 978-0-07-811289-8
MHID 0-07-811289-3

Senior Vice President, Products & Markets: *Kurt L. Strand*
Vice President, Content Production & Technology Services: *Kimberly Meriwether David*
Managing Director: *Paul Ducham*
Executive Brand Manager: *Michael Ablassmeir*
Executive Director of Development: *Ann Torbert*
Development Editor: *Andrea Heirendt*
Editorial Coordinator: *Claire Wood*
Marketing Manager: *Elizabeth Trepkowski*
Marketing Specialist: *Elizabeth Steiner*
Director, Content Production: *Terri Schiesl*
Content Project Manager: *Harvey Yep*
Content Project Manager: *Susan Lombardi*
Senior Buyer: *Debra R. Sylvester*
Design: *Matt Diamond*
Cover Image: *Getty Images / Courtney Keating*
Lead Content Licensing Specialist: *Keri Johnson*
Typeface: *10.5/13 Palatino Roman*
Compositor: *Laserwords Private Limited*
Printer: *R. R. Donnelley*

All credits appearing on page or at the end of the book are considered to be an extension of the copyright page.

Library of Congress Cataloging-in-Publication Data

Gamble, John (John E.)
    Essentials of strategic management : the quest for competitive advantage/John E. Gamble,
Arthur A. Thompson, Jr., Margaret A. Peteraf.—4e [edition].
        pages cm
    Includes bibliographical references and index.
    ISBN 978-0-07-811289-8 (alk. paper)—ISBN 0-07-811289-3 (alk. paper)
    1. Strategic planning. 2. Business planning. 3. Competition. 4. Strategic planning—Case studies.
    I. Thompson, Arthur A., 1940- II. Peteraf, Margaret Ann. III. Title.
HD30.28.G353 2015
658.4'012—dc23

2013045409

The Internet addresses listed in the text were accurate at the time of publication. The inclusion of a website does not indicate an endorsement by the authors or McGraw-Hill Education, and McGraw-Hill Education does not guarantee the accuracy of the information presented at these sites.

www.mhhe.com

ABOUT THE AUTHORS

John E. Gamble is a Professor of Management and Dean of the College of Business at Texas A&M University–Corpus Christi. His teaching and research for nearly 20 years has focused on strategic management at the undergraduate and graduate levels. He has conducted courses in strategic management in Germany since 2001, which have been sponsored by the University of Applied Sciences in Worms.

Dr. Gamble's research has been published in various scholarly journals and he is the author or co-author of more than 75 case studies published in an assortment of strategic management and strategic marketing texts. He has done consulting on industry and market analysis for clients in a diverse mix of industries.

Professor Gamble received his Ph.D., Master of Arts, and Bachelor of Science degrees from The University of Alabama and was a faculty member in the Mitchell College of Business at the University of South Alabama before his appointment to the faculty at Texas A&M University–Corpus Christi.

Margaret A. Peteraf is the Leon E. Williams Professor of Management at the Tuck School of Business at Dartmouth College. She is an internationally recognized scholar of strategic management, with a long list of publications in top management journals. She has earned myriad honors and prizes for her contributions, including the 1999 Strategic Management Society Best Paper Award recognizing the deep influence of her work on the field of strategic management. Professor Peteraf is on the Board of Directors of the Strategic Management Society and has been elected as a Fellow of the Society. She served previously as a member of the Academy of Management's Board of Governors and as Chair of the Business Policy and Strategy Division of the Academy. She has also served in various editorial roles and is presently on nine editorial boards, including the *Strategic Management Journal*, the *Academy of Management Review*, and *Organization Science*. She has taught in Executive Education programs around the world and has won teaching awards at the MBA and Executive level.

Professor Peteraf earned her Ph.D., M.A., and M.Phil. at Yale University and held previous faculty appointments at Northwestern University's Kellogg Graduate School of Management and at the University of Minnesota's Carlson School of Management.

Arthur A. Thompson, Jr., earned his B.S. and Ph.D. degrees in economics from The University of Tennessee, spent three years on the economics faculty at Virginia Tech, and served on the faculty of The University of Alabama's College of Commerce and Business Administration for 25 years. In 1974 and again in 1982, Dr. Thompson spent semester-long sabbaticals as a visiting scholar at the Harvard Business School.

His areas of specialization are business strategy, competition and market analysis, and the economics of business enterprises. In addition to publishing over 30 articles in some 25 different professional and trade publications, he has authored or co-authored five textbooks and six computer-based simulation exercises that are used in colleges and universities worldwide.

Dr. Thompson spends much of his off-campus time giving presentations, putting on management development programs, working with companies, and helping operate a business simulation enterprise in which he is a major partner.

Dr. Thompson and his wife of 52 years have two daughters, two grandchildren, and a Yorkshire terrier.

BRIEF CONTENTS

PREFACE

The standout features of this fourth edition of *Essentials of Strategic Management* are its concisely written and robust coverage of strategic management concepts and its compelling collection of cases. The text presents a conceptually strong treatment of strategic management principles and analytic approaches that features straight-to-the-point discussions, timely examples, and a writing style that captures the interest of students. While this edition retains the 10-chapter structure of the prior edition, every chapter has been reexamined, refined, and refreshed. New content has been added to keep the material in line with the latest developments in the theory and practice of strategic management. Also, scores of new examples have been added, along with fresh Concepts & Connections illustrations, to make the content come alive and to provide students with a ringside view of strategy in action. The fundamental character of the fourth edition of *Essentials of Strategic Management* is very much in step with the best academic thinking and contemporary management practice. The chapter content continues to be solidly mainstream and balanced, mirroring *both* the penetrating insight of academic thought and the pragmatism of real-world strategic management.

Complementing the text presentation is a truly appealing lineup of 12 diverse, timely, and thoughtfully crafted cases. All of the cases are tightly linked to the content of the 10 chapters, thus pushing students to apply the concepts and analytical tools they have read about. Eight of the 12 cases were written by the coauthors to illustrate specific tools of analysis or distinct strategic management theories. The four cases not written by the coauthors were chosen because of their exceptional linkage to strategic management concepts presented in the text. We are confident you will be impressed with how well each of the 12 cases in the collection will work in the classroom and the amount of student interest they will spark.

For some years now, growing numbers of strategy instructors at business schools worldwide have been transitioning from a purely text-cases course structure to a more robust and energizing text-cases-simulation course structure. Incorporating a competition-based strategy simulation has the strong appeal of providing class members with *an immediate and engaging opportunity to apply the concepts and analytical tools covered in the chapters in a head-to-head competition with companies run by other class members.* Two widely used and pedagogically effective online strategy simulations, *The Business Strategy Game* and *GLO-BUS,* are optional companions for this text. Both simulations, like the cases, are closely linked to the content of each chapter in the text. The Exercises for Simulation Participants, found at the end of each chapter, provide clear guidance to class members in applying the concepts and analytical tools covered in the chapters to the issues and decisions that they have to wrestle with in managing their simulation company.

Through our experiences as business school faculty members, we also fully understand the assessment demands on faculty teaching strategic management and business policy courses. In many institutions, capstone courses have emerged as the logical home for assessing student achievement of program learning objectives. The fourth edition includes Assurance of Learning Exercises at the end of each chapter that link to the specific Learning Objectives appearing at the beginning of each chapter and highlighted throughout the text. *An important instructional feature of this edition is the linkage of selected chapter-end Assurance of Learning Exercises and cases to the publisher's Connect Management web-based assignment and assessment platform.* Your students will be able to use the online *Connect* supplement to (1) complete two of the Assurance of Learning Exercises appearing at the end of each of the 10 chapters, (2) complete chapter-end quizzes, and (3) complete case tutorials based upon the suggested assignment questions for all 12 cases in this edition. With the exception of some of the chapter-end Assurance of Learning exercises, all of the *Connect* exercises are automatically graded, thereby enabling you to easily assess the learning that has occurred.

In addition, both of the companion strategy simulations have a built-in Learning Assurance Report that quantifies how well each member of your class performed on nine skills/learning measures *versus tens of thousands of other students worldwide* who completed the simulation in the past 12 months. We believe the chapter-end Assurance of Learning Exercises, the all-new online and automatically graded Connect exercises, and the Learning Assurance Report generated at the conclusion of *The Business Strategy Game* and *GLO-BUS* simulations provide you with easy-to-use, empirical measures of student learning in your course. All can be used in conjunction with other instructor-developed or school-developed scoring rubrics and assessment tools to comprehensively evaluate course or program learning outcomes and measure compliance with AACSB accreditation standards.

Taken together, the various components of the fourth edition package and the supporting set of Instructor Resources provide you with enormous course design flexibility and a powerful kit of teaching/learning tools. We've done our very best to ensure that the elements comprising this edition will work well for you in the classroom, help you economize on the time needed to be well prepared for each class, and cause students to conclude that your course is one of the very best they have ever taken—from the standpoint of both enjoyment and learning.

Differentiation from Other Texts

Five noteworthy traits strongly differentiate this text and the accompanying instructional package from others in the field:

1. *Our integrated coverage of the two most popular perspectives on strategic management positioning theory and resource-based theory is unsurpassed by any other leading strategy text.* Principles and concepts from both the positioning perspective and the resource-based perspective are prominently and comprehensively integrated into our coverage of crafting both single-business and multibusiness strategies. By highlighting the relationship between a firm's

resources and capabilities to the activities it conducts along its value chain, we show explicitly how these two perspectives relate to one another. Moreover, in Chapters 3 through 8 it is emphasized repeatedly that a company's strategy must be matched not only to its external market circumstances but also to its internal resources and competitive capabilities.

2. *Our coverage of business ethics, core values, social responsibility, and environmental sustainability is unsurpassed by any other leading strategy text.* Chapter 9, "Ethics, Corporate Social Responsibility, Environmental Sustainability, and Strategy," is embellished with fresh content so that it can better fulfill the important functions of (1) alerting students to the role and importance of ethical and socially responsible decision making and (2) addressing the accreditation requirements that business ethics be visibly and thoroughly embedded in the core curriculum. Moreover, discussions of the roles of values and ethics are integrated into portions of other chapters to further reinforce why and how considerations relating to ethics, values, social responsibility, and sustainability should figure prominently into the managerial task of crafting and executing company strategies.

3. *The caliber of the case collection in the fourth edition is truly unrivaled* from the standpoints of student appeal, teachability, and suitability for drilling students in the use of the concepts and analytical treatments in Chapters 1 through 10. The 12 cases included in this edition are the very latest, the best, and the most on-target that we could find. The ample information about the cases in the Instructor's Manual makes it effortless to select a set of cases each term that will capture the interest of students from start to finish.

4. *The publisher's Connect Management assignment and assessment platform is tightly linked to the text chapters and case lineup.* The *Connect* package for the fourth edition allows professors to assign autograded quizzes and select chapter-end Assurance of Learning Exercises to assess class members' understanding of chapter concepts. In addition, our texts have pioneered the extension of the *Connect Management* platform to case analysis. The autograded case exercises for each of the 12 cases in this edition are robust and extensive and will better enable students to make meaningful contributions to class discussions. The autograded *Connect* case exercises may also be used as graded assignments in the course.

5. The two cutting-edge and widely used strategy simulations—*The Business Strategy Game* and *GLO-BUS*—that are optional companions to the fourth edition give you unmatched capability to employ a text-case-simulation model of course delivery.

Organization, Content, and Features of the Fourth Edition Text Chapters

The following rundown summarizes the noteworthy features and topical emphasis in this new edition:

- Chapter 1 focuses on the importance of developing a clear understanding of why a company exists and why it matters in the marketplace. In developing such an understanding, management must define its approach to creating superior value for customers and how capabilities and resources will be employed to deliver the desired value to customers. We introduce students to the primary approaches to building competitive advantage and the key elements of business-level strategy. Following Henry Mintzberg's pioneering research, we also stress why a company's strategy is partly planned and partly reactive and why this strategy tends to evolve. The chapter also discusses why it is important for a company to have a *viable business model* that outlines the company's customer value proposition and its profit formula. This brief chapter is the perfect accompaniment to your opening-day lecture on what the course is all about and why it matters.

- Chapter 2 delves more deeply into the managerial process of actually crafting and executing a strategy—it makes a great assignment for the second day of class and provides a smooth transition into the heart of the course. The focal point of the chapter is the five-stage managerial process of crafting and executing strategy: (1) forming a strategic vision of where the company is headed and why, (2) developing strategic as well as financial objectives with which to measure the company's progress, (3) crafting a strategy to achieve these targets and move the company toward its market destination, (4) implementing and executing the strategy, and (5) evaluating a company's situation and performance to identify corrective adjustments that are needed. Students are introduced to such core concepts as strategic visions, mission statements and core values, the balanced scorecard, and business-level versus corporate-level strategies. There's a robust discussion of why *all managers are on a company's strategy-making, strategy-executing team* and why a company's strategic plan is a collection of strategies devised by different managers at different levels in the organizational hierarchy. The chapter winds up with a section on how to exercise good corporate governance and examines the conditions that led to recent high-profile corporate governance failures.

- Chapter 3 sets forth the now-familiar analytical tools and concepts of industry and competitive analysis and demonstrates the importance of tailoring strategy to fit the circumstances of a company's industry and competitive environment. The standout feature of this chapter is a presentation of Michael Porter's "five forces model of competition" *that has long been the clearest, most straightforward discussion of any text in the field.* New to this edition is the recasting of the discussion of the macro-environment to include the use of the PESTEL analysis framework for assessing the political, economic, social, technological, environmental, and legal factors in a company's macro-environment.

- Chapter 4 presents the resource-based view of the firm, showing why resource and capability analysis is such a powerful tool for sizing up a company's competitive assets. It offers a simple framework for identifying a company's resources and capabilities and another for determining whether they can provide the company with a sustainable competitive advantage over its competitors. New to this edition is a more explicit reference to the widely used VRIN framework. Other topics covered in this chapter include dynamic capabilities, SWOT analysis, value chain analysis, benchmarking, and competitive strength assessments, thus enabling a solid appraisal of a company's relative cost position and customer value proposition vis-à-vis its rivals.

- Chapter 5 deals with the basic approaches used to compete successfully and gain a competitive advantage over market rivals. This discussion is framed around the five generic competitive strategies—low-cost leadership, differentiation, best-cost provider, focused differentiation, and focused low-cost. It describes when each of these approaches works best and what pitfalls to avoid. It explains the role of *cost drivers* and *uniqueness drivers* in reducing a company's costs and enhancing its differentiation, respectively.

- Chapter 6 deals with the *strategy options* available to complement a company's competitive approach and maximize the power of its overall strategy. These include a variety of offensive or defensive competitive moves, and their timing, such as blue ocean strategy and first-mover advantages and disadvantages. It also includes choices concerning the breadth of a company's activities (or its scope of operations along an industry's entire value chain), ranging from horizontal mergers and acquisitions, to vertical integration, outsourcing, and strategic alliances. This material serves to segue into that covered in the next two chapters on international and diversification strategies.

- Chapter 7 explores the full range of strategy options for competing in international markets: export strategies; licensing; franchising; establishing a subsidiary in a foreign market; and using strategic alliances and joint ventures to build competitive strength in foreign markets. There's also a discussion of how to best tailor a company's international strategy to cross-country differences in market conditions and buyer preferences, how to use international operations to improve overall competitiveness, and the unique characteristics of competing in emerging markets.

- Chapter 8 introduces the topic of corporate-level strategy—a topic of concern for multibusiness companies pursuing diversification. This chapter begins by explaining why successful diversification strategies must create shareholder value and lays out the three essential tests that a strategy must pass to achieve this goal (*the industry attractiveness, cost of entry, and better-off tests*). Corporate strategy topics covered in the chapter include methods of entering new businesses, related diversification, unrelated diversification, combined related and unrelated diversification approaches, and strategic options for improving the overall performance of an already diversified company. The chapter's analytical spotlight is trained on the techniques and procedures for assessing a diversified company's business portfolio—the relative attractiveness of the various businesses the company has diversified into, the company's competitive strength in each of its business lines, and the *strategic fit* and *resource fit* among a diversified company's different businesses. The chapter concludes with a brief survey of a company's four main postdiversification strategy alternatives: (1) sticking closely with the existing business lineup,

(2) broadening the diversification base, (3) divesting some businesses and retrenching to a narrower diversification base, and (4) restructuring the makeup of the company's business lineup.

- Although the topic of ethics and values comes up at various points in this textbook, Chapter 9 brings more direct attention to such issues and may be used as a stand-alone assignment in either the early, middle, or late part of a course. It concerns the themes of ethical standards in business, approaches to ensuring consistent ethical standards for companies with international operations, corporate social responsibility, and environmental sustainability. The contents of this chapter are sure to give students some things to ponder, rouse lively discussion, and help to make students more ethically aware and conscious of *why all companies should conduct their business in a socially responsible and sustainable manner.*

- Chapter 10 is anchored around a pragmatic, compelling conceptual framework: (1) building dynamic capabilities, core competencies, resources, and structure necessary for proficient strategy execution; (2) allocating ample resources to strategy-critical activities; (3) ensuring that policies and procedures facilitate rather than impede strategy execution; (4) pushing for continuous improvement in how value chain activities are performed; (5) installing information and operating systems that enable company personnel to better carry out essential activities; (6) tying rewards and incentives directly to the achievement of performance targets and good strategy execution; (7) shaping the work environment and corporate culture to fit the strategy; and (8) exerting the internal leadership needed to drive execution forward. The recurring theme throughout the chapter is that implementing and executing strategy entails figuring out the specific actions, behaviors, and conditions that are needed for a smooth strategy-supportive operation—the goal here is to ensure that students understand that the strategy-implementing/strategy-executing phase is a make-it-happen-right kind of managerial exercise that leads to operating excellence and good performance.

In this latest edition, we have put our utmost effort into ensuring that the 10 chapters are consistent with the latest and best thinking of academics and practitioners in the field of strategic management and hit the bull's-eye in topical coverage for senior- and MBA-level strategy courses. The ultimate test of the text, of course, is the positive pedagogical impact it has in the classroom. If this edition sets a more effective stage for your lectures and does a better job of helping you persuade students that the discipline of strategy merits their rapt attention, then it will have fulfilled its purpose.

The Case Collection

The 12-case lineup in this edition is flush with interesting companies and valuable lessons for students in the art and science of crafting and executing strategy. There's a good blend of cases from a length perspective—about one-third are under 12 pages, yet offer plenty for students to chew on; about a third are medium-length cases; and the remaining one-third are detail-rich cases that call for sweeping analysis.

At least 10 of the 12 cases involve companies, products, people, or activities that students will have heard of, know about from personal experience, or can easily identify with. The lineup includes at least four cases that will provide students with insight into the special demands of competing in industry environments where technological developments are an everyday event, product life cycles are short, and competitive maneuvering among rivals comes fast and furious. All of the cases involve situations where the role of company resources and competitive capabilities in the strategy formulation, strategy execution scheme is emphasized. Scattered throughout the lineup are eight cases concerning non-U.S. companies, globally competitive industries, and/or cross-cultural situations; these cases, in conjunction with the globalized content of the text chapters, provide abundant material for linking the study of strategic management tightly to the ongoing globalization of the world economy. You'll also find four cases dealing with the strategic problems of family-owned or relatively small entrepreneurial businesses and 10 cases involving public companies and situations where students can do further research on the Internet. A number of the cases have accompanying videotape segments.

The Two Strategy Simulation Supplements: *The Business Strategy Game* and *GLO-BUS*

The Business Strategy Game and *GLO-BUS: Developing Winning Competitive Strategies*—two competition-based strategy simulations that are delivered online and that feature automated processing and grading of performance—are being marketed by the publisher as companion supplements for use with the fourth edition (and other texts in the field). *The Business Strategy Game* is the world's most popular strategy simulation, having been used by nearly 2,000 instructors in courses involving over 700,000 students at 900 university campuses in 60 countries. *GLO-BUS*, a somewhat simpler strategy simulation introduced in 2004, has been used by more than 1,100 instructors at 500+ university campuses in 40 countries. Both simulations allow students to apply strategy-making and analysis concepts presented in the text and may be used as part of a comprehensive effort to assess undergraduate or graduate program learning objectives.

The Compelling Case for Incorporating Use of a Strategy Simulation

There are *three exceptionally important benefits* associated with using a competition-based simulation in strategy courses taken by seniors and MBA students:

- *A three-pronged text-case-simulation course model delivers significantly more teaching and learning power than the traditional text-case model.* Using *both* cases and a strategy simulation to drill students in thinking strategically and applying what they read in the text chapters is a stronger, more effective means of helping them connect theory with practice and develop better business judgment. What cases do that a simulation cannot is give class members broad exposure to a variety of companies and industry situations and insight into the kinds of strategy-related problems managers face. But what a competition-based strategy simulation does far better than case analysis is thrust class members squarely into *an active, hands-on managerial role* where they are totally responsible for assessing market conditions, determining how to respond to the actions of competitors, forging a long-term direction and strategy for their company, and making all kinds of operating decisions. Because they are held fully accountable for their decisions and their company's performance, *co-managers are strongly motivated* to dig deeply into company operations, probe for ways to be more cost-efficient and competitive, and ferret out strategic moves and decisions calculated to boost company performance. *Consequently, incorporating both case assignments and a strategy simulation to develop the skills of class members in thinking strategically and applying the concepts and tools of strategic analysis turns out to be more pedagogically powerful than relying solely on case assignments—there's stronger retention of the lessons learned and better achievement of course learning objectives.*

- *The competitive nature of a strategy simulation arouses positive energy and steps up the whole tempo of the course by a notch or two.* Nothing sparks class excitement quicker or better than the concerted efforts on the part of class members during each decision round to achieve a high industry ranking and avoid the perilous consequences of being outcompeted by other class members. Students really enjoy taking on the role of a manager, running their own company, crafting strategies, making all kinds of operating decisions, trying to outcompete rival companies, and getting immediate feedback on the resulting company performance. Co-managers become *emotionally invested* in running their company and figuring out what strategic moves to make to boost their company's performance. All this stimulates learning and causes students to see the practical relevance of the subject matter and the benefits of taking your course.

- *Use of a fully automated online simulation reduces the time instructors spend on course preparation, course administration, and grading.* Since the simulation exercise involves a 20- to 30-hour workload for student-teams (roughly 2 hours per decision round times 10-12 rounds, plus optional assignments), simulation adopters often compensate by trimming the number of assigned cases from, say, 10 to 12 to perhaps 4 to 6. This significantly reduces the time instructors spend reading cases, studying teaching notes, and otherwise getting ready to lead class discussion of a case or grade oral team presentations. Course preparation time is further cut because you can use several class days to have students meet in the computer lab to work on upcoming decision rounds or a three-year strategic plan (in lieu of lecturing on a chapter or covering an additional assigned case). Not only does use of a simulation permit assigning fewer cases, but it also permits you to eliminate at least one assignment that entails considerable grading on your part. Grading one less written case or essay exam or other written assignment saves enormous time. With *BSG* and *GLO-BUS*, grading is effortless and takes only minutes; once you enter percentage weights for each assignment in your online grade book, a suggested overall grade is calculated for you. You'll be pleasantly surprised—and quite pleased—at how little time it takes to gear up for and to administer *The Business Strategy Game* or *GLO-BUS*.

In sum, incorporating use of a strategy simulation turns out to be *a win-win proposition for both students and instructors.* Moreover, a very convincing argument can be made that a competition-based strategy simulation is *the single most effective teaching/learning tool that instructors can employ to teach the discipline of business and competitive strategy, to make learning more enjoyable, and to promote better achievement of course learning objectives.*

Administration and Operating Features of the Two Simulations

The Internet delivery and user-friendly designs of both *BSG* and *GLO-BUS* make them incredibly easy to administer, even for first-time users. And the menus and controls are so similar that you can readily switch between the two simulations or use one in your undergraduate class and the other in a graduate class. If you have not yet used either of the two simulations, you may find the following of particular interest:

- Setting up the simulation for your course is done online and takes about 10 to 15 minutes. Once setup is completed, no other administrative actions are required beyond that of moving participants to a different team (should the need arise) and monitoring the progress of the simulation (to whatever extent desired).

- Participant's Guides are delivered electronically to class members at the website—students can read it on their monitors or print out a copy, as they prefer.

- There are two- to four-minute Video Tutorials scattered throughout the software (including each decision screen and each page of each report) that provide on-demand guidance to class members who may be uncertain about how to proceed.

- Complementing the video tutorials are detailed and clearly written Help sections explaining "all there is to know" about (a) each decision entry and the relevant cause-effect relationships, (b) the information on each page of the Industry Reports, and (c) the numbers presented in the Company Reports. *The Video Tutorials and the Help screens allow company co-managers to figure things out for themselves, thereby curbing the need for students to ask the instructor "how things work."*

- Team members running the same company who are logged-in simultaneously on different computers at different locations can click a button to enter Collaboration Mode, enabling them to work collaboratively from the same screen in viewing reports and making decision entries, and click a second button to enter Audio Mode, letting them talk to one another.

  - When in "Collaboration Mode," each team member sees the same screen at the same time as all other team members who are logged in and have joined Collaboration Mode. If one team member chooses to view a particular decision screen, that same screen appears on the monitors for all team members in Collaboration Mode.

- Team members each control their own color-coded mouse pointer (with their first-name appearing in a color-coded box linked to their mouse pointer) and can make a decision entry or move the mouse to point to particular on-screen items.

- A decision entry change made by one team member is seen by all, in real time, and all team members can immediately view the on-screen calculations that result from the new decision entry.

- If one team member wishes to view a report page and clicks on the menu link to the desired report, that same report page will immediately appear for the other team members engaged in collaboration.

- Use of Audio Mode capability requires that team members work from a computer with a built-in microphone (if they want to be heard by their team members) and speakers (so they may hear their teammates) or else have a headset with a microphone that they can plug into their desktop or laptop. A headset is recommended for best results, but most laptops now are equipped with a built-in microphone and speakers that will support use of our new voice chat feature.

- Real-time VoIP audio chat capability among team members who have entered both the Audio Mode and the Collaboration Mode is a tremendous boost in functionality that enables team members to go online simultaneously on computers at different locations and conveniently and effectively collaborate in running their simulation company.

- In addition, instructors have the capability to join the online session of any company and speak with team members, thus circumventing the need for team members to arrange for and attend a meeting in the instructor's office. Using the standard menu for administering a particular industry, instructors can connect with the company desirous of assistance. Instructors who wish not only to talk but also enter Collaboration (highly recommended because all attendees are then viewing the same screen) have a red-colored mouse pointer linked to a red box labeled Instructor.

  Without a doubt, the Collaboration and Voice-Chat capabilities are hugely valuable for students enrolled in online and distance-learning courses where meeting face-to-face is impractical or time-consuming. Likewise, the instructors of online and distance-learning courses will appreciate having the capability to join the online meetings of particular company teams when their advice or assistance is requested.

- Both simulations are quite suitable for use in distance-learning or online courses (and are currently being used in such courses on numerous campuses).

- Participants and instructors are notified via e-mail when the results are ready (usually about 15 to 20 minutes after the decision round deadline specified by the instructor/game administrator).

- Following each decision round, participants are provided with a complete set of reports—a six-page Industry Report, a one-page Competitive Intelligence report for each geographic region that includes strategic group maps and bulleted lists of competitive strengths and weaknesses, and a set of Company Reports (income statement, balance sheet, cash flow statement, and assorted production, marketing, and cost statistics).

- Two "open-book" multiple-choice tests of 20 questions are built into each simulation. The quizzes, which you can require or not as you see fit, are taken online and automatically graded, with scores reported instantaneously to participants and automatically recorded in the instructor's electronic grade book. Students are automatically provided with three sample questions for each test.

- Both simulations contain a three-year strategic plan option that you can assign. Scores on the plan are automatically recorded in the instructor's online grade book.

- At the end of the simulation, you can have students complete online peer evaluations (again, the scores are automatically recorded in your online grade book).

- Both simulations have a Company Presentation feature that enables each team of company co-managers to easily prepare PowerPoint slides for use in describing their strategy and summarizing their company's performance in a presentation to either the class, the instructor, or an "outside" board of directors.

- *A Learning Assurance Report provides you with hard data concerning how well your students performed vis-à-vis students playing the simulation worldwide over the past 12 months.* The report is based on nine measures of student proficiency, business know-how, and decision-making skill and can also be used in evaluating the extent to which your school's academic curriculum produces the desired degree of student learning insofar as accreditation standards are concerned.

For more details on either simulation, please consult Section 2 of the Instructor's Manual accompanying this text or register as an instructor at the simulation websites (www.bsg-online.com and www.globus.com) to access even more comprehensive information. You should also consider signing up for one of the webinars that the simulation authors conduct several times each month (sometimes several times weekly) to demonstrate how the software works, walk you through the various features and menu options, and answer any questions. You have an open invitation to call the senior author of this text at (205) 722-9145 to arrange a personal demonstration or talk about how one of the simulations might work in one of your courses. We think you'll be quite impressed with the cutting-edge capabilities that have been programmed into *The Business Strategy Game* and *GLO-BUS*, the simplicity with which both simulations can be administered, and their exceptionally tight connection to the text chapters, core concepts, and standard analytical tools.

Resources and Support Materials for the Fourth Edition for Students

Key Points Summaries

At the end of each chapter is a synopsis of the core concepts, analytical tools, and other key points discussed in the chapter. These chapter-end synopses, along with the core concept definitions and margin notes scattered throughout each chapter, help students focus on basic strategy principles, digest the messages of each chapter, and prepare for tests.

Two Sets of Chapter-End Exercises

Each chapter concludes with two sets of exercises. The Assurance of Learning Exercises can be used as the basis for class discussion, oral presentation assignments, short written reports, and substitutes for case assignments. The Exercises for Simulation Participants are designed expressly for use by adopters who have incorporated use of a simulation and wish to go a step further in tightly and explicitly connecting the chapter content to the simulation company their students are running. The questions in both sets of exercises (along with those Concepts & Connections illustrations that qualify as "mini cases") can be used to round out the rest of a 75-minute class period should your lecture on a chapter only last for 50 minutes.

A Value-Added Website

The student version of the Online Learning Center (OLC) or website www.mhhe.com/gamble4e contains a number of helpful aids:

- 20-question self-scoring chapter tests that students can take to measure their grasp of the material presented in each of the 10 chapters.
- A "Guide to Case Analysis" containing sections on what a case is, why cases are a standard part of courses in strategy, preparing a case for class discussion, doing a written case analysis, doing an oral presentation, and using financial ratio analysis to assess a company's financial condition. We suggest having students read this guide prior to the first class discussion of a case.
- PowerPoint slides for each chapter.

The *Connect Management* Web-Based Assignment and Assessment Platform

We have taken advantage of the publisher's innovative *Connect Management* assignment and assessment platform and created several robust and valuable features that simplify the task of assigning and grading three types of exercises for students:

- There are self-scoring chapter tests consisting of 20 multiple-choice questions that students can take to measure their grasp of the material presented in each of the 10 chapters.
- *Connect Management* includes interactive versions of two Assurance of Learning Exercises for each chapter that drill students in the use and application of the concepts and tools of strategic analysis.
- The *Connect Management* platform also includes fully autograded interactive application exercises for each of the 12 cases in this edition. The exercises require students to work through tutorials based upon the analysis set forth in the assignment questions for the case; these exercises have multiple components such as resource and capability analysis, financial

ratio analysis, identifcation of a company's strategy, or analysis of the five competitive forces. The content of these case exercises is tailored to match the circumstances presented in each case, calling upon students to do whatever strategic thinking and strategic analysis is called for to arrive at pragmatic, analysis-based action recommendations for improving company performance. The entire exercise is autograded, allowing instructors to focus on grading only the students' strategic recommendations.

All of the *Connect* exercises are automatically graded (with the exception of a few exercise components that entail student entry of essay answers), thereby simplifying the task of evaluating each class member's performance and monitoring the learning outcomes. The progress-tracking function built into the *Connect* system enables you to

- View scored work immediately and track individual or group performance with assignment and grade reports.
- Access an instant view of student or class performance relative to learning objectives.
- Collect data and generate reports required by many accreditation organizations, such as AACSB.

For Instructors

Online Learning Center (OLC)

In addition to the student resources, the instructor section of www.mhhe .com/gamble4e includes an Instructor's Manual and other support materials. Your McGraw-Hill representative can arrange delivery of instructor support materials in a format-ready Standard Cartridge for Blackboard, WebCT, and other web-based educational platforms.

Instructor's Manual

The accompanying IM contains:

- A section on suggestions for organizing and structuring your course.
- Sample syllabi and course outlines.
- A set of lecture notes on each chapter.
- Answers to the chapter-end Assurance of Learning Exercises.
- A comprehensive case teaching note for each of the 12 cases—these teaching notes are filled with suggestions for using the case effectively, have very thorough, analysis-based answers to the suggested assignment questions for the case, and contain an epilogue detailing any important developments since the case was written.

Test Bank and EZ Test Online

There is a test bank containing over 700 multiple-choice questions and short-answer/essay questions. It has been tagged with AACSB and Bloom's Taxonomy criteria. All of the test bank questions are also accessible within a computerized test bank powered by McGraw-Hill's flexible electronic testing program EZ Test Online (www.eztestonline.com). Using EZ Test Online allows you to create paper and online tests or quizzes. With EZ Test Online, instructors can select questions from multiple McGraw-Hill test banks or author their own, and then either print the test for paper distribution or give it online.

PowerPoint Slides

To facilitate delivery preparation of your lectures and to serve as chapter outlines, you'll have access to approximately 350 colorful and professional-looking slides displaying core concepts, analytical procedures, key points, and all the figures in the text chapters.

The Business Strategy Game and GLO-BUS Online Simulations

Using one of the two companion simulations is a powerful and constructive way of emotionally connecting students to the subject matter of the course. We know of no more effective way to arouse the competitive energy of students and prepare them for the challenges of real-world business decision making than to have them match strategic wits with classmates in running a company in head-to-head competition for global market leadership.

Acknowledgments

We heartily acknowledge the contributions of the case researchers whose case-writing efforts appear herein and the companies whose cooperation made the cases possible. To each one goes a very special thank-you. We cannot overstate the importance of timely, carefully researched cases in contributing to a substantive study of strategic management issues and practices. From a research standpoint, strategy-related cases are invaluable in exposing the generic kinds of strategic issues that companies face in forming hypotheses about strategic behavior and in drawing experienced-based generalizations about the practice of strategic management. From an instructional standpoint, strategy cases give students essential practice in diagnosing and evaluating the strategic situations of companies and organizations, in applying the concepts and tools of strategic analysis, in weighing strategic options and crafting strategies, and in tackling the challenges of successful strategy execution. Without a continuing stream of fresh, well-researched, and well-conceived cases, the discipline of strategic management would lose its close ties to the very institutions whose strategic actions and behavior it is aimed at explaining. There's no question, therefore, that first-class case research constitutes a valuable scholarly contribution to the theory and practice of strategic management.

A great number of colleagues and students at various universities, business acquaintances, and people at McGraw-Hill provided inspiration, encouragement, and counsel during the course of this project. Like all text authors in the strategy field, we are intellectually indebted to the many academics whose research and writing have blazed new trails and advanced the discipline of strategic management.

We also express our thanks to Todd M. Alessandri, Michael Anderson, Gerald D. Baumgardner, Edith C. Busija, Gerald E. Calvasina, Sam D. Cappel, Richard Churchman, John W. Collis, Connie Daniel, Christine DeLaTorre, Vickie Cox Edmondson, Diane D. Galbraith, Naomi A. Gardberg, Sanjay Goel, Les Jankovich, Jonatan Jelen, William Jiang, Bonnie Johnson, Roy Johnson, John J. Lawrence, Robert E. Ledman, Mark Lehrer, Fred Maidment, Frank Markham, Renata Mayrhofer, Simon Medcalfe, Elouise Mintz, Michael Monahan, Gerry Nkombo Muuka, Cori J. Myers, Jeryl L. Nelson, David Olson, John Perry, L. Jeff Seaton, Charles F. Seifert, Eugene S. Simko, Karen J. Smith, Susan Steiner, Troy V. Sullivan, Elisabeth J. Teal, Lori Tisher, Vincent Weaver, Jim Whitlock, and Beth Woodard. These reviewers provided valuable guidance in steering our efforts to improve earlier editions.

As always, we value your recommendations and thoughts about the book. Your comments regarding coverage and contents will be taken to heart, and we always are grateful for the time you take to call our attention to printing errors, deficiencies, and other shortcomings. Please e-mail us at john.gamble@tamucc.edu, or athompso@cba.ua.edu, or margaret.a.peteraf@ tuck.dartmouth.edu.

John E. Gamble

Margaret A. Peteraf

Arthur A. Thompson

CONTENTS

Section B: Core Concepts and Analytical Tools

Chapter 3 Evaluating a Company's External Environment 37

Chapter 7 Strategies for Competing in International Markets **137**

PART TWO CASES IN CRAFTING AND EXECUTING STRATEGY
Cases

Strategy, Business Models, and Competitive Advantage

chapter 1

LEARNING OBJECTIVES

LO1 Understand why every company needs a distinctive strategy to compete successfully, manage its business operations, and strengthen its prospects for long-term success.

LO2 Learn why it is important for a company to have a viable business model that outlines the company's customer value proposition and its profit formula.

LO3 Develop an awareness of the five most dependable strategic approaches for setting a company apart from rivals and winning a sustainable competitive advantage.

LO4 Understand that a company's strategy tends to evolve over time because of changing circumstances and ongoing management efforts to improve the company's strategy.

LO5 Learn the three tests of a winning strategy.

Learning Objectives are listed at the beginning of each chapter; corresponding numbered indicators in the margins show where learning objectives are covered in the text.

CONCEPTS & CONNECTIONS 1.1

PANDORA, SIRIUS XM, AND OVER-THE-AIR BROADCAST RADIO: THREE CONTRASTING BUSINESS MODELS

The strategies of rival companies are often predicated on strikingly different business models. Consider, for example, the business models for over-the-air radio broadcasters, Sirius XM, and Pandora Media.

The business model of over-the-air broadcast radio—provide listeners with free programming and charging advertisers fees—is a proven moneymaker. Sirius XM's business model is proving to be viable with the company recording three consecutive years of profitability after recording losses for its first seven years. But the jury is still out on Pandora's business model of offering streaming Internet radio. Even though Pandora had established itself as the leading Internet radio service with more than 200 million users in the United States, the company ended fiscal 2013 with a $38 million loss.

	Pandora	Sirius XM	Over-the-Air Radio Broadcasters
Customer value proposition	Internet radio service that allowed PC, tablet computer, and smartphone users to create up to 100 personalized music and comedy stations. Users could create a new station by entering the name of a song, artist, or genre. Pandora utilized algorithms to generate playlists based upon the users' predicted music preferences. Programming for the free service was interrupted by brief, occasional ads, while advertising was eliminated for Pandora One subscribers.	Satellite-based music, news, sports, national and regional weather, traffic reports in limited areas, and talk radio programming provided for a monthly subscription fee. Programming was interrupted only by brief, occasional ads. The company also offered subscribers streaming Internet channels and the ability to create personalized commercial-free stations for online and mobile listening.	Free-of-charge music, national and local news, local traffic reports, national and local weather, and talk radio programming. Listeners could expect frequent programming interruption for ads.
Profit formula	*Revenue generation:* Display, audio, and video ads sold to local and national advertisers. Ads could be targeted to listeners based on age, gender, zip code, and content preferences. Subscription revenues were generated from an advertising-free option called Pandora One. *Cost structure:* Fixed costs associated with developing software for computers, smartphones, and tablet computer. Fixed and variable costs related to operating data centers to support	*Revenue generation:* Monthly subscription fees, sales of satellite radio equipment, and advertising revenues. *Cost structure:* Fixed costs associated with operating a satellite-based music delivery service and streaming Internet service. Fixed and variable costs related to programming and content royalties, marketing, and support activities.	*Revenue generation:* Advertising sales to national and local businesses. *Cost structure:* Fixed costs associated with terrestrial broadcasting operations. Fixed and variable costs related to local news reporting, advertising sales operations, network affiliate fees, programming and content royalties, commercial production activities.

Concepts & Connections appear in boxes throughout each chapter to provide in-depth examples, connect the text presentation to real-world companies, and convincingly demonstrate "strategy in action." Some are appropriate for use as mini cases.

Margin Notes define core concepts and call attention to important ideas and principles.

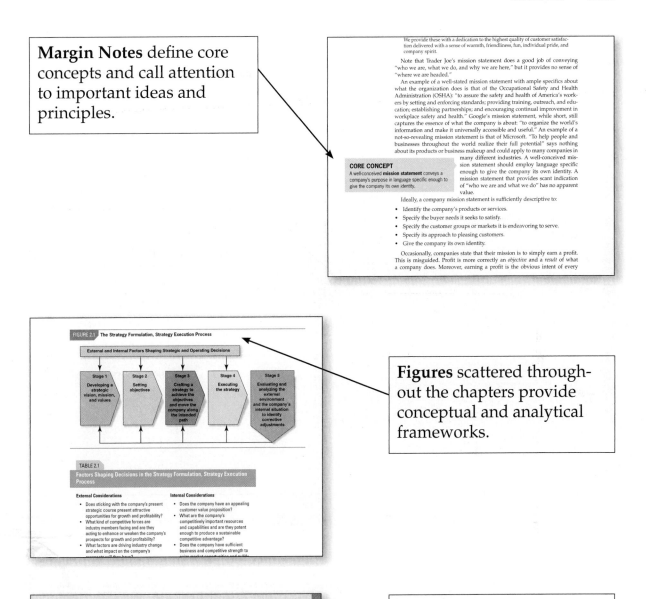

We provide these with a dedication to the highest quality of customer satisfaction delivered with a sense of warmth, friendliness, fun, individual pride, and company spirit.

Note that Trader Joe's mission statement does a good job of conveying "who we are, what we do, and why we are here," but it provides no sense of "where we are headed."

An example of a well-stated mission statement with ample specifics about what the organization does is that of the Occupational Safety and Health Administration (OSHA): "to assure the safety and health of America's workers by setting and enforcing standards; providing training, outreach, and education; establishing partnerships; and encouraging continual improvement in workplace safety and health." Google's mission statement, while short, still captures the essence of what the company is about: "to organize the world's information and make it universally accessible and useful." An example of a not-so-revealing mission statement is that of Microsoft. "To help people and businesses throughout the world realize their full potential" says nothing about its products or business makeup and could apply to many companies in many different industries. A well-conceived mission statement should employ language specific enough to give the company its own identity. A mission statement that provides scant indication of "who we are and what we do" has no apparent value.

CORE CONCEPT
A well-conceived **mission statement** conveys a company's purpose in language specific enough to give the company its own identity.

Ideally, a company mission statement is sufficiently descriptive to:

- Identify the company's products or services.
- Specify the buyer needs it seeks to satisfy.
- Specify the customer groups or markets it is endeavoring to serve.
- Specify its approach to pleasing customers.
- Give the company its own identity.

Occasionally, companies state that their mission is to simply earn a profit. This is misguided. Profit is more correctly an *objective* and a *result* of what a company does. Moreover, earning a profit is the obvious intent of every

---

FIGURE 2.1 The Strategy Formulation, Strategy Execution Process

External and Internal Factors Shaping Strategic and Operating Decisions

Stage 1 Developing a strategic vision, mission, and values → Stage 2 Setting objectives → Stage 3 Crafting a strategy to achieve the objectives and move the company along the intended path → Stage 4 Executing the strategy → Stage 5 Evaluating and analyzing the external environment and the company's internal situation to identify corrective adjustments

TABLE 2.1
Factors Shaping Decisions in the Strategy Formulation, Strategy Execution Process

External Considerations	Internal Considerations
• Does sticking with the company's present strategic course present attractive opportunities for growth and profitability?	• Does the company have an appealing customer value proposition?
• What kind of competitive forces are industry members facing and are they acting to enhance or weaken the company's prospects for growth and profitability?	• What are the company's competitively important resources and capabilities and are they potent enough to produce a sustainable competitive advantage?
• What factors are driving industry change and what impact on the company's	• Does the company have sufficient business and competitive strength to

Figures scattered throughout the chapters provide conceptual and analytical frameworks.

▶ **KEY POINTS**

Thinking strategically about a company's external situation involves probing for answers to the following eight questions:

1. *What are the strategically relevant factors in the macro-environment?* Industries differ as to how they are affected by conditions in the broad macro-environment. PESTEL analysis of the political, economic, sociocultural, technological, environmental/ecological, and legal/regulatory factors provides a framework for approaching this issue systematically.

2. *What are the industry's dominant economic features?* Industries may also differ significantly on such factors as market size and growth rate, the number and relative sizes of both buyers and sellers, the geographic scope of competitive rivalry, the degree of product differentiation, the speed of product innovation, demand–supply conditions, the extent of vertical integration, and the extent of scale economies and learning curve effects.

3. *What kinds of competitive forces are industry members facing, and how strong is each force?* The strength of competition is a composite of five forces: (1) competitive pressures stemming from buyer bargaining power and seller-buyer collaboration, (2) competitive pressures associated with the sellers of substitutes, (3) competitive pressures stemming from supplier bargaining power and supplier-seller collaboration, (4) competitive pressures associated with the threat of new entrants into the market, and (5) competitive pressures stemming from the competitive jockeying among industry rivals.

4. *What forces are driving changes in the industry, and what impact will these changes have on competitive intensity and industry profitability?* Industry and competitive conditions change because forces are in motion that create incentives or pressures for change. The first phase is to identify the forces that are driving industry change. The second phase of driving forces analysis is to determine whether the driving forces, taken together, are acting to make the industry environment more or less attractive.

5. *What market positions do industry rivals occupy—who is strongly positioned and who is not?* Strategic group mapping is a valuable tool for understanding the similarities and differences inherent in the market positions of rival companies. Rivals in the same or nearby strategic groups are close competitors, whereas companies in

Key Points at the end of each chapter provide a handy summary of essential ideas and things to remember.

> ASSURANCE OF LEARNING EXERCISES

LO1 1. The heart of Toyota's strategy in motor vehicles is to outcompete rivals by manufacturing world-class, quality vehicles at lower costs and selling them at competitive price levels. Executing this strategy requires top-notch manufacturing capability and super-efficient management of people, equipment, and materials. Concepts & Connections 10.1, discusses the principles, practices, and techniques grounded in Toyota's famed Toyota Production System. How does Toyota's philosophy of dealing with defects, empowering employees, and developing capabilities impact strategy execution? Why are its slogans such as "Never be satisfied" and "Ask yourself 'Why?' five times" important?

LO2 2. Implementing and executing a new or different strategy call for new resource allocations. Using your university's access to LexisNexis or EBSCO, search for recent articles that discuss how a company has revised its pattern of resource allocation and divisional budgets to support new strategic initiatives.

LO3 3. Policies and procedures facilitate strategy execution when they are designed to fit the company's strategy and objectives. Using your university's access to LexisNexis or EBSCO, search for recent articles that discuss how a company has revised its policies and procedures to provide better top-down guidance to company personnel about how certain things should be done.

LO4 4. Concepts & Connections 10.2 discusses Whirlpool Corporation's Operational Excellence initiative and its use of Six Sigma practices. How did the implementation of the program change the culture and mind-set of the company's personnel? List three tangible benefits provided by the program. Explain why a commitment to quality control is important in the appliance industry.

connect

LO5 5. Company strategies can't be implemented or executed well without a number of support systems to carry on business operations. Using your university's access to LexisNexis or EBSCO, search for recent articles that discuss how a company has used real-time information systems and control systems to aid the cause of good strategy execution.

LO6 6. Concepts & Connections 10.3, provides a sampling of motivational tactics employed by several companies (many of which appear on *Fortune*'s list of the "100 Best Companies to Work For" in America. Discuss how rewards at Google, JM Family Enterprises, Wegmans, and Ukrop's Supermarkets aid in the strategy execution of each company.

LO7 7. Concepts & Connections 10.4 discusses W. L. Gore's strategy-supportive corporate culture. What are the standout features of Gore's corporate culture? How does W. L. Gore's culture contribute to innovation and creativity at the company? How does the company's culture make W. L. Gore a good place to work?

connect

LO8 8. Leading the strategy execution process involves staying on top of the situation and monitoring progress, putting constructive pressure on the organization to achieve operating excellence, and initiating corrective actions to improve the execution effort. Using your university's access to business periodicals, discuss a recent example of how a company's managers have demonstrated the kind of effective internal leadership needed for superior strategy execution.

236

Exercises at the end of each chapter, linked to learning objectives, provide a basis for class discussion, oral presentations, and written assignments. Two exercises in each chapter are linked to the *Connect* online assignment and assessment platform for the text.

---

case
1   Mystic Monk Coffee

connect   DAVID L. TURNIPSEED University of South Alabama

As Father Daniel Mary, the prior of the Carmelite Order of monks in Clark, Wyoming, walked to chapel to preside over Mass, he noticed the sun glistening across the four-inch snowfall from the previous evening. Snow in June was not unheard of in Wyoming, but the late snowfall and the bright glow of the rising sun made him consider the opposing forces accompanying change and how he might best prepare his monastery to achieve his vision of creating a new Mount Carmel in the Rocky Mountains. His vision of transforming the small brotherhood of 13 monks living in a small home used as makeshift rectory into a 500-acre monastery that would include accommodations for 30 monks, a Gothic church, a convent for Carmelite nuns, a retreat center for lay visitors, and a hermitage presented a formidable challenge. However, as a former high school football player, boxer, bull rider, and man of great faith, Father Prior Daniel Mary was unaccustomed to shrinking from a challenge.

Father Prior had identified a nearby ranch for sale that met the requirements of his vision perfectly, but its current listing price of $8.9 million presented a financial obstacle to creating a place of prayer, worship, and solitude in the Rockies. The Carmelites had received a $250,000 donation that could be used toward the purchase, and the monastery had earned nearly $75,000 during the first year of its Mystic Monk coffee-roasting operations, but more money would be needed. The coffee roaster used to produce packaged coffee sold to Catholic consumers

at the Mystic Monk Coffee website was reaching its capacity, but a larger roaster could be purchased for $35,000. Also, local Cody, Wyoming, business owners had begun a foundation for those wishing to donate to the monks' cause. Father Prior Daniel Mary did not have a great deal of experience in business matters but considered to what extent the monastery could rely on its Mystic Monk Coffee operations to fund the purchase of the ranch. If Mystic Monk Coffee was capable of making the vision a reality, what were the next steps in turning the coffee into land?

The Carmelite Monks of Wyoming

Carmelites are a religious order of the Catholic Church that was formed by men who traveled to the Holy Land as pilgrims and crusaders and had chosen to remain near Jerusalem to seek God. The men established their hermitage at Mount Carmel because of its beauty, seclusion, and biblical importance as the site where Elijah stood against King Ahab and the false prophets of Jezebel to prove Jehovah to be the one true God. The Carmelites led a life of solitude, silence, and prayer at Mount Carmel before eventually returning to Europe and becoming a recognized order of the Catholic Church. The size of the Carmelite Order varied widely

Copyright © 2011 by David L. Turnipseed. All rights reserved.

Twelve cases detail the strategic circumstances of actual companies and provide practice in applying the concepts and tools of strategic analysis. An autograded tutorial for each of the 12 cases in the text is included in *Connect*.

FOR STUDENTS: AN ASSORTMENT OF SUPPORT MATERIALS

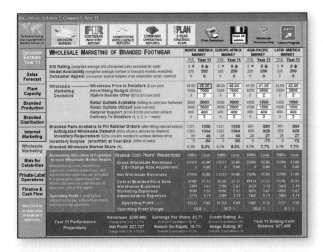

The Business Strategy Game **or** *GLO-BUS* **Simulation Exercises** Either one of these text supplements involves teams of students managing companies in a head-to-head contest for global market leadership. Company co-managers have to make decisions relating to product quality, production, workforce compensation and training, pricing and marketing, and financing of company operations. The challenge is to craft and execute a strategy that is powerful enough to deliver good financial performance despite the competitive efforts of rival companies. Each company competes in America, Latin America, Europe-Africa, and Asia-Pacific.

MCGRAW-HILL *CONNECT MANAGEMENT*

Less Managing. More Teaching. Greater Learning.

McGraw-Hill *Connect Management* is an online assignment and assessment solution that connects students with the tools and resources they'll need to achieve success.

McGraw-Hill *Connect Management* helps prepare students for their future by enabling faster learning, more efficient studying, and higher retention of knowledge.

McGraw-Hill *Connect Management* features

Connect Management offers a number of powerful tools and features to make managing assignments easier, so faculty can spend more time teaching. With *Connect Management,* students can engage with their coursework anytime and anywhere, making the learning process more accessible and efficient. *Connect Management* offers you the features described below.

Simple assignment management

With *Connect Management,* creating assignments is easier than ever, so you can spend more time teaching and less time managing. The assignment management function enables you to:

- Create and deliver assignments easily with selectable end-of-chapter questions and test bank items.
- Streamline lesson planning, student progress reporting, and assignment grading to make classroom management more efficient than ever.
- Go paperless with the e-book and online submission and grading of student assignments.

Smart grading

When it comes to studying, time is precious. *Connect Management* helps students learn more efficiently by providing feedback and practice material when they need it, where they need it. When it comes to teaching, your time also is precious. The grading function enables you to:

- Have assignments scored automatically, giving students immediate feedback on their work and side-by-side comparisons with correct answers.
- Access and review each response; manually change grades or leave comments for students to review.
- Reinforce classroom concepts with practice tests and instant quizzes.

Instructor library

The *Connect Management* Instructor Library is your repository for additional resources to improve student engagement in and out of class. You can select and use any asset that enhances your lecture. The *Connect Management* Instructor Library includes:

- e-book
- Instructor's Manual

- PowerPoint files
- Videos and Instructional Notes

Student study center

The *Connect Management* Student Study Center is the place for students to access additional resources. The Student Study Center:

- Offers students quick access to lectures, practice materials, e-books, and more.
- Provides instant practice material and study questions, easily accessible on the go.
- Gives students access to the Personalized Learning Plan described below.

Student progress tracking

Connect Management keeps instructors informed about how each student, section, and class is performing, allowing for more productive use of lecture and office hours. The progress-tracking function enables you to:

- View scored work immediately and track individual or group performance with assignment and grade reports.
- Access an instant view of student or class performance relative to learning objectives.
- Collect data and generate reports required by many accreditation organizations, such as AACSB.

Lecture capture

Increase the attention paid to lecture discussion by decreasing the attention paid to note taking. For an additional charge, Lecture Capture offers new ways for students to focus on the in-class discussion, knowing they can revisit important topics later. Lecture Capture enables you to:

- Record and distribute your lecture with a click of button.
- Record and index PowerPoint presentations and anything shown on your computer so it is easily searchable, frame by frame.
- Offer access to lectures anytime and anywhere by computer, iPod, or mobile device.
- Increase intent listening and class participation by easing students' concerns about note taking. Lecture Capture will make it more likely you will see students' faces, not the tops of their heads.

McGraw-Hill *Connect Plus* Management

McGraw-Hill reinvents the textbook learning experience for the modern student with *Connect Plus Management*. A seamless integration of an e-book and *Connect Management*, *Connect Plus Management* provides all of the *Connect Management* features plus the following:

- An integrated e-book, allowing for anytime, anywhere access to the textbook.
- Dynamic links between the problems or questions you assign to your students and the location in the e-book where that problem or question is covered.
- A powerful search function to pinpoint and connect key concepts in a snap.

In short, *Connect Management* offers you and your students powerful tools and features that optimize your time and energies, enabling you to focus on course content, teaching, and student learning. *Connect Management* also offers a wealth of content resources for both instructors and students. This state-of-the-art, thoroughly tested system supports you in preparing students for the world that awaits.

For more information about Connect, go to **www.mcgrawhillconnect.com**, or contact your local McGraw-Hill sales representative.

TEGRITY CAMPUS: LECTURES 24/7

Tegrity Campus is a service that makes class time available 24/7 by automatically capturing every lecture in a searchable format for students to review when they study and complete assignments. With a simple one-click start-and-stop process, you capture all computer screens and corresponding audio. Students can replay any part of any class with easy-to-use browser-based viewing on a PC or Mac.

Educators know that the more students can see, hear, and experience class resources, the better they learn. In fact, studies prove it. With Tegrity Campus, students quickly recall key moments by using Tegrity Campus's unique search feature. This search helps students efficiently find what they need, when they need it, across an entire semester of class recordings. Help turn all your students' study time into learning moments immediately supported by your lecture.

To learn more about Tegrity, watch a two-minute Flash demo at **http://tegritycampus.mhhe.com**.

ASSURANCE OF LEARNING READY

Many educational institutions today are focused on the notion of *assurance of learning,* an important element of some accreditation standards. *Essentials of Strategic Management* is designed specifically to support your assurance of learning initiatives with a simple, yet powerful solution.

Each test bank question for *Essentials of Strategic Management* maps to a specific chapter learning outcome/objective listed in the text. You can use our test bank software, EZ Test and EZ Test Online, or *Connect Management* to easily query for learning outcomes/objectives that directly relate to the learning objectives for your course. You can then use the reporting features of EZ Test to aggregate student results in similar fashion, making the collection and presentation of assurance of learning data simple and easy.

MCGRAW-HILL HIGHER EDUCATION AND BLACKBOARD

McGraw-Hill Higher Education and Blackboard have teamed up. What does this mean for you?

1. **Your life, simplified.** Now you and your students can access McGraw-Hill's Connect™ and Create™ right from within your Blackboard course—all with one single sign-on. Say good-bye to the days of logging in to multiple applications.

2. **Deep integration of content and tools.** Not only do you get single sign-on with Connect™ and Create™, you also get deep integration of McGraw-Hill content and content engines right in Blackboard. Whether you're choosing a book for your course or building Connect™ assignments, all the tools you need are right where you want them—inside of Blackboard.

The **Best** of **Both Worlds**

3. **Seamless Gradebooks.** Are you tired of keeping multiple gradebooks and manually synchronizing grades into Blackboard? We thought so. When a student completes an integrated Connect™ assignment, the grade for that assignment automatically (and instantly) feeds your Blackboard grade center.

4. **A solution for everyone.** Whether your institution is already using Blackboard or you just want to try Blackboard on your own, we have a solution for you. McGraw-Hill and Blackboard can now offer you easy access to industry leading technology and content, whether your campus hosts it, or we do. Be sure to ask your local McGraw-Hill representative for details.

AACSB STATEMENT

The McGraw-Hill Companies is a proud corporate member of AACSB International. Understanding the importance and value of AACSB accreditation, *Essentials of Strategic Management*, Fourth Edition, recognizes the curricula guidelines detailed in the AACSB standards for business accreditation by connecting selected questions in the test bank to the six general knowledge and skill guidelines in the AACSB standards.

The statements contained in *Essentials of Strategic Management*, Fourth Edition, are provided only as a guide for the users of this textbook. The AACSB leaves content coverage and assessment within the purview of individual schools, the mission of the school, and the faculty. While *Essentials of Strategic Management*, Fourth Edition, and the teaching package make no claim of any specific AACSB qualification or evaluation, we have within *Essentials of Strategic Management*, Fourth Edition, labeled selected questions according to the six general knowledge and skills areas.

MCGRAW-HILL EDUCATION CUSTOMER CARE CONTACT INFORMATION

At McGraw-Hill, we understand that getting the most from new technology can be challenging. That's why our services don't stop after you purchase our products. You can e-mail our Product Specialists 24 hours a day to get product-training online. Or you can search our knowledge bank of Frequently Asked Questions on our support website. For Customer Support, call **800-331-5094,** e-mail **hmsupport@mcgraw-hill.com,** or visit **www.mhhe.com/support**. One of our Technical Support Analysts will be able to assist you in a timely fashion.

e-BOOK OPTIONS

e-books are an innovative way for students to save money and to "go green." McGraw-Hill's e-books are typically 40% off the bookstore price. Students have the choice between an online and a downloadable CourseSmart e-book.

Through CourseSmart, students have the flexibility to access an exact replica of their textbook from any computer that has Internet service without plug-ins or special software via the online version, or to create a library of books on their hard drive via the downloadable version. Access to the CourseSmart e-books lasts for one year.

Features CourseSmart e-books allow students to highlight, take notes, organize notes, and share the notes with other CourseSmart users. Students can also search for terms across all e-books in their purchased CourseSmart library. CourseSmart e-books can be printed (five pages at a time).

More info and purchase Please visit **www.coursesmart.com** for more information and to purchase access to our e-books. CourseSmart allows students to try one chapter of the e-book, free of charge, before purchase.

Strategy, Business Models, and Competitive Advantage

LEARNING OBJECTIVES

LO1   Understand why every company needs a distinctive strategy to compete successfully, manage its business operations, and strengthen its prospects for long-term success.

LO2   Learn why it is important for a company to have a viable business model that outlines the company's customer value proposition and its profit formula.

LO3   Develop an awareness of the five most dependable strategic approaches for setting a company apart from rivals and winning a sustainable competitive advantage.

LO4   Understand that a company's strategy tends to evolve over time because of changing circumstances and ongoing management efforts to improve the company's strategy.

LO5   Learn the three tests of a winning strategy.

In thinking strategically about a company, *managers of all types of businesses must develop a clear understanding of why a company exists and why the company matters in the marketplace.* Do the company's products or services offer customers value in ways that competitors cannot match? Is the company's approach to doing business different from that of rivals and thereby allows the company to offer superior customer value? What is it about the company's offering that is distinctive and makes it important in the minds of customers? How would customers be affected if the company did not exist? A company's **strategy** spells out why the company matters in the marketplace by defining its approach to creating superior value for customers and how capabilities and resources will be employed to deliver the desired value to customers. In effect, the crafting of a strategy represents a managerial commitment to pursuing an array of choices about how to compete. These include choices about:

- *How* to create products or services that attract and please customers.
- *How* to position the company in the industry.
- *How* to develop and deploy resources to build valuable competitive capabilities.
- *How* each functional piece of the business (R&D, supply chain activities, production, sales and marketing, distribution, finance, and human resources) will be operated.
- *How* to achieve the company's performance targets.

In most industries companies have considerable freedom in choosing the *hows* of strategy. Thus some rivals strive to create superior value for customers by achieving lower costs than rivals while others pursue product superiority or personalized customer service or the development of capabilities that rivals cannot match. Some competitors position themselves in only one part of the industry's chain of production/distribution activities, while others are partially or fully integrated, with operations ranging from components production to manufacturing and assembly to wholesale distribution or retailing. Some competitors deliberately confine their operations to local or regional markets; others opt to compete nationally, internationally (several countries), or globally. Some companies decide to operate in only one industry, while others diversify broadly or narrowly, into related or unrelated industries.

> **CORE CONCEPT**
>
> A company's **strategy** explains why the company matters in the marketplace by specifying an approach to creating superior value for customers and determining how capabilities and resources will be utilized to deliver the desired value to customers.

The role of this chapter is to define the concepts of strategy and competitive advantage, the relationship between a company's strategy and its business model, why strategies are partly proactive and partly reactive, and why company strategies evolve over time. Particular attention will be paid to what sets a winning strategy apart from a ho-hum or flawed strategy and why the caliber of a company's strategy determines whether it will enjoy a competitive advantage or be burdened by competitive disadvantage. By the end of this chapter, you will have a clear idea of why the tasks of crafting and executing strategy are core management functions and why excellent execution of an excellent strategy is the most reliable recipe for turning a company into a standout performer.

The Importance of Strategic Uniqueness

For a company to matter in the minds of customers, its strategy needs a distinctive element that sets it apart from rivals and produces a competitive edge. A strategy must tightly fit a company's own particular situation, but there is no shortage of opportunity to fashion a strategy that is discernibly different from the strategies of rivals. In fact, competitive success requires a company's managers to make strategic choices about the key building blocks of its strategy that differ from the choices made by competitors—not 100 percent different but at least different in several important respects. A strategy stands a chance of succeeding only when it is predicated on actions, business approaches, and competitive moves aimed at appealing to buyers *in ways that set a company apart from rivals.* Simply trying to mimic the strategies of the industry's successful companies rarely works. Rather, every company's strategy needs to have some distinctive element that draws in customers and produces a competitive edge. Strategy, at its essence, is about competing differently—doing what rival firms *don't* do or, better yet, what rival firms *can't* do.[1]

LO1 Understand why every company needs a distinctive strategy to compete successfully, manage its business operations, and strengthen its prospects for long-term success.

> Mimicking the strategies of successful industry rivals—with either copycat product offerings or efforts to stake out the same market position—rarely works. A creative, distinctive strategy that sets a company apart from rivals and yields a competitive advantage is a company's most reliable ticket for earning above-average profits.

Strategy and a Company's Business Model

Closely related to the concept of strategy is the concept of a company's **business model**. While the company's strategy sets forth an approach to offering superior value, a company's business model is management's blueprint for delivering a valuable product or service to customers in a manner that will yield an attractive profit.[2] The two elements of a company's business model are (1) its *customer value proposition* and (2) its *profit formula.* The customer value proposition is established by the company's overall strategy and lays out the company's approach to satisfying buyer wants and needs at a price customers will consider a good value. The greater the value provided and the lower the price, the more attractive the value proposition is to customers. The profit formula describes the company's approach to determining a cost structure that will allow for acceptable profits given the pricing tied to its customer value proposition. The lower the costs given the customer value proposition, the greater the ability of the business model to be a moneymaker. The nitty-gritty issue surrounding a company's business model is whether it can execute its customer value proposition profitably. Just because company managers have crafted a strategy for competing and running the business does not automatically mean the strategy will lead to profitability—it may or it may not.[3]

LO2 Learn why it is important for a company to have a viable business model that outlines the company's customer value proposition and its profit formula.

> **CORE CONCEPT**
> A company's **business model** sets forth how its strategy and operating approaches will create value for customers, while at the same time generate ample revenues to cover costs and realize a profit. The two elements of a company's business model are its (1) customer value proposition and (2) its profit formula.

Cable television providers utilize a business model, keyed to delivering news and entertainment that viewers will find valuable, to secure sufficient revenues from subscriptions and advertising to cover operating expenses and

CONCEPTS & CONNECTIONS 1.1

PANDORA, SIRIUS XM, AND OVER-THE-AIR BROADCAST RADIO: THREE CONTRASTING BUSINESS MODELS

The strategies of rival companies are often predicated on strikingly different business models. Consider, for example, the business models for over-the-air radio broadcasters, Sirius XM, and Pandora Media.

The business model of over-the-air broadcast radio—providing listeners with free programming and charging advertisers fees—is a proven moneymaker. Sirius XM's business model is proving to be viable with the company recording three consecutive years of profitability after recording losses for its first seven years. But the jury is still out on Pandora's business model of offering streaming Internet radio. Even though Pandora had established itself as the leading Internet radio service with more than 200 million users in the United States, the company ended fiscal 2013 with a $38 million loss.

	Pandora	**Sirius XM**	**Over-the-Air Radio Broadcasters**
Customer value proposition	Internet radio service that allowed PC, tablet computer, and smartphone users to create up to 100 personalized music and comedy stations. Users could create a new station by entering the name of a song, artist, or genre. Pandora utilized algorithms to generate playlists based upon the users' predicted music preferences. Programming for the free service was interrupted by brief, occasional ads, while advertising was eliminated for Pandora One subscribers.	Satellite-based music, news, sports, national and regional weather, traffic reports in limited areas, and talk radio programming provided for a monthly subscription fee. Programming was interrupted only by brief, occasional ads. The company also offered subscribers streaming Internet channels and the ability to create personalized commercial-free stations for online and mobile listening.	Free-of-charge music, national and local news, local traffic reports, national and local weather, and talk radio programming. Listeners could expect frequent programming interruption for ads.
Profit formula	*Revenue generation:* Display, audio, and video ads sold to local and national advertisers. Ads could be targeted to listeners based on age, gender, zip code, and content preferences. Subscription revenues were generated from an advertising-free option called Pandora One. *Cost structure:* Fixed costs associated with developing software for computers, smartphones, and tablet computers. Fixed and variable costs related to operating data centers to support streaming network, content royalties, marketing, and support activities. *Profit margin:* Pandora Media's profitability was dependent on generating sufficient advertising revenues and subscription revenues to cover its costs and provide attractive profits.	*Revenue generation:* Monthly subscription fees, sales of satellite radio equipment, and advertising revenues. *Cost structure:* Fixed costs associated with operating a satellite-based music delivery service and streaming Internet service. Fixed and variable costs related to programming and content royalties, marketing, and support activities. *Profit margin:* Sirius XM's profitability was dependent on attracting a sufficiently large number of subscribers to cover its costs and provide attractive profits.	*Revenue generation:* Advertising sales to national and local businesses. *Cost structure:* Fixed costs associated with terrestrial broadcasting operations. Fixed and variable costs related to local news reporting, advertising sales operations, network affiliate fees, programming and content royalties, commercial production activities, and support activities. *Profit margin:* The profitability of over-the-air radio stations was dependent on generating sufficient advertising revenues to cover costs and provide attractive profits.

Sources: Company documents, 10-Ks, and information posted on their websites.

allow for profits. The business model of automobile dealerships entails generating revenues from automobile sales and after-the-sale service. The cost structure of automobile dealerships allows for healthy profit margins as long as the dealership represents a brand that is valued by consumers and it is able to provide quality service during the warranty period and after warranties expire. Gillette's business model in razor blades involves achieving economies of scale in the production of its shaving products, selling razors at an attractively low price, and then making money on repeat purchases of razor blades. Printer manufacturers such as Hewlett-Packard, Lexmark, and Epson pursue much the same business model as Gillette—achieving economies of scale in production and selling printers at a low (virtually break-even) price and making large profit margins on the repeat purchases of printer supplies, especially ink cartridges. Concepts & Connections 1.1 discusses three contrasting business models in radio broadcasting.

Strategy and the Quest for Competitive Advantage

The heart and soul of any strategy is the actions and moves in the marketplace that managers are taking to gain a competitive edge over rivals.[4] Five of the most frequently used and dependable strategic approaches to setting a company apart from rivals and winning a sustainable competitive advantage are:

LO3 Develop an awareness of the five most dependable strategic approaches for setting a company apart from rivals and winning a sustainable competitive advantage.

1. *A low-cost provider strategy*—achieving a cost-based advantage over rivals. Walmart and Southwest Airlines have earned strong market positions because of the low-cost advantages they have achieved over their rivals. Low-cost provider strategies can produce a durable competitive edge when rivals find it hard to match the low-cost leader's approach to driving costs out of the business.

2. *A broad differentiation strategy*—seeking to differentiate the company's product or service from rivals' in ways that will appeal to a broad spectrum of buyers. Successful adopters of broad differentiation strategies include Johnson & Johnson in baby products (product reliability) and Apple (innovative products). Differentiation strategies can be powerful so long as a company is sufficiently innovative to thwart rivals' attempts to copy or closely imitate its product offering.

3. *A focused low-cost strategy*—concentrating on a narrow buyer segment (or market niche) and outcompeting rivals by having lower costs than rivals and thus being able to serve niche members at a lower price. Private-label manufacturers of food, health and beauty products, and nutritional supplements use their low-cost advantage to offer supermarket buyers lower prices than those demanded by producers of branded products.

4. *A focused differentiation strategy*—concentrating on a narrow buyer segment (or market niche) and outcompeting rivals by offering niche members customized attributes that meet their tastes and requirements better than rivals' products. Louis Vuitton and Rolex have sustained their advantage in the luxury goods industry through a focus on affluent consumers demanding luxury and prestige.

5. *A best-cost provider strategy*—giving customers more value for the money by satisfying buyers' expectations on key quality/features/ performance/service attributes, while beating their price expectations. This approach is a hybrid strategy that blends elements of low-cost provider and differentiation strategies; the aim is to have the lowest (best) costs and prices among sellers offering products with comparable differentiating attributes. Target's best-cost advantage allows it to give discount store shoppers more value for the money by offering an attractive product lineup and an appealing shopping ambience at low prices.

In Concepts & Connections 1.2, it's evident that Starbucks has gained a competitive advantage over rivals through its efforts to offer the highest quality coffee-based beverages, create an emotional attachment with customers, expand its global presence, expand the product line, and ensure consistency in store operations. A creative, distinctive strategy such as that used by Starbucks is a company's most reliable ticket for developing a sustainable competitive advantage and earning above-average profits. A **sustainable competitive advantage** allows a company to attract sufficiently large numbers of buyers who have a lasting preference for its products or services over those offered by rivals, despite the efforts of competitors to offset that appeal and overcome the company's advantage. The bigger and more durable the competitive advantage, the better a company's prospects for winning in the marketplace and earning superior long-term profits relative to rivals.

> **CORE CONCEPT**
>
> A company achieves **sustainable competitive advantage** when an attractively large number of buyers develop a durable preference for its products or services over the offerings of competitors, despite the efforts of competitors to overcome or erode its advantage.

The Importance of Capabilities in Building and Sustaining Competitive Advantage

Winning a *sustainable* competitive edge over rivals with any of the above five strategies generally hinges as much on building competitively valuable capabilities that rivals cannot readily match as it does on having a distinctive product offering. Clever rivals can nearly always copy the attributes of a popular product or service, but it is substantially more difficult for rivals to match the know-how and specialized capabilities a company has developed and perfected over a long period. FedEx, for example, has superior capabilities in next-day delivery of small packages. And Hyundai has become the world's fastest-growing automaker as a result of its advanced manufacturing processes and unparalleled quality control system. The capabilities of both of these companies have proven difficult for competitors to imitate or best and have allowed each to build and sustain competitive advantage.

CONCEPTS & CONNECTIONS 1.2

STARBUCKS' STRATEGY IN THE SPECIALTY COFFEE MARKET

Since its founding in 1985 as a modest nine-store operation in Seattle, Washington, Starbucks had become the premier roaster and retailer of specialty coffees in the world, with over 18,800 store locations in more than 60 countries as of April 2013 and annual sales that were expected to exceed $15 billion in fiscal 2013. The sharp economic downturn that plagued much of the world's economy in late 2008 and all of 2009 hit Starbucks hard, but the strength of the company's strategy allowed it to rebound and set an earnings record in 2010. The company set new earnings records in 2011 and 2012 and was expected to record all-time high revenues and net earnings in fiscal 2013. The key elements of Starbucks' strategy in specialty coffees included:

- **Emphasis on store ambience and elevating the customer experience at Starbucks stores.** Starbucks management viewed each store as a billboard for the company and as a contributor to building the company's brand and image. Each detail was scrutinized to enhance the mood and ambience of the store, to make sure everything signaled "best-of-class" and reflected the personality of the community and the neighborhood. The thesis was "everything mattered." The company went to great lengths to make sure the store fixtures, the merchandise displays, the colors, the artwork, the banners, the music, and the aromas all blended to create a consistent, inviting, stimulating environment that evoked the romance of coffee, that signaled the company's passion for coffee, and that rewarded customers with ceremony, stories, and surprise.

- **Purchase and roast only top-quality coffee beans.** The company purchased only the highest quality arabica beans and carefully roasted coffee to exacting standards of quality and flavor. Starbucks did not use chemicals or artificial flavors when preparing its roasted coffees.

- **Commitment to corporate responsibility.** Starbucks was protective of the environment and contributed positively to the communities where Starbucks stores were located. In addition, Starbucks promoted fair trade practices and paid above-market prices for coffee beans to provide its growers/suppliers with sufficient funding to sustain their operations and provide for their families.

- **Continue the drive to make Starbucks a global brand.** Starbucks had increased its store openings in Latin America, Europe, the Middle East, Africa, and Asia to expand its reach to more than 60 countries in 2013. Most of the company's international locations were operated by partners/licensees that had strong retail and restaurant experience and values that were compatible with Starbucks' corporate culture.

- **Expansion of the number of Starbucks stores domestically and internationally.** Starbucks operated stores in high-traffic, high-visibility locations in the United States and abroad. The company's ability to vary store size and format made it possible to locate stores in settings such as downtown and suburban shopping areas, office buildings, and university campuses. Starbucks added 161 new company-owned locations in the United States and another 237 company-owned stores internationally in fiscal 2012. Starbucks also added 101 licensed store locations in the United States and 275 licensed stores internationally in 2012. The company planned to open 1,650 new stores globally in fiscal 2013, which would include 350 Teavana tea emporiums selling premium loose-leaf teas and tea accessories.

- **Broaden and periodically refresh in-store product offerings.** Noncoffee products offered by Starbucks included teas, fresh pastries and other food items, candy, juice drinks, music CDs, and coffee mugs and coffee accessories.

- **Fully exploit the growing power of the Starbucks name and brand image with out-of-store sales.** Starbucks consumer packaged goods division included domestic and international sales of Frappuccino, coffee ice creams, and Starbucks coffees.

Sources: Company documents, 10-Ks, and information posted on Starbucks' website.

Why a Company's Strategy Evolves over Time

LO4 Understand that a company's strategy tends to evolve over time because of changing circumstances and ongoing management efforts to improve the company's strategy.

The appeal of a strategy that yields a sustainable competitive advantage is that it offers the potential for an enduring edge over rivals. However, managers of every company must be willing and ready to modify the strategy in response to the unexpected moves of competitors, shifting buyer needs and preferences, emerging market opportunities, new ideas for improving the strategy, and mounting evidence that the strategy is not working well. Most of the time, a company's strategy evolves incrementally as management fine-tunes various pieces of the strategy and adjusts the strategy to respond to unfolding events. However, on occasion, major strategy shifts are called for, such as when the strategy is clearly failing or when industry conditions change in dramatic ways.

Regardless of whether a company's strategy changes gradually or swiftly, the important point is that the task of crafting strategy is not a onetime event, but is always a work in progress.[5] The evolving nature of a company's strategy means the typical company strategy is a blend of (1) *proactive* moves to improve the company's financial performance and secure a competitive edge and (2) *adaptive* reactions to unanticipated developments and fresh market conditions—see Figure 1.1.[6] The biggest portion of a company's current strategy flows from ongoing actions that have proven themselves in the marketplace and newly launched initiatives aimed at building a larger lead over rivals and further boosting financial performance. This part of management's action plan for running the company is its proactive, **deliberate strategy**.

> Changing circumstances and ongoing management efforts to improve the strategy cause a company's strategy to evolve over time—a condition that makes the task of crafting a strategy a work in progress, not a onetime event.

At times, certain components of a company's deliberate strategy will fail in the marketplace and become **abandoned strategy elements**. Also, managers must always be willing to supplement or modify planned, deliberate strategy elements with as-needed reactions to unanticipated developments. Inevitably, there will be occasions when market and competitive conditions take unexpected turns that call for some kind of strategic reaction. Novel strategic moves

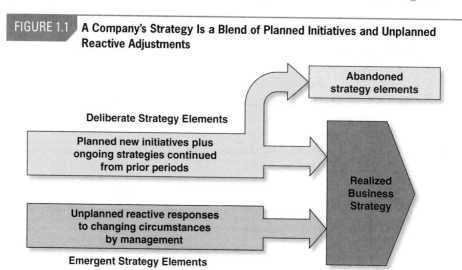

FIGURE 1.1 **A Company's Strategy Is a Blend of Planned Initiatives and Unplanned Reactive Adjustments**

Deliberate Strategy Elements

Planned new initiatives plus ongoing strategies continued from prior periods

Unplanned reactive responses to changing circumstances by management

Emergent Strategy Elements

Abandoned strategy elements

Realized Business Strategy

on the part of rival firms, unexpected shifts in customer preferences, fast-changing technological developments, and new market opportunities call for unplanned, reactive adjustments that form the company's **emergent strategy**. As shown in Figure 1.1, a company's **realized strategy** tends to be a *combination* of deliberate planned elements and unplanned, emergent elements.

> **CORE CONCEPT**
> A company's **realized strategy** is a combination of *deliberate planned elements* and *unplanned, emergent elements*. Some components of a company's deliberate strategy will fail in the marketplace and become *abandoned strategy elements*.

The Three Tests of a Winning Strategy

Three questions can be used to distinguish a winning strategy from a so-so or flawed strategy:

LO5 Learn the three tests of a winning strategy.

1. *How well does the strategy fit the company's situation?* To qualify as a winner, a strategy has to be well matched to the company's external and internal situations. The strategy must fit competitive conditions in the industry and other aspects of the enterprise's external environment. At the same time, it should be tailored to the company's collection of competitively important resources and capabilities. It's unwise to build a strategy upon the company's weaknesses or pursue a strategic approach that requires resources that are deficient in the company. Unless a strategy exhibits tight fit with both the external and internal aspects of a company's overall situation, it is unlikely to produce respectable first-rate business results.

   > A winning strategy must fit the company's external and internal situation, build sustainable competitive advantage, and improve company performance.

2. *Is the strategy helping the company achieve a sustainable competitive advantage?* Strategies that fail to achieve a durable competitive advantage over rivals are unlikely to produce superior performance for more than a brief period of time. Winning strategies enable a company to achieve a competitive advantage over key rivals that is long lasting. The bigger and more durable the competitive edge that the strategy helps build, the more powerful it is.

3. *Is the strategy producing good company performance?* The mark of a winning strategy is strong company performance. Two kinds of performance improvements tell the most about the caliber of a company's strategy: (1) gains in profitability and financial strength and (2) advances in the company's competitive strength and market standing.

   Strategies that come up short on one or more of the above tests are plainly less appealing than strategies passing all three tests with flying colors. Managers should use the same questions when evaluating either proposed or existing strategies. New initiatives that don't seem to match the company's internal and external situation should be scrapped before they come to fruition, while existing strategies must be scrutinized on a regular basis to ensure they have good fit, offer a competitive advantage, and have contributed to above-average performance or performance improvements.

Why Crafting and Executing Strategy Are Important Tasks

High-achieving enterprises are nearly always the product of astute, creative, and proactive strategy making. Companies don't get to the top of the industry rankings or stay there with illogical strategies, copycat strategies, or timid attempts to try to do better. Among all the things managers do, nothing affects a company's ultimate success or failure more fundamentally than how well its management team charts the company's direction, develops competitively effective strategic moves and business approaches, and pursues what needs to be done internally to produce good day-in, day-out strategy execution and operating excellence. Indeed, *good strategy and good strategy execution are the most telling signs of good management.* The rationale for using the twin standards of good strategy making and good strategy execution to determine whether a company is well managed is therefore compelling: *The better conceived a company's strategy and the more competently it is executed, the more likely that the company will be a standout performer in the marketplace.* In stark contrast, a company that lacks clear-cut direction, has a flawed strategy, or can't execute its strategy competently is a company whose financial performance is probably suffering, whose business is at long-term risk, and whose management is sorely lacking.

> How well a company performs is directly attributable to the caliber of its strategy and the proficiency with which the strategy is executed.

The Road Ahead

Throughout the chapters to come and the accompanying case collection, the spotlight is trained on the foremost question in running a business enterprise: *What must managers do, and do well, to make a company a winner in the marketplace?* The answer that emerges is that doing a good job of managing inherently requires good strategic thinking and good management of the strategy formulation, strategy execution process.

The mission of this book is to provide a solid overview of what every business student and aspiring manager needs to know about crafting and executing strategy. We will explore what good strategic thinking entails, describe the core concepts and tools of strategic analysis, and examine the ins and outs of crafting and executing strategy. The accompanying cases will help build your skills in both diagnosing how well the strategy formulation, strategy execution task is being performed and prescribing actions for how the strategy in question or its execution can be improved. The strategic management course that you are enrolled in may also include a strategy simulation exercise where you will run a company in head-to-head competition with companies run by your classmates. Your mastery of the strategic management concepts presented in the following chapters will put you in a strong position to craft a winning strategy for your company and figure out how to execute it in a cost-effective and profitable manner. As you progress through the chapters of the text and the activities assigned during the term, we hope to convince you that first-rate capabilities in crafting and executing strategy are essential to good management.

KEY POINTS

1. A company's strategy is management's game plan to attract and please customers, compete successfully, conduct operations, and achieve targeted levels of performance. The essence of the strategy explains why the company matters to its customers. It outlines an approach to creating superior customer value and determining how capabilities and resources will be utilized to deliver the desired value to customers.

2. Closely related to the concept of strategy is the concept of a company's business model. A company's business model is management's blueprint for delivering customer value in a manner that will generate revenues sufficient to cover costs and yield an attractive profit. The two elements of a company's business model are its (1) customer value proposition and (2) its profit formula.

3. The central thrust of a company's strategy is undertaking moves to build and strengthen the company's long-term competitive position and financial performance by competing differently from rivals and gaining a sustainable competitive advantage over them.

4. A company's strategy typically evolves over time, arising from a blend of (1) proactive and deliberate actions on the part of company managers and (2) adaptive emergent responses to unanticipated developments and fresh market conditions.

5. A winning strategy fits the circumstances of a company's external and internal situations, builds competitive advantage, and boosts company performance.

ASSURANCE OF LEARNING EXERCISES

1. Based on your experiences as a coffee consumer, does Starbucks' strategy as described in Concepts & Connections 1.2 seem to set the company apart from rivals? Does the strategy seem to be keyed to a cost-based advantage, differentiating features, serving the unique needs of a niche, or some combination of these? What is there about Starbucks' strategy that can lead to sustainable competitive advantage?

   LO1, LO3

2. Go to www.nytco.com/investors and check whether *The New York Times'* recent financial reports indicate that its business model is working. Does the company's business model remain sound as more consumers go to the Internet to find general information and stay abreast of current events and news stories? Is its revenue stream from advertisements growing or declining? Are its subscription fees and circulation increasing or declining? Does its cost structure allow for acceptable profit margins?

   LO2

3. Elements of eBay's strategy have evolved in meaningful ways since the company's founding in 1995. After reviewing all of the links at the company's investor relations site, which can be found at investor.ebayinc.com, prepare a one-to two-page report that discusses how its strategy has evolved. Your report should also assess how well eBay's strategy passes the three tests of a winning strategy.

   LO4, LO5

▶ EXERCISES FOR SIMULATION PARTICIPANTS

After you have read the Participant's Guide or Player's Manual for the strategy simulation exercise that you will participate in this academic term, you and your co-managers should come up with brief one- or two-paragraph answers to the questions that follow *before* entering your first set of decisions. While your answers to the first of the four questions can be developed from your reading of the manual, the remaining questions will require a collaborative discussion among the members of your company's management team about how you intend to manage the company you have been assigned to run.

LO5 1. What is your company's current situation? A substantive answer to this question should cover the following issues:

- Does your company appear to be in sound financial condition?
- What problems does your company have that need to be addressed?

LO1, LO3 2. Why will your company matter to customers? A complete answer to this question should say something about each of the following:

- How will you create customer value?
- What will be distinctive about the company's products or services?
- How will capabilities and resources be deployed to deliver customer value?

LO2 3. What are the primary elements of your company's business model?

- Describe your customer value proposition.
- Discuss the profit formula tied to your business model.
- What level of revenues is required for your company's business model to become a moneymaker?

LO3, LO4, LO5 4. How will you build and sustain competitive advantage?

- Which of the basic strategic and competitive approaches discussed in this chapter do you think makes the most sense to pursue?
- What kind of competitive advantage over rivals will you try to achieve?
- How do you envision that your strategy might evolve as you react to the competitive moves of rival firms?
- Does your strategy have the ability to pass the three tests of a winning strategy? Explain.

▶ ENDNOTES

1. Michael E. Porter, "What Is Strategy?" *Harvard Business Review* 74, no. 6 (November–December 1996).
2. Mark W. Johnson, Clayton M. Christensen, and Henning Kagermann, "Reinventing Your Business Model," *Harvard Business Review* 86, no. 12 (December 2008); and Joan Magretta, "Why Business Models Matter," *Harvard Business Review* 80, no. 5 (May 2002).
3. W. Chan Kim and Renée Mauborgne, "How Strategy Shapes Structure," *Harvard Business Review* 87, no. 9 (September 2009).
4. Porter, "What Is Strategy?"
5. Cynthia A. Montgomery, "Putting Leadership Back Into Strategy," *Harvard Business Review* 86, no. 1 (January 2008).
6. Henry Mintzberg and Joseph Lampel, "Reflecting on the Strategy Process," *Sloan Management Review* 40, no. 3 (Spring 1999); Henry Mintzberg and J. A. Waters, "Of Strategies, Deliberate and Emergent," *Strategic Management Journal* 6 (1985); Costas Markides, "Strategy as Balance: From 'Either-Or' to 'And,'" *Business Strategy Review* 12, no. 3 (September 2001); Henry Mintzberg, Bruce Ahlstrand, and Joseph Lampel, *Strategy Safari: A Guided Tour through the Wilds of Strategic Management* (New York: Free Press, 1998); and C. K. Prahalad and Gary Hamel, "The Core Competence of the Corporation," *Harvard Business Review* 70, no. 3 (May–June 1990).

Charting a Company's Direction: Vision and Mission, Objectives, and Strategy

LEARNING OBJECTIVES

LO1 Grasp why it is critical for company managers to have a clear strategic vision of where a company needs to head and why.

LO2 Understand the importance of setting both strategic and financial objectives.

LO3 Understand why the strategic initiatives taken at various organizational levels must be tightly coordinated to achieve companywide performance targets.

LO4 Learn what a company must do to achieve operating excellence and to execute its strategy proficiently.

LO5 Become aware of the role and responsibility of a company's board of directors in overseeing the strategic management process.

Crafting and executing strategy are the heart and soul of managing a business enterprise. But exactly what is involved in developing a strategy and executing it proficiently? What are the various components of the strategy formulation, strategy execution process and to what extent are company personnel—aside from senior management—involved in the process? This chapter presents an overview of the ins and outs of crafting and executing company strategies. Special attention will be given to management's direction-setting responsibilities—charting a strategic course, setting performance targets, and choosing a strategy capable of producing the desired outcomes. We will also explain why strategy formulation is a task for a company's entire management team and discuss which kinds of strategic decisions tend to be made at which levels of management. The chapter concludes with a look at the roles and responsibilities of a company's board of directors and how good corporate governance protects shareholder interests and promotes good management.

What Does the Strategy Formulation, Strategy Execution Process Entail?

The managerial process of crafting and executing a company's strategy is an ongoing, continuous process consisting of five integrated stages:

1. *Developing a strategic vision* that charts the company's long-term direction, a *mission statement* that describes the company's business, and a set of *core values* to guide the pursuit of the strategic vision and mission.
2. *Setting objectives* for measuring the company's performance and tracking its progress in moving in the intended long-term direction.
3. *Crafting a strategy* for advancing the company along the path to management's envisioned future and achieving its performance objectives.
4. *Implementing and executing the chosen strategy* efficiently and effectively.
5. *Evaluating and analyzing the external environment and the company's internal situation and performance* to identify corrective adjustments that are needed in the company's long-term direction, objectives, strategy, or approach to strategy execution.

Figure 2.1 displays this five-stage process. The model illustrates the need for management to evaluate a number of external and internal factors in deciding upon a strategic direction, appropriate objectives, and approaches to crafting and executing strategy (see Table 2.1). Management's decisions that are made in the strategic management process must be shaped by the prevailing economic conditions and competitive environment and the company's own internal resources and competitive capabilities. These strategy-shaping conditions will be the focus of Chapters 3 and 4.

The model shown in Figure 2.1 also illustrates the need for management to evaluate the company's performance on an ongoing basis. Any indication that the company is failing to achieve its objectives calls for corrective adjustments in one of the first four stages of the process. The company's implementation efforts might have fallen short and new tactics must be devised to fully exploit

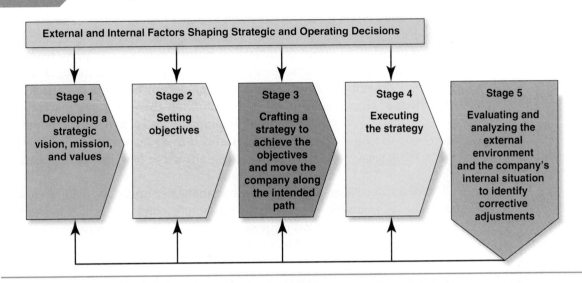

FIGURE 2.1 The Strategy Formulation, Strategy Execution Process

TABLE 2.1

Factors Shaping Decisions in the Strategy Formulation, Strategy Execution Process

External Considerations

- Does sticking with the company's present strategic course present attractive opportunities for growth and profitability?
- What kind of competitive forces are industry members facing and are they acting to enhance or weaken the company's prospects for growth and profitability?
- What factors are driving industry change and what impact on the company's prospects will they have?
- How are industry rivals positioned and what strategic moves are they likely to make next?
- What are the key factors of future competitive success and does the industry offer good prospects for attractive profits for companies possessing those capabilities?

Internal Considerations

- Does the company have an appealing customer value proposition?
- What are the company's competitively important resources and capabilities and are they potent enough to produce a sustainable competitive advantage?
- Does the company have sufficient business and competitive strength to seize market opportunities and nullify external threats?
- Are the company's costs competitive with those of key rivals?
- Is the company competitively stronger or weaker than key rivals?

the potential of the company's strategy. If management determines that the company's execution efforts are sufficient, it should challenge the assumptions underlying the company's business strategy and alter the strategy to better fit competitive conditions and the company's internal capabilities. If the company's strategic approach to competition is rated as sound, then perhaps management set overly ambitious targets for the company's performance.

The evaluation stage of the strategic management process shown in Figure 2.1 also allows for a change in the company's vision, but this should be necessary only when it becomes evident to management that the industry has changed in a significant way that renders its vision obsolete. Such occasions can be referred to as **strategic inflection points.** When a company reaches a strategic inflection point, management has tough decisions to make about the company's direction because abandoning an established course carries considerable risk. However, responding to unfolding changes in the marketplace in a timely fashion lessens a company's chances of becoming trapped in a stagnant or declining business or letting attractive new growth opportunities slip away.

> A company's **strategic plan** lays out its future direction, performance targets, and strategy.

The first three stages of the strategic management process make up a strategic plan. A **strategic plan** maps out where a company is headed, establishes strategic and financial targets, and outlines the competitive moves and approaches to be used in achieving the desired business results.[1]

Stage 1: Developing a Strategic Vision, a Mission, and Core Values

LO1 Grasp why it is critical for company managers to have a clear strategic vision of where a company needs to head and why.

At the outset of the strategy formulation, strategy execution process, a company's senior managers must wrestle with the issue of what directional path the company should take and whether its market positioning and future performance prospects could be improved by changing the company's product offerings and/or the markets in which it participates and/or the customers it caters to and/or the technologies it employs. Top management's views about the company's direction and future product-customer-market-technology focus constitute a **strategic vision** for the company. A clearly articulated strategic vision communicates management's aspirations to stakeholders about "where we are going" and helps steer the energies of company personnel in a common direction. For instance, Henry Ford's vision of a car in every garage had power because it captured the imagination of others, aided internal efforts to mobilize the Ford Motor Company's resources, and served as a reference point for gauging the merits of the company's strategic actions.

> **CORE CONCEPT**
>
> A **strategic vision** describes "where we are going"—the course and direction management has charted and the company's future product-customer-market-technology focus.

Well-conceived visions are *distinctive* and *specific* to a particular organization; they avoid generic, feel-good statements like "We will become a global leader and the first choice of customers in every market we choose to serve"—which could apply to any of hundreds of organizations.[2] And they are not the product of a committee charged with coming up with an innocuous but well-meaning one-sentence vision that wins consensus approval from various stakeholders. Nicely worded vision statements with no specifics about the company's product-market-customer-technology focus fall well short of what it takes for a vision to measure up.

For a strategic vision to function as a valuable managerial tool, it must provide understanding of what management wants its business to look like and provide managers with a reference point in making strategic decisions. It must say something definitive about how the company's leaders intend to position the company beyond where it is today. Table 2.2 lists some characteristics of effective vision statements.

A surprising number of the vision statements found on company websites and in annual reports are vague and unrevealing, saying very little about the company's future product-market-customer-technology focus. Some could apply to most any company in any industry. Many read like a public relations statement—lofty words that someone came up with because it is fashionable for companies to have an official vision statement.[3] Table 2.3

TABLE 2.2

Characteristics of Effectively Worded Vision Statements

Graphic—Paints a picture of the kind of company that management is trying to create and the market position(s) the company is striving to stake out.

Directional—Is forward-looking; describes the strategic course that management has charted and the kinds of product-market-customer-technology changes that will help the company prepare for the future.

Focused—Is specific enough to provide managers with guidance in making decisions and allocating resources.

Flexible—Is not so focused that it makes it difficult for management to adjust to changing circumstances in markets, customer preferences, or technology.

Feasible—Is within the realm of what the company can reasonably expect to achieve.

Desirable—Indicates why the directional path makes good business sense.

Easy to communicate—Is explainable in 5 to 10 minutes and, ideally, can be reduced to a simple, memorable "slogan" (like Henry Ford's famous vision of "a car in every garage").

Source: Based partly on John P. Kotter, *Leading Change* (Boston: Harvard Business School Press, 1996), p. 72.

TABLE 2.3

Common Shortcomings in Company Vision Statements

Vague or incomplete—Short on specifics about where the company is headed or what the company is doing to prepare for the future.

Not forward-looking—Doesn't indicate whether or how management intends to alter the company's current product-market-customer-technology focus.

Too broad—So all-inclusive that the company could head in most any direction, pursue most any opportunity, or enter most any business.

Bland or uninspiring—Lacks the power to motivate company personnel or inspire shareholder confidence about the company's direction.

Not distinctive—Provides no unique company identity; could apply to companies in any of several industries (including rivals operating in the same market arena).

Too reliant on superlatives—Doesn't say anything specific about the company's strategic course beyond the pursuit of such distinctions as being a recognized leader, a global or worldwide leader, or the first choice of customers.

Sources: Based on information in Hugh Davidson, *The Committed Enterprise* (Oxford: Butterworth Heinemann, 2002), chap. 2; and Michel Robert, *Strategy Pure and Simple II* (New York: McGraw-Hill, 1998), chaps. 2, 3, and 6.

provides a list of the most common shortcomings in company vision statements. Like any tool, vision statements can be used properly or improperly, either clearly conveying a company's strategic course or not. Concepts & Connections 2.1 provides a critique of the strategic visions of several prominent companies.

The Importance of Communicating the Strategic Vision

A strategic vision has little value to the organization unless it's effectively communicated down the line to lower-level managers and employees. It would be difficult for a vision statement to provide direction to decision makers and energize employees toward achieving long-term strategic intent unless they know of the vision and observe management's commitment to that vision. Communicating the vision to organization members nearly always means putting "where we are going and why" in writing, distributing the statement organization-wide, and having executives personally explain the vision and its rationale to as many people as feasible. Ideally, executives should present their vision for the company in a manner that reaches out and grabs people's attention. An engaging and convincing strategic vision has enormous motivational value—for the same reason that a stonemason is inspired by building a great cathedral for the ages. Therefore, an executive's ability to paint a convincing and inspiring picture of a company's journey to a future destination is an important element of effective strategic leadership.[4]

Expressing the Essence of the Vision in a Slogan

The task of effectively conveying the vision to company personnel is assisted when management can capture the vision of where to head in a catchy or easily remembered slogan. A number of organizations have summed up their vision in a brief phrase. Nike's vision slogan is "To bring innovation and inspiration to every athlete in the world." The Mayo Clinic's vision is to provide "The best care to every patient every day," while Greenpeace's envisioned future is "To halt environmental abuse and promote environmental solutions." Creating a short slogan to illuminate an organization's direction and then using it repeatedly as a reminder of "where we are headed and why" helps rally organization members to hurdle whatever obstacles lie in the company's path and maintain their focus.

> An effectively communicated vision is a valuable management tool for enlisting the commitment of company personnel to engage in actions that move the company in the intended direction.

Why a Sound, Well-Communicated Strategic Vision Matters

A well-thought-out, forcefully communicated strategic vision pays off in several respects: (1) it crystallizes senior executives' own views about the firm's long-term direction; (2) it reduces the risk of rudderless decision making by management at all levels; (3) it is a tool for winning the support of employees to help make the vision a reality; (4) it provides a beacon for lower-level managers in forming departmental missions; and (5) it helps an organization prepare for the future.

CONCEPTS & CONNECTIONS 2.1

EXAMPLES OF STRATEGIC VISIONS—HOW WELL DO THEY MEASURE UP?

Vision Statement	Effective Elements	Shortcomings
Coca-Cola Our vision serves as the framework for our roadmap and guides every aspect of our business by describing what we need to accomplish in order to continue achieving sustainable, quality growth. • People: Be a great place to work where people are inspired to be the best they can be. • Portfolio: Bring to the world a portfolio of quality beverage brands that anticipate and satisfy people's desires and needs. • Partners: Nurture a winning network of customers and suppliers; together we create mutual, enduring value. • Planet: Be a responsible citizen that makes a difference by helping build and support sustainable communities. • Profit: Maximize long-term return to shareowners while being mindful of our overall responsibilities. • Productivity: Be a highly effective, lean and fast-moving organization.	• Focused • Flexible • Feasible • Desirable	• Long • Not forward-looking
UBS We are determined to be the best global financial services company. We focus on wealth and asset management, and on investment banking and securities businesses. We continually earn recognition and trust from clients, shareholders, and staff through our ability to anticipate, learn and shape our future. We share a common ambition to succeed by delivering quality in what we do. Our purpose is to help our clients make financial decisions with confidence. We use our resources to develop effective solutions and services for our clients. We foster a distinctive, meritocratic culture of ambition, performance and learning as this attracts, retains and develops the best talent for our company. By growing both our client and our talent franchises, we add sustainable value for our shareholders.	• Focused • Feasible • Desirable	• Not forward-looking • Bland or uninspiring
Heinz We define a compelling, sustainable future and create the path to achieve it.	• Directional • Flexible	• Bland and uninspiring • Too broad • Vague • Not distinctive
Procter & Gamble We will provide branded products and services of superior quality and value that improve the lives of the world's consumers, now and for generations to come. As a result, consumers will reward us with leadership sales, profit and value creation, allowing our people, our shareholders, and the communities in which we live and work to prosper.	• Directional • Flexible • Desirable	• Too broad • Too reliant on superlatives

Sources: Company documents and websites.

Developing a Company Mission Statement

The defining characteristic of a well-conceived **strategic vision** is what it says about the company's *future strategic course—"where we are headed and what our future product-customer-market-technology focus will be."* The **mission statements** of most companies say much more about the enterprise's *present* business scope and purpose—"who we are, what we do, and why we are here." Very few mission statements are forward-looking in content or emphasis. Consider, for example, the mission statement of Trader Joe's (a specialty grocery chain):

> The distinction between a **strategic vision** and a **mission statement** is fairly clear-cut: A strategic vision portrays a company's *future business scope* ("where we are going") whereas a company's mission statement typically describes its *present business and purpose* ("who we are, what we do, and why we are here").

The mission of Trader Joe's is to give our customers the best food and beverage values that they can find anywhere and to provide them with the information required for informed buying decisions. We provide these with a dedication to the highest quality of customer satisfaction delivered with a sense of warmth, friendliness, fun, individual pride, and company spirit.

Note that Trader Joe's mission statement does a good job of conveying "who we are, what we do, and why we are here," but it provides no sense of "where we are headed."

An example of a well-stated mission statement with ample specifics about what the organization does is that of the Occupational Safety and Health Administration (OSHA): "to assure the safety and health of America's workers by setting and enforcing standards; providing training, outreach, and education; establishing partnerships; and encouraging continual improvement in workplace safety and health." Google's mission statement, while short, still captures the essence of what the company is about: "to organize the world's information and make it universally accessible and useful." An example of a not-so-revealing mission statement is that of Microsoft. "To help people and businesses throughout the world realize their full potential" says nothing about its products or business makeup and could apply to many companies in many different industries. A well-conceived mission statement should employ language specific enough to give the company its own identity. A mission statement that provides scant indication of "who we are and what we do" has no apparent value.

> **CORE CONCEPT**
>
> A well-conceived **mission statement** conveys a company's purpose in language specific enough to give the company its own identity.

Ideally, a company mission statement is sufficiently descriptive to:

- Identify the company's products or services.
- Specify the buyer needs it seeks to satisfy.
- Specify the customer groups or markets it is endeavoring to serve.
- Specify its approach to pleasing customers.
- Give the company its own identity.

Occasionally, companies state that their mission is to simply earn a profit. This is misguided. Profit is more correctly an *objective* and a *result* of what a company does. Moreover, earning a profit is the obvious intent of every commercial enterprise. Such companies as BMW, Netflix, Shell Oil, Procter & Gamble, Google, and McDonald's are each striving to earn a profit for shareholders, but the fundamentals of their businesses are substantially different when it comes to "who we are and what we do."

Linking the Strategic Vision and Mission with Company Values

Many companies have developed a statement of **values** (sometimes called *core values*) to guide the actions and behavior of company personnel in conducting the company's business and pursuing its strategic vision and mission. These values are the designated beliefs and desired ways of doing things at the company and frequently relate to such things as fair treatment, honor and integrity, ethical behavior, innovativeness, teamwork, a passion for excellence, social responsibility, and community citizenship.

> **CORE CONCEPT**
>
> A company's **values** are the beliefs, traits, and behavioral norms that company personnel are expected to display in conducting the company's business and pursuing its strategic vision and mission.

Most companies normally have four to eight core values. At Kodak, the core values are respect for the dignity of the individual, uncompromising integrity, unquestioned trust, constant credibility, continual improvement and personal renewal, and open celebration of individual and team achievements. Home Depot embraces eight values—entrepreneurial spirit, excellent customer service, giving back to the community, respect for all people, doing the right thing, taking care of people, building strong relationships, and creating shareholder value—in its quest to be the world's leading home improvement retailer.

Do companies practice what they preach when it comes to their professed values? Sometimes no, sometimes yes—it runs the gamut. At one extreme are companies with window-dressing values; the professed values are given lip service by top executives but have little discernible impact on either how company personnel behave or how the company operates. At the other extreme are companies whose executives are committed to grounding company operations on sound values and principled ways of doing business. Executives at these companies deliberately seek to ingrain the designated core values into the corporate culture—the core values thus become an integral part of the company's DNA and what makes it tick. At such values-driven companies, executives "walk the talk" and company personnel are held accountable for displaying the stated values. Concepts & Connections 2.2 describes how core values drive the company's mission at Zappos, a widely known and quite successful online shoe and apparel retailer.

Stage 2: Setting Objectives

The managerial purpose of setting **objectives** is to convert the strategic vision into specific performance targets. Objectives reflect management's aspirations for company performance in light of the industry's prevailing economic and competitive conditions and the company's internal capabilities. Well-stated objectives are *quantifiable*, or *measurable*, and contain a *deadline for achievement*. Concrete, measurable objectives are managerially valuable because they serve

LO2 Understand the importance of setting both strategic and financial objectives.

CONCEPTS & CONNECTIONS 2.2

ZAPPOS MISSION AND CORE VALUES

We've been asked by a lot of people how we've grown so quickly, and the answer is actually really simple. . . . We've aligned the entire organization around one mission: *to provide the best customer service possible.* Internally, we call this our **WOW** philosophy.

These are the 10 core values that we live by:

Deliver Wow through Service. At Zappos, anything worth doing is worth doing with WOW. WOW is such a short, simple word, but it really encompasses a lot of things. To WOW, you must differentiate yourself, which means doing something a little unconventional and innovative. You must do something that's above and beyond what's expected. And whatever you do must have an emotional impact on the receiver. We are not an average company, our service is not average, and we don't want our people to be average. We expect every employee to deliver WOW.

Embrace and Drive Change. Part of being in a growing company is that change is constant. For some people, especially those who come from bigger companies, the constant change can be somewhat unsettling at first. If you are not prepared to deal with constant change, then you probably are not a good fit for the company.

Create Fun and a Little Weirdness. At Zappos, We're Always Creating Fun and A Little Weirdness! One of the things that makes Zappos different from a lot of other companies is that we value being fun and being a little weird. We don't want to become one of those big companies that feels corporate and boring. We want to be able to laugh at ourselves. We look for both fun and humor in our daily work.

Be Adventurous, Creative, and Open Minded. At Zappos, we think it's important for people and the company as a whole to be bold and daring (but not reckless). We do not want people to be afraid to take risks and make mistakes. We believe if people aren't making mistakes, then that means they're not taking enough risks. Over time, we want everyone to develop his/her gut about business decisions. We want people to develop and improve their decision-making skills. We encourage people to make mistakes as long as they learn from them.

Pursue Growth and Learning. At Zappos, we think it's important for employees to grow both personally and professionally. It's important to constantly challenge and stretch yourself and not be stuck in a job where you don't feel like you are growing or learning.

Build Open and Honest Relationships with Communication. Fundamentally, we believe that openness and honesty make for the best relationships because that leads to trust and faith. We value strong relationships in all areas: with managers, direct reports, customers (internal and external), vendors, business partners, team members, and co-workers.

Build a Positive Team and Family Spirit. At Zappos, we place a lot of emphasis on our culture because we are both a team and a family. We want to create an environment that is friendly, warm, and exciting. We encourage diversity in ideas, opinions, and points of view.

Do More with Less. Zappos has always been about being able to do more with less. While we may be casual in our interactions with each other, we are focused and serious about the operations of our business. We believe in working hard and putting in the extra effort to get things done.

Be Passionate and Determined. Passion is the fuel that drives us and our company forward. We value passion, determination, perseverance, and the sense of urgency. We are inspired because we believe in what we are doing and where we are going. We don't take "no" or "that'll never work" for an answer because if we had, then Zappos would have never started in the first place.

Be Humble. While we have grown quickly in the past, we recognize that there are always challenges ahead to tackle. We believe that no matter what happens we should always be respectful of everyone.

Source: Information posted at www.zappos.com, accessed June 6, 2010.

as yardsticks for tracking a company's performance and progress toward its vision. Vague targets such as "maximize profits," "reduce costs," "become more efficient," or "increase sales," which specify neither how much nor when, offer little value as a management tool to improve company performance. Ideally, managers should develop *challenging,* yet *achievable* objectives that *stretch an organization to perform at its full potential.* As Mitchell Leibovitz, former CEO of the auto parts and service retailer Pep Boys, once said, "If you want to have ho-hum results, have ho-hum objectives."

> **CORE CONCEPT**
>
> **Objectives** are an organization's performance targets—the results management wants to achieve.

What Kinds of Objectives to Set

Two very distinct types of performance yardsticks are required: those relating to financial performance and those relating to strategic performance. **Financial objectives** communicate management's targets for financial performance. Common financial objectives relate to revenue growth, profitability, and return on investment. **Strategic objectives** are related to a company's marketing standing and competitive vitality. The importance of attaining financial objectives is intuitive. Without adequate profitability and financial strength, a company's long-term health and ultimate survival is jeopardized. Furthermore, subpar earnings and a weak balance sheet alarm shareholders and creditors and put the jobs of senior executives at risk. However, good financial performance, by itself, is not enough.

> **CORE CONCEPT**
>
> **Financial objectives** relate to the financial performance targets management has established for the organization to achieve.
>
> **Strategic objectives** relate to target outcomes that indicate a company is strengthening its market standing, competitive vitality, and future business prospects.

A company's financial objectives are really *lagging indicators* that reflect the results of past decisions and organizational activities.[5] The results of past decisions and organizational activities are not reliable indicators of a company's future prospects. Companies that have been poor financial performers are sometimes able to turn things around, and good financial performers on occasion fall upon hard times. Hence, the best and most reliable predictors of a company's success in the marketplace and future financial performance are strategic objectives. Strategic outcomes are *leading indicators* of a company's future financial performance and business prospects. The accomplishment of strategic objectives signals the company is well positioned to sustain or improve its performance. For instance, if a company is achieving ambitious strategic objectives, then there's reason to expect that its *future* financial performance will be better than its current or past performance. If a company begins to lose competitive strength and fails to achieve important strategic objectives, then its ability to maintain its present profitability is highly suspect.

Consequently, utilizing a performance measurement system that strikes a *balance* between financial objectives and strategic objectives is optimal.[6] Just tracking a company's financial performance overlooks the fact that what ultimately enables a company to deliver better financial results is the achievement of strategic objectives that improve its competitiveness and market strength.

TABLE 2.4

The Balanced Scorecard Approach to Performance Measurement

Financial Objectives	Strategic Objectives	
• An x percent increase in annual revenues	• Win an x percent market share	• Increase percentage of sales coming from new products to x percent
• Annual increases in earnings per share of x percent	• Achieve customer satisfaction rates of x percent	
• An x percent return on capital employed (ROCE) or shareholder investment (ROE)	• Achieve a customer retention rate of x percent	• Improve information systems capabilities to give frontline managers defect information in x minutes
• Bond and credit ratings of x	• Acquire x number of new customers	
• Internal cash flows of x to fund new capital investment	• Introduce x number of new products in the next three years	• Improve teamwork by increasing the number of projects involving more than one business unit to x
	• Reduce product development times to x months	

Representative examples of financial and strategic objectives that companies often include in a **balanced scorecard** approach to measuring their performance are displayed in Table 2.4.[7]

In 2010, nearly 50 percent of global companies used a balanced scorecard approach to measuring strategic and financial performance.[8] Examples of organizations that have adopted a balanced scorecard approach to setting objectives and measuring performance include SAS Institute, UPS, Ann Taylor Stores, Fort Bragg Army Garrison, Caterpillar, Daimler AG, Hilton Hotels, Susan G. Komen for the Cure, and Siemens AG.[9] Concepts & Connections 2.3 provides selected strategic and financial objectives of three prominent companies.

CORE CONCEPT

The **balanced scorecard** is a widely used method for combining the use of both strategic and financial objectives, tracking their achievement, and giving management a more complete and balanced view of how well an organization is performing.

Short-Term and Long-Term Objectives

A company's set of financial and strategic objectives should include both near-term and long-term performance targets. Short-term objectives focus attention on delivering performance improvements in the current period, while long-term targets force the organization to consider how actions currently under way will affect the company later. Specifically, long-term objectives stand as a barrier to an undue focus on short-term results by nearsighted management. When trade-offs have to be made between achieving long-run and short-run objectives, long-run objectives should take precedence (unless the achievement of one or more short-run performance targets has unique importance).

The Need for Objectives at All Organizational Levels

Objective setting should not stop with the establishment of companywide performance targets. Company objectives need to be broken into performance targets for each of the organization's separate businesses, product lines, functional departments, and individual work units. Employees within various functional areas

CONCEPTS & CONNECTIONS 2.3

EXAMPLES OF COMPANY OBJECTIVES

PEPSICO

Accelerate top-line growth; build and expand our better-for-your snacks and beverages and nutrition businesses; improve our water use efficiency by 20 percent per unit of production by 2015; improve our electricity use efficiency by 20 percent per unit of production by 2015; maintain appropriate financial flexibility with ready access to global capital and credit markets at favorable interest rates.

WALGREENS

Increase revenues from $72 billion in 2012 to more than $130 billion in 2016; increase operating income from $3.5 billion in 2012 to $8.5 billion to $9.0 billion by 2016; increase operating cash flow from $4.4 billion in 2012 to approximately $8 billion in 2016; generate $1 billion in cost savings from combined pharmacy and general merchandise purchasing synergies by 2016.

YUM! BRANDS (KFC, PIZZA HUT, TACO BELL, LONG JOHN SILVER'S)

Increase operating profit derived from operations in emerging markets from 48 percent in 2010 to 57 percent in 2015; increase number of KFC units in Africa from 655 in 2010 to 2,100 in 2020; increase KFC revenues in Africa from $865 million in 2010 to $1.94 billion in 2014; increase number of KFC units in India from 101 in 2010 to 1,250 in 2020; increase number of KFC units in Vietnam from 87 in 2010 to 500 in 2020; increase number of KFC units in Russia from 150 in 2010 to 500 in 2020; open 100+ new Taco Bell units in international markets in 2015; increase annual cash flows from operations from $1.5 billion in 2010 to $2+ billion in 2015.

Source: Information posted on company websites.

and operating levels will be guided much better by narrow objectives relating directly to their departmental activities than broad organizational-level goals. Objective setting is thus a top-down process that must extend to the lowest organizational levels. And it means that each organizational unit must take care to set performance targets that support—rather than conflict with or negate—the achievement of companywide strategic and financial objectives.

Stage 3: Crafting a Strategy

As indicated earlier, the task of stitching a strategy together entails addressing a series of *hows: how* to attract and please customers, *how* to compete against rivals, *how* to position the company in the marketplace and capitalize on attractive opportunities to grow the business, *how* best to respond to changing economic and market conditions, *how* to manage each functional piece of the business, and *how* to achieve the company's performance targets. It also means choosing among the various strategic alternatives and proactively searching for opportunities to do new things or to do existing things in new or better ways.[10]

LO3 Understand why the strategic initiatives taken at various organizational levels must be tightly coordinated to achieve companywide performance targets.

Strategy Formulation Involves Managers at All Organizational Levels

In some enterprises, the CEO or owner functions as strategic visionary and chief architect of the strategy, personally deciding what the key elements of the company's strategy will be, although the CEO may seek the advice of key subordinates in fashioning an overall strategy and deciding on important strategic moves. However, it is a mistake to view strategy making as a *top* management function—the exclusive province of owner-entrepreneurs, CEOs, high-ranking executives, and board members. The more a company's operations cut across different products, industries, and geographical areas, the more that headquarters executives have little option but to delegate considerable strategy-making authority to down-the-line managers. On-the-scene managers who oversee specific operating units are likely to have a more detailed command of the strategic issues and choices for the particular operating unit under their supervision—knowing the prevailing market and competitive conditions, customer requirements and expectations, and all the other relevant aspects affecting the several strategic options available.

> In most companies, crafting strategy is a *collaborative team effort* that includes managers in various positions and at various organizational levels. Crafting strategy is rarely something only high-level executives do.

A Company's Strategy-Making Hierarchy

The larger and more diverse the operations of an enterprise, the more points of strategic initiative it will have and the more managers at different organizational levels will have a relevant strategy-making role. In diversified companies, where multiple and sometimes strikingly different businesses have to be managed, crafting a full-fledged strategy involves four distinct types of strategic actions and initiatives, each undertaken at different levels of the organization and partially or wholly crafted by managers at different organizational levels, as shown in Figure 2.2. A company's overall strategy is therefore *a collection of strategic initiatives and actions* devised by managers up and down the whole organizational hierarchy. Ideally, the pieces of a company's strategy up and down the strategy hierarchy should be cohesive and mutually reinforcing, fitting together like a jigsaw puzzle.

> **Corporate strategy** establishes an overall game plan for managing a *set of businesses* in a diversified, multibusiness company.
>
> **Business strategy** is primarily concerned with strengthening the company's market position and building competitive advantage in a single business company or a single business unit of a diversified multibusiness corporation.

As shown in Figure 2.2, **corporate strategy** is orchestrated by the CEO and other senior executives and establishes an overall game plan for managing a *set of businesses* in a diversified, multibusiness company. Corporate strategy addresses the questions of how to capture cross-business synergies, what businesses to hold or divest, which new markets to enter, and how to best enter new markets—by acquisition, by creation of a strategic alliance, or through internal development. Corporate strategy and business diversification are the subject of Chapter 8, where they are discussed in detail.

Business strategy is primarily concerned with building competitive advantage in a single business unit of a diversified company or strengthening the market position of a nondiversified single business company. Business strategy is also the responsibility of the CEO and other senior executives, but key business-unit heads may also be influential, especially in strategic decisions

FIGURE 2.2   **A Company's Strategy-Making Hierarchy**

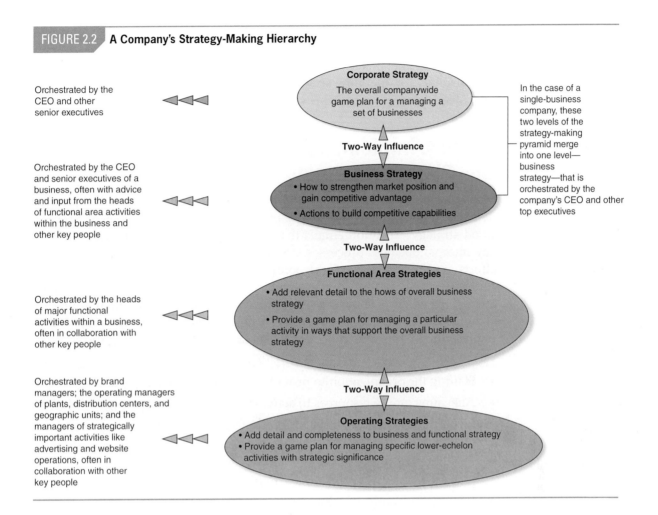

Orchestrated by the CEO and other senior executives

Corporate Strategy
The overall companywide game plan for a managing a set of businesses

In the case of a single-business company, these two levels of the strategy-making pyramid merge into one level—business strategy—that is orchestrated by the company's CEO and other top executives

Two-Way Influence

Orchestrated by the CEO and senior executives of a business, often with advice and input from the heads of functional area activities within the business and other key people

Business Strategy
• How to strengthen market position and gain competitive advantage
• Actions to build competitive capabilities

Two-Way Influence

Orchestrated by the heads of major functional activities within a business, often in collaboration with other key people

Functional Area Strategies
• Add relevant detail to the hows of overall business strategy
• Provide a game plan for managing a particular activity in ways that support the overall business strategy

Two-Way Influence

Orchestrated by brand managers; the operating managers of plants, distribution centers, and geographic units; and the managers of strategically important activities like advertising and website operations, often in collaboration with other key people

Operating Strategies
• Add detail and completeness to business and functional strategy
• Provide a game plan for managing specific lower-echelon activities with strategic significance

affecting the businesses they lead. *In single-business companies, the corporate and business levels of the strategy-making hierarchy merge into a single level—business strategy—because the strategy for the entire enterprise involves only one distinct business.* So, a single-business company has three levels of strategy: business strategy, functional-area strategies, and operating strategies.

Functional-area strategies concern the actions related to particular functions or processes within a business. A company's product development strategy, for example, represents the managerial game plan for creating new products that are in tune with what buyers are looking for. Lead responsibility for functional strategies within a business is normally delegated to the heads of the respective functions, with the general manager of the business having final approval over functional strategies. For the overall business strategy to have maximum impact, a company's marketing strategy, production strategy, finance strategy, customer service strategy, product development strategy, and human resources strategy should be compatible and mutually reinforcing rather than each serving its own narrower purpose.

Operating strategies concern the relatively narrow strategic initiatives and approaches for managing key operating units (plants, distribution centers, geographic units) and specific operating activities such as materials purchasing or Internet sales. Operating strategies are limited in scope, but add further detail to functional-area strategies and the overall business strategy. Lead responsibility for operating strategies is usually delegated to frontline managers, subject to review and approval by higher-ranking managers.

Stage 4: Implementing and Executing the Chosen Strategy

LO4 Learn what a company must do to achieve operating excellence and to execute its strategy proficiently.

Managing the implementation and execution of strategy is easily the most demanding and time-consuming part of the strategic management process. Good strategy execution entails that managers pay careful attention to how key internal business processes are performed and see to it that employees' efforts are directed toward the accomplishment of desired operational outcomes. The task of implementing and executing the strategy also necessitates an ongoing analysis of the efficiency and effectiveness of a company's internal activities and a managerial awareness of new technological developments that might improve business processes. In most situations, managing the strategy execution process includes the following principal aspects:

- Staffing the organization to provide needed skills and expertise.
- Allocating ample resources to activities critical to good strategy execution.
- Ensuring that policies and procedures facilitate rather than impede effective execution.
- Installing information and operating systems that enable company personnel to perform essential activities.
- Pushing for continuous improvement in how value chain activities are performed.
- Tying rewards and incentives directly to the achievement of performance objectives.
- Creating a company culture and work climate conducive to successful strategy execution.
- Exerting the internal leadership needed to propel implementation forward.

Stage 5: Evaluating Performance and Initiating Corrective Adjustments

The fifth stage of the strategy management process—evaluating and analyzing the external environment and the company's internal situation and performance to identify needed corrective adjustments—is the trigger point for deciding whether to continue or change the company's vision, objectives, strategy, and/or strategy execution methods. So long as the company's direction and strategy seem well matched to industry and competitive conditions and performance targets are being met, company executives may well decide to stay the course. Simply fine-tuning the strategic plan and continuing with efforts to improve strategy execution are sufficient.

But whenever a company encounters disruptive changes in its environment, questions need to be raised about the appropriateness of its direction and strategy. If a company experiences a downturn in its market position or persistent shortfalls in performance, then company managers are obligated to ferret out the causes—do they relate to poor strategy, poor strategy execution, or both?—and take timely corrective action. A company's direction, objectives, and strategy have to be revisited any time external or internal conditions warrant.

> A company's vision, objectives, strategy, and approach to strategy execution are never final; managing strategy is an ongoing process, not an every-now-and-then task.

Also, it is not unusual for a company to find that one or more aspects of its strategy implementation and execution are not going as well as intended. Proficient strategy execution is always the product of much organizational learning. It is achieved unevenly—coming quickly in some areas and proving nettlesome in others. Successful strategy execution entails vigilantly searching for ways to improve and then making corrective adjustments whenever and wherever it is useful to do so.

Corporate Governance: The Role of the Board of Directors in the Strategy Formulation, Strategy Execution Process

Although senior managers have *lead responsibility* for crafting and executing a company's strategy, it is the duty of the board of directors to exercise strong oversight and see that the five tasks of strategic management are done in a manner that benefits shareholders (in the case of investor-owned enterprises) or stakeholders (in the case of not-for-profit organizations). In watching over management's strategy formulation, strategy execution actions, a company's board of directors has four important corporate governance obligations to fulfill:

LO5 Become aware of the role and responsibility of a company's board of directors in overseeing the strategic management process.

1. *Oversee the company's financial accounting and financial reporting practices.* While top management, particularly the company's CEO and CFO (chief financial officer), is primarily responsible for seeing that the company's financial statements accurately report the results of the company's operations, board members have a fiduciary duty to protect shareholders by exercising oversight of the company's financial practices. In addition, corporate boards must ensure that generally acceptable accounting principles (GAAP) are properly used in preparing the company's financial statements and determine whether proper financial controls are in place to prevent fraud and misuse of funds. Virtually all boards of directors monitor the financial reporting activities by appointing an audit committee, always composed entirely of *outside directors* (*inside directors* hold management positions in the company and either directly or indirectly report to the CEO). The members of the audit committee have lead responsibility

for overseeing the decisions of the company's financial officers and consulting with both internal and external auditors to ensure that financial reports are accurate and adequate financial controls are in place. Faulty oversight of corporate accounting and financial reporting practices by audit committees and corporate boards during the early 2000s resulted in the federal investigation of more than 20 major corporations between 2000 and 2002. The investigations of such well-known companies as AOL Time Warner, Global Crossing, Enron, Qwest Communications, and WorldCom found that upper management had employed fraudulent or unsound accounting practices to artificially inflate revenues, overstate assets, and reduce expenses. The scandals resulted in the conviction of a number of corporate executives and the passage of the Sarbanes-Oxley Act of 2002, which tightened financial reporting standards and created additional compliance requirements for public boards.

2. *Diligently critique and oversee the company's direction, strategy, and business approaches.* Even though board members have a legal obligation to warrant the accuracy of the company's financial reports, directors must set aside time to guide management in choosing a strategic direction and to make independent judgments about the validity and wisdom of management's proposed strategic actions. Many boards have found that meeting agendas become consumed by compliance matters and little time is left to discuss matters of strategic importance. The board of directors and management at Philips Electronics hold annual two- to three-day retreats devoted to evaluating the company's long-term direction and various strategic proposals. The company's exit from the semiconductor business and its increased focus on medical technology and home health care resulted from management–board discussions during such retreats.[11]

3. *Evaluate the caliber of senior executives' strategy formulation and strategy execution skills.* The board is always responsible for determining whether the current CEO is doing a good job of strategic leadership and whether senior management is actively creating a pool of potential successors to the CEO and other top executives.[12] Evaluation of senior executives' strategy formulation and strategy execution skills is enhanced when outside directors go into the field to personally evaluate how well the strategy is being executed. Independent board members at GE visit operating executives at each major business unit once per year to assess the company's talent pool and stay abreast of emerging strategic and operating issues affecting the company's divisions. Home Depot board members visit a store once per quarter to determine the health of the company's operations.[13]

4. *Institute a compensation plan for top executives that rewards them for actions and results that serve shareholder interests.* A basic principle of corporate governance is that the owners of a corporation delegate operating authority and managerial control to top management in return for compensation. In their role as an *agent* of shareholders, top executives have a clear and unequivocal duty to make decisions and operate the company in

CONCEPTS & CONNECTIONS 2.4

CORPORATE GOVERNANCE FAILURES AT FANNIE MAE AND FREDDIE MAC

Executive compensation in the financial services industry during the mid-2000s ranks high among examples of failed corporate governance. Corporate governance at the government-sponsored mortgage giants Fannie Mae and Freddie Mac was particularly weak. The politically appointed boards at both enterprises failed to understand the risks of the sub-prime loan strategies being employed, did not adequately monitor the decisions of the CEO, did not exercise effective oversight of the accounting principles being employed (which led to inflated earnings), and approved executive compensation systems that allowed management to manipulate earnings to receive lucrative performance bonuses. The audit and compensation committees at Fannie Mae were particularly ineffective in protecting shareholder interests, with the audit committee allowing the government-sponsored enterprise's financial officers to audit reports prepared under their direction and used to determine performance bonuses. Fannie Mae's audit committee also was aware of management's use of questionable accounting practices that reduced losses and recorded onetime gains to achieve EPS targets linked to bonuses. In addition, the audit committee failed to investigate formal charges of accounting improprieties filed by a manager in the Office of the Controller.

Fannie Mae's compensation committee was equally ineffective. The committee allowed the company's CEO, Franklin Raines, to select the consultant employed to design the mortgage firm's executive compensation plan and agreed to a tiered bonus plan that would permit Raines and other senior managers to receive maximum bonuses without great difficulty. The compensation plan allowed Raines to earn performance-based bonuses of $52 million and total compensation of $90 million between 1999 and 2004. Raines was forced to resign in December 2004 when the Office of Federal Housing Enterprise Oversight found that Fannie Mae

executives had fraudulently inflated earnings to receive bonuses linked to financial performance. Securities and Exchange Commission investigators also found evidence of improper accounting at Fannie Mae and required it to restate its earnings between 2002 and 2004 by $6.3 billion.

Poor governance at Freddie Mac allowed its CEO and senior management to manipulate financial data to receive performance-based compensation as well. Freddie Mac CEO Richard Syron received 2007 compensation of $19.8 million while the mortgage company's share price declined from a high of $70 in 2005 to $25 at year-end 2007. During Syron's tenure as CEO the company became embroiled in a multibillion-dollar accounting scandal, and Syron personally disregarded internal reports dating to 2004 that warned of an impending financial crisis at the company. Forewarnings within Freddie Mac and by federal regulators and outside industry observers proved to be correct, with loan underwriting policies at Freddie Mac and Fannie Mae leading to combined losses at the two firms in 2008 of more than $100 billion. The price of Freddie Mac's shares had fallen to below $1 by Syron's resignation in September 2008.

Both organizations were placed into a conservatorship under the direction of the U.S. government in September 2008 and were provided bailout funds of nearly $200 billion by 2013.

Sources: Chris Isidore, "Fannie, Freddie Bailout: $153 Billion . . . and Counting," *CNNMoney*, February 11, 2011; "Adding Up the Government's Total Bailout Tab," *The New York Times Online*, February 4, 2009; Eric Dash, "Fannie Mae to Restate Results by $6.3 Billion Because of Accounting," *The New York Times Online*, www.nytimes.com, December 7, 2006; Annys Shin, "Fannie Mae Sets Executive Salaries," *The Washington Post*, February 9, 2006, p. D4; and Scott DeCarlo, Eric Weiss, Mark Jickling, and James R. Cristie, *Fannie Mae and Freddie Mac: Scandal in U.S. Housing.* (Hauppauge, NY: Nova Publishers, 2006), pp. 266–86.

accord with shareholder interests (but this does not mean disregarding the interests of other stakeholders, particularly those of employees, with whom they also have an agency relationship). Most boards of directors have a compensation committee, composed entirely of directors from outside the company, to develop a salary and incentive compensation plan that rewards senior executives for boosting the company's *long-term* performance and growing the economic value of the enterprise on behalf of shareholders; the compensation committee's recommendations are presented to the full board for approval. But during the past 10 to 15 years, many boards of directors have done a poor job of ensuring that executive salary increases, bonuses, and stock option awards are tied tightly to performance measures that are truly in the long-term interests of shareholders. Rather, compensation packages at many companies have increasingly rewarded executives for short-term performance improvements—most notably, achieving quarterly and annual earnings targets and boosting the stock price by specified percentages. This has had the perverse effect of causing company managers to become preoccupied with actions to improve a company's near-term performance, often motivating them to take unwise business risks to boost short-term earnings by amounts sufficient to qualify for multimillion-dollar bonuses and stock option awards (that, in the view of many people, were obscenely large). The greater weight being placed on short-term performance improvements has worked against shareholders since, in many cases, the excessive risk-taking has proved damaging to long-term company performance—witness the huge loss of shareholder wealth that occurred at many financial institutions in 2008–2009 because of executive risk-taking in subprime loans, credit default swaps, and collateralized mortgage securities in 2006–2007. As a consequence, the need to overhaul and reform executive compensation has become a hot topic in both public circles and corporate boardrooms. Concepts & Connections 2.4 discusses how weak governance at Fannie Mae and Freddie Mac allowed opportunistic senior managers to secure exorbitant bonuses, while making decisions that imperiled the futures of the companies they managed.

Every corporation should have a strong, independent board of directors that (1) is well informed about the company's performance, (2) guides and judges the CEO and other top executives, (3) has the courage to curb management actions it believes are inappropriate or unduly risky, (4) certifies to shareholders that the CEO is doing what the board expects, (5) provides insight and advice to management, and (6) is intensely involved in debating the pros and cons of key decisions and actions.[14] Boards of directors that lack the backbone to challenge a strong-willed or "imperial" CEO or that rubber-stamp most anything the CEO recommends without probing inquiry and debate abandon their duty to represent and protect shareholder interests.

KEY POINTS

The strategic management process consists of five interrelated and integrated stages:

1. *Developing a strategic vision* of where the company needs to head and what its future product-customer-market-technology focus should be. This managerial step provides long-term direction, infuses the organization with a sense of purposeful action, and communicates to stakeholders management's aspirations for the company.

2. *Setting objectives* and using the targeted results as yardsticks for measuring the company's performance. Objectives need to spell out *how much* of *what kind* of performance *by when*. A *balanced scorecard* approach for measuring company performance entails setting both *financial objectives and strategic objectives.*

3. *Crafting a strategy to achieve the objectives* and move the company along the strategic course that management has charted. The total strategy that emerges is really a collection of strategic actions and business approaches initiated partly by senior company executives, partly by the heads of major business divisions, partly by functional-area managers, and partly by operating managers on the frontlines. A single business enterprise has three levels of strategy—business strategy for the company as a whole, functional-area strategies for each main area within the business, and operating strategies undertaken by lower-echelon managers. In diversified, multibusiness companies, the strategy-making task involves four distinct types or levels of strategy: corporate strategy for the company as a whole, business strategy (one for each business the company has diversified into), functional-area strategies within each business, and operating strategies. Typically, the strategy-making task is more top-down than bottom-up, with higher-level strategies serving as the guide for developing lower-level strategies.

4. *Implementing and executing the chosen strategy efficiently and effectively.* Managing the implementation and execution of strategy is an operations-oriented, make-things-happen activity aimed at shaping the performance of core business activities in a strategy supportive manner. Management's handling of the strategy implementation process can be considered successful if things go smoothly enough that the company meets or beats its strategic and financial performance targets and shows good progress in achieving management's strategic vision.

5. *Evaluating and analyzing the external environment and the company's internal situation and performance to identify corrective adjustments* in vision, objectives, strategy, or execution. This stage of the strategy management process is the trigger point for deciding whether to continue or change the company's vision, objectives, strategy, and/or strategy execution methods.

The sum of a company's strategic vision, objectives, and strategy constitutes a *strategic plan.*

Boards of directors have a duty to shareholders to play a vigilant role in overseeing management's handling of a company's strategy formulation, strategy execution process. A company's board is obligated to (1) ensure that the company issues accurate financial reports and has adequate financial controls, (2) critically appraise and ultimately approve strategic action plans, (3) evaluate the strategic leadership skills of the CEO, and (4) institute a compensation plan for top executives that rewards them for actions and results that serve stakeholder interests, most especially those of shareholders.

ASSURANCE OF LEARNING EXERCISES

1. Using the information in Tables 2.2 and 2.3, critique the adequacy and merit of the following vision statements, listing effective elements and shortcomings. Rank the vision statements from best to worst once you complete your evaluation.

LO1

 connect

Wells Fargo

We want to satisfy all of our customers' financial needs, help them succeed financially, be the premier provider of financial services in every one of our markets, and be known as one of America's great companies.

Hilton Hotels Corporation

Our vision is to be the first choice of the world's travelers. Hilton intends to build on the rich heritage and strength of our brands by:

- Consistently delighting our customers
- Investing in our team members
- Delivering innovative products and services
- Continuously improving performance
- Increasing shareholder value
- Creating a culture of pride
- Strengthening the loyalty of our constituents

BASF

We are "The Chemical Company" successfully operating in all major markets.

- Our customers view BASF as their partner of choice.
- Our innovative products, intelligent solutions and services make us the most competent worldwide supplier in the chemical industry.
- We generate a high return on assets.
- We strive for sustainable development.
- We welcome change as an opportunity.
- We, the employees of BASF, together ensure our success.

Source: Company websites and annual reports.

LO2 2. Go to the company investor relations websites for ExxonMobil (ir.exxonmobil.com), Pfizer (www.pfizer.com/investors), and Intel (www.intc.com) to find examples of strategic and financial objectives. List four objectives for each company and indicate which of these are strategic and which are financial.

LO3 3. American Airlines' Chapter 11 reorganization plan filed in 2012 involved the company reducing operating expenses by $2 billion, while increasing revenues by $1 billion. The company's strategy to increase revenues included expanding the number of international flights and destinations and increasing daily departures for its five largest markets by 20 percent. The company also intended to upgrade its fleet by spending $2 billion to purchase new aircraft and refurbish the first-class cabins for planes not replaced. A final component of the restructuring plan included a merger with US Airways to create a global airline with more than 56,700 daily flights to 336 destinations in 56 countries. The merger was expected to produce cost savings from synergies of more than $1 billion and result in a stronger airline capable of paying creditors and rewarding employees and shareholders. Explain why the strategic initiatives at various organizational levels and functions require tight coordination to achieve the results desired by American Airlines.

4. Go to the investor relations website for Wal-Mart Stores, Inc., (http://investors. walmartstores.com) and review past presentations it has made during various investor conferences by clicking on the Events option in the navigation bar. Prepare a one- to two-page report that outlines what Wal-Mart has said to investors about its approach to strategy execution. Specifically, what has management discussed concerning staffing, resource allocation, policies and procedures, information and operating systems, continuous improvement, rewards and incentives, corporate culture, and internal leadership at the company? **LO4**

5. Based on the information provided in Concepts & Connections 2.4, explain how corporate governance at Freddie Mac failed the enterprise's shareholders and other stakeholders. Which important obligations to shareholders were fulfilled by Fannie Mae's board of directors? What is your assessment of how well Fannie Mae's compensation committee handled executive compensation at the government-sponsored mortgage giant? **LO5**

McGraw Hill connect

EXERCISES FOR SIMULATION PARTICIPANTS

1. Meet with your co-managers and prepare a strategic vision statement for your company. It should be at least one sentence long and no longer than a brief paragraph. When you are finished, check to see if your vision statement meets the conditions for an effectively worded strategic vision set forth in Table 2.2 and avoids the shortcomings set forth in Table 2.3. If not, then revise it accordingly. What would be a good slogan that captures the essence of your strategic vision and that could be used to help communicate the vision to company personnel, shareholders, and other stakeholders? **LO1**

2. What are your company's financial objectives? What are your company's strategic objectives? **LO2**

3. What are the three or four key elements of your company's strategy? **LO3**

ENDNOTES

1. Gordon Shaw, Robert Brown, and Philip Bromiley, "Strategic Stories: How 3M Is Rewriting Business Planning," *Harvard Business Review* 76, no. 3 (May–June 1998); and David J. Collins and Michael G. Rukstad, "Can You Say What Your Strategy Is?" *Harvard Business Review* 86, no. 4 (April 2008).

2. Hugh Davidson, *The Committed Enterprise: How to Make Vision and Values Work* (Oxford: Butterworth Heinemann, 2002); W. Chan Kim and Renée Mauborgne, "Charting Your Company's Future," *Harvard Business Review* 80, no. 6 (June 2002); James C. Collins and Jerry I. Porras, "Building Your Company's Vision," *Harvard Business Review* 74, no. 5 (September–October 1996); Jim Collins and Jerry Porras, *Built to Last: Successful Habits of Visionary Companies* (New York: HarperCollins, 1994); Michel Robert, *Strategy Pure and Simple II: How Winning Companies Dominate Their Competitors* (New York: McGraw-Hill, 1998).

3. Hugh Davidson, *The Committed Enterprise* (Oxford: Butterworth Heinemann, 2002).

4. Ibid.

5. Robert S. Kaplan and David P. Norton, *The Strategy-Focused Organization* (Boston: Harvard Business School Press, 2001).

6. Ibid. Also, see Robert S. Kaplan and David P. Norton, *The Balanced Scorecard: Translating Strategy into Action* (Boston: Harvard Business School Press, 1996); Kevin B. Hendricks,

Larry Menor, and Christine Wiedman, "The Balanced Scorecard: To Adopt or Not to Adopt," *Ivey Business Journal* 69, no. 2 (November–December 2004); and Sandy Richardson, "The Key Elements of Balanced Scorecard Success," *Ivey Business Journal* 69, no. 2 (November–December 2004).

7. Kaplan and Norton, *The Balanced Scorecard: Translating Strategy into Action,* pp. 25—29. Kaplan and Norton classify strategic objectives under the categories of customer-related, business processes, and learning and growth. In practice, companies using the balanced scorecard may choose categories of strategic objectives that best reflect the organization's value-creating activities and processes.

8. Information posted on the website of Bain and Company, www.bain.com, accessed May 27, 2011.

9. Information posted on the website of Balanced Scorecard Institute, accessed May 27, 2011.

10. Henry Mintzberg, Bruce Ahlstrand, and Joseph Lampel, *Strategy Safari: A Guided Tour through the Wilds of Strategic Management* (New York: Free Press, 1998); Bruce Barringer and Allen C. Bluedorn, "The Relationship between Corporate Entrepreneurship and Strategic Management," *Strategic Management Journal* 20 (1999); Jeffrey G. Covin and Morgan P. Miles, "Corporate Entrepreneurship and the Pursuit of Competitive Advantage," *Entrepreneurship: Theory and Practice* 23, no. 3 (Spring 1999); and David A. Garvin and Lynne C. Levesque, "Meeting the Challenge of Corporate Entrepreneurship," *Harvard Business Review* 84, no. 10 (October 2006).

11. Jay W. Lorsch and Robert C. Clark, "Leading from the Boardroom," *Harvard Business Review* 86, no. 4 (April 2008).

12. Ibid., p. 110.

13. Stephen P. Kaufman, "Evaluating the CEO," *Harvard Business Review* 86, no. 10 (October 2008).

14. David A. Nadler, "Building Better Boards," *Harvard Business Review* 82, no. 5 (May 2004); Cynthia A. Montgomery and Rhonda Kaufman, "The Board's Missing Link," *Harvard Business Review* 81, no. 3 (March 2003); John Carver, "What Continues to Be Wrong with Corporate Governance and How to Fix It," *Ivey Business Journal* 68, no. 1 (September/October 2003); and Gordon Donaldson, "A New Tool for Boards: The Strategic Audit," *Harvard Business Review* 73, no. 4 (July–August 1995).

Evaluating a Company's External Environment

LEARNING OBJECTIVES

LO1 Identify factors in a company's broad macro-environment that may have strategic significance.

LO2 Recognize the factors that cause competition in an industry to be fierce, more or less normal, or relatively weak.

LO3 Become adept at mapping the market positions of key groups of industry rivals.

LO4 Learn how to determine whether an industry's outlook presents a company with sufficiently attractive opportunities for growth and profitability.

In Chapter 2, we learned that the strategy formulation, strategy execution process begins with an appraisal of the company's present situation. The company's situation includes two facets: (1) the competitive conditions in the industry in which the company operates—its external environment; and (2) its resources and organizational capabilities—its internal environment.

Charting a company's long-term direction, conceiving its customer value proposition, setting objectives, or crafting a strategy without first gaining an understanding of the company's external and internal environments hamstrings attempts to build competitive advantage and boost company performance. Indeed, the first test of a winning strategy inquires, *"How well does the strategy fit the company's situation?"*

This chapter presents the concepts and analytical tools for zeroing in on a single-business company's external environment. Attention centers on the competitive arena in which the company operates, the drivers of market change, the market positions of rival companies, and the factors that determine competitive success. Chapter 4 explores the methods of evaluating a company's internal circumstances and competitiveness.

Evaluating the Strategically Relevant Components of a Company's Macro-Environment

LO1 Identify factors in a company's broad macro-environment that may have strategic significance.

A company's external environment includes the immediate industry and competitive environment and broader macro-environmental factors such as general economic conditions, societal values and cultural norms, political factors, the legal and regulatory environment, ecological considerations, and technological factors. These two levels of a company's external environment—the broad outer ring macro-environment and immediate inner ring industry and competitive environment—are illustrated in Figure 3.1. Strictly speaking, a company's **macro-environment** encompasses all of the *relevant factors* making up the broad environmental context in which a company operates; by *relevant*, we mean the factors are important enough that they should shape management's decisions regarding the company's long-term direction, objectives, strategy, and business model. The relevance of macro-environmental factors can be evaluated using **PESTEL analysis**, an acronym for the six principal components of the macro-environment: political factors, economic conditions in the firm's general environment, sociocultural forces, technological factors, environmental forces, and legal/regulatory factors. Table 3.1 provides a description of each of the six PESTEL components of the macro-environment.

> **CORE CONCEPT**
>
> The **macro-environment** encompasses the broad environmental context in which a company is situated and is comprised of six principal components: political factors, economic conditions, sociocultural forces, technological factors, environmental factors, and legal/regulatory conditions.
>
> **PESTEL analysis** can be used to assess the strategic relevance of the six principal components of the macro-environment: political, economic, social, technological, environmental, and legal forces.

The impact of outer ring macro-environmental factors on a company's choice of strategy can be big or small. But even if the factors of the macro-environment change slowly or are likely to have a low impact on the company's

FIGURE 3.1 **The Components of a Company's External Environment**

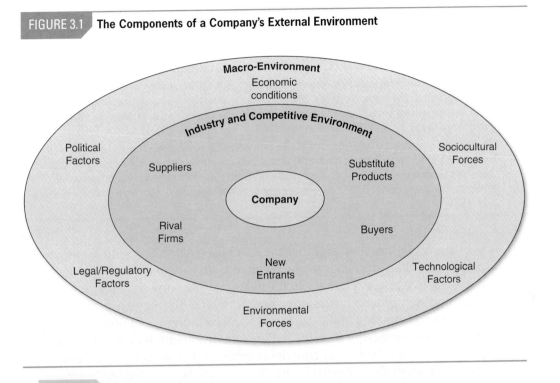

TABLE 3.1

The Six Components of the Macro-Environment Included in a PESTEL Analysis

Component	Description
Political factors	These factors include political policies and processes, including the extent to which a government intervenes in the economy. They include such matters as tax policy, fiscal policy, tariffs, the political climate, and the strength of institutions such as the federal banking system. Some political factors, such as bailouts, are industry-specific. Others, such as energy policy, affect certain types of industries (energy producers and heavy users of energy) more than others.
Economic conditions	Economic conditions include the general economic climate and specific factors such as interest rates, exchange rates, the inflation rate, the unemployment rate, the rate of economic growth, trade deficits or surpluses, savings rates, and per capita domestic product. Economic factors also include conditions in the markets for stocks and bonds, which can affect consumer confidence and discretionary income. Some industries, such as construction, are particularly vulnerable to economic downturns but are positively affected by factors such as low interest rates. Others, such as discount retailing, may benefit when general economic conditions weaken, as consumers become more price-conscious.
Sociocultural forces	Sociocultural forces include the societal values, attitudes, cultural factors, and lifestyles that impact businesses, as well as demographic factors such as the population size, growth rate, and age distribution. Sociocultural forces vary by locale and change over time. An example is the trend toward healthier lifestyles, which can shift spending toward exercise equipment and health clubs and away from alcohol and snack foods. Population demographics can have large implications for industries such as health care, where costs and service needs vary with demographic factors such as age and income distribution.
Technological factors	Technological factors include the pace of technological change and technical developments that have the potential for wide-ranging effects on society, such as genetic engineering and nanotechnology. They include institutions involved in creating knowledge and controlling the use of technology, such as R&D consortia, university-sponsored technology incubators, patent and copyright laws, and government control over the Internet. Technological change can encourage the birth of new industries, such as those based on nanotechnology, and disrupt others, such as the recording industry.

(continued)

TABLE 3.1   *(continued)*

Component	Description
Environmental forces	These include ecological and environmental forces such as weather, climate, climate change, and associated factors like water shortages. These factors can directly impact industries such as insurance, farming, energy production, and tourism. They may have an indirect but substantial effect on other industries such as transportation and utilities.
Legal and regulatory factors	These factors include the regulations and laws with which companies must comply such as consumer laws, labor laws, antitrust laws, and occupational health and safety regulation. Some factors, such as banking deregulation, are industry-specific. Others, such as minimum wage legislation, affect certain types of industries (low-wage, labor-intensive industries) more than others.

business situation, they still merit a watchful eye. Motor vehicle companies must adapt their strategies to customer concerns about carbon emissions and high gasoline prices. Changes in lifestyles, attitudes toward nutrition and fitness, and leisure preferences have begun to have strategy-shaping effects on companies competing in the processed food, restaurant, and fitness industries. As company managers scan the external environment, they must be alert for potentially important outer ring developments, assess their impact and influence, and adapt the company's direction and strategy as needed.

However, the factors and forces in a company's macro-environment that have the *biggest* strategy-shaping impact typically pertain to the company's immediate inner ring industry and competitive environment—competitive pressures, the actions of rival firms, buyer behavior, supplier-related considerations, and so on. Consequently, this chapter concentrates on a company's industry and competitive environment.

Assessing the Company's Industry and Competitive Environment

Thinking strategically about a company's industry and competitive environment entails using some well-validated concepts and analytical tools to get clear answers to seven questions:

1. Do the dominant economic characteristics of the industry offer sellers opportunities for growth and attractive profits?
2. What kinds of competitive forces are industry members facing, and how strong is each force?
3. What forces are driving industry change, and what impact will these changes have on competitive intensity and industry profitability?
4. What market positions do industry rivals occupy—who is strongly positioned and who is not?
5. What strategic moves are rivals likely to make next?
6. What are the key factors of competitive success?
7. Does the industry outlook offer good prospects for profitability?

Analysis-based answers to these questions are prerequisites for a strategy offering good fit with the external situation. The remainder of this chapter is devoted to describing the methods of obtaining solid answers to the seven questions above.

Question 1: What Are the Industry's Dominant Economic Characteristics?

Analyzing a company's industry and competitive environment begins with identifying the industry's dominant economic characteristics. While the general economic conditions of the macro-environment identified through PESTEL analysis may prove to be strategically relevant, it is the economic characteristics of the industry that will have a greater bearing on the industry's prospects for growth and attractive profits. An industry's dominant economic characteristics include such factors as market size and growth rate, the geographic boundaries of the market (which can extend from local to worldwide), market demand-supply conditions, market segmentation, and the pace of technological change. Table 3.2 summarizes analytical questions that define the industry's dominant economic features.

Getting a handle on an industry's distinguishing economic features not only provides a broad overview of the attractiveness of the industry, but also

TABLE 3.2

What to Consider in Identifying an Industry's Dominant Economic Features

Economic Characteristic	Questions to Answer
Market size and growth rate	• How big is the industry and how fast is it growing? • What does the industry's position in the life cycle (early development, rapid growth and takeoff, early maturity and slowing growth, saturation and stagnation, decline) reveal about the industry's growth prospects?
Scope of competitive rivalry	• Is the geographic area over which most companies compete local, regional, national, multinational, or global?
Demand-supply conditions	• Is a surplus of capacity pushing prices and profit margins down? • Is the industry overcrowded with too many competitors?
Market segmentation	• Is the industry characterized by various product characteristics or customer wants, needs, or preferences that divide the market into distinct segments?
Pace of technological change	• What role does advancing technology play in this industry? • Do most industry members have or need strong technological capabilities? Why?

promotes understanding of the kinds of strategic moves that industry members are likely to employ. For example, industries that are characterized by rapid technological change may require substantial investments in R&D and the development of strong product innovation capabilities—continuous product innovation is primarily a survival strategy in such industries as video games, computers, and pharmaceuticals.

Question 2: How Strong Are the Industry's Competitive Forces?

LO2 Recognize the factors that cause competition in an industry to be fierce, more or less normal, or relatively weak.

After gaining an understanding of the industry's general economic characteristics, industry and competitive analysis should focus on the competitive dynamics of the industry. The nature and subtleties of competitive forces are never the same from one industry to another and must be wholly understood to accurately assess the company's current situation. Far and away the most powerful and widely used tool for assessing the strength of the industry's competitive forces is the *five-forces model of competition*.[1] This model, as depicted in Figure 3.2, holds that competitive forces affecting industry attractiveness go beyond rivalry among competing sellers and include pressures stemming from four coexisting sources. The five competitive forces affecting industry attractiveness are listed below.

1. Competitive pressures stemming from *buyer* bargaining power.
2. Competitive pressures coming from companies in other industries to win buyers over to *substitute products*.
3. Competitive pressures stemming from *supplier* bargaining power.
4. Competitive pressures associated with the threat of *new entrants* into the market.
5. Competitive pressures associated with *rivalry among competing sellers* to attract customers. This is usually the strongest of the five competitive forces.

The Competitive Force of Buyer Bargaining Power

Whether seller-buyer relationships represent a minor or significant competitive force depends on (1) whether some or many buyers have sufficient bargaining leverage to obtain price concessions and other favorable terms, and (2) the extent to which buyers are price sensitive. Buyers with strong bargaining power can limit industry profitability by demanding price concessions, better payment terms, or additional features and services that increase industry members' costs. Buyer price sensitivity limits the profit potential of industry members by restricting the ability of sellers to raise prices without losing volume or unit sales.

The leverage that buyers have in negotiating favorable terms of the sale can range from weak to strong. Individual consumers, for example, rarely have much bargaining power in negotiating price concessions or other favorable terms with sellers. The primary exceptions involve situations in which price

FIGURE 3.2	The Five-Forces Model of Competition

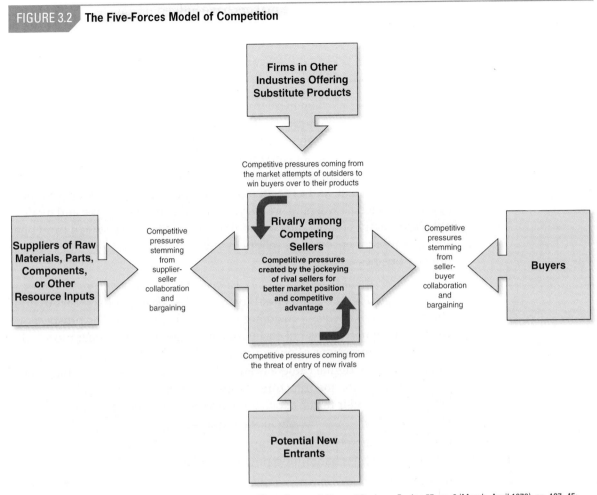

Sources: Based on Michael E. Porter, "How Competitive Forces Shape Strategy," *Harvard Business Review* 57, no. 2 (March–April 1979), pp. 137–45; and Michael E. Porter, "The Five Competitive Forces That Shape Strategy," *Harvard Business Review* 86, no. 1 (January 2008), pp. 80–86.

haggling is customary, such as the purchase of new and used motor vehicles, homes, and other big-ticket items such as jewelry and pleasure boats. For most consumer goods and services, individual buyers have no bargaining leverage—their option is to pay the seller's posted price, delay their purchase until prices and terms improve, or take their business elsewhere.

In contrast, large retail chains such as Walmart, Best Buy, Staples, and Home Depot typically have considerable negotiating leverage in purchasing products from manufacturers because retailers usually stock just two or three competing brands of a product and rarely carry all competing brands. In addition, the strong bargaining power of major supermarket chains such as Kroger, Safeway, and Albertsons allows them to demand promotional allowances and lump-sum payments (called slotting fees) from food products manufacturers in return for stocking certain brands or putting them in the best shelf locations. Motor vehicle manufacturers have strong bargaining power in negotiating to buy original equipment tires from Goodyear, Michelin, Bridgestone/Firestone, Continental, and Pirelli not only because they buy in large quantities, but also because tire makers have judged original equipment tires to be important contributors to brand awareness and brand loyalty.

Even if buyers do not purchase in large quantities or offer a seller important market exposure or prestige, they gain a degree of bargaining leverage in the following circumstances:

- *If buyers' costs of switching to competing brands or substitutes are relatively low.* Buyers who can readily switch between several sellers have more negotiating leverage than buyers who have high switching costs. When the products of rival sellers are virtually identical, it is relatively easy for buyers to switch from seller to seller at little or no cost. For example, the screws, rivets, steel, and capacitors used in the production of large home appliances such as washers and dryers are all commodity-like and available from many sellers. The potential for buyers to easily switch from one seller to another encourages sellers to make concessions to win or retain a buyer's business.

- *If the number of buyers is small or if a customer is particularly important to a seller.* The smaller the number of buyers, the less easy it is for sellers to find alternative buyers when a customer is lost to a competitor. The prospect of losing a customer who is not easily replaced often makes a seller more willing to grant concessions of one kind or another. Because of the relatively small number of digital camera brands, the sellers of lenses and other components used in the manufacture of digital cameras are in a weak bargaining position in their negotiations with buyers of their components.

- *If buyer demand is weak.* Weak or declining demand creates a "buyers' market"; conversely, strong or rapidly growing demand creates a "sellers' market" and shifts bargaining power to sellers.

- *If buyers are well informed about sellers' products, prices, and costs.* The more information buyers have, the better bargaining position they are in. The mushrooming availability of product information on the Internet is giving added bargaining power to individuals. It has become common for automobile shoppers to arrive at dealerships armed with invoice prices, dealer holdback information, a summary of incentives, and manufacturers' financing terms.

- *If buyers pose a credible threat of integrating backward into the business of sellers.* Companies such as Anheuser-Busch, Coors, and Heinz have integrated backward into metal can manufacturing to gain bargaining power in obtaining the balance of their can requirements from otherwise powerful metal can manufacturers.

Figure 3.3 summarizes factors causing buyer bargaining power to be strong or weak.

Not all buyers of an industry's product have equal degrees of bargaining power with sellers, and some may be less sensitive than others to price, quality, or service differences. For example, apparel manufacturers confront significant bargaining power when selling to big retailers such as Macy's, T. J. Maxx, or Target, but they can command much better prices selling to small owner-managed apparel boutiques.

FIGURE 3.3 **Factors Affecting the Strength of Buyer Bargaining Power**

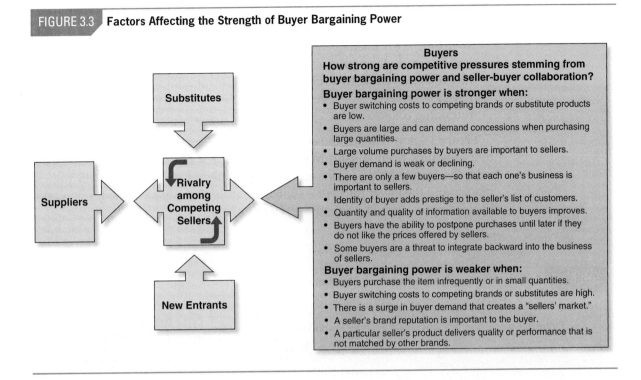

The Competitive Force of Substitute Products

Companies in one industry are vulnerable to competitive pressure from the actions of companies in another industry whenever buyers view the products of the two industries as good substitutes. For instance, the producers of sugar experience competitive pressures from the sales and marketing efforts of the makers of Equal, Splenda, and Sweet'N Low. Newspapers are struggling to maintain their relevance to subscribers who can watch the news on numerous television channels or go to the Internet for updates, blogs, and articles. Similarly, the producers of eyeglasses and contact lenses face competitive pressures from doctors who do corrective laser surgery.

Just how strong the competitive pressures are from the sellers of substitute products depends on three factors:

1. *Whether substitutes are readily available and attractively priced.* The presence of readily available and attractively priced substitutes creates competitive pressure by placing a ceiling on the prices industry members can charge. When substitutes are cheaper than an industry's product, industry members come under heavy competitive pressure to reduce their prices and find ways to absorb the price cuts with cost reductions.

2. *Whether buyers view the substitutes as comparable or better in terms of quality, performance, and other relevant attributes.* Customers are prone to compare performance and other attributes as well as price. For example, consumers have found digital cameras to be a superior substitute to film cameras because of the superior ease of use, the ability to download images to a home computer, and the ability to delete bad shots without paying for film developing.

3. *Whether the costs that buyers incur in switching to the substitutes are high or low.* High switching costs deter switching to substitutes while low switching costs make it easier for the sellers of attractive substitutes to lure buyers to their products. Typical switching costs include the inconvenience of switching to a substitute, the costs of additional equipment, the psychological costs of severing old supplier relationships, and employee retraining costs.

Figure 3.4 summarizes the conditions that determine whether the competitive pressures from substitute products are strong, moderate, or weak. As a rule, the lower the price of substitutes, the higher their quality and performance, and the lower the user's switching costs, the more intense the competitive pressures posed by substitute products.

FIGURE 3.4   **Factors Affecting Competition from Substitute Products**

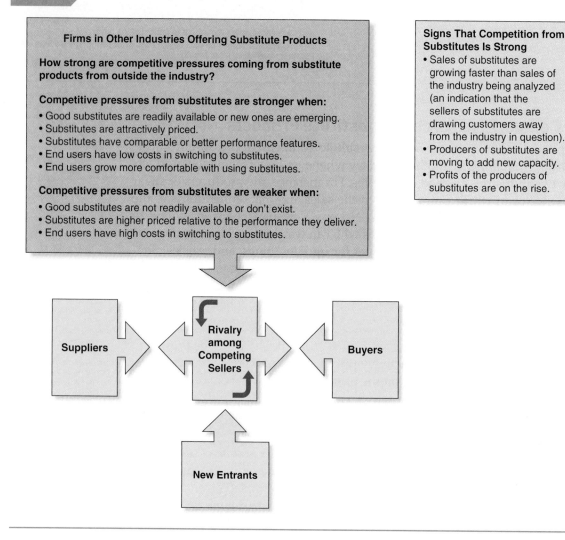

Firms in Other Industries Offering Substitute Products

How strong are competitive pressures coming from substitute products from outside the industry?

Competitive pressures from substitutes are stronger when:
• Good substitutes are readily available or new ones are emerging.
• Substitutes are attractively priced.
• Substitutes have comparable or better performance features.
• End users have low costs in switching to substitutes.
• End users grow more comfortable with using substitutes.

Competitive pressures from substitutes are weaker when:
• Good substitutes are not readily available or don't exist.
• Substitutes are higher priced relative to the performance they deliver.
• End users have high costs in switching to substitutes.

Signs That Competition from Substitutes Is Strong
• Sales of substitutes are growing faster than sales of the industry being analyzed (an indication that the sellers of substitutes are drawing customers away from the industry in question).
• Producers of substitutes are moving to add new capacity.
• Profits of the producers of substitutes are on the rise.

Suppliers

Rivalry among Competing Sellers

Buyers

New Entrants

The Competitive Force of Supplier Bargaining Power

Whether the suppliers of industry members represent a weak or strong competitive force depends on the degree to which suppliers have sufficient *bargaining power* to influence the terms and conditions of supply in their favor. Suppliers with strong bargaining power can erode industry profitability by charging industry members higher prices, passing costs on to them, and limiting their opportunities to find better deals. For instance, Microsoft and Intel, both of which supply PC makers with essential components, have been known to use their dominant market status not only to charge PC makers premium prices but also to leverage PC makers in other ways. The bargaining power possessed by Microsoft and Intel when negotiating with customers is so great that both companies have faced antitrust charges on numerous occasions. Before a legal agreement ending the practice, Microsoft pressured PC makers to load only Microsoft products on the PCs they shipped. Intel has also defended against antitrust charges resulting from its bargaining strength, but continues to give PC makers that use the biggest percentages of Intel chips in their PC models top priority in filling orders for newly introduced Intel chips. Being on Intel's list of preferred customers helps a PC maker get an early allocation of Intel's latest chips and thus allows a PC maker to get new models to market ahead of rivals.

The factors that determine whether any of the industry suppliers are in a position to exert substantial bargaining power or leverage are fairly clear-cut:

- *If the item being supplied is a commodity that is readily available from many suppliers.* Suppliers have little or no bargaining power or leverage whenever industry members have the ability to source from any of several alternative and eager suppliers.

- *The ability of industry members to switch their purchases from one supplier to another or to switch to attractive substitutes.* High switching costs increase supplier bargaining power, whereas low switching costs and the ready availability of good substitute inputs weaken supplier bargaining power.

- *If certain inputs are in short supply.* Suppliers of items in short supply have some degree of pricing power.

- *If certain suppliers provide a differentiated input that enhances the performance, quality, or image of the industry's product.* The greater the ability of a particular input to enhance a product's performance, quality, or image, the more bargaining leverage its suppliers are likely to possess.

- *Whether certain suppliers provide equipment or services that deliver cost savings to industry members in conducting their operations.* Suppliers who provide cost-saving equipment or services are likely to possess some degree of bargaining leverage.

- *The fraction of the costs of the industry's product accounted for by the cost of a particular input.* The bigger the cost of a specific part or component, the more opportunity for competition in the marketplace to be affected by the actions of suppliers to raise or lower their prices.

- *If industry members are major customers of suppliers.* As a rule, suppliers have less bargaining leverage when their sales to members of this one industry

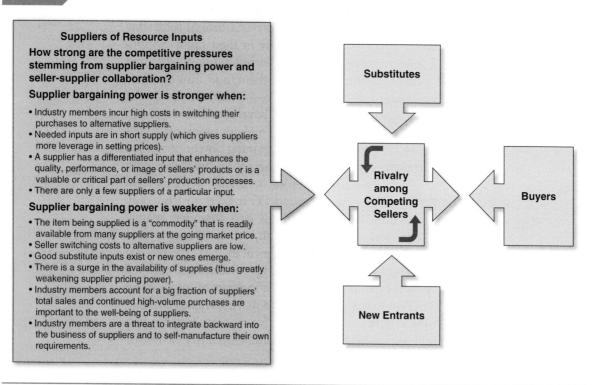

FIGURE 3.5   **Factors Affecting the Strength of Supplier Bargaining Power**

constitute a big percentage of their total sales. In such cases, the well-being of suppliers is closely tied to the well-being of their major customers.

- *Whether it makes good economic sense for industry members to vertically integrate backward.* The make-or-buy decision generally boils down to whether suppliers are able to supply a particular component at a lower cost than industry members could achieve if they were to integrate backward.

Figure 3.5 summarizes the conditions that tend to make supplier bargaining power strong or weak.

The Competitive Force of Potential New Entrants

Several factors determine whether the threat of new companies entering the marketplace presents a significant competitive pressure. One factor relates to the size of the pool of likely entry candidates and the resources at their command. As a rule, the bigger the pool of entry candidates, the stronger the threat of potential entry. This is especially true when some of the likely entry candidates have ample resources to support entry into a new line of business. Frequently, the strongest competitive pressures associated with potential entry come not from outsiders but from current industry participants looking for growth opportunities. *Existing industry members are often strong candidates to enter market segments or geographic areas where they currently do not have a market presence.*

A second factor concerns whether the likely entry candidates face high or low entry barriers. High barriers reduce the competitive threat of potential entry, while low barriers make entry more likely, especially if the industry is growing and offers attractive profit opportunities. The most widely encountered barriers that entry candidates must hurdle include:[2]

- *The presence of sizable economies of scale in production or other areas of operation.* When incumbent companies enjoy cost advantages associated with large-scale operations, outsiders must either enter on a large scale (a costly and perhaps risky move) or accept a cost disadvantage and consequently lower profitability.

- *Cost and resource disadvantages not related to scale of operation.* Aside from enjoying economies of scale, industry incumbents can have cost advantages that stem from the possession of proprietary technology, partnerships with the best and cheapest suppliers, low fixed costs (because they have older facilities that have been mostly depreciated), and experience/learning curve effects. The microprocessor industry is an excellent example of how learning/experience curves put new entrants at a substantial cost disadvantage. Manufacturing unit costs for microprocessors tend to decline about 20 percent each time *cumulative* production volume doubles. With a 20 percent experience curve effect, if the first 1 million chips cost $100 each, once production volume reaches 2 million the unit cost would fall to $80 (80 percent of $100), and by a production volume of 4 million the unit cost would be $64 (80 percent of $80).[3] The bigger the learning or experience curve effect, the bigger the cost advantage of the company with the largest *cumulative* production volume.

- *Strong brand preferences and high degrees of customer loyalty.* The stronger the attachment of buyers to established brands, the harder it is for a newcomer to break into the marketplace.

- *High capital requirements.* The larger the total dollar investment needed to enter the market successfully, the more limited the pool of potential entrants. The most obvious capital requirements for new entrants relate to manufacturing facilities and equipment, introductory advertising and sales promotion campaigns, working capital to finance inventories and customer credit, and sufficient cash to cover start-up costs.

- *The difficulties of building a network of distributors-retailers and securing adequate space on retailers' shelves.* A potential entrant can face numerous distribution channel challenges. Wholesale distributors may be reluctant to take on a product that lacks buyer recognition. Retailers have to be recruited and convinced to give a new brand ample display space and an adequate trial period. Potential entrants sometimes have to "buy" their way into wholesale or retail channels by cutting their prices to provide dealers and distributors with higher markups and profit margins or by giving them big advertising and promotional allowances.

- *Restrictive regulatory policies.* Government agencies can limit or even bar entry by requiring licenses and permits. Regulated industries such as cable TV, telecommunications, electric and gas utilities, and radio and television broadcasting entail government-controlled entry.

- *Tariffs and international trade restrictions.* National governments commonly use tariffs and trade restrictions (antidumping rules, local content requirements, local ownership requirements, quotas, etc.) to raise entry barriers for foreign firms and protect domestic producers from outside competition.

- *The ability and willingness of industry incumbents to launch vigorous initiatives to block a newcomer's successful entry.* Even if a potential entrant has or can acquire the needed competencies and resources to attempt entry, it must still worry about the reaction of existing firms.[4] Sometimes, there's little that incumbents can do to throw obstacles in an entrant's path. But there are times when incumbents use price cuts, increase advertising, introduce product improvements, and launch legal attacks to prevent the entrant from building a clientele. Cable TV companies have vigorously fought the entry of satellite TV into the industry by seeking government intervention to delay satellite providers in offering local stations, offering satellite customers discounts to switch back to cable, and charging satellite customers high monthly rates for cable Internet access.

Figure 3.6 summarizes conditions making the threat of entry strong or weak.

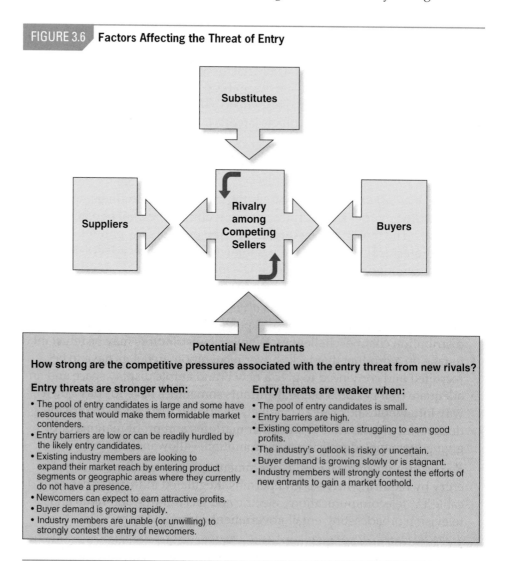

FIGURE 3.6 **Factors Affecting the Threat of Entry**

Potential New Entrants

How strong are the competitive pressures associated with the entry threat from new rivals?

Entry threats are stronger when:
- The pool of entry candidates is large and some have resources that would make them formidable market contenders.
- Entry barriers are low or can be readily hurdled by the likely entry candidates.
- Existing industry members are looking to expand their market reach by entering product segments or geographic areas where they currently do not have a presence.
- Newcomers can expect to earn attractive profits.
- Buyer demand is growing rapidly.
- Industry members are unable (or unwilling) to strongly contest the entry of newcomers.

Entry threats are weaker when:
- The pool of entry candidates is small.
- Entry barriers are high.
- Existing competitors are struggling to earn good profits.
- The industry's outlook is risky or uncertain.
- Buyer demand is growing slowly or is stagnant.
- Industry members will strongly contest the efforts of new entrants to gain a market foothold.

The Competitive Force of Rivalry among Competing Sellers

The strongest of the five competitive forces is nearly always the rivalry among competing sellers of a product or service. In effect, *a market is a competitive battlefield* where there's no end to the campaign for buyer patronage. Rival sellers are prone to employ whatever weapons they have in their business arsenal to improve their market positions, strengthen their market position with buyers, and earn good profits. The strategy formulation challenge is to craft a competitive strategy that, at the very least, allows a company to hold its own against rivals and that, ideally, *produces a competitive edge over rivals.* But competitive contests are ongoing and dynamic. When one firm makes a strategic move that produces good results, its rivals typically respond with offensive or defensive countermoves of their own. This pattern of action and reaction produces a continually evolving competitive landscape where the market battle ebbs and flows and produces winners and losers. But the current market leaders have no guarantees of continued leadership. In every industry, the ongoing jockeying of rivals leads to one or more companies gaining or losing momentum in the marketplace according to whether their latest strategic maneuvers succeed or fail.[5]

Figure 3.7 shows a sampling of competitive weapons that firms can deploy in battling rivals and indicates the factors that influence the intensity of their rivalry. Some factors that influence the tempo of rivalry among industry competitors include:

- *Rivalry intensifies when competing sellers regularly launch fresh actions to boost their market standing and business performance.* Normally, competitive jockeying among rival sellers is fairly intense. Indicators of strong competitive rivalry include lively price competition, the rapid introduction of next-generation products, and moves to differentiate products by offering better performance features, higher quality, improved customer service, or a wider product selection. Other common tactics used to temporarily boost sales include special sales promotions, heavy advertising, rebates, or low-interest-rate financing.

- *Rivalry is stronger in industries where competitors are equal in size and capability.* Competitive rivalry in the quick-service restaurant industry is particularly strong where there are numerous relatively equal-sized hamburger, deli sandwich, chicken, and taco chains. For the most part, McDonald's, Burger King, Taco Bell, KFC, Arby's, and other national fast-food chains have comparable capabilities and are required to compete aggressively to hold their own in the industry.

- *Rivalry is usually stronger in slow-growing markets and weaker in fast-growing markets.* Rapidly expanding buyer demand produces enough new business for all industry members to grow. But in markets where growth is sluggish or where buyer demand drops off unexpectedly, it is not uncommon for competitive rivalry to intensify significantly as rivals battle for market share and volume gains.

- *Rivalry is usually weaker in industries comprised of vast numbers of small rivals; likewise, it is often weak when there are fewer than five competitors.*

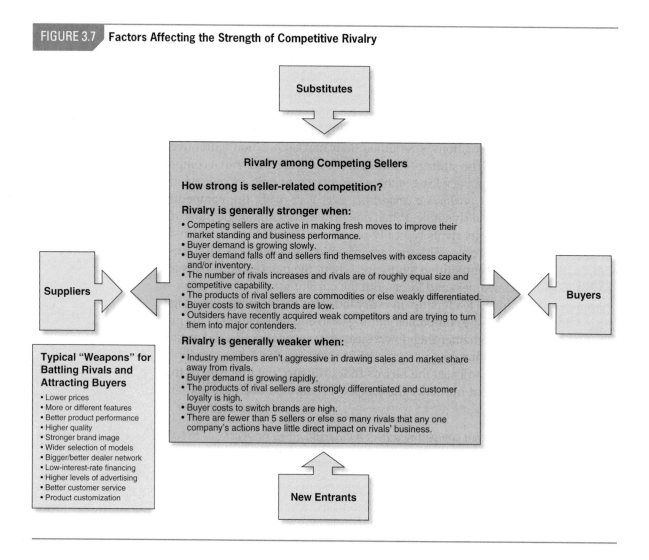

FIGURE 3.7 Factors Affecting the Strength of Competitive Rivalry

Head-to-head rivalry tends to be weak once an industry becomes populated with so many rivals that the strategic moves of any one competitor have little discernible impact on the success of rivals. Rivalry also *tends* to be weak if an industry consists of just two to four sellers. In a market with few rivals, each competitor soon learns that aggressive moves to grow its sales and market share can have an immediate adverse impact on rivals' businesses, almost certainly provoking vigorous retaliation. However, some caution must be exercised in concluding that rivalry is weak just because there are only a few competitors. The fierceness of the current battle between Google and Microsoft and the decades-long war between Coca-Cola and Pepsi are prime examples.

• *Rivalry increases when buyer demand falls off and sellers find themselves with excess capacity and/or inventory.* Excess supply conditions create a "buyers' market," putting added competitive pressure on industry rivals to scramble for profitable sales levels (often by price discounting).

- *Rivalry increases as it becomes less costly for buyers to switch brands.* The less expensive it is for buyers to switch their purchases from the seller of one brand to the seller of another brand, the easier it is for sellers to steal customers away from rivals.

- *Rivalry increases as the products of rival sellers become more standardized and diminishes as the products of industry rivals become more differentiated.* When the offerings of rivals are identical or weakly differentiated, buyers have less reason to be brand loyal—a condition that makes it easier for rivals to persuade buyers to switch to their offering. On the other hand, strongly differentiated product offerings among rivals breed high brand loyalty on the part of buyers.

- *Rivalry is more intense when industry conditions tempt competitors to use price cuts or other competitive weapons to boost unit volume.* When a product is perishable, seasonal, or costly to hold in inventory, competitive pressures build quickly any time one or more firms decide to cut prices and dump supplies on the market. Likewise, whenever fixed costs account for a large fraction of total cost, so that unit costs tend to be lowest at or near full capacity, firms come under significant pressure to cut prices or otherwise try to boost sales whenever they are operating below full capacity.

- *Rivalry increases when one or more competitors become dissatisfied with their market position.* Firms that are losing ground or are in financial trouble often pursue aggressive (or perhaps desperate) turnaround strategies that can involve price discounts, greater advertising, or merger with other rivals. Such strategies can turn competitive pressures up a notch.

- *Rivalry increases when strong companies outside the industry acquire weak firms in the industry and launch aggressive, well-funded moves to build market share.* A concerted effort to turn a weak rival into a market leader nearly always entails launching well-financed strategic initiatives to dramatically improve the competitor's product offering, excite buyer interest, and win a much bigger market share—actions that, if successful, put added pressure on rivals to counter with fresh strategic moves of their own.

Rivalry can be characterized as *cutthroat* or *brutal* when competitors engage in protracted price wars or habitually employ other aggressive tactics that are mutually destructive to profitability. Rivalry can be considered *fierce* to *strong* when the battle for market share is so vigorous that the profit margins of most industry members are squeezed to bare-bones levels. Rivalry can be characterized as *moderate* or *normal* when the maneuvering among industry members, while lively and healthy, still allows most industry members to earn acceptable profits. Rivalry is *weak* when most companies in the industry are relatively well satisfied with their sales growth and market share and rarely undertake offensives to steal customers away from one another.

The Collective Strengths of the Five Competitive Forces and Industry Profitability

Scrutinizing each of the five competitive forces one by one provides a powerful diagnosis of what competition is like in a given market. Once the strategist has gained an understanding of the competitive pressures associated with each of the five forces, the next step is to evaluate the collective strength of the five forces and determine if companies in this industry should reasonably expect to earn decent profits.

As a rule, the stronger the collective impact of the five competitive forces, the lower the combined profitability of industry participants. The most extreme case of a "competitively unattractive" industry is when all five forces are producing strong competitive pressures: Rivalry among sellers is vigorous, low entry barriers allow new rivals to gain a market foothold, competition from substitutes is intense, and both suppliers and customers are able to exercise considerable bargaining leverage. Fierce to strong competitive pressures coming from all five directions nearly always drive industry profitability to unacceptably low levels, frequently producing losses for many industry members and forcing some out of business. But an industry can be competitively unattractive without all five competitive forces being strong. Fierce competitive pressures from just one of the five forces, such as brutal price competition among rival sellers, may suffice to destroy the conditions for good profitability.

> The stronger the forces of competition, the harder it becomes for industry members to earn attractive profits.

In contrast, when the collective impact of the five competitive forces is moderate to weak, an industry is competitively attractive in the sense that industry members can reasonably expect to earn good profits and a nice return on investment. The ideal competitive environment for earning superior profits is one in which both suppliers and customers are in weak bargaining positions, there are no good substitutes, high barriers block further entry, and rivalry among present sellers generates only moderate competitive pressures. Weak competition is the best of all possible worlds for companies with mediocre strategies and second-rate implementation because even they can expect a decent profit.

Question 3: What Are the Industry's Driving Forces of Change and What Impact Will They Have?

The intensity of competitive forces and the level of industry attractiveness are almost always fluid and subject to change. It is essential for strategy makers to understand the current competitive dynamics of the industry, but it is equally important for strategy makers to consider how the industry is changing and the effect of industry changes that are under way. Any strategies devised by management will play out in a dynamic industry environment, so it's imperative that such plans consider what the industry environment might look like during the near term.

The Concept of Industry Driving Forces

Industry and competitive conditions change because forces are enticing or pressuring certain industry participants (competitors, customers, suppliers) to alter their actions in important ways. The most powerful of the change agents are called **driving forces** because they have the biggest influences in reshaping the industry landscape and altering competitive conditions. Some driving forces originate in the outer ring of the company's macro-environment (see Figure 3.1), but most originate in the company's more immediate industry and competitive environment.

> ### CORE CONCEPT
> **Driving forces** are the major underlying causes of change in industry and competitive conditions.

Driving forces analysis has three steps: (1) identifying what the driving forces are, (2) assessing whether the drivers of change are, individually or collectively, acting to make the industry more or less attractive, and (3) determining what strategy changes are needed to prepare for the impact of the driving forces.

Identifying an Industry's Driving Forces

Many developments can affect an industry powerfully enough to qualify as driving forces, but most drivers of industry and competitive change fall into one of the following categories:

- *Changes in an industry's long-term growth rate.* Shifts in industry growth have the potential to affect the balance between industry supply and buyer demand, entry and exit, and the character and strength of competition. An upsurge in buyer demand triggers a race among established firms and newcomers to capture the new sales opportunities. A slowdown in the growth of demand nearly always brings an increase in rivalry and increased efforts by some firms to maintain their high rates of growth by taking sales and market share away from rivals.

- *Increasing globalization.* Competition begins to shift from primarily a regional or national focus to an international or global focus when industry members begin seeking customers in foreign markets or when production activities begin to migrate to countries where costs are lowest. The forces of globalization are sometimes such a strong driver that companies find it highly advantageous, if not necessary, to spread their operating reach into more and more country markets. Globalization is very much a driver of industry change in such industries as credit cards, mobile phones, digital cameras, motor vehicles, steel, petroleum, personal computers, and video games.

- *Changes in who buys the product and how they use it.* Shifts in buyer demographics and the ways products are used can alter competition by affecting how customers perceive value, how customers make purchasing decisions, and where customers purchase the product. The burgeoning popularity of streaming video has affected broadband providers, wireless phone carriers, and television broadcasters and created opportunities for such new entertainment businesses as Hulu and Netflix.

- *Product innovation.* An ongoing stream of product innovations tends to alter the pattern of competition in an industry by attracting more first-time buyers, rejuvenating industry growth, and/or creating wider or narrower product differentiation among rival sellers. Product innovation has been a key driving force in such industries as computers, digital cameras, televisions, video games, and prescription drugs.

- *Technological change and manufacturing process innovation.* Advances in technology can dramatically alter an industry's landscape, making it possible to produce new and better products at lower cost and opening new industry frontiers. For instance, Voice over Internet Protocol technology (VoIP) has spawned low-cost, Internet-based phone networks that have begun competing with traditional telephone companies worldwide (whose higher-cost technology depends on hard-wire connections via overhead and underground telephone lines).

- *Marketing innovation.* When firms are successful in introducing *new ways* to market their products, they can spark a burst of buyer interest, widen industry demand, increase product differentiation, and lower unit costs— any or all of which can alter the competitive positions of rival firms and force strategy revisions.

- *Entry or exit of major firms.* The entry of one or more foreign companies into a geographic market once dominated by domestic firms nearly always shakes up competitive conditions. Likewise, when an established domestic firm from another industry attempts entry either by acquisition or by launching its own start-up venture, it usually pushes competition in new directions.

- *Diffusion of technical know-how across more companies and more countries.* As knowledge about how to perform a particular activity or execute a particular manufacturing technology spreads, the competitive advantage held by firms originally possessing this know-how erodes. Knowledge diffusion can occur through scientific journals, trade publications, on-site plant tours, word of mouth among suppliers and customers, employee migration, and Internet sources.

- *Changes in cost and efficiency.* Widening or shrinking differences in the costs among key competitors tend to dramatically alter the state of competition. Declining costs to produce PCs have enabled price cuts and spurred PC sales (especially lower-priced models) by making them more affordable to lower-income households worldwide.

- *Growing buyer preferences for differentiated products instead of a commodity product (or for a more standardized product instead of strongly differentiated products).* When a shift from standardized to differentiated products occurs, rivals must adopt strategies to outdifferentiate one another. However, buyers sometimes decide that a standardized, budget-priced product suits their requirements as well as a premium-priced product with lots of snappy features and personalized services.

- *Regulatory influences and government policy changes.* Government regulatory actions can often force significant changes in industry practices and strategic approaches. New rules and regulations pertaining to government-sponsored health insurance programs are driving changes in the health care industry. In international markets, host governments can drive competitive changes by opening their domestic markets to foreign participation or closing them.

TABLE 3.3

Common Driving Forces

1. Changes in the long-term industry growth rate.
2. Increasing globalization.
3. Emerging new Internet capabilities and applications.
4. Changes in who buys the product and how they use it.
5. Product innovation.
6. Technological change and manufacturing process innovation.
7. Marketing innovation.
8. Entry or exit of major firms.
9. Diffusion of technical know-how across more companies and more countries.
10. Changes in cost and efficiency.
11. Growing buyer preferences for differentiated products instead of a standardized commodity product (or for a more standardized product instead of strongly differentiated products).
12. Regulatory influences and government policy changes.
13. Changing societal concerns, attitudes, and lifestyles.

- *Changing societal concerns, attitudes, and lifestyles.* Emerging social issues and changing attitudes and lifestyles can be powerful instigators of industry change. Consumer concerns about the use of chemical additives and the nutritional content of food products have forced food producers to revamp food-processing techniques, redirect R&D efforts into the use of healthier ingredients, and compete in developing nutritious, good-tasting products.

While many forces of change may be at work in a given industry, *no more than three or four* are likely to be true driving forces powerful enough to qualify as the *major determinants* of why and how the industry is changing. Thus, company strategists must resist the temptation to label every change they see as a driving force. Table 3.3 lists the most common driving forces.

Assessing the Impact of the Industry Driving Forces

The second step in driving forces analysis is to determine whether the prevailing driving forces are acting to make the industry environment more or less attractive. Getting a handle on the collective impact of the driving forces usually requires looking at the likely effects of each force separately, because the driving forces may not all be pushing change in the same direction. For example, two driving forces may be acting to spur demand for the industry's product while one driving force may be working to curtail demand. Whether the net effect on industry demand is up or down hinges on which driving forces are the more powerful.

> An important part of driving forces analysis is to determine whether the individual or collective impact of the driving forces will be to increase or decrease market demand, make competition more or less intense, and lead to higher or lower industry profitability.

Determining Strategy Changes Needed to Prepare for the Impact of Driving Forces

The third step of driving forces analysis—where the real payoff for strategy making comes—is for managers to draw some conclusions about what

> The real payoff of driving forces analysis is to help managers understand what strategy changes are needed to prepare for the impacts of the driving forces.

strategy adjustments will be needed to deal with the impact of the driving forces. Without understanding the forces driving industry change and the impacts these forces will have on the industry environment over the next one to three years, managers are ill prepared to craft a strategy tightly matched to emerging conditions. Similarly, if managers are uncertain about the implications of one or more driving forces, or if their views are off-base, it will be difficult for them to craft a strategy that is responsive to the consequences of driving forces. So driving forces analysis is not something to take lightly; it has practical value and is basic to the task of thinking strategically about where the industry is headed and how to prepare for the changes ahead.

Question 4: How Are Industry Rivals Positioned?

LO3 Become adept at mapping the market positions of key groups of industry rivals.

The nature of competitive strategy inherently positions companies competing in an industry into strategic groups with diverse price/quality ranges, different distribution channels, varying product features, and different geographic coverages. The best technique for revealing the market positions of industry competitors is **strategic group mapping.** This analytical tool is useful for comparing the market positions of industry competitors or for grouping industry combatants into like positions.

CORE CONCEPT

Strategic group mapping is a technique for displaying the different market or competitive positions that rival firms occupy in the industry.

Using Strategic Group Maps to Assess the Positioning of Key Competitors

A **strategic group** consists of those industry members with similar competitive approaches and positions in the market. Companies in the same strategic group can resemble one another in any of several ways—they may have comparable product-line breadth, sell in the same price/quality range, emphasize the same distribution channels, use essentially the same product attributes to appeal to similar types of buyers, depend on identical technological approaches, or offer buyers similar services and technical assistance.[6] An industry with a commodity-like product may contain only one strategic group whereby all sellers pursue essentially identical strategies and have comparable market positions. But even with commodity products, there is likely some attempt at differentiation occurring in the form of varying delivery times, financing terms, or levels of customer service. Most industries offer a host of competitive approaches that allow companies to find unique industry positioning and avoid fierce competition in a crowded strategic group. Evaluating strategy options entails examining what strategic groups exist, identifying which companies exist within each group, and determining if a

CORE CONCEPT

A **strategic group** is a cluster of industry rivals that have similar competitive approaches and market positions.

competitive "white space" exists where industry competitors are able to create and capture altogether new demand.

The procedure for constructing a *strategic group map* is straightforward:

- Identify the competitive characteristics that delineate strategic approaches used in the industry. Typical variables used in creating strategic group maps are the price/quality range (high, medium, low), geographic coverage (local, regional, national, global), degree of vertical integration (none, partial, full), product-line breadth (wide, narrow), choice of distribution channels (retail, wholesale, Internet, multiple channels), and degree of service offered (no-frills, limited, full).

- Plot firms on a two-variable map based upon their strategic approaches.

- Assign firms occupying the same map location to a common strategic group.

- Draw circles around each strategic group, making the circles proportional to the size of the group's share of total industry sales revenues.

This produces a two-dimensional diagram like the one for the retail chain store industry in Concepts & Connections 3.1.

Several guidelines need to be observed in creating strategic group maps. First, the two variables selected as axes for the map should *not* be highly correlated; if they are, the circles on the map will fall along a diagonal and strategy makers will learn nothing more about the relative positions of competitors than they would by considering just one of the variables. For instance, if companies with broad product lines use multiple distribution channels while companies with narrow lines use a single distribution channel, then looking at product line-breadth reveals just as much about industry positioning as looking at the two competitive variables. Second, the variables chosen as axes for the map should reflect key approaches to offering value to customers and expose big differences in how rivals position themselves in the marketplace. Third, the variables used as axes don't have to be either quantitative or continuous; rather, they can be discrete variables or defined in terms of distinct classes and combinations. Fourth, drawing the sizes of the circles on the map proportional to the combined sales of the firms in each strategic group allows the map to reflect the relative sizes of each strategic group. Fifth, if more than two good competitive variables can be used as axes for the map, multiple maps can be drawn to give different exposures to the competitive positioning in the industry. Because there is not necessarily one best map for portraying how competing firms are positioned in the market, it is advisable to experiment with different pairs of competitive variables.

The Value of Strategic Group Maps

Strategic group maps are revealing in several respects. The *most important* has to do with identifying which rivals are similarly positioned and are thus close rivals and which are distant rivals. Generally, *the closer strategic groups are to each other on the map, the stronger the cross-group competitive rivalry tends to be.* Although firms in the same strategic group are the closest rivals, the next closest rivals are in the immediately adjacent groups.[7] Often, firms in strategic groups

CONCEPTS & CONNECTIONS 3.1

COMPARATIVE MARKET POSITIONS OF SELECTED RETAIL CHAINS: A STRATEGIC GROUP MAP APPLICATION

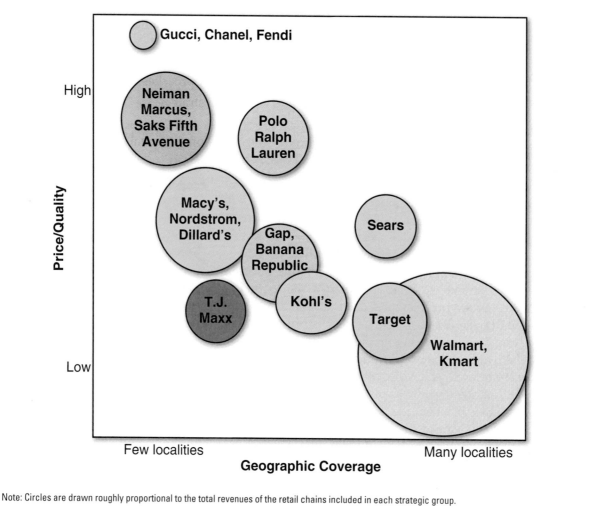

Note: Circles are drawn roughly proportional to the total revenues of the retail chains included in each strategic group.

> Some strategic groups are more favorably positioned than others because they confront weaker competitive forces and/or because they are more favorably impacted by industry driving forces.

that are far apart on the map hardly compete. For instance, Walmart's clientele, merchandise selection, and pricing points are much too different to justify calling them close competitors of Neiman Marcus or Saks Fifth Avenue in retailing. For the same reason, Timex is not a meaningful competitive rival of Rolex, and Kia is not a close competitor of Porsche or Lexus.

The second thing to be gleaned from strategic group mapping is that *not all positions on the map are equally attractive.* Two reasons account for why some positions can be more attractive than others:

1. *Industry driving forces may favor some strategic groups and hurt others.* Driving forces in an industry may be acting to grow the demand for the products of firms in some strategic groups and shrink the demand for the products of firms in other strategic groups—as is the case in the news industry where Internet news services and cable news networks are gaining ground at the expense of newspapers and network television. The industry driving forces of emerging Internet capabilities and applications, changes in who buys the product and how they use it, and changing societal concerns, attitudes, and lifestyles are making it increasingly difficult for traditional media to increase audiences and attract new advertisers.

2. *Competitive pressures may cause the profit potential of different strategic groups to vary.* The profit prospects of firms in different strategic groups can vary from good to poor because of differing degrees of competitive rivalry within strategic groups, differing degrees of exposure to competition from substitute products outside the industry, and differing degrees of supplier or customer bargaining power from group to group. For instance, the competitive battle between Walmart and Target is more intense (with consequently smaller profit margins) than the rivalry among Versace, Chanel, Fendi, and other high-end fashion retailers.

Thus, part of strategic group analysis always entails drawing conclusions about where on the map is the "best" place to be and why. Which companies or strategic groups are in the best positions to prosper and which might be expected to struggle? And equally important, how might firms in poorly positioned strategic groups reposition themselves to improve their prospects for good financial performance?

Question 5: What Strategic Moves Are Rivals Likely to Make Next?

As in sports, scouting the business opposition is an essential part of game plan development. **Competitive intelligence** about rivals' strategies, their latest actions and announcements, their resources and organizational capabilities, and the thinking and leadership styles of their executives is valuable for predicting the strategic moves competitors are likely to make next. Having good information to predict the likely moves of key competitors allows a company to prepare defensive countermoves and to exploit any openings that arise from competitors' missteps.

Considerations in trying to predict what strategic moves rivals are likely to make next include the following:

- What executives are saying about where the industry is headed, the firm's situation, and their past actions and leadership styles.
- Identifying trends in the timing of product launches or new marketing promotions.
- Determining which rivals badly need to increase unit sales and market share.
- Considering which rivals have a strong incentive, along with the resources, to make major strategic changes.

CONCEPTS & CONNECTIONS 3.2

BUSINESS ETHICS AND COMPETITIVE INTELLIGENCE

Those who gather competitive intelligence on rivals can sometimes cross the fine line between honest inquiry and unethical or even illegal behavior. For example, calling rivals to get information about prices, the dates of new-product introductions, or wage and salary levels is legal, but misrepresenting one's company affiliation during such calls is unethical. Pumping rivals' representatives at trade shows is ethical only if one wears a name tag with accurate company affiliation indicated. Avon Products at one point secured information about its biggest rival, Mary Kay Cosmetics (MKC), by having its personnel search through the garbage bins outside MKC's headquarters.[8] When MKC officials learned of the action and sued, Avon claimed it did nothing illegal because a 1988 Supreme Court ruling declared that trash left on public property (in this case, a sidewalk) was anyone's for the taking. Avon even produced a videotape of its removal of the trash at the MKC site. Avon won the lawsuit—but Avon's action, while legal, scarcely qualifies as ethical.

- Knowing which rivals are likely to enter new geographic markets.
- Deciding which rivals are strong candidates to expand their product offerings and enter new product segments.

To succeed in predicting a competitor's next moves, company strategists need to have a good understanding of each rival's situation, its pattern of behavior and preferences in responding to prior strategic attacks, what its best strategic options are, and how rival management measures success. Doing the necessary detective work can be tedious and time-consuming, but scouting competitors well enough to anticipate their next moves allows managers to prepare effective countermoves and to take rivals' probable actions into account in crafting their own offensive strategies.[9] Concepts & Connections 3.2 discusses the ethical limits to gathering competitive intelligence.

> Studying competitors' past behavior and preferences provides a valuable assist in anticipating what moves rivals are likely to make next and outmaneuvering them in the marketplace.

Question 6: What Are the Industry Key Success Factors?

An industry's **key success factors (KSFs)** are those competitive factors that most affect industry members' ability to prosper in the marketplace. Key success factors may include particular strategy elements, product attributes, resources, competitive capabilities, or intangible assets. KSFs by their very nature are so important to future competitive success that *all firms* in the industry must pay close attention to them or risk an eventual exit from the industry.

In the ready-to-wear apparel industry, the KSFs are appealing designs and color combinations, low-cost manufacturing, a strong network of retailers or company-owned stores, distribution capabilities that allow stores to keep the best-selling items in stock, and advertisements that effectively convey the brand's image. These attributes and capabilities apply

CORE CONCEPT

Key success factors are the strategy elements, product attributes, competitive capabilities, or intangible assets with the greatest impact on future success in the marketplace.

to all brands of apparel ranging from private-label brands sold by discounters to premium-priced ready-to-wear brands sold by upscale department stores. Table 3.4 lists the most common types of industry key success factors.

TABLE 3.4
Common Types of Industry Key Success Factors

Technology-related KSFs	• Expertise in a particular technology or in scientific research (important in pharmaceuticals, Internet applications, mobile communications, and most high-tech industries) • Proven ability to improve production processes (important in industries where advancing technology opens the way for higher manufacturing efficiency and lower production costs)
Manufacturing-related KSFs	• Ability to achieve scale economies and/or capture experience curve effects (important to achieving low production costs) • Quality control know-how (important in industries where customers insist on product reliability) • High utilization of fixed assets (important in capital-intensive/high-fixed-cost industries) • Access to attractive supplies of skilled labor • High labor productivity (important for items with high labor content) • Low-cost product design and engineering (reduces manufacturing costs) • Ability to manufacture or assemble products that are customized to buyer specifications
Distribution-related KSFs	• A strong network of wholesale distributors/dealers • Strong direct sales capabilities via the Internet and/or having company-owned retail outlets • Ability to secure favorable display space on retailer shelves
Marketing-related KSFs	• Breadth of product line and product selection • A well-known and well-respected brand name • Fast, accurate technical assistance • Courteous, personalized customer service • Accurate filling of buyer orders (few back orders or mistakes) • Customer guarantees and warranties (important in mail-order and online retailing, big-ticket purchases, and new-product introductions) • Clever advertising
Skills- and capability-related KSFs	• A talented workforce (superior talent is important in professional services such as accounting and investment banking) • National or global distribution capabilities • Product innovation capabilities (important in industries where rivals are racing to be first to market with new product attributes or performance features) • Design expertise (important in fashion and apparel industries) • Short delivery time capability • Supply chain management capabilities • Strong e-commerce capabilities—a user-friendly website and/or skills in using Internet technology applications to streamline internal operations
Other types of KSFs	• Overall low costs (not just in manufacturing) to be able to meet low-price expectations of customers • Convenient locations (important in many retailing businesses) • Ability to provide fast, convenient, after-the-sale repairs and service • A strong balance sheet and access to financial capital (important in newly emerging industries with high degrees of business risk and in capital-intensive industries) • Patent protection

An industry's key success factors can usually be deduced through identifying the industry's dominant characteristics, assessing the five competitive forces, considering the impacts of the driving forces, comparing the market positions of industry members, and forecasting the likely next moves of key rivals. In addition, the answers to the following three questions help identify an industry's key success factors:

1. On what basis do buyers of the industry's product choose between the competing brands of sellers? That is, what product attributes are crucial?

2. Given the nature of the competitive forces prevailing in the marketplace, what resources and competitive capabilities does a company need to have to be competitively successful?

3. What shortcomings are almost certain to put a company at a significant competitive disadvantage?

Only rarely are there more than five or six key factors for future competitive success. Managers should therefore resist the temptation to label a factor that has only minor importance a KSF. To compile a list of every factor that matters even a little bit defeats the purpose of concentrating management attention on the factors truly critical to long-term competitive success.

Question 7: Does the Industry Offer Good Prospects for Attractive Profits?

LO4 Learn how to determine whether an industry's outlook presents a company with sufficiently attractive opportunities for growth and profitability.

The final step in evaluating the industry and competitive environment is boiling down the results of the analyses performed in Questions 1–6 to determine if the industry offers a company strong prospects for attractive profits.

The important factors on which to base such a conclusion include:

- The industry's growth potential.
- Whether powerful competitive forces are squeezing industry profitability to subpar levels and whether competition appears destined to grow stronger or weaker.
- Whether industry profitability will be favorably or unfavorably affected by the prevailing driving forces.
- The company's competitive position in the industry vis-à-vis rivals. (Well-entrenched leaders or strongly positioned contenders have a much better chance of earning attractive margins than those fighting a steep uphill battle.)
- How competently the company performs industry key success factors.

> The degree to which an industry is attractive or unattractive is not the same for all industry participants and potential new entrants. The attractiveness of an industry depends on the degree of fit between a company's competitive capabilities and industry key success factors.

It is a mistake to think of a particular industry as being equally attractive or unattractive to all industry participants and all potential entrants. Conclusions have to be drawn from the perspective of a particular company. Industries attractive to insiders may be unattractive to outsiders. Industry environments unattractive to weak competitors may be attractive to strong competitors. A favorably positioned company may survey a business environment and see a host of opportunities that weak competitors cannot capture.

When a company decides an industry is fundamentally attractive, a strong case can be made that it should invest aggressively to capture the opportunities it sees. When a strong competitor concludes an industry is relatively unattractive, it may elect to simply protect its present position, investing cautiously if at all, and begin looking for opportunities in other industries. A competitively weak company in an unattractive industry may see its best option as finding a buyer, perhaps a rival, to acquire its business.

KEY POINTS

Thinking strategically about a company's external situation involves probing for answers to the following eight questions:

1. *What are the strategically relevant factors in the macro-environment?* Industries differ as to how they are affected by conditions in the broad macro-environment. PESTEL analysis of the political, economic, sociocultural, technological, environmental/ecological, and legal/regulatory factors provides a framework for approaching this issue systematically.

2. *What are the industry's dominant economic features?* Industries may also differ significantly on such factors as market size and growth rate, the number and relative sizes of both buyers and sellers, the geographic scope of competitive rivalry, the degree of product differentiation, the speed of product innovation, demand-supply conditions, the extent of vertical integration, and the extent of scale economies and learning curve effects.

3. *What kinds of competitive forces are industry members facing, and how strong is each force?* The strength of competition is a composite of five forces: (1) competitive pressures stemming from buyer bargaining power and seller-buyer collaboration, (2) competitive pressures associated with the sellers of substitutes, (3) competitive pressures stemming from supplier bargaining power and supplier-seller collaboration, (4) competitive pressures associated with the threat of new entrants into the market, and (5) competitive pressures stemming from the competitive jockeying among industry rivals.

4. *What forces are driving changes in the industry, and what impact will these changes have on competitive intensity and industry profitability?* Industry and competitive conditions change because forces are in motion that create incentives or pressures for change. The first phase is to identify the forces that are driving industry change. The second phase of driving forces analysis is to determine whether the driving forces, taken together, are acting to make the industry environment more or less attractive.

5. *What market positions do industry rivals occupy—who is strongly positioned and who is not?* Strategic group mapping is a valuable tool for understanding the similarities and differences inherent in the market positions of rival companies. Rivals in the same or nearby strategic groups are close competitors, whereas companies in distant strategic groups usually pose little or no immediate threat. Some strategic groups are more favorable than others. The profit potential of different strategic

groups may not be the same because industry driving forces and competitive forces likely have varying effects on the industry's distinct strategic groups.

6. *What strategic moves are rivals likely to make next?* Scouting competitors well enough to anticipate their actions can help a company prepare effective countermoves (perhaps even beating a rival to the punch) and allows managers to take rivals' probable actions into account in designing their own company's best course of action.

7. *What are the key factors for competitive success?* An industry's key success factors (KSFs) are the particular product attributes, competitive capabilities, and intangible assets that spell the difference between being a strong competitor and a weak competitor—and sometimes between profit and loss. KSFs by their very nature are so important to competitive success that *all firms* in the industry must pay close attention to them or risk being driven out of the industry.

8. *Does the outlook for the industry present the company with sufficiently attractive prospects for profitability?* Conclusions regarding industry attractiveness are a major driver of company strategy. When a company decides an industry is fundamentally attractive and presents good opportunities, a strong case can be made that it should invest aggressively to capture the opportunities it sees. When a strong competitor concludes an industry is relatively unattractive and lacking in opportunity, it may elect to simply protect its present position, investing cautiously if at all and looking for opportunities in other industries. A competitively weak company in an unattractive industry may see its best option as finding a buyer, perhaps a rival, to acquire its business. On occasion, an industry that is unattractive overall is still very attractive to a favorably situated company with the skills and resources to take business away from weaker rivals.

ASSURANCE OF LEARNING EXERCISES

LO2 1. Prepare a brief analysis of the coffee industry using the information provided on industry trade association websites. Based upon information provided on the websites of these associations, draw a five-forces diagram for the coffee industry and briefly discuss the nature and strength of each of the five competitive forces.

LO3 2. Based on the strategic group map in Concepts & Connections 3.1, who are Nordstrom's closest competitors? Between which two strategic groups is competition the strongest? Why do you think no retail chains are positioned in the upper-right corner of the map? Which company/strategic group faces the weakest competition from the members of other strategic groups?

LO1, LO4 3. The National Restaurant Association publishes an annual industry factbook that can be found at www.restaurant.org. Based on information in the latest report, does it appear that macro-environmental factors and the economic characteristics of the industry will present industry participants with attractive opportunities for growth and profitability? Explain.

EXERCISES FOR SIMULATION PARTICIPANTS

1. Which of the five competitive forces is creating the strongest competitive pressures for your company?

2. What are the "weapons of competition" that rival companies in your industry can use to gain sales and market share? See Figure 3.7 to help you identify the various competitive factors.

3. What are the factors affecting the intensity of rivalry in the industry in which your company is competing? Use Figure 3.7 and the accompanying discussion to help you in pinpointing the specific factors most affecting competitive intensity. Would you characterize the rivalry and jockeying for better market position, increased sales, and market share among the companies in your industry as fierce, very strong, strong, moderate, or relatively weak? Why?

4. Are there any driving forces in the industry in which your company is competing? What impact will these driving forces have? Will they cause competition to be more or less intense? Will they act to boost or squeeze profit margins? List at least two actions your company should consider taking to combat any negative impacts of the driving forces.

5. Draw a strategic group map showing the market positions of the companies in your industry. Which companies do you believe are in the most attractive position on the map? Which companies are the most weakly positioned? Which companies do you believe are likely to try to move to a different position on the strategic group map?

6. What do you see as the key factors for being a successful competitor in your industry? List at least three.

7. Does your overall assessment of the industry suggest that industry rivals have sufficiently attractive opportunities for growth and profitability? Explain.

ENDNOTES

1. Michael E. Porter, *Competitive Strategy: Techniques for Analyzing Industries and Competitors* (New York: Free Press, 1980), chap. 1; Michael E. Porter, "The Five Competitive Forces That Shape Strategy," *Harvard Business Review* 86, no. 1 (January 2008).

2. J. S. Bain, *Barriers to New Competition* (Cambridge, MA: Harvard University Press, 1956); F. M. Scherer, *Industrial Market Structure and Economic Performance* (Chicago: Rand McNally & Co., 1971).

3. Pankaj Ghemawat, "Building Strategy on the Experience Curve," *Harvard Business Review* 64, no. 2 (March–April 1985).

4. Michael E. Porter, "How Competitive Forces Shape Strategy," *Harvard Business Review* 57, no. 2 (March–April 1979).

5. Pamela J. Derfus, Patrick G. Maggitti, Curtis M. Grimm, and Ken G. Smith, "The Red Queen Effect: Competitive Actions and Firm Performance," *Academy of Management Journal* 51, no. 1 (February 2008).

6. Mary Ellen Gordon and George R. Milne, "Selecting the Dimensions That Define Strategic Groups: A Novel Market-Driven Approach," *Journal of Managerial Issues* 11, no. 2 (Summer 1999).

7. Avi Fiegenbaum and Howard Thomas, "Strategic Groups as Reference Groups: Theory, Modeling and Empirical Examination of Industry and Competitive Strategy," *Strategic Management Journal* 16 (1995); and S. Ade Olusoga, Michael P. Mokwa, and Charles H. Noble, "Strategic Groups, Mobility Barriers, and Competitive Advantage," *Journal of Business Research* 33 (1995).

8. Larry Kahaner, *Competitive Intelligence* (New York: Simon and Schuster, 1996).

9. Kevin P. Coyne and John Horn, "Predicting Your Competitor's Reaction," *Harvard Business Review* 87, no. 4 (April 2009).

Evaluating a Company's Resources, Capabilities, and Competitiveness

LEARNING OBJECTIVES

LO1 Learn how to assess how well a company's strategy is working.

LO2 Understand why a company's resources and capabilities are central to its strategic approach and how to evaluate their potential for giving the company a competitive edge over rivals.

LO3 Grasp how a company's value chain activities can affect the company's cost structure and customer value proposition.

LO4 Learn how to evaluate a company's competitive strength relative to key rivals.

LO5 Understand how a comprehensive evaluation of a company's external and internal situations can assist managers in making critical decisions about their next strategic moves.

Chapter 3 described how to use the tools of industry and competitive analysis to assess a company's external environment and lay the groundwork for matching a company's strategy to its external situation. This chapter discusses the techniques of evaluating a company's internal situation, including its collection of resources and capabilities, its cost structure and customer value proposition, and its competitive strength versus its rivals. The analytical spotlight will be trained on five questions:

1. How well is the company's strategy working?
2. What are the company's competitively important resources and capabilities?
3. Are the company's cost structure and customer value proposition competitive?
4. Is the company competitively stronger or weaker than key rivals?
5. What strategic issues and problems merit front-burner managerial attention?

The answers to these five questions complete management's understanding of the company's overall situation and position the company for a good strategy-situation fit required by the "The Three Tests of a Winning Strategy" (see Chapter 1, page 9).

Question 1: How Well Is the Company's Strategy Working?

The two best indicators of how well a company's strategy is working are (1) whether the company is recording gains in financial strength and profitability and (2) whether the company's competitive strength and market standing are improving. Persistent shortfalls in meeting company financial performance targets and weak performance relative to rivals are reliable warning signs that the company suffers from poor strategy making, less-than-competent strategy execution, or both. Other indicators of how well a company's strategy is working include:

LO1 Learn how to assess how well a company's strategy is working.

- Trends in the company's sales and earnings growth.
- Trends in the company's stock price.
- The company's overall financial strength.
- The company's customer retention rate.
- The rate at which new customers are acquired.
- Changes in the company's image and reputation with customers.
- Evidence of improvement in internal processes such as defect rate, order fulfillment, delivery times, days of inventory, and employee productivity.

The stronger a company's current overall performance, the less likely the need for radical changes in strategy. The weaker a company's financial performance and market standing, the more its current strategy must be questioned. (A compilation of financial ratios most commonly used to evaluate a company's financial performance and balance sheet strength is presented in the Appendix on pages 240–241.)

Question 2: What Are the Company's Competitively Important Resources and Capabilities?

LO2 Understand why a company's resources and capabilities are central to its strategic approach and how to evaluate their potential for giving the company a competitive edge over rivals.

As discussed in Chapter 1, a company's business model and strategy must be well matched to its collection of resources and capabilities. An attempt to create and deliver customer value in a manner that depends on resources or capabilities that are deficient and cannot be readily acquired or developed is unwise and positions the company for failure. A company's competitive approach requires a tight fit with a company's internal situation and is strengthened when it exploits resources that are competitively valuable, rare, hard to copy, and not easily trumped by rivals' substitute resources. In addition, long-term competitive advantage requires the ongoing development and expansion of resources and capabilities to pursue emerging market opportunities and defend against future threats to its market standing and profitability.[1]

Sizing up the company's collection of resources and capabilities and determining whether they can provide the foundation for competitive success can be achieved through **resource and capability analysis.** This is a two-step process: (1) identify the company's resources and capabilities, and (2) examine them more closely to ascertain which are the most competitively important and whether they can support a sustainable competitive advantage over rival firms.[2] This second step involves applying the *four tests of a resource's competitive power.*

Resource and capability analysis is a powerful tool for sizing up a company's competitive assets and determining if the assets can support a sustainable competitive advantage over market rivals.

Identifying Competitively Important Resources and Capabilities

A company's **resources** are competitive assets that are owned or controlled by the company and may either be *tangible resources* such as plants, distribution centers, manufacturing equipment, patents, information systems, and capital reserves or creditworthiness or *intangible assets* such as a well-known brand or a results-oriented organizational culture. Table 4.1 lists the common types of tangible and intangible resources that a company may possess.

A **capability** is the capacity of a firm to competently perform some internal activity. A capability may also be referred to as a **competence.** Capabilities or competences also vary in form, quality, and competitive importance, with some being more competitively valuable than others. *Organizational capabilities are developed and enabled through the deployment of a company's resources or some combination of its resources.*[3] Some capabilities rely heavily on a company's intangible

CORE CONCEPT

A **resource** is a competitive asset that is owned or controlled by a company; a **capability** is the capacity of a company to competently perform some internal activity. Capabilities are developed and enabled through the deployment of a company's resources.

TABLE 4.1

Common Types of Tangible and Intangible Resources

Tangible Resources

- *Physical resources*—state-of-the-art manufacturing plants and equipment, efficient distribution facilities, attractive real estate locations, or ownership of valuable natural resource deposits.
- *Financial resources*—cash and cash equivalents, marketable securities, and other financial assets such as a company's credit rating and borrowing capacity.
- *Technological assets*—patents, copyrights, superior production technology, and technologies that enable activities.
- *Organizational resources*—information and communication systems (servers, workstations, etc.), proven quality control systems, and strong network of distributors or retail dealers.

Intangible Resources

- *Human assets and intellectual capital*—an experienced and capable workforce, talented employees in key areas, collective learning embedded in the organization, or proven managerial know-how.
- *Brand, image, and reputational assets*—brand names, trademarks, product or company image, buyer loyalty, and reputation for quality, superior service.
- *Relationships*—alliances or joint ventures that provide access to technologies, specialized know-how, or geographic markets, and trust established with various partners.
- *Company culture*—the norms of behavior, business principles, and ingrained beliefs within the company.

resources, such as human assets and intellectual capital. For example, General Mills' brand management capabilities draw upon the knowledge of the company's brand managers, the expertise of its marketing department, and the company's relationships with retailers. Electronic Arts' video game design capabilities result from the creative talents and technological expertise of its game developers and the company's culture that encourages creative thinking.

Determining the Competitive Power of a Company's Resources and Capabilities

What is most telling about a company's aggregation of resources and capabilities is how powerful they are in the marketplace. The competitive power of a resource or capability is measured by how many of the following four tests it can pass.[4]

> **CORE CONCEPT**
>
> The **VRIN tests for sustainable competitive advantage** ask if a resource or capability is *valuable, rare, inimitable,* and *nonsubstitutable.*

The tests are often referred to as the **VRIN tests for sustainable competitive advantage**—an acronym for *valuable, rare, inimitable,* and *nonsubstitutable.* The first two tests determine whether the resource or capability may contribute to a competitive advantage. The last two determine the degree to which the competitive advantage potential can be sustained.

1. *Is the resource or capability competitively **valuable**?* All companies possess a collection of resources and capabilities—some have the potential

to contribute to a competitive advantage while others may not. Apple's operating system for its personal computers by some accounts is superior to Windows 8, but Apple has failed in converting its resources devoted to operating system design into anything more than moderate competitive success in the global PC market.

> **CORE CONCEPT**
>
> A **core competence** is a proficiently performed internal activity that is *central* to a company's strategy and competitiveness. A core competence that is performed with a very high level of proficiency is referred to as a **distinctive competence**.

A capability that passes the "competitively valuable" test and is *central* to a company's strategy and competitiveness is frequently referred to as a **core competence.** A competitively valuable capability that is performed with a very high level of proficiency is sometimes known as a **distinctive competence.** Most often, *a core competence or distinctive competence is knowledge-based, residing in people and in a company's intellectual capital and not in its assets on the balance sheet.*

2. *Is the resource or capability **rare**—is it something rivals lack?* Resources and capabilities that are common among firms and widely available cannot be a source of competitive advantage. All makers of branded cookies and sweet snacks have valuable marketing capabilities and brands. Therefore, these skills are not rare or unique in the industry. However, the brand strength of Oreo is uncommon and has provided Kraft Foods with greater market share as well as the opportunity to benefit from brand extensions such as Double Stuf Oreo cookies and Mini Oreo cookies.

3. *Is the resource or capability **inimitable** or hard to copy?* The more difficult and more expensive it is to imitate a company's resource or capability, the more likely that it can also provide a *sustainable* competitive advantage. Resources tend to be difficult to copy when they are unique (a fantastic real estate location, patent protection), when they must be built over time (a brand name, a strategy-supportive organizational culture), and when they carry big capital requirements (a cost-effective plant to manufacture cutting-edge microprocessors). Imitation by rivals is most challenging when capabilities reflect a high level of *social complexity* (for example, a stellar team-oriented culture or unique trust-based relationships with employees, suppliers, or customers) and *causal ambiguity,* a term that signifies the hard-to-disentangle nature of complex processes, such as the web of intricate activities enabling a new drug discovery.

4. *Is the resource or capability **nonsubstitutable** or is it vulnerable to the threat of substitution from different types of resources and capabilities?* Resources that are competitively valuable, rare, and costly to imitate may lose much of their ability to offer competitive advantage if rivals possess equivalent substitute resources. For example, manufacturers relying on automation to gain a cost-based advantage in production activities may find their technology-based advantage nullified by rivals' use of low-wage offshore manufacturing. Resources can contribute to a competitive advantage only when resource substitutes don't exist.

Understanding the nature of competitively important resources allows managers to identify resources or capabilities that should be further developed to play an important role in the company's future strategies. In addition, management may determine that it doesn't possess a resource that independently passes all four tests listed here with high marks, but that it does have a **bundle of resources** that can pass the tests. Although Nike's resources dedicated to research and development, marketing research, and product design are matched relatively well by rival Adidas, its cross-functional design process allows it to set the pace for innovation in athletic apparel and footwear and consistently outperform Adidas and other rivals in the marketplace. Nike's footwear designers get ideas for new performance features from the professional athletes who endorse its products and then work alongside footwear materials researchers, consumer trend analysts, color designers, and marketers to design new models that are presented to a review committee. Nike's review committee is made up of hundreds of individuals who evaluate prototype details such as shoe proportions and color designs, the size of the swoosh, stitching patterns, sole color and tread pattern, and insole design. About 400 models are approved by the committee each year, which are sourced from contract manufacturers and marketed in more than 180 countries. The bundling of Nike's professional endorsements, R&D activities, marketing research efforts, styling expertise, and managerial know-how has become an important source of the company's competitive advantage and has allowed it to remain number one in the athletic footwear and apparel industry for more than 20 years.

> **CORE CONCEPT**
>
> Companies that lack a stand-alone resource that is competitively powerful may nonetheless develop a competitive advantage through **resource bundles** that enable the superior performance of important cross-functional capabilities.

Companies lacking certain resources needed for competitive success in an industry may be able to adopt strategies directed at eroding or at least neutralizing the competitive potency of a particular rival's resources and capabilities by identifying and developing **substitute resources** to accomplish the same purpose. For example, Amazon.com lacks a big network of retail stores to compete with those operated by rival Barnes & Noble, but Amazon's much larger, readily accessible, and searchable book inventory—coupled with its short delivery times and free shipping on orders over $25—are more attractive to many busy consumers than visiting a big-box bookstore. In other words, Amazon has carefully and consciously developed a set of competitively valuable resources that are proving to be effective substitutes for competing head-to-head against Barnes & Noble without having to invest in hundreds of brick-and-mortar retail stores.[5]

> Rather than try to match the resources possessed by a rival company, a company may develop entirely different resources that substitute for the strengths of the rival.

The Importance of Dynamic Capabilities in Sustaining Competitive Advantage

Resources and capabilities must be continually strengthened and nurtured to sustain their competitive power and, at times, may need to be broadened and deepened to allow the company to position itself to pursue emerging market opportunities.[6] Organizational resources and capabilities that grow stale can impair competitiveness unless they are refreshed, modified, or even phased out and replaced in response to ongoing market changes and shifts in company strategy. In addition, disruptive environmental change may destroy the value of key strategic assets, turning *static* resources and capabilities "from diamonds to rust."[7] Management's organization-building challenge has two elements: (1) attending to ongoing recalibration of existing capabilities and resources, and (2) casting a watchful eye for opportunities to develop totally new capabilities for delivering better customer value and/or outcompeting rivals. Companies that know the importance of recalibrating and upgrading resources and capabilities make it a routine management function to build new resource configurations and capabilities. Such a managerial approach allows a company to prepare for market changes and pursue emerging opportunities. This ability to build and integrate new competitive assets becomes a capability in itself—a **dynamic capability.** A dynamic capability is the ability to modify, deepen, or reconfigure the company's existing resources and capabilities in response to its changing environment or market opportunities.[8]

Management at Toyota has aggressively upgraded the company's capabilities in fuel-efficient hybrid engine technology and constantly fine-tuned the famed Toyota Production System to enhance the company's already proficient capabilities in manufacturing top-quality vehicles at relatively low costs. Likewise, management at Honda has recently accelerated the company's efforts to broaden its expertise and capabilities in hybrid engines to stay close to Toyota. Resources and capabilities can also be built and augmented through alliances and acquisitions.[9] Cisco Systems has greatly expanded its engineering capabilities and its ability to enter new product categories through frequent acquisitions. Strategic alliances are a commonly used approach to developing and reconfiguring capabilities in the biotech and pharmaceutical industries.

> **CORE CONCEPT**
>
> A **dynamic capability** is the ability to modify, deepen, or reconfigure the company's existing resources and capabilities in response to its changing environment or market opportunities.

> A company requires a dynamically evolving portfolio of resources and capabilities in order to sustain its competitiveness and position itself to pursue future market opportunities.

Is the Company Able to Seize Market Opportunities and Nullify External Threats?

An essential element in evaluating a company's overall situation entails examining the company's resources and competitive capabilities in terms of the degree to which they enable it to pursue its best market opportunities and defend against the external threats to its future well-being. The simplest and most easily applied tool for conducting this examination is widely known as *SWOT analysis,* so named because it zeros in on a company's internal **S**trengths and **W**eaknesses, market **O**pportunities, and external **T**hreats. *A company's internal strengths should always serve as the basis of its strategy—placing heavy reliance on a company's best competitive*

> **CORE CONCEPT**
>
> **SWOT analysis** is a simple but powerful tool for sizing up a company's internal strengths and competitive deficiencies, its market opportunities, and the external threats to its future well-being.

assets is the soundest route to attracting customers and competing successfully against rivals.[10] As a rule, strategies that place heavy demands on areas where the company is weakest or has unproven competencies should be avoided. Plainly, managers must look toward correcting competitive

> Basing a company's strategy on its strengths resulting from most competitively valuable resources and capabilities gives the company its best chance for market success.

weaknesses that make the company vulnerable, hold down profitability, or disqualify it from pursuing an attractive opportunity. Furthermore, a company's strategy should be aimed squarely at capturing those market opportunities that are most attractive and suited to the company's collection of capabilities. How much attention to devote to defending against external threats to the company's future performance hinges on how vulnerable the company is, whether defensive moves can be taken to lessen their impact, and whether the costs of undertaking such moves represent the best use of company resources. A first-rate SWOT analysis provides the basis for crafting a strategy that capitalizes on the company's strengths, aims squarely at capturing the company's best opportunities, and defends against the threats to its well-being. Table 4.2 lists the kinds of factors to consider in compiling a company's resource strengths and weaknesses.

The Value of a SWOT Analysis   A SWOT analysis involves more than making four lists. The most important parts of SWOT analysis are:

1. Drawing conclusions from the SWOT listings about the company's overall situation.

2. Translating these conclusions into strategic actions to better match the company's strategy to its strengths and market opportunities, correcting problematic weaknesses, and defending against worrisome external threats.

> Simply listing a company's strengths, weaknesses, opportunities, and threats is not enough; the payoff from SWOT analysis comes from the conclusions about a company's situation and the implications for strategy improvement that flow from the four lists.

Question 3: Are the Company's Cost Structure and Customer Value Proposition Competitive?

Company managers are often stunned when a competitor cuts its prices to "unbelievably low" levels or when a new market entrant comes on strong with a great new product offered at a surprisingly low price. Such competitors may not, however, be buying market positions with prices that are below costs. They may simply have substantially lower costs and therefore are able to offer prices that result in more appealing customer value propositions. One of the most telling signs of whether a company's business position is strong or precarious is whether its cost structure and customer value proposition are competitive with industry rivals.

LO3 Grasp how a company's value chain activities can affect the company's cost structure and customer value proposition.

Cost comparisons are especially critical in industries where price competition is typically the ruling market force. But even in industries where products are differentiated, rival companies have to keep their costs in line with rivals offering value propositions based upon a similar mix of differentiating features.

TABLE 4.2

Factors to Consider When Identifying a Company's Strengths, Weaknesses, Opportunities, and Threats

Potential Internal Strengths and Competitive Capabilities

- Core competencies in _____.
- A strong financial condition; ample financial resources to grow the business.
- Strong brand-name image/company reputation.
- Economies of scale and/or learning and experience curve advantages over rivals.
- Proprietary technology/superior technological skills/important patents.
- Cost advantages over rivals.
- Product innovation capabilities.
- Proven capabilities in improving production processes.
- Good supply chain management capabilities.
- Good customer service capabilities.
- Better product quality relative to rivals.
- Wide geographic coverage and/or strong global distribution capability.
- Alliances/joint ventures with other firms that provide access to valuable technology, competencies, and/or attractive geographic markets.

Potential Internal Weaknesses and Competitive Deficiencies

- No clear strategic direction.
- No well-developed or proven core competencies.
- A weak balance sheet; burdened with too much debt.
- Higher overall unit costs relative to key competitors.
- A product/service with features and attributes that are inferior to those of rivals.
- Too narrow a product line relative to rivals.
- Weak brand image or reputation.
- Weaker dealer network than key rivals.
- Behind on product quality, R&D, and/or technological know-how.
- Lack of management depth.
- Short on financial resources to grow the business and pursue promising initiatives.

Potential Market Opportunities

- Serving additional customer groups or market segments.
- Expanding into new geographic markets.
- Expanding the company's product line to meet a broader range of customer needs.
- Utilizing existing company skills or technological know-how to enter new product lines or new businesses.
- Falling trade barriers in attractive foreign markets.
- Acquiring rival firms or companies with attractive technological expertise or capabilities.

Potential External Threats to a Company's Future Prospects

- Increasing intensity of competition among industry rivals—may squeeze profit margins.
- Slowdowns in market growth.
- Likely entry of potent new competitors.
- Growing bargaining power of customers or suppliers.
- A shift in buyer needs and tastes away from the industry's product.
- Adverse demographic changes that threaten to curtail demand for the industry's product.
- Vulnerability to unfavorable industry driving forces.
- Restrictive trade policies on the part of foreign governments.
- Costly new regulatory requirements.

But a company must also remain competitive in terms of its customer value proposition. Tiffany's value proposition, for example, remains attractive to people who want customer service, the assurance of quality, and a high-status brand despite the availability of cut-rate diamond jewelry online. Target's customer value proposition has withstood the Walmart low-price juggernaut by attention to product design, image, and attractive store layouts in addition to efficiency. The key for managers is to keep close track of how *cost effectively* the company can deliver value to customers relative to its competitors. *If the company can deliver the same amount of value with lower expenditures (or more value at a similar cost), it will maintain a competitive edge.* Two analytical tools are particularly useful in determining whether a company's value proposition and costs are competitive: value chain analysis and benchmarking.

> Competitive advantage hinges on how cost effectively a company can execute its customer value proposition.

Company Value Chains

Every company's business consists of a collection of activities undertaken in the course of designing, producing, marketing, delivering, and supporting its product or service. All of the various activities that a company performs internally combine to form a **value chain,** so called because the underlying intent of a company's activities is to do things that ultimately *create value for buyers.*

As shown in Figure 4.1, a company's value chain consists of two broad categories of activities that drive costs and create customer value: the *primary activities* that are foremost in creating value for customers and the requisite *support activities*

> **CORE CONCEPT**
>
> A company's **value chain** identifies the primary activities that create customer value and related support activities.

that facilitate and enhance the performance of the primary activities.[11] For example, the primary activities and cost drivers for a big-box retailer such as Target include merchandise selection and buying, store layout and product display, advertising, and customer service; its support activities that affect customer value and costs include site selection, hiring and training, store maintenance, plus the usual assortment of administrative activities. A hotel chain's primary activities and costs are mainly comprised of reservations and hotel operations (check-in and check-out, maintenance and housekeeping, dining and room service, and conventions and meetings); principal support activities that drive costs and impact customer value include accounting, hiring and training hotel staff, and general administration. Supply chain management is a crucial activity for Nissan or Amazon.com but is not a value chain component at Google or CBS. Sales and marketing are dominant activities at Procter & Gamble and Sony but have minor roles at oil-drilling companies and natural gas pipeline companies. With its focus on value-creating activities, the value chain is an ideal tool for examining how a company delivers on its customer value proposition. It permits a deep look at the company's cost structure and ability to offer low prices. It reveals the emphasis that a company places on activities that enhance differentiation and support higher prices, such as service and marketing.

The value chain also includes a profit margin component; profits are necessary to compensate the company's owners/shareholders and investors,

FIGURE 4.1　**A Representative Company Value Chain**

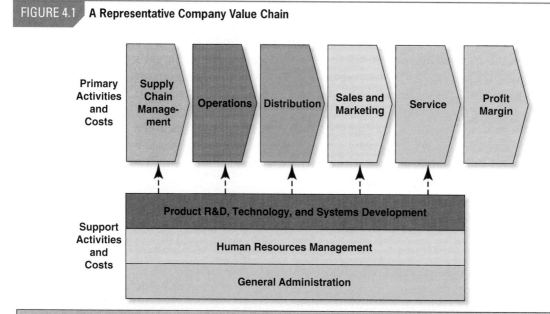

PRIMARY ACTIVITIES

• **Supply Chain Management**—Activities, costs, and assets associated with purchasing fuel, energy, raw materials, parts and components, merchandise, and consumable items from vendors; receiving, storing, and disseminating inputs from suppliers; inspection; and inventory management.

• **Operations**—Activities, costs, and assets associated with converting inputs into final product form (production, assembly, packaging, equipment maintenance, facilities, operations, quality assurance, environmental protection).

• **Distribution**—Activities, costs, and assets dealing with physically distributing the product to buyers (finished goods warehousing, order processing, order picking and packing, shipping, delivery vehicle operations, establishing and maintaining a network of dealers and distributors).

• **Sales and Marketing**—Activities, costs, and assets related to sales force efforts, advertising and promotion, market research and planning, and dealer/distributor support.

• **Service**—Activities, costs, and assets associated with providing assistance to buyers, such as installation, spare parts delivery, maintenance and repair, technical assistance, buyer inquiries, and complaints.

SUPPORT ACTIVITIES

• **Product R&D, Technology, and Systems Development**—Activities, costs, and assets relating to product R&D, process R&D, process design improvement, equipment design, computer software development, telecommunications systems, computer-assisted design and engineering, database capabilities, and development of computerized support systems.

• **Human Resources Management**—Activities, costs, and assets associated with the recruitment, hiring, training, development, and compensation of all types of personnel; labor relations activities; and development of knowledge-based skills and core competencies.

• **General Administration**—Activities, costs, and assets relating to general management, accounting and finance, legal and regulatory affairs, safety and security, management information systems, forming strategic alliances and collaborating with strategic partners, and other "overhead" functions.

Source: Based on the discussion in Michael E. Porter, *Competitive Advantage* (New York: Free Press, 1985), pp. 37–43.

who bear risks and provide capital. Tracking the profit margin along with the value-creating activities is critical because unless an enterprise succeeds in delivering customer value profitably (with a sufficient return on invested capital), it can't survive for long. Attention to a company's profit formula in

CONCEPTS & CONNECTIONS 4.1

THE VALUE CHAIN FOR KP MACLANE, A PRODUCER OF POLO SHIRTS

Value Chain Activities and Costs in Producing and Selling a Women's Polo Shirt

1. Cotton-blend fabric from France	$ 6.80
2. Fabric for placket and vent	$ 0.99
3. 4 buttons, including 1 extra	$ 0.12
4. Thread	$ 0.09
5. Labels	$ 1.10
6. Hang tag	$ 0.40
7. Waste fabric	$ 0.85
8. Labor	$ 11.05
9. Packing materials	$ 0.17
10. Shipping materials to factory; shirt to store	$ 5.00
11. Hand-embroidered linen bag	$ 3.00
12. Total company costs	$ 29.57
13. Wholesale markup over company costs (company operating profit)	$ 35.43
14. Wholesale price	$ 65.00
15. Retailer's markup	$ 90.00
16. Retail price	$155.00

Source: Christina Binkley, "What Goes into a $155 Price Tag," *The Wall Street Journal,* U.S. Home Edition, On Style, February 2, 2012, http://online.wsj.com/article_email/SB10001424052970204652904577195252388913754-IMyQjAxMTAyMDAwMzEwNDMyWj.html?mod=wsj_share_email.

addition to its customer value proposition is the essence of a sound business model, as described in Chapter 1. Concepts & Connections 4.1 shows representative costs for various activities performed by KP MacLane, a maker of upscale polo shirts.

Benchmarking: A Tool for Assessing Whether a Company's Value Chain Activities Are Competitive

Benchmarking entails comparing how different companies perform various value chain activities—how materials are purchased, how inventories are managed, how products are assembled, how customer orders are filled and shipped, and how maintenance is performed—and then making cross-company comparisons of the costs and effectiveness of these activities.[12] The objectives of benchmarking are to identify the best practices in performing an activity and to emulate those best practices when they are possessed by others.

> **CORE CONCEPT**
>
> **Benchmarking** is a potent tool for learning which companies are best at performing particular activities and then using their techniques (or "best practices") to improve the cost and effectiveness of a company's own internal activities.

Xerox led the way in the use of benchmarking to become more cost-competitive by deciding not to restrict its benchmarking efforts to its office equipment rivals, but by comparing itself to *any company* regarded as "world class" in performing activities relevant to Xerox's business. Other companies quickly picked up on Xerox's approach. Toyota managers got their idea for just-in-time inventory deliveries by studying how U.S. supermarkets replenished their shelves. Southwest Airlines reduced the turnaround time of its aircraft at each scheduled stop by studying pit crews on the auto-racing circuit. More than 80 percent of Fortune 500 companies reportedly use benchmarking for comparing themselves against rivals on cost and other competitively important measures.

The tough part of benchmarking is not whether to do it, but rather how to gain access to information about other companies' practices and costs. Sometimes benchmarking can be accomplished by collecting information from published reports, trade groups, and industry research firms and by talking to knowledgeable industry analysts, customers, and suppliers. Sometimes field trips to the facilities of competing or noncompeting companies can be arranged to observe how things are done, compare practices and processes, and perhaps exchange data on productivity and other cost components. However, such companies, even if they agree to host facilities tours and answer questions, are unlikely to share competitively sensitive cost information. Furthermore, comparing two companies' costs may not involve comparing apples to apples if the two companies employ different cost accounting principles to calculate the costs of particular activities.

However, a fairly reliable source of benchmarking information has emerged. The explosive interest of companies in benchmarking costs and identifying best practices has prompted consulting organizations (e.g., Accenture, A. T. Kearney, Benchnet—The Benchmarking Exchange, Towers Watson, and Best Practices, LLC) and several councils and associations (e.g., the APQC, the Qualserve Benchmarking Clearinghouse, and the Strategic Planning Institute's Council on Benchmarking) to gather benchmarking data, distribute information about best practices, and provide comparative cost data without identifying the names of particular companies. Having an independent group gather the information and report it in a manner that disguises the names of individual companies avoids the disclosure of competitively sensitive data and lessens the potential for unethical behavior on the part of company personnel in gathering their own data about competitors.

The Value Chain System for an Entire Industry

A company's value chain is embedded in a larger system of activities that includes the value chains of its suppliers and the value chains of whatever distribution channel allies it utilizes in getting its product or service to end users. The value chains of forward channel partners are relevant because (1) the costs and margins of a company's distributors and retail dealers are part of the price the consumer ultimately pays, and (2) the activities that distribution allies perform affect the company's customer value proposition. For these reasons, companies normally work closely with their suppliers and forward channel allies to perform value chain activities in mutually beneficial ways. For instance, motor vehicle manufacturers work closely with their forward channel allies (local automobile dealers) to ensure that owners are satisfied with dealers' repair and maintenance services.[13] Also, many automotive parts suppliers

> A company's customer value proposition and cost competitiveness depend not only on internally performed activities (its own company value chain), but also on the value chain activities of its suppliers and forward channel allies.

have built plants near the auto assembly plants they supply to facilitate just-in-time deliveries, reduce warehousing and shipping costs, and promote close collaboration on parts design and production scheduling. Irrigation equipment companies, suppliers of grape-harvesting and winemaking equipment, and firms making barrels, wine bottles, caps, corks, and labels all have facilities in the California wine country to be close to the nearly 700 winemakers they supply.[14] The lesson here is that a company's value chain activities are often closely linked to the value chains of its suppliers and the forward allies.

As a consequence, *accurately assessing the competitiveness of a company's cost structure and customer value proposition requires that company managers understand an industry's entire value chain system for delivering a product or service to customers, not just the company's own value chain.* A typical industry value chain that incorporates the value-creating activities, costs, and margins of suppliers and forward channel allies (if any) is shown in Figure 4.2. However, industry value chains vary significantly by industry. For example, the primary value chain activities in the bottled water industry (spring operation or water purification, processing of basic ingredients used in flavored or vitamin-enhanced water, bottling, wholesale distribution, advertising, and retail merchandising) differ from those for the computer software industry (programming, disk loading, marketing, distribution). Producers of bathroom and kitchen faucets depend heavily on the activities of wholesale distributors and building supply retailers in winning sales to home builders and do-it-yourselfers, but producers of papermaking machines internalize their distribution activities by selling directly to the operators of paper plants.

Strategic Options for Remedying a Cost or Value Disadvantage

The results of value chain analysis and benchmarking may disclose cost or value disadvantages relative to key rivals. These competitive disadvantages are likely to lower a company's relative profit margin or weaken its customer value proposition. In such instances, actions to improve a company's value chain are called for to boost profitability or to allow for the addition of new

FIGURE 4.2 Representative Value Chain for an Entire Industry

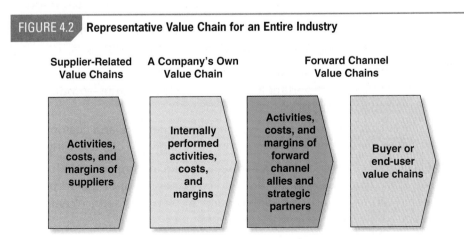

Source: Based in part on the single-industry value chain displayed in Michael E. Porter, *Competitive Advantage* (New York: Free Press, 1985), p. 35.

features that drive customer value. There are three main areas in a company's overall value chain where important differences between firms in costs and value can occur: a company's own internal activities, the suppliers' part of the industry value chain, and the forward channel portion of the industry chain.

Improving Internally Performed Value Chain Activities

Managers can pursue any of several strategic approaches to reduce the costs of internally performed value chain activities and improve a company's cost competitiveness.

1. *Implement the use of best practices* throughout the company, particularly for high-cost activities.

2. *Try to eliminate some cost-producing activities* by revamping the value chain. Many retailers have found that donating returned items to charitable organizations and taking the appropriate tax deduction results in a smaller loss than incurring the costs of the value chain activities involved in reverse logistics.

3. *Relocate high-cost activities* (such as manufacturing) to geographic areas such as China, Latin America, or Eastern Europe where they can be performed more cheaply.

4. *Outsource certain internally performed activities* to vendors or contractors if they can perform them more cheaply than can be done in-house.

5. *Invest in productivity-enhancing, cost-saving technological improvements* (robotics, flexible manufacturing techniques, state-of-the-art electronic networking).

6. *Find ways to detour around the activities or items where costs are high*—computer chip makers regularly design around the patents held by others to avoid paying royalties; automakers have substituted lower-cost plastic for metal at many exterior body locations.

7. *Redesign the product* and/or some of its components to facilitate speedier and more economical manufacture or assembly.

8. *Try to make up the internal cost disadvantage* by reducing costs in the supplier or forward channel portions of the industry value chain—usually a last resort.

Rectifying a weakness in a company's customer value proposition can be accomplished by applying one or more of the following approaches:

1. Implement the use of best practices throughout the company, particularly for activities that are important for creating customer value—product design, product quality, or customer service.

2. Adopt best practices for marketing, brand management, and customer relationship management to improve brand image and customer loyalty.

3. Reallocate resources to activities having a significant impact on value delivered to customers—larger R&D budgets, new state-of-the-art production facilities, new distribution centers, modernized service centers, or enhanced budgets for marketing campaigns.

Additional approaches to managing value chain activities that drive costs, uniqueness, and value are discussed in Chapter 5.

Improving Supplier-Related Value Chain Activities   Supplier-related cost disadvantages can be attacked by pressuring suppliers for lower prices, switching to lower-priced substitute inputs, and collaborating closely with suppliers to identify mutual cost-saving opportunities.[15] For example, just-in-time deliveries from suppliers can lower a company's inventory and internal logistics costs, eliminate capital expenditures for additional warehouse space, and improve cash flow and financial ratios by reducing accounts payable. In a few instances, companies may find that it is cheaper to integrate backward into the business of high-cost suppliers and make the item in-house instead of buying it from outsiders.

Similarly, a company can enhance its customer value proposition through its supplier relationships. Some approaches include selecting and retaining suppliers that meet higher-quality standards, providing quality-based incentives to suppliers, and integrating suppliers into the design process. When fewer defects exist in components provided by suppliers this not only improves product quality and reliability, but it can also lower costs because there is less disruption to production processes and lower warranty expenses.

Improving Value Chain Activities of Forward Channel Allies   There are three main ways to combat a cost disadvantage in the forward portion of the industry value chain: (1) Pressure dealer-distributors and other forward channel allies to reduce their costs and markups; (2) work closely with forward channel allies to identify win-win opportunities to reduce costs—for example, a chocolate manufacturer learned that by shipping its bulk chocolate in liquid form in tank cars instead of 10-pound molded bars, it could not only save its candy bar manufacturing customers the costs associated with unpacking and melting but also eliminate its own costs of molding bars and packing them; and (3) change to a more economical distribution strategy or perhaps integrate forward into company-owned retail outlets. Dell Computer's direct sales model eliminated all activities, costs, and margins of distributors, dealers, and retailers by allowing buyers to purchase customized PCs directly from Dell.

A company can improve its customer value proposition through the activities of forward channel partners by the use of (1) cooperative advertising and promotions with forward channel allies; (2) training programs for dealers, distributors, or retailers to improve the purchasing experience or customer service; and (3) creating and enforcing operating standards for resellers or franchisees to ensure consistent store operations. Harley-Davidson, for example, enhances the shopping experience and perceptions of buyers by selling through dealers that represent Harley-Davidson motorcycles exclusively and operate under strict operating guidelines developed by Harley-Davidson.

How Value Chain Activities Relate to Resources and Capabilities

A close relationship exists between the value-creating activities that a company performs and its resources and capabilities. When companies engage in a value-creating activity, they do so by drawing on specific company resources and capabilities that underlie and enable the activity. For example, brand-building activities that enhance a company's customer value proposition can depend on human resources, such as experienced brand managers, as well as organizational capabilities related to developing and executing effective marketing campaigns. Distribution activities that lower costs may derive from organizational capabilities in inventory management and resources such as cutting-edge inventory tracking systems.

Because of the linkage between activities and enabling resources and capabilities, value chain analysis complements resource and capability analysis as another tool for assessing a company's competitive advantage. Resources and capabilities that are *both valuable and rare* provide a company with the *necessary preconditions* for competitive advantage. When these assets are deployed in the form of a value-creating activity, *that potential is realized.* Resource analysis is a valuable tool for assessing the competitive advantage potential of resources and capabilities. But the actual competitive benefit provided by resources and capabilities can only be assessed objectively after they are deployed in the form of activities.

Question 4: What Is the Company's Competitive Strength Relative to Key Rivals?

LO4 Learn how to evaluate a company's competitive strength relative to key rivals.

An additional component of evaluating a company's situation is developing a comprehensive assessment of the company's overall competitive strength. Making this determination requires answers to two questions:

1. How does the company rank relative to competitors on each of the important factors that determine market success?

2. All things considered, does the company have a net competitive advantage or disadvantage versus major competitors?

Step 1 in doing a competitive strength assessment is to list the industry's key success factors and other telling measures of competitive strength or weakness (6 to 10 measures usually suffice). Step 2 is to assign a weight to each measure of competitive strength based on its perceived importance in shaping competitive success. (The sum of the weights for each measure must add up to 1.0.) Step 3 is to calculate weighted strength ratings by scoring each competitor on each strength measure (using a 1 to 10 rating scale where 1 is very weak and 10 is very strong) and multiplying the assigned rating by the assigned weight. Step 4 is to sum the weighted strength ratings on each factor to get an overall measure of competitive strength for each company being rated. Step 5 is to use the overall strength ratings to draw conclusions about the size and extent of the company's net competitive advantage or disadvantage and to take specific note of areas of strength and weakness. Table 4.3 on page 86 provides an example of a competitive strength assessment, using the hypothetical ABC Company against four rivals. ABC's total score of 5.95 signals a net competitive advantage over Rival 3 (with a score of 2.10) and Rival 4 (with a score of 3.70), but indicates a net competitive disadvantage against Rival 1 (with a score of 7. 70) and Rival 2 (with an overall score of 6.85).

Interpreting the Competitive Strength Assessments

Competitive strength assessments provide useful conclusions about a company's competitive situation. The ratings show how a company compares against rivals, factor by factor or capability by capability, thus revealing where it is strongest and weakest. Moreover, the overall competitive strength scores indicate whether the company is at a net competitive advantage or disadvantage against each rival.

> A company's competitive strength scores pinpoint its strengths and weaknesses against rivals and point to offensive and defensive strategies capable of producing first-rate results.

In addition, the strength ratings provide guidelines for designing wise offensive and defensive strategies. For example, consider the ratings and weighted scores in Table 4.3. If ABC Co. wants to go on the offensive to win additional sales and market share, such an offensive probably needs to be aimed directly at winning customers away from Rivals 3 and 4 (which have lower overall strength scores) rather than Rivals 1 and 2 (which have higher overall strength scores). ABC's advantages over Rival 4 tend to be in areas that are moderately important to competitive success in the industry, but ABC outclasses Rival 3 on the two most heavily weighted strength factors—relative cost position and customer service capabilities. Therefore, Rival 3 should be viewed as the primary target of ABC's offensive strategies, with Rival 4 being a secondary target.

A competitively astute company should utilize the strength scores in deciding what strategic moves to make. When a company has important competitive strengths in areas where one or more rivals are weak, it makes sense to consider offensive moves to exploit rivals' competitive weaknesses. When a company has competitive weaknesses in important areas where one or more rivals are strong, it makes sense to consider defensive moves to curtail its vulnerability.

Question 5: What Strategic Issues and Problems Must Be Addressed by Management?

The final and most important analytical step is to zero in on exactly what strategic issues company managers need to address. This step involves drawing on the results of both industry and competitive analysis and the evaluations of the company's internal situation. The task here is to get a clear fix on exactly what industry and competitive challenges confront the company, which of the company's internal weaknesses need fixing, and what specific problems merit front-burner attention by company managers. *Pinpointing the precise things that management needs to worry about sets the agenda for deciding what actions to take next to improve the company's performance and business outlook.*

LO5 Understand how a comprehensive evaluation of a company's external and internal situations can assist managers in making critical decisions about their next strategic moves.

If the items on management's "worry list" are relatively minor, which suggests the company's strategy is mostly on track and reasonably well matched to the company's overall situation, company managers seldom need to go much beyond fine-tuning the present strategy. If, however, the issues and problems confronting the company are serious and indicate the present strategy is not well suited for the road ahead, the task of crafting a better strategy has got to go to the top of management's action agenda.

> Compiling a "worry list" of problems and issues creates an agenda for managerial strategy making.

TABLE 4.3

Illustration of a Competitive Strength Assessment

Key Success Factor/Strength Measure	Importance Weight	ABC CO. Strength Rating	ABC CO. Score	RIVAL 1 Strength Rating	RIVAL 1 Score	RIVAL 2 Strength Rating	RIVAL 2 Score	RIVAL 3 Strength Rating	RIVAL 3 Score	RIVAL 4 Strength Rating	RIVAL 4 Score
Quality/product performance	0.10	8	0.80	5	0.50	10	1.00	1	0.10	6	0.60
Reputation/image	0.10	8	0.80	7	0.70	10	1.00	1	0.10	6	0.60
Manufacturing capability	0.10	2	0.20	10	1.00	4	0.40	5	0.50	1	0.10
Technological skills	0.05	10	0.50	1	0.05	7	0.35	3	0.15	8	0.40
Dealer network/distribution capability	0.05	9	0.45	4	0.20	10	0.50	5	0.25	1	0.05
New-product innovation capability	0.05	9	0.45	4	0.20	10	0.50	5	0.25	1	0.05
Financial resources	0.10	5	0.50	10	1.00	7	0.70	3	0.30	1	0.10
Relative cost position	0.30	5	1.50	10	3.00	3	0.95	1	0.30	4	1.20
Customer service capabilities	0.15	5	0.75	7	1.05	10	1.50	1	0.15	4	0.60
Sum of importance weights	1.00										
Weighted overall strength rating			**5.95**		**7.70**		**6.85**		**2.10**		**3.70**

(Rating scale: 1 = very weak; 10 = very strong)

KEY POINTS

In analyzing a company's own particular competitive circumstances and its competitive position vis-à-vis key rivals, consider five key questions:

1. *How well is the present strategy working?* This involves evaluating the strategy in terms of the company's financial performance and competitive strength and market standing. The stronger a company's current overall performance, the less likely the need for radical strategy changes. The weaker a company's performance and/or the faster the changes in its external situation (which can be gleaned from industry and competitive analysis), the more its current strategy must be questioned.

2. *Do the company's resources and capabilities have sufficient competitive power to give it a sustainable advantage over competitors?* The answer to this question comes from conducting the four tests of a resource's competitive power—the VRIN tests. If a company has resources and capabilities that are competitively *valuable* and *rare*, the firm will have the potential for a competitive advantage over market rivals. If its resources and capabilities are also hard to copy (*inimitable*) with no good substitutes (*nonsubstitutable*), then the firm may be able to sustain this advantage even in the face of active efforts by rivals to overcome it.

   SWOT analysis can be used to assess if a company's resources and capabilities are sufficient to seize market opportunities and overcome external threats to its future well-being. The two most important parts of SWOT analysis are (1) drawing conclusions about what story the compilation of strengths, weaknesses, opportunities, and threats tells about the company's overall situation, and (2) acting on the conclusions to better match the company's strategy to its internal strengths and market opportunities, to correct the important internal weaknesses, and to defend against external threats. A company's strengths and competitive assets are strategically relevant because they are the most logical and appealing building blocks for strategy; internal weaknesses are important because they may represent vulnerabilities that need correction. External opportunities and threats come into play because a good strategy necessarily aims at capturing a company's most attractive opportunities and at defending against threats to its well-being.

3. *Are the company's cost structure and customer value proposition competitive?* One telling sign of whether a company's situation is strong or precarious is whether its costs are competitive with those of industry rivals. Another sign is how it compares with rivals in terms of its customer value proposition. Value chain analysis and benchmarking are essential tools in determining whether the company is performing particular functions and activities well, whether its costs are in line with competitors, whether it is able to offer an attractive value proposition to customers, and whether particular internal activities and business processes need improvement. Value chain analysis complements resource and capability analysis because of the tight linkage between activities and enabling resources and capabilities.

4. *Is the company competitively stronger or weaker than key rivals?* The key appraisals here involve how the company matches up against key rivals on industry key success factors and other chief determinants of competitive success and whether and why the company has a competitive advantage or disadvantage. Quantitative competitive strength assessments, using the method presented in Table 4.3, indicate where a company is competitively strong and weak and provide insight into the company's ability to defend or enhance its market position. As a rule a company's

competitive strategy should be built around its competitive strengths and should aim at shoring up areas where it is competitively vulnerable. When a company has important competitive strengths in areas where one or more rivals are weak, it makes sense to consider offensive moves to exploit rivals' competitive weaknesses. When a company has important competitive weaknesses in areas where one or more rivals are strong, it makes sense to consider defensive moves to curtail its vulnerability.

5. *What strategic issues and problems merit front-burner managerial attention?* This analytical step zeros in on the strategic issues and problems that stand in the way of the company's success. It involves using the results of both industry and competitive analysis and company situation analysis to identify a "worry list" of issues to be resolved for the company to be financially and competitively successful in the years ahead. Actually deciding upon a strategy and what specific actions to take comes after the list of strategic issues and problems that merit front-burner management attention has been developed.

Good company situation analysis, like good industry and competitive analysis, is a valuable precondition for good strategy making.

ASSURANCE OF LEARNING EXERCISES

LO1

1. Using the financial ratios provided in the Appendix and the financial statement information for Macy's, Inc., below, calculate the following ratios for Macy's for both 2011 and 2012.

   a. Gross profit margin.
   b. Operating profit margin.
   c. Net profit margin.
   d. Times interest earned coverage.
   e. Return on shareholders' equity.
   f. Return on assets.
   g. Debt-to-equity ratio.
   h. Days of inventory.
   i. Inventory turnover ratio.
   j. Average collection period.

   Based on these ratios, did Macy's financial performance improve, weaken, or remain about the same from 2011 to 2012?

Consolidated Statements of Income for Macy's, Inc., 2011–2012 (in millions, except per share data)		
	2012	**2011**
Net sales	$ 27,686	$ 26,405
Cost of sales	(16,538)	(15,738)
Gross margin	11,148	10,667
Selling, general, and administrative expenses	(8,482)	(8,281)
Impairments, store closing costs and gain on sale of leases	(5)	25
Operating income	2,661	2,411
		(continued)

Consolidated Statements of Income for Macy's, Inc., 2011–2012
(in millions, except per share data)

	2012	2011
Interest expense	(425)	(447)
Premium on early retirement of debt	(137)	—
Interest income	3	4
Income before income taxes	2,102	1,968
Federal, state, and local income tax expense	(767)	(712)
Net income	$ 1,335	$ 1,256
Basic earnings per share	$ 3.29	$ 2.96
Diluted earnings per share	$ 3.24	$ 2.92

Consolidated Balance Sheets for Macy's, Inc., 2011–2012
(in millions, except per share data)

ASSETS	FEBRUARY 2, 2013	JANUARY 28, 2012
Current Assets:		
Cash and cash equivalents	$ 1,836	$ 2,827
Receivables	371	368
Merchandise inventories	5,308	5,117
Prepaid expenses and other current assets	361	465
Total Current Assets	7,876	8,777
Property and Equipment – net	8,196	8,420
Goodwill	3,743	3,743
Other Intangible Assets – net	561	598
Other Assets	615	557
Total Assets	$ 20,991	$ 22,095
LIABILITIES AND SHAREHOLDERS' EQUITY		
Current Liabilities:		
Short-term debt	$ 124	$ 1,103
Merchandise accounts payable	1,579	1,593
Accounts payable and accrued liabilities	2,610	2,788
Income taxes	355	371
Deferred income taxes	407	408
Total Current Liabilities	5,075	6,263
Long-Term Debt	6,806	6,655
Deferred Income Taxes	1,238	1,141
Other Liabilities	1,821	2,103
Shareholders' Equity:		
Common stock (387.7 and 414.2 shares outstanding)	4	5
Additional paid-in capital	3,872	5,408
Accumulated equity	5,108	4,015
Treasury stock	(2,002)	(2,434)
Accumulated other comprehensive loss	(931)	(1,061)
Total Shareholders' Equity	6,051	5,933
Total Liabilities and Shareholders' Equity	$ 20,991	$ 22,095

Source: Macy's, Inc., 2012 10-K.

connect

LO2 2. Panera Bread operates more than 1,600 bakery-cafés in 44 states and Canada. How many of the four tests of the competitive power of a resource does the store network pass? Explain your answer.

LO3 3. Review the information in Concepts & Connections 4.1 concerning the value chain average costs of producing and selling an upscale polo shirt and compare this with the representative value chain depicted in Figure 4.1. Then answer the following questions:

   a. Which of the company's primary value chain activities account for the largest percentage of its operating expenses?

   b. What support activities described in Figure 4.1 would be necessary at KP MacLane?

   c. What value chain activities might be important in securing or maintaining a competitive advantage for a producer of upscale, branded shirts like KP MacLane?

LO4 4. Using the methodology illustrated in Table 4.3 and your knowledge as an automobile owner, prepare a competitive strength assessment for General Motors and its rivals Ford, Chrysler, Toyota, and Honda. Each of the five automobile manufacturers should be evaluated on the key success factors/strength measures of cost competitiveness, product-line breadth, product quality and reliability, financial resources and profitability, and customer service. What does your competitive strength assessment disclose about the overall competitiveness of each automobile manufacturer? What factors account most for Toyota's competitive success? Does Toyota have competitive weaknesses that were disclosed by your analysis? Explain.

▶ EXERCISES FOR SIMULATION PARTICIPANTS

LO1 1. Using the formulas in the Appendix and the data in your company's latest financial statements, calculate the following measures of financial performance for your company:

   a. Operating profit margin

   b. Return on total assets

   c. Current ratio

   d. Working capital

   e. Long-term debt-to-capital ratio

   f. Price-earnings ratio

LO1 2. Based on your company's latest financial statements and all of the other available data regarding your company's performance that appear in the Industry Report, list the three measures of financial performance on which your company did "best" and the three measures on which your company's financial performance was "worst."

LO1 3. What hard evidence can you cite that indicates your company's strategy is working fairly well (or perhaps not working so well, if your company's performance is lagging that of rival companies)?

LO2 4. What internal strengths and weaknesses does your company have? What external market opportunities for growth and increased profitability exist for your company? What external threats to your company's future well-being and profitability do you and your co-managers see? What does the preceding SWOT analysis indicate about your company's present situation and future prospects—where on the scale from "exceptionally strong" to "alarmingly weak" does the attractiveness of your company's situation rank?

5. Does your company have any core competencies? If so, what are they? **LO2**

6. What are the key elements of your company's value chain? Refer to Figure 4.1 in developing your answer. **LO3**

7. Using the methodology illustrated in Table 4.3, do a weighted competitive strength assessment for your company and two other companies that you and your co-managers consider to be very close competitors. **LO4**

◢ ENDNOTES

1. Birger Wernerfelt, "A Resource-Based View of the Firm," *Strategic Management Journal* 5, no. 5 (September–October 1984); Jay Barney, "Firm Resources and Sustained Competitive Advantage," *Journal of Management* 17, no. 1 (1991); Margaret A. Peteraf, "The Cornerstones of Competitive Advantage: A Resource-Based View," *Strategic Management Journal* 14, no. 3 (March 1993).

2. Birger Wernerfelt, "A Resource-Based View of the Firm," *Strategic Management Journal* 5, no. 5 (September–October 1984), pp. 171–80; Jay Barney, "Firm Resources and Sustained Competitive Advantage," *Journal of Management* 17, no. 1 (1991); and Margaret A. Peteraf, "The Cornerstones of Competitive Advantage: A Resource-Based View," *Strategic Management Journal* 14, no. 3 (March 1993).

3. R. Amit and P. Schoemaker, "Strategic Assets and Organizational Rent," *Strategic Management Journal* 14, no. 1 (1993).

4. David J. Collis and Cynthia A. Montgomery, "Competing on Resources: Strategy in the 1990s," *Harvard Business Review* 73, no. 4 (July–August 1995).

5. George Stalk, Philip Evans, and Lawrence E. Schulman, "Competing on Capabilities: The New Rules of Corporate Strategy," *Harvard Business Review* 70, no. 2 (March–April 1992).

6. David J. Teece, Gary Pisano, and Amy Shuen, "Dynamic Capabilities and Strategic Management," *Strategic Management Journal* 18, no. 7 (1997); and Constance E. Helfat and Margaret A. Peteraf, "The Dynamic Resource-Based View: Capability Lifecycles," *Strategic Management Journal* 24, no. 10 (2003).

7. C. Montgomery, "Of Diamonds and Rust: A New Look at Resources" in *Resource-Based and Evolutionary Theories of the Firm*, ed. C. Montgomery (Boston: Kluwer Academic Publishers, 1995), pp. 251–68.

8. D. Teece, G. Pisano, and A. Shuen, "Dynamic Capabilities and Strategic Management," *Strategic Management Journal* 18, no. 7 (1997); K. Eisenhardt and J. Martin, "Dynamic Capabilities: What Are They?" *Strategic Management Journal* 21, nos. 10–11 (2000); M. Zollo and S. Winter, "Deliberate Learning and the Evolution of Dynamic Capabilities," *Organization Science* 13 (2002); and C. Helfat et al., *Dynamic Capabilities: Understanding Strategic Change in Organizations* (Malden, MA: Blackwell, 2007).

9. W. Powell, K. Koput, and L. Smith-Doerr, "Interorganizational Collaboration and the Locus of Innovation," *Administrative Science Quarterly* 41, no. 1 (1996).

10. M. Peteraf, "The Cornerstones of Competitive Advantage: A Resource-Based View," *Strategic Management Journal*, March 1993, pp. 179–91.

11. Michael E. Porter, *Competitive Advantage* (New York: Free Press, 1985).

12. Gregory H. Watson, *Strategic Benchmarking: How to Rate Your Company's Performance Against the World's Best* (New York: John Wiley & Sons, 1993); Robert C. Camp, *Benchmarking: The Search for Industry Best Practices That Lead to Superior Performance* (Milwaukee: ASQC Quality Press, 1989); Christopher E. Bogan and Michael J. English, *Benchmarking for Best Practices: Winning through Innovative Adaptation* (New York: McGraw-Hill, 1994); and Dawn Iacobucci and Christie Nordhielm, "Creative Benchmarking," *Harvard Business Review* 78, no. 6 (November–December 2000).

13. M. Hegert and D. Morris, "Accounting Data for Value Chain Analysis," *Strategic Management Journal* 10 (1989); Robin Cooper and Robert S. Kaplan, "Measure Costs Right: Make the Right Decisions," *Harvard Business Review* 66, no. 5 (September–October 1988); and John K. Shank and Vijay Govindarajan, *Strategic Cost Management* (New York: Free Press, 1993).

14. Michael E. Porter, "Clusters and the New Economics of Competition," *Harvard Business Review* 76, no. 6 (November–December 1998).

15. Reuben E. Stone, "Leading a Supply Chain Turnaround," *Harvard Business Review* 82, no. 10 (October 2004).

The Five Generic Competitive Strategies

LEARNING OBJECTIVES

LO1   Understand what distinguishes each of the five generic strategies and why some of these strategies work better in certain kinds of industry and competitive conditions than in others.

LO2   Learn the major avenues for achieving a competitive advantage based on lower costs.

LO3   Gain command of the major avenues for developing a competitive advantage based on differentiating a company's product or service offering from the offerings of rivals.

LO4   Recognize the required conditions for delivering superior value to customers through the use of a hybrid of low-cost provider and differentiation strategies.

There are several basic approaches to competing successfully and gaining a competitive advantage, but they all involve giving buyers what they perceive as superior value compared to the offerings of rival sellers. A superior value proposition can be based on offering a good product at a lower price, a superior product that is worth paying more for, or a best-value offering that represents an attractive combination of price, features, quality, service, and other appealing attributes.

This chapter describes the five *generic competitive strategy options* for building competitive advantage and delivering superior value to customers. Which of the five to employ is a company's first and foremost choice in crafting an overall strategy and beginning its quest for competitive advantage.

The Five Generic Competitive Strategies

A company's **competitive strategy** *deals exclusively with the specifics of management's game plan for competing successfully*—its specific efforts to please customers, strengthen its market position, counter the maneuvers of rivals, respond to shifting market conditions, and achieve a particular competitive advantage. The chances are remote that any two companies—even companies in the same industry—will employ competitive strategies that are exactly alike. However, when one strips away the details to get at the real substance, the two biggest factors that distinguish one competitive strategy from another boil down to (1) whether a company's market target is broad or narrow, and (2) whether the company is pursuing a competitive advantage linked to lower costs or differentiation. These two factors give rise to the five competitive strategy options shown in Figure 5.1 and listed below.[1]

LO1 Understand what distinguishes each of the five generic strategies and why some of these strategies work better in certain kinds of industry and competitive conditions than in others.

1. *A low-cost provider strategy*—striving to achieve lower overall costs than rivals and appealing to a broad spectrum of customers, usually by underpricing rivals.

2. *A broad differentiation strategy*—seeking to differentiate the company's product or service from rivals' in ways that will appeal to a broad spectrum of buyers.

> **CORE CONCEPT**
> A **competitive strategy** concerns the specifics of management's game plan for competing successfully and securing a competitive advantage over rivals in the marketplace.

3. *A focused low-cost strategy*—concentrating on a narrow buyer segment (or market niche) and outcompeting rivals by having lower costs than rivals and thus being able to serve niche members at a lower price.

4. *A focused differentiation strategy*—concentrating on a narrow buyer segment (or market niche) and outcompeting rivals by offering niche members customized attributes that meet their tastes and requirements better than rivals' products.

5. *A best-cost provider strategy*—giving customers more value for the money by satisfying buyers' expectations on key quality/features/performance/service attributes while beating their price expectations. This option is a *hybrid* strategy that blends elements of low-cost provider and differentiation strategies; the aim is to have the lowest (best) costs and prices among sellers offering products with comparable differentiating attributes.

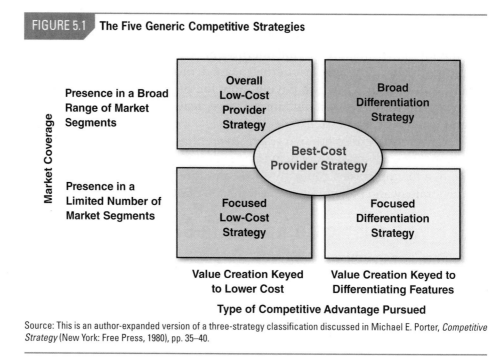

FIGURE 5.1   **The Five Generic Competitive Strategies**

Source: This is an author-expanded version of a three-strategy classification discussed in Michael E. Porter, *Competitive Strategy* (New York: Free Press, 1980), pp. 35–40.

The remainder of this chapter explores the ins and outs of the five generic competitive strategies and how they differ.

Low-Cost Provider Strategies

Striving to be the industry's overall low-cost provider is a powerful competitive approach in markets with many price-sensitive buyers. A company achieves low-cost leadership when it becomes the industry's lowest-cost provider rather than just being one of perhaps several competitors with low costs. Successful low-cost providers boast meaningfully lower costs than rivals, but not necessarily the absolutely lowest possible cost. In striving for a cost advantage over rivals, managers must include features and services that buyers consider essential. A product offering that is too frills-free can be viewed by consumers as offering little value, regardless of its pricing.

> **CORE CONCEPT**
>
> A **low-cost leader**'s basis for competitive advantage is lower overall costs than competitors. Success in achieving a low-cost edge over rivals comes from eliminating and/or curbing "nonessential" activities and/or outmanaging rivals in performing essential activities.

A company has two options for translating a low-cost advantage over rivals into attractive profit performance. Option 1 is to use the lower-cost edge to underprice competitors and attract price-sensitive buyers in great enough numbers to increase total profits. Option 2 is to maintain the present price, be content with the present market share, and use the lower-cost edge to earn a higher profit margin on each unit sold, thereby raising the firm's total profits and overall return on investment.

The Two Major Avenues for Achieving Low-Cost Leadership

LO2 Learn the major avenues for achieving a competitive advantage based on lower costs.

To achieve a low-cost edge over rivals, a firm's cumulative costs across its overall value chain must be lower than competitors' cumulative costs. There are two major avenues for accomplishing this:[2]

1. Performing essential value chain activities more cost-effectively than rivals.
2. Revamping the firm's overall value chain to eliminate or bypass some cost-producing activities.

Cost-Efficient Management of Value Chain Activities   For a company to do a more cost-efficient job of managing its value chain than rivals, managers must launch a concerted, ongoing effort to ferret out cost-saving opportunities in every part of the value chain. No activity can escape cost-saving scrutiny, and all company personnel must be expected to use their talents and ingenuity to come up with innovative and effective ways to keep costs down. Particular attention needs to be paid to **cost drivers**, which are factors that have an especially strong effect on the costs of a company's value chain activities. The number of products in a company's product line, its capacity utilization, the type of components used in the assembly of its products, and the extent of its employee benefits package are all factors affecting the company's overall cost position. Figure 5.2 shows the most important cost drivers. Cost-saving approaches that demonstrate effective management of the cost drivers in a company's value chain include:

> **CORE CONCEPT**
>
> A **cost driver** is a factor having a strong effect on the cost of a company's value chain activities and cost structure.

- *Striving to capture all available economies of scale.* Economies of scale stem from an ability to lower unit costs by increasing the scale of operation. For example, occasions may arise when a large plant is more economical to operate than a small or medium-sized plant or when a large distribution center is more cost efficient than a small one.
- *Taking full advantage of experience and learning curve effects.* The cost of performing an activity can decline over time as the learning and experience of company personnel build.
- *Trying to operate facilities at full capacity.* Whether a company is able to operate at or near full capacity has a big impact on unit costs when its value chain contains activities associated with substantial fixed costs. Higher rates of capacity utilization allow depreciation and other fixed costs to be spread over a larger unit volume, thereby lowering fixed costs per unit.
- *Substituting lower-cost inputs whenever there's little or no sacrifice in product quality or product performance.* If the costs of certain raw materials and parts are "too high," a company can switch to using lower-cost alternatives when they exist.

FIGURE 5.2   **Important Cost Drivers in a Company's Value Chain**

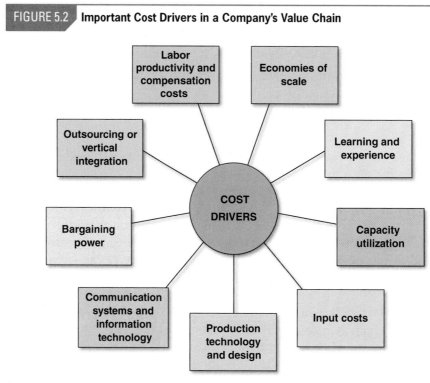

Sources: Adapted by the authors from M. Porter, *The Competitive Advantage: Creating and Sustaining Superior Performance* (New York: Free Press, 1985).

- *Employing advanced production technology and process design to improve overall efficiency.* Often production costs can be cut by utilizing design for manufacture (DFM) procedures and computer-assisted design (CAD) techniques that enable more integrated and efficient production methods, investing in highly automated robotic production technology, and shifting to production processes that enable manufacturing multiple versions of a product as cost efficiently as mass producing a single version. A number of companies are ardent users of total quality management systems, business process reengineering, Six Sigma methodology, and other business process management techniques that aim at boosting efficiency and reducing costs.
- *Using communication systems and information technology to achieve operating efficiencies.* For example, sharing data and production schedules with suppliers, coupled with the use of enterprise resource planning (ERP) and manufacturing execution system (MES) software, can reduce parts inventories, trim production times, and lower labor requirements.
- *Using the company's bargaining power vis-à-vis suppliers to gain concessions.* A company may have sufficient bargaining clout with suppliers to win price discounts on large-volume purchases or realize other cost as on p. 97 savings.
- *Being alert to the cost advantages of outsourcing and vertical integration.* Outsourcing the performance of certain value chain activities can be more economical than performing them in-house if outside specialists, by virtue of their expertise and volume, can perform the activities at lower cost.

- *Pursuing ways to boost labor productivity and lower overall compensation costs.* A company can economize on labor costs by using incentive compensation systems that promote high productivity, installing labor-saving equipment, shifting production from geographic areas where pay scales are high to geographic areas where pay scales are low, and avoiding the use of union labor where possible (because costly work rules can stifle productivity and because of union demands for above-market pay scales and costly fringe benefits).

Revamping the Value Chain   Dramatic cost advantages can often emerge from reengineering the company's value chain in ways that eliminate costly work steps and bypass certain cost-producing value chain activities. Such value chain revamping can include:

- *Selling directly to consumers and cutting out the activities and costs of distributors and dealers.* To circumvent the need for distributors–dealers, a company can (1) create its own direct sales force (which adds the costs of maintaining and supporting a sales force but may be cheaper than utilizing independent distributors and dealers to access buyers), and/or (2) conduct sales operations at the company's website (costs for website operations and shipping may be a substantially cheaper way to make sales to customers than going through distributor–dealer channels). Costs in the wholesale/retail portions of the value chain frequently represent 35 to 50 percent of the price final consumers pay, so establishing a direct sales force or selling online may offer big cost savings.

- *Streamlining operations by eliminating low-value-added or unnecessary work steps and activities.* Southwest Airlines has achieved considerable cost savings by reconfiguring the traditional value chain of commercial airlines to eliminate low-value-added activities and work steps. Southwest does not offer assigned seating, baggage transfer to connecting airlines, or first-class seating and service, thereby eliminating all the cost-producing activities associated with these features. Also, the company's carefully designed point-to-point route system minimizes connections, delays, and total trip time for passengers, allowing about 75 percent of Southwest passengers to fly nonstop to their destinations and at the same time helping reduce Southwest's costs for flight operations.

- *Improving supply chain efficiency to reduce materials handling and shipping costs.* Collaborating with suppliers to streamline the ordering and purchasing process, to reduce inventory carrying costs via just-in-time inventory practices, to economize on shipping and materials handling, and to ferret out other cost-saving opportunities is a much-used approach to cost reduction. A company with a distinctive competence in cost-efficient supply chain management, such as BASF (the world's leading chemical company), can sometimes achieve a sizable cost advantage over less adept rivals.

Concepts & Connections 5.1 describes Walmart's broad approach to managing its value chain in the retail grocery portion of its business to achieve a dramatic cost advantage over rival supermarket chains and become the world's biggest grocery retailer.

CONCEPTS & CONNECTIONS 5.1

HOW WALMART MANAGED ITS VALUE CHAIN TO ACHIEVE A LOW-COST ADVANTAGE OVER RIVAL SUPERMARKET CHAINS

Walmart has achieved a very substantial cost and pricing advantage over rival supermarket chains by both revamping portions of the grocery retailing value chain and outmanaging its rivals in efficiently performing various value chain activities. Its cost advantage stems from a series of initiatives and practices:

- Instituting extensive information sharing with vendors via online systems that relay sales at its checkout counters directly to suppliers of the items, thereby providing suppliers with real-time information on customer demand and preferences (creating an estimated 6 percent cost advantage).

- Pursuing global procurement of some items and centralizing most purchasing activities so as to leverage the company's buying power (creating an estimated 2.5 percent cost advantage).

- Investing in state-of-the-art automation at its distribution centers, efficiently operating a truck fleet that makes daily deliveries to Walmart's stores, and putting assorted other cost-saving practices into place at its headquarters, distribution centers, and stores (resulting in an estimated 4 percent cost advantage).

- Striving to optimize the product mix and achieve greater sales turnover (resulting in about a 2 percent cost advantage).

- Installing security systems and store operating procedures that lower shrinkage rates (producing a cost advantage of about 0.5 percent).

- Negotiating preferred real estate rental and leasing rates with real estate developers and owners of its store sites (yielding a cost advantage of 2 percent).

- Managing and compensating its workforce in a manner that produces lower labor costs (yielding an estimated 5 percent cost advantage).

Altogether, these value chain initiatives give Walmart an approximately 22 percent cost advantage over Kroger, Safeway, and other leading supermarket chains. With such a sizable cost advantage, Walmart has been able to underprice its rivals and become the world's leading supermarket retailer.

Sources: www.walmart.com; and Marco Iansiti and Roy Levien, "Strategy as Ecology," *Harvard Business Review* 82, no. 3 (March 2004), p. 70.

When a Low-Cost Provider Strategy Works Best

A competitive strategy predicated on low-cost leadership is particularly powerful when:

1. *Price competition among rival sellers is especially vigorous.* Low-cost providers are in the best position to compete offensively on the basis of price and to survive price wars.

2. *The products of rival sellers are essentially identical and are readily available from several sellers.* Commodity-like products and/or ample supplies set the stage for lively price competition; in such markets, it is the less efficient, higher-cost companies that are most vulnerable.

3. *There are few ways to achieve product differentiation that have value to buyers.* When the product or service differences between brands do not matter much to buyers, buyers nearly always shop the market for the best price.

4. *Buyers incur low costs in switching their purchases from one seller to another.* Low switching costs give buyers the flexibility to shift purchases to lower-priced sellers having equally good products. A low-cost leader is

well positioned to use low price to induce its customers not to switch to rival brands.

5. *The majority of industry sales are made to a few, large-volume buyers.* Low-cost providers are in the best position among sellers in bargaining with high-volume buyers because they are able to beat rivals' pricing to land a high-volume sale while maintaining an acceptable profit margin.

6. *Industry newcomers use introductory low prices to attract buyers and build a customer base.* The low-cost leader can use price cuts of its own to make it harder for a new rival to win customers.

As a rule, the more price-sensitive buyers are, the more appealing a low-cost strategy becomes. A low-cost company's ability to set the industry's price floor and still earn a profit erects protective barriers around its market position.

Pitfalls to Avoid in Pursuing a Low-Cost Provider Strategy

Perhaps the biggest pitfall of a low-cost provider strategy is getting carried away with *overly aggressive price cutting* and ending up with lower, rather than higher, profitability. A low-cost/low-price advantage results in superior profitability only if (1) prices are cut by less than the size of the cost advantage or (2) the added volume is large enough to bring in a bigger total profit despite lower margins per unit sold. Thus, a company with a 5 percent cost advantage cannot cut prices 20 percent, end up with a volume gain of only 10 percent, and still expect to earn higher profits!

A second big pitfall is *relying on an approach to reduce costs that can be easily copied by rivals.* The value of a cost advantage depends on its sustainability. Sustainability, in turn, hinges on whether the company achieves its cost advantage in ways difficult for rivals to replicate or match. If rivals find it relatively easy or inexpensive to imitate the leader's low-cost methods, then the leader's advantage will be too short-lived to yield a valuable edge in the marketplace.

A third pitfall is becoming *too fixated on cost reduction.* Low costs cannot be pursued so zealously that a firm's offering ends up being too features-poor to gain the interest of buyers. Furthermore, a company driving hard to push its costs down has to guard against misreading or ignoring increased buyer preferences for added features or declining buyer price sensitivity. Even if these mistakes are avoided, a low-cost competitive approach still carries risk. Cost-saving technological breakthroughs or process improvements by rival firms can nullify a low-cost leader's hard-won position.

Broad Differentiation Strategies

Differentiation strategies are attractive whenever buyers' needs and preferences are too diverse to be fully satisfied by a standardized product or service. A company attempting to succeed through differentiation must study buyers' needs and behavior carefully to learn what buyers think has value and what they are willing to

> **CORE CONCEPT**
>
> The essence of a **broad differentiation strategy** is to offer unique product or service attributes that a wide range of buyers find appealing and worth paying for.

pay for. Then the company must include these desirable features to clearly set itself apart from rivals lacking such product or service attributes.

Successful differentiation allows a firm to:

- Command a premium price, and/or
- Increase unit sales (because additional buyers are won over by the differentiating features), and/or
- Gain buyer loyalty to its brand (because some buyers are strongly attracted to the differentiating features and bond with the company and its products).

Differentiation enhances profitability whenever the extra price the product commands outweighs the added costs of achieving the differentiation. Company differentiation strategies fail when buyers don't value the brand's uniqueness and/or when a company's approach to differentiation is easily copied or matched by its rivals.

Approaches to Differentiation

LO3 Gain command of the major avenues for developing a competitive advantage based on differentiating a company's product or service offering from the offerings of rivals.

Companies can pursue differentiation from many angles: a unique taste (Red Bull, Listerine), multiple features (Microsoft Office, Apple iPad), wide selection and one-stop shopping (Home Depot, Amazon.com), superior service (Ritz-Carlton, Nordstrom), spare parts availability (Caterpillar guarantees 48-hour spare parts delivery to any customer anywhere in the world or else the part is furnished free), engineering design and performance (Mercedes-Benz, BMW), luxury and prestige (Rolex, Gucci, Chanel), product reliability (Whirlpool and Bosch in large home appliances), quality manufacturing (Michelin in tires, Toyota and Honda in automobiles), technological leadership (3M Corporation in bonding and coating products), a full range of services (Charles Schwab in stock brokerage), and a complete line of products (Campbell soups, Frito-Lay snack foods).

The most appealing approaches to differentiation are those that are hard or expensive for rivals to duplicate. Resourceful competitors can, in time, clone almost any product or feature or attribute. If Coca-Cola introduces a vitamin-enhanced bottled water, so can Pepsi; if Firestone offers customers attractive financing terms, so can Goodyear. As a rule, differentiation yields a longer-lasting and more profitable competitive edge when it is based on product innovation, technical superiority, product quality and reliability, comprehensive customer service, and unique competitive capabilities. Such differentiating attributes tend to be tough for rivals to copy or offset profitably, and buyers widely perceive them as having value.

> Easy-to-copy differentiating features cannot produce sustainable competitive advantage; differentiation based on hard-to-copy competencies and capabilities tends to be more sustainable.

Managing the Value Chain in Ways That Enhance Differentiation

Success in employing a differentiation strategy results from management's ability to offer superior customer value through the addition of product/service attributes and features that differentiate a company's offering from the offerings of rivals. Differentiation opportunities can exist in activities all along an industry's value chain and particularly in activities and factors that meaningfully impact customer value. Such activities are referred to as **uniqueness drivers**—analogous to cost drivers—but have a high impact on differentiation rather than a company's overall cost position. Figure 5.3 lists important uniqueness drivers found in a company's value chain. Ways that managers can enhance differentiation through the systematic management of uniqueness drivers include the following:

- *Seeking out high-quality inputs.* Input quality can ultimately spill over to affect the performance or quality of the company's end product. Starbucks, for example, gets high ratings on its coffees partly because it has very strict specifications on the coffee beans purchased from suppliers.

> **CORE CONCEPT**
> A **uniqueness driver** is a value chain activity or factor that can have a strong effect on customer value and creating differentiation.

- *Striving for innovation and technological advances.* Successful innovation is the route to more frequent first-on-the-market victories and is a powerful differentiator. If the innovation proves hard to replicate, through patent protection or other means, it can provide a company with a first-mover advantage that is sustainable.

- *Creating superior product features, design, and performance.* The physical and functional features of a product have a big influence on differentiation. Styling and appearance are big differentiating factors in the apparel and

FIGURE 5.3 | **Important Uniqueness Drivers in a Company's Value Chain**

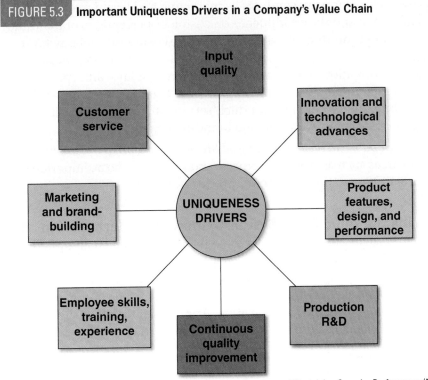

Source: Adapted from M. Porter, *The Competitive Advantage: Creating and Sustaining Superior Performance* (New York: Free Press, 1985).

motor vehicle industries. Size and weight matter in binoculars and smartphones. Most companies employing broad differentiation strategies make a point of incorporating innovative and novel features in their product/service offering, especially those that improve performance.

- *Investing in production-related R&D activities.* Engaging in production R&D may permit custom-order manufacture at an efficient cost, provide wider product variety and selection, or improve product quality. Many manufacturers have developed flexible manufacturing systems that allow different models and product versions to be made on the same assembly line. Being able to provide buyers with made-to-order products can be a potent differentiating capability.

- *Pursuing continuous quality improvement.* Quality control processes reduce product defects, prevent premature product failure, extend product life, make it economical to offer longer warranty coverage, improve economy of use, result in more end-user convenience, enhance product appearance, or improve customer service.

- *Emphasizing human resource management activities that improve the skills, expertise, and knowledge of company personnel.* A company with high-caliber intellectual capital often has the capacity to generate the kinds of ideas that drive product innovation, technological advances, better product design and product performance, improved production techniques, and higher product quality.

- *Increasing emphasis on marketing and brand-building activities.* The manner in which a company conducts its marketing and brand management activities has a significant influence on customer perceptions of the value of a company's product offering and the price customers will pay for it. A highly skilled and competent sales force, effectively communicated product information, eye-catching ads, in-store displays, and special promotional campaigns can all cast a favorable light on the differentiating attributes of a company's product/service offering and contribute to greater brand-name awareness and brand-name power.

- *Improving customer service or adding additional services.* Better customer service, in areas such as delivery, returns, and repair, can be as important in creating differentiation as superior product features.

Revamping the Value Chain System to Increase Differentiation

Just as pursuing a cost advantage can involve the entire value chain system, the same is true for a differentiation advantage. As was discussed in Chapter 4, activities performed upstream by suppliers or downstream by distributors and retailers can have a meaningful effect on customers' perceptions of a company's offerings and its value proposition. Approaches to enhancing differentiation through changes in the value chain system include:

- *Coordinating with channel allies to enhance customer value.* Coordinating with downstream partners such as distributors, dealers, brokers, and retailers can contribute to differentiation in a variety of ways. Many manufacturers work directly with retailers on in-store displays and signage, joint advertising campaigns, and providing sales clerks with product knowledge and tips on sales techniques—all to enhance customer buying experiences. Companies can work with distributors and shippers to ensure fewer "out-of-stock" annoyances, quicker delivery to customers, more-accurate order filling, lower shipping costs, and a variety of shipping choices to customers.

- *Coordinating with suppliers to better address customer needs.* Collaborating with suppliers can also be a powerful route to a more effective differentiation strategy. This is particularly true for companies that engage only in assembly operations, such as Dell in PCs and Ducati in motorcycles. Close coordination with suppliers can also enhance differentiation by speeding up new-product development cycles or speeding delivery to end customers. Strong relationships with suppliers can also mean that the company's supply requirements are prioritized when industry supply is insufficient to meet overall demand.

Delivering Superior Value via a Differentiation Strategy

While it is easy enough to grasp that a successful differentiation strategy must offer value in ways unmatched by rivals, a big issue in crafting a differentiation strategy is deciding what is valuable to customers. Typically, value can be delivered to customers in three basic ways.

1. *Include product attributes and user features that lower the buyer's costs.* Commercial buyers value products that can reduce their cost of doing business. For example, making a company's product more economical for a buyer to use can be done by reducing the buyer's raw materials waste (providing cut-to-size components), reducing a buyer's inventory requirements (providing just-in-time deliveries), increasing product reliability to lower a buyer's repair and maintenance costs, and providing free technical support. Similarly, consumers find value in differentiating features that will reduce their expenses. Rising costs for gasoline prices have spurred the efforts of motor vehicle manufacturers worldwide to introduce models with better fuel economy.

2. *Incorporate tangible features that improve product performance.* Commercial buyers and consumers alike value higher levels of performance in many types of products. Product reliability, output, durability, convenience, and ease of use are aspects of product performance that differentiate products offered to buyers. Mobile phone manufacturers are currently in a race to improve the performance of their products through the introduction of next-generation phones with added functionality and greater ease of use.

3. *Incorporate intangible features that enhance buyer satisfaction in noneconomic ways.* Toyota's Prius appeals to environmentally conscious motorists who wish to help reduce global carbon dioxide emissions. Bentley, Ralph Lauren, Louis Vuitton, Tiffany, Cartier, and Rolex have differentiation-based competitive advantages linked to buyer desires for status, image, prestige, upscale fashion, superior craftsmanship, and the finer things in life.

> Differentiation can be based on *tangible* or *intangible* features and attributes.

Perceived Value and the Importance of Signaling Value

The price premium commanded by a differentiation strategy reflects *the value actually delivered* to the buyer and *the value perceived* by the buyer. The value of certain differentiating features is rather easy for buyers to detect, but in some instances buyers may have trouble assessing what their experience with the product will be. Successful differentiators go to great lengths to make buyers knowledgeable about a product's value and incorporate signals of value such as attractive packaging; extensive ad campaigns; the quality of brochures and sales presentations; the seller's list of customers; the length of time the firm has been in business; and the professionalism, appearance, and personality of the seller's employees. Such signals of value may be as important as actual value (1) when the nature of differentiation is subjective or hard to quantify, (2) when buyers are making a first-time purchase, (3) when repurchase is infrequent, and (4) when buyers are unsophisticated.

When a Differentiation Strategy Works Best

Differentiation strategies tend to work best in market circumstances where:

1. *Buyer needs and uses of the product are diverse.* Diverse buyer preferences allow industry rivals to set themselves apart with product attributes that appeal to particular buyers. For instance, the diversity of consumer preferences for menu selection, ambience, pricing, and customer service gives restaurants exceptionally wide latitude in creating differentiated concepts. Other industries offering opportunities for differentiation based upon diverse buyer needs and uses include magazine publishing, automobile manufacturing, footwear, kitchen appliances, and computers.

2. *There are many ways to differentiate the product or service that have value to buyers.* Industries that allow competitors to add features to product attributes are well suited to differentiation strategies. For example, hotel chains can differentiate on such features as location, size of room, range of guest services, in-hotel dining, and the quality and luxuriousness of bedding and furnishings. Similarly, cosmetics producers are able to differentiate based upon prestige and image, formulations that fight the signs of aging, UV light protection, exclusivity of retail locations, the inclusion of antioxidants and natural ingredients, or prohibitions against animal testing.

3. *Few rival firms are following a similar differentiation approach.* The best differentiation approaches involve trying to appeal to buyers on the basis of attributes that rivals are not emphasizing. A differentiator encounters less head-to-head rivalry when it goes its own separate way to create uniqueness and does not try to outdifferentiate rivals on the very same attributes. When many rivals are all claiming "ours tastes better than theirs" or "ours gets your clothes cleaner than theirs," competitors tend to end up chasing the same buyers with very similar product offerings.

4. *Technological change is fast-paced and competition revolves around rapidly evolving product features.* Rapid product innovation and frequent introductions of next-version products heighten buyer interest and provide space for companies to pursue distinct differentiating paths. In video game

hardware and video games, golf equipment, PCs, mobile phones, and automobile navigation systems, competitors are locked into an ongoing battle to set themselves apart by introducing the best next-generation products; companies that fail to come up with new and improved products and distinctive performance features quickly lose out in the marketplace.

Pitfalls to Avoid in Pursuing a Differentiation Strategy

Differentiation strategies can fail for any of several reasons. *A differentiation strategy keyed to product or service attributes that are easily and quickly copied is always suspect.* Rapid imitation means that no rival achieves meaningful differentiation, because whatever new feature one firm introduces that strikes the fancy of buyers is almost immediately added by rivals. This is why a firm must search out sources of uniqueness that are time-consuming or burdensome for rivals to match if it hopes to use differentiation to win a sustainable competitive edge over rivals.

Differentiation strategies can also falter when buyers see little value in the unique attributes of a company's product. Thus, even if a company sets the attributes of its brand apart from its rivals' brands, its strategy can fail because of trying to differentiate on the basis of something that does not deliver adequate value to buyers. Any time many potential buyers look at a company's differentiated product offering and conclude "so what," the company's differentiation strategy is in deep trouble; buyers will likely decide the product is not worth the extra price and sales will be disappointingly low.

Overspending on efforts to differentiate is a strategy flaw that can erode profitability. Company efforts to achieve differentiation nearly always raise costs. The trick to profitable differentiation is either to keep the costs of achieving differentiation below the price premium the differentiating attributes can command in the marketplace or to offset thinner profit margins by selling enough additional units to increase total profits. If a company goes overboard in pursuing costly differentiation, it could be saddled with unacceptably thin profit margins or even losses. The need to contain differentiation costs is why many companies add little touches of differentiation that add to buyer satisfaction but are inexpensive to institute.

Other common pitfalls and mistakes in crafting a differentiation strategy include:

- *Overdifferentiating so that product quality or service levels exceed buyers' needs.* Buyers are unlikely to pay extra for features and attributes that will go unused. For example, consumers are unlikely to purchase programmable large appliances such as washers, dryers, and ovens if they are satisfied with manually controlled appliances.

- *Trying to charge too high a price premium.* Even if buyers view certain extras or deluxe features as "nice to have," they may still conclude that the added benefit or luxury is not worth the price differential over that of lesser differentiated products.

- *Being timid and not striving to open up meaningful gaps in quality or service or performance features vis-à-vis the products of rivals.* Tiny differences between rivals' product offerings may not be visible or important to buyers.

A low-cost provider strategy can always defeat a differentiation strategy when buyers are satisfied with a basic product and don't think "extra" attributes are worth a higher price.

Focused (or Market Niche) Strategies

What sets focused strategies apart from low-cost leadership or broad differentiation strategies is a concentration on a narrow piece of the total market. The targeted segment, or niche, can be defined by geographic uniqueness or by special product attributes that appeal only to niche members. The advantages of focusing a company's entire competitive effort on a single market niche are considerable, especially for smaller and medium-sized companies that may lack the breadth and depth of resources to tackle going after a national customer base with a "something for everyone" lineup of models, styles, and product selection. Community Coffee, the largest family-owned specialty coffee retailer in the United States, has a geographic focus on the state of Louisiana and communities across the Gulf of Mexico. Community holds only a 1.1 percent share of the national coffee market, but has recorded sales in excess of $100 million and has won a 50 percent share of the coffee business in the 11-state region where its coffee is distributed. Examples of firms that concentrate on a well-defined market niche keyed to a particular product or buyer segment include Discovery Channel and Comedy Central (in cable TV), Google (in Internet search engines), Porsche (in sports cars), and CGA, Inc. (a specialist in providing insurance to cover the cost of lucrative hole-in-one prizes at golf tournaments). Microbreweries, local bakeries, bed-and-breakfast inns, and local owner-managed retail boutiques are all good examples of enterprises that have scaled their operations to serve narrow or local customer segments.

A Focused Low-Cost Strategy

A focused strategy based on low cost aims at securing a competitive advantage by serving buyers in the target market niche at a lower cost and a lower price than rival competitors. This strategy has considerable attraction when a firm can lower costs significantly by limiting its customer base to a well-defined buyer segment. The avenues to achieving a cost advantage over rivals also serving the target market niche are the same as for low-cost leadership—outmanage rivals in keeping the costs to a bare minimum and searching for innovative ways to bypass or reduce nonessential activities. The only real difference between a low-cost provider strategy and a focused low-cost strategy is the size of the buyer group to which a company is appealing.

Focused low-cost strategies are fairly common. Producers of private-label goods are able to achieve low costs in product development, marketing, distribution, and advertising by concentrating on making generic items similar to name-brand merchandise and selling directly to retail chains wanting a low-priced store brand. The Perrigo Company has become a leading manufacturer of over-the-counter health care products with 2012 sales of more than

CONCEPTS & CONNECTIONS 5.2

ARAVIND EYE CARE SYSTEM'S FOCUSED LOW-COST STRATEGY

Cataracts, the largest cause of preventable blindness, can be treated with a quick surgical procedure that restores sight; however, poverty and limited access to care prevent millions worldwide from obtaining surgery. The Aravind Eye Care System has found a way to address this problem, with a focused low-cost strategy that has made cataract surgery not only affordable for more people in India, but also free for the very poorest. On the basis of this strategy, Aravind has achieved world renown and become the largest provider of eye care in the world.

High volume and high efficiency are at the cornerstone of Aravind's strategy. The Aravind network of five eye hospitals in India has become one of the most productive systems in the world, conducting about 300,000 surgeries a year in addition to seeing more than 2.6 million outpatients each year. Using the unique model of screenings at camps all over the country, Aravind reaches a broad cross-section of the market for surgical treatment. Additionally, Aravind attains very high staff productivity with each surgeon performing more than 2,500 surgeries annually, compared to 125 for a comparable American surgeon.

This level of productivity (with no loss in quality of care) was achieved through the development of a standardized system of surgical treatment, capitalizing on the fact that cataract removal is a fairly routine process. Aravind streamlined as much of the process as possible, reducing discretionary elements to a minimum, and tracking outcomes to ensure continuous process improvement. At Aravind's hospitals, no time is wasted between surgeries as different teams of support staff prepare patients for surgery and bring them to the operating theater; surgeons simply turn from one table to another to perform surgery on the next prepared patient. Aravind also drove costs down through the creation of its own manufacturing division, Aurolab, to produce intraocular lenses, suture needles, pharmaceuticals, and surgical blades in India.

Aravind's low costs allow it to keep prices for cataract surgery very low—about $10 per patient, compared to an average cost of $1,500 for surgery in the United States. Nevertheless, the system provides surgical outcomes and quality comparable to clinics in the United States. As a result of its unique fee system and effective management, Aravind is also able to provide free eye care to 60 percent of its patients from the revenue generated from paying patients.

Sources: Developed with Avni V. Patel. G. Natchiar, A. L. Robin, R. Thulasiraj, et al., "Attacking the Backlog of India's Curable Blind; The Aravind Eye Hospital Model," *Archives of Ophthalmology* 112, no. 7 (July 1994), pp. 987–93; D. F. Chang, "Tackling the Greatest Challenge in Cataract Surgery," *British Journal of Ophthalmology* 89, no. 9 (September 2005), pp. 1073–77; and McKinsey & Co., "Driving Down the Cost of High-Quality Care," *Health International,* December 2011.

$3.2 billion by focusing on producing private-label brands for retailers such as Walmart, CVS, Walgreens, Rite Aid, and Safeway. Even though Perrigo doesn't make branded products, a focused low-cost strategy is appropriate for the makers of branded products as well. Concepts & Connections 5.2 describes how Aravind's focus on lowering the costs of cataract removal allowed the company to address the needs of the "bottom of the pyramid" in India's population where blindness due to cataracts is an endemic problem.

A Focused Differentiation Strategy

Focused differentiation strategies are keyed to offering carefully designed products or services to appeal to the unique preferences and needs of a narrow, well-defined group of buyers (as opposed to a broad differentiation strategy aimed at many buyer groups and market segments). Companies such as Four Seasons Hotels and Resorts, Chanel, Gucci, and Louis Vuitton employ successful differentiation-based focused strategies targeted at affluent buyers wanting products and services with world-class attributes. Indeed, most markets contain a buyer segment willing to pay a price premium for the very finest items available, thus opening the strategic window for some competitors to pursue differentiation-based focused strategies aimed at the very top of the market pyramid.

Another successful focused differentiator is "fashion food retailer" Trader Joe's, a 369-store, 33-state chain that is a combination gourmet deli and food warehouse. Customers shop Trader Joe's as much for entertainment as for conventional grocery items; the store stocks out-of-the-ordinary culinary treats such as raspberry salsa, salmon burgers, and jasmine fried rice, as well as the standard goods normally found in supermarkets. What sets Trader Joe's apart is not just its unique combination of food novelties and competitively priced grocery items but also its capability to turn an otherwise mundane grocery excursion into a whimsical treasure hunt that is just plain fun. Concepts & Connections 5.3 describes the focused differentiation strategy of Popchips in the snack food industry.

When a Focused Low-Cost or Focused Differentiation Strategy Is Viable

A focused strategy aimed at securing a competitive edge based on either low cost or differentiation becomes increasingly attractive as more of the following conditions are met:

- The target market niche is big enough to be profitable and offers good growth potential.
- Industry leaders have chosen not to compete in the niche—focusers can avoid battling head-to-head against the industry's biggest and strongest competitors.
- It is costly or difficult for multisegment competitors to meet the specialized needs of niche buyers and at the same time satisfy the expectations of mainstream customers.
- The industry has many different niches and segments, thereby allowing a focuser to pick a niche suited to its resource strengths and capabilities.
- Few, if any, rivals are attempting to specialize in the same target segment.

The Risks of a Focused Low-Cost or Focused Differentiation Strategy

Focusing carries several risks. The *first major risk* is the chance that competitors will find effective ways to match the focused firm's capabilities in serving the target niche. In the lodging business, large chains such as Marriott and Hilton have launched multibrand strategies that allow them to compete effectively in several lodging segments simultaneously. Marriott has flagship hotels with a full complement of services and amenities that allow it to attract travelers and vacationers going to major resorts; it has J.W. Marriott and Ritz-Carlton hotels that provide deluxe comfort and service to business and leisure travelers; it

CONCEPTS & CONNECTIONS 5.3

POPCHIPS'S FOCUSED DIFFERENTIATION STRATEGY

Potato chips are big business: Americans spend $7 billion annually on their consumption. But the industry is a hard one to break into; it's a mature, slow-growth industry dominated by a few large competitors. Frito-Lay, maker of Lays and Ruffles, has a commanding 60 percent market share. These characteristics are enough to dissuade most potential entrants, but not Popchips, a small potato chip start-up. Despite difficult odds, Popchips has made impressive inroads into the industry with the help of a *focused differentiation strategy.* Popchips was founded in 2007 by Keith Belling, a serial entrepreneur, and Pat Turpin, a former Costco snack executive. Their idea was simple: Take advantage of high-income purchasers' growing desire for tasty, low-fat snacks. Using an innovative cooking method, they found a way to halve the fat content in potato chips while preserving the flavor.

Popchips has a differentiated product. But its real point of differentiation is in its brand and distribution strategy. Most potato chips have mass distribution and a broad buyer base. Belling and Turpin decided from the outset to narrow their distribution and their targeted buyers. They hoped that focusing on a market niche would allow their product to stand out from the bags of Lays and cans of Pringles in aisles all over America. Popchips's target: upper-income, health-conscious urban and suburban consumers.

To that end, the firm signed distribution deals with Whole Foods, Target, and, reflecting Turpin's roots, Costco. Popchips marketing emphasizes social marketing and word-of-mouth recommendations. The company sends samples to key tastemakers who tweet, blog, or recommend the product in traditional media. Ashton Kutcher, MTV's former *Punk'd* host, was so impressed with the chips that he volunteered to promote them. Like *Punk'd,* Popchips advertising is irreverent, with taglines like "love. without the handles."

Popchips's differentiation strategy is succeeding. Between 2009 and 2011, the company's sales accounted for nearly all potato chip sales growth at natural supermarket stores, such as Whole Foods. Popchips now has nearly 15 percent market share in this niche distribution channel. The company's 2010 sales were $45.7 million, more than double the 2009 figure. That's particularly impressive given that the industry growth rate has been a paltry 4 percent. In 2011, Forbes put Popchips on its list of America's most promising companies.

Developed with Dennis L. Huggins.

Sources: Molly *Maier,* "Chips, Pretzels and Corn Snacks - US - January 2012," Mintel, January 2012, www.oxygen.mintel.com (accessed February 1, 2012); Lindsay Blakely and Caitlin Elsaesser, "One Snacker at a Time: How Popchips Grew without Losing Its Character," *CBS News,* January 2011, www.cbsnews.com (accessed February 1, 2012; Laura Petrecca, "Popchips CEO Keith Belling Is 'Poptimist' on Healthy Snacks," *USA Today,* March 2010, www.usatoday.com (accessed February 13, 2012); http://www.forbes.com/sites/brettnelson/2011/11/30/americas-most-promising-companies-the-top-20/, accessed February 28, 2012; Popchips website.

has Courtyard by Marriott and SpringHill Suites brands for business travelers looking for moderately priced lodging; it has Marriott Residence Inns and TownePlace Suites designed as a "home away from home" for travelers staying five or more nights; and it has more than 670 Fairfield Inn locations that cater to travelers looking for quality lodging at an "affordable" price. Multibrand strategies are attractive to large companies such as Marriott precisely because they enable a company to enter a market niche and siphon business away from companies that employ a focus strategy.

A *second risk* of employing a focus strategy is the potential for the preferences and needs of niche members to shift over time toward the product attributes desired by the majority of buyers. An erosion of the differences across buyer segments lowers entry barriers into a focuser's market niche and provides an open invitation for rivals in adjacent segments to begin competing for the focuser's customers. A *third risk* is that the segment may become so attractive it is soon inundated with competitors, intensifying rivalry and splintering segment profits.

Best-Cost Provider Strategies

LO4 Recognize the required conditions for delivering superior value to customers through the use of a hybrid of low-cost provider and differentiation strategies.

As Figure 5.1 indicates, **best-cost provider strategies** are a *hybrid* of low-cost provider and differentiation strategies that aim at satisfying buyer expectations on key quality/features/performance/service attributes and beating customer expectations on price. Companies pursuing best-cost strategies aim squarely at the sometimes great mass of value-conscious buyers looking for a good-to-very-good product or service at an economical price. The essence of a best-cost provider strategy is giving customers *more value for the money* by satisfying buyer desires for appealing features/performance/quality/service and charging a lower price for these attributes compared to rivals with similar-caliber product offerings.[3]

To profitably employ a best-cost provider strategy, a company *must have the capability to incorporate attractive or upscale attributes at a lower cost than rivals.* This capability is contingent on (1) a superior value chain configuration that eliminates or minimizes activities that do not add value, (2) unmatched efficiency in managing essential value chain activities, and (3) core competencies that allow differentiating attributes to be incorporated at a low cost. When a company can incorporate appealing features, good-to-excellent product performance or quality, or more satisfying customer service into its product offering *at a lower cost than rivals,* then it enjoys "best-cost" status—it is the low-cost provider of a product or service with *upscale attributes.* A best-cost provider can use its low-cost advantage to underprice rivals whose products or services have similar upscale attributes and still earn attractive profits.

Concepts & Connections 5.4 describes how Toyota has applied the principles of a best-cost provider strategy in producing and marketing its Lexus brand.

> ## CORE CONCEPT
>
> **Best-cost provider strategies** are a *hybrid* of low-cost provider and differentiation strategies that aim at satisfying buyer expectations on key quality/features/performance/service attributes and beating customer expectations on price.

When a Best-Cost Provider Strategy Works Best

A best-cost provider strategy works best in markets where product differentiation is the norm and attractively large numbers of value-conscious buyers can be induced to purchase midrange products rather than the basic products of low-cost producers or the expensive products of top-of-the-line differentiators. A best-cost provider usually needs to position itself near the middle of the market with either a medium-quality product at a below-average price or a high-quality product at an average or slightly higher-than-average price. Best-cost provider strategies also work well in recessionary times when great masses of buyers become value-conscious and are attracted to economically priced products and services with especially appealing attributes.

The Danger of an Unsound Best-Cost Provider Strategy

A company's biggest vulnerability in employing a best-cost provider strategy is not having the requisite core competencies and efficiencies in managing value chain activities to support the addition of differentiating features without significantly increasing costs. A company with a modest degree of

CONCEPTS & CONNECTIONS 5.4

TOYOTA'S BEST-COST PRODUCER STRATEGY FOR ITS LEXUS LINE

Toyota Motor Company is widely regarded as a low-cost producer among the world's motor vehicle manufacturers. Despite its emphasis on product quality, Toyota has achieved low-cost leadership because it has developed considerable skills in efficient supply chain management and low-cost assembly capabilities, and because its models are positioned in the low-to-medium end of the price spectrum, where high production volumes are conducive to low unit costs. But when Toyota decided to introduce its new Lexus models to compete in the luxury-car market, it employed a classic best-cost provider strategy. Toyota took the following four steps in crafting and implementing its Lexus strategy:

- Designing an array of high-performance characteristics and upscale features into the Lexus models so as to make them comparable in performance and luxury to other high-end models and attractive to Mercedes-Benz, BMW, Audi, Jaguar, Cadillac, and Lincoln buyers.

- Transferring its capabilities in making high-quality Toyota models at low cost to making premium-quality Lexus models at costs below other luxury-car makers. Toyota's supply chain capabilities and low-cost assembly know-how allowed it to incorporate high-tech performance features

and upscale quality into Lexus models at substantially less cost than comparable Mercedes and BMW models.

- Using its relatively lower manufacturing costs to underprice comparable Mercedes and BMW models. Toyota believed that with its cost advantage it could price attractively equipped Lexus cars low enough to draw price-conscious buyers away from Mercedes and BMW. Toyota's pricing policy also allowed it to induce Toyota, Honda, Ford, or GM owners desiring more luxury to switch to a Lexus. Lexus's pricing advantage over Mercedes and BMW was sometimes quite significant. For example, in 2013 the Lexus RX 350, a midsize SUV, carried a sticker price in the $39,000–$54,000 range (depending on how it was equipped), whereas variously equipped Mercedes ML 350 SUVs had price tags in the $47,000–$96,000 range, and a BMW X5 SUV could range anywhere from $47,000 to $89,000, depending on the optional equipment chosen.

- Establishing a new network of Lexus dealers, separate from Toyota dealers, dedicated to providing a level of personalized, attentive customer service unmatched in the industry.

differentiation and no real cost advantage will most likely find itself squeezed between the firms using low-cost strategies and those using differentiation strategies. Low-cost providers may be able to siphon customers away with the appeal of a lower price (despite having marginally less appealing product attributes). High-end differentiators may be able to steal customers away with the appeal of appreciably better product attributes (even though their products carry a somewhat higher price tag). Thus, a successful best-cost provider must offer buyers *significantly* better product attributes to justify a price above what low-cost leaders are charging. Likewise, it has to achieve significantly lower costs in providing upscale features so that it can outcompete high-end differentiators on the basis of a *significantly* lower price.

Successful Competitive Strategies Are Resource Based

For a company's competitive strategy to succeed in delivering good performance and the intended competitive edge over rivals, it has to be well matched to a company's internal situation and underpinned by an appropriate set of

A company's competitive strategy should be well matched to its internal situation and predicated on leveraging its collection of competitively valuable resources and competencies.

resources, know-how, and competitive capabilities. To succeed in employing a low-cost provider strategy, a company has to have the resources and capabilities to keep its costs below those of its competitors; this means having the expertise to cost-effectively manage value chain activities better than rivals and/or the innovative capability to bypass certain value chain activities being performed by rivals. To succeed in strongly differentiating its product in ways that are appealing to buyers, a company must have the resources and capabilities (such as better technology, strong skills in product innovation, expertise in customer service) to incorporate unique attributes into its product offering that a broad range of buyers will find appealing and worth paying for. Strategies focusing on a narrow segment of the market require the capability to do an outstanding job of satisfying the needs and expectations of niche buyers. Success in employing a strategy keyed to a best-value offering requires the resources and capabilities to incorporate upscale product or service attributes at a lower cost than rivals.

KEY POINTS

1. Early in the process of crafting a strategy, company managers have to decide which of the five basic competitive strategies to employ—overall low-cost, broad differentiation, focused low-cost, focused differentiation, or best-cost provider.

2. In employing a low-cost provider strategy, a company must do a better job than rivals of cost-effectively managing internal activities and/or it must find innovative ways to eliminate or bypass cost-producing activities. Particular attention should be paid to cost drivers, which are factors having a strong effect on the cost of a company's value chain activities and cost structure. Low-cost provider strategies work particularly well when price competition is strong and the products of rival sellers are very weakly differentiated. Other conditions favoring a low-cost provider strategy are when supplies are readily available from eager sellers, when there are not many ways to differentiate that have value to buyers, when the majority of industry sales are made to a few large buyers, when buyer switching costs are low, and when industry newcomers are likely to use a low introductory price to build market share.

3. Broad differentiation strategies seek to produce a competitive edge by incorporating attributes and features that set a company's product/service offering apart from rivals in ways that buyers consider valuable and worth paying for. Such features and attributes are best integrated through the systematic management of uniqueness—value chain activities or factors that can have a strong effect on customer value and creating differentiation. Successful differentiation allows a firm to (1) command a premium price for its product, (2) increase unit sales (because additional buyers are won over by the differentiating features), and/or (3) gain buyer loyalty to its brand (because some buyers are strongly attracted to the differentiating features and bond with the company and its products).

Differentiation strategies work best in markets with diverse buyer preferences where there are big windows of opportunity to strongly differentiate a company's product offering from those of rival brands, in situations where few other rivals are pursuing a similar differentiation approach, and in circumstances where technological change is fast-paced and competition centers on rapidly evolving product features. A differentiation strategy is doomed when competitors are able to quickly copy most or all of the appealing product attributes a company comes up with, when a company's differentiation efforts meet with a ho-hum or so-what market reception, or when a company erodes profitability by overspending on efforts to differentiate its product offering.

4. A focus strategy delivers competitive advantage either by achieving lower costs than rivals in serving buyers comprising the target market niche or by offering niche buyers an appealingly differentiated product or service that meets their needs better than rival brands. A focused strategy becomes increasingly attractive when the target market niche is big enough to be profitable and offers good growth potential, when it is costly or difficult for multisegment competitors to put capabilities in place to meet the specialized needs of the target market niche and at the same time satisfy the expectations of their mainstream customers, when there are one or more niches that present a good match with a focuser's resource strengths and capabilities, and when few other rivals are attempting to specialize in the same target segment.

5. Best-cost provider strategies stake out a middle ground between pursuing a low-cost advantage and a differentiation-based advantage and between appealing to the broad market as a whole and a narrow market niche. The aim is to create competitive advantage by giving buyers more value for the money—satisfying buyer expectations on key quality/features/performance/service attributes while beating customer expectations on price. To profitably employ a best-cost provider strategy, a company *must have the capability to incorporate attractive or upscale attributes at a lower cost than rivals.* This capability is contingent on (1) a superior value chain configuration, (2) unmatched efficiency in managing essential value chain activities, and (3) resource strengths and core competencies that allow differentiating attributes to be incorporated at a low cost. A best-cost provider strategy works best in markets where opportunities to differentiate exist and where many buyers are sensitive to price and value.

6. Deciding which generic strategy to employ is perhaps the most important strategic commitment a company makes—it tends to drive the rest of the strategic actions a company decides to undertake and it sets the whole tone for the pursuit of a competitive advantage over rivals.

ASSURANCE OF LEARNING EXERCISES

1. Best Buy is the largest consumer electronics retailer in the United States with 2012 sales of almost $50 billion. The company competes aggressively on price with rivals such as Costco Wholesale, Sam's Club, Walmart, and Target, but is also known by consumers for its first-rate customer service. Best Buy customers have commented that the retailer's sales staff is exceptionally knowledgeable about products and can direct them to the exact location of difficult-to-find items. Best Buy customers also appreciate that demonstration models of PC monitors, digital

LO1, LO2, LO3, LO4

media players, and other electronics are fully powered and ready for in-store use. Best Buy's Geek Squad tech support and installation services are additional customer service features valued by many customers.

How would you characterize Best Buy's competitive strategy? Should it be classified as a low-cost provider strategy? a differentiation strategy? a best-cost strategy? Explain your answer.

LO2

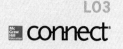

2. Concepts & Connections 5.1 discusses Walmart's low-cost advantage in the supermarket industry. Based on information provided in the illustration, explain how Walmart has built its low-cost advantage in the supermarket industry and why a low-cost provider strategy is well suited to the industry.

LO1, LO2, LO3, LO4

3. Stihl is the world's leading manufacturer and marketer of chain saws with annual sales exceeding $2 billion. With innovations dating to its 1929 invention of the gasoline-powered chain saw, the company holds more than 1,000 patents related to chain saws and outdoor power tools. The company's chain saws, leaf blowers, and hedge trimmers sell at price points well above competing brands and are sold only by its network of some 8,000 independent dealers.

How would you characterize Stihl's competitive strategy? Should it be classified as a low-cost provider strategy? a differentiation strategy? a best-cost strategy? Also, has the company chosen to focus on a narrow piece of the market or does it appear to pursue a broad market approach? Explain your answer.

LO3

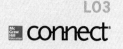

4. Explore BMW's website at www.bmwgroup.com and see if you can identify at least three ways in which the company seeks to differentiate itself from rival automakers. Is there reason to believe that BMW's differentiation strategy has been successful in producing a competitive advantage? Why or why not?

EXERCISES FOR SIMULATION PARTICIPANTS

LO1, LO2, LO3, LO4

1. Which one of the five generic competitive strategies best characterizes your company's strategic approach to competing successfully?

2. Which rival companies appear to be employing a low-cost provider strategy?

3. Which rival companies appear to be employing a broad differentiation strategy?

4. Which rival companies appear to be employing a best-cost provider strategy?

5. Which rival companies appear to be employing some type of focus strategy?

6. What is your company's action plan to achieve a sustainable competitive advantage over rival companies? List at least three (preferably more than three) specific kinds of decision entries on specific decision screens that your company has made or intends to make to win this kind of competitive edge over rivals.

ENDNOTES

1. Michael E. Porter, *Competitive Strategy: Techniques for Analyzing Industries and Competitors* (New York: Free Press, 1980), chap. 2; and Michael E. Porter, "What Is Strategy?"

Harvard Business Review 74, no. 6 (November–December 1996).

2. Michael E. Porter, *Competitive Advantage* (New York: Free Press, 1985).

3. Peter J. Williamson and Ming Zeng, "Value-for-Money Strategies for Recessionary Times," *Harvard Business Review* 87, no. 3 (March 2009).

Strengthening a Company's Competitive Position: Strategic Moves, Timing, and Scope of Operations

LEARNING OBJECTIVES

LO1 Learn whether and when to pursue offensive or defensive strategic moves to improve a company's market position.

LO2 Recognize when being a first mover or a fast follower or a late mover can lead to competitive advantage.

LO3 Become aware of the strategic benefits and risks of expanding a company's horizontal scope through mergers and acquisitions.

LO4 Learn the advantages and disadvantages of extending a company's scope of operations via vertical integration.

LO5 Understand the conditions that favor farming out certain value chain activities to outside parties.

LO6 Gain an understanding of how strategic alliances and collaborative partnerships can bolster a company's collection of resources and capabilities.

Once a company has settled on which of the five generic competitive strategies to employ, attention turns to what *other strategic actions* it can take to complement its competitive approach and maximize the power of its overall strategy. Several decisions regarding the company's operating scope and how to best strengthen its market standing must be made:

- Whether and when to go on the offensive and initiate aggressive strategic moves to improve the company's market position.
- Whether and when to employ defensive strategies to protect the company's market position.
- When to undertake strategic moves based upon whether it is advantageous to be a first mover or a fast follower or a late mover.
- Whether to integrate backward or forward into more stages of the industry value chain.
- Which value chain activities, if any, should be outsourced.
- Whether to enter into strategic alliances or partnership arrangements with other enterprises.
- Whether to bolster the company's market position by merging with or acquiring another company in the same industry.

This chapter presents the pros and cons of each of these measures that round out a company's overall strategy.

Launching Strategic Offensives to Improve a Company's Market Position

LO1 Learn whether and when to pursue offensive or defensive strategic moves to improve a company's market position.

No matter which of the five generic competitive strategies a company employs, there are times when a company *should be aggressive and go on the offensive.* Strategic offensives are called for when a company spots opportunities to gain profitable market share at the expense of rivals or when a company has no choice but to try to whittle away at a strong rival's competitive advantage. Companies such as Walmart, Apple, Southwest Airlines, and Google play hardball, aggressively pursuing competitive advantage and trying to reap the benefits a competitive edge offers—a leading market share, excellent profit margins, and rapid growth.[1]

Choosing the Basis for Competitive Attack

Generally, strategic offensives should be grounded in a company's competitive assets and strong points and should be aimed at exploiting competitor weaknesses.[2] Ignoring the need to tie a strategic offensive to a company's competitive strengths is like going to war with a popgun—the prospects for success are dim. For instance, it is foolish for a company with relatively high costs to employ a price-cutting offensive. Likewise, it is ill advised to pursue a product innovation offensive without having proven expertise in R&D, new-product development, and speeding new or improved products to market.

The best offensives use a company's most competitively potent resources to attack rivals in those competitive areas where they are weakest.

The principal offensive strategy options include the following:

1. *Attacking the competitive weaknesses of rivals.* For example, a company with especially good customer service capabilities can make special sales pitches to the customers of those rivals who provide subpar customer service. Aggressors with a recognized brand name and strong marketing skills can launch efforts to win customers away from rivals with weak brand recognition.

2. *Offering an equally good or better product at a lower price.* Lower prices can produce market share gains if competitors offering similarly performing products don't respond with price cuts of their own. Price-cutting offensives are best initiated by companies that have *first achieved a cost advantage.*[3]

3. *Pursuing continuous product innovation to draw sales and market share away from less innovative rivals.* Ongoing introductions of new/improved products can put rivals under tremendous competitive pressure, especially when rivals' new-product development capabilities are weak.

4. *Leapfrogging competitors by being the first to market with next-generation technology or products.* Microsoft got its next-generation Xbox 360 to market 12 months ahead of Sony's PlayStation 3 and Nintendo's Wii, helping it build a sizable market share and develop a reputation for cutting-edge innovation in the video game industry.

5. *Adopting and improving on the good ideas of other companies (rivals or otherwise).* The idea of warehouse-type home improvement centers did not originate with Home Depot co-founders Arthur Blank and Bernie Marcus; they got the "big box" concept from their former employer, Handy Dan Home Improvement. But they were quick to improve on Handy Dan's business model and strategy and take Home Depot to a higher plateau in terms of product-line breadth and customer service.

6. *Deliberately attacking those market segments where a key rival makes big profits.* Toyota has launched a hardball attack on General Motors, Ford, and Chrysler in the U.S. market for light trucks and SUVs, the very market arena where the Detroit automakers typically earn their big profits (roughly $10,000 to $15,000 per vehicle). Toyota's pickup trucks and SUVs have weakened the Big 3 U.S. automakers by taking away sales and market share that they desperately need.

7. *Maneuvering around competitors to capture unoccupied or less contested market territory.* Examples include launching initiatives to build strong positions in geographic areas or product categories where close rivals have little or no market presence.

8. *Using hit-and-run or guerrilla warfare tactics to grab sales and market share from complacent or distracted rivals.* Options for "guerrilla offensives" include occasional lowballing on price (to win a big order or steal a key account from a rival) or surprising key rivals with sporadic but intense bursts of promotional activity (offering a 20 percent discount for one week to draw customers away from rival brands).[4] Guerrilla offensives are particularly well suited to small challengers who have neither the resources nor the market visibility to mount a full-fledged attack on industry leaders.

9. *Launching a preemptive strike to capture a rare opportunity or secure an industry's limited resources.*[5] What makes a move preemptive is its one-of-a-kind nature—whoever strikes first stands to acquire competitive assets that rivals can't readily match. Examples of preemptive moves include (1) securing the best distributors in a particular geographic region or country; (2) moving to obtain the most favorable site at a new interchange or intersection, in a new shopping mall, and so on; and (3) tying up the most reliable, high-quality suppliers via exclusive partnerships, long-term contracts, or even acquisition. To be successful, a preemptive move doesn't have to totally block rivals from following or copying; it merely needs to give a firm a prime position that is not easily circumvented.

Choosing Which Rivals to Attack

Offensive-minded firms need to analyze which of their rivals to challenge as well as how to mount that challenge. The following are the best targets for offensive attacks:

- *Market leaders that are vulnerable.* Offensive attacks make good sense when a company that leads in terms of size and market share is not a true leader in terms of serving the market well. Signs of leader vulnerability include unhappy buyers, an inferior product line, a weak competitive strategy with regard to low-cost leadership or differentiation, a preoccupation with diversification into other industries, and mediocre or declining profitability.

- *Runner-up firms with weaknesses in areas where the challenger is strong.* Runner-up firms are an especially attractive target when a challenger's resource strengths and competitive capabilities are well suited to exploiting their weaknesses.

- *Struggling enterprises that are on the verge of going under.* Challenging a hard-pressed rival in ways that further sap its financial strength and competitive position can hasten its exit from the market.

- *Small local and regional firms with limited capabilities.* Because small firms typically have limited expertise and resources, a challenger with broader capabilities is well positioned to raid their biggest and best customers.

Blue Ocean Strategy—A Special Kind of Offensive

A **blue ocean strategy** seeks to gain a dramatic and durable competitive advantage *by abandoning efforts to beat out competitors in existing markets and, instead, inventing a new industry or distinctive market segment that renders existing competitors largely irrelevant and allows a company to create and capture altogether new demand.*[6] This strategy views the business universe as consisting of two distinct types of market space. One is where industry boundaries are defined and accepted, the competitive rules of the game are well understood by all industry members, and companies try to outperform rivals by capturing a bigger share of existing demand; in such markets, lively competition constrains a company's prospects for rapid growth and superior profitability since rivals move quickly to either imitate or counter the successes of competitors. The second type of market space is a "blue ocean" where the industry does not really exist yet, is untainted by competition, and offers wide-open opportunity for profitable and rapid growth if a company can come up with a product offering and strategy that allows it to create new demand rather than fight over existing demand. A terrific example of such wide-open or blue ocean market space is the online auction industry that eBay created and now dominates.

> **CORE CONCEPT**
> **Blue ocean strategies** offer growth in revenues and profits by discovering or inventing new industry segments that create altogether new demand.

Other examples of companies that have achieved competitive advantages by creating blue ocean market spaces include Starbucks in the coffee shop industry, Dollar General in extreme discount retailing, FedEx in overnight package delivery, and Cirque du Soleil in live entertainment. Cirque du Soleil "reinvented the circus" by creating a distinctively different market space for its performances (Las Vegas nightclubs and theater-type settings) and pulling in a whole new group of customers—adults and corporate clients—who were willing to pay several times more than the price of a conventional circus ticket to have an "entertainment experience" featuring sophisticated clowns and star-quality acrobatic acts in a comfortable atmosphere.

Blue ocean strategies provide a company with a great opportunity in the short run. But they don't guarantee a company's long-term success, which depends more on whether a company can protect the market position it opened up. Concepts & Connections 6.1 discusses how Gilt Groupe used a blue ocean strategy to open a new competitive space in online luxury retailing.

Using Defensive Strategies to Protect a Company's Market Position and Competitive Advantage

In a competitive market, all firms are subject to offensive challenges from rivals. The purposes of defensive strategies are to lower the risk of being attacked, weaken the impact of any attack that occurs, and influence challengers to aim their efforts at other rivals. While defensive strategies usually don't enhance a firm's competitive advantage, they can definitely help fortify its competitive position. Defensive strategies can take either of two forms: actions to block challengers and actions signaling the likelihood of strong retaliation.

> Good defensive strategies can help protect competitive advantage but rarely are the basis for creating it.

Blocking the Avenues Open to Challengers

The most frequently employed approach to defending a company's present position involves actions to restrict a competitive attack by a challenger. A number of obstacles can be put in the path of would-be challengers.[7] A defender can introduce new features, add new models, or broaden its product

CONCEPTS & CONNECTIONS 6.1

GILT GROUPE'S BLUE OCEAN STRATEGY IN THE U.S. FLASH SALE INDUSTRY

Luxury fashion flash sales exploded onto the U.S. e-commerce scene when Gilt Groupe launched its business in 2007. Flash sales offer limited quantities of high-end designer brands at steep discounts to site members over a very narrow time frame: The opportunity to snap up an incredible bargain is over in a "flash." The concept of online time-limited, designer-brand sale events, available to members only, had been invented six years earlier by the French company Vente Privée. But since Vente Privée operated in Europe and the United Kingdom, the U.S. market represented a wide-open, blue ocean of uncontested opportunity. Gilt Groupe's only rival was Ideeli, another U.S. start-up that had launched in the same year.

Gilt Groupe grew rapidly in the calm waters of the early days of the U.S. industry. Its tremendous growth stemmed from its recognition of an underserved segment of the population—the web-savvy, value-conscious fashionista—and also from fortuitous timing. The Great Recession hit the United States in December 2007, causing a sharp decline in consumer buying and leaving designers with unforeseen quantities of luxury items they could not sell. The fledgling flash sale industry was the perfect channel to off-load excess inventory, while it still maintained the cachet of exclusivity, through members-only sales and limited-time availability.

Gilt's revenue grew exponentially from $25 million in 2008 to upward of $700 million by 2012. But the company's success prompted an influx of fast followers into the luxury flash sale

industry, including HauteLook and Rue La La, which entered the market in December 2007 and April 2008, respectively. Competition among rival sites became especially strong since memberships were free and online customers could switch easily from site to site. Competition also heightened as larger retailers entered the luxury flash sale industry, with Nordstrom acquiring HauteLook, eBay purchasing Rue La La, and Amazon acquiring MyHabit.com. In late 2011, Vente Privée announced the launch of its U.S. online site, via a joint venture with American Express.

As the competitive waters roiled and turned increasingly red, Gilt Groupe began looking for new ways to compete, expanding into a variety of online luxury product and services niches, venturing overseas, eliminating 10 percent of its workforce, and replacing its founder as CEO in 2013. As of year-end 2012, the company had not yet become profitable. Can Gilt Groupe survive and prosper in a more crowded competitive space? Only time will tell.

Developed with Judith H. Lin.

Sources: Matthew Carroll, "The Rise of Gilt Groupe," Forbes. com, January 2012, www.forbes.com (accessed February 26, 2012); Mark Brohan, "The Top 500 Guide," *Internet Retailer,* June 2011, www.internetretailer.com (accessed February 26, 2012); Colleen Debaise, "Launching Gilt Groupe, A Fashionable Enterprise," *The Wall Street Journal,* October 2010, www.wsj.com (accessed February 26, 2012); http://about.americanexpress.com/news/pr/2011/vente_usa.aspx, accessed March 3, 2012.

line to close vacant niches to opportunity-seeking challengers. It can thwart the efforts of rivals to attack with a lower price by maintaining economy-priced options of its own. It can try to discourage buyers from trying competitors' brands by making early announcements about upcoming new products or planned price changes. Finally, a defender can grant volume discounts or better financing terms to dealers and distributors to discourage them from experimenting with other suppliers.

Signaling Challengers That Retaliation Is Likely

The goal of signaling challengers that strong retaliation is likely in the event of an attack is either to dissuade challengers from attacking or to divert them to less threatening options. Either goal can be achieved by letting challengers know the battle will cost more than it is worth. Would-be challengers can be signaled by:

- Publicly announcing management's commitment to maintain the firm's present market share.
- Publicly committing the company to a policy of matching competitors' terms or prices.
- Maintaining a war chest of cash and marketable securities.
- Making an occasional strong counterresponse to the moves of weak competitors to enhance the firm's image as a tough defender.

Timing a Company's Offensive and Defensive Strategic Moves

When to make a strategic move is often as crucial as *what* move to make. Timing is especially important when **first-mover advantages** or **disadvantages** exist. Being first to initiate a strategic move can have a high payoff when (1) pioneering helps build a firm's image and reputation with buyers; (2) early commitments to new technologies, new-style components, new or emerging distribution channels, and so on, can produce an absolute cost advantage over rivals; (3) first-time customers remain strongly loyal to pioneering firms in making repeat purchases; and (4) moving first constitutes a preemptive strike, making imitation extra hard or unlikely. The bigger the first-mover advantages, the more attractive making the first move becomes.[8]

LO2 Recognize when being a first mover or a fast follower or a late mover can lead to competitive advantage.

> **CORE CONCEPT**
> Because of **first-mover advantages and disadvantages,** competitive advantage can spring from *when* a move is made as well as from *what* move is made.

Sometimes, though, markets are slow to accept the innovative product offering of a first mover, in which case a fast follower with substantial resources and marketing muscle can overtake a first mover (as Fox News has done in competing against CNN to become the leading cable news network). Sometimes furious technological change or product innovation makes a first mover vulnerable to quickly appearing next-generation technology or products. For instance, former market leaders in mobile phones Nokia and BlackBerry have been victimized by Apple's far more innovative iPhone models and new smartphones based on Google's Android operating system. Hence, there are no guarantees that a first mover will win sustainable competitive advantage.[9]

To sustain any advantage that may initially accrue to a pioneer, a first mover needs to be a fast learner and continue to move aggressively to capitalize on any initial pioneering advantage. If a first mover's skills, know-how, and actions are easily copied or even surpassed, then followers and even late movers can catch or overtake the first mover in a relatively short period. What makes being a first mover strategically important is not being the first company to do something but rather being the first competitor to put together the precise combination of features, customer value, and sound revenue/cost/profit economics that gives it an edge over rivals in the battle for market leadership.[10] If the marketplace quickly takes to a first mover's innovative product offering, a first mover must have large-scale production, marketing, and distribution capabilities if it is to stave off fast followers that possess similar resources capabilities. If technology is advancing at a torrid pace, a first mover cannot hope to sustain its lead without having strong capabilities in R&D, design, and new-product development, along with the financial strength to fund these activities.

The Potential for Late-Mover Advantages or First-Mover Disadvantages

There are instances when there are actually *advantages* to being an adept follower rather than a first mover. Late-mover advantages (or *first-mover disadvantages*) arise in four instances:

- When pioneering leadership is more costly than followership and only negligible experience or learning curve benefits accrue to the leader—a condition that allows a follower to end up with lower costs than the first mover.

- When the products of an innovator are somewhat primitive and do not live up to buyer expectations, thus allowing a clever follower to win disenchanted buyers away from the leader with better-performing products.

- When potential buyers are skeptical about the benefits of a new technology or product being pioneered by a first mover.

- When rapid market evolution (due to fast-paced changes in either technology or buyer needs and expectations) gives fast followers and maybe even cautious late movers the opening to leapfrog a first mover's products with more attractive next-version products.

Deciding Whether to Be an Early Mover or Late Mover

In weighing the pros and cons of being a first mover versus a fast follower versus a slow mover, it matters whether the race to market leadership in a particular industry is a marathon or a sprint. In marathons, a slow mover is not unduly penalized—first-mover advantages can be fleeting, and there's ample time for fast followers and sometimes even late movers to catch up.[11] Thus the speed at which the pioneering innovation is likely to catch on matters considerably as companies struggle with whether to pursue a particular emerging market opportunity aggressively or cautiously. For instance, it took 5.5 years for worldwide mobile phone use to grow from 10 million to 100 million worldwide and close to 10 years for the number of at-home broadband subscribers to grow to 100 million worldwide. The lesson here is that there is a market-penetration curve for every emerging opportunity; typically, the curve has an inflection point at which all the pieces of the business model fall into place, buyer demand explodes, and the market takes off. The inflection point can come early on a fast-rising curve (like use of e-mail) or farther on up a slow-rising curve (such as use of broadband). Any company that seeks competitive advantage by being a first mover thus needs to ask some hard questions:

- Does market takeoff depend on the development of complementary products or services that currently are not available?
- Is new infrastructure required before buyer demand can surge?
- Will buyers need to learn new skills or adopt new behaviors? Will buyers encounter high switching costs?
- Are there influential competitors in a position to delay or derail the efforts of a first mover?

When the answers to any of these questions are yes, then a company must be careful not to pour too many resources into getting ahead of the market opportunity—the race is likely going to be more of a 10-year marathon than a 2-year sprint.

Strengthening a Company's Market Position Via Its Scope of Operations

Apart from considerations of offensive and defensive competitive moves and their timing, another set of managerial decisions can affect the strength of a company's market position. These decisions concern the **scope of the firm**—the breadth of a company's activities and the extent of its market reach. For example, Ralph Lauren Corporation designs, markets, and distributes fashionable apparel and other merchandise to more than 10,000 major department stores and specialty retailers around the world, plus it also operates nearly 400 Ralph Lauren retail stores, 200-plus factory stores, and seven e-commerce sites. Scope decisions also concern which segments of the market to serve—decisions that can include geographic market segments as well as product and service segments. Almost 40 percent of Ralph Lauren's sales are made outside the United States, and its product line includes apparel, fragrances, home furnishings, eyewear, watches and jewelry, and handbags and other leather goods. The company has also expanded its brand lineup through the acquisitions of Chaps menswear and casual retailer Club Monaco.

LO3 Become aware of the strategic benefits and risks of expanding a company's horizontal scope through mergers and acquisitions.

> **CORE CONCEPT**
> The **scope of the firm** refers to the range of activities the firm performs internally, the breadth of its product and service offerings, the extent of its geographic market presence, and its mix of businesses.

Four dimensions of firm scope have the capacity to strengthen a company's position in a given market—the breadth of its product and service offerings, the range of activities the firm performs internally, the extent of its geographic market presence, and its mix of businesses. In this chapter, we discuss horizontal and vertical scope decisions in relation to its breadth of offerings and range of internally performed activities. A company's **horizontal scope,** which is the range of product and service segments that it serves, can be expanded through new-business development or mergers and acquisitions of other companies in the marketplace.

> **CORE CONCEPT**
> **Horizontal scope** is the range of product and service segments that a firm serves within its focal market.

The company's **vertical scope** is the extent to which it engages in the various activities that make up the industry's entire value chain system—from raw-material or component production all the way to retailing and after-sales service. Expanding a company's vertical scope by means of vertical integration can also affect the strength of a company's market position.

Additional dimensions of a firm's scope are discussed in the two following chapters; Chapter 7 focuses on the company's geographic scope and expansion into foreign markets, while Chapter 8 takes up the topic of business diversification and corporate strategy.

> **CORE CONCEPT**
> **Vertical scope** is the extent to which a firm's internal activities encompass one, some, many, or all of the activities that make up an industry's entire value chain system, ranging from raw-material production to final sales and service activities.

Horizontal Merger and Acquisition Strategies

Mergers and acquisitions are much-used strategic options to strengthen a company's market position. A *merger* is the combining of two or more companies into a single corporate entity, with the newly created company often taking on a new name. An *acquisition* is a combination in which one company, the acquirer, purchases and absorbs the operations of another, the acquired.

> Combining the operations of two companies, via merger or acquisition, is an attractive strategic option for achieving operating economies, strengthening the resulting company's competencies and competitiveness, and opening avenues of new market opportunity.

The difference between a merger and an acquisition relates more to the details of ownership, management control, and financial arrangements than to strategy and competitive advantage. The resources and competitive capabilities of the newly created enterprise end up much the same whether the combination is the result of an acquisition or merger.

Horizontal mergers and acquisitions, which involve combining the operations of companies within the same product or service market, allow companies to rapidly increase scale and horizontal scope. For example, the United–Continental merger has increased the airlines' scale of operations and extended their reach geographically.

Merger and acquisition strategies typically set sights on achieving any of five objectives:[12]

1. *Extending the company's business into new product categories.* Many times a company has gaps in its product line that need to be filled. Acquisition can be a quicker and more potent way to broaden a company's product line than going through the exercise of introducing a company's own new product to fill the gap. PepsiCo acquired Quaker Oats chiefly to bring Gatorade into the Pepsi family of beverages. While Coca-Cola has expanded its beverage lineup by introducing its own new products (such as Powerade and Dasani), it has also expanded its offerings by acquiring Minute Maid, Glacéau VitaminWater, and Hi-C.

2. *Creating a more cost-efficient operation out of the combined companies.* When a company acquires another company in the same industry, there's usually enough overlap in operations that certain inefficient plants can be closed or distribution and sales activities can be partly combined and

downsized. The combined companies may also be able to reduce supply chain costs because of buying in greater volume from common suppliers. Likewise, it is usually feasible to squeeze out cost savings in administrative activities, again by combining and downsizing such activities as finance and accounting, information technology, human resources, and so on.

3. *Expanding a company's geographic coverage.* One of the best and quickest ways to expand a company's geographic coverage is to acquire rivals with operations in the desired locations. Food products companies such as Nestlé, Kraft, Unilever, and Procter & Gamble have made acquisitions an integral part of their strategies to expand internationally.

4. *Gaining quick access to new technologies or complementary resources and capabilities.* Making acquisitions to bolster a company's technological know-how or to expand its skills and capabilities allows a company to bypass a time-consuming and expensive internal effort to build desirable new resources and capabilities. From 2000 through May 2013, Cisco Systems purchased 106 companies to give it more technological reach and product breadth, thereby enhancing its standing as the world's largest provider of hardware, software, and services for building and operating Internet networks.

5. *Leading the convergence of industries whose boundaries are being blurred by changing technologies and new market opportunities.* Such acquisitions are the result of a company's management betting that two or more distinct industries are converging into one and deciding to establish a strong position in the consolidating markets by bringing together the resources and products of several different companies. News Corporation has prepared for the convergence of media services with the purchase of satellite TV companies to complement its media holdings in TV broadcasting (the Fox network and TV stations in various countries), cable TV (Fox News, Fox Sports, and FX), filmed entertainment (Twentieth Century Fox and Fox Studios), newspapers, magazines, and book publishing.

Concepts & Connections 6.2 describes how Bristol-Myers Squibb developed its "string-of-pearls" horizontal acquisition strategy to fill in its pharmaceutical product development gaps.

Why Mergers and Acquisitions Sometimes Fail to Produce Anticipated Results

Despite many successes, mergers and acquisitions do not always produce the hoped-for outcomes.[13] Cost savings may prove smaller than expected. Gains in competitive capabilities may take substantially longer to realize or, worse, may never materialize. Efforts to mesh the corporate cultures can stall due to formidable resistance from organization members. Key employees at the acquired company can quickly become disenchanted and leave; the morale of company personnel who remain can drop to disturbingly low levels because they disagree with newly instituted changes. Differences in management styles and operating procedures can prove hard to resolve. In addition, the managers appointed to oversee the integration of a newly acquired company

CONCEPTS & CONNECTIONS 6.2

BRISTOL-MYERS SQUIBB'S "STRING-OF-PEARLS" HORIZONTAL ACQUISITION STRATEGY

In 2007, the pharmaceutical company Bristol-Myers Squibb had a problem: Its top-selling drugs, Plavix and Abilify, would go off patent by 2012 and its drug pipeline was nearly empty. Together these drugs (the first for heart attacks, the second for depression) accounted for nearly half of the company's sales. Not surprisingly, the company's stock price had stagnated and was underperforming that of its peers.

Developing new drugs is difficult: New drugs must be identified, tested in increasingly sophisticated trials, and approved by the Food and Drug Administration. On average, this process takes 13 years and costs $2 billion. The success rate is low; only one drug in eight manages to pass through clinical testing. In 2007, Bristol-Myers Squibb had only six new drugs at the clinical testing stage.

At the time, many drug companies were diversifying into new markets such as over-the-counter drugs to better manage drug development risk. Bristol-Myers Squibb's management pursued a different strategy: product diversification through horizontal acquisitions. Bristol-Myers Squibb targeted small companies in new treatment areas, with the objective of reducing new-product development risk by betting on pre-identified drugs. The small companies it targeted, with one or two drugs in development, needed cash; Bristol-Myers Squibb needed new drugs. The firm's management called this its "string-of-pearls" strategy.

To implement its approach and obtain the cash it needed, Bristol-Myers Squibb sold its stake in Mead Johnson, a nutritional supplement manufacturer. Then, it went on a shopping spree. Starting in 2007, the company spent over $8 billion on 18 transactions, including 12 horizontal acquisitions. In the process, the company acquired many promising new drug candidates for common diseases such as cancer, cardiovascular disease, rheumatoid arthritis, and hepatitis C.

By early 2012, the company's string-of-pearls acquisitions were estimated to have added more than $4 billion of new revenue to the company's coffers. Analysts reported that Bristol-Myers Squibb had one of the best pipelines among drugmakers. Investors agreed: Between 2007 and 2012, the company's stock price climbed 20 percent, substantially outperforming that of its peers.

Developed with Dennis L. Huggins.

Sources: D. Armstrong and M. Tirrell, "Bristol's Buy of Inhibitex for Hepatitis Drug Won't Be Last," *Bloomberg Businessweek,* January 9, 2012, www.bloomberg.com (accessed January 30, 2012); S. M. Paul, et al., "How to Improve R&D Productivity: The Pharmaceutical Industry's Grand Challenge," *Nature Reviews,* March 2010, pp. 203–14; and Bristol-Myers Squibb 2007 and 2011 Annual Reports.

can make mistakes in deciding which activities to leave alone and which activities to meld into their own operations and systems.

A number of mergers/acquisitions have been notably unsuccessful. eBay's $2.6 billion acquisition of Skype in 2005 proved to be a mistake—eBay wrote off $900 million of its Skype investment in 2007 and sold 70 percent of its ownership in Skype in September 2009 to a group of investors. While the company finally found a white knight in Microsoft in 2011, the jury is out as to whether or not Microsoft can make this acquisition work. A number of recent mergers and acquisitions failed to live up to expectations—prominent examples include the merger of Sprint and Nextel, the Fiat–Chrysler deal, and Bank of America's acquisition of Countrywide Financial.

LO4 Learn the advantages and disadvantages of extending a company's scope of operations via vertical integration.

Vertical Integration Strategies

Vertical integration extends a firm's competitive and operating scope within the same industry. It involves expanding the firm's range of value chain activities backward into sources of supply and/or forward toward end users. Thus, if a manufacturer invests in facilities to produce certain component parts that it formerly purchased from outside suppliers or if it opens its own chain of retail stores to market its products to consumers, it remains in essentially the same industry as before. The only change is that it has operations in two stages of the industry value chain. For example, paint manufacturer Sherwin-Williams remains in the paint business even though it has integrated forward into retailing by operating nearly 4,000 retail stores that market its paint products directly to consumers.

> **CORE CONCEPT**
>
> A **vertically integrated** firm is one that performs value chain activities along more than one stage of an industry's overall value chain.

A firm can pursue vertical integration by starting its own operations in other stages of the vertical activity chain, by acquiring a company already performing the activities it wants to bring in-house, or by means of a strategic alliance or joint venture. Vertical integration strategies can aim at *full integration* (participating in all stages of the vertical chain) or *partial integration* (building positions in selected stages of the vertical chain). Companies may choose to pursue *tapered integration,* a strategy that involves both outsourcing and performing the activity internally. Oil companies' practice of supplying their refineries with both crude oil produced from their own wells and crude oil supplied by third-party operators and well owners is an example of tapered backward integration. Boston Beer Company, the maker of Samuel Adams, engages in tapered forward integration since it operates brew pubs, but sells the majority of its products through third-party distributors.

> **CORE CONCEPT**
>
> **Backward integration** involves performing industry value chain activities previously performed by suppliers or other enterprises engaged in earlier stages of the industry value chain; **forward integration** involves performing industry value chain activities closer to the end user.

The Advantages of a Vertical Integration Strategy

The two best reasons for investing company resources in vertical integration are to strengthen the firm's competitive position and/or to boost its profitability.[14] Vertical integration has no real payoff unless it produces sufficient cost savings to justify the extra investment, adds materially to a company's technological and competitive strengths, and/or helps differentiate the company's product offering.

Integrating Backward to Achieve Greater Competitiveness It is harder than one might think to generate cost savings or boost profitability by integrating backward into activities such as parts and components manufacture. For backward integration to be a viable and profitable strategy, a company must be able to (1) achieve the same scale economies as outside suppliers and (2) match or beat suppliers' production efficiency with no decline in quality. Neither outcome is easily achieved. To begin with, a company's in-house requirements are often too small to reach the optimum size for low-cost operation—for instance, if it takes a minimum production volume of 1 million units to achieve scale economies and a company's in-house requirements are just 250,000 units, then it falls way short of being able to match the costs of outside suppliers (who may readily find buyers for 1 million or more units).

But that said, there are still occasions when a company can improve its cost position and competitiveness by performing a broader range of value chain activities in-house rather than having these activities performed by outside suppliers. The best potential for being able to reduce costs via a backward integration strategy exists in situations where suppliers have very large profit margins, where the item being supplied is a major cost component, and where the requisite technological skills are easily mastered or acquired. Backward vertical integration can produce a differentiation-based competitive advantage when performing activities internally contributes to a better-quality product/service offering, improves the caliber of customer service, or in other ways enhances the performance of a final product. Other potential advantages of backward integration include sparing a company the uncertainty of being dependent on suppliers for crucial components or support services and lessening a company's vulnerability to powerful suppliers inclined to raise prices at every opportunity. Apple recently decided to integrate backward into producing its own chips for iPhones, chiefly because chips are a major cost component, have big profit margins, and in-house production would help protect Apple's proprietary iPhone technology.

Integrating Forward to Enhance Competitiveness   Vertical integration into forward stages of the industry value chain allows manufacturers to gain better access to end users, improve market visibility, and include the end user's purchasing experience as a differentiating feature. In many industries, independent sales agents, wholesalers, and retailers handle competing brands of the same product and have no allegiance to any one company's brand—they tend to push whatever offers the biggest profits. An independent insurance agency, for example, represents a number of different insurance companies and tries to find the best match between a customer's insurance requirements and the policies of alternative insurance companies. Under this arrangement, it is possible an agent will develop a preference for one company's policies or underwriting practices and neglect other represented insurance companies. An insurance company may conclude, therefore, that it is better off integrating forward and setting up its own local sales offices. The insurance company also has the ability to make consumers' interactions with local agents and office personnel a differentiating feature. Likewise, apparel manufacturers as varied as Polo Ralph Lauren, Ann Taylor, and Nike have integrated forward into retailing by operating full-price stores, factory outlet stores, and Internet retailing websites.

Forward Vertical Integration and Internet Retailing   Bypassing regular wholesale/retail channels in favor of direct sales and Internet retailing can have appeal if it lowers distribution costs, produces a relative cost advantage over certain rivals, offers higher margins, or results in lower selling prices to end users. In addition, sellers are compelled to include the Internet as a retail channel when a sufficiently large number of buyers in an industry prefer to make purchases online. However, a company that is vigorously pursuing online sales to consumers at the same time that it is also heavily promoting sales to consumers through its network of wholesalers and retailers *is competing directly against its distribution allies.* Such actions constitute *channel conflict* and create a tricky route to negotiate. A company that is actively trying to grow

CONCEPTS & CONNECTIONS 6.3

AMERICAN APPAREL'S VERTICAL INTEGRATION STRATEGY

American Apparel—known for its hip line of basic garments and its provocative advertisements—is no stranger to the concept of "doing it all." The Los Angeles–based casual wear company has made both forward and backward vertical integration a central part of its strategy, making it a rarity in the fashion industry. Not only does it do all its own fabric cutting and sewing, but it also owns several knitting and dyeing facilities in Southern California, as well as a distribution warehouse, a wholesale operation, and more than 270 retail stores in 20 countries. American Apparel even does its own clothing design, marketing, and advertising, often using its employees as photographers and clothing models.

Founder and CEO Dov Charney claims the company's vertical integration strategy lets American Apparel respond more quickly to rapid market changes, allowing the company to bring an item from design to its stores worldwide in the span of a week. End-to-end coordination also improves inventory control, helping prevent common problems in the fashion business such as stock-outs and steep markdowns. The company capitalizes on its California-based vertically integrated operations by using taglines such as "Sweatshop Free. Made in the USA" to bolster its "authentic" image.

However, this strategy is not without risks and costs. In an industry where 97 percent of goods are imported, American Apparel pays its workers wages and benefits above the relatively high mandated American minimum. Furthermore, operating in so many key vertical chain activities makes it impossible to be expert in all of them, and creates optimal scale and capacity mismatches—problems with which the firm has partly dealt by tapering its backward integration into knitting and dyeing. Lastly, while the company can respond quickly to new fashion trends, its vertical integration strategy may make it more difficult for the company to scale back in an economic downturn or respond to radical change in the industry environment. Ultimately, only time will tell whether American Apparel will dilute or capitalize on its vertical integration strategy in its pursuit of profitable growth.

Developed with John R. Moran.

Sources: American Apparel website, www.americanapparel.net, accessed June 16, 2010; American Apparel investor presentation, June 2009, http://files.shareholder.com/downloads/APP/938846703x0x300331/3dd0b7ca-e458-45b8-8516-e25ca272016d/NYC%20JUNE%202009.pdf; YouTube, "American Apparel—Dov Charney Interview," CBS News, http://youtube.com/watch?v=hYqR8UlI8A4; and Christopher Palmeri, "Living on the Edge at American Apparel," *BusinessWeek*, June 27, 2005.

online sales to consumers is signaling *a weak strategic commitment to its dealers* and *a willingness to cannibalize dealers' sales and growth potential.* The likely result is angry dealers and loss of dealer goodwill. Quite possibly, a company may stand to lose more sales by offending its dealers than it gains from its own online sales effort. Consequently, in industries where the strong support and goodwill of dealer networks is essential, companies may conclude that it is important to avoid channel conflict and that *their website should be designed to partner with dealers rather than compete with them.*

The Disadvantages of a Vertical Integration Strategy

Vertical integration has some substantial drawbacks beyond the potential for channel conflict.[15] The most serious drawbacks to vertical integration include:

- Vertical integration *increases a firm's capital investment* in the industry.
- Integrating into more industry value chain segments *increases business risk* if industry growth and profitability sour.
- Vertically integrated companies are often *slow to embrace technological advances* or more-efficient production methods when they are saddled with older technology or facilities.

- Integrating backward potentially results in less flexibility in accommodating shifting buyer preferences when a new product design doesn't include parts and components that the company makes in-house.

- Vertical integration poses all kinds of *capacity matching problems.* In motor vehicle manufacturing, for example, the most efficient scale of operation for making axles is different from the most economic volume for radiators, and different yet again for both engines and transmissions. Consequently, integrating across several production stages in ways that achieve the lowest feasible costs can be a monumental challenge.

- Integration forward or backward often requires the *development of new skills and business capabilities.* Parts and components manufacturing, assembly operations, wholesale distribution and retailing, and direct sales via the Internet are different businesses with different key success factors.

> A vertical integration strategy has appeal *only* if it significantly strengthens a firm's competitive position and/or boosts its profitability.

American Apparel, the largest U.S. clothing manufacturer, has made vertical integration a central part of its strategy, as described in Concepts & Connections 6.3.

Outsourcing Strategies: Narrowing the Scope of Operations

LO5 Understand the conditions that favor farming out certain value chain activities to outside parties.

Outsourcing forgoes attempts to perform certain value chain activities internally and instead farms them out to outside specialists and strategic allies. Outsourcing makes strategic sense whenever:

- *An activity can be performed better or more cheaply by outside specialists.* A company should generally *not* perform any value chain activity internally that can be performed more efficiently or effectively by outsiders. The chief exception is when a particular activity is strategically crucial and internal control over that activity is deemed essential.

> **CORE CONCEPT**
>
> **Outsourcing** involves contracting out certain value chain activities to outside specialists and strategic allies.

- *The activity is not crucial to the firm's ability to achieve sustainable competitive advantage and won't hollow out its capabilities, core competencies, or technical know-how.* Outsourcing of support activities such as maintenance services, data processing and data storage, fringe benefit management, and website operations has become common. Colgate-Palmolive, for instance, has been able to reduce its information technology operational costs by more than 10 percent per year through an outsourcing agreement with IBM.

- *It improves organizational flexibility and speeds time to market.* Outsourcing gives a company the flexibility to switch suppliers in the event that its present supplier falls behind competing suppliers. Also, to the extent that its suppliers can speedily get next-generation parts and components into production, a company can get its own next-generation product offerings into the marketplace quicker.

- *It reduces the company's risk exposure to changing technology and/or buyer preferences.* When a company outsources certain parts, components, and services, its suppliers must bear the burden of incorporating state-of-the-art technologies and/or undertaking redesigns and upgrades to accommodate a company's plans to introduce next-generation products.

- *It allows a company to concentrate on its core business, leverage its key resources and core competencies, and do even better what it already does best.* A company is better able to build and develop its own competitively valuable competencies and capabilities when it concentrates its full resources and energies on performing those activities. Nike, for example, devotes its energy to designing, marketing, and distributing athletic footwear, sports apparel, and sports equipment, while outsourcing the manufacture of all its products to some 600 contract factories in 46 countries. Apple also outsources production of its iPod, iPhone, and iPad models to Chinese contract manufacturer Foxconn. Hewlett-Packard and others have sold some of their manufacturing plants to outsiders and contracted to repurchase the output from the new owners.

> A company should guard against outsourcing activities that hollow out the resources and capabilities that it needs to be a master of its own destiny.

The Big Risk of an Outsourcing Strategy   The biggest danger of outsourcing is that a company will farm out the wrong types of activities and thereby hollow out its own capabilities.[16] In such cases, a company loses touch with the very activities and expertise that over the long run determine its success. But most companies are alert to this danger and take actions to protect against being held hostage by outside suppliers. Cisco Systems guards against loss of control and protects its manufacturing expertise by designing the production methods that its contract manufacturers must use. Cisco keeps the source code for its designs proprietary, thereby controlling the initiation of all improvements and safeguarding its innovations from imitation. Further, Cisco uses the Internet to monitor the factory operations of contract manufacturers around the clock and can know immediately when problems arise and decide whether to get involved.

Strategic Alliances and Partnerships

Companies in all types of industries have elected to form strategic alliances and partnerships to complement their accumulation of resources and capabilities and strengthen their competitiveness in domestic and international markets. A **strategic alliance** is a formal agreement between two or more separate companies in which there is strategically relevant collaboration of some sort, joint contribution of resources, shared risk, shared control, and mutual dependence. Collaborative relationships between partners may entail a contractual agreement, but they commonly stop short of formal ownership ties between the partners (although there are a few strategic alliances where one or more allies have minority ownership in certain of the

> **LO6** Gain an understanding of how strategic alliances and collaborative partnerships can bolster a company's collection of resources and capabilities.

CORE CONCEPT

A **strategic alliance** is a formal agreement between two or more companies to work cooperatively toward some common objective.

other alliance members). Collaborative arrangements involving shared ownership are called joint ventures. A **joint venture** is a partnership involving the establishment of an independent corporate entity that is jointly owned and controlled by two or more companies. Since joint ventures involve setting up a mutually owned business, they tend to be more durable but also riskier than other arrangements.

The most common reasons companies enter into strategic alliances are to expedite the development of promising new technologies or products, to overcome deficits in their own technical and manufacturing expertise, to bring together the personnel and expertise needed to create desirable new skill sets and capabilities, to improve supply chain efficiency, to gain economies of scale in production and/or marketing, and to acquire or improve market access through joint marketing agreements.[17] Because of the varied benefits of strategic alliances, many large corporations have become involved in 30 to 50 alliances, and a number have formed hundreds of alliances.

Genentech, a leader in biotechnology and human genetics, has formed R&D alliances with more than 30 companies to boost its prospects for developing new cures for various diseases and ailments. Most automakers have forged a variety of long-term strategic partnerships with suppliers of automotive parts and components, both to achieve lower costs and to improve the quality and reliability of their vehicles. Daimler AG's 2010 joint venture with Chinese automaker BYD is intended to help Daimler make and sell electric cars for the Chinese market. Companies that have formed a host of alliances need to manage their alliances like a portfolio—terminating those that no longer serve a useful purpose or that have produced meager results, forming promising new alliances, and restructuring existing alliances to correct performance problems and/or redirect the collaborative effort.

CORE CONCEPT

A **joint venture** is a type of strategic alliance that involves the establishment of an independent corporate entity that is jointly owned and controlled by the two partners.

Failed Strategic Alliances and Cooperative Partnerships

Most alliances with an objective of technology sharing or providing market access turn out to be temporary, fulfilling their purpose after a few years because the benefits of mutual learning have occurred. Although long-term alliances sometimes prove mutually beneficial, most partners don't hesitate to terminate the alliance and go it alone when the payoffs run out. Alliances are more likely to be long lasting when (1) they involve collaboration with partners that do not compete directly, (2) a trusting relationship has been established, and (3) both parties conclude that continued collaboration is in their mutual interest, perhaps because new opportunities for learning are emerging.

A surprisingly large number of alliances never live up to expectations. In 2004, McKinsey & Co. estimated the overall success rate of alliances was about 50 percent, based on whether the alliance achieved the stated objectives. Another study, published in 2007, found that while the number of strategic alliances was increasing about 25 percent annually, some 60 to 70 percent of alliances failed each year. The high "divorce rate" among strategic allies has several causes, the most common of which are:[18]

- Diverging objectives and priorities.
- An inability to work well together.
- Changing conditions that make the purpose of the alliance obsolete.
- The emergence of more attractive technological paths.
- Marketplace rivalry between one or more allies.

Experience indicates that *alliances stand a reasonable chance of helping a company reduce competitive disadvantage but very rarely have they proved a strategic option for gaining a durable competitive edge over rivals.*

The Strategic Dangers of Relying on Alliances for Essential Resources and Capabilities

The Achilles' heel of alliances and cooperative strategies is becoming dependent on other companies for *essential* expertise and capabilities. To be a market leader (and perhaps even a serious market contender), a company must ultimately develop its own resources and capabilities in areas where internal strategic control is pivotal to protecting its competitiveness and building competitive advantage. Moreover, some alliances hold only limited potential because the partner guards its most valuable skills and expertise; in such instances, acquiring or merging with a company possessing the desired know-how and resources is a better solution.

 KEY POINTS

Once a company has selected which of the five basic competitive strategies to employ in its quest for competitive advantage, then it must decide whether and how to supplement its choice of a basic competitive strategy approach.

1. Companies have a number of offensive strategy options for improving their market positions and trying to secure a competitive advantage: (1) attacking competitors' weaknesses, (2) offering an equal or better product at a lower price, (3) pursuing sustained product innovation, (4) leapfrogging competitors by being first to adopt next-generation technologies or the first to introduce next-generation products, (5) adopting and improving on the good ideas of other companies, (6) deliberately attacking those market segments where key rivals make big profits, (7) going after less contested or unoccupied market territory, (8) using hit-and-run tactics to steal sales away from unsuspecting rivals, and (9) launching preemptive strikes. A blue ocean offensive strategy seeks to gain a dramatic and durable competitive advantage by abandoning efforts to beat out competitors in existing markets and, instead, inventing a new industry or distinctive market segment that renders existing competitors largely irrelevant and allows a company to create and capture altogether new demand.

2. Defensive strategies to protect a company's position usually take the form of making moves that put obstacles in the path of would-be challengers and fortify

the company's present position while undertaking actions to dissuade rivals from even trying to attack (by signaling that the resulting battle will be more costly to the challenger than it is worth).

3. The timing of strategic moves also has relevance in the quest for competitive advantage. Company managers are obligated to carefully consider the advantages or disadvantages that attach to being a first mover versus a fast follower versus a wait-and-see late mover.

4. Decisions concerning the scope of a company's operations can also affect the strength of a company's market position. The scope of the firm refers to the range of its activities, the breadth of its product and service offerings, the extent of its geographic market presence, and its mix of businesses. Companies can expand their scope horizontally (more broadly within their focal market) or vertically (up or down the industry value chain system that starts with raw-materials production and ends with sales and service to the end consumer). Horizontal mergers and acquisitions (combinations of market rivals) provide a means for a company to expand its horizontal scope. Vertical integration expands a firm's vertical scope.

5. Horizontal mergers and acquisitions can be an attractive strategic option for strengthening a firm's competitiveness. When the operations of two companies are combined via merger or acquisition, the new company's competitiveness can be enhanced in any of several ways—lower costs; stronger technological skills; more or better competitive capabilities; a more attractive lineup of products and services; wider geographic coverage; and/or greater financial resources with which to invest in R&D, add capacity, or expand into new areas.

6. Vertically integrating forward or backward makes strategic sense only if it strengthens a company's position via either cost reduction or creation of a differentiation-based advantage. Otherwise, the drawbacks of vertical integration (increased investment, greater business risk, increased vulnerability to technological changes, and less flexibility in making product changes) are likely to outweigh any advantages.

7. Outsourcing pieces of the value chain formerly performed in-house can enhance a company's competitiveness whenever (1) an activity can be performed better or more cheaply by outside specialists; (2) the activity is not crucial to the firm's ability to achieve sustainable competitive advantage and won't hollow out its core competencies, capabilities, or technical know-how; (3) it improves a company's ability to innovate; and/or (4) it allows a company to concentrate on its core business and do what it does best.

8. Many companies are using strategic alliances and collaborative partnerships to help them in the race to build a global market presence or be a leader in the industries of the future. Strategic alliances are an attractive, flexible, and often cost-effective means by which companies can gain access to missing technology, expertise, and business capabilities.

ASSURANCE OF LEARNING EXERCISES

LO1, LO2, LO3

McGraw Hill connect

1. Live Nation operates music venues, provides management services to music artists, and promotes more than 22,000 live music events annually. The company merged with Ticketmaster and acquired concert and festival promoters in the United States, Australia, and Great Britain. How has the company used

horizontal mergers and acquisitions to strengthen its competitive position? Are these moves primarily offensive or defensive? Has either Live Nation or Ticketmaster achieved any type of advantage based on the timing of its strategic moves?

2. American Apparel, known for its hip line of basic garments and its provocative advertisements, is no stranger to the concept of "doing it all." Concepts & Connections 6.3 on page 129 describes how American Apparel has made vertical integration a central part of its strategy. What value chain segments has American Apparel chosen to enter and perform internally? How has vertical integration aided the company in building competitive advantage? Has vertical integration strengthened its market position? Explain why or why not.

LO4

connect

3. Perform an Internet search to identify at least two companies in different industries that have entered into outsourcing agreements with firms with specialized services. In addition, describe what value chain activities the companies have chosen to outsource. Do any of these outsourcing agreements seem likely to threaten any of the companies' competitive capabilities?

LO5

4. Using your university library's subscription to Lexis-Nexis, EBSCO, or a similar database, find two examples of how companies have relied on strategic alliances or joint ventures to substitute for horizontal or vertical integration.

LO6

▶ EXERCISES FOR SIMULATION PARTICIPANTS

1. Has your company relied more on offensive or defensive strategies to achieve your rank in the industry? What options for being a first mover does your company have? Do any of these first-mover options hold competitive advantage potential?

LO1, LO2

2. Does your company have the option to merge with or acquire other companies? If so, which rival companies would you like to acquire or merge with?

LO3

3. Is your company vertically integrated? Explain.

LO4

4. Is your company able to engage in outsourcing? If so, what do you see as the pros and cons of outsourcing?

LO5

▶ ENDNOTES

1. George Stalk, Jr., and Rob Lachenauer, "Hardball: Five Killer Strategies for Trouncing the Competition," *Harvard Business Review* 82, no. 4 (April 2004); Richard D'Aveni, "The Empire Strikes Back: Counterrevolutionary Strategies for Industry Leaders," *Harvard Business Review* 80, no. 11 (November 2002); and David J. Bryce and Jeffrey H. Dyer, "Strategies to Crack Well-Guarded Markets," *Harvard Business Review* 85, no. 5 (May 2007).

2. David B. Yoffie and Mary Kwak, "Mastering Balance: How to Meet and Beat a Stronger Opponent," *California Management Review* 44, no. 2 (Winter 2002).

3. Ian C. MacMillan, Alexander B. van Putten, and Rita Gunther McGrath, "Global Gamesmanship," *Harvard Business Review* 81, no. 5 (May 2003); and Askay R. Rao, Mark E. Bergen, and Scott Davis, "How to Fight a Price War," *Harvard Business Review* 78, no. 2 (March–April 2000).

4. Ming-Jer Chen and Donald C. Hambrick, "Speed, Stealth, and Selective Attack: How Small Firms Differ from Large Firms in Competitive Behavior," *Academy of Management Journal* 38, no. 2 (April 1995); Ian MacMillan, "How Business Strategists Can Use Guerrilla Warfare Tactics," *Journal of Business Strategy* 1, no. 2 (Fall 1980); William E. Rothschild, "Surprise and the Competitive Advantage," *Journal of Business Strategy* 4, no. 3

(Winter 1984); Kathryn R. Harrigan, *Strategic Flexibility* (Lexington, MA: Lexington Books, 1985); and Liam Fahey, "Guerrilla Strategy: The Hit-and-Run Attack," in *The Strategic Management Planning Reader,* ed. Liam Fahey (Englewood Cliffs, NJ: Prentice Hall, 1989).

5. Ian MacMillan, "Preemptive Strategies," *Journal of Business Strategy* 14, no. 2 (Fall 1983).

6. W. Chan Kim and Renée Mauborgne, "Blue Ocean Strategy," *Harvard Business Review* 82, no. 10 (October 2004).

7. Michael E. Porter, *Competitive Advantage* (New York: Free Press, 1985).

8. Jeffrey G. Covin, Dennis P. Slevin, and Michael B. Heeley, "Pioneers and Followers: Competitive Tactics, Environment, and Growth," *Journal of Business Venturing* 15, no. 2 (March 1999); and Christopher A. Bartlett and Sumantra Ghoshal, "Going Global: Lessons from Late-Movers," *Harvard Business Review* 78, no. 2 (March–April 2000).

9. Fernando Suarez and Gianvito Lanzolla, "The Half-Truth of First-Mover Advantage," *Harvard Business Review* 83 no. 4 (April 2005).

10. Gary Hamel, "Smart Mover, Dumb Mover," *Fortune,* September 3, 2001.

11. Costas Markides and Paul A. Geroski, "Racing to Be 2nd: Conquering the Industries of the Future," *Business Strategy Review* 15, no. 4 (Winter 2004).

12. Joseph L. Bower, "Not All M&As Are Alike—and That Matters," *Harvard Business Review* 79, no. 3 (March 2001); and O. Chatain and P. Zemsky, "The Horizontal Scope of the Firm: Organizational Tradeoffs vs. Buyer–Supplier Relationships," *Management Science* 53, no. 4 (April 2007), pp. 550–65.

13. Jeffrey H. Dyer, Prashant Kale, and Harbir Singh, "When to Ally and When to Acquire," *Harvard Business Review* 82, no. 4 (July–August 2004), pp. 109–10.

14. Kathryn R. Harrigan, "Matching Vertical Integration Strategies to Competitive Conditions," *Strategic Management Journal* 7, no. 6 (November–December 1986); and John Stuckey and David White, "When and When Not to Vertically Integrate," *Sloan Management Review,* Spring 1993.

15. Thomas Osegowitsch and Anoop Madhok, "Vertical Integration Is Dead, or Is It?" *Business Horizons* 46, no. 2 (March–April 2003).

16. Jérôme Barthélemy, "The Seven Deadly Sins of Outsourcing,"

Academy of Management Executive 17, no. 2 (May 2003); Gary P. Pisano and Willy C. Shih, "Restoring American Competitiveness," *Harvard Business Review* 87, no. 7/8 (July–August 2009); and Ronan McIvor, "What Is the Right Outsourcing Strategy for Your Process?" *European Management Journal* 26, no. 1 (February 2008).

17. Michael E. Porter, *The Competitive Advantage of Nations* (New York: Free Press, 1990); K. M. Eisenhardt and C. B. Schoonhoven, "Resource-Based View of Strategic Alliance Formation: Strategic and Social Effects in Entrepreneurial Firms," *Organization Science* 7, no. 2 (March–April 1996); Nancy J. Kaplan and Jonathan Hurd, "Realizing the Promise of Partnerships," *Journal of Business Strategy* 23, no. 3 (May–June 2002); Salvatore Parise and Lisa Sasson, "Leveraging Knowledge Management across Strategic Alliances," *Ivey Business Journal* 66, no. 4 (March–April 2002); and David Ernst and James Bamford, "Your Alliances Are Too Stable," *Harvard Business Review* 83, no. 6 (June 2005).

18. Yves L. Doz and Gary Hamel, *Alliance Advantage; The Art of Creating Value through Partnering* (Boston: Harvard Business School Press, 1998).

Strategies for Competing in International Markets

LEARNING OBJECTIVES

LO1 Develop an understanding of the primary reasons companies choose to compete in international markets.

LO2 Learn why and how differing market conditions across countries influence a company's strategy choices in international markets.

LO3 Gain familiarity with the five general modes of entry into foreign markets.

LO4 Learn the three main options for tailoring a company's international strategy to cross-country differences in market conditions and buyer preferences.

LO5 Understand how multinational companies are able to use international operations to improve overall competitiveness.

LO6 Gain an understanding of the unique characteristics of competing in developing-country markets.

Any company that aspires to industry leadership in the twenty-first century must think in terms of global, not domestic, market leadership. The world economy is globalizing at an accelerating pace as countries previously closed to foreign companies open their markets, as countries with previously planned economies embrace market or mixed economies, as information technology shrinks the importance of geographic distance, and as ambitious, growth-minded companies race to build stronger competitive positions in the markets of more and more countries. The forces of globalization are changing the competitive landscape in many industries, offering companies attractive new opportunities but at the same time introducing new competitive threats. Companies in industries where these forces are greatest are under considerable pressure to develop strategies for competing successfully in international markets.

This chapter focuses on strategy options for expanding beyond domestic boundaries and competing in the markets of either a few or many countries. We will discuss the factors that shape the choice of strategy in international markets and the specific market circumstances that support the adoption of multidomestic, transnational, and global strategies. The chapter also includes sections on strategy options for entering foreign markets; how international operations may be used to improve overall competitiveness; and the special circumstances of competing in such emerging markets as China, India, Brazil, Russia, and Eastern Europe.

Why Companies Expand into International Markets

LO1 Develop an understanding of the primary reasons companies choose to compete in international markets.

A company may opt to expand outside its domestic market for any of five major reasons:

1. *To gain access to new customers.* Expanding into foreign markets offers potential for increased revenues, profits, and long-term growth and becomes an especially attractive option when a company's home markets are mature. Honda has done this with its classic 50-cc motorcycle, the Honda Cub, which is still selling well in developing markets, more than 50 years after it was introduced in Japan.

2. *To achieve lower costs and enhance the firm's competitiveness.* Many companies are driven to sell in more than one country because domestic sales volume alone is not large enough to fully capture manufacturing economies of scale or learning curve effects. The relatively small size of country markets in Europe explains why companies such as Michelin, BMW, and Nestlé long ago began selling their products all across Europe and then moved into markets in North America and Latin America.

3. *To further exploit its core competencies.* A company may be able to leverage its competencies and capabilities into a position of competitive advantage in foreign markets as well as domestic markets. Walmart is capitalizing on its considerable expertise in discount retailing to expand into the United Kingdom, Japan, China, and Latin America. Walmart executives are particularly excited about the company's growth opportunities in China.

4. *To gain access to resources and capabilities located in foreign markets.* An increasingly important motive for entering foreign markets is to acquire resources and capabilities that cannot be accessed as readily in a company's home market. Companies often enter into cross-border alliances, make acquisitions abroad, or establish operations in foreign countries to access local resources such as distribution networks, low-cost labor, natural resources, or specialized technical knowledge.[1]

5. *To spread its business risk across a wider market base.* A company spreads business risk by operating in a number of foreign countries rather than depending entirely on operations in its domestic market. Thus, if the economies of North American countries turn down for a period of time, a company with operations across much of the world may be sustained by buoyant sales in Latin America, Asia, or Europe.

Factors That Shape Strategy Choices in International Markets

Four important factors shape a company's strategic approach to competing in foreign markets: (1) the degree to which there are important cross-country differences in demographic, cultural, and market conditions; (2) whether opportunities exist to gain a location-based advantage based on wage rates, worker productivity, inflation rates, energy costs, tax rates, and other factors that impact cost structure; (3) the risks of adverse shifts in currency exchange rates; and (4) the extent to which governmental policies affect the local business climate.

LO2 Learn why and how differing market conditions across countries influence a company's strategy choices in international markets.

Cross-Country Differences in Demographic, Cultural, and Market Conditions

Buyer tastes for a particular product or service sometimes differ substantially from country to country. For example, Italian coffee drinkers prefer espressos, but in North America the preference is for milder-roasted coffees. In parts of Asia, refrigerators are a status symbol and may be placed in the living room, leading to preferences for stylish designs and colors; bright blue and red are popular colors in India. People in Hong Kong and Japan prefer compact appliances, but in Taiwan large appliances are more popular. Consequently, companies operating in a global marketplace must wrestle with *whether and how much to customize their offerings in each different country market to match the tastes and preferences of local buyers or whether to pursue a strategy of offering a mostly standardized product worldwide.* While making products that are closely matched to local tastes makes them more appealing to local buyers, customizing a company's products country by country may raise production and distribution costs. Greater standardization of a global company's product offering, on the other hand, can lead to scale economies and learning curve effects, thus contributing to the achievement of a low-cost advantage. *The tension between the market pressures to localize a company's product offerings country by country and the competitive pressures to lower costs is one of the big strategic issues that participants in foreign markets have to resolve.*

Understandably, differing population sizes, income levels, and other demographic factors give rise to considerable differences in market size and growth rates from country to country. In emerging markets such as India, China, Brazil, and Malaysia, market growth potential is far higher for such products as PCs, mobile phones, steel, credit cards, and electric energy than in the more mature economies of Britain, Canada, and Japan. The potential for market growth in automobiles is explosive in China, where 2010 sales of new vehicles amounted to 18 million, surpassing U.S. sales of 11.6 million and making China the world's largest market for the second year in a row.[2] Owing to widely differing population demographics and income levels, there is a far bigger market for luxury automobiles in the United States and Germany than in Argentina, India, Mexico, and Thailand. Cultural influences can also affect consumer demand for a product. For instance, in China, many parents are reluctant to purchase PCs even when they can afford them because of concerns that their children will be distracted from their schoolwork by surfing the web, playing PC-based video games, and downloading and listening to pop music.

Market growth can be limited by the lack of infrastructure or established distribution and retail networks in emerging markets. India has well-developed national channels for distribution of goods to the nation's 3 million retailers, whereas in China distribution is primarily local. Also, the competitive rivalry in some country marketplaces is only moderate, while others are characterized by strong or fierce competition. The managerial challenge at companies with international or global operations is how best to tailor a company's strategy to take all these cross-country differences into account.

Opportunities for Location-Based Cost Advantages

Differences from country to country in wage rates, worker productivity, energy costs, environmental regulations, tax rates, inflation rates, and the like are often so big that *a company's operating costs and profitability are significantly impacted by where its production, distribution, and customer service activities are located.* Wage rates, in particular, vary enormously from country to country. For example, in 2011, hourly compensation for manufacturing workers averaged about $1.36 in China, $2.01 in the Philippines, $6.48 in Mexico, $9.17 in Hungary, $9.34 in Taiwan, $11.65 in Brazil, $12.91 in Portugal, $18.91 in South Korea, $35.53 in the United States, $35.71 in Japan, $36.56 in Canada, $47.38 in Germany, and $64.15 in Norway.[3] Not surprisingly, China has emerged as the manufacturing capital of the world—virtually all of the world's major manufacturing companies now have facilities in China. A manufacturer can also gain cost advantages by locating its manufacturing and assembly plants in countries with less costly government regulations, low taxes, low energy costs, and cheaper access to essential natural resources.

The Risks of Adverse Exchange Rate Shifts

When companies produce and market their products and services in many different countries, they are subject to the impacts of sometimes favorable and sometimes unfavorable changes in currency exchange rates. The rates of exchange between different currencies can vary by as much as 20 to

40 percent annually, with the changes occurring sometimes gradually and sometimes swiftly. Sizable shifts in exchange rates, which tend to be hard to predict because of the variety of factors involved and the uncertainties surrounding when and by how much these factors will change, *shuffle the global cards of which countries represent the low-cost manufacturing location* and *which rivals have the upper hand in the marketplace.*

To illustrate the competitive risks associated with fluctuating exchange rates, consider the case of a U.S. company that has located manufacturing facilities in Brazil (where the currency is reals—pronounced *ray-alls*) and that exports most of its Brazilian-made goods to markets in the European Union (where the currency is euros). To keep the numbers simple, assume the exchange rate is 4 Brazilian reals for 1 euro and that the product being made in Brazil has a manufacturing cost of 4 Brazilian reals (or 1 euro). Now suppose that for some reason the exchange rate shifts from 4 reals per euro to 5 reals per euro (meaning the real has declined in value and the euro is stronger). Making the product in Brazil is now more cost-competitive because a Brazilian good costing 4 reals to produce has fallen to only 0.8 euro at the new exchange rate (4 reals divided by 5 reals per euro = 0.8 euro). On the other hand, should the value of the Brazilian real grow stronger in relation to the euro—resulting in an exchange rate of 3 reals to 1 euro—the same Brazilian-made good formerly costing 4 reals to produce now has a cost of 1.33 euros (4 reals divided by 3 reals per euro = 1.33). This increase in the value of the real has eroded the cost advantage of the Brazilian manufacturing facility for goods shipped to Europe and affects the ability of the U.S. company to underprice European producers of similar goods. Thus, *the lesson of fluctuating exchange rates is that companies that export goods to foreign countries always gain in competitiveness when the currency of the country in which the goods are manufactured is weak. Exporters are disadvantaged when the currency of the country where goods are being manufactured grows stronger.*

The Impact of Government Policies on the Business Climate in Host Countries

National governments enact all kinds of measures affecting business conditions and the operation of foreign companies in their markets. It matters whether these measures create a favorable or unfavorable business climate. Governments of countries eager to spur economic growth, create more jobs, and raise living standards for their citizens usually make a special effort to create a business climate that outsiders will view favorably. They may provide such incentives as reduced taxes, low-cost loans, and site-development assistance to companies agreeing to construct or expand production and distribution facilities in the host country.

On the other hand, governments sometimes enact policies that, from a business perspective, make locating facilities within a country's borders less attractive. For example, the nature of a company's operations may make it particularly costly to achieve compliance with environmental regulations in certain countries. Some governments, wishing to discourage foreign imports, may enact deliberately burdensome customs procedures and requirements or impose tariffs or quotas on imported goods. Host-country governments may also specify that products contain a certain percentage of locally produced parts and components, require prior approval of capital spending projects, limit withdrawal of funds from the country, and require local ownership stakes in foreign-company operations in the host country. Such governmental actions make a country's business climate unattractive, and in some cases may be sufficiently onerous as to discourage a company from locating facilities in that country or sell its products there.

A country's business climate is also a function of the political and economic risks associated with operating within its borders. **Political risks** have to do with the instability of weak governments or the potential for future elections to produce government leaders hostile to foreign-owned businesses. **Economic risks** have to do with the threat of piracy and lack of protection for the company's intellectual property and the stability of a country's economy—whether inflation rates might skyrocket or whether uncontrolled deficit spending on the part of government could lead to a breakdown of the country's monetary system and prolonged economic distress.

> **CORE CONCEPT**
>
> **Political risks** stem from instability or weakness in national governments and hostility to foreign business; **economic risks** stem from the stability of a country's monetary system, economic and regulatory policies, and the lack of property rights protections.

Strategy Options for Entering Foreign Markets

LO3 Gain familiarity with the five general modes of entry into foreign markets.

A company choosing to expand outside its domestic market may elect one of the following five general modes of entry into a foreign market:

1. *Maintain a national (one-country) production base and export goods to foreign markets.*

2. *License foreign firms to produce and distribute the company's products abroad.*

3. *Employ a franchising strategy.*

4. *Establish a subsidiary in a foreign market via acquisition or internal development.*

5. *Rely on strategic alliances or joint ventures with foreign partners to enter new country markets.*

The following sections discuss the five general options in more detail.

Export Strategies

Using domestic plants as a production base for exporting goods to foreign markets is an excellent initial strategy for pursuing international sales. It is a conservative way to test the international waters. The amount of capital needed to begin exporting is often quite minimal, and existing production capacity may be sufficient to make goods for export. With an export-based entry strategy, a manufacturer can limit its involvement in foreign markets by contracting with foreign wholesalers experienced in importing to handle the entire distribution and marketing function in their countries or regions of the world. If it is more advantageous to maintain control over these functions, however, a manufacturer can establish its own distribution and sales organizations in some or all of the target foreign markets. Either way, a home-based production and export strategy helps the firm minimize its direct investments in foreign countries.

An export strategy is vulnerable when (1) manufacturing costs in the home country are substantially higher than in foreign countries where rivals have plants, (2) the costs of shipping the product to distant foreign markets are relatively high, or (3) adverse shifts occur in currency exchange rates. Unless an exporter can both keep its production and shipping costs competitive with rivals and successfully hedge against unfavorable changes in currency exchange rates, its success will be limited.

Licensing Strategies

Licensing as an entry strategy makes sense when a firm with valuable technical know-how or a unique patented product has neither the internal organizational capability nor the resources to enter foreign markets. Licensing also has the advantage of avoiding the risks of committing resources to country markets that are unfamiliar, politically volatile, economically unstable, or otherwise risky. By licensing the technology or the production rights to foreign-based firms, the firm does not have to bear the costs and risks of entering foreign markets on its own, yet it is able to generate income from royalties. The big disadvantage of licensing is the risk of providing valuable technological know-how to foreign companies and thereby losing some degree of control over its use. Also, monitoring licensees and safeguarding the company's proprietary know-how can prove quite difficult in some circumstances. But if the royalty potential is considerable and the companies to whom the licenses are being granted are both trustworthy and reputable, then licensing can be a very attractive option. Many software and pharmaceutical companies use licensing strategies.

Franchising Strategies

While licensing works well for manufacturers and owners of proprietary technology, franchising is often better suited to the global expansion efforts of service and retailing enterprises. McDonald's, Yum! Brands (the parent of A&W, Pizza Hut, KFC, Long John Silver's, and Taco Bell), the UPS Store, 7-Eleven, and Hilton Hotels have all used franchising to build a presence in international markets. Franchising has much the same advantages as licensing. The franchisee bears most of the costs and risks of establishing foreign locations, so a franchisor has to expend only the resources to recruit, train, support, and monitor franchisees. The big problem a franchisor faces is maintaining quality control. In many cases, foreign franchisees do not always exhibit strong commitment to consistency and standardization, especially when the local culture does not stress the same kinds of quality concerns. Another problem that can arise is whether to allow foreign franchisees to modify the franchisor's product offering to better satisfy the tastes and expectations of local buyers. Should McDonald's allow its franchised units in Japan to modify Big Macs slightly to suit Japanese tastes? Should the franchised KFC units in China be permitted to substitute spices that appeal to Chinese consumers? Or should the same menu offerings be rigorously and unvaryingly required of all franchisees worldwide?

Foreign Subsidiary Strategies

While exporting, licensing, and franchising rely upon the resources and capabilities of allies in international markets to deliver goods or services to buyers, companies pursuing international expansion may elect to take responsibility for the performance of all essential value chain activities in foreign markets. Companies that prefer direct control over all aspects of operating in a foreign market can establish a wholly owned subsidiary, either by acquiring a foreign company or by establishing operations from the ground up via internal development.

Acquisition is the quicker of the two options, and it may be the least risky and cost-efficient means of hurdling such entry barriers as gaining access to local distribution channels, building supplier relationships, and establishing working relationships with key government officials and other constituencies. Buying an ongoing operation allows the acquirer to move directly to the task of transferring resources and personnel to the newly acquired business, integrating and redirecting the activities of the acquired business into its own operation, putting its own strategy into place, and accelerating efforts to build a strong market position.[4]

The big issue an acquisition-minded firm must consider is whether to pay a premium price for a successful local company or to buy a struggling competitor at a bargain price. If the buying firm has little knowledge of the local market but ample capital, it is often better off purchasing a capable, strongly positioned firm—unless the acquisition price is prohibitive. However, when the acquirer sees promising ways to transform a weak firm into a strong one and has the resources and managerial know-how to do it, a struggling company can be the better long-term investment.

Entering a new foreign country via internal development and building a foreign subsidiary from scratch makes sense when a company already operates in a number of countries, has experience in getting new subsidiaries up and running and overseeing their operations, and has a sufficiently large pool of resources and competencies to rapidly equip a new subsidiary with the personnel and capabilities it needs to compete successfully and profitably. Four other conditions make an internal start-up strategy appealing:

- When creating an internal start-up is cheaper than making an acquisition.
- When adding new production capacity will not adversely impact the supply–demand balance in the local market.
- When a start-up subsidiary has the ability to gain good distribution access (perhaps because of the company's recognized brand name).
- When a start-up subsidiary will have the size, cost structure, and resources to compete head-to-head against local rivals.

Alliance and Joint Venture Strategies

Strategic alliances, joint ventures, and other cooperative agreements with foreign companies are a favorite and potentially fruitful means for entering a foreign market or strengthening a firm's competitiveness in world markets.[5] Historically, export-minded firms in industrialized nations sought alliances with firms in less-developed countries to import and market their products locally—such arrangements were often necessary to win approval for entry from the host country's government. Both Japanese and American companies are actively forming alliances with European companies to strengthen their ability to compete in the 28-nation European Union (and the three countries that are candidates to become EU members) and to capitalize on the opening of Eastern European markets. Many U.S. and European companies are allying with Asian companies in their efforts to enter markets in China, India, Malaysia, Thailand, and other Asian countries. Many foreign companies, of course, are particularly interested in strategic partnerships that will strengthen their ability to gain a foothold in the U.S. market.

However, cooperative arrangements between domestic and foreign companies have strategic appeal for reasons besides gaining better access to attractive country markets.[6] A second big appeal of cross-border alliances is to capture economies of scale in production and/or marketing. By joining forces in producing components, assembling models, and marketing their products, companies can realize cost savings not achievable with their own small volumes. A third motivation for entering into a cross-border alliance is to fill gaps in technical expertise and/or knowledge of local markets (buying habits and product preferences of consumers, local customs, and so on). A fourth motivation for cross-border alliances is to share distribution facilities and dealer networks, and to mutually strengthen each partner's access to buyers.

A fifth benefit is that cross-border allies can direct their competitive energies more toward mutual rivals and less toward one another; teaming up may help them close the gap on leading companies. A sixth driver of cross-border alliances comes into play when companies wanting to enter a new foreign market conclude that alliances with local companies are an effective way to establish working relationships with key officials in the host-country government.[7] And, finally, alliances can be a particularly useful way for companies across the world to gain agreement on important technical standards—they have been used to arrive at standards for assorted PC devices, Internet-related technologies, high-definition televisions, and mobile phones.

What makes cross-border alliances an attractive strategic means of gaining the aforementioned types of benefits (as compared to acquiring or merging with foreign-based companies) is that entering into alliances and strategic partnerships allows a company to preserve its independence and avoid using perhaps scarce financial resources to fund acquisitions. Furthermore, an alliance offers the flexibility to readily disengage once its purpose has been served or if the benefits prove elusive, whereas an acquisition is a more permanent sort of arrangement.[8] Concepts & Connections 7.1 discusses how California-based Solazyme, a maker of biofuels and other green products, has used cross-border strategic alliances to fuel its growth.

CONCEPTS & CONNECTIONS 7.1

SOLAZYME'S CROSS-BORDER ALLIANCES WITH UNILEVER, SEPHORA, QANTAS, AND ROQUETTE

Solazyme, a California-based company that produces oils from algae for nutritional, cosmetic, and biofuel products, was named "America's Fastest-Growing Manufacturing Company" by *Inc.* magazine in 2011. The company has fueled its rapid growth through a variety of cross-border strategic alliances with much larger partners. These partnerships have not only facilitated Solazyme's entry into new markets, but they have also created value through resource sharing and risk spreading.

Its partnership with Unilever, a British–Dutch consumer goods company, has focused on collaborative R&D. Projects under way are aimed at meeting the growing demand for completely renewable, natural, and sustainable personal care products through the use of algal oils. By further developing Solazyme's technology platform, the partnership will enable the production of Solazyme's oils and other biomaterials efficiently and at large scale.

Solazyme has entered into a variety of marketing and distribution agreements with French cosmetics company Sephora (now part of LVMH). In March 2011, Solazyme launched its luxury skin care brand, Algenist, with Sephora's help. Sephora has also agreed to distribute Solazyme's anti-aging skin care line, making it available in Sephora stores and at Sephora.com.

In 2011, Solazyme also signed a contract with Australian airline Qantas to supply, test, and refine Solazyme's jet fuel product, SolaJet. Solazyme stands to gain valuable input on how to design and distribute its product while receiving media attention and the marketing advantage of a well-known customer. On the other hand, Qantas hopes to better understand how it will achieve its sustainability goals while building its reputation as a sustainability leader in the airline industry.

Because its algae require sugar to produce oil, Solazyme has an interest in securing a stable supply of this feedstock. For this purpose, Solazyme created a 50/50 joint venture with French starch processor Roquette to develop, produce, and market food products globally. By working with Roquette to source feedstock and manufacture final food products, Solazyme lowered its exposure to sugar price fluctuations while taking advantage of Roquette's manufacturing infrastructure and expertise. In return, Roquette gained access to Solazyme's innovative technological resources.

Developed with John L. Gardner.

Sources: Company website; http://gigaom.com/cleantech/solazyme-draws-richard-branson-unilever-to-algae/; www.businessgreen.com/bg/news/2026103/qantas-inks-solazyme-algae-biofuel-deal; www.reuters.com/article/2012/02/22/us-smallbiz-solazyme-feb-idUSTRE81L1ZO20120222; www.foodnavigator-usa.com/Business/Solazyme-Roquette-JV-prepares-for-January-2012-launch-of-unique-algal-flour, accessed March 4, 2012.

The Risks of Strategic Alliances with Foreign Partners   Alliances and joint ventures with foreign partners have their pitfalls, however. Cross-border allies typically have to overcome language and cultural barriers and figure out how to deal with diverse (or perhaps conflicting) operating practices. The communication, trust-building, and coordination costs are high in terms of management time.[9] It is not unusual for partners to discover they have conflicting objectives and strategies, deep differences of opinion about how to proceed, or important differences in corporate values and ethical standards. Tensions build, working relationships cool, and the hoped-for benefits never materialize. The recipe for successful alliances requires many meetings of many people working in good faith over a period of time to iron out what is to be shared, what is to remain proprietary, and how the cooperative arrangements will work.[10]

Even if the alliance becomes a win-win proposition for both parties, there is the danger of becoming overly dependent on foreign partners for essential expertise and competitive capabilities. If a company is aiming for global market leadership and needs to develop capabilities of its own, then at some juncture cross-border merger or acquisition may have to be substituted for cross-border alliances and joint ventures. One of the lessons about cross-border alliances is that they are more effective in helping a company establish a beachhead of new opportunity in world markets than they are in enabling a company to achieve and sustain global market leadership.

International Strategy: The Three Principal Options

Broadly speaking, a company's **international strategy** is simply its strategy for competing in two or more countries simultaneously. Typically, a company will start to compete internationally by entering just one or perhaps a select few foreign markets, selling its products or services in countries where there is a ready market for them. But as it expands further internationally, it will have to confront head-on the conflicting pressures of local responsiveness versus efficiency gains from standardizing its product offering globally. As discussed earlier in the chapter, deciding upon the degree to vary its competitive approach to fit the specific market conditions and buyer preferences in each host country is perhaps the foremost strategic issue that must be addressed when operating in two or more foreign markets.[11] Figure 7.1 shows a company's three strategic approaches for competing internationally and resolving this issue.

> **CORE CONCEPT**
> A company's **international strategy** is its strategy for competing in two or more countries simultaneously.

LO4 Learn the three main options for tailoring a company's international strategy to cross-country differences in market conditions and buyer preferences.

Multidomestic Strategy—A Think Local, Act Local Approach to Strategy Making

A **multidomestic strategy** or **think local, act local** approach to strategy making is essential when there are significant country-to-country differences in customer preferences and buying habits, when there are significant cross-country differences in distribution channels and marketing methods, when host governments enact regulations requiring that products sold locally meet strict manufacturing specifications or performance standards, and when the trade restrictions of host governments are so diverse and complicated that they preclude a uniform, coordinated worldwide market approach. With localized strategies, a company often has different product versions for different countries and sometimes sells the products under different brand names. Government requirements for gasoline additives that help reduce carbon monoxide, smog, and other emissions are almost never the same from country to country. BP utilizes localized strategies in its gasoline and service station

> **CORE CONCEPT**
> A **multidomestic strategy** calls for varying a company's product offering and competitive approach from country to country in an effort to be responsive to significant cross-country differences in customer preferences, buyer purchasing habits, distribution channels, or marketing methods. **Think local, act local** strategy-making approaches are also essential when host-government regulations or trade policies preclude a uniform, coordinated worldwide market approach.

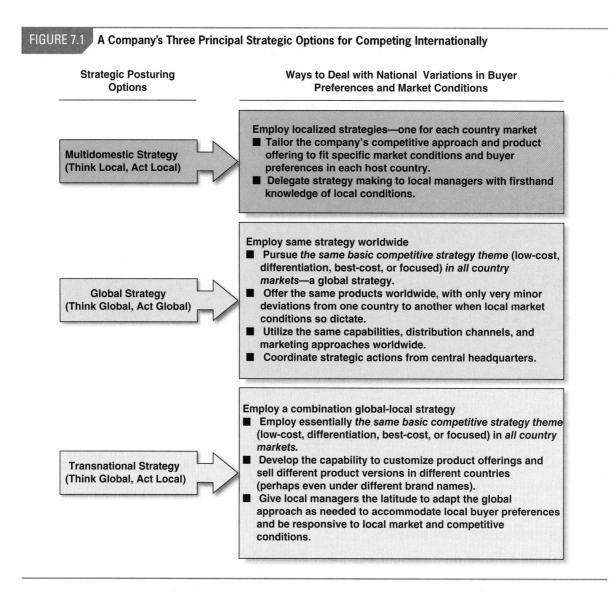

FIGURE 7.1 A Company's Three Principal Strategic Options for Competing Internationally

Strategic Posturing Options

Ways to Deal with National Variations in Buyer Preferences and Market Conditions

Multidomestic Strategy (Think Local, Act Local)

Employ localized strategies—one for each country market
- Tailor the company's competitive approach and product offering to fit specific market conditions and buyer preferences in each host country.
- Delegate strategy making to local managers with firsthand knowledge of local conditions.

Global Strategy (Think Global, Act Global)

Employ same strategy worldwide
- Pursue *the same basic competitive strategy theme* (low-cost, differentiation, best-cost, or focused) *in all country markets*—a global strategy.
- Offer the same products worldwide, with only very minor deviations from one country to another when local market conditions so dictate.
- Utilize the same capabilities, distribution channels, and marketing approaches worldwide.
- Coordinate strategic actions from central headquarters.

Transnational Strategy (Think Global, Act Local)

Employ a combination global-local strategy
- Employ essentially *the same basic competitive strategy theme* (low-cost, differentiation, best-cost, or focused) in *all country markets.*
- Develop the capability to customize product offerings and sell different product versions in different countries (perhaps even under different brand names).
- Give local managers the latitude to adapt the global approach as needed to accommodate local buyer preferences and be responsive to local market and competitive conditions.

business segment because of these cross-country formulation differences and because of customer familiarity with local brand names. For example, the company markets gasoline in the United States under its BP and Arco brands, but markets gasoline in Germany, Belgium, Poland, Hungary, and the Czech Republic under the Aral brand. Companies in the food products industry often vary the ingredients in their products and sell the localized versions under local brand names to cater to country-specific tastes and eating preferences. The strength of employing a set of localized or multidomestic strategies is that the company's actions and business approaches are deliberately crafted to appeal to the tastes and expectations of buyers in each country and to stake out the most attractive market positions vis-à-vis local competitors.[12]

However, think local, act local strategies have two big drawbacks: (1) They hinder transfer of a company's competencies and resources across country boundaries because the strategies in different host countries can be grounded in varying competencies and capabilities; and (2) they do not promote building a single, unified competitive advantage, especially one based on low cost. Companies employing highly localized or multidomestic strategies face big hurdles in achieving low-cost leadership *unless* they find ways to customize their products and *still* be in a position to capture scale economies and learning curve effects. Toyota's unique mass customization production capability has been key to its ability to effectively adapt product offerings to local buyer tastes, while maintaining low-cost leadership.

Global Strategy—A Think Global, Act Global Approach to Strategy Making

While multidomestic strategies are best suited for industries where a fairly high degree of local responsiveness is important, global strategies are best suited for globally standardized industries. A **global strategy** is one in which the company's approach is predominantly the same in all countries—it sells the same products under the same brand names everywhere, utilizes much the same distribution channels in all countries, and competes on the basis of the same capabilities and marketing approaches worldwide. Although the company's strategy or product offering may be adapted in very minor ways to accommodate specific situations in a few host countries, the company's fundamental competitive approach (low-cost, differentiation, or focused) remains very much intact worldwide and local managers stick close to the global strategy. A **think global, act global** strategic theme prompts company managers to integrate and coordinate the company's strategic moves worldwide and to expand into most if not all nations where there is significant buyer demand. It puts considerable strategic emphasis on building a *global* brand name and aggressively pursuing opportunities to transfer ideas, new products, and capabilities from one country to another.

> **CORE CONCEPT**
>
> **Global strategies** employ the same basic competitive approach in all countries where a company operates and are best suited to industries that are globally standardized in terms of customer preferences, buyer purchasing habits, distribution channels, or marketing methods. This is the **think global, act global** strategic theme.

Ford's global design strategy is a move toward a think global, act global strategy by the company and involves the development and production of standardized models with country-specific modifications limited primarily to what is required to meet local country emission and safety standards. The 2010 Ford Fiesta and 2011 Ford Focus were the company's first global design models to be marketed in Europe, North America, Asia, and Australia. Whenever country-to-country differences are small enough to be accommodated within the framework of a global strategy, a global strategy is preferable to localized strategies because a company can more readily unify its operations and focus on establishing a brand image and reputation that is uniform from country to country. Moreover, with a global strategy a company is better able to focus its full resources on securing a sustainable low-cost or differentiation-based competitive advantage over both domestic rivals and global rivals.

Transnational Strategy—A Think Global, Act Local Approach to Strategy Making

A **transnational strategy** is a **think global, act local** approach to developing strategy that accommodates cross-country variations in buyer tastes, local customs, and market conditions while also striving for the benefits of standardization. This middle-ground approach entails utilizing the same basic competitive theme (low-cost, differentiation, or focused) in each country but allows local managers the latitude to (1) incorporate whatever country-specific variations in product attributes are needed to best satisfy local buyers and (2) make whatever adjustments in production, distribution, and marketing are needed to respond to local market conditions and compete successfully against local rivals. Both McDonald's and KFC have discovered ways to customize their menu offerings in various countries without compromising costs, product quality, and operating effectiveness. Otis Elevator found that a transnational strategy delivers better results than a global strategy when competing in countries such as China where local needs are highly differentiated. In 2000, it switched from its customary single-brand approach to a multibrand strategy aimed at serving different segments of the market. By 2009, it had doubled its market share in China and increased its revenues sixfold.[13]

> **CORE CONCEPT**
>
> A **transnational strategy** is a **think global, act local** approach to strategy making that involves employing essentially the same strategic theme (low-cost, differentiation, focused, best-cost) in all country markets, while allowing some country-to-country customization to fit local market conditions.

As a rule, most companies that operate multinationally endeavor to employ as global a strategy as customer needs and market conditions permit. Electronic Arts has two major design studios—one in Vancouver, British Columbia, and one in Los Angeles—and smaller design studios in San Francisco, Orlando, London, and Tokyo. This dispersion of design studios helps EA to design games that are specific to different cultures—for example, the London studio took the lead in designing the popular FIFA Soccer game to suit European tastes and to replicate the stadiums, signage, and team rosters; the U.S. studio took the lead in designing games involving NFL football, NBA basketball, and NASCAR racing.

Using International Operations to Improve Overall Competitiveness

LO5 Understand how multinational companies are able to use international operations to improve overall competitiveness.

A firm can gain competitive advantage by expanding outside its domestic market in two important ways. One, it can use location to lower costs or help achieve greater product differentiation. And two, it can use cross-border coordination in ways that a domestic-only competitor cannot.

Using Location to Build Competitive Advantage

To use location to build competitive advantage, a company must consider two issues: (1) whether to concentrate each internal process in a few countries or to disperse performance of each process to many nations, and (2) in which countries to locate particular activities.

When to Concentrate Internal Processes in a Few Locations

Companies tend to concentrate their activities in a limited number of locations in the following circumstances:

- *When the costs of manufacturing or other activities are significantly lower in some geographic locations than in others.* For example, much of the world's athletic footwear is manufactured in Asia (China and Korea) because of low labor costs; much of the production of circuit boards for PCs is located in Taiwan because of both low costs and the high-caliber technical skills of the Taiwanese labor force.

- *When there are significant scale economies.* The presence of significant economies of scale in components production or final assembly means a company can gain major cost savings from operating a few super-efficient plants as opposed to a host of small plants scattered across the world. Makers of digital cameras and LED TVs located in Japan, South Korea, and Taiwan have used their scale economies to establish a low-cost advantage.

- *When there is a steep learning curve associated with performing an activity.* In some industries, learning curve effects in parts manufacture or assembly are so great that a company establishes one or two large plants from which it serves the world market. The key to riding down the learning curve is to concentrate production in a few locations to increase the accumulated volume at a plant (and thus the experience of the plant's workforce) as rapidly as possible.

- *When certain locations have superior resources, allow better coordination of related activities, or offer other valuable advantages.* A research unit or a sophisticated production facility may be situated in a particular nation because of its pool of technically trained personnel. Samsung became a leader in memory chip technology by establishing a major R&D facility in Silicon Valley and transferring the know-how it gained back to headquarters and its plants in South Korea.

> Companies that compete multinationally can pursue competitive advantage in world markets by locating their value chain activities in whichever nations prove most advantageous.

When to Disperse Internal Processes Across Many Locations

There are several instances when dispersing a process is more advantageous than concentrating it in a single location. Buyer-related activities, such as distribution to dealers, sales and advertising, and after-sale service, usually must take place close to buyers. This makes it necessary to physically locate the capability to perform such activities in every country market where a global firm has major customers. For example, large public accounting firms have numerous international offices to service the foreign operations of their multinational corporate clients. Dispersing activities to many locations is also competitively important when high transportation costs, diseconomies of large size, and trade barriers make it too expensive to operate from a central location. In addition, it is strategically advantageous to disperse activities to hedge against the risks of fluctuating exchange rates and adverse political developments.

Using Cross-Border Coordination to Build Competitive Advantage

Multinational and global competitors are able to coordinate activities across different countries to build competitive advantage.[14] If a firm learns how to assemble its product more efficiently at, say, its Brazilian plant, the accumulated expertise and knowledge can be shared with assembly plants in other world locations. Also, knowledge gained in marketing a company's product in Great Britain, for instance, can readily be exchanged with company personnel in New Zealand or Australia. Other examples of cross-border coordination include shifting production from a plant in one country to a plant in another to take advantage of exchange rate fluctuations and to respond to changing wage rates, energy costs, or changes in tariffs and quotas.

Efficiencies can also be achieved by shifting workloads from where they are unusually heavy to locations where personnel are underutilized. Whirlpool's efforts to link its product R&D and manufacturing operations in North America, Latin America, Europe, and Asia allowed it to accelerate the discovery of innovative appliance features, coordinate the introduction of these features in the appliance products marketed in different countries, and create a cost-efficient worldwide supply chain. Whirlpool's conscious efforts to integrate and coordinate its various operations around the world have helped it become a low-cost producer and also speed product innovations to market, thereby giving Whirlpool an edge over rivals worldwide.

Strategies for Competing in the Markets of Developing Countries

LO6 Gain an understanding of the unique characteristics of competing in developing-country markets.

Companies racing for global leadership have to consider competing in developing-economy markets such as China, India, Brazil, Indonesia, Thailand, Poland, Russia, and Mexico—countries where the business risks are considerable but where the opportunities for growth are huge, especially as their economies develop and living standards climb toward levels in the industrialized world.[15] For example, in 2010 China was the world's second-largest economy (behind the United States) based upon purchasing power, and its population of 1.3 billion people made it the world's largest market for many commodities and types of consumer goods. China's growth in demand for consumer goods put it on track to become the world's largest market for luxury goods by 2014.[16] Thus, no company pursuing global market leadership can afford to ignore the strategic importance of establishing competitive market positions in China, India, other parts of the Asian-Pacific region, Latin America, and Eastern Europe. Concepts & Connections 7.2 describes Yum! Brands' strategy to boost its sales and market share in China.

Tailoring products to fit conditions in an emerging country market such as China, however, often involves more than making minor product changes and becoming more familiar with local cultures. McDonald's has had to offer vegetable burgers in parts of Asia and to rethink its prices, which are often high by local standards and affordable only by the well-to-do. Kellogg has struggled to introduce its cereals successfully because consumers in many

CONCEPTS & CONNECTIONS 7.2

YUM! BRANDS' STRATEGY FOR BECOMING THE LEADING FOOD SERVICE BRAND IN CHINA

In 2013, Yum! Brands operated more than 38,000 restaurants in more than 117 countries. Its best-known brands were KFC, Taco Bell, Pizza Hut, A&W, and Long John Silver's. In 2012, its fastest growth in revenues came from its 5,700-plus restaurants in China, which recorded operating profits of $963 million during the year. KFC was the largest quick-service chain in China, with 4,260 units in 2012, while Pizza Hut was the largest casual-dining chain, with 987 units. Yum! Brands planned to open at least 700 new restaurant locations annually in China, including new Little Sheep units and East Dawning units, which had menus offering traditional Chinese food. All Yum! Brands menu items for China were developed in its R&D facility in Shanghai.

In addition to adapting its menu to local tastes and adding new units at a rapid pace, Yum! Brands adapted the restaurant ambience and decor to appeal to local consumer preferences and behavior. The company changed its KFC store formats to provide educational displays that supported parents' priorities for their children and to make KFC a fun place for children to visit. The typical KFC outlet in China averaged two birthday parties per day.

In 2012, Yum! Brands operated 58 KFC, Taco Bell, Pizza Hut, A&W, and Long John Silver's restaurants for every 1 million Americans. The company's more than 5,700 units in China represented only two restaurants per 1 million Chinese. Yum! Brands management believed that its strategy keyed to continued expansion in the number of units in China, and additional menu refinements would allow its operating profits from restaurants located in China to account for nearly 50 percent of systemwide operating profits by 2017.

Sources: Yum! Brands 2012 10K; information posted at www.yum.com.

less-developed countries do not eat cereal for breakfast—changing habits is difficult and expensive. Single-serving packages of detergents, shampoos, pickles, cough syrup, and cooking oils are very popular in India because they allow buyers to conserve cash by purchasing only what they need immediately. Thus, many companies find that trying to employ a strategy akin to that used in the markets of developed countries is hazardous.[17] Experimenting with some, perhaps many, local twists is usually necessary to find a strategy combination that works.

Strategy Options for Competing in Developing-Country Markets

Several strategy options for tailoring a company's strategy to fit the sometimes unusual or challenging circumstances presented in developing-country markets are the following:

- *Prepare to compete on the basis of low price.* Consumers in emerging markets are often highly focused on price, which can give low-cost local competitors the edge unless a company can find ways to attract buyers with bargain prices as well as better products. For example, when Unilever entered the market for laundry detergents in India, it developed a low-cost detergent (named Wheel) that was not harsh to the skin, constructed new super-efficient production facilities, distributed the product to local merchants by handcarts, and crafted an economical marketing campaign that included painted signs on buildings and demonstrations near stores—the new brand quickly captured $100 million in sales and was the top detergent brand in India in 2011 based on dollar sales. Unilever later replicated the strategy with low-price shampoos and deodorants in India and in South America with a detergent brand named Ala.

- *Modify aspects of the company's business model or strategy to accommodate local circumstances (but not so much that the company loses the advantage of global scale and global branding).* For instance when Dell entered China, it discovered that individuals and businesses were not accustomed to placing orders via the Internet. To adapt, Dell modified its direct sales model to rely more heavily on phone and fax orders and decided to be patient in getting Chinese customers to place Internet orders. Further, because numerous Chinese government departments and state-owned enterprises insisted that hardware vendors make their bids through distributors and systems integrators (as opposed to dealing directly with Dell salespeople as did large enterprises in other countries), Dell opted to use third parties in marketing its products to this buyer segment (although it did sell through its own sales force where it could). But Dell was careful not to abandon those parts of its business model that gave it a competitive edge over rivals.

- *Try to change the local market to better match the way the company does business elsewhere.* A multinational company often has enough market clout to drive major changes in the way a local country market operates. When Japan's Suzuki entered India in 1981, it triggered a quality revolution among Indian auto parts manufacturers. Local parts and components suppliers teamed up with Suzuki's vendors in Japan and worked with Japanese experts to produce higher-quality products. Over the next two decades, Indian companies became very proficient in making top-notch parts and components for vehicles, won more prizes for quality than companies in any country other than Japan, and broke into the global market as suppliers to many automakers in Asia and other parts of the world. Mahindra and Mahindra, one of India's premier automobile manufacturers, has been recognized by a number of organizations for its product quality. Among its most noteworthy awards was its number-one ranking by J.D. Power Asia Pacific for new-vehicle overall quality.

- *Stay away from those emerging markets where it is impractical or uneconomical to modify the company's business model to accommodate local circumstances.* Home Depot expanded into Mexico in 2001 and China in 2006, but has avoided entry into other emerging countries because its value proposition of good quality, low prices, and attentive customer service relies on (1) good highways and logistical systems to minimize store inventory costs, (2) employee stock ownership to help motivate store personnel to provide good customer service, and (3) high labor costs for housing construction and home repairs to encourage homeowners to engage in do-it-yourself projects. Relying on these factors in the U.S. and Canadian markets has worked spectacularly for Home Depot, but Home Depot has found that it cannot count on these factors in nearby Latin America.

Company experiences in entering developing markets such as China, India, Russia, and Brazil indicate that profitability seldom comes quickly or easily. Building a market for the company's products can often turn into a long-term process that involves reeducation of consumers, sizable investments in advertising and promotion to alter tastes and buying habits, and upgrades of the local infrastructure (the supplier base, transportation systems, distribution channels, labor markets, and capital markets).

In such cases, a company must be patient, work within the system to improve the infrastructure, and lay the foundation for generating sizable revenues and profits once conditions are ripe for market takeoff.

> Profitability in emerging markets rarely comes quickly or easily—new entrants have to adapt their business models and strategies to local conditions and be patient in earning a profit.

KEY POINTS

1. Competing in international markets allows multinational companies to (1) gain access to new customers, (2) achieve lower costs and enhance the firm's competitiveness by more easily capturing scale economies or learning curve effects, (3) leverage core competencies refined domestically in additional country markets, (4) gain access to resources and capabilities located in foreign markets, and (5) spread business risk across a wider market base.

2. Companies electing to expand into international markets must consider cross-country differences in buyer tastes, market sizes, and growth potential; location-based cost drivers; adverse exchange rates; and host-government policies when evaluating strategy options.

3. Options for entering foreign markets include maintaining a national (one-country) production base and exporting goods to foreign markets, licensing foreign firms to use the company's technology or produce and distribute the company's products, employing a franchising strategy, establishing a foreign subsidiary, and using strategic alliances or other collaborative partnerships.

4. In posturing to compete in foreign markets, a company has three basic options: (1) a multidomestic or think local, act local approach to crafting a strategy, (2) a global or think global, act global approach to crafting a strategy, and (3) a transnational strategy or combination think global, act local approach. A "think local, act local" or multicountry strategy is appropriate for industries or companies that must vary their product offerings and competitive approaches from country to country to accommodate differing buyer preferences and market conditions. A "think global, act global" approach (or global strategy) works best in markets that support employing the same basic competitive approach (low-cost, differentiation, focused) in all country markets and marketing essentially the same products under the same brand names in all countries where the company operates. A "think global, act local" approach can be used when it is feasible for a company to employ essentially the same basic competitive strategy in all markets, but still customize its product offering and some aspect of its operations to fit local market circumstances.

5. There are two general ways in which a firm can gain competitive advantage (or offset domestic disadvantages) in global markets. One way involves locating various value chain activities among nations in a manner that lowers costs or achieves greater product differentiation. A second way draws on a multinational or global competitor's ability to deepen or broaden its resources and capabilities and to coordinate its dispersed activities in ways that a domestic-only competitor cannot.

6. Companies racing for global leadership have to consider competing in emerging markets such as China, India, Brazil, Indonesia, and Mexico—countries where the business risks are considerable but the opportunities for growth are huge. To succeed in these markets, companies often have to (1) compete on the basis of low price, (2) be prepared to modify aspects of the company's business model or strategy to accommodate local circumstances (but not so much that the company loses the advantage of global scale and global branding), and/or (3) try to change the local market to better match the way the company does business elsewhere. Profitability is unlikely to come quickly or easily in emerging markets, typically because of the investments needed to alter buying habits and tastes and/or the need for infrastructure upgrades. And there may be times when a company should simply stay away from certain emerging markets until conditions for entry are better suited to its business model and strategy.

▶ ASSURANCE OF LEARNING EXERCISES

LO1, LO3 1. Chile's largest producer of wine, Concha y Toro, chooses to compete in Europe, North America, the Caribbean, and Asia using an export strategy. Go to the investor relations section of the company's website (www.conchaytoro.com/the-company/investor-relations/) to review the company's press releases, annual reports, and presentations. Why does it seem that the company has avoided developing vineyards and wineries in wine growing regions outside of South America? For what reasons does Concha y Toro likely have to pursue exporting rather than stick to a domestic-only sales and distribution strategy?

LO1, LO3 2. Collaborative agreements with foreign companies in the form of strategic alliances or joint ventures are widely used as a means of entering foreign markets.

connect They are also used as a means of acquiring resources and capabilities by learning from foreign partners. And they are used to put together powerful combinations of complementary resources and capabilities by accessing the complementary resources and capabilities of a foreign partner. Concepts & Connections 7.1 provides examples of four cross-border strategic alliances in which Solazyme has participated. What were each of these partnerships (with Unilever, Sephora, Qantas, and Roquette) designed to achieve, and why would they make sense for a company such as Solazyme? (Analyze each partnership separately based on the information provided in the capsule.)

LO2, LO4 3. Assume you are in charge of developing the strategy for a multinational company selling products in some 50 countries around the world. One of the issues you face

connect is whether to employ a multidomestic, a transnational, or a global strategy.

    a. If your company's product is mobile phones, do you think it would make better strategic sense to employ a multidomestic strategy, a transnational strategy, or a global strategy? Why?

b. If your company's product is dry soup mixes and canned soups, would a multidomestic strategy seem to be more advisable than a transnational or global strategy? Why or why not?

c. If your company's product is large home appliances such as washing machines, ranges, ovens, and refrigerators, would it seem to make more sense to pursue a multidomestic strategy or a transnational strategy or a global strategy? Why?

4. Using your university library's subscription to Lexis-Nexis, EBSCO, or a similar database, identify and discuss three key strategies that Volkswagen is using to compete in China.   **LO5, LO6**

EXERCISES FOR SIMULATION PARTICIPANTS

The questions below are for simulation participants whose companies operate in an international market arena. If your company competes only in a single country, then skip the questions in this section.

1. To what extent, if any, have you and your co-managers adapted your company's strategy to take shifting exchange rates into account? In other words, have you undertaken any actions to try to minimize the impact of adverse shifts in exchange rates?   **LO2**

2. To what extent, if any, have you and your co-managers adapted your company's strategy to consider geographic differences in import tariffs or import duties?   **LO2**

3. Which one of the following best describes the strategic approach your company is taking to try to compete successfully on an international basis?   **LO4**

   - Multidomestic or think local, act local approach.
   - Global or think global, act global approach.
   - Transnational or think global, act local approach.

   Explain your answer and indicate two or three chief elements of your company's strategy for competing in two or more different geographic regions.

ENDNOTES

1. A. C. Inkpen and A. Dinur, "Knowledge Management Processes and International Joint Ventures," *Organization Science* 9, no. 4 (July–August 1998); P. Dussauge, B. Garrette, and W. Mitchell, "Learning from Competing Partners: Outcomes and Durations of Scale and Link Alliances in Europe, North America and Asia," *Strategic Management Journal* 21, no. 2 (February 2000); C. Dhanaraj, M. A. Lyles, H. K. Steensma, et al., "Managing Tacit and Explicit Knowledge Transfer in IJVS: The Role of Relational Embeddedness and the Impact on Performance," *Journal of International Business Studies* 35, no. 5 (September 2004); K. W. Glaister and P. J. Buckley, "Strategic Motives for International Alliance Formation," *Journal of Management Studies* 33, no. 3 (May 1996); J. Anand and B. Kogut, "Technological Capabilities of Countries, Firm Rivalry and Foreign Direct Investment," *Journal of International Business Studies* 28, no. 3 (1997); J. Anand and A. Delios, "Absolute and Relative Resources as Determinants of International Acquisitions," *Strategic Management Journal* 23, no. 2 (February 2002); A. Seth, K. Song, and A. Pettit, "Value Creation and Destruction in Cross-Border Acquisitions: An Empirical Analysis of Foreign Acquisitions of U.S. Firms," *Strategic Management Journal* 23, no. 10 (October 2002); J. Anand, L. Capron, and W. Mitchell, "Using Acquisitions to Access Multinational Diversity: Thinking Beyond the Domestic Versus Cross-Border M&A Comparison," *Industrial & Corporate Change* 14, no. 2 (April 2005).

2. "China Car Sales 'Overtook the US' in 2009," *BBC News,* January 11, 2010, http://news.bbc.co.uk/2/hi/8451887.stm.

3. News release by U.S. Department of Labor, Bureau of Labor Statistics, "International Comparisons of Hourly Compensation Costs in Manufacturing, 2011," December 19, 2012.

4. E. Pablo, "Determinants of Cross-Border M&As in Latin America," *Journal of Business Research* 62, no. 9 (2009); R. Olie, "Shades of Culture and Institutions in International Mergers," *Organization Studies* 15, no. 3 (1994); and K. E. Meyer, M. Wright, and S. Pruthi, "Institutions, Resources, and Entry Strategies in Emerging Economies," *Strategic Management Journal* 30, no. 5 (2009).

5. Joel Bleeke and David Ernst, "The Way to Win in Cross-Border Alliances," *Harvard Business Review* 69, no. 6 (November–December 1991); and Gary Hamel, Yves L. Doz, and C. K. Prahalad, "Collaborate with Your Competitors—and Win," *Harvard Business Review* 67, no. 1 (January–February 1989).

6. Yves L. Doz and Gary Hamel, *Alliance Advantage* (Boston: Harvard Business School Press, 1998); Bleeke and Ernst, "The Way to Win in Cross-Border Alliances"; Hamel, Doz, and Prahalad, "Collaborate with Your Competitors—and Win"; and Michael Porter, *The Competitive Advantage of Nations* (New York: Free Press, 1990).

7. H. Kurt Christensen, "Corporate Strategy: Managing a Set of Businesses," in *The Portable MBA in Strategy,* ed. Liam Fahey and Robert M. Randall (New York: John Wiley & Sons, 2001).

8. Jeffrey H. Dyer, Prashant Kale, and Harbir Singh, "When to Ally and When to Acquire," *Harvard Business Review* 82, no. 7/8 (July–August 2004).

9. Rosabeth Moss Kanter, "Collaborative Advantage: The Art of the Alliance," *Harvard Business Review* 72, no. 4 (July–August 1994).

10. Jeremy Main, "Making Global Alliances Work," *Fortune,* December 19, 1990, p. 125.

11. Pankaj Ghemawat, "Managing Differences: The Central Challenge of Global Strategy," *Harvard Business Review* 85, no. 3 (March 2007).

12. C. A. Bartlett and S. Ghoshal, *Managing Across Borders: The Transnational Solution,* 2nd ed. (Boston: Harvard Business School Press, 1998).

13. Lynn S. Paine, "The China Rules," *Harvard Business Review* 88, no. 6 (June 2010) pp. 103-8.

14. C. K. Prahalad and Yves L. Doz, *The Multinational Mission* (New York: Free Press, 1987), pp. 58–60.

15. David J. Arnold and John A. Quelch, "New Strategies in Emerging Markets," *Sloan Management Review* 40, no. 1 (Fall 1998); and C. K. Prahalad, *The Fortune at the Bottom of the Pyramid: Eradicating Poverty through Profits* (Upper Saddle River, NJ: Wharton, 2005).

16. Brenda Cherry, "What China Eats (and Drinks and . . .)," *Fortune,* October 4, 2004, pp. 152–53; "A Ravenous Dragon," *The Economist* 386, no. 8571 (March 15, 2008), online edition; and "China: Just the Facts," *Journal of Commerce,* June 2, 2008, p. 24.

17. Tarun Khanna, Krishna G. Palepu, and Jayant Sinha, "Strategies That Fit Emerging Markets," *Harvard Business Review* 83, no. 6 (June 2005); and Arindam K. Bhattacharya and David C. Michael, "How Local Companies Keep Multinationals at Bay," *Harvard Business Review* 86, no. 3 (March 2008).

Corporate Strategy: Diversification and the Multibusiness Company

LEARNING OBJECTIVES

LO1 Understand when and how diversifying into multiple businesses can enhance shareholder value.

LO2 Gain an understanding of how related diversification strategies can produce cross-business strategic fit capable of delivering competitive advantage.

LO3 Become aware of the merits and risks of corporate strategies keyed to unrelated diversification.

LO4 Gain command of the analytical tools for evaluating a company's diversification strategy.

LO5 Understand a diversified company's four main corporate strategy options for solidifying its diversification strategy and improving company performance.

This chapter moves up one level in the strategy-making hierarchy, from strategy making in a single-business enterprise to strategy making in a diversified enterprise. Because a diversified company is a collection of individual businesses, the strategy-making task is more complicated. In a one-business company, managers have to come up with a plan for competing successfully in only a single industry environment—the result is what Chapter 2 labeled as *business strategy* (or *business-level strategy*). But in a diversified company, the strategy-making challenge involves assessing multiple industry environments and developing a *set* of business strategies, one for each industry arena in which the diversified company operates. And top executives at a diversified company must still go one step further and devise a companywide or *corporate strategy* for improving the attractiveness and performance of the company's overall business lineup and for making a rational whole out of its diversified collection of individual businesses.

In most diversified companies, corporate-level executives delegate considerable strategy-making authority to the heads of each business, usually giving them the latitude to craft a business strategy suited to their particular industry and competitive circumstances and holding them accountable for producing good results. But the task of crafting a diversified company's overall corporate strategy falls squarely in the lap of top-level executives and involves four distinct facets:

1. *Picking new industries to enter and deciding on the means of entry.* The decision to pursue business diversification requires that management decide what new industries offer the best growth prospects and whether to enter by starting a new business from the ground up, acquiring a company already in the target industry, or forming a joint venture or strategic alliance with another company.

2. *Pursuing opportunities to leverage cross-business value chain relationships into competitive advantage.* Companies that diversify into businesses with strategic fit across the value chains of their business units have a much better chance of gaining a 1 + 1 = 3 effect than multibusiness companies lacking strategic fit.

3. *Establishing investment priorities and steering corporate resources into the most attractive business units.* A diversified company's business units are usually not equally attractive, and it is incumbent on corporate management to channel resources into areas where earnings potentials are higher.

4. *Initiating actions to boost the combined performance of the corporation's collection of businesses.* Corporate strategists must craft moves to improve the overall performance of the corporation's business lineup and sustain increases in shareholder value. Strategic options for diversified corporations include (a) sticking closely with the existing business lineup and pursuing opportunities presented by these businesses, (b) broadening the scope of diversification by entering additional industries, (c) retrenching to a narrower scope of diversification by divesting poorly performing businesses, and (d) broadly restructuring the business lineup with multiple divestitures and/or acquisitions.

The first portion of this chapter describes the various means a company can use to diversify and explores the pros and cons of related versus unrelated diversification strategies. The second part of the chapter looks at how to evaluate the attractiveness of a diversified company's business lineup, decide whether it has a good diversification strategy, and identify ways to improve its future performance.

When Business Diversification Becomes a Consideration

As long as a single-business company can achieve profitable growth opportunities in its present industry, there is no urgency to pursue diversification. However, a company's opportunities for growth can become limited if the industry becomes competitively unattractive. Consider, for example, what the growing use of debit cards and online bill payment have done to the check printing business and what mobile phone companies and marketers of Voice over Internet Protocol (VoIP) have done to the revenues of long-distance providers such as AT&T, British Telecommunications, and NTT in Japan. Thus, *diversifying into new industries always merits strong consideration whenever a single-business company encounters diminishing market opportunities and stagnating sales in its principal business.*[1]

LO1 Understand when and how diversifying into multiple businesses can enhance shareholder value.

Building Shareholder Value: The Ultimate Justification for Business Diversification

Diversification must do more for a company than simply spread its business risk across various industries. In principle, diversification cannot be considered a success unless it results in *added shareholder value*—value that shareholders cannot capture on their own by spreading their investments across the stocks of companies in different industries.

Business diversification stands little chance of building shareholder value without passing the following three tests:[2]

1. *The industry attractiveness test.* The industry to be entered through diversification must offer an opportunity for profits and return on investment that is equal to or better than that of the company's present business(es).

2. *The cost-of-entry test.* The cost to enter the target industry must not be so high as to erode the potential for good profitability. A Catch-22 can prevail here, however. The more attractive an industry's prospects are for growth and good long-term profitability, the more expensive it can be to enter. It's easy for acquisitions of companies in highly attractive industries to fail the cost-of-entry test.

3. *The better-off test.* Diversifying into a new business must offer potential for the company's existing businesses and the new business to perform better together under a single corporate umbrella than they would perform operating as independent, stand-alone businesses. For example, let's say company A diversifies by purchasing company B in another industry.

If A and B's consolidated profits in the years to come prove no greater than what each could have earned on its own, then A's diversification won't provide its shareholders with added value. Company A's shareholders could have achieved the same $1 + 1 = 2$ result by merely purchasing stock in company B. Shareholder value is not created by diversification unless it produces a $1 + 1 = 3$ effect.

> Creating added value for shareholders via diversification requires building a multibusiness company where the whole is greater than the sum of its parts.

Diversification moves that satisfy all three tests have the greatest potential to grow shareholder value over the long term. Diversification moves that can pass only one or two tests are suspect.

Approaches to Diversifying the Business Lineup

The means of entering new industries and lines of business can take any of three forms: acquisition, internal development, or joint ventures with other companies.

Diversification by Acquisition of an Existing Business

Acquisition is a popular means of diversifying into another industry. Not only is it quicker than trying to launch a new operation, but it also offers an effective way to hurdle such entry barriers as acquiring technological know-how, establishing supplier relationships, achieving scale economies, building brand awareness, and securing adequate distribution. Buying an ongoing operation allows the acquirer to move directly to the task of building a strong market position in the target industry, rather than getting bogged down in the fine points of launching a start-up.

The big dilemma an acquisition-minded firm faces is whether to pay a premium price for a successful company or to buy a struggling company at a bargain price.[3] If the buying firm has little knowledge of the industry but has ample capital, it is often better off purchasing a capable, strongly positioned firm—unless the price of such an acquisition is prohibitive and flunks the cost-of-entry test. However, when the acquirer sees promising ways to transform a weak firm into a strong one, a struggling company can be the better long-term investment.

Entering a New Line of Business through Internal Development

Achieving diversification through *internal development* involves starting a new business subsidiary from scratch. Generally, forming a start-up subsidiary to enter a new business has appeal only when (1) the parent company already has in-house most or all of the skills and resources needed to compete effectively; (2) there is ample time to launch the business; (3) internal entry has lower costs than entry via acquisition; (4) the targeted industry is populated with many relatively small firms such that the new start-up does not have to compete against large, powerful rivals; (5) adding new production capacity will not adversely impact the supply–demand balance in the industry; and

(6) incumbent firms are likely to be slow or ineffective in responding to a new entrant's efforts to crack the market.

Using Joint Ventures to Achieve Diversification

A joint venture to enter a new business can be useful in at least two types of situations.[4] First, a joint venture is a good vehicle for pursuing an opportunity that is too complex, uneconomical, or risky for one company to pursue alone. Second, joint ventures make sense when the opportunities in a new industry require a broader range of competencies and know-how than an expansion-minded company can marshal. Many of the opportunities in biotechnology call for the coordinated development of complementary innovations and tackling an intricate web of technical, political, and regulatory factors simultaneously. In such cases, pooling the resources and competencies of two or more companies is a wiser and less risky way to proceed.

However, as discussed in Chapters 6 and 7, partnering with another company—in the form of either a joint venture or a collaborative alliance—has significant drawbacks due to the potential for conflicting objectives, disagreements over how to best operate the venture, culture clashes, and so on. Joint ventures are generally the least durable of the entry options, usually lasting only until the partners decide to go their own ways.

Choosing the Diversification Path: Related versus Unrelated Businesses

> **CORE CONCEPT**
> **Related businesses** possess competitively valuable cross-business value chain and resource matchups; **unrelated businesses** have dissimilar value chains and resources requirements, with no competitively important cross-business value chain relationships.

Once a company decides to diversify, its first big corporate strategy decision is whether to diversify into **related businesses, unrelated businesses**, or some mix of both (see Figure 8.1). *Businesses are said to be related when their value chains possess competitively valuable cross-business relationships.* These value chain matchups present opportunities for the businesses to perform better under the same corporate umbrella than they could by operating as stand-alone entities. *Businesses are said to be unrelated when the activities comprising their respective value chains and resource requirements are so dissimilar that no competitively valuable cross-business relationships are present.*

LO2 Gain an understanding of how related diversification strategies can produce cross-business strategic fit capable of delivering competitive advantage.

The next two sections explore the ins and outs of related and unrelated diversification.

Diversifying into Related Businesses

A related diversification strategy involves building the company around businesses whose value chains possess competitively valuable strategic fit, as shown in Figure 8.2. **Strategic fit** exists whenever one or more activities comprising the

> **CORE CONCEPT**
> **Strategic fit** exists when value chains of different businesses present opportunities for cross-business skills transfer, cost sharing, or brand sharing.

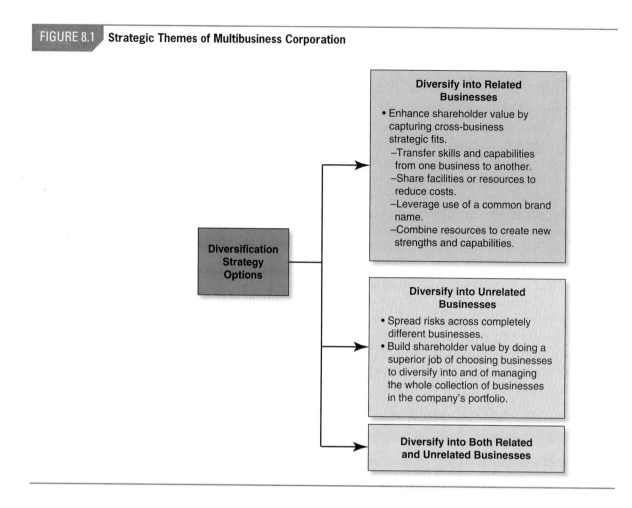

FIGURE 8.1 **Strategic Themes of Multibusiness Corporation**

value chains of different businesses are sufficiently similar to present opportunities for:[5]

- *Transferring competitively valuable resources, expertise, technological know-how, or other capabilities from one business to another.* Google's technological know-how and innovation capabilities refined in its Internet search business have aided considerably in the development of its Android mobile operating system and Chrome operating system for computers. After acquiring Marvel Comics in 2009, Walt Disney Company shared Marvel's iconic characters such as Spider-Man, Iron Man, and the Black Widow with many of the other Disney businesses, including its theme parks, retail stores, motion picture division, and video game business.

- *Cost sharing between separate businesses where value chain activities can be combined.* For instance, it is often feasible to manufacture the products of different businesses in a single plant or have a single sales force for the products of different businesses if they are marketed to the same types of customers.

- *Brand sharing between business units that have common customers or that draw upon common core competencies.* For example, Yamaha's name in motorcycles gave it instant credibility and recognition in entering the personal watercraft business, allowing it to achieve a significant market share

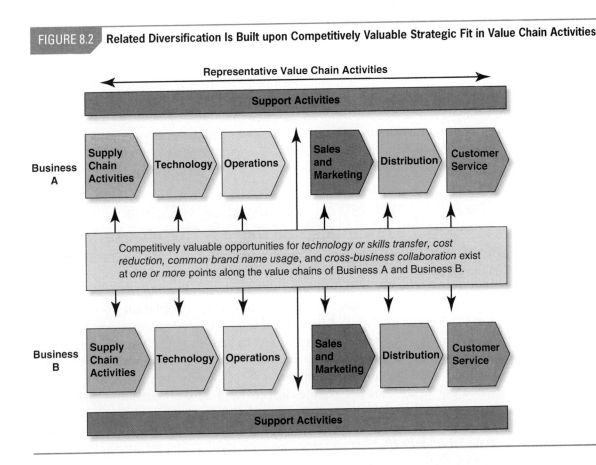

FIGURE 8.2   Related Diversification Is Built upon Competitively Valuable Strategic Fit in Value Chain Activities

Representative Value Chain Activities

Support Activities

Business A: Supply Chain Activities | Technology | Operations | Sales and Marketing | Distribution | Customer Service

Competitively valuable opportunities for *technology or skills transfer, cost reduction, common brand name usage,* and *cross-business collaboration* exist at *one or more* points along the value chains of Business A and Business B.

Business B: Supply Chain Activities | Technology | Operations | Sales and Marketing | Distribution | Customer Service

Support Activities

without spending large sums on advertising to establish a brand identity for the WaveRunner. Likewise, Apple's reputation for producing easy-to-operate computers was a competitive asset that facilitated the company's diversification into digital music players and smartphones.

Cross-business strategic fit can exist anywhere along the value chain—in R&D and technology activities, in supply chain activities, in manufacturing, in sales and marketing, or in distribution activities. Likewise, different businesses can often use the same administrative and customer service infrastructure. For instance, a cable operator that diversifies as a broadband provider can use the same customer data network, the same customer call centers and local offices, the same billing and customer accounting systems, and the same customer service infrastructure to support all its products and services.[6]

Strategic Fit and Economies of Scope

Strategic fit in the value chain activities of a diversified corporation's different businesses opens up opportunities for economies of scope— a concept distinct from *economies of scale.* Economies of *scale* are cost savings that accrue directly from a larger operation; for example, unit costs may be lower in a large plant than in a small

> **CORE CONCEPT**
>
> **Economies of scope** are cost reductions stemming from strategic fit along the value chains of related businesses (thereby, a larger scope of operations), whereas *economies of scale* accrue from a larger operation.

plant. **Economies of scope,** however, stem directly from cost-saving strategic fit along the value chains of related businesses. Such economies are open only to a multibusiness enterprise and are the result of a related diversification strategy that allows sibling businesses to share technology, perform R&D together, use common manufacturing or distribution facilities, share a common sales force or distributor/dealer network, and/or share the same administrative infrastructure. *The greater the cross-business economies associated with cost-saving strategic fit, the greater the potential for a related diversification strategy to yield a competitive advantage based on lower costs than rivals.*

The Ability of Related Diversification to Deliver Competitive Advantage and Gains in Shareholder Value

Economies of scope and the other strategic-fit benefits provide a dependable basis for earning higher profits and returns than what a diversified company's businesses could earn as stand-alone enterprises. Converting the competitive advantage potential into greater profitability is what fuels $1 + 1 = 3$ gains in shareholder value—the necessary outcome for satisfying the *better-off test.* There are three things to bear in mind here: (1) Capturing cross-business strategic fit via related diversification builds shareholder value in ways that shareholders cannot replicate by simply owning a diversified portfolio of stocks; (2) the capture of cross-business strategic-fit benefits is possible only through related diversification; and (3) the benefits of cross-business strategic fit are not automatically realized—*the benefits materialize only after management has successfully pursued internal actions to capture them.*[7]

Diversifying into Unrelated Businesses

LO3 Become aware of the merits and risks of corporate strategies keyed to unrelated diversification.

An unrelated diversification strategy discounts the importance of pursuing cross-business strategic fit and, instead, focuses squarely on entering and operating businesses in industries that allow the company as a whole to increase its earnings. Companies that pursue a strategy of unrelated diversification generally exhibit a willingness to diversify into *any industry* where senior managers see opportunity to realize improved financial results. Such companies are frequently labeled *conglomerates* because their business interests range broadly across diverse industries.

Companies that pursue unrelated diversification nearly always enter new businesses by acquiring an established company rather than by internal development. The premise of acquisition-minded corporations is that growth by acquisition can deliver enhanced shareholder value through upward-trending corporate revenues and earnings and a stock price that *on average* rises enough year after year to amply reward and please shareholders. Three types of acquisition candidates are usually of particular interest: (1) businesses that have bright growth prospects but are short on investment capital, (2) undervalued companies that can be acquired at a bargain price, and (3) struggling companies whose operations can be turned around with the aid of the parent company's financial resources and managerial know-how.

Building Shareholder Value through Unrelated Diversification

Given the absence of cross-business strategic fit with which to capture added competitive advantage, the task of building shareholder value via unrelated diversification ultimately hinges on the ability of the parent company to improve its businesses via other means. To succeed with a corporate strategy keyed to unrelated diversification, corporate executives must:

- Do a superior job of identifying and acquiring new businesses that can produce consistently good earnings and returns on investment.
- Do an excellent job of negotiating favorable acquisition prices.
- Do such a good job *overseeing* and *parenting* the firm's businesses that they perform at a higher level than they would otherwise be able to do through their own efforts alone. The parenting activities of corporate executives can take the form of providing expert problem-solving skills, creative strategy suggestions, and first-rate advice and guidance on how to improve competitiveness and financial performance to the heads of the various business subsidiaries.[8]

The Pitfalls of Unrelated Diversification

Unrelated diversification strategies have two important negatives that undercut the pluses: very demanding managerial requirements and limited competitive advantage potential.

Demanding Managerial Requirements   Successfully managing a set of fundamentally different businesses operating in fundamentally different industry and competitive environments is an exceptionally difficult proposition for corporate-level managers. The greater the number of businesses a company is in and the more diverse they are, the more difficult it is for corporate managers to:

1. Stay abreast of what's happening in each industry and each subsidiary.
2. Pick business-unit heads having the requisite combination of managerial skills and know-how to drive gains in performance.
3. Tell the difference between those strategic proposals of business-unit managers that are prudent and those that are risky or unlikely to succeed.
4. Know what to do if a business unit stumbles and its results suddenly head downhill.[9]

As a rule, the more unrelated businesses that a company has diversified into, the more corporate executives are forced to "manage by the numbers"—that is, keep a close track on the financial and operating results of each subsidiary and assume that the heads of the various subsidiaries have most everything under control so long as the latest key financial and operating measures look good. Managing by the numbers works if the heads of the various business units are quite capable and consistently meet their numbers. But problems arise when things start

> Unrelated diversification requires that corporate executives rely on the skills and expertise of business-level managers to build competitive advantage and boost the performance of individual businesses.

to go awry and corporate management has to get deeply involved in turning around a business it does not know much about.

Limited Competitive Advantage Potential   The second big negative associated with unrelated diversification is that such a strategy *offers limited potential for competitive advantage beyond what each individual business can generate on its own.* Unlike a related diversification strategy, there is no cross-business strategic fit to draw on for reducing costs; transferring capabilities, skills, and technology; or leveraging use of a powerful brand name and thereby adding to the competitive advantage possessed by individual businesses. *Without the competitive advantage potential of strategic fit, consolidated performance of an unrelated group of businesses is unlikely to be better than the sum of what the individual business units could achieve independently in most instances.*

Misguided Reasons for Pursuing Unrelated Diversification

Competently overseeing a set of widely diverse businesses can turn out to be much harder than it sounds. In practice, comparatively few companies have proved that they have top management capabilities that are up to the task. Far more corporate executives have failed than been successful at delivering consistently good financial results with an unrelated diversification strategy.[10] Odds are that the result of unrelated diversification will be $1 + 1 = 2$ or less. In addition, management sometimes undertakes a strategy of unrelated diversification for the wrong reasons.

- *Risk reduction.* Managers sometimes pursue unrelated diversification to reduce risk by spreading the company's investments over a set of diverse industries. But this cannot create long-term shareholder value alone since the company's shareholders can more efficiently reduce their exposure to risk by investing in a diversified portfolio of stocks and bonds.

- *Growth.* While unrelated diversification may enable a company to achieve rapid or continuous growth in revenues, only profitable growth can bring about increases in shareholder value and justify a strategy of unrelated diversification.

- *Earnings stabilization.* In a broadly diversified company, there's a chance that market downtrends in some of the company's businesses will be partially offset by cyclical upswings in its other businesses, thus producing somewhat less earnings volatility. In actual practice, however, there's no convincing evidence that the consolidated profits of firms with unrelated diversification strategies are more stable than the profits of firms with related diversification strategies.

- *Managerial motives.* Unrelated diversification can provide benefits to managers such as higher compensation, which tends to increase with firm size and degree of diversification. Diversification for this reason alone is far more likely to reduce shareholder value than to increase it.

Diversifying into Both Related and Unrelated Businesses

There's nothing to preclude a company from diversifying into both related and unrelated businesses. Indeed, the business makeup of diversified companies varies considerably. Some diversified companies are really *dominant-business enterprises*—one major "core" business accounts for 50 to 80 percent of total revenues and a collection of small related or unrelated businesses accounts for the remainder. Some diversified companies are *narrowly diversified* around a few (two to five) related or unrelated businesses. Others are *broadly diversified* around a wide-ranging collection of related businesses, unrelated businesses, or a mixture of both. And a number of multibusiness enterprises have diversified into *several unrelated groups of related businesses.* There's ample room for companies to customize their diversification strategies to incorporate elements of both related and unrelated diversification.

Evaluating the Strategy of a Diversified Company

Strategic analysis of diversified companies builds on the methodology used for single-business companies discussed in Chapters 3 and 4 but utilizes tools that streamline the overall process. The procedure for evaluating the pluses and minuses of a diversified company's strategy and deciding what actions to take to improve the company's performance involves six steps:

LO4 Gain command of the analytical tools for evaluating a company's diversification strategy.

1. Assessing the attractiveness of the industries the company has diversified into.
2. Assessing the competitive strength of the company's business units.
3. Evaluating the extent of cross-business strategic fit along the value chains of the company's various business units.
4. Checking whether the firm's resources fit the requirements of its present business lineup.
5. Ranking the performance prospects of the businesses from best to worst and determining a priority for allocating resources.
6. Crafting new strategic moves to improve overall corporate performance.

The core concepts and analytical techniques underlying each of these steps are discussed further in this section of the chapter.

Step 1: Evaluating Industry Attractiveness

A principal consideration in evaluating the caliber of a diversified company's strategy is the attractiveness of the industries in which it has business operations. The more attractive the industries (both individually and as a group) a diversified company is in, the better its prospects for good long-term performance. A simple and reliable analytical tool for gauging industry attractiveness involves calculating quantitative industry attractiveness scores based upon the following measures:

- *Market size and projected growth rate.* Big industries are more attractive than small industries, and fast-growing industries tend to be more attractive than slow-growing industries, other things being equal.

- *The intensity of competition.* Industries where competitive pressures are relatively weak are more attractive than industries with strong competitive pressures.

- *Emerging opportunities and threats.* Industries with promising opportunities and minimal threats on the near horizon are more attractive than industries with modest opportunities and imposing threats.

- *The presence of cross-industry strategic fit.* The more the industry's value chain and resource requirements match up well with the value chain activities of other industries in which the company has operations, the more attractive the industry is to a firm pursuing related diversification. However, cross-industry strategic fit may be of no consequence to a company committed to a strategy of unrelated diversification.

- *Resource requirements.* Industries having resource requirements within the company's reach are more attractive than industries where capital and other resource requirements could strain corporate financial resources and organizational capabilities.

- *Seasonal and cyclical factors.* Industries where buyer demand is relatively steady year-round and not unduly vulnerable to economic ups and downs tend to be more attractive than industries with wide seasonal or cyclical swings in buyer demand.

- *Social, political, regulatory, and environmental factors.* Industries with significant problems in such areas as consumer health, safety, or environmental pollution or that are subject to intense regulation are less attractive than industries where such problems are not burning issues.

- *Industry profitability.* Industries with healthy profit margins are generally more attractive than industries where profits have historically been low or unstable.

- *Industry uncertainty and business risk.* Industries with less uncertainty on the horizon and lower overall business risk are more attractive than industries whose prospects for one reason or another are quite uncertain.

Each attractiveness measure should be assigned a weight reflecting its relative importance in determining an industry's attractiveness; it is weak methodology to assume that the various attractiveness measures are equally important. The intensity of competition in an industry should nearly always carry a high weight (say, 0.20 to 0.30). Strategic-fit considerations should be assigned a high weight in the case of companies with related diversification strategies; but for companies with an unrelated diversification strategy, strategic fit with other industries may be given a low weight or even dropped from the list of attractiveness measures. Seasonal and cyclical factors generally are assigned a low weight (or maybe even eliminated from the analysis) unless a company has diversified into industries strongly characterized by seasonal demand and/or heavy vulnerability to cyclical upswings and downswings. The importance weights must add up to 1.0.

Next, each industry is rated on each of the chosen industry attractiveness measures, using a rating scale of 1 to 10 (where 10 signifies *high* attractiveness and 1 signifies *low* attractiveness). Weighted attractiveness scores are then calculated by multiplying the industry's rating on each measure by the

TABLE 8.1

Calculating Weighted Industry Attractiveness Scores

Rating scale: 1 = Very unattractive to company; 10 = Very attractive to company

Industry Attractiveness Measure	Importance Weight	Industry A Rating/Score	Industry B Rating/Score	Industry C Rating/Score	Industry D Rating/Score
Market size and projected growth rate	0.10	8/0.80	5/0.50	2/0.20	3/0.30
Intensity of competition	0.25	8/2.00	7/1.75	3/0.75	2/0.50
Emerging opportunities and threats	0.10	2/0.20	9/0.90	4/0.40	5/0.50
Cross-industry strategic fit	0.20	8/1.60	4/0.80	8/1.60	2/0.40
Resource requirements	0.10	9/0.90	7/0.70	5/0.50	5/0.50
Seasonal and cyclical influences	0.05	9/0.45	8/0.40	10/0.50	5/0.25
Societal, political, regulatory, and environmental factors	0.05	10/0.50	7/0.35	7/0.35	3/0.15
Industry profitability	0.10	5/0.50	10/1.00	3/0.30	3/0.30
Industry uncertainty and business risk	0.05	5/0.25	7/0.35	10/0.50	1/0.05
Sum of the assigned weights	1.00				
Overall weighted industry attractiveness scores		**7.20**	**6.75**	**5.10**	**2.95**

corresponding weight. For example, a rating of 8 times a weight of 0.25 gives a weighted attractiveness score of 2.00. The sum of the weighted scores for all the attractiveness measures provides an overall industry attractiveness score. This procedure is illustrated in Table 8.1.

Calculating Industry Attractiveness Scores
Two conditions are necessary for producing valid industry attractiveness scores using this method. One is deciding on appropriate weights for the industry attractiveness measures. This is not always easy because different analysts have different views about which weights are most appropriate. Also, different weightings may be appropriate for different companies—based on their strategies, performance targets, and financial circumstances. For instance, placing a low weight on financial resource requirements may be justifiable for a cash-rich company, whereas a high weight may be more appropriate for a financially strapped company.

The second requirement for creating accurate attractiveness scores is to have sufficient knowledge to rate the industry on each attractiveness measure. It's usually rather easy to locate statistical data needed to compare industries on market size, growth rate, seasonal and cyclical influences, and industry profitability. Cross-industry fit and resource requirements are also fairly easy to judge. But the attractiveness measure that is toughest to rate is that of intensity of competition. It is not always easy to conclude whether competition in one industry is stronger or weaker than in another industry. In the event that the available information is too skimpy to confidently assign a rating value to an industry on a particular attractiveness measure, then it is usually best to use a score of 5, which avoids biasing the overall attractiveness score either up or down.

Despite the hurdles, calculating industry attractiveness scores is a systematic and reasonably reliable method for ranking a diversified company's industries from most to least attractive.

Step 2: Evaluating Business-Unit Competitive Strength

The second step in evaluating a diversified company is to determine how strongly positioned its business units are in their respective industries. Doing an appraisal of each business unit's strength and competitive position in its industry not only reveals its chances for industry success but also provides a basis for ranking the units from competitively strongest to weakest. Quantitative measures of each business unit's competitive strength can be calculated using a procedure similar to that for measuring industry attractiveness. The following factors may be used in quantifying the competitive strengths of a diversified company's business subsidiaries:

- *Relative market share.* A business unit's *relative market share* is defined as the ratio of its market share to the market share held by the largest rival firm in the industry, with market share measured in unit volume, not dollars. For instance, if business A has a market-leading share of 40 percent and its largest rival has 30 percent, A's relative market share is 1.33. If business B has a 15 percent market share and B's largest rival has 30 percent, B's relative market share is 0.5.

- *Costs relative to competitors' costs.* There's reason to expect that business units with higher relative market shares have lower unit costs than competitors with lower relative market shares because of the possibility of scale economies and experience or learning curve effects. Another indicator of low cost can be a business unit's supply chain management capabilities.

- *Products or services that satisfy buyer expectations.* A company's competitiveness depends in part on being able to offer buyers appealing features, performance, reliability, and service attributes.

- *Ability to benefit from strategic fit with sibling businesses.* Strategic fit with other businesses within the company enhances a business unit's competitive strength and may provide a competitive edge.

- *Number and caliber of strategic alliances and collaborative partnerships.* Well-functioning alliances and partnerships may be a source of potential competitive advantage and thus add to a business's competitive strength.

- *Brand image and reputation.* A strong brand name is a valuable competitive asset in most industries.

- *Competitively valuable capabilities.* All industries contain a variety of important competitive capabilities related to product innovation, production capabilities, distribution capabilities, or marketing prowess.

- *Profitability relative to competitors.* Above-average returns on investment and large profit margins relative to rivals are usually accurate indicators of competitive advantage.

After settling on a set of competitive strength measures that are well matched to the circumstances of the various business units, weights indicating each

TABLE 8.2

Calculating Weighted Competitive Strength Scores for a Diversified Company's Business Units

Rating scale: 1 = Very weak; 10 = Very strong

Competitive Strength Measure	Importance Weight	Business A in Industry A Rating/Score	Business B in Industry B Rating/Score	Business C in Industry C Rating/Score	Business D in Industry D Rating/Score
Relative market share	0.15	10/1.50	1/0.15	6/0.90	2/0.30
Costs relative to competitors' costs	0.20	7/1.40	2/0.40	5/1.00	3/0.60
Ability to match or beat rivals on key product attributes	0.05	9/0.45	4/0.20	8/0.40	4/0.20
Ability to benefit from strategic fit with sister businesses	0.20	8/1.60	4/0.80	4/0.80	2/0.60
Bargaining leverage with suppliers/ buyers; caliber of alliances	0.05	9/0.45	3/0.15	6/0.30	2/0.10
Brand image and reputation	0.10	9/0.90	2/0.20	7/0.70	5/0.50
Competitively valuable capabilities	0.15	7/1.05	2/0.30	5/0.75	3/0.45
Profitability relative to competitors	0.10	5/0.50	1/0.10	4/0.40	4/0.40
Sum of the assigned weights	1.00				
Overall weighted competitive strength scores		**7.85**	**2.30**	**5.25**	**3.15**

measure's importance need to be assigned. As in the assignment of weights to industry attractiveness measures, the importance weights must add up to 1.0. Each business unit is then rated on each of the chosen strength measures, using a rating scale of 1 to 10 (where 10 signifies competitive *strength* and a rating of 1 signifies competitive *weakness*). If the available information is too skimpy to confidently assign a rating value to a business unit on a particular strength measure, then it is usually best to use a score of 5. Weighted strength ratings are calculated by multiplying the business unit's rating on each strength measure by the assigned weight. For example, a strength score of 6 times a weight of 0.15 gives a weighted strength rating of 0.90. The sum of weighted ratings across all the strength measures provides a quantitative measure of a business unit's overall market strength and competitive standing. Table 8.2 provides sample calculations of competitive strength ratings for four businesses.

Using a Nine-Cell Matrix to Evaluate the Strength of a Diversified Company's Business Lineup   The industry attractiveness and business strength scores can be used to portray the strategic positions of each business in a diversified company. Industry attractiveness is plotted on the vertical axis and competitive strength on the horizontal axis. A nine-cell grid emerges from dividing the vertical axis into three regions (high, medium, and low attractiveness) and the horizontal axis into three regions (strong, average, and weak competitive strength). As shown in Figure 8.3, high attractiveness is associated with scores of 6.7 or greater on a rating scale of 1 to 10, medium attractiveness to scores of 3.3 to 6.7, and low attractiveness to scores below 3.3. Likewise, high competitive strength is defined as a score greater than 6.7, average strength as scores of 3.3 to 6.7, and low strength as scores below 3.3. *Each business unit is plotted on the nine-cell matrix according to its overall attractiveness and strength scores, and then shown as a "bubble."* The size of each bubble is scaled to what percentage of revenues the business generates relative to total corporate revenues. The bubbles in Figure 8.3 were located on the grid using the four industry attractiveness scores from Table 8.1 and the strength scores for the four business units in Table 8.2.

The locations of the business units on the attractiveness–competitive strength matrix provide valuable guidance in deploying corporate resources.

FIGURE 8.3 A Nine-Cell Industry Attractiveness–Competitive Strength Matrix

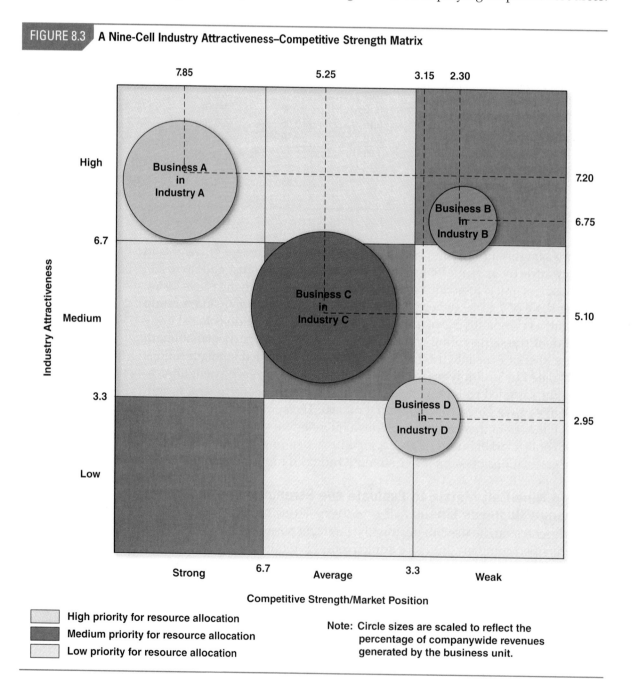

Note: Circle sizes are scaled to reflect the percentage of companywide revenues generated by the business unit.

High priority for resource allocation
Medium priority for resource allocation
Low priority for resource allocation

In general, *a diversified company's best prospects for good overall performance involve concentrating corporate resources on business units having the greatest competitive strength and industry attractiveness.* Businesses plotted in the three cells in the upper left portion of the attractiveness–competitive strength matrix have both favorable industry attractiveness and competitive strength and should receive a high investment priority. Business units plotted in these three cells (such as business A in Figure 8.3) are referred to as "grow and build" businesses because of their capability to drive future increases in shareholder value.

Next in priority come businesses positioned in the three diagonal cells stretching from the lower left to the upper right (businesses B and C in Figure 8.3). Such businesses usually merit medium or intermediate priority in the parent's resource allocation ranking. However, some businesses in the medium-priority diagonal cells may have brighter or dimmer prospects than others. For example, a small business in the upper right cell of the matrix (like business B), despite being in a highly attractive industry, may occupy too weak a competitive position in its industry to justify the investment and resources needed to turn it into a strong market contender. If, however, a business in the upper right cell has attractive opportunities for rapid growth and a good potential for winning a much stronger market position over time, management may designate it as a grow and build business—the strategic objective here would be to move the business leftward in the attractiveness–competitive strength matrix over time.

Businesses in the three cells in the lower right corner of the matrix (business D in Figure 8.3) typically are weak performers and have the lowest claim on corporate resources. Such businesses are typically good candidates for being divested or else managed in a manner calculated to squeeze out the maximum cash flows from operations. The cash flows from low-performing/low-potential businesses can then be diverted to financing expansion of business units with greater market opportunities. In exceptional cases where a business located in the three lower right cells is nonetheless fairly profitable or has the potential for good earnings and return on investment, the business merits retention and the allocation of sufficient resources to achieve better performance.

The nine-cell attractiveness–competitive strength matrix provides clear, strong logic for why a diversified company needs to consider both industry attractiveness and business strength in allocating resources and investment capital to its different businesses. A good case can be made for concentrating resources in those businesses that enjoy higher degrees of attractiveness and competitive strength, being very selective in making investments in businesses with intermediate positions on the grid, and withdrawing resources from businesses that are lower in attractiveness and strength unless they offer exceptional profit or cash flow potential.

Step 3: Determining the Competitive Value of Strategic Fit in Multibusiness Companies

The potential for competitively important strategic fit is central to making conclusions about the effectiveness of a company's related diversification strategy. This step can be bypassed for diversified companies whose businesses are all unrelated (because, by design, no cross-business strategic fit is present). Checking the competitive advantage potential of cross-business strategic fit involves evaluating how much benefit a diversified company can gain from value chain matchups that present:

> The greater the value of cross-business strategic fit in enhancing a company's performance in the marketplace or the bottom line, the more powerful is its strategy of related diversification.

1. Opportunities to combine the performance of certain activities, thereby reducing costs and capturing economies of scope.

2. Opportunities to transfer skills, technology, or intellectual capital from one business to another.

3. Opportunities to share use of a well-respected brand name across multiple product and/or service categories.

But more than just strategic-fit identification is needed. The real test is what competitive value can be generated from this fit. To what extent can cost savings be realized? How much competitive value will come from cross-business transfer of skills, technology, or intellectual capital? Will transferring a potent brand name to the products of sibling businesses grow sales significantly? Absent significant strategic fit and dedicated company efforts to capture the benefits, one has to be skeptical about the potential for a diversified company's businesses to perform better together than apart.

Step 4: Evaluating Resource Fit

The businesses in a diversified company's lineup need to exhibit good resource fit. **Resource fit** exists when (1) businesses, individually, strengthen a company's overall mix of resources and capabilities and (2) the parent company has sufficient resources that add customer value to support its entire group of businesses without spreading itself too thin.

> **CORE CONCEPT**
>
> A diversified company exhibits **resource fit** when its businesses add to a company's overall mix of resources and capabilities and when the parent company has sufficient resources to support its entire group of businesses without spreading itself too thin.

> **CORE CONCEPT**
>
> A strong **internal capital market** allows a diversified company to add value by shifting capital from business units generating *free cash flow* to those needing additional capital to expand and realize their growth potential.

Financial Resource Fit   One important dimension of resource fit concerns whether a diversified company can generate the internal cash flows sufficient to fund the capital requirements of its businesses, pay its dividends, meet its debt obligations, and otherwise remain financially healthy. While additional capital can usually be raised in financial markets, it is also important for a diversified firm to have a healthy **internal capital market** that can support the financial requirements of its business lineup. The greater the extent to which a diversified company is able to fund investment in its businesses through internally generated free cash flows rather than from equity issues or borrowing, the more powerful its financial resource fit and the less dependent the firm is on external financial resources.

A *portfolio approach* to ensuring financial fit among the firm's businesses is based on the fact that different businesses have different cash flow and investment characteristics. For example, business units in rapidly growing industries are often **cash hogs**—so labeled because the cash flows they generate from internal operations aren't big enough to fund their expansion. To keep pace with rising buyer demand, rapid-growth businesses frequently need sizable annual capital infusions—for new facilities and equipment, for technology improvements, and for additional working capital to support inventory expansion. Because a cash hog's financial resources must be provided by the corporate parent, corporate managers have to decide whether it makes good financial and strategic sense to keep pouring new money into a cash hog business.

> **CORE CONCEPT**
>
> A **cash hog** generates operating cash flows that are too small to fully fund its operations and growth; a cash hog must receive cash infusions from outside sources to cover its working capital and investment requirements.

In contrast, business units with leading market positions in mature industries may be **cash cows**—businesses that generate substantial cash surpluses over what is needed to adequately fund their operations. Market leaders in slow-growth industries often generate sizable positive cash flows *over and above what is needed for growth and reinvestment* because the slow-growth nature of their industry often entails relatively modest annual investment requirements. Cash cows, though not always attractive from a growth standpoint, are

> **CORE CONCEPT**
>
> A **cash cow** generates operating cash flows over and above its internal requirements, thereby providing financial resources that may be used to invest in cash hogs, finance new acquisitions, fund share buyback programs, or pay dividends.

valuable businesses from a financial resource perspective. The surplus cash flows they generate can be used to pay corporate dividends, finance acquisitions, and provide funds for investing in the company's promising cash hogs. It makes good financial and strategic sense for diversified companies to keep cash cows in healthy condition, fortifying and defending their market position to preserve their cash-generating capability over the long term and thereby have an ongoing source of financial resources to deploy elsewhere.

A diversified company has good financial resource fit when the excess cash generated by its cash cow businesses is sufficient to fund the investment requirements of promising cash hog businesses. Ideally, investing in promising cash hog businesses over time results in growing the hogs into self-supporting *star businesses* that have strong or market-leading competitive positions in attractive, high-growth markets and high levels of profitability. Star businesses are often the cash cows of the future—when the markets of star businesses begin to mature and their growth slows, their competitive strength should produce self-generated cash flows more than sufficient to cover their investment needs. The "success sequence" is thus cash hog to young star (but perhaps still a cash hog) to self-supporting star to cash cow.

If, however, a cash hog has questionable promise (because of either low industry attractiveness or a weak competitive position), then it becomes a logical candidate for divestiture. Aggressively investing in a cash hog with an uncertain future seldom makes sense because it requires the corporate parent to keep pumping more capital into the business with only a dim hope of turning the cash hog into a future star. Such businesses are a financial drain and fail the resource-fit test because they strain the corporate parent's ability to adequately fund its other businesses. Divesting a less-attractive cash hog business is usually the best alternative unless (1) it has highly valuable strategic fit with other business units or (2) the capital infusions needed from the corporate parent are modest relative to the funds available, and (3) there's a decent chance of growing the business into a solid bottom-line contributor.

Aside from cash flow considerations, two other factors to consider in assessing the financial resource fit for businesses in a diversified firm's portfolio are:

- *Do individual businesses adequately contribute to achieving companywide performance targets?* A business exhibits poor financial fit if it soaks up a disproportionate share of the company's financial resources, while making subpar or insignificant contributions to the bottom line. Too many underperforming businesses reduce the company's overall performance and ultimately limit growth in shareholder value.

- *Does the corporation have adequate financial strength to fund its different businesses and maintain a healthy credit rating?* A diversified company's strategy fails the resource fit test when the resource needs of its portfolio unduly stretch the company's financial health and threaten to impair its credit rating. Many of the world's largest banks, including Royal Bank of Scotland, Citigroup, and HSBC, recently found themselves so undercapitalized and financially overextended that they were forced to sell some of their business assets to meet regulatory requirements and restore public confidence in their solvency.

Examining a Diversified Company's Nonfinancial Resource Fit

A diversified company must also ensure that the nonfinancial resource needs of its portfolio of businesses are met by its corporate capabilities. Just as a diversified company must avoid allowing an excessive number of cash hungry businesses to jeopardize its financial stability, it should also avoid adding to the business lineup in ways that overly stretch such nonfinancial resources as managerial talent, technology and information systems, and marketing support.

- *Does the company have or can it develop the specific resources and competitive capabilities needed to be successful in each of its businesses?*[11] Sometimes the resources a company has accumulated in its core business prove to be a poor match with the competitive capabilities needed to succeed in businesses into which it has diversified. For instance, BTR, a multibusiness company in Great Britain, discovered that the company's resources and managerial skills were quite well suited for parenting industrial manufacturing businesses but not for parenting its distribution businesses (National Tyre Services and Texas-based Summers Group). As a result, BTR decided to divest its distribution businesses and focus exclusively on diversifying around small industrial manufacturing.

> Resource fit extends beyond financial resources to include a good fit between the company's resources and core competencies and the key success factors of each industry it has diversified into.

- *Are the company's resources being stretched too thinly by the resource requirements of one or more of its businesses?* A diversified company has to guard against overtaxing its resources, a condition that can arise when (1) it goes on an acquisition spree and management is called upon to assimilate and oversee many new businesses very quickly or (2) when it lacks sufficient resource depth to do a creditable job of transferring skills and competencies from one of its businesses to another.

Step 5: Ranking Business Units and Setting a Priority for Resource Allocation

Once a diversified company's businesses have been evaluated from the standpoints of industry attractiveness, competitive strength, strategic fit, and resource fit, the next step is to use this information to rank the performance prospects of the businesses from best to worst. Such rankings help top-level executives assign each business a priority for corporate resource support and new capital investment.

The locations of the different businesses in the nine-cell industry attractiveness/competitive strength matrix provide a solid basis for identifying high-opportunity businesses and low-opportunity businesses. Normally, competitively strong businesses in attractive industries have significantly better performance prospects than competitively weak businesses in unattractive industries. Also, normally, the revenue and earnings outlook for businesses in fast-growing businesses is better than for businesses in slow-growing businesses. As a rule, *business subsidiaries with the brightest profit and growth prospects, attractive positions in the nine-cell matrix, and solid strategic and resource fit should receive top priority for allocation of corporate resources.* However, in ranking the prospects of the different businesses from best to worst, it is usually wise to also consider each business's past performance as concerns sales growth, profit growth, contribution to company earnings, return on capital invested in the business, and cash flow from operations. While past performance is not always a reliable predictor of future performance, it does signal whether a business already has good to excellent performance or has problems to overcome.

Allocating Financial Resources   Figure 8.4 shows the chief strategic and financial options for allocating a diversified company's financial resources. Divesting businesses with the weakest future prospects and businesses that lack adequate strategic fit and/or resource fit is one of the best ways of generating additional funds for redeployment to businesses with better opportunities and better strategic and resource fit. Free cash flows from cash cow businesses also add to the pool of funds that can be usefully redeployed. *Ideally, a diversified company will have sufficient financial resources to strengthen or grow its existing businesses, make any new acquisitions that are desirable, fund other promising business opportunities, pay off existing debt, and periodically increase dividend payments to shareholders and/or repurchase shares of stock. But, as a practical matter, a company's financial resources are limited. Thus, for top executives to make the best use of the available funds, they must steer resources to those businesses with the best opportunities and performance prospects and allocate little if any resources to businesses with marginal or dim prospects—this is why ranking the performance prospects of the various businesses from best to worst is so crucial. Strategic uses of

FIGURE 8.4   **The Chief Strategic and Financial Options for Allocating a Diversified Company's Financial Resources**

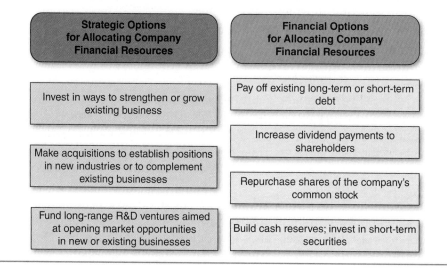

corporate financial resources (see Figure 8.4) should usually take precedence unless there is a compelling reason to strengthen the firm's balance sheet or better reward shareholders.

Step 6: Crafting New Strategic Moves to Improve the Overall Corporate Performance

LO5 Understand a diversified company's four main corporate strategy options for solidifying its diversification strategy and improving company performance.

The conclusions flowing from the five preceding analytical steps set the agenda for crafting strategic moves to improve a diversified company's overall performance. The strategic options boil down to four broad categories of actions:

1. Sticking closely with the existing business lineup and pursuing the opportunities these businesses present.

2. Broadening the company's business scope by making new acquisitions in new industries.

3. Divesting some businesses and retrenching to a narrower base of business operations.

4. Restructuring the company's business lineup and putting a whole new face on the company's business makeup.

Sticking Closely with the Existing Business Lineup   The option of sticking with the current business lineup makes sense when the company's present businesses offer attractive growth opportunities and can be counted on to generate good earnings and cash flows. As long as the company's set of existing businesses puts it in a good position for the future and these businesses have good strategic and/or resource fit, then rocking the boat with major changes in the company's business mix is usually unnecessary. Corporate executives can concentrate their attention on getting the best performance from each of the businesses, steering corporate resources into those areas of greatest potential and profitability. However, in the event that corporate executives are not entirely satisfied with the opportunities they see in the company's present set of businesses, they can opt for any of the three strategic alternatives listed in the following sections.

Broadening the Diversification Base Diversified companies sometimes find it desirable to add to the diversification base for any one of the same reasons a single-business company might pursue initial diversification. Sluggish growth in revenues or profits, vulnerability to seasonality or recessionary influences, potential for transferring resources and capabilities to other related businesses, or unfavorable driving forces facing core businesses are all reasons management of a diversified company might choose to broaden diversification. An additional, and often very important, motivating factor for adding new businesses is to complement and strengthen the market position and competitive capabilities of one or more of its present businesses. Procter & Gamble's acquisition of Gillette strengthened and extended P&G's reach into personal care and household products—Gillette's businesses included Oral-B toothbrushes, Gillette razors and razor blades, Duracell batteries, Braun shavers and small appliances (coffeemakers, mixers, hair dryers, and electric toothbrushes), and toiletries (Right Guard, Foamy, Soft & Dry, White Rain, and Dry Idea).

Divesting Some Businesses and Retrenching to a Narrower Diversification Base A number of diversified firms have had difficulty managing a diverse group of businesses and have elected to get out of some of them. Selling a business outright to another company is far and away the most frequently used option for divesting a business. Ford divested its Jaguar and Land Rover brands to the Tata Group of India in 2009

> Focusing corporate resources on a few core and mostly related businesses avoids the mistake of diversifying so broadly that resources and management attention are stretched too thin.

and then sold its Volvo brand to a Chinese conglomerate in 2010. But sometimes a business selected for divestiture has ample resources and capabilities to compete successfully on its own. In such cases, a corporate parent may elect to spin off the unwanted business as a financially and managerially independent company, either by selling shares to the public via an initial public offering or by distributing shares in the new company to shareholders of the corporate parent. Online travel company Expedia, Inc., spun off Trip Advisor as a public company in 2011, distributing shares to its shareholders. Expedia itself was spun off from IAC/InterActiveCorp in 2005.

Retrenching to a narrower diversification base is usually undertaken when top management concludes that its diversification strategy has ranged too far afield and that the company can improve long-term performance by concentrating on building stronger positions in a smaller number of core businesses and industries. But there are other important reasons for divesting one or more of a company's present businesses. Sometimes divesting a business has to be considered because market conditions in a once-attractive industry have badly deteriorated. A business can become a prime candidate for divestiture because it lacks adequate strategic or resource fit, because it is a cash hog with questionable long-term potential, or because it is weakly positioned in its industry with little prospect of earning a decent return on investment. Sometimes a company acquires businesses that, down the road, just do not work out as expected even though management has tried all it can think of to make them profitable. Other business units, despite adequate financial performance, may not mesh as well with the rest of the firm as was originally thought. For instance, PepsiCo divested its group of fast-food restaurant businesses to focus its resources on its core soft drink and snack foods businesses, where its resources and capabilities could add more value.

Evidence indicates that pruning businesses and narrowing a firm's diversification base improves corporate performance.[12] Corporate parents often end up selling businesses too late and at too low a price, sacrificing shareholder value.[13] A useful guide to determine whether or when to divest a business subsidiary is to ask, "If we were not in this business today, would we want to get into it now?"[14] When the answer is no or probably not, divestiture should be considered. Another signal that a business should become a divestiture candidate is whether it is worth more to another company than to the present parent; in such cases, shareholders would be well served if the company were to sell the business and collect a premium price from the buyer for whom the business is a valuable fit.[15]

Selling a business outright to another company is far and away the most frequently used option for divesting a business. But sometimes a business selected for divestiture has ample resources to compete successfully on its own. In such cases, a corporate parent may elect to spin the unwanted business off as a financially and managerially independent company, either by selling shares to the investing public via an initial public offering or by distributing shares in the new company to existing shareholders of the corporate parent.

Broadly Restructuring the Business Lineup through a Mix of Divestitures and New Acquisitions

Corporate **restructuring** strategies involve divesting some businesses and acquiring others so as to put a new face on the company's business lineup. Performing radical surgery on a company's group of businesses is an appealing corporate strategy when its financial performance is squeezed or eroded by:

> **CORE CONCEPT**
>
> **Corporate restructuring** involves radically altering the business lineup by divesting businesses that lack strategic fit or are poor performers and acquiring new businesses that offer better promise for enhancing shareholder value.

- Too many businesses in slow-growth, declining, low-margin, or otherwise unattractive industries.
- Too many competitively weak businesses.
- An excessive debt burden with interest costs that eat deeply into profitability.
- Ill-chosen acquisitions that haven't lived up to expectations.

Candidates for divestiture in a corporate restructuring effort typically include not only weak or up-and-down performers or those in unattractive industries but also business units that lack strategic fit with the businesses to be retained, businesses that are cash hogs or that lack other types of resource fit, and businesses incompatible with the company's revised diversification strategy (even though they may be profitable or in an attractive industry).

CONCEPTS & CONNECTIONS 8.1

KRAFT FOODS' CORPORATE RESTRUCTURING PLAN TO PURSUE GROWTH AND BOOST SHAREHOLDER VALUE

In 2012, Kraft Foods, the 90-year-old darling of the consumer packaged goods industry, moved to improve its long-term performance by *restructuring* the corporation—the latest move in a series by CEO Irene Rosenfeld, who was brought in to turn around the company's performance. In addition to trimming operations, the restructuring plan called for dividing the enterprise into two separate units: a $32 billion fast-growing global snacks business that included Oreo and Cadbury (the British confectionary acquired in 2010), and a North American grocery unit that included Kraft Macaroni and Cheese, Oscar Mayer, and other nonsnack brands. With this radical new operational structure in place, Kraft hoped to improve its ability to focus on new opportunities and pursue profitable growth.

Managing these two large and very different businesses jointly had made it difficult for Kraft to act nimbly and adapt to changing market conditions. It also inhibited the company from executing new strategies free from significant portfolio-wide considerations. In announcing her intention to split the company in September 2011, CEO Irene Rosenfeld said, "Simply put, we have now reached a point where North American grocery and global snacks will each benefit from standing on its own and focusing on its unique drivers for success." She noted that as separate businesses, "each will have the leadership, resources, and mandate to realize its full potential."

Before the split, Kraft undertook additional restructuring efforts in its U.S. sales operations, including reducing the number of management centers and selling some underperforming brands. Although in refashioning the company Kraft loses some of the operational benefits it enjoyed as a single entity, managers and investors hope the move will ultimately improve the company's ability to sustain profitable growth and increase shareholder value.

Developed with Maximilian A. Pinto.

Sources: Sam Webb, "New Reality Makes Kraft Split Vital," *Food Global News,* September 2011; E. J. Schultz, "Could Kraft Split Be a Blueprint for Blue Chips?" *Advertising Age* 82, no. 29 (August 8, 2011); www.nytimes.com/2007/02/21/business/21kraft.html (accessed March 2, 2012); http://stocks.investopedia.com/stock-analysis/2012/Cozying-Up-To-Kraft-KFT-CPB-K-HNZ0227.aspx#axzz1nzOMjDex (accessed March 2, 2012).

As businesses are divested, corporate restructuring generally involves aligning the remaining business units into groups with the best strategic fit and then redeploying the cash flows from the divested business to either pay down debt or make new acquisitions.

Over the past decade, corporate restructuring has become a popular strategy at many diversified companies, especially those that had diversified broadly into many different industries and lines of business. VF Corporation, maker of North Face and other popular "lifestyle" apparel brands, has used a restructuring strategy to provide its shareholders with returns that are more than five times greater than shareholder returns for competing apparel makers. Since its acquisition and turnaround of North Face in 2000, VF has spent nearly $5 billion to acquire 19 additional businesses, including about $2 billion in 2011 for Timberland. New apparel brands acquired by VF Corporation include 7 For All Mankind sportswear, Vans skateboard shoes, Nautica, John Varvatos, Reef surf wear, and Lucy athletic wear. By 2012, VF Corporation had become one of the most profitable apparel and footwear companies in the world, with net earnings of nearly $1.1 billion on revenues of $10.9 billion. It was listed as number 277 on *Fortune*'s 2012 list of the 500 largest U.S. companies. Concepts & Connections 8.1 discusses how Kraft Foods underwent a major restructuring that split the corporation into two companies in an attempt to boost shareholder value.

1. The purpose of diversification is to build shareholder value. Diversification builds shareholder value when a diversified group of businesses can perform better under the auspices of a single corporate parent than they would as independent, stand-alone businesses—the goal is to achieve not just a $1 + 1 = 2$ result but rather to realize important $1 + 1 = 3$ performance benefits. Whether getting into a new business has potential to enhance shareholder value hinges on whether a company's entry into that business can pass the attractiveness test, the cost-of-entry test, and the better-off test.

2. Entry into new businesses can take any of three forms: acquisition, internal development, or joint venture/strategic partnership. Each has its pros and cons, but acquisition usually provides quickest entry into a new entry; internal development takes the longest to produce home-run results; and joint venture/strategic partnership tends to be the least durable.

3. There are two fundamental approaches to diversification—into related businesses and into unrelated businesses. The rationale for *related* diversification is based on cross-business *strategic fit:* Diversify into businesses with strategic fit along their respective value chains, capitalize on strategic-fit relationships to gain competitive advantage, and then use competitive advantage to achieve the desired $1 + 1 = 3$ impact on shareholder value.

4. *Unrelated diversification* strategies surrender the competitive advantage potential of strategic fit. Given the absence of cross-business strategic fit, the task of building shareholder value through a strategy of unrelated diversification hinges on the ability of the parent company to (1) do a superior job of identifying and acquiring new businesses that can produce consistently good earnings and returns on investment; (2) do an excellent job of negotiating favorable acquisition prices; and (3) do such a good job of overseeing and parenting the collection of businesses that they perform at a higher level than they would on their own efforts. The greater the number of businesses a company has diversified into and the more diverse these businesses are, the harder it is for corporate executives to select capable managers to run each business, know when the major strategic proposals of business units are sound, or decide on a wise course of recovery when a business unit stumbles.

5. Evaluating a company's diversification strategy is a six-step process:
    *   Step 1: *Evaluate the long-term attractiveness of the industries into which the firm has diversified.* Determining industry attractiveness involves developing a list of industry attractiveness measures, each of which might have a different importance weight.
    *   Step 2: *Evaluate the relative competitive strength of each of the company's business units.* The purpose of rating each business's competitive strength is to gain clear understanding of which businesses are strong contenders in their industries, which are weak contenders, and the underlying reasons for their strength or weakness. The conclusions about industry attractiveness can be joined with the conclusions about competitive strength by drawing an industry attractiveness–competitive strength matrix that helps identify the prospects of each business and what priority each business should be given in allocating corporate resources and investment capital.
    *   Step 3: *Check for cross-business strategic fit.* A business is more attractive strategically when it has value chain relationships with sibling business units

that offer the potential to (1) realize economies of scope or cost-saving efficiencies; (2) transfer technology, skills, know-how, or other resources and
capabilities from one business to another; and/or (3) leverage use of a well-
known and trusted brand name. Cross-business strategic fit represents a
significant avenue for producing competitive advantage beyond what any
one business can achieve on its own.

- Step 4: *Check whether the firm's resources fit the requirements of its present business lineup.* Resource fit exists when (1) businesses, individually, strengthen
a company's overall mix of resources and capabilities and (2) a company has
sufficient resources to support its entire group of businesses without spreading
itself too thin. One important test of financial resource fit involves determining
whether a company has ample cash cows and not too many cash hogs.

- Step 5: *Rank the performance prospects of the businesses from best to worst and
determine what the corporate parent's priority should be in allocating resources to
its various businesses.* The most important considerations in judging business-
unit performance are sales growth, profit growth, contribution to company
earnings, cash flow characteristics, and the return on capital invested in the
business. Normally, strong business units in attractive industries should
head the list for corporate resource support.

- Step 6: *Crafting new strategic moves to improve overall corporate performance.*
This step entails using the results of the preceding analysis as the basis for
selecting one of four different strategic paths for improving a diversified
company's performance: *(a)* Stick closely with the existing business lineup
and pursue opportunities presented by these businesses, *(b)* broaden the
scope of diversification by entering additional industries, *(c)* retrench to a
narrower scope of diversification by divesting poorly performing businesses,
and *(d)* broadly restructure the business lineup with multiple divestitures
and/or acquisitions.

▶ ASSURANCE OF LEARNING EXERCISES

1. See if you can identify the value chain relationships that make the businesses of
the following companies related in competitively relevant ways. In particular, you
should consider whether there are cross-business opportunities for *(a)* transferring
competitively valuable resources, expertise, technological know-how and other
capabilities, *(b)* cost sharing where value chain activities can be combined, and/or
(c) leveraging use of a well-respected brand name.

LO1, LO2,
LO3, LO4

Mc Graw Hill Education **connect**

OSI Restaurant Partners

- Outback Steakhouse.
- Carrabba's Italian Grill.
- Roy's Restaurant (Hawaiian fusion cuisine).
- Bonefish Grill (market-fresh fine seafood).
- Fleming's Prime Steakhouse & Wine Bar.
- Lee Roy Selmon's (Southern comfort food).
- Cheeseburger in Paradise.
- Blue Coral Seafood & Spirits (fine seafood).

L'Oréal

- Maybelline, Lancôme, Helena Rubinstein, Kiehl's, Garner, and Shu Uemura cosmetics.
- L'Oréal and Soft Sheen/Carson hair care products.
- Redken, Matrix, L'Oréal Professional, and Kerastase Paris professional hair care and skin care products.
- Ralph Lauren and Giorgio Armani fragrances.
- Biotherm skin care products.
- La Roche–Posay and Vichy Laboratories dermocosmetics.

Johnson & Johnson

- Baby products (powder, shampoo, oil, lotion).
- Band-Aids and other first-aid products.
- Women's health and personal care products (Stayfree, Carefree, Sure & Natural).
- Neutrogena and Aveeno skin care products.
- Nonprescription drugs (Tylenol, Motrin, Pepcid AC, Mylanta, Monistat).
- Prescription drugs.
- Prosthetic and other medical devices.
- Surgical and hospital products.
- Acuvue contact lenses.

LO1, LO2, LO3, LO4

2. Peruse the business group listings for United Technologies shown below and listed at its website (www.utc.com). How would you characterize the company's corporate strategy? Related diversification, unrelated diversification, or a combination related-unrelated diversification strategy? Explain your answer.

Carrier—the world's largest provider of air-conditioning, heating, and refrigeration solutions.

Hamilton Sundstrand—technologically advanced aerospace and industrial products.

Otis—the world's leading manufacturer, installer, and maintainer of elevators, escalators, and moving walkways.

Pratt & Whitney—designs, manufactures, services, and supports aircraft engines, industrial gas turbines, and space propulsion systems.

Sikorsky—a world leader in helicopter design, manufacture, and service.

UTC Fire & Security—fire and security systems developed for commercial, industrial, and residential customers.

UTC Power—a full-service provider of environmentally advanced power solutions.

LO1, LO2, LO3, LO4, LO5

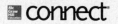

3. ITT is a technology-oriented engineering and manufacturing company with the following business divisions and products:

Industrial Process Division—industrial pumps, valves, and monitoring and control systems; aftermarket services for the chemical, oil and gas, mining, pulp and paper, power, and biopharmaceutical markets.

Motion Technologies Division—durable brake pads, shock absorbers, and damping technologies for the automotive and rail markets.

Interconnect Solutions—connectors and fittings for the production of automobiles, aircraft, railcars and locomotives, oil field equipment, medical equipment, and industrial equipment.

Control Technologies—energy absorption and vibration dampening equipment, transducers and regulators, and motion controls used in the production of robotics, medical equipment, automobiles, sub-sea equipment, industrial equipment, aircraft, and military vehicles.

Based on the above listing, would you say that ITT's business lineup reflects a strategy of related diversification, unrelated diversification, or a combination of related and unrelated diversification? What benefits are generated from any strategic fit existing between ITT's businesses? Also, what types of companies should ITT consider acquiring that might improve shareholder value? Justify your answer.

EXERCISES FOR SIMULATION PARTICIPANTS

1. In the event that your company had the opportunity to diversify into other products or businesses of your choosing, would you opt to pursue related diversification, unrelated diversification, or a combination of both? Explain why.   **LO1, LO2, LO3**

2. What specific resources and capabilities does your company possess that would make it attractive to diversify into related businesses? Indicate what kinds of strategic fit benefits could be captured by transferring these resources and competitive capabilities to newly acquired related businesses.   **LO1, LO2**

3. If your company opted to pursue a strategy of related diversification, what industries or product categories could your company diversify into that would allow it to achieve economies of scope? Name at least two or three such industries/product categories and indicate the specific kinds of cost savings that might accrue from entry into each of these businesses/product categories.   **LO1, LO2**

4. If your company opted to pursue a strategy of related diversification, what industries or product categories could your company diversify into that would allow your company to capitalize on using your company's present brand name and corporate image to good advantage in these newly entered businesses or product categories? Name at least two or three such industries or product categories and indicate *the specific benefits* that might be captured by transferring your company's brand name to each of these other businesses/product categories.   **LO1, LO2, LO3, LO4, LO5**

   Would you prefer to pursue a strategy of related or unrelated diversification? Why?

ENDNOTES

1. Constantinos C. Markides, "To Diversify or Not to Diversify," *Harvard Business Review* 75, no. 6 (November–December 1997).

2. Michael E. Porter, "From Competitive Advantage to Corporate Strategy," *Harvard Business Review* 45, no. 3 (May–June 1987).

3. Michael E. Porter, *Competitive Strategy: Techniques for Analyzing Industries and Competitors* (New York: Free Press, 1980).

4. Yves L. Doz and Gary Hamel, *Alliance Advantage: The Art of Creating Value through Partnering* (Boston: Harvard Business School Press, 1998).

5. Michael E. Porter, *Competitive Advantage* (New York: Free Press, 1985); and Constantinos C. Markides and Peter J. Williamson, "Corporate Diversification and Organization Structure: A Resource-Based View," *Academy of Management Journal* 39, no. 2 (April 1996).

6. Jeanne M. Liedtka, "Collaboration across Lines of Business for Competitive Advantage," *Academy of Management Executive* 10, no. 2 (May 1996).

7. Kathleen M. Eisenhardt and D. Charles Galunic, "Coevolving: At Last, a Way to Make Synergies Work," *Harvard Business Review* 78, no. 1 (January–February 2000); and Constantinos C. Markides and Peter J. Williamson, "Related Diversification, Core Competencies and Corporate Performance," *Strategic Management Journal* 15 (Summer 1994).

8. A. Campbell, M. Goold, and M. Alexander, "Corporate Strategy: The Quest for Parenting Advantage,"

Harvard Business Review 73, no. 2 (March–April 1995); and Cynthia A. Montgomery and Birger Wernerfelt, "Diversification, Ricardian Rents, and Tobin-Q," *RAND Journal of Economics* 19, no. 4 (1988).

9. Patricia L. Anslinger and Thomas E. Copeland, "Growth through Acquisitions: A Fresh Look," *Harvard Business Review* 74, no. 1 (January–February 1996).

10. Lawrence G. Franko, "The Death of Diversification? The Focusing of the World's Industrial Firms, 1980–2000," *Business Horizons* 47, no. 4 (July–August 2004).

11. Andrew Campbell, Michael Gould, and Marcus Alexander, "Corporate

Strategy: The Quest for Parenting Advantage," *Harvard Business Review* 73, no. 2 (March–April 1995).

12. Constantinos C. Markides, "Diversification, Restructuring, and Economic Performance," *Strategic Management Journal* 16 (February 1995).

13. Lee Dranikoff, Tim Koller, and Antoon Schneider, "Divestiture: Strategy's Missing Link," *Harvard Business Review* 80, no. 5 (May 2002).

14. Peter F. Drucker, *Management: Tasks, Responsibilities, Practices* (New York: Harper & Row, 1974).

15. David J. Collis and Cynthia A. Montgomery, "Creating Corporate Advantage," *Harvard Business Review* 76, no. 3 (May–June 1998).

Ethics, Corporate Social Responsibility, Environmental Sustainability, and Strategy

LEARNING OBJECTIVES

LO1 Understand why the standards of ethical behavior in business are no different from ethical standards in general.

LO2 Recognize conditions that give rise to unethical business strategies and behavior.

LO3 Gain an understanding of the costs of business ethics failures.

LO4 Learn the concepts of corporate social responsibility and environmental sustainability and how companies balance these duties with economic responsibilities to shareholders.

Clearly, a company has a responsibility to make a profit and grow the business, but just as clearly, a company and its personnel also have a duty to obey the law and play by the rules of fair competition. But does a company have a duty to go beyond legal requirements and operate according to the ethical norms of the societies in which it operates? And does it have a duty or obligation to contribute to the betterment of society independent of the needs and preferences of the customers it serves? Should a company display a social conscience and devote a portion of its resources to bettering society? Should its strategic initiatives be screened for possible negative effects on future generations of the world's population?

This chapter focuses on whether a company, in the course of trying to craft and execute a strategy that delivers value to both customers and shareholders, also has a duty to (1) act in an ethical manner, (2) demonstrate socially responsible behavior by being a committed corporate citizen, and (3) adopt business practices that conserve natural resources, protect the interest of future generations, and preserve the well-being of the planet.

What Do We Mean by *Business Ethics?*

LO1 Understand why the standards of ethical behavior in business are no different from ethical standards in general.

Business ethics is the application of ethical principles and standards to the actions and decisions of business organizations and the conduct of their personnel.[1] Ethical principles in business are not materially different from ethical principles in general because business actions have to be judged in the context of society's standards of right and wrong. There is not a special set of rules that businesspeople decide to apply to their own conduct. If dishonesty is considered unethical and immoral, then dishonest behavior in business—whether it relates to customers, suppliers, employees, or shareholders—qualifies as equally unethical and immoral. If being ethical entails adhering to generally accepted norms about conduct that is right and wrong, then managers must consider such norms when crafting and executing strategy.

CORE CONCEPT

Business ethics involves the application of general ethical principles to the actions and decisions of businesses and the conduct of their personnel.

While most company managers are careful to ensure that a company's strategy is within the bounds of what is legal, evidence indicates they are not always so careful to ensure that their strategies are within the bounds of what is considered ethical. In recent years, there have been revelations of ethical misconduct on the part of managers at such companies as Enron, Tyco International, HealthSouth, Adelphia, Royal Dutch/Shell, Parmalat (an Italy-based food products company), Rite Aid, Mexican oil giant Pemex, AIG, Citigroup, several leading brokerage houses, mutual fund companies and investment banking firms, and a host of mortgage lenders. The consequences of crafting strategies that cannot pass the test of moral scrutiny are manifested in sharp drops in stock price that cost shareholders billions of dollars, devastating public relations hits, sizable fines, and criminal indictments and convictions of company executives.

Drivers of Unethical Strategies and Business Behavior

Apart from "the business of business is business, not ethics" kind of thinking apparent in recent high-profile business scandals, three other main drivers of unethical business behavior also stand out:[2]

LO2 Recognize conditions that give rise to unethical business strategies and behavior.

- *Overzealous pursuit of wealth and other selfish interests.* People who are obsessed with wealth accumulation, greed, power, status, and other selfish interests often push ethical principles aside in their quest for self-gain. Driven by their ambitions, they exhibit few qualms in skirting the rules or doing whatever is necessary to achieve their goals. The first and only priority of such corporate "bad apples" is to look out for their own best interests, and if climbing the ladder of success means having few scruples and ignoring the welfare of others, so be it. The U.S. government has been conducting a multiyear investigation of insider trading, the illegal practice of exchanging confidential information to gain an advantage in the stock market. Focusing on the hedge fund industry and nicknamed "Operation Perfect Hedge," the investigation has brought to light scores of violations and led to more than 60 guilty pleas or convictions by early 2012. Among the most prominent of those convicted was Raj Rajaratnam, the former head of Galleon Group, who was sentenced to 11 years in prison and fined $10 million. In January 2012, seven hedge fund managers, described as a "circle of friends who formed a criminal club," were charged with reaping nearly $62 million in illegal profits on trades of Dell Inc.[3]

- *Heavy pressures on company managers to meet or beat performance targets.* When key personnel find themselves scrambling to meet the quarterly and annual sales and profit expectations of investors and financial analysts or to hit other ambitious performance targets, they often feel enormous pressure to *do whatever it takes* to protect their reputation for delivering good results. As the pressure builds, they start stretching the rules further and further, until the limits of ethical conduct are overlooked.[4] Once people cross ethical boundaries to "meet or beat their numbers," the threshold for making more extreme ethical compromises becomes lower. In 2010, ATM maker Diebold, Inc., was fined $25 million for engaging in a fraudulent accounting scheme to inflate the company's earnings. Three of Diebold's former financial executives were also charged with manipulating the company's books to meet earnings forecasts.[5] More recently, an investigation into a decade-long cover-up of investment losses by the Japanese camera maker Olympus resulted in the 2012 arrest of seven executives on suspicion of violation of Japanese securities laws.

- *A company culture that puts profitability and good business performance ahead of ethical behavior.* When a company's culture spawns an ethically corrupt or amoral work climate, people have a company-approved license to ignore "what's right" and engage in most any behavior or employ most any strategy they think they can get away with. Such cultural norms as "everyone else does it" and "it is OK to bend the rules to get the job done" permeate the work environment. At such companies, ethically immoral or amoral people are certain to play down observance of ethical strategic actions and business conduct. Moreover, cultural pressures to utilize unethical means if circumstances become challenging can prompt otherwise honorable people to behave unethically. Enron's leaders created a culture that pressured company personnel to be innovative and aggressive in figuring out how to grow current earnings—regardless of the methods. Enron's annual "rank and yank" performance evaluation process, in which the lowest-ranking 15 to 20 percent of employees were let go, made it abundantly clear that bottom-line results were what mattered most. The name of the game at Enron became devising clever ways to boost revenues and earnings, even if this sometimes meant operating outside established policies. In fact, outside-the-lines behavior was celebrated if it generated profitable new business.

The Business Case for Ethical Strategies

LO3 Gain an understanding of the costs of business ethics failures.

While it is undoubtedly true that unethical business behavior may sometimes contribute to higher company profits (*so long as such behavior escapes public scrutiny*), deliberate pursuit of unethical strategies and tolerance of unethical conduct is a risky practice from both a shareholder perspective and a reputational standpoint. Figure 9.1 shows the wide-ranging costs a company can incur when unethical behavior is discovered and it is forced to make amends for its behavior. The more egregious a company's ethical violations, the higher are the costs and the bigger the damage to its reputation (and to the reputations of the company personnel involved). In high-profile instances, the costs of ethical misconduct can easily run into the hundreds of millions and even billions of dollars, especially if they provoke widespread public outrage and many people were harmed.

The fallout of ethical misconduct on the part of a company goes well beyond just the costs of making amends for the misdeeds. Buyers shun companies known for their shady behavior. Companies known to have engaged in unethical conduct have difficulty recruiting and retaining talented employees.[6] Most ethically upstanding people don't want to get entrapped in a compromising situation, nor do they want their personal reputations tarnished by the actions of an unsavory employer. A company's unethical behavior risks considerable damage to shareholders in the form of lost revenues, higher costs, lower profits, lower stock prices, and a diminished business reputation. To a significant degree, therefore, ethical strategies and ethical conduct are *good business*. Many companies have a code of ethics governing how they will conduct business—in the United States, the Sarbanes-Oxley Act, enacted in 2002, requires that

> Shareholders suffer major damage when a company's unethical behavior is discovered and punished. Making amends for unethical business conduct is costly, and it takes years to rehabilitate a tarnished company reputation.

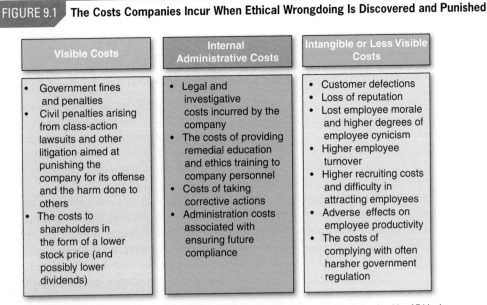

FIGURE 9.1 The Costs Companies Incur When Ethical Wrongdoing Is Discovered and Punished

Visible Costs	Internal Administrative Costs	Intangible or Less Visible Costs
• Government fines and penalties • Civil penalties arising from class-action lawsuits and other litigation aimed at punishing the company for its offense and the harm done to others • The costs to shareholders in the form of a lower stock price (and possibly lower dividends)	• Legal and investigative costs incurred by the company • The costs of providing remedial education and ethics training to company personnel • Costs of taking corrective actions • Administration costs associated with ensuring future compliance	• Customer defections • Loss of reputation • Lost employee morale and higher degrees of employee cynicism • Higher employee turnover • Higher recruiting costs and difficulty in attracting employees • Adverse effects on employee productivity • The costs of complying with often harsher government regulation

Source: Adapted from Terry Thomas, John R. Schermerhorn, and John W. Dienhart, "Strategic Leadership of Ethical Behavior," *Academy of Management Executive* 18, no. 2 (May 2004), p. 58.

companies whose stock is publicly traded have a code of ethics or else explain in writing to the Securities and Exchange Commission why they do not.

Ensuring a Strong Commitment to Business Ethics in Companies with International Operations

Notions of right and wrong, fair and unfair, moral and immoral, ethical and unethical are present in all societies, organizations, and individuals. But there are three schools of thought about the extent to which the ethical standards travel across cultures and whether multinational companies can apply the same set of ethical standards in all of the locations where they operate. Concepts & Connections 9.1 describes the difficulties Apple has faced in trying to enforce a common set of ethical standards across its vast global supplier network.

The School of Ethical Universalism

According to the school of **ethical universalism**, some concepts of what is right and what is wrong are *universal* and transcend most all cultures, societies, and religions.[7] For instance, being truthful strikes a chord of what's right in the peoples of all nations. Ethical norms considered universal by many ethicists include honesty, trustworthiness, respecting the rights of others, practicing the Golden Rule, and avoiding

> **CORE CONCEPT**
>
> According to the school of **ethical universalism,** the same standards of what's ethical and what's unethical resonate with peoples of most societies regardless of local traditions and cultural norms; hence, common ethical standards can be used to judge employee conduct in a variety of country markets and cultural circumstances.

CONCEPTS & CONNECTIONS 9.1

APPLE'S CHALLENGES IN ENFORCING ITS SUPPLIER CODE OF CONDUCT

Apple requires its suppliers to comply with the company's Supplier Code of Conduct as a condition of being awarded contracts. To ensure compliance, Apple has a monitoring program that includes audits of supplier factories, corrective action plans, and verification measures. In the company's 26-page 2012 progress report on supplier responsibility, Apple reported that in 2011 it conducted 229 audits of supplier facilities in such countries as China, the Czech Republic, Malaysia, the Philippines, Singapore, South Korea, Taiwan, Thailand, and the United States. More than 100 of these audits were first-time audits.

Apple distinguishes among the seriousness of infractions, designating "core violations" as those that go directly against the core principles of its Supplier Code of Conduct and must be remedied immediately. During the 2011 audits, core violations were discovered in 35 facilities, including cases of underage labor, excessive recruitment fees, improper hazardous waste disposal, and deliberately falsified audit records. Apple responded by ensuring that immediate corrective actions were taken, placing violators on probation, and planning to audit them again in a year's time.

While Apple's final-assembly manufacturers had high compliance scores for most categories, suppliers did not fare very well in terms of working hours. At 93 of the audited facilities, workers were required to work more than 60 hours per week—Apple sets a maximum of 60 hours per week (except in unusual or emergency circumstances). In 90 of the audited facilities, workers were found to have been required to work more than six consecutive days a week at least once per month—Apple requires at least one day of rest per seven days of work (except in unusual or emergency circumstances). At 108 facilities, Apple also found that overtime wages had been calculated improperly, resulting in underpayment of overtime compensation.

Apple requires suppliers to provide a safe working environment and to eliminate physical hazards to employees where possible. But the 2011 audits revealed that workers were not wearing appropriate protective personal equipment at 58 facilities. Violations were found at 126 facilities where unlicensed workers were operating equipment. Moreover, the audits revealed that 74 supplier facilities did not have any personnel assigned to ensuring compliance with Apple's Supplier Code of Conduct.

For Apple, the audits represent a starting point for bringing its suppliers into compliance, through greater scrutiny, education and training of suppliers' personnel, and incentives. Apple collects quarterly data to hold its suppliers accountable for their actions and makes procurement decisions based, in part, on these numbers. Suppliers that are unable to meet Apple's high standards of conduct ultimately end up losing Apple's business.

Sources: Apple, *Apple Supplier Responsibility 2012 Progress Report,* January 13, 2012, http://images.apple.com/supplierresponsibility/pdf/Apple_SR_2012_Progress_Report.pdf (accessed June 25, 2013); Nick Wingfield and Charles Duhigg, "Apple Lists Its Suppliers for 1st Time," *Nytimes.com*, January 13, 2012, www.nytimes.com/2012/01/14/technology/apple-releases-list-of-its-suppliers-for-the-first-time.html (accessed March 2, 2012).

unnecessary harm to workers or to the users of the company's product or service.[8] *To the extent there is common moral agreement about right and wrong actions and behaviors across multiple cultures and countries, there exists a set of universal ethical standards to which all societies, companies, and individuals can be held accountable.* The strength of ethical universalism is that it draws upon the collective views of multiple societies and cultures to put some clear boundaries on what constitutes ethical business behavior no matter what country market its personnel are operating in. This means that in those instances where basic moral standards really do not vary significantly according to local cultural beliefs, traditions, or religious convictions, a multinational company can develop a code of ethics that it applies more or less evenly across its worldwide operations.

The School of Ethical Relativism

Beyond widely accepted ethical norms, many ethical standards likely vary from one country to another because of divergent religious beliefs, social customs, and prevailing political and economic doctrines (whether a country leans more toward a capitalistic market economy or one heavily dominated by socialistic or communistic principles). The school of **ethical relativism** holds that when there are national or cross-cultural differences in what is deemed an ethical or unethical business situation, it is appropriate for local moral standards to take precedence over what the ethical standards may be in a company's home market. The thesis is that whatever a culture thinks is right or wrong really is right or wrong for that culture.[9]

> **CORE CONCEPT**
>
> According to the school of **ethical relativism**, different societal cultures and customs create divergent standards of right and wrong—thus, what is ethical or unethical must be judged in the light of local customs and social mores and can vary from one culture or nation to another.

A company that adopts the principle of ethical relativism and holds company personnel to local ethical standards necessarily assumes that what prevails as local morality is an adequate guide to ethical behavior. This can be ethically dangerous; it leads to the conclusion that if a country's culture generally accepts bribery or environmental degradation or exposing workers to dangerous conditions, then managers working in that country are free to engage in such activities. Adopting such a position places a company in a perilous position if it is required to defend these activi-

> Codes of conduct based upon ethical relativism can be *ethically dangerous* by creating a maze of conflicting ethical standards for multinational companies.

ties to its stakeholders in countries with higher ethical expectations. Moreover, from a global markets perspective, ethical relativism results in a maze of conflicting ethical standards for multinational companies. Imagine, for example, that a multinational company in the name of ethical relativism takes the position that it is acceptable for company personnel to pay bribes and kickbacks in countries where such payments are customary but forbids company personnel from making such payments in those countries where bribes and kickbacks are considered unethical or illegal. Having thus adopted conflicting ethical standards for operating in different countries, company managers have little moral basis for enforcing ethical standards companywide—rather, the clear message to employees would be that the company has no ethical standards or principles of its own, preferring to let its practices be governed by the countries in which it operates.

Integrative Social Contracts Theory

Integrative social contracts theory provides a middle position between the opposing views of universalism and relativism.[10] According to **integrative social contracts theory**, the ethical standards a company should try to uphold are governed both by (1) a limited number of universal ethical principles that are widely recognized as putting legitimate ethical boundaries on actions and behavior in *all* situations and (2) the circumstances of local cultures, traditions, and shared values that further prescribe what constitutes ethically permissible

CORE CONCEPT

According to **integrative social contracts theory,** universal ethical principles based on collective views of multiple cultures combine to form a "social contract" that all employees in all country markets have a duty to observe. Within the boundaries of this social contract, there is room for host-country cultures to exert *some* influence in setting their own moral and ethical standards. However, *"first-order"* universal ethical norms always take precedence over *"second-order"* local ethical norms in circumstances where local ethical norms are more permissive.

behavior and what does not. This "social contract" by which managers in all situations have a duty to serve provides that *"first-order" universal ethical norms always take precedence over "second-order" local ethical norms in circumstances where local ethical norms are more permissive.* Integrative social contracts theory offers managers in multinational companies clear guidance in resolving cross-country ethical differences: Those parts of the company's code of ethics that involve universal ethical norms must be enforced worldwide, but within these boundaries there is room for ethical diversity and opportunity for host-country cultures to exert *some* influence in setting their own moral and ethical standards.

A good example of the application of integrative social contracts theory involves the payment of bribes and kickbacks. Bribes and kickbacks seem to be common in some countries, but does this justify paying them? Just because bribery flourishes in a country does not mean that it is an authentic or legitimate ethical norm. Virtually all of the world's major religions (Buddhism, Christianity, Confucianism, Hinduism, Islam, Judaism, Sikhism, and Taoism) and all moral schools of thought condemn bribery and corruption.[11] Therefore, a multinational company might reasonably conclude that the right ethical standard is one of refusing to condone bribery and kickbacks on the part of company personnel no matter what the second-order local norm is and no matter what the sales consequences are. An example of the application of integrative social contracts theory that allows second-order local customs to set ethical boundaries involves employee recruiting and selection practices. A company that has adopted a first-order universal norm of equal opportunity in the workplace might allow applicants to include photographs with résumés in countries where such is the norm. Managers in the United States are prohibited by law from accepting employment applications including a photograph, but managers in Europe would find it very unusual for an application to not be accompanied by a photograph of the applicant. A policy that prohibited managers from accepting applications containing a photo of the applicant would result in almost all applications being rejected. But even with the guidance provided by integrative social contracts theory, there are many instances where cross-country differences in ethical norms create "gray areas" where it is tough to draw a line in the sand between right and wrong decisions, actions, and business practices.

LO4 Learn the concepts of corporate social responsibility and environmental sustainability and how companies balance these duties with economic responsibilities to shareholders.

Strategy, Corporate Social Responsibility, and Environmental Sustainability

The idea that businesses have an obligation to foster social betterment, a much-debated topic in the past 50 years, took root in the nineteenth century when progressive companies in the aftermath of the industrial revolution began to provide workers with housing and other amenities. The notion that corporate executives should balance the interests of all stakeholders—shareholders, employees, customers, suppliers, the communities in which they operated, and society at large—began to blossom in the 1960s.

What Do We Mean by *Corporate Social Responsibility?*

The essence of socially responsible business behavior is that a company should balance strategic actions to benefit shareholders against the *duty* to be a good corporate citizen. The underlying thesis is that company managers should display a *social conscience* in operating the business and specifically consider how management decisions and company actions affect the well-being of employees, local communities, the environment, and society at large.[12] Acting in a socially responsible manner thus encompasses more than just participating in community service projects and donating monies to charities and other worthy social causes. Demonstrating **corporate social responsibility (CSR)** also entails undertaking actions that earn trust and respect from all stakeholders—operating in an honorable and ethical manner, striving to make the company a great place to work, demonstrating genuine respect for the environment, and trying to make a difference in bettering society. Corporate social responsibility programs commonly involve:

> **CORE CONCEPT**
>
> **Corporate social responsibility (CSR)** refers to a company's *duty* to operate in an honorable manner, provide good working conditions for employees, encourage workforce diversity, be a good steward of the environment, and actively work to better the quality of life in the local communities where it operates and in society at large.

- *Efforts to employ an ethical strategy and observe ethical principles in operating the business.* A sincere commitment to observing ethical principles is a necessary component of a CSR strategy simply because unethical conduct is incompatible with the concept of good corporate citizenship and socially responsible business behavior.

- *Making charitable contributions, supporting community service endeavors, engaging in broader philanthropic initiatives, and reaching out to make a difference in the lives of the disadvantaged.* Some companies fulfill their philanthropic obligations by spreading their efforts over a multitude of charitable and community activities—for instance, Microsoft and Johnson & Johnson support a broad variety of community, art, and social welfare programs. Others prefer to focus their energies more narrowly. McDonald's, for example, concentrates on sponsoring the Ronald McDonald House program (which provides a home away from home for the families of seriously ill children receiving treatment at nearby hospitals). British Telecom gives 1 percent of its profits directly to communities, largely for education—teacher training, in-school workshops, and digital technology. Leading prescription drug maker GlaxoSmithKline and other pharmaceutical companies either donate or heavily discount medicines for distribution in the least-developed nations. Companies frequently reinforce their philanthropic efforts by encouraging employees to support charitable causes and participate in community affairs, often through programs that match employee contributions.

- *Actions to protect the environment and, in particular, to minimize or eliminate any adverse impact on the environment stemming from the company's own business activities.* Corporate social responsibility as it applies to environmental protection entails actively striving to be good stewards of the environment. This means using the best available science and technology to reduce environmentally harmful aspects of its operations *below the levels required by prevailing environmental regulations.* It also means putting time and money into improving the environment in ways that extend past a company's own industry boundaries—such as participating in recycling projects, adopting energy conservation practices, and supporting efforts to clean up local water supplies.

- *Actions to create a work environment that enhances the quality of life for employees.* Numerous companies exert extra effort to enhance the quality of life for their employees, both at work and at home. This can include on-site day care, flexible work schedules, workplace exercise facilities, special leaves to care for sick family members, work-at-home opportunities, career development programs and education opportunities, special safety programs, and the like.

- *Actions to build a workforce that is diverse with respect to gender, race, national origin, and other aspects that different people bring to the workplace.* Most large companies in the United States have established workforce diversity programs, and some go the extra mile to ensure that their workplaces are attractive to ethnic minorities and inclusive of all groups and perspectives.

The particular combination of socially responsible endeavors a company elects to pursue defines its **corporate social responsibility strategy.** Concepts & Connections 9.2 describes Burt's Bees' approach to corporate social responsibility. But the specific components emphasized in a CSR strategy vary from company to company and are typically linked to a company's core values. General Mills, for example, builds its CSR strategy around the theme of "nourishing lives" to emphasize its commitment to good nutrition as well as philanthropy, community building, and environmental protection.[13] Starbucks's CSR strategy includes four main elements (ethical sourcing, community service, environmental stewardship, and farmer support), all of which have touch points with the way that the company procures its coffee—a key aspect of its product differentiation strategy.[14]

> **CORE CONCEPT**
>
> A company's **corporate social responsibility strategy** is defined by the specific combination of socially beneficial activities it opts to support with its contributions of time, money, and other resources.

Corporate Social Responsibility and the Triple Bottom Line

CSR initiatives undertaken by companies are frequently directed at improving the company's "triple bottom line"—a reference to three types of performance metrics: *economic, social, environmental.* The goal is for a company to succeed simultaneously in all three dimensions.[15] The three dimensions of performance are often referred to in terms of the three pillars of "people, planet, and profit." The term *people* refers to the various social initiatives that make up CSR strategies, such as corporate giving and community involvement. *Planet* refers to a firm's ecological impact and environmental practices. The term *profit* has a

CONCEPTS & CONNECTIONS 9.2

BURT'S BEES: A STRATEGY BASED ON CORPORATE SOCIAL RESPONSIBILITY

Burt's Bees is a leading company in natural personal care, offering nearly 200 products including its popular beeswax lip balms and skin care creams. The brand has enjoyed tremendous success as consumers have begun to embrace all-natural, environmentally friendly products, boosting Burt's Bees' revenues to more than $160 million in 2012. Much of Burt's Bees' success can be attributed to its skillful use of corporate social responsibility (CSR) as a strategic tool to engage customers and differentiate itself from competitors.

While many companies have embraced corporate social responsibility, few companies have managed to integrate CSR as fully and seamlessly throughout their organizations as Burt's Bees. The company's business model is centered on a principle refered to as "The Greater Good," which specifies that all company practices must be socially responsible. The execution of this strategy is managed by a special committee dedicated to leading the organization to attain its CSR goals with respect to three primary areas: natural well-being, humanitarian responsibility, and environmental sustainability.

Natural well-being is focused on the ingredients used to create Burt's Bees products. Today, the average Burt's Bees product contains over 99 percent natural ingredients; by 2020, the brand expects to produce only 100 percent natural products.

Burt's Bees' humanitarian focus is centered on its relationships with employees and suppliers. A key part of this effort involves a mandatory employee training program that focuses on four key areas: outreach, wellness, world-class leadership, and the environment. Another is the company's responsible sourcing mission, which lays out a carefully prescribed set of guidelines for sourcing responsible suppliers and managing supplier relationships.

A focus on caring for the environment is clearly interwoven into all aspects of Burt's Bees. By focusing on environmentally efficient processes, the company uses its in-house manufacturing capability as a point of strategic differentiation.

Burt's Bees faced some consumer backlash when it was purchased in 2007 by The Clorox Company, whose traditional image is viewed in sharp contrast to Burt's Bees' values. But while Burt's Bees is still only a small part of Clorox's total revenue, it has become its fastest-growing division.

Developed with Ross M. Templeton.

Sources: Company websites; Louise Story, "Can Burt's Bees Turn Clorox Green?" *The New York Times,* January 6, 2008; Bill Chameides, "Burt's Bees Are Busy on the Sustainability Front," *Huffington Post,* June 25, 2010; Katie Bird, "Burt's Bees' International Performance Weaker Than Expected," *CosmeticsDesign.com,* January 6, 2011; "Burt's Bees, Marks & Spencer Share Staff Engagement Tactics," *EnvironmentalLeader.com,* May 31, 2011; http://blogs.newsobserver.com/business/investor-icahn-pushes-for-sale-of-burts-bees-parent-clorox#storylink=cpy (accessed March 1, 2012).

broader meaning with respect to the triple bottom line than it does otherwise. It encompasses not only the profit a firm earns for its shareholders but also the economic impact the company has on society more generally. Triple-bottom-line (TBL) reporting is emerging as an increasingly important way for companies to make the results of their CSR strategies apparent to stakeholders.

What Do We Mean by *Sustainability* and *Sustainable Business Practices?*

The term *sustainability* is used in a variety of ways. In many firms, it is synonymous with corporate social responsibility; it is seen by some as a term that is gradually replacing CSR in the business lexicon. Indeed, sustainability reporting and TBL reporting are often one and the same. More often, however, the term takes on a more focused meaning, concerned with the relationship of a company to its *environment* and its use of *natural resources,* including land, water, air, minerals, and fossil fuels. Since corporations are the biggest users of finite natural resources, managing and maintaining these resources is critical for the long-term economic interests of corporations.

For some companies, this issue has direct and obvious implications for the continued viability of their business model and strategy. Pacific Gas and Electric has begun measuring the full carbon footprint of its supply chain to become not only "greener" but also a more efficient energy producer.[16] For other companies, the connection is less direct, but all companies are part of a business ecosystem whose economic health depends on the availability of natural resources. In response, most major companies have begun to change *how* they do business, emphasizing the use of **sustainable business practices**, defined as those capable of meeting the needs of the present without compromising the ability to meet the needs of the future.[17] Many have also begun to incorporate a consideration of environmental sustainability into their strategy-making activities.

> **CORE CONCEPT**
>
> **Sustainable business practices** are those that meet the needs of the present without compromising the ability to meet the needs of the future.

Environmental sustainability strategies entail deliberate and concerted actions to operate businesses in a manner that protects and maybe even enhances natural resources and ecological support systems, guards against outcomes that will ultimately endanger the planet, and is therefore sustainable for centuries.[18] Sustainability initiatives undertaken by companies are directed at improving the company's triple bottom line— its performance on economic, environment, and social metrics.[19] Unilever, a diversified producer of processed foods, personal care, and home cleaning products, is among the most committed corporations pursuing environmentally sustainable business practices. The company tracks 11 sustainable agricultural indicators in its processed-foods business and has launched a variety of programs to improve the environmental performance of its suppliers. Examples of such programs include special low-rate financing for tomato suppliers choosing to switch to water-conserving irrigation systems and training programs in India that have allowed contract cucumber growers to reduce pesticide use by 90 percent, while improving yields by 78 percent.

> **CORE CONCEPT**
>
> **Environmental sustainability** involves deliberate actions to protect the environment, provide for the longevity of natural resources, maintain ecological support systems for future generations, and guard against the ultimate endangerment of the planet.

Unilever has also reengineered many internal processes to improve the company's overall performance on sustainability measures. For example, the company's factories have reduced water usage by 50 percent and manufacturing waste by 14 percent through the implementation of sustainability initiatives. Unilever has also redesigned packaging for many of its products to conserve natural resources and reduce the volume of consumer waste. The company's Suave shampoo bottles in the United States were reshaped to save almost 150 tons of plastic resin per year, which is the equivalent of 15 million fewer empty bottles. As the producer of Lipton Tea, Unilever is the world's largest purchaser of tea leaves; the company has committed to sourcing all of its tea from Rainforest Alliance Certified farms by 2015, due to Unilever's comprehensive triple-bottom-line approach toward sustainable farm management. Because 40 percent of Unilever's sales are made to consumers in developing countries, the company also is committed to addressing societal needs of consumers in those countries. Examples of the company's social performance include free laundries in poor neighborhoods in developing countries, start-up assistance for women-owned micro businesses in India, and free drinking water provided to villages in Ghana.

Sometimes cost savings and improved profitability are drivers of corporate sustainability strategies. DuPont's sustainability initiatives regarding energy usage have resulted in energy conservation savings of more than $2 billion between 1990 and 2005. Procter & Gamble's Swiffer cleaning system, one of the company's best-selling new products, was developed as a sustainable product; not only does the Swiffer system have an earth-friendly design, but it also outperforms less ecologically friendly alternatives. Although most consumers probably aren't aware that the Swiffer mop reduces demands on municipal water sources, saves electricity that would be needed to heat water, and doesn't add to the amount of detergent making its way into waterways and waste treatment facilities, they are attracted to purchasing Swiffer mops because they prefer Swiffer's disposable cleaning sheets to filling and refilling a mop bucket and wringing out a wet mop until the floor is clean.

Crafting Corporate Social Responsibility and Sustainability Strategies

While striving to be socially responsible and to engage in environmentally sustainable business practices, there's plenty of room for every company to make its own statement about what charitable contributions to make, what kinds of community service projects to emphasize, what environmental actions to support, how to make the company a good place to work, where and how workforce diversity fits into the picture, and what else it will do to support worthy causes and projects that benefit society. A company may choose to focus its social responsibility strategy on generic social issues, but social responsibility strategies linked to its customer value proposition or key value chain activities may also help build competitive advantage.[20] For example, while carbon emissions may be a generic social issue for a

> CSR strategies that have the effect of both providing valuable social benefits and fulfilling customer needs in a superior fashion can lead to competitive advantage. Corporate social agendas that address generic social issues may help boost a company's reputation, but are unlikely to improve its competitive strength in the marketplace.

financial institution such as Wells Fargo, Toyota's social responsibility strategy aimed at reducing carbon emissions has produced both competitive advantage and environmental benefits. Its Prius hybrid electric/gasoline-powered automobile not only is among the least polluting automobiles, but also is the best-selling hybrid vehicle in the United States and has earned the company the loyalty of fuel-conscious buyers and given Toyota a green image.

The Business Case for Socially Responsible Behavior

It has long been recognized that it is in the enlightened self-interest of companies to be good citizens and devote some of their energies and resources to the betterment of employees, the communities in which they operate, and society in general. In short, there are several reasons the exercise of corporate social responsibility is good business:

- *Such actions can lead to increased buyer patronage.* A strong visible social responsibility strategy gives a company an edge in differentiating itself from rivals and in appealing to those consumers who prefer to do business with companies that are good corporate citizens. Ben & Jerry's, Whole Foods Market, Stonyfield Farm, and The Body Shop have definitely expanded their customer bases because of their visible and well-publicized activities as socially conscious companies.

- *A strong commitment to socially responsible behavior reduces the risk of reputation-damaging incidents.* Companies that place little importance on operating in a socially responsible manner are more prone to scandal and embarrassment. Consumer, environmental, and human rights activist groups are quick to criticize businesses whose behavior they consider to be out of line, and they are adept at getting their message into the media and onto the Internet. For many years, Nike received stinging criticism for not policing sweatshop conditions in the Asian factories that produced Nike footwear, causing Nike co-founder and former CEO Phil Knight to observe, "Nike has become synonymous with slave wages, forced overtime, and arbitrary abuse."[21] In 1997, Nike began an extensive effort to monitor conditions in the 800 factories of the contract manufacturers that produced Nike shoes. As Knight said, "Good shoes come from good factories and good factories have good labor relations." Nonetheless, Nike has continually been plagued by complaints from human rights activists that its monitoring procedures are flawed and that it is not doing enough to correct the plight of factory workers.

- *Socially responsible actions yield internal benefits (particularly for employee recruiting, workforce retention, and training costs) and can improve operational efficiency.* Companies with deservedly good reputations for contributing time and money to the betterment of society are better able to attract and retain employees compared to companies with tarnished reputations. Some employees just feel better about working for a company committed to improving society.[22] This can contribute to lower turnover and better worker productivity. Other direct and indirect economic benefits include lower costs for staff recruitment and training. For example, Starbucks is said to enjoy much lower rates of employee turnover because of its full benefits package for both full-time and part-time employees, management efforts to make Starbucks a great place to work, and the company's socially responsible practices. When a U.S. manufacturer of recycled paper, taking eco-efficiency to heart, discovered how to increase its fiber recovery rate, it saved the equivalent of 20,000 tons of waste paper—a factor that helped the company become the industry's lowest-cost producer. By helping two-thirds of its employees stop smoking and investing in a number of wellness programs for employees, Johnson & Johnson has saved $250 million on its health care costs over the past decade.[23]

- *Well-conceived social responsibility strategies work to the advantage of shareholders.* A two-year study of leading companies found that improving environmental compliance and developing environmentally friendly products can enhance earnings per share, profitability, and the likelihood of winning contracts. The stock prices of companies that rate high on social and environmental performance criteria have been found to perform 35 to 45 percent better than the average of the 2,500 companies comprising the Dow Jones Global Index.[24] A review of some 135 studies indicated there is a positive, but small, correlation between good corporate behavior and good financial performance; only 2 percent of the studies showed that dedicating corporate resources to social responsibility harmed the interests of shareholders.[25]

In sum, companies that take social responsibility seriously can improve their business reputations and operational efficiency while also reducing their risk exposure and encouraging loyalty and innovation. Overall, companies that take special pains to protect the environment (beyond what is required by law), are active in community affairs, and are generous supporters of charitable causes and projects that benefit society are more likely to be seen as good investments and as good companies to work for or do business with. Shareholders are likely to view the business case for social responsibility as a strong one, even though they certainly have a right to be concerned about whether the time and money their company spends to carry out its social responsibility strategy outweigh the benefits and reduce the bottom line by an unjustified amount.

 **KEY POINTS**

1. Business ethics concerns the application of ethical principles and standards to the actions and decisions of business organizations and the conduct of their personnel. Ethical principles in business are not materially different from ethical principles in general.

2. The three main drivers of unethical business behavior stand out:
   - Overzealous or obsessive pursuit of personal gain, wealth, and other selfish interests.
   - Heavy pressures on company managers to meet or beat earnings targets.
   - A company culture that puts profitability and good business performance ahead of ethical behavior.

3. Business ethics failures can result in visible costs (fines, penalties, civil penalties arising from lawsuits, stock price declines), the internal administrative or "cleanup" costs, and intangible or less visible costs (customer defections, loss of reputation, higher turnover, harsher government regulations).

4. There are three schools of thought about ethical standards for companies with international operations:
   - According to the *school of ethical universalism,* the same standards of what's ethical and unethical resonate with peoples of most societies regardless of local traditions and cultural norms; hence, common ethical standards can be used to judge the conduct of personnel at companies operating in a variety of international markets and cultural circumstances.

- According to the *school of ethical relativism,* different societal cultures and customs have divergent values and standards of right and wrong—thus, what is ethical or unethical must be judged in the light of local customs and social mores and can vary from one culture or nation to another.

- According to *integrative social contracts theory,* universal ethical principles or norms based on the collective views of multiple cultures and societies combine to form a "social contract" that all individuals in all situations have a duty to observe. Within the boundaries of this social contract, local cultures can specify other impermissible actions; however, universal ethical norms always take precedence over local ethical norms.

5. The term *corporate social responsibility* concerns a company's *duty* to operate in an honorable manner, provide good working conditions for employees, encourage workforce diversity, be a good steward of the environment, and support philanthropic endeavors in local communities where it operates and in society at large. The particular combination of socially responsible endeavors a company elects to pursue defines its corporate social responsibility (CSR) strategy.

6. The triple bottom line refers to company performance in three realms: economic, social, environmental. Increasingly, companies are reporting their performance with respect to all three performance dimensions.

7. Sustainability is a term that is used variously, but most often it concerns a firm's relationship to the environment and its use of natural resources. Environmentally sustainable business practices are those capable of meeting the needs of the present without compromising the world's ability to meet future needs. A company's environmental sustainability strategy consists of its deliberate actions to protect the environment, provide for the longevity of natural resources, maintain ecological support systems for future generations, and guard against ultimate endangerment of the planet.

8. There are also solid reasons CSR and environmental sustainability strategies may be good business—they can be conducive to greater buyer patronage, reduce the risk of reputation-damaging incidents, provide opportunities for revenue enhancement, and lower costs. Well-crafted CSR and environmental sustainability strategies are in the best long-term interest of shareholders, for the reasons above and because they can avoid or preempt costly legal or regulatory actions.

ASSURANCE OF LEARNING EXERCISES

LO1, LO4 1. Ikea is widely known for its commitment to business ethics and environmental sustainability. After reviewing the About Ikea section of its website (www.ikea.com/ms/en_US/about_ikea/index.html), prepare a list of 10 specific policies and programs that help the company achieve its vision of creating a better everyday life for people around the world.

LO2, LO3 2. Prepare a one- to two-page analysis of a recent ethics scandal using your university library's access to Lexis-Nexis or other Internet resources. Your report should (*a*) discuss the conditions that gave rise to unethical business strategies and behavior and (*b*) provide an overview of the costs resulting from the company's business ethics failure.

3. Based on the information provided in Concepts & Connections 9.2 explain how Burt's Bees' CSR strategy has contributed to its success in the marketplace. How are its various stakeholder groups affected by its commitment to social responsibility? How would you evaluate its triple- bottom-line performance?

LO4

4. Go to www.nestle.com and read the company's latest sustainability report. What are Nestlé's key environmental sustainability policies? How do these initiatives relate to the company's principles, values, and culture? How do these initiatives help build competitive advantage in the food industry?

LO4

▶ EXERCISES FOR SIMULATION PARTICIPANTS

1. Is your company's strategy ethical? Why or why not? Is there anything that your company has done or is now doing that could legitimately be considered as "shady" by your competitiors?

LO1

2. In what ways, if any, is your company exercising corporate social responsibility? What are the elements of your company's CSR strategy? What changes to this strategy would you suggest?

LO4

3. If some shareholders complained that you and your co-managers have been spending too little or too much on corporate social responsibility, what would you tell them?

LO3, LO4

4. Is your company striving to conduct its business in an environmentally sustainable manner? What specific *additional* actions could your company take that would make an even greater contribution to environmental sustainability?

LO4

5. In what ways is your company's environmental sustainability strategy in the best long-term interest of shareholders? Does it contribute to your company's competitive advantage or profitability?

LO4

▶ ENDNOTES

1. James E. Post, Anne T. Lawrence, and James Weber, *Business and Society: Corporate Strategy, Public Policy, Ethics,* 10th ed. (New York: McGraw-Hill Irwin, 2002).

2. John F. Veiga, Timothy D. Golden, and Kathleen Dechant, "Why Managers Bend Company Rules," *Academy of Management Executive* 18, no. 2 (May 2004).

3. Basil Katz and Grant McCool, "US Charges 7 in $62 Million Dell Insider-Trading Case," Reuters, January 18, 2012, www.reuters.com/ article/2012/01/18/us-insidertrading-arrests-idUSTRE80H18920120118 (accessed February 15, 2012).

4. Ronald R. Sims and Johannes Brinkmann, "Enron Ethics (Or: Culture Matters More Than Codes)," *Journal of Business Ethics* 45, no. 3 (July 2003).

5. Marcy Gordon, "Diebold-SEC Fraud Settlement Reached: Former Voting Machine Maker to Pay $25 Million," *HuffPost Business,* June 2, 2010, http://www.huffmgtonpost.com/2010/06/02/diebold-sec-fraud-settleme_n_598627.html (accessed February 16, 2012).

6. Archie B. Carroll, "The Four Faces of Corporate Citizenship," *Business and Society Review* 100/101 (September 1998).

7. Mark S. Schwartz, "Universal Moral Values for Corporate Codes of Ethics," *Journal of Business Ethics* 59, no. 1 (June 2005).

8. Mark S. Schwartz, "A Code of Ethics for Corporate Codes of Ethics," *Journal of Business Ethics* 41, nos. 1–2 (November–December 2002).

9. T. L. Beauchamp and N. E. Bowie, *Ethical Theory and Business* (Upper Saddle River, NJ: Prentice Hall, 2001).

10. Thomas Donaldson and Thomas W. Dunfee, "Towards a Unified Conception of Business Ethics: Integrative Social Contracts Theory," *Academy of Management Review* 19, no. 2 (April 1994); Thomas Donaldson and Thomas W. Dunfee, *Ties That Bind: A Social Contracts Approach*

to *Business Ethics* (Boston: Harvard Business School Press, 1999); and Andrew Spicer, Thomas W. Dunfee, and Wendy J. Bailey, "Does National Context Matter in Ethical Decision Making? An Empirical Test of Integrative Social Contracts Theory," *Academy of Management Journal* 47, no. 4 (August 2004).

11. P. M. Nichols, "Outlawing Transnational Bribery through the World Trade Organization," *Law and Policy in International Business* 28, no. 2 (1997).

12. Timothy M. Devinney, "Is the Socially Responsible Corporation a Myth? The Good, the Bad, and the Ugly of Corporate Social Responsibility," *Academy of Management Perspectives* 23, no. 2 (May 2009).

13. "General Mills' 2010 Corporate Social Responsibility Report Highlights New and Longstanding Achievements in the Areas of Health, Community, and Environment," *CSRwire*, April 15, 2010, www.csrwire.com/press_releases/29347-General-Mills-2010-Corporate-Social-Responsibility-report-now-available.html.

14. Arthur A. Thompson and Amit J. Shah, "Starbucks' Strategy and Internal Initiatives to Return to Profitable Growth," 2010.

15. Gerald I.J.M. Zwetsloot and Marcel N. A. van Marrewijk, "From Quality to Sustainability," *Journal of Business Ethics* 55 (December 2004), pp. 79–82.

16. Tilde Herrera, "PG&E Claims Industry First with Supply Chain Footprint Project," *GreenBiz.com*, June 30, 2010, www.greenbiz.com/news/2010/06/30/pge-claims-industry-first-supply-chain-carbon-footprint-project.

17. This definition is based on the Brundtland Commission's report, which described sustainable development in a like manner: United Nations General Assembly, "Report of the World Commission on Environment and Development: Our Common Future," 1987, www.un-documents.net/wced-ocf.htm, transmitted to the General Assembly as an annex to document A/42/427—"Development and International Cooperation: Environment" (accessed February 15, 2009).

18. Robert Goodland, "The Concept of Environmental Sustainability," *Annual Review of Ecology and Systematics* 26 (1995); and J. G. Speth, *The Bridge at the End of the World: Capitalism, the Environment, and Crossing from Crisis to Sustainability* (New Haven, CT: Yale University Press, 2008).

19. Gerald I. J. M. Zwetsloot and Marcel N. A. van Marrewijk, "From Quality to Sustainability," *Journal of Business Ethics* 55 (December 2004); and John B. Elkington, *Cannibals with Forks: The Triple Bottom Line of 21st Century Business* (Oxford: Capstone Publishing, 1997).

20. Michael E. Porter and Mark R. Kramer, "Strategy & Society: The Link between Competitive Advantage and Corporate Social Responsibility," *Harvard Business Review* 84, no. 12 (December 2006).

21. Tom McCawley, "Racing to Improve Its Reputation: Nike Has Fought to Shed Its Image as an Exploiter of Third-World Labor Yet It Is Still a Target of Activists," *Financial Times*, December 2000.

22. N. Craig Smith, "Corporate Responsibility: Whether and How," *California Management Review* 45, no. 4 (Summer 2003), p. 63; see also World Economic Forum, "Findings of a Survey on Global Corporate Leadership," www.weforum.org/corporatecitizenship (accessed October 11, 2003).

23. Michael E. Porter and Mark Kramer, "Creating Shared Value," *Harvard Business Review* 89, nos. 1–2 (January–February 2011).

24. James C. Collins and Jerry I. Porras, *Built to Last: Successful Habits of Visionary Companies*, 3rd ed. (London: HarperBusiness, 2002).

25. Joshua D. Margolis and Hillary A. Elfenbein, "Doing Well by Doing Good: Don't Count on It," *Harvard Business Review* 86, no. 1 (January 2008); Lee E. Preston and Douglas P. O'Bannon, "The Corporate Social-Financial Performance Relationship," *Business and Society* 36, no. 4 (December 1997); Ronald M. Roman, Sefa Hayibor, and Bradley R. Agle, "The Relationship between Social and Financial Performance: Repainting a Portrait," *Business and Society* 38, no. 1 (March 1999); and Joshua D. Margolis and James P. Walsh, *People and Profits* (Mahwah, NJ: Lawrence Erlbaum, 2001).

Superior Strategy Execution—Another Path to Competitive Advantage

LEARNING OBJECTIVES

LO1   Gain command of what managers must do to build an organization capable of good strategy execution.

LO2   Learn why resource allocation should always be based on strategic priorities.

LO3   Understand why policies and procedures should be designed to facilitate good strategy execution.

LO4   Understand how process management programs that drive continuous improvement help an organization achieve operating excellence.

LO5   Recognize the role of information and operating systems in enabling company personnel to carry out their strategic roles proficiently.

LO6   Learn how and why the use of well-designed incentives and rewards can be management's single most powerful tool for promoting operating excellence.

LO7   Gain an understanding of how and why a company's culture can aid the drive for proficient strategy execution.

LO8   Understand what constitutes effective managerial leadership in achieving superior strategy execution.

Once managers have decided on a strategy, the emphasis turns to converting it into actions and good results. Putting the strategy into place and getting the organization to execute it well call for different sets of managerial skills. Whereas crafting strategy is largely a market-driven and resource-driven activity, strategy implementation is an operations-driven activity primarily involving the management of people and business processes. Successful strategy execution depends on management's ability to direct organizational change and do a good job of allocating resources, building and strengthening competitive capabilities, instituting strategy-supportive policies, improving processes and systems, motivating and rewarding people, creating and nurturing a strategy-supportive culture, and consistently meeting or beating performance targets. While an organization's chief executive officer and other senior managers are ultimately responsible for ensuring that the strategy is executed successfully, it is middle and lower-level managers who must see to it that frontline employees and work groups competently perform the strategy-critical activities that allow companywide performance targets to be met. *Hence, strategy execution requires every manager to think through the answer to the question "What does my area have to do to implement its part of the strategic plan, and what should I do to get these things accomplished effectively and efficiently?"*

> **CORE CONCEPT**
>
> Good strategy execution requires a *team effort*. All managers have strategy execution responsibility in their areas of authority, and all employees are active participants in the strategy execution.

The Principal Managerial Components of Strategy Execution

Executing strategy entails figuring out the specific techniques, actions, and behaviors that are needed to get things done and deliver results. The exact items that need to be placed on management's action agenda always have to be customized to fit the particulars of a company's situation. The hot buttons for successfully executing a low-cost provider strategy are different from those in executing a differentiation strategy. Implementing a new strategy for a struggling company in the midst of a financial crisis is different from improving strategy execution in a company where the execution is already pretty good. While there's no definitive managerial recipe for successful strategy execution that cuts across all company situations and all types of strategies, certain managerial bases have to be covered no matter what the circumstances. Eight managerial tasks crop up repeatedly in company efforts to execute strategy (see Figure 10.1).

1. Building an organization with the capabilities, people, and structure needed to execute the strategy successfully.

2. Allocating ample resources to strategy-critical activities.

3. Ensuring that policies and procedures facilitate rather than impede effective strategy execution.

4. Adopting process management programs that drive continuous improvement in how strategy execution activities are performed.

FIGURE 10.1 **The Eight Components of Strategy Execution**

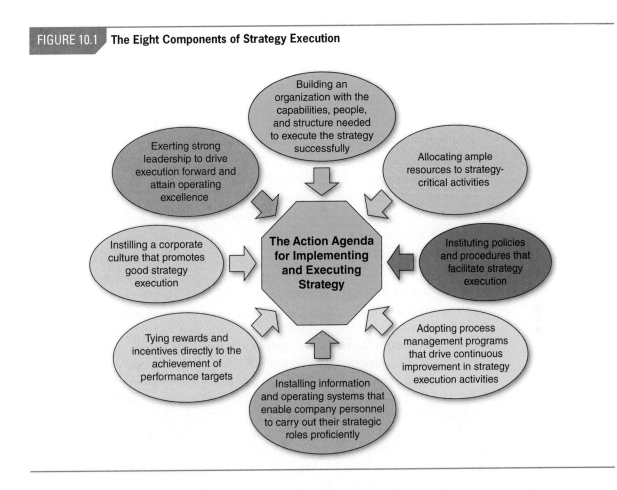

5. Installing information and operating systems that enable company personnel to perform essential activities.

6. Tying rewards directly to the achievement of performance objectives.

7. Fostering a corporate culture that promotes good strategy execution.

8. Exerting the internal leadership needed to propel implementation forward.

How well managers perform these eight tasks has a decisive impact on whether the outcome is a spectacular success, a colossal failure, or something in between. In the remainder of this chapter, we will discuss what is involved in performing the eight key managerial tasks that shape the process of implementing and executing strategy.

Building an Organization Capable of Good Strategy Execution: Three Key Actions

Proficient strategy execution depends heavily on competent personnel, better-than-adequate competitive capabilities, and an effective internal organization. Building a capable organization is thus always a top priority in strategy execution. Three types of organization building actions are paramount.

LO1 Gain command of what managers must do to build an organization capable of good strategy execution.

1. *Staffing the organization*—putting together a strong management team and recruiting and retaining employees with the needed experience, technical skills, and intellectual capital.

2. *Acquiring, developing, and strengthening strategy-supportive resources and capabilities*—accumulating the required resources, developing proficiencies in performing strategy-critical value chain activities, and updating them to match changing market conditions and customer expectations.

3. *Structuring the organization and work effort*—organizing value chain activities and business processes, establishing lines of authority and reporting relationships, and deciding how much decision-making authority to push down to lower-level managers and frontline employees.

Staffing the Organization

No company can hope to perform the activities required for successful strategy execution without attracting and retaining talented managers and employees with suitable skills and intellectual capital.

Building Managerial Talent   Assembling a capable management team is a cornerstone of the organization-building task.[1] While company circumstances sometimes call for different mixes of backgrounds, experiences, management styles, and know-how, *the most important consideration is to fill key managerial slots with people who are good at figuring out what needs to be done and skilled in "making it happen" and delivering good results.*[2] Without a capable, results-oriented management team, the implementation–execution process ends up being hampered by missed deadlines, misdirected or wasteful efforts, and/or managerial ineptness.[3] Weak executives are serious impediments to getting optimal results because they are unable to differentiate between ideas that have merit and those that are misguided. In contrast, managers with strong strategy-implementing capabilities have a talent for asking tough, incisive questions. They know enough about the details of the business to be able to challenge and ensure the soundness of the approaches of the people around them, and they can discern whether the resources people are asking for make sense strategically. They are good at getting things done through others, typically by making sure they have the right people under them and that these people are put in the right jobs. They consistently follow through on issues and do not let important details slip through the cracks.

Sometimes a company's existing management team is suitable; at other times it may need to be strengthened or expanded by promoting qualified people from within or by bringing in outsiders. The overriding aim in building a management team should be to assemble a *critical mass* of talented managers who can function as agents of change and further the cause of first-rate strategy execution. When a first-rate manager enjoys the help and support of other first-rate managers, it's possible to create a managerial whole that is greater than the sum of individual efforts—talented managers who work well together as a team can produce organizational results that are dramatically better than what one or two star managers acting individually can achieve.[4]

Recruiting and Retaining a Capable Workforce   Assembling a capable management team is not enough. Staffing the organization with the right kinds of people must go much deeper than managerial jobs in order for value chain activities to be performed competently. *The quality of an organization's people is always an essential ingredient of successful strategy execution—knowledgeable, engaged employees are a company's best source of creative ideas for the nuts-and-bolts operating improvements that lead to operating excellence.* Companies such as Mercedes-Benz, Google, Boston Consulting Group, and Procter & Gamble make a concerted effort to recruit the best and brightest people they can find and then retain them with excellent compensation packages, opportunities for rapid advancement and professional growth, and challenging and interesting assignments. Having a pool of "A players" with strong skill sets and lots of brainpower is essential to their business. Facebook makes a point of hiring the very brightest and most talented programmers it can find and motivating them with both good monetary incentives and the challenge of working on cutting-edge technology projects. The leading global accounting firms screen candidates not only on the basis of their accounting expertise but also on whether they possess the people skills needed to relate well with clients and colleagues. Southwest Airlines goes to considerable lengths to hire people who can have fun and be fun on the job; it uses special interviewing and screening methods to gauge whether applicants for customer-contact jobs have outgoing personality traits that match its strategy of creating a high-spirited, fun-loving, in-flight atmosphere for passengers. Southwest Airlines is so selective that only about 3 percent of the people who apply are offered jobs.

The tactics listed below are common among companies dedicated to staffing jobs with the best people they can find:

1. Putting forth considerable effort in screening and evaluating job applicants—selecting only those with suitable skill sets, energy, initiative, judgment, aptitudes for learning, and adaptability to the company's culture.

2. Investing in training programs that continue throughout employees' careers.

3. Providing promising employees with challenging, interesting, and skill-stretching assignments.

4. Rotating people through jobs that span functional and geographic boundaries.

5. Striving to retain talented, high-performing employees via promotions, salary increases, performance bonuses, stock options and equity ownership, fringe benefit packages, and other perks.

6. Coaching average performers to improve their skills and capabilities, while weeding out underperformers and benchwarmers.

Acquiring, Developing, and Strengthening Key Resources and Capabilities

High among the organization-building priorities in the strategy execution process is the need to build and strengthen competitively valuable resources and capabilities. As explained in Chapter 4, a company's ability to perform value-creating activities and realize its strategic objectives depends upon its resources and capabilities. In the course of crafting strategy, it is important for managers to identify the resources and capabilities that will enable the firm's strategy to succeed. Good strategy execution requires putting those resources and capabilities into place, refreshing and strengthening them as needed, and then modifying them as market conditions evolve.

Three Approaches to Building and Strengthening Capabilities
Building core competencies and competitive capabilities is a time-consuming, managerially challenging exercise. But with deliberate effort and continued practice, it is possible for a firm to become proficient at capability building. Indeed, by making capability-building activities a routine part of their strategy execution, some firms are able to develop *dynamic capabilities* that assist them in managing resource and capability change, as discussed in Chapter 4. The most common approaches to capability building include (1) internal development, (2) acquiring capabilities through mergers and acquisitions, and (3) accessing capabilities via collaborative partnerships.[5]

> Building new competencies and capabilities is a multistage process that occurs over a period of months and years. It is not something that is accomplished overnight.

Developing Capabilities Internally
Capabilities develop incrementally along an evolutionary path as organizations search for solutions to their problems. The process is complex because capabilities are the product of bundles of skills and know-how. In addition, capabilities tend to require the combined efforts of teams that are often cross-functional in nature, spanning a variety of departments and locations. For instance, the capability of speeding new products to market involves the collaborative efforts of personnel in R&D, engineering and design, purchasing, production, marketing, and distribution.

Because the process is incremental, the first step is to develop the *ability* to do something, however imperfectly or inefficiently. This entails selecting people with the requisite skills and experience, upgrading or expanding individual abilities as needed, and then molding the efforts of individuals into a collaborative effort to create an organizational ability. At this stage, progress can be fitful since it depends on experimentation, active search for alternative solutions, and learning through trial and error.[6] As experience grows and company personnel learn how to perform the activities consistently well and at an acceptable cost, the ability evolves into a tried-and-true competence.

> A company's capabilities must be continually refreshed and renewed to remain aligned with changing customer expectations, altered competitive conditions, and new strategic initiatives.

It is generally much easier and less time-consuming to update and remodel a company's existing capabilities as external conditions and company strategy change than it is to create them from scratch. Maintaining capabilities in top form may simply require exercising them continually and fine-tuning them as necessary. Similarly, augmenting a capability may require less effort if it involves the recombination of well-established company capabilities and draws on existing company resources.[7] For example, Canon combined miniaturization capabilities that it developed in producing calculators with its existing capabilities in precision optics to revolutionize the 35-mm camera market.[8]

Toyota, en route to overtaking General Motors as the global leader in motor vehicles, aggressively upgraded its capabilities in fuel-efficient hybrid engine technology and constantly fine-tuned its famed Toyota Production System to enhance its already proficient capabilities in manufacturing top-quality vehicles at relatively low costs—see Concepts & Connections 10.1.

Acquiring Capabilities through Mergers and Acquisitions

Sometimes a company can build and refresh its competencies by acquiring another company with attractive resources and capabilities.[9] An acquisition aimed at building a stronger portfolio of resources and capabilities can be every bit as valuable as an acquisition aimed at adding new products or services to the company's lineup of offerings. The advantage of this mode of acquiring new capabilities is primarily one of speed, since developing new capabilities internally can take many years. Capabilities-motivated acquisitions are essential (1) when a market opportunity can slip by faster than a needed capability can be created internally and (2) when industry conditions, technology, or competitors are moving at such a rapid clip, that time is of the essence.

At the same time, acquiring capabilities in this way is not without difficulty. Capabilities tend to involve tacit knowledge and complex routines that cannot be transferred readily from one organizational unit to another. This may limit the extent to which the new capability can be utilized by the acquiring organization. For example, the Newell Company acquired Rubbermaid in part for its famed product-innovation capabilities. Transferring these capabilities to other parts of the Newell organization proved easier said than done, however, contributing to a slump in the firm's stock prices that lasted for some time.

Accessing Capabilities through Collaborative Partnerships

Another method of acquiring capabilities from an external source is to access them via collaborative partnerships with suppliers, competitors, or other companies having the cutting-edge expertise. There are three basic ways to pursue this course of action:

1. *Outsource the function or activity requiring new capabilities to an outside provider.* As discussed in Chapter 6, outsourcing has the advantage of conserving resources so the firm can focus its energies on those activities most central to its strategy. It may be a good choice for firms that are too small and resource-constrained to execute all the parts of their strategy internally.

2. *Collaborate with a firm that has complementary resources and capabilities in a joint venture, strategic alliance, or other type of partnership to achieve a shared strategic objective.* Since the success of the venture will depend on how well the partners work together, potential partners should be selected as much for their management style, culture, and goals as for their resources and capabilities.

3. *Engage in a collaborative partnership for the purpose of learning how the partner performs activities, internalizing its methods, and thereby acquiring its capabilities.* This may be a viable method when each partner has something to learn from the other. But in other cases, it involves an abuse of trust and puts the cooperative venture at risk.

CONCEPTS & CONNECTIONS 10.1

TOYOTA'S LEGENDARY PRODUCTION SYSTEM—A CAPABILITY THAT TRANSLATES INTO COMPETITIVE ADVANTAGE

The heart of Toyota's strategy in motor vehicles is to outcompete rivals by manufacturing world-class, quality vehicles at lower costs and selling them at competitive price levels. Executing this strategy requires top-notch manufacturing capability and super-efficient management of people, equipment, and materials. Toyota began conscious efforts to improve its manufacturing competence more than 50 years ago. Through tireless trial and error, the company gradually took what started as a loose collection of techniques and practices and integrated them into a full-fledged process that has come to be known as the Toyota Production System (TPS). The TPS drives all plant operations and the company's supply chain management practices. TPS is grounded in the following principles, practices, and techniques:

- *Use just-in-time delivery of parts and components to the point of vehicle assembly.* The idea here is to cut out all the bits and pieces of transferring materials from place to place and to discontinue all activities on the part of workers that don't add value (particularly activities where nothing ends up being made or assembled).

- *Develop people who can come up with unique ideas for production improvements.* Toyota encourages employees at all levels to question existing ways of doing things—even if it means challenging a boss on the soundness of a directive. Former Toyota President Katsuaki Watanabe encouraged the company's employees to "pick a friendly fight." Also, Toyota doesn't fire its employees who, at first, have little judgment for improving work flows; instead, the company gives them extensive training to become better problem solvers.

- *Emphasize continuous improvement.* Workers are expected to use their heads and develop better ways of doing things, rather than mechanically follow instructions. Toyota managers tout messages such as "Never be satisfied" and "There's got to be a better way." Another mantra at Toyota is that the *T* in TPS also stands for "Thinking." The thesis is that a work environment where people have to think generates the wisdom to spot opportunities for making tasks simpler and easier to perform, increasing the speed and efficiency with which activities are performed, and constantly improving product quality.

- *Empower workers to stop the assembly line when there's a problem or a defect is spotted.* Toyota views worker efforts to purge defects and sort out the problem immediately as critical to the whole concept of building quality into the production process. According to TPS, "If the line doesn't stop, useless defective items will move on to the next stage. If you don't know where the problem occurred, you can't do anything to fix it."

- *Deal with defects only when they occur.* TPS philosophy holds that when things are running smoothly, they should not be subject to control; if attention is directed to fixing problems that are found, quality control along the assembly line can be handled with fewer personnel.

- *Ask yourself "Why?" five times.* While errors need to be fixed whenever they occur, the value of asking "Why?" five times enables identifying the root cause of the error and correcting it so that the error won't recur.

- *Organize all jobs around human motion to create a production/assembly system with no wasted effort.* Work organized in this fashion is called "standardized work," and people are trained to observe standardized work procedures (which include supplying parts to each process on the assembly line at the proper time, sequencing the work in an optimal manner, and allowing workers to do their jobs continuously in a set sequence of subprocesses).

- *Find where a part is made cheaply and use that price as a benchmark.*

The TPS utilizes a unique vocabulary of terms (such as *kanban, takt-time, jikoda, kaizen, heijunka, monozukuri, poka yoke,* and *muda*) that facilitates precise discussion of specific TPS elements. In 2003, Toyota established a Global Production Center to efficiently train large numbers of shop-floor experts in the latest TPS methods and better operate an increasing number of production sites worldwide. Since then, additional upgrades and refinements have been introduced, some in response to the large number of defects in Toyota vehicles that surfaced in 2009–2010.

There's widespread agreement that Toyota's ongoing effort to refine and improve on its renowned TPS gives it important manufacturing capabilities that are the envy of other motor vehicle manufacturers. Not only have such auto manufacturers as Ford, Daimler, Volkswagen, and General Motors attempted to emulate key elements of TPS, but elements of Toyota's production philosophy also have been adopted by hospitals and postal services.

Sources: Information posted at www.toyotageorgetown.com; Hirotaka Takeuchi, Emi Osono, and Norihiko Shimizu, "The Contradictions that Drive Toyota's Success," *Harvard Business Review* 86, no. 6 (June 2008), pp. 96–104; and Taiichi Ohno, *Toyota Production System: Beyond Large-Scale Production* (New York: Sheridan Books, 1988).

Matching Organizational Structure to the Strategy

Building an organization capable of good strategy execution also relies on an organizational structure that lays out lines of authority and reporting relationships in a manner that supports the company's key strategic initiatives. The best approach to settling on an organizational structure is to first consider the key value chain activities that deliver value to the customer. In any business, some activities in the value chain are always more critical than others. For instance, hotel/motel enterprises have to be good at fast check-in/check-out, housekeeping, food service, and creating a pleasant ambience. In specialty chemicals, the strategy-critical activities include R&D, product innovation, getting new products onto the market quickly, effective marketing, and expertise in assisting customers. It is important for management to build its organization structure around proficient performance of these activities, making them the centerpieces or main building blocks on the organization chart.

The rationale for making strategy-critical activities the main building blocks in structuring a business is compelling: If activities crucial to strategic success are to have the resources, decision-making influence, and organizational impact they need, they have to be centerpieces in the organizational scheme. In addition, a new or changed strategy is likely to entail new or different key activities or capabilities and therefore to require a new or different organizational structure.[10] Attempting to carry out a new strategy with an old organizational structure is usually unwise.

Types of Organizational Structures   It is common for companies engaged in a single line of business to utilize a **functional (or departmental) organizational structure** that organizes strategy-critical activities into distinct *functional, product, geographic, process,* or *customer* groups. For instance, a technical instruments manufacturer may be organized around research and development, engineering, supply chain management, assembly, quality control, marketing technical services, and corporate administration. A company with operations scattered across a large geographic area or many countries may organize activities and reporting relationships by geography. Many diversified companies utilize a **multidivisional (or divisional) organizational structure.** A multidivisional structure is appropriate for a diversified building materials company that designs, produces, and markets cabinets, plumbing fixtures, windows, and paints and stains. The divisional structure organizes all of the value chain activities involved with making each type of home construction product available to home builders and do-it-yourselfers into a common division and makes each division an independent profit center. **Matrix organizational structures** allow companies to specify dual reporting relationships for various value-creating building blocks. For example, in the diversified building materials company just mentioned, a matrix structure could require the marketing department for the plumbing fixtures division to report to both the corporate marketing department and the chief manager of the plumbing equipment division.

Organizational Structure and Authority in Decision Making   Responsibility for results of decisions made throughout the organization ultimately lies with managers at the top of the organizational structure, but in practice, lower-level managers might possess a great deal of authority in decision making. Companies vary in the degree of authority delegated to managers of each organization unit and how much decision-making latitude is given to individual employees in performing their jobs. The two extremes are to *centralize decision making* at the top (the CEO and a few close lieutenants) or to *decentralize decision making* by giving managers and employees considerable decision-making latitude in their areas of responsibility. The two approaches are based on sharply different underlying principles and beliefs, with each having its pros and cons. *In a highly decentralized organization, decision-making authority is pushed down to the lowest organizational level capable of making timely, informed, competent decisions.* The objective is to put adequate decision-making authority in the hands of the people closest to and most familiar with the situation and train them to weigh all the factors and exercise good judgment. Decentralized decision making means that the managers of each organizational unit are delegated lead responsibility for deciding how best to execute strategy.

The case for empowering down-the-line managers and employees to make decisions related to daily operations and executing the strategy is based on the belief that a company that draws on the combined intellectual capital of all its employees can outperform a command-and-control company.[11] Decentralized decision making means, for example, employees with customer contact may be empowered to do what it takes to please customers. At Starbucks, for example, employees are encouraged to exercise initiative in promoting customer satisfaction—there's the story of a store employee who, when the computerized cash register system went offline, enthusiastically offered free coffee to waiting customers.

> The ultimate goal of decentralized decision making is to put decision-making authority in the hands of those persons or teams closest to and most knowledgeable about the situation.

Pushing decision-making authority deep down into the organization structure and empowering employees presents its own organizing challenge: *how to exercise adequate control over the actions of empowered employees so that the business is not put at risk at the same time that the benefits of empowerment are realized.* Maintaining adequate organizational control over empowered employees is generally accomplished by placing limits on the authority that empowered personnel can exercise, holding people accountable for their decisions, instituting compensation incentives that reward people for doing their jobs in a manner that contributes to good company performance, and creating a corporate culture where there's strong peer pressure on individuals to act responsibly.

In a highly centralized organization structure, top executives retain authority for most strategic and operating decisions and keep a tight rein on business-unit heads, department heads, and the managers of key operating units; comparatively little discretionary authority is granted to frontline supervisors and rank-and-file employees. The command-and-control paradigm of centralized structures is based on the underlying assumption that frontline personnel have neither the time nor the inclination to direct and properly control the work they are performing, and that they lack the knowledge and judgment to make wise decisions about how best to do it.

The big advantage of an authoritarian structure is that it is easy to know who is accountable when things do not go well. But there are some serious disadvantages. Hierarchical command-and-control structures make an organization sluggish in responding to changing conditions because of the time it takes for the review/approval process to run up all the layers of the management bureaucracy. Also, centralized decision making is often impractical—the larger the company and the more scattered its operations, the more that decision-making authority has to be delegated to managers closer to the scene of the action.

Facilitating Collaboration with External Partners and Strategic Allies

Strategic alliances, outsourcing arrangements, joint ventures, and cooperative partnerships can contribute little of value without active management of the relationship. Building organizational bridges with external partners and strategic allies can be accomplished by appointing "relationship managers" with responsibility for fostering the success of strategic partnerships. Relationship managers have many roles and functions: getting the right people together, promoting good rapport, facilitating the flow of information, nurturing interpersonal communication and cooperation, and ensuring effective coordination.[12] Communication and coordination are particularly important since information sharing is required to make the relationship work and to address conflicts, trouble spots, and changing situations.

Communication and coordination are also aided by the adoption of a **network structure** that links independent organizations involved in cooperative arrangements to achieve some common undertaking. A well-managed network structure typically includes one firm in a more central role, with the responsibility of ensuring that the right partners are included and the activities across the network are coordinated. The high-end Italian motorcycle company Ducati operates in this manner, assembling its motorcycles from parts obtained from a hand-picked integrated network of parts suppliers.

> **CORE CONCEPT**
> A **network structure** is the arrangement linking a number of independent organizations involved in some common undertaking.

Allocating Resources to Strategy-Critical Activities

Early in the process of implementing and executing a new or different strategy, top management must determine what funding is needed to execute new strategic initiatives, to bolster value-creating processes, and to strengthen the company's capabilities and competencies. This includes careful screening of requests for more people and new facilities and equipment, approving those that hold promise for making a contribution to strategy execution, and turning down those that don't. Should internal cash flows prove insufficient to fund the planned strategic initiatives, then management must raise additional funds through borrowing or selling additional shares of stock to willing investors.

LO2 Learn why resource allocation should always be based on strategic priorities.

A company's ability to marshal the resources needed to support new strategic initiatives has a major impact on the strategy execution process. Too little funding slows progress and impedes the efforts of organizational units to execute their pieces of the strategic plan proficiently. Too much funding wastes organizational resources and reduces financial performance. Both outcomes argue for managers to be deeply involved in reviewing budget proposals and directing the proper amounts of resources to strategy-critical organization units.

A change in strategy nearly always calls for budget reallocations and resource shifting. Previously important units having a lesser role in the new strategy may need downsizing. Units that now have a bigger strategic role may need more people, new equipment, additional facilities, and above-average increases in their operating budgets. Strategy implementers have to exercise their power to put enough resources behind new strategic initiatives to make things happen, and they have to make the tough decisions to kill projects and activities that are no longer justified. Honda's strong support of R&D activities allowed it to develop the first low-polluting four-stroke outboard marine engine, a wide range of ultra-low-emission cars, the first hybrid car (Honda Insight) in the U.S. market, and the first hydrogen fuel cell car (Honda Clarity). However, Honda managers had no trouble stopping production of the Insight in 2006 when its sales failed to take off and then shifting resources to the development and manufacture of other promising hybrid models, including a redesigned Insight that was launched in the United States in 2009.

> A company's strategic priorities must drive how capital allocations are made and the size of each unit's operating budgets.

Instituting Strategy-Supportive Policies and Procedures

LO3 Understand why policies and procedures should be designed to facilitate good strategy execution.

A company's policies and procedures can either assist or become a barrier to good strategy execution. Anytime a company makes changes to its business strategy, managers are well advised to carefully review existing policies and procedures and revise or discard those that are out of sync. Well-conceived policies and operating procedures act to facilitate organizational change and good strategy execution in three ways:

> Well-conceived policies and procedures aid strategy execution; out-of-sync ones are barriers to effective implementation.

1. *Policies and procedures help enforce needed consistency in how particular strategy-critical activities are performed.* Standardization and strict conformity are sometimes desirable components of good strategy execution. Eliminating significant differences in the operating practices of different plants, sales regions, or customer service centers helps a company deliver consistent product quality and service to customers.

2. *Policies and procedures support change programs by providing top-down guidance regarding how certain things now need to be done.* Asking people to alter established habits and procedures always upsets the internal order of things. It is normal for pockets of resistance to develop and for people to exhibit some degree of stress and anxiety about how the changes will affect them. Policies are a particularly useful way to counteract tendencies for some people to resist change—most people refrain from violating company policy or going against recommended practices and procedures without first gaining clearance or having strong justification.

3. *Well-conceived policies and procedures promote a work climate that facilitates good strategy execution.* Managers can use the policy-changing process as a powerful lever for changing the corporate culture in ways that produce a stronger fit with the new strategy.

McDonald's policy manual spells out detailed procedures that personnel in each McDonald's unit are expected to observe to ensure consistent quality across its 31,000 units. For example, "Cooks must turn, never flip, hamburgers. If they haven't been purchased, Big Macs must be discarded in 10 minutes after being cooked and French fries in 7 minutes." To get store personnel to dedicate themselves to outstanding customer service, Nordstrom has a policy of promoting only those people whose personnel records contain evidence of "heroic acts" to please customers, especially customers who may have made "unreasonable requests" that require special efforts.

One of the big policy-making issues concerns what activities need to be rigidly prescribed and what activities allow room for independent action on the part of empowered personnel. Few companies need thick policy manuals to prescribe exactly how daily operations are to be conducted. Too much policy can be confusing and erect obstacles to good strategy implementation. There is wisdom in a middle approach: *Prescribe enough policies to place boundaries on employees' actions; then empower them to act within these boundaries in whatever way they think makes sense.* Allowing company personnel to act anywhere between the "white lines" is especially appropriate when individual creativity and initiative are more essential to good strategy execution than standardization and strict conformity.

Striving for Continuous Improvement in Processes and Activities

Company managers can significantly advance the cause of superior strategy execution by pushing organization units and company personnel to strive for continuous improvement in how value chain activities are performed. In aiming for operating excellence, many companies have come to rely on three potent management tools: business process reengineering, total quality management (TQM) programs, and Six Sigma quality control techniques. *Business process reengineering* involves pulling the pieces of strategy-critical activities out of different departments and unifying their performance in a single department or cross-functional work group.[13] When done properly, business process reengineering can produce dramatic operating benefits. In the order-processing section of General Electric's circuit breaker division, elapsed time from order receipt to delivery was cut from three weeks to three days by consolidating six production units into one, reducing a variety of former inventory and handling steps, automating the design system to replace a human custom-design process, and cutting the organizational layers between managers and workers from three to one. Productivity rose 20 percent in one year, and unit manufacturing costs dropped 30 percent.[14]

Total quality management (TQM) is a philosophy of managing a set of business practices that emphasizes continuous improvement in all phases of

LO4 Understand how process management programs that drive continuous improvement help an organization achieve operating excellence.

operations, 100 percent accuracy in performing tasks, involvement and empowerment of employees at all levels, team-based work design, benchmarking, and total customer satisfaction.[15] While TQM concentrates on the production of quality goods and fully satisfying customer expectations, it achieves its biggest successes when it is extended to employee efforts in *all departments*—human resources, billing, R&D, engineering, accounting and records, and information systems. It involves reforming the corporate culture and shifting to a total quality/continuous improvement business philosophy that permeates every facet of the organization.[16] TQM doctrine preaches that there's no such thing as "good enough" and that everyone has a responsibility to participate in continuous improvement. TQM is thus a race without a finish. Success comes from making little steps forward each day, a process that the Japanese call *kaizen.*

Six Sigma quality control consists of a disciplined, statistics-based system aimed at producing not more than 3.4 defects per million iterations for any business process—from manufacturing to customer transactions.[17] The Six Sigma process of define, measure, analyze, improve, and control (DMAIC, pronounced *Dee-may-ic*) is an improvement system for existing processes falling below specification. The Six Sigma DMADV (define, measure, analyze, design, and verify) methodology is used to develop *new* processes or products at Six Sigma quality levels.[18] DMADV is sometimes referred to as Design for Six Sigma (DFSS). The statistical thinking underlying Six Sigma is based on the following three principles: All work is a process, all processes have variability, and all processes create data that explain variability.[19] To illustrate how these three principles work, consider the case of a Milwaukee hospital that used Six Sigma to map the prescription-filling process. Prescriptions written in the hospital originated with a doctor's write-up, were filled by the hospital pharmacy, and then administered by nurses. DMAIC analysis revealed that most mistakes came from misreading the doctor's handwriting.[20] The hospital implemented a program requiring doctors to type the prescription into a computer, which slashed the number of errors dramatically. Concepts & Connections 10.2 describes Whirlpool's use of Six Sigma in its appliance business.

While Six Sigma programs often improve the efficiency of many operating activities and processes, evidence shows that Six Sigma programs can stifle innovation. The essence of Six Sigma is to reduce variability in processes, but creative processes, by nature, include quite a bit of variability. In many instances, breakthrough innovations occur only after thousands of ideas have been abandoned and promising ideas have gone through multiple iterations and extensive prototyping. Google CEO Eric Schmidt has commented that the innovation process is "anti–Six Sigma" and applying Six Sigma principles to those performing creative work at Google would choke off innovation at the company.[21]

A blended approach to Six Sigma implementation that is gaining in popularity pursues incremental improvements in operating efficiency, while R&D and other processes that allow the company to develop new ways of offering value to customers are given more free rein. Managers of these *ambidextrous organizations* are adept at employing continuous improvement in operating

CONCEPTS & CONNECTIONS 10.2

WHIRLPOOL'S USE OF SIX SIGMA TO PROMOTE OPERATING EXCELLENCE

Top management at Whirlpool Corporation (with 66 manufacturing and technology centers around the globe and sales in some 170 countries totaling more than $18 billion in 2012) has a vision of Whirlpool appliances in "Every Home . . . Everywhere with Pride, Passion, and Performance." One of management's chief objectives in pursuing this vision is to build unmatched customer loyalty to the Whirlpool brand. Whirlpool's strategy to win the hearts and minds of appliance buyers the world over has been to produce and market appliances with top-notch quality and innovative features that users will find appealing. In addition, Whirlpool's strategy has been to offer a wide selection of models (recognizing that buyer tastes and needs differ) and to strive for low-cost production efficiency, thereby enabling Whirlpool to price its products very competitively. Executing this strategy at Whirlpool's operations in North America (where it is the market leader), Latin America (where it is also the market leader), Europe (where it ranks third), and Asia (where it is number one in India and has a foothold with huge growth opportunities elsewhere) has involved a strong focus on continuous improvement, lean manufacturing capabilities, and a drive for operating excellence. To marshal the efforts of its 68,000 employees in executing the strategy successfully, management developed a comprehensive Operational Excellence program with Six Sigma as one of the centerpieces.

The Operational Excellence initiative, which began in the 1990s, incorporated Six Sigma techniques to improve the quality of Whirlpool products and, at the same time, lower costs and trim the time it took to get product innovations into the marketplace. The Six Sigma program helped Whirlpool save $175 million in manufacturing costs in its first three years.

To sustain the productivity gains and cost savings, Whirlpool embedded Six Sigma practices within each of its manufacturing facilities and instilled a culture based on Six Sigma and lean manufacturing skills and capabilities. In 2002, each of Whirlpool's operating units began taking the Six Sigma initiative to a higher level by first placing the needs of the customer at the center of every function—R&D, technology, manufacturing, marketing, and administrative support—and then striving to consistently improve quality levels while eliminating all unnecessary costs. The company systematically went through every aspect of its business with the view that company personnel should perform every activity at every level in a manner that delivers value to the customer and leads to continuous improvement on how things are done.

Whirlpool management believes that the company's Operational Excellence process has been a major contributor in sustaining the company's position as the leading global manufacturer and marketer of home appliances.

Source: www.whirlpool.com, accessed June 27, 2013; LexisNexis Edgar Online, exhibit type: exhibit 99, additional exhibits, filing date: June 21, 2010.

---

processes but allowing R&D to operate under a set of rules that allows for the development of breakthrough innovations. Ciba Vision, a global leader in contact lenses, dramatically reduced operating expenses through the use of continuous improvement programs, while simultaneously and harmoniously developing new series of contact lens products that grew its revenues by 300 percent over a 10-year period.[22]

The Difference between Business Process Reengineering and Continuous Improvement Programs

Business process reengineering and continuous improvement efforts such as TQM and Six Sigma both aim at improved efficiency, better product quality, and greater customer satisfaction. The essential difference between business process reengineering and continuous improvement programs is that reengineering aims at *quantum gains* on the order of 30 to 50 percent or more whereas total quality programs stress *incremental progress*—striving for inch-by-inch gains again and again in a never-ending stream. The two approaches to improved performance of value chain activities and operating excellence are not mutually exclusive; it makes sense to use them in tandem. Reengineering can be used first to produce a good basic design that yields quick, dramatic improvements in performing a business process. Total quality programs can then be used as a follow-up to deliver continuing improvements.

> The purpose of using benchmarking, best practices, business process reengineering, TQM, Six Sigma, or other operational improvement programs is to improve the performance of strategy-critical activities and promote superior strategy execution.

Installing Information and Operating Systems

LO5 Recognize the role of information and operating systems in enabling company personnel to carry out their strategic roles proficiently.

Company strategies and value-creating internal processes can't be executed well without a number of internal operating systems. FedEx has internal communication systems that allow it to coordinate its more than 90,000 vehicles in handling a daily average of 8.5 million shipments to 220 countries. Its leading-edge flight operations systems allow a single controller to direct as many as 200 of FedEx's 690 aircraft simultaneously, overriding their flight plans should weather problems or other special circumstances arise. In addition, FedEx has created a series of e-business tools for customers that allow them to track packages online, create address books, review shipping history, generate custom reports, simplify customer billing, reduce internal warehousing and inventory management costs, purchase goods and services from suppliers, and respond to quickly changing customer demands. All of FedEx's systems support the company's strategy of providing businesses and individuals with a broad array of package delivery services and enhancing its competitiveness against United Parcel Service, DHL, and the U.S. Postal Service.

Telephone companies have elaborate information systems to measure signal quality, connection times, interrupts, wrong connections, billing errors, and other measures of reliability that affect customer service and satisfaction. British Petroleum (BP) has outfitted railcars carrying hazardous materials with sensors and global-positioning systems so that it can track the status, location, and other information about these shipments via satellite and relay the data to its corporate intranet. At eBay, there are systems for real-time monitoring of new listings, bidding activity, website traffic, and page views.

> Having state-of-the-art operating systems, information systems, and real-time data is integral to competent strategy execution and operating excellence.

Information systems need to cover five broad areas: (1) customer data, (2) operations data, (3) employee data, (4) supplier/partner/collaborative ally data, and (5) financial performance data. All key strategic performance indicators have to be tracked and reported as often as practical. Long the norm, monthly profit-and-loss statements and monthly statistical summaries are fast being replaced with daily statistical updates and even up-to-the-minute performance monitoring. Many retail companies have automated online systems that generate daily sales reports for each store and maintain up-to-the-minute inventory and sales records on each item. Manufacturing plants typically generate daily production reports and track labor productivity on every shift. Many retailers and manufacturers have online data systems connecting them with their suppliers that monitor the status of inventories, track shipments and deliveries, and measure defect rates. Regardless of the industry, real-time information systems permit company managers to stay on top of implementation initiatives and daily operations, and to intervene if things seem to be drifting off course.

Using Rewards and Incentives to Promote Better Strategy Execution

To create a strategy-supportive system of rewards and incentives, a company must emphasize rewarding people for accomplishing results related to creating value for customers, not for just dutifully performing assigned tasks. Focusing jobholders' attention and energy on what to *achieve* as opposed to what to *do* makes the work environment results-oriented. It is flawed management to tie incentives and rewards to satisfactory performance of duties and activities instead of desired business outcomes and company achievements.[23] In any job, performing assigned tasks is not equivalent to achieving intended outcomes.

LO6   Learn how and why the use of well-designed incentives and rewards can be management's single most powerful tool for promoting operating excellence.

Diligently showing up for work and attending to job assignment does not, by itself, guarantee results. As any student knows, the fact that an instructor teaches and students go to class doesn't necessarily mean that the students are learning.

> A properly designed reward structure is management's most powerful tool for gaining employee commitment to superior strategy execution and excellent operating results.

Motivation and Reward Systems

It is important for both organization units and individuals to be properly aligned with strategic priorities and enthusiastically committed to executing strategy. *To get employees' sustained, energetic commitment, management has to be resourceful in designing and using motivational incentives—both monetary and nonmonetary.* The more a manager understands what motivates subordinates and is able to use appropriate motivational incentives, the greater will be employees' commitment to good day-in, day-out strategy execution and achievement of performance targets.

Guidelines for Designing Monetary Incentive Systems

Guidelines for creating incentive compensation systems that link employee behavior to organizational objectives include:

1. *Make the performance payoff a major, not minor, piece of the total compensation package.* The payoff for high-performing individuals and teams must be meaningfully greater than the payoff for average performers, and the payoff for average performers meaningfully bigger than for below-average performers.

2. *Have incentives that extend to all managers and all workers, not just top management.* Lower-level managers and employees are just as likely as senior executives to be motivated by the possibility of lucrative rewards.

3. *Administer the reward system with scrupulous objectivity and fairness.* If performance standards are set unrealistically high or if individual/ group performance evaluations are not accurate and well documented, dissatisfaction with the system will overcome any positive benefits.

4. *Tie incentives to performance outcomes directly linked to good strategy execution and financial performance.* Incentives should never be paid just because people are thought to be "doing a good job" or because they "work hard." An argument can be presented that exceptions should be made in giving rewards to people who've come up short because of circumstances beyond their control. The problem with making exceptions for unknowable, uncontrollable, or unforeseeable circumstances is that once good excuses start to creep into justifying rewards for subpar results, the door is open for all kinds of reasons actual performance has failed to match targeted performance.

5. *Make sure the performance targets that each individual or team is expected to achieve involve outcomes that the individual or team can personally affect.* The role of incentives is to enhance individual commitment and channel behavior in beneficial directions.

6. *Keep the time between achieving the target performance outcome and the payment of the reward as short as possible.* Weekly or monthly payments for good performance work much better than annual payments for employees in most job categories. Annual bonus payouts work best for higher-level managers and for situations where target outcome relates to overall company profitability or stock price performance.

Once the incentives are designed, they have to be communicated and explained. Everybody needs to understand how their incentive compensation is calculated and how individual/group performance targets contribute to organizational performance targets.

Nonmonetary Rewards

Financial incentives generally head the list of motivating tools for trying to gain wholehearted employee commitment to good strategy execution and operating excellence. But most successful companies also make extensive use of nonmonetary incentives. Some of the most important nonmonetary approaches used to enhance motivation are listed below:[24]

- *Provide attractive perks and fringe benefits.* The various options include full coverage of health insurance premiums; college tuition reimbursement; paid vacation time; on-site child care; on-site fitness centers; telecommuting; and compressed workweeks (four 10-hour days instead of five 8-hour days).

- *Adopt promotion-from-within policies.* This practice helps bind workers to their employers and employers to their workers, plus it is an incentive for good performance.

CONCEPTS & CONNECTIONS 10.3

WHAT COMPANIES DO TO MOTIVATE AND REWARD EMPLOYEES

Companies have come up with an impressive variety of motivational and reward practices to help create a work environment that energizes employees and promotes better strategy execution. Here's a sampling of what companies are doing:

- Google has a sprawling 20-building headquarters complex known as the Googleplex where its several thousand employees have access to 19 cafés and 60 snack centers, unlimited ice cream, four gyms, heated swimming pools, ping-pong and pool tables, and community bicycles to go from building to building. Management built the Googleplex to be "a dream workplace" and a showcase for environmentally correct building design and construction.

- At JM Family Enterprises, a Toyota distributor in Florida, employees get attractive lease options on new Toyotas and enjoy on-site amenities such as a heated lap pool, a fitness center, a free nail salon, free prescriptions delivered by a "pharmacy concierge," and professionally made take-home dinners. Exceptionally high performers are flown to the Bahamas for cruises on the 172-foot company yacht.

- Wegmans, a family-owned grocer with 75 stores on the East Coast of the United States, provides employees with flexible schedules and benefits that include on-site fitness centers. The company's approach to managing people allows it to provide a very high level of customer service not found in other grocery chains. Employees ranging from cashiers to butchers to store managers are all treated equally and viewed as experts in their jobs. Employees receive 50 hours of formal training per year and are allowed to make decisions that they believe are appropriate for their jobs. The company's 2012 annual turnover rate is only 4 percent, which is less than one-fourth the 19 percent average turnover rate in the U.S. supermarket industry.

- At Ukrop's Super Markets, a family-owned chain, stores are closed on Sunday; the company pays out 20 percent of pretax profits to employees in the form of quarterly bonuses; and the company picks up the membership tab for employees if they visit their health club 30 times a quarter.

Sources: http://money.cnn.com/magazines/fortune/best-companies/2013/, accessed June 27, 2013; Jefferson Graham, "The Search Engine That Could," *USA Today,* August 26, 2003, p. B3; and company websites.

- *Act on suggestions from employees.* Research indicates that the moves of many companies to push decision making down the line and empower employees increases employee motivation and satisfaction, as well as boosting productivity.

- *Create a work atmosphere in which there is genuine sincerity, caring, and mutual respect among workers and between management and employees.* A "family" work environment where people are on a first-name basis and there is strong camaraderie promotes teamwork and cross-unit collaboration.

- *Share information with employees about financial performance, strategy, operational measures, market conditions, and competitors' actions.* Broad disclosure and prompt communication send the message that managers trust their workers.

- *Have attractive office spaces and facilities.* A workplace environment with appealing features and amenities usually has decidedly positive effects on employee morale and productivity.

Concepts & Connections 10.3 presents specific examples of the motivational tactics employed by several prominent companies that have appeared on *Fortune*'s list of the "100 Best Companies to Work For" in America.

Instilling a Corporate Culture That Promotes Good Strategy Execution

LO7 Gain an understanding of how and why a company's culture can aid the drive for proficient strategy execution.

Every company has its own unique culture. The character of a company's culture or work climate defines "how we do things around here," its approach to people management, and the "chemistry" that permeates its work environment. The meshing of shared core values, beliefs, ingrained behaviors and attitudes, and business principles constitutes a company's **corporate culture.** A company's culture is important because it influences the organization's actions and approaches to conducting business—in a very real sense, the culture is the company's organizational DNA.[25]

> ## CORE CONCEPT
>
> **Corporate culture** is a company's internal work climate and is shaped by its core values, beliefs, and business principles. A company's culture is important because it influences its traditions, work practices, and style of operating.

The psyche of corporate cultures varies widely. For instance, the bedrock of Walmart's culture is dedication to customer satisfaction, zealous pursuit of low costs and frugal operating practices, a strong work ethic, ritualistic Saturday-morning headquarters meetings to exchange ideas and review problems, and company executives' commitment to visiting stores, listening to customers, and soliciting suggestions from employees. At Nordstrom, the corporate culture is centered on delivering exceptional service to customers, where the company's motto is "Respond to unreasonable customer requests," and each out-of-the-ordinary request is seen as an opportunity for a "heroic" act by an employee that can further the company's reputation for unparalleled customer service. Nordstrom makes a point of promoting employees noted for their heroic acts and dedication to outstanding service. The company motivates its salespeople with a commission-based compensation system that enables Nordstrom's best salespeople to earn more than double what other department stores pay. Concepts & Connections 10.4 describes the corporate culture at W.L. Gore & Associates—the inventor of Gore-Tex.

High-Performance Cultures

Some companies have so-called "high-performance" cultures where the standout cultural traits are a "can-do" spirit, pride in doing things right, no-excuses accountability, and a pervasive results-oriented work climate where people go the extra mile to meet or beat stretch objectives. In high-performance cultures, there's a strong sense of involvement on the part of company personnel and emphasis on individual initiative and creativity. Performance expectations are clearly stated for the company as a whole, for each organizational unit, and for each individual. Issues and problems are promptly addressed—there's a razor-sharp focus on what needs to be done. A high-performance culture where there's constructive pressure to achieve good results is a valuable contributor to good strategy execution and operating excellence. Results-oriented cultures are permeated with a spirit of achievement and have a good track record in meeting or beating performance targets.[26]

The challenge in creating a high-performance culture is to inspire high loyalty and dedication on the part of employees, such that they are energized to

CONCEPTS & CONNECTIONS 10.4

THE CULTURE THAT DRIVES INNOVATION AT W.L. GORE & ASSOCIATES

W.L. Gore & Associates is best known for Gore-Tex, the waterproof/breathable fabric so highly prized by outdoor enthusiasts. But the company has developed a wide variety of other revolutionary products, including Elixir guitar strings, Ride-On bike cables, and a host of medical devices such as cardiovascular patches and synthetic blood vessels. As a result, it is now one of the largest privately held companies in the United States, with roughly $3 billion in revenue and more than 9,500 employees in 30 countries worldwide.

When the company developed the core technology on which most of its more than 2,000 worldwide patents is based, its unique culture played a crucial role in allowing it to pursue multiple end-market applications simultaneously, enabling rapid growth from a niche business into a diversified multinational company. The company's culture is team-based and designed to foster personal initiative. It is described on the company's website as follows:

> There are no traditional organizational charts, no chains of command, nor predetermined channels of communication. Instead, we communicate directly with each other and are accountable to fellow members of our multi-disciplines teams. We encourage hands-on innovation, involving those closest to a project in decision making. Teams organize around opportunities and leaders emerge.

Personal stories posted on the website describe the discovery process behind a number of breakthrough products developed by particular teams at W.L. Gore & Associates. Employees are encouraged to use 10 percent of their time to tinker with new ideas and to take the long view regarding the idea's development. Promising ideas attract more people who are willing to work on them without orders from higher-ups. Instead, self-managing associates operating in self-developed teams are simply encouraged to pursue novel applications of Gore technology until they are fully commercialized or have had their potential exhausted. The encouragement comes from both the culture (norms and practices) of the organization and from a profit-sharing arrangement that allows employees to benefit directly from their successes.

This approach makes Gore a great place to work and has helped it attract, retain, and motivate top talent globally. Gore has been on *Fortune* magazine's list of the "100 Best Companies to Work For" in America for the past 15 years. It places similarly on the lists of other countries in which it operates, including the United Kingdom, Germany, France, Italy, and Sweden.

Developed with Kenneth P. Fraser.

Sources: Company websites; www.gore.com/en_xx/news/FORTUNE-2011.html; www.director.co.uk/magazine/2010/2_Feb/WLGore_63_06.html; www.fastcompany.com/magazine/89/open_gore.html.

put forth their very best efforts to do things right. Managers have to take pains to reinforce constructive behavior, reward top performers, and purge habits and behaviors that stand in the way of good results. They must work at knowing the strengths and weaknesses of their subordinates, so as to better match talent with task. In sum, there has to be an overall disciplined, performance-focused approach to managing the organization.

Adaptive Cultures

The hallmark of adaptive corporate cultures is willingness on the part of organizational members to accept change and take on the challenge of introducing and executing new strategies. In direct contrast to change-resistant cultures, **adaptive cultures** are very supportive of managers and employees at all ranks who propose or help initiate useful change. Internal entrepreneurship on the part of individuals and groups is encouraged and rewarded. Senior executives seek out, support, and promote individuals who exercise initiative,

> As a company's strategy evolves, an adaptive culture is a definite ally in the strategy execution process.

spot opportunities for improvement, and display the skills to take advantage of them. As in high-performance cultures, the company exhibits a proactive approach to identifying issues, evaluating the implications and options, and quickly moving ahead with workable solutions.

Technology companies, software companies, and Internet-based companies are good illustrations of organizations with adaptive cultures. Such companies thrive on change—driving it, leading it, and capitalizing on it (but sometimes also succumbing to change when they make the wrong move or are swamped by better technologies or the superior business models of rivals). Companies such as Twitter, Groupon, Apple, Google, and Intel cultivate the capability to act and react rapidly. They are avid practitioners of entrepreneurship and innovation, with a demonstrated willingness to take bold risks to create new products, new businesses, and new industries. To create and nurture a culture that can adapt rapidly to changing or shifting business conditions, they staff their organizations with people who are proactive, who rise to the challenge of change, and who have an aptitude for adapting.

In fast-changing business environments, a corporate culture that is receptive to altering organizational practices and behaviors is a virtual necessity. However, adaptive cultures work to the advantage of all companies, not just those in rapid-change environments. Every company operates in a market and business climate that is changing to one degree or another. *As a company's strategy evolves, an adaptive culture is a definite ally in the strategy implementation, strategy execution process as compared to cultures that have to be coaxed and cajoled to change.*

Unhealthy Corporate Cultures

The distinctive characteristic of an unhealthy corporate culture is the presence of counterproductive cultural traits that adversely impact the work climate and company performance.[27] Five particularly unhealthy cultural traits are a heavily politicized internal environment, hostility to change, an insular "not invented here" mind-set, a disregard for high ethical standards, and the presence of incompatible, clashing subcultures.

Politicized Cultures A politicized internal environment is unhealthy because political infighting consumes a great deal of organizational energy and often results in the company's strategic agenda taking a backseat to political maneuvering. In companies where internal politics pervades the work climate, empire-building managers pursue their own agendas, and the positions they take on issues are usually aimed at protecting or expanding their turf. The support or opposition of politically influential executives and/or coalitions among departments with vested interests in a particular outcome typically weighs heavily in deciding what actions the company takes. All this maneuvering detracts from efforts to execute strategy with real proficiency and frustrates company personnel who are less political and more inclined to do what is in the company's best interests.

Change-Resistant Cultures Change-resistant cultures encourage a number of undesirable or unhealthy behaviors—avoiding risks, hesitation in pursuing emerging opportunities, and widespread aversion to continuous improvement in performing value chain activities. Change-resistant companies have little appetite for being first movers or fast followers, believing that being in the forefront of change is too risky and that acting too quickly increases vulnerability to costly mistakes. They are more inclined to adopt a wait-and-see posture, learn from the missteps of early movers, and then move forward cautiously with initiatives that are deemed safe. Hostility to change is most often found in companies with multilayered management bureaucracies that have enjoyed considerable market success in years past and that are wedded to the "We have done it this way for years" syndrome.

General Motors, IBM, Sears, and Eastman Kodak are classic examples of companies whose change-resistant bureaucracies have damaged their market standings and financial performance; clinging to what made them successful, they were reluctant to alter operating practices and modify their business approaches when signals of market change first sounded. As strategies of gradual change won out over bold innovation, all four lost market share to rivals that quickly moved to institute changes more in tune with evolving market conditions and buyer preferences. While IBM has made strides in building a culture needed for market success, Sears, GM, and Kodak are still struggling to recoup lost ground.

Insular, Inwardly Focused Cultures Sometimes a company reigns as an industry leader or enjoys great market success for so long that its personnel start to believe they have all the answers or can develop them on their own. Such confidence breeds arrogance—company personnel discount the merits of what outsiders are doing and what can be learned by studying best-in-class performers. Benchmarking and a search for the best practices of outsiders are seen as offering little payoff. The big risk of a must-be-invented-here mind-set and insular cultural thinking is that the company can underestimate the competencies and accomplishments of rival companies and overestimate its own progress—with a resulting loss of competitive advantage over time.

Unethical and Greed-Driven Cultures Companies that have little regard for ethical standards or that are run by executives driven by greed and ego gratification are scandals waiting to happen. Executives exude the negatives of arrogance, ego, greed, and an "ends-justify-the-means" mentality in pursuing overambitious revenue and profitability targets.[28] Senior managers wink at unethical behavior and may cross the line to unethical (and sometimes criminal) behavior themselves. They are prone to adopt accounting principles that make financial performance look better than it really is. Legions of companies have fallen prey to unethical behavior and greed, most notably WorldCom, Enron, Quest, HealthSouth, Adelphia, Tyco, Parmalat, Marsh & McLennan, Countrywide Financial, World Savings Bank, and Stanford Financial Group, with executives being indicted and/or convicted of criminal behavior.

Incompatible Subcultures It is not unusual for companies to have multiple subcultures with values, beliefs, and ingrained behaviors and attitudes varying to some extent by department, geographic location, division, or business unit. These subcultures within a company don't pose a problem as long as the subcultures don't conflict with the overarching corporate work climate and are supportive of the strategy execution effort. Multiple subcultures become unhealthy when they are incompatible with each other or the overall corporate culture. The existence of conflicting business philosophies and values eventually leads to inconsistent strategy execution. Incompatible subcultures arise most commonly because of important cultural differences between a company's culture and those of a recently acquired company or because of a merger between companies with cultural differences. Cultural due diligence is often as important as financial due diligence in deciding whether to go forward on an acquisition or merger. On a number of occasions, companies have decided to pass on acquiring particular companies because of culture conflicts they believed would be hard to resolve.

Changing a Problem Culture

Changing a company culture that impedes proficient strategy execution is among the toughest management tasks. It is natural for company personnel to cling to familiar practices and to be wary, if not hostile, to new approaches toward how things are to be done. Consequently, it takes concerted management action over a period of time to root out certain unwanted behaviors and replace an out-of-sync culture with more effective ways of doing things. *The single most visible factor that distinguishes successful culture-change efforts from failed attempts is competent leadership at the top.* Great power is needed to force major cultural change and overcome the unremitting resistance of entrenched cultures—and great power is possessed only by the most senior executives, especially the CEO. However, while top management must lead the culture-change effort, instilling new cultural behaviors is a job for the whole management team. Middle managers and frontline supervisors play a key role in implementing the new work practices and operating approaches, helping win rank-and-file acceptance of and support for the changes, and instilling the desired behavioral norms.

As shown in Figure 10.2, the first step in fixing a problem culture is for top management to identify those facets of the present culture that pose obstacles to executing new strategic initiatives. Second, managers have to clearly define the desired new behaviors and features of the culture they want to create. Third, managers have to convince company personnel why the present culture poses problems and why and how new behaviors and operating approaches will improve company performance. Finally, all the talk about remodeling the present culture has to be followed swiftly by visible, forceful actions on the part of management to promote the desired new behaviors and work practices.

Making a Compelling Case for a Culture Change The place for management to begin a major remodeling of the corporate culture is by selling company personnel on the need for new-style behaviors and work practices. This means making a compelling case for why the company's new strategic direction and culture-remodeling efforts are in the organization's best

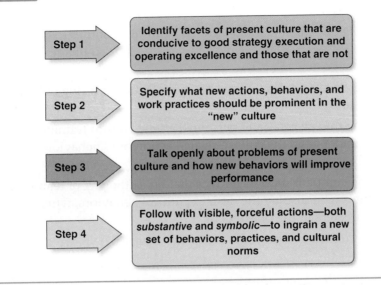

FIGURE 10.2   **Steps in Changing a Problem Culture**

interests and why company personnel should wholeheartedly join the effort to do things somewhat differently. This can be done by:

- Citing reasons the current strategy has to be modified and why new strategic initiatives are being undertaken. The case for altering the old strategy usually needs to be predicated on its shortcomings—why sales are growing slowly, why too many customers are opting to go with the products of rivals, why costs are too high, and so on. There may be merit in holding events where managers and other key personnel are forced to listen to dissatisfied customers or the complaints of strategic allies.

- Citing why and how certain behavioral norms and work practices in the current culture pose obstacles to good execution of new strategic initiatives.

- Explaining why new behaviors and work practices have important roles in the new culture and will produce better results.

Management's efforts to make a persuasive case for changing what is deemed to be a problem culture must be *quickly followed* by forceful, high-profile actions across several fronts. The actions to implant the new culture must be both substantive and symbolic.

Substantive Culture-Changing Actions   No culture-change effort can get very far when leaders merely talk about the need for different actions, behaviors, and work practices. Company executives have to give the culture-change effort some teeth by initiating *a series of actions* that company personnel will see as *unmistakable support* for the change program. The strongest signs that management is truly committed to instilling a new culture include:

1. Replacing key executives who stonewall needed organizational and cultural changes.

2. Promoting individuals who have stepped forward to advocate the shift to a different culture and who can serve as role models for the desired cultural behavior.

3. Appointing outsiders with the desired cultural attributes to high-profile positions—bringing in new-breed managers sends an unambiguous message that a new era is dawning.

4. Screening all candidates for new positions carefully, hiring only those who appear to fit in with the new culture.

5. Mandating that all company personnel attend culture-training programs to better understand the culture-related actions and behaviors that are expected.

6. Designing compensation incentives that boost the pay of teams and individuals who display the desired cultural behaviors, while hitting change-resisters in the pocketbook.

7. Revising policies and procedures in ways that will help drive cultural change.

Symbolic Culture-Changing Actions

There's also an important place for symbolic managerial actions to alter a problem culture and tighten the strategy–culture fit. The most important symbolic actions are those that top executives take to *lead by example*. For instance, if the organization's strategy involves a drive to become the industry's low-cost producer, senior managers must display frugality in their own actions and decisions: inexpensive decorations in the executive suite, conservative expense accounts and entertainment allowances, a lean staff in the corporate office, few executive perks, and so on. At Walmart, all the executive offices are simply decorated; executives are habitually frugal in their own actions, and they are zealous in their own efforts to control costs and promote greater efficiency. At Nucor, one of the world's low-cost producers of steel products, executives fly coach class and use taxis at airports rather than limousines. Top executives must be alert to the fact that company personnel will be watching their actions and decisions to see if they are walking the talk.[29]

Another category of symbolic actions includes holding ceremonial events to single out and honor people whose actions and performance exemplify what is called for in the new culture. A point is made of holding events to celebrate each culture-change success. Executives sensitive to their role in promoting the strategy–culture fit make a habit of appearing at ceremonial functions to praise individuals and groups that get with the program. They show up at employee training programs to stress strategic priorities, values, ethical principles, and cultural norms. Every group gathering is seen as an opportunity to repeat and ingrain values, praise good deeds, and cite instances of how the new work practices and operating approaches have led to improved results.

LO8 Understand what constitutes effective managerial leadership in achieving superior strategy execution.

Leading the Strategy Execution Process

For an enterprise to execute its strategy in truly proficient fashion and approach operating excellence, top executives have to take the lead in the implementation/execution process and personally drive the pace of progress. They have to be out in the field, seeing for themselves how well operations are going, gathering information firsthand, and gauging the progress being made. Proficient strategy execution requires company managers to be diligent and adept in spotting problems, learning what obstacles lie in the path of good execution, and then clearing the way for progress—the goal must be to produce better results speedily and productively.[30] In general, leading the drive for good strategy execution and operating excellence calls for three actions on the part of the manager:

- Staying on top of what is happening and closely monitoring progress.
- Putting constructive pressure on the organization to execute the strategy well and achieve operating excellence.
- Initiating corrective actions to improve strategy execution and achieve the targeted performance results.

Staying on Top of How Well Things Are Going

One of the best ways for executives to stay on top of strategy execution is by regularly visiting the field and talking with many different people at many different levels—a technique often labeled *managing by walking around* (MBWA). Walmart executives have had a long-standing practice of spending two to three days every week visiting stores and talking with store managers and employees. Jeff Bezos, Amazon.com's CEO, is noted for his frequent facilities visits and his insistence that other Amazon managers spend time in the trenches with their people to prevent overly abstract thinking and getting disconnected from the reality of what's happening.[31]

Most managers practice MBWA, attaching great importance to gathering information from people at different organizational levels about how well various aspects of the strategy execution are going. They believe facilities visits and face-to-face contacts give them a good feel for what progress is being made, what problems are being encountered, and whether additional resources or different approaches may be needed. Just as important, MBWA provides opportunities to give encouragement, lift spirits, shift attention from old to new priorities, and create excitement—all of which help mobilize organizational efforts behind strategy execution.

Putting Constructive Pressure on Organizational Units to Achieve Good Results and Operating Excellence

Managers have to be out front in mobilizing the effort for good strategy execution and operating excellence. Part of the leadership requirement here entails fostering a results-oriented work climate, where performance standards are high and a spirit of achievement is pervasive. Successfully leading the effort to foster a results-oriented, high-performance culture generally entails such leadership actions and managerial practices as:

- *Treating employees with dignity and respect.*
- *Encouraging employees to use initiative and creativity in performing their work.*
- *Setting stretch objectives* and clearly communicating an expectation that company personnel are to give their best in achieving performance targets.

- *Focusing attention on continuous improvement.*
- *Using the full range of motivational techniques and compensation incentives to reward high performance.*
- *Celebrating individual, group, and company successes.* Top management should miss no opportunity to express respect for individual employees and show appreciation of extraordinary individual and group effort.[32]

While leadership efforts to instill a spirit of high achievement into the culture usually accentuate the positive, there are negative reinforcers too. Low-performing workers and people who reject the results-oriented cultural emphasis have to be weeded out or at least moved to out-of-the-way positions. Average performers have to be candidly counseled that they have limited career potential unless they show more progress in the form of additional effort, better skills, and improved ability to deliver good results. In addition, managers whose units consistently perform poorly have to be replaced.

Pushing Corrective Actions to Improve Both the Company's Strategy and Its Execution

The leadership challenge of making corrective adjustments is twofold: deciding when adjustments are needed and deciding what adjustments to make. Both decisions are a normal and necessary part of managing the strategic management process, since no scheme for implementing and executing strategy can foresee all the events and problems that will arise.[33] There comes a time at every company when managers have to fine-tune or overhaul the company's strategy or its approaches to strategy execution and push for better results. Clearly, when a company's strategy or its execution efforts are not delivering good results, it is the leader's responsibility to step forward and push corrective actions.

KEY POINTS

Implementing and executing strategy is an operations-driven activity revolving around the management of people and business processes. The managerial emphasis is on converting strategic plans into actions and good results. *Management's handling of the process of implementing and executing the chosen strategy can be considered successful if and when the company achieves the targeted strategic and financial performance and shows good progress in making its strategic vision a reality.*

Like crafting strategy, executing strategy is a job for a company's whole management team, not just a few senior managers. Top-level managers have to rely on the active support and cooperation of middle and lower-level managers to push strategy changes into functional areas and operating units and to see that the organization actually operates in accordance with the strategy on a daily basis.

Eight managerial tasks crop up repeatedly in company efforts to execute strategy:

1. *Building an organization capable of executing the strategy successfully.* Building an organization capable of good strategy execution entails three types of organization-building actions: *(a) staffing the organization*—assembling a

EXERCISES FOR SIMULATION PARTICIPANTS

1. How would you describe the organization of your company's top management team? Is some decision making decentralized and delegated to individual managers? If so, explain how the decentralization works. Or are decisions made more by consensus, with all co-managers having input? What do you see as the advantages and disadvantages of the decision-making approach your company is employing?

   LO1

2. Have you and your co-managers allocated ample resources to strategy-critical areas? If so, explain how these investments have contributed to good strategy execution and improved company performance.

   LO2

3. Does your company have opportunities to use incentive compensation techniques? If so, explain your company's approach to incentive compensation. Is there any hard evidence you can cite that indicates your company's use of incentive compensation techniques has worked? For example, have your company's compensation incentives actually boosted productivity? Can you cite evidence indicating the productivity gains have resulted in lower labor costs? If the productivity gains have *not* translated into lower labor costs, then is it fair to say that your company's use of incentive compensation is a failure?

   LO6

4. If you were making a speech to company personnel, what would you tell them about the kind of corporate culture you would like to have at your company? What specific cultural traits would you like your company to exhibit? Explain.

   LO7

5. Following each decision round, do you and your co-managers make corrective adjustments in either your company's strategy or how well the strategy is being executed? List at least three such adjustments you made in the most recent decision round. What hard evidence (in the form of results relating to your company's performance in the most recent year) can you cite that indicates the various corrective adjustments you made either succeeded or failed to improve your company's performance?

   LO8

ENDNOTES

1. Christopher A. Bartlett and Sumantra Ghoshal, "Building Competitive Advantage through People," *MIT Sloan Management Review* 43, no. 2 (Winter 2002).

2. Justin Menkes, "Hiring for Smarts," *Harvard Business Review* 83, no. 11 (November 2005); and Justin Menkes, *Executive Intelligence* (New York: HarperCollins, 2005).

3. Larry Bossidy and Ram Charan, *Execution: The Discipline of Getting Things Done* (New York: Crown Business, 2002).

4. Jim Collins, *Good to Great* (New York: HarperBusiness, 2001).

5. C. Helfat et al., *Dynamic Capabilities: Understanding Strategic Change in Organizations* (Malden, MA: Blackwell, 2007); and R. Grant, *Contemporary Strategy Analysis*, 6th ed. (Malden, MA: Blackwell, 2008).

6. G. Dosi, R. Nelson, and S. Winter, eds., *The Nature and Dynamics of Organizational Capabilities* (Oxford, England: Oxford University Press, 2001).

7. B. Kogut and U. Zander, "Knowledge of the Firm, Combinative Capabilities, and the Replication of Technology," *Organization Science* 3, no. 3 (August 1992), pp. 383–97.

8. C. Helfat and R. Raubitschek, "Product Sequencing: Co-Evolution of Knowledge, Capabilities and Products," *Strategic Management Journal* 21, nos. 10–11 (October–November 2000), pp. 961–80.

9. S. Karim and W. Mitchell, "Path-Dependent and Path-Breaking Change: Reconfiguring Business Resources Following Business," *Strategic Management Journal* 21, nos. 10–11 (October–November 2000), pp. 1061–82; L. Capron, P. Dussauge, and W. Mitchell, "Resource Redeployment Following Horizontal Acquisitions in Europe and North America, 1988-1992,"

Strategic Management Journal 19, no. 7 (July 1998), pp. 631–62.

10. Alfred Chandler, *Strategy and Structure* (Cambridge, MA: MIT Press, 1962).

11. Stanley E. Fawcett, Gary K. Rhoads, and Phillip Burnah, "People as the Bridge to Competitiveness: Benchmarking the 'ABCs' of an Empowered Workforce," *Benchmarking: An International Journal* 11, no. 4 (2004).

12. Rosabeth Moss Kanter, "Collaborative Advantage: The Art of the Alliance," *Harvard Business Review* 72, no. 4 (July–August 1994), pp. 96–108.

13. Michael Hammer and James Champy, *Reengineering the Corporation* (New York: HarperBusiness, 1993).

14. Gene Hall, Jim Rosenthal, and Judy Wade, "How to Make Reengineering Really Work," *Harvard Business Review* 71, no. 6 (November–December 1993).

15. M. Walton, *The Deming Management Method* (New York: Pedigree, 1986); J. Juran, *Juran on Quality by Design* (New York: Free Press, 1992); Philip Crosby, *Quality Is Free: The Act of Making Quality Certain* (New York: McGraw-Hill, 1979); S. George, *The Baldrige Quality System* (New York: John Wiley & Sons, 1992); and Mark J. Zbaracki, "The Rhetoric and Reality of Total Quality Management," *Administrative Science Quarterly* 43, no. 3 (September 1998).

16. Robert T. Amsden, Thomas W. Ferratt, and Davida M. Amsden, "TQM: Core Paradigm Changes," *Business Horizons* 39, no. 6 (November–December 1996).

17. Peter S. Pande and Larry Holpp, *What Is Six Sigma?* (New York: McGraw-Hill, 2002); Jiju Antony, "Some Pros and Cons of Six Sigma: An Academic Perspective," *The TQM Magazine* 16, no. 4 (2004); Peter S. Pande, Robert P. Neuman, and Roland R. Cavanagh, *The Six Sigma Way: How GE, Motorola and Other Top Companies Are Honing Their Performance* (New York: McGraw-Hill, 2000); Joseph Gordon and M. Joseph Gordon, Jr., *Six Sigma Quality for Business and Manufacture* (New York: Elsevier, 2002); and Godecke Wessel and Peter Burcher, "Six Sigma for Small and Medium-Sized Enterprises," *The TQM Magazine* 16, no. 4 (2004).

18. Based on information posted at www.sixsigma.com, November 4, 2002.

19. Kennedy Smith, "Six Sigma for the Service Sector," *Quality Digest Magazine,* May 2003, www.quality-digest.com, accessed September 28, 2003.

20. Del Jones, "Taking the Six Sigma Approach," *USA Today,* October 31, 2002.

21. As quoted in "A Dark Art No More," *The Economist* 385, no. 8550 (October 13, 2007).

22. Charles A. O'Reilly and Michael L. Tushman, "The Ambidextrous Organization," *Harvard Business Review* 82, no. 4 (April 2004).

23. See Steven Kerr, "On the Folly of Rewarding A while Hoping for B," *Academy of Management Executive* 9, no. 1 (February 1995); Steven Kerr, "Risky Business: The New Pay Game," *Fortune,* July 22, 1996; and Doran Twer, "Linking Pay to Business Objectives," *Journal of Business Strategy* 15, no. 4 (July–August 1994).

24. Jeffrey Pfeffer and John F. Veiga, "Putting People First for Organizational Success," *Academy of Management Executive* 13, no. 2 (May 1999); Linda K. Stroh and Paula M. Caliguiri, "Increasing Global Competitiveness through Effective People Management," *Journal of World Business* 33, no. 1 (Spring 1998); and articles in *Fortune* on the 100 best companies to work for (various issues).

25. Joanne Reid and Victoria Hubbell, "Creating a Performance Culture," *Ivey Business Journal* 69, no. 4 (March–April 2005).

26. Jay B. Barney and Delwyn N. Clark, *Resource-Based Theory: Creating and Sustaining Competitive Advantage* (New York: Oxford University Press, 2007).

27. John P. Kotter and James L. Heskett, *Corporate Culture and Performance* (New York: Free Press, 1992).

28. Kurt Eichenwald, *Conspiracy of Fools: A True Story* (New York: Broadway Books, 2005).

29. Judy D. Olian and Sara L. Rynes, "Making Total Quality Work: Aligning Organizational Processes, Performance Measures, and Stakeholders," *Human Resource Management* 30, no. 3 (Fall 1991).

30. Larry Bossidy and Ram Charan, *Confronting Reality: Doing What Matters to Get Things Right* (New York: Crown Business, 2004); Larry Bossidy and Ram Charan, *Execution: The Discipline of Getting Things Done* (New York: Crown Business, 2002); John P. Kotter, "Leading Change: Why Transformation Efforts Fail," *Harvard Business Review* 73, no. 2 (March–April 1995); Thomas M. Hout and John C. Carter, "Getting It Done: New Roles for Senior Executives," *Harvard Business Review* 73, no. 6 (November–December 1995); and Sumantra Ghoshal and Christopher A. Bartlett, "Changing the Role of Top Management: Beyond Structure to Processes," *Harvard Business Review* 73, no. 1 (January–February 1995).

31. Fred Vogelstein, "Winning the Amazon Way," *Fortune,* May 26, 2003.

32. Jeffrey Pfeffer, "Producing Sustainable Competitive Advantage through the Effective Management of People," *Academy of Management Executive* 9, no. 1 (February 1995).

33. Cynthia A. Montgomery, "Putting Leadership Back into Strategy," *Harvard Business Review* 86, no. 1 (January 2008).

APPENDIX

Ratio	How Calculated	What It Shows
Profitability Ratios		
1. Gross profit margin	$$\frac{\text{Sales revenues} - \text{Cost of goods sold}}{\text{Sales revenues}}$$	Shows the percentage of revenues available to cover operating expenses and yield a profit. Higher is better and the trend should be upward.
2. Operating profit margin (or return on sales)	$$\frac{\text{Sales revenues} - \text{Operating expenses}}{\text{Sales revenues}}$$ or $$\frac{\text{Operating income}}{\text{Sales revenues}}$$	Shows the profitability of current operations without regard to interest charges and income taxes. Higher is better and the trend should be upward.
3. Net profit margin (or net return on sales)	$$\frac{\text{Profits after taxes}}{\text{Sales revenues}}$$	Shows after-tax profits per dollar of sales. Higher is better and the trend should be upward.
4. Total return on assets	$$\frac{\text{Profits after taxes} + \text{Interest}}{\text{Total assets}}$$	A measure of the return on total monetary investment in the enterprise. Interest is added to after-tax profits to form the numerator since total assets are financed by creditors as well as by stockholders. Higher is better and the trend should be upward.
5. Net return on total assets (ROA)	$$\frac{\text{Profits after taxes}}{\text{Total assets}}$$	A measure of the return earned by stockholders on the firm's total assets. Higher is better, and the trend should be upward.
6. Return on stockholder's equity	$$\frac{\text{Profits after taxes}}{\text{Total stockholders' equity}}$$	Shows the return stockholders are earning on their capital investment in the enterprise. A return in the 12–15% range is "average," and the trend should be upward.
7. Return on invested capital (ROIC) — sometimes referred to as return on capital (ROCE)	$$\frac{\text{Profits after taxes}}{\text{Long term debt} + \text{Total stockholders' equity}}$$	A measure of the return shareholders are earning on the long-term monetary capital invested in the enterprise. Higher is better and the trend should be upward.
8. Earnings per share (EPS)	$$\frac{\text{Profits after taxes}}{\text{Number of shares of common stock outstanding}}$$	Shows the earnings for each share of common stock outstanding. The trend should be upward, and the bigger the annual percentage gains, the better.
Liquidity Ratios		
1. Current ratio	$$\frac{\text{Current assets}}{\text{Current liabilities}}$$	Shows a firm's ability to pay current liabilities using assets that can be converted to cash in the near term. Ratio should definitely be higher than 1.0; ratios of 2 or higher are better still.
2. Working capital	$$\text{Current assets} - \text{Current liabilities}$$	Bigger amounts are better because the company has more internal funds available to (1) pay its current liabilities on a timely basis and (2) finance inventory expansion, additional accounts receivable, and a larger base of operations without resorting to borrowing or raising more equity capital.
Leverage Ratios		
1. Total debt-to-assets ratio	$$\frac{\text{Total debt}}{\text{Total assets}}$$	Measures the extent to which borrowed funds (both short-term loans and long-term debt) have been used to finance the firm's operations. A low fraction or ratio is better—a high fraction indicates overuse of debt and greater risk of bankruptcy.

Ratio	How Calculated	What It Shows
2. Long-term debt-to-capital ratio	$$\frac{\text{Long-term debt}}{\text{Long-term debt + Total stockholders' equity}}$$	An important measure of creditworthiness and balance sheet strength. It indicates the percentage of capital investment in the enterprise that has been financed by both long-term lenders and stockholders. A ratio below 0.25 is usually preferable since monies invested by stockholders account for 75% or more of the company's total capital. The lower the ratio, the greater the capacity to borrow additional funds. Debt-to-capital ratios above 0.50 and certainly above 0.75 indicate a heavy and perhaps excessive reliance on long-term borrowing, lower creditworthiness, and weak balance sheet strength.
3. Debt-to-equity ratio	$$\frac{\text{Total debt}}{\text{Total stockholders' equity}}$$	Shows the balance between debt (funds borrowed both short-term and long-term) and the amount that stockholders have invested in the enterprise. The further the ratio is below 1.0, the greater the firm's ability to borrow additional funds. Ratios above 1.0 and definitely above 2.0 put creditors at greater risk, signal weaker balance sheet strength, and often result in lower credit ratings.
4. Long-term debt-to-equity ratio	$$\frac{\text{Long-term debt}}{\text{Total stockholders' equity}}$$	Shows the balance between long-term debt and stockholders' equity in the firm's *long-term* capital structure. Low ratios indicate greater capacity to borrow additional funds if needed.
5. Times-interest-earned (or coverage) ratio	$$\frac{\text{Operating income}}{\text{Interest expenses}}$$	Measures the ability to pay annual interest charges. Lenders usually insist on a minimum ratio of 2.0, but ratios progressively above 3.0 signal progressively better creditworthiness.

Activity Ratios

1. Days of inventory	$$\frac{\text{Inventory}}{\text{Cost of goods sold} \div 365}$$	Measures inventory management efficiency. Fewer days of inventory are usually better.
2. Inventory turnover	$$\frac{\text{Cost of goods sold}}{\text{Inventory}}$$	Measures the number of inventory turns per year. Higher is better.
3. Average collection period	$$\frac{\text{Accounts receivable}}{\text{Total sales} \div 365}$$ or $$\frac{\text{Accounts receivable}}{\text{Average daily sales}}$$	Indicates the average length of time the firm must wait after making a sale to receive cash payment. A shorter collection time is better.

Other Important Measures of Financial Performance

1. Dividend yield on common stock	$$\frac{\text{Annual dividends per share}}{\text{Current market price per share}}$$	A measure of the return that shareholders receive in the form of dividends. A "typical" dividend yield is 2–3%. The dividend yield for fast-growth companies is often below 1% (maybe even 0); the dividend yield for slow-growth companies can run 4–5%.
2. Price-earnings ratio	$$\frac{\text{Current market price per share}}{\text{Earnings per share}}$$	P-e ratios above 20 indicate strong investor confidence in a firm's outlook and earnings growth; firms whose future earnings are at risk or likely to grow slowly typically have ratios below 12.
3. Dividend payout ratio	$$\frac{\text{Annual dividends per share}}{\text{Earnings per share}}$$	Indicates the percentage of after-tax profits paid out as dividends.
4. Internal cash flow	After tax profits + Depreciation	A quick and rough estimate of the cash a company's business is generating after payment of operating expenses, interest, and taxes. Such amounts can be used for dividend payments or funding capital expenditures.
5. Free cash flow	After tax profits + Depreciation – Capital expenditures – Dividends	A quick and rough estimate of the cash a company's business is generating after payment of operating expenses, interest, taxes, dividends, and desirable reinvestments in the business. The larger a company's free cash flow, the greater is its ability to internally fund new strategic initiatives, repay debt, make new acquisitions, repurchase shares of stock, or increase dividend payments.

connect   DAVID L. TURNIPSEED   University of South Alabama

As Father Daniel Mary, the prior of the Carmelite Order of monks in Clark, Wyoming, walked to chapel to preside over Mass, he noticed the sun glistening across the four-inch snowfall from the previous evening. Snow in June was not unheard of in Wyoming, but the late snowfall and the bright glow of the rising sun made him consider the opposing forces accompanying change and how he might best prepare his monastery to achieve his vision of creating a new Mount Carmel in the Rocky Mountains. His vision of transforming the small brotherhood of 13 monks living in a small home used as makeshift rectory into a 500-acre monastery that would include accommodations for 30 monks, a Gothic church, a convent for Carmelite nuns, a retreat center for lay visitors, and a hermitage presented a formidable challenge. However, as a former high school football player, boxer, bull rider, and man of great faith, Father Prior Daniel Mary was unaccustomed to shrinking from a challenge.

Father Prior had identified a nearby ranch for sale that met the requirements of his vision perfectly, but its current listing price of $8.9 million presented a financial obstacle to creating a place of prayer, worship, and solitude in the Rockies. The Carmelites had received a $250,000 donation that could be used toward the purchase, and the monastery had earned nearly $75,000 during the first year of its Mystic Monk coffee-roasting operations, but more money would be needed. The coffee roaster used to produce packaged coffee sold to Catholic consumers at the Mystic Monk Coffee website was reaching its capacity, but a larger roaster could be purchased for $35,000. Also, local Cody, Wyoming, business owners had begun a foundation for those wishing to donate to the monks' cause. Father Prior Daniel Mary did not have a great deal of experience in business matters but considered to what extent the monastery could rely on its Mystic Monk Coffee operations to fund the purchase of the ranch. If Mystic Monk Coffee was capable of making the vision a reality, what were the next steps in turning the coffee into land?

The Carmelite Monks of Wyoming

Carmelites are a religious order of the Catholic Church that was formed by men who traveled to the Holy Land as pilgrims and crusaders and had chosen to remain near Jerusalem to seek God. The men established their hermitage at Mount Carmel because of its beauty, seclusion, and biblical importance as the site where Elijah stood against King Ahab and the false prophets of Jezebel to prove Jehovah to be the one true God. The Carmelites led a life of solitude, silence, and prayer at Mount Carmel before eventually returning to Europe and becoming a recognized order of the Catholic Church. The size of the Carmelite Order varied widely

Copyright © 2011 by David L. Turnipseed. All rights reserved.

throughout the centuries with its peak in the 1600s and stood at approximately 2,200 friars living on all inhabited continents at the beginning of the 21st century.

The Wyoming Carmelite monastery was founded by Father Daniel Mary, who lived as a Carmelite hermit in Minnesota before moving to Clark, Wyoming, to establish the new monastery. The Wyoming Carmelites were a cloistered order and were allowed to leave the monastery only by permission of the bishop for medical needs or the death of a family member. The Wyoming monastery's abbey bore little resemblance to the great stone cathedrals and monasteries of Europe and was confined to a rectory that had once been a four-bedroom ranch-style home and an adjoining 42 acres of land that had been donated to the monastery.

There were 13 monks dedicated to a life of prayer and worship in the Wyoming Carmelite monastery. Since the founding of the monastery six years ago, there had been more than 500 inquiries from young men considering becoming a Wyoming Carmelite. Father Prior Daniel Mary wished to eventually have 30 monks who would join the brotherhood at age 19 to 30 and live out their lives in the monastery. However, the selection criteria for acceptance into the monastery were rigorous, with the monks making certain that applicants understood the reality of the vows of obedience, chastity, and poverty and the sacrifices associated with living a cloistered religious life.

The Daily Activities of a Carmelite Monk

The Carmelite monks' day began at 4:10 a.m., when they arose and went to chapel for worship wearing traditional brown habits and handmade sandals. At about 6:00 a.m., the monks rested and contemplated in silence for one hour before Father Prior began morning Mass. After Mass, the monks went about their manual labors. In performing their labors, each brother had a special set of skills that enabled the monastery to independently maintain its

operations. Brother Joseph Marie was an excellent mechanic, Brother Paul was a carpenter, Brother Peter Joseph (Brother Cook) worked in the kitchen, and five-foot, four-inch Brother Simon Mary (Little Monk) was the secretary to Father Daniel Mary. Brother Elias, affectionately known as Brother Java, was Mystic Monk Coffee's master roaster, although he was not a coffee drinker.

Each monk worked up to six hours per day; however, the monks' primary focus was spiritual, with eight hours of each day spent in prayer. At 11:40 a.m., the monks stopped work and went to Chapel. Afterward they had lunch, cleaned the dishes, and went back to work. At 3:00 p.m., the hour that Jesus was believed to have died on the cross, work stopped again for prayer and worship. The monks then returned to work until the bell was rung for Vespers (evening prayer). After Vespers, the monks had an hour of silent contemplation, an evening meal, and more prayers before bedtime.

The New Mount Carmel

Soon after arriving in Wyoming, Father Daniel Mary had formed the vision of acquiring a large parcel of land—a new Mount Carmel—and building a monastery with accommodations for 30 monks, a retreat center for lay visitors, a Gothic church, a convent for Carmelite nuns, and a hermitage. In a letter to supporters posted on the monastery's website, Father Daniel Mary succinctly stated his vision: "We beg your prayers, your friendship and your support that this vision, our vision may come to be that Mount Carmel may be refounded in Wyoming's Rockies for the glory of God."

The brothers located a 496-acre ranch for sale that would satisfy all of the requirements to create a new Mount Carmel. The Irma Lake Ranch was located about 21 miles outside Cody, Wyoming, and included a remodeled 17,800-square-foot residence, a 1,700-square-foot caretaker house, a 2,950-square-foot guesthouse, a hunting cabin, a dairy and horse barn, and forested land. The ranch was at the end of a seven-mile-long private gravel road and was bordered on one side by the private Hoodoo Ranch (100,000 acres) and on the other by the Shoshone National Park (2.4 million acres). Although the asking price was $8.9 million, the monks believed they would be able to acquire the property through donations and the profits generated by the monastery's Mystic Monk Coffee operations. The $250,000 donation they had received from an individual wishing to support the Carmelites could be applied toward whatever purpose the monks chose. Additionally, a group of Cody business owners had formed the New Mount Carmel Foundation to help the monks raise funds.

Overview of the Coffee Industry

About 150 million consumers in the United States drank coffee, with 89 percent of U.S. coffee drinkers brewing their own coffee at home rather than purchasing ready-to-drink coffee at coffee shops and restaurants such as Starbucks, Dunkin' Donuts, or McDonald's. Packaged coffee for home brewing was easy to find in any grocery store and typically carried a retail price of $4 to $6 for a 12-ounce package. About 30 million coffee drinkers in the United States preferred premium-quality specialty coffees that sold for $7 to $10 per 12-ounce package. Specialty coffees are made from high-quality Arabica beans instead of the mix of low-quality Arabica beans and bitter, less flavorful Robusta beans that makers of value brands use. The wholesale price of Robusta coffee beans averaged $1.15 per pound, while mild Colombian Arabica wholesale prices averaged $1.43 per pound.

Prior to the 1990s, the market for premium-quality specialty coffees barely existed in the United States, but Howard Schultz's vision for Starbucks of bringing the Italian espresso bar experience to America helped specialty coffees become a large and thriving segment of the industry. The company's pursuit of its mission "To inspire and nurture the human spirit—one person, one cup, and one neighborhood at a time" had allowed Starbucks to become an iconic brand in most parts of the world. The company's success had given rise to a number of competing specialty coffee shops and premium brands of packaged specialty coffee, including Seattle's Best, Millstone, Green Mountain Coffee Roasters, and First Colony Coffee and Tea. Some producers such as First Colony had difficulty gaining shelf space in supermarkets and concentrated on private-label roasting and packaging for fine department stores and other retailers wishing to have a proprietary brand of coffee.

Specialty coffees sold under premium brands might be made from shade-grown or organically grown coffee beans, or have been purchased from a grower belonging to a World Fair Trade Organization (WFTO) cooperative. WFTO cooperative growers were paid above-market prices to better support the cost of operating their farms—for example, WFTO-certified organic wholesale prices averaged $1.55 per pound. Many consumers who purchased specialty coffees were willing to pay a higher price for organic, shade-grown, or fair trade coffee because of their personal health or social concerns—organic coffees are grown without the use of synthetic fertilizers or pesticides, shade-grown coffee plants are allowed to grow beneath the canopies of larger indigenous trees, and fair trade pricing makes it easier for farmers in developing countries to pay workers a living wage. The specialty coffee segment of the retail coffee industry had grown dramatically in the United States, with retail sales increasing from $8.3 billion to $13.5 billion during the last seven years. The retail sales of organic coffee accounted for about $1 billion of industry sales and had grown at an annual rate of 32 percent for each of the last seven years.

Mystic Monk Coffee

Mystic Monk Coffee was produced using high-quality fair trade Arabica and fair trade/organic Arabica beans. The monks produced whole-bean and ground caffeinated and decaffeinated varieties in dark, medium, and light roasts and in different flavors. The most popular Mystic Monk flavors were Mystical Chants of Carmel, Cowboy Blend, Royal Rum Pecan, and Mystic Monk Blend. With the exception of sample bags, which carried a retail price of $2.99, all varieties of Mystic Monk Coffee were sold via the monastery's website (www.mysticmonkcoffee.com) in 12-ounce bags at a price of $9.95. All purchases from the website were delivered by United Parcel Service (UPS) or the U.S. Postal Service. Frequent customers were given the option of joining a "coffee club," which offered monthly delivery of one to six bags of preselected coffee. Purchases of three or more bags qualified for free shipping. The Mystic Monk Coffee website also featured T-shirts, gift cards, CDs featuring the monastery's Gregorian chants, and coffee mugs.

Mystic Monk Coffee's target market was the segment of the U.S. Catholic population who drank coffee and wished to support the monastery's mission. More than 69 million Americans were members of the Catholic Church—making it four times larger than the second-largest Christian denomination in the United States. An appeal to Catholics to "use their Catholic coffee dollar for Christ and his Catholic church" was published on the Mystic Monk Coffee website.

Mystic Monk Coffee-Roasting Operations

After the morning religious services and breakfast, Brother Java roasted the green coffee beans delivered each week from a coffee broker in Seattle, Washington. The monks paid the Seattle broker the prevailing wholesale price per pound, which fluctuated daily with global supply and demand. The capacity of Mystic Monk Coffee's roaster limited production to 540 pounds per day; production was also limited by time devoted to prayer, silent meditation, and worship. Demand for Mystic Monk Coffee had not yet exceeded the roaster's capacity,

but the monastery planned to purchase a larger, 130-pound-per-hour-roaster when demand further approached the current roaster's capacity. The monks had received a quote of $35,000 for the new larger roaster.

Marketing and Website Operations

Mystic Monk Coffee was promoted primarily by word of mouth among loyal customers in Catholic parishes across the United States. The majority of Mystic Monk's sales were made through its website, but on occasion telephone orders were placed with the monks' secretary, who worked outside the cloistered part of the monastery. Mystic Monk also offered secular website operators commissions on its sales through its Mystic Monk Coffee Affiliate Program, which placed banner ads and text ads on participating websites. Affiliate sites earned an 18 percent commission on sales made to customers who were directed to the Mystic Monk site from their site. The affiliate program's ShareASale participation level allowed affiliates to refer new affiliates to Mystic Monk and earn 56 percent of the new affiliate's commission. The monks had also just recently expanded Mystic Monk's business model to include wholesale sales to churches and local coffee shops.

Mystic Monk's Financial Performance

At the conclusion of Mystic Monk Coffee's first year in operation, its sales of coffee and coffee accessories averaged about $56,500 per month. Its cost of sales averaged about 30 percent of revenues, inbound shipping costs accounted for 19 percent of revenues, and broker fees were 3 percent of revenues—for a total cost of goods sold of 52 percent. Operating expenses such as utilities, supplies, telephone, and website maintenance averaged 37 percent of revenues. Thus, Mystic Monk's net profit margin averaged 11 percent of revenues.

Realizing the Vision

During a welcome period of solitude before his evening meal, Father Prior Daniel Mary again contemplated the purchase of the Irma Lake Ranch. He realized that his vision of purchasing the ranch would require careful planning and execution. For the Wyoming Carmelites, coffee sales were a means of support from the outside world that might provide the financial resources to purchase the land. Father Prior understood that the cloistered monastic environment offered unique challenges to operating a business enterprise, but it also provided opportunities that were not available to secular businesses. He resolved to develop an execution plan that would enable Mystic Monk Coffee to minimize the effect of its cloistered monastic constraints, maximize the potential of monastic opportunities, and realize his vision of buying the Irma Lake Ranch.

Under Armour's Strategy in 2013—Good Enough to Win Market Share from Nike and adidas?

Mc Graw Hill Education **connect**

ARTHUR A. THOMPSON   The University of Alabama

Founded in 1996 by former University of Maryland football player Kevin Plank, Under Armour was the originator of performance apparel—gear engineered to keep athletes cool, dry, and light throughout the course of a game, practice, or workout. It started with a simple plan to make a T-shirt that provided compression and wicked perspiration off the wearer's skin, thereby regulating body temperature and avoiding the discomfort of sweat-absorbed apparel.

Some 15 years later, with 2012 sales of $1.8 billion, Under Armour had a growing brand presence in the roughly $60 billion multi-segment retail market for sports apparel, activewear, and athletic footwear in the United States. Its interlocking "U" and "A" logo had become almost as familiar and well-known as industry-leader Nike's swoosh. According to SportsOneSource data, in 2012 Under Armour had a 7 percent share of the U.S. market for lightweight running shoes (up from 3 percent in 2011) and a 13.7 percent share of the sports apparel segment (versus 11.1 percent in 2011). Across all segments, Under Armour had boosted its domestic market share from 0.6 percent in 2003 to an estimated 3.0 percent in 2012, while industry leader Nike's share had remained relatively flat at about 7.0 percent; second-ranked adidas had a market share of about 5.4 percent in 2012.[1]

Founder and CEO Kevin Plank believed Under Armour's potential for long-term growth was exceptional for three reasons: (1) the company had built an incredibly powerful and authentic brand in a relatively short time, (2) there were significant opportunities to expand the company's narrow product lineup and brand-name appeal into product categories where it currently had little or no market presence, and (3) the company was only in the early stages of establishing its brand and penetrating markets outside North America.

Company Background

Kevin Plank honed his competitive instinct growing up with four older brothers and playing football. As a young teenager, he squirmed under the authority of his mother, who was the town mayor of Kensington, Maryland. When he was a sophomore, he was tossed out of Georgetown Prep for poor academic performance and ended up at Fork Union Military Academy, where he learned to accept discipline and resumed playing high school football. After graduation, Plank became a walk-on special-teams football player for the University of Maryland in the early 1990s, ending his college career as the special-teams' captain in 1995.

Copyright © 2013 by Arthur A. Thompson. All rights reserved.

Throughout his football career, he regularly experienced the discomfort of practicing on hot days and the unpleasantness of peeling off sweat-soaked cotton T-shirts after practice. At the University of Maryland, Plank sometimes changed the cotton T-shirt under his jersey as it became wet and heavy during the course of a game.

During his later college years and in classic entrepreneurial fashion, Plank hit upon the idea of using newly available moisture-wicking, polyester-blend fabrics to make next-generation, tighter-fitting shirts and undergarments that would make it cooler and more comfortable to engage in strenuous activities during high-temperature conditions.[2] While Plank had a job offer from Prudential Life Insurance at the end of his college days in 1995, he couldn't see himself being happy working in a corporate environment—he told the author of a 2011 *Fortune* article on Under Armour, "I would have killed myself."[3] Despite a lack of business training, Plank opted to try to make a living selling high-tech microfiber shirts. Plank's vision was to sell innovative, technically advanced apparel products engineered with a special fabric construction that provided supreme moisture management. A year of fabric and product testing produced a synthetic compression T-shirt that was suitable for wear beneath an athlete's uniform or equipment, provided a snug fit (like a second skin), and remained drier and lighter than a traditional cotton shirt. Plank formed KP Sports as a subchapter S corporation in Maryland in 1996 and commenced selling the shirt to athletes and sports teams.

The Company's Early Years

Plank's former teammates at high school, military school, and the University of Maryland included some 40 National Football League players that he knew well enough to call and offer them the shirt he had designed. He worked the phone and, with a trunk full of shirts in the back of his car, visited schools and training camps in person to show his products. Within a short time, Plank's sales successes were good enough that he convinced Kip Fulks, who played lacrosse at Maryland, to become a partner in his enterprise. Fulks's initial role was to leverage his connections to promote use of the company's shirts by lacrosse players. Their sales strategy was predicated on networking and referrals. But Fulks had another critical role—he had good credit and was able to obtain 17 credit cards that were used to make purchases from suppliers and charge expenses.[4] Operations were conducted on a shoestring budget out of the basement of Plank's grandmother's house in Georgetown, a Washington, D.C., suburb. Plank and Fulks generated sufficient cash from their sales efforts that Fulks never missed a minimum payment on any of his credit cards. When cash flows became particularly tight, Plank's older brother Scott made loans to the company to help keep KP Sports afloat (in 2011 Scott owned 4 percent of the company's stock). It didn't take long for Plank and Fulks to learn that it was more productive to direct their sales efforts more toward equipment managers than to individual players. Getting a whole team to adopt use of the T-shirts that KP Sports was marketing meant convincing equipment managers that it was more economical to provide players with a pricey $25 high-performance T-shirt that would hold up better in the long-run than a cheap cotton T-shirt.

In 1998, the company's sales revenues and growth prospects were sufficient to secure a $250,000 small-business loan from a tiny bank in Washington, D.C.; the loan enabled the company to move its basement operation to a facility on Sharp Street in nearby Baltimore.[5] As sales continued to gain momentum, the bank later granted KP Sports additional small loans from time to time to help fund its needs for more working capital. Then Ryan Wood, one of Plank's acquaintances from high school, joined the company in 1999 and became a partner. The company consisted of three jocks trying to gain a foothold in a growing, highly competitive industry against more than 25 brands, including those of Nike, adidas, Columbia, and Patagonia. Plank functioned as president and CEO; Kip Fulks was vice president of sourcing and quality assurance; and Ryan Wood was vice president of sales.

Nonetheless, KP Sports sales grew briskly as the company expanded its product line to include high-tech undergarments tailored for athletes in different sports and for cold temperatures as well as hot temperatures, plus jerseys, team uniforms, socks, and other accessories. Increasingly, the company was able to secure deals not just to provide gear for a particular team but also for most or all of a school's sports teams. However, the company's partners came to recognize the merits of tapping the retail market for high-performance apparel and began making sales calls on sports apparel retailers. In 2000, Galyan's, a large retail chain since acquired by Dick's Sporting Goods, signed on to carry KP Sports' expanding line of performance apparel for men, women, and youth. Sales to other sports apparel retailers began to explode, quickly making the retail segment of the sports apparel market the biggest component of the company's revenue stream. Revenues totaled $5.3 million in 2000, with operating income of $0.7 million. The company's products were available in some 500 retail stores. Beginning in 2000, Scott Plank, Kevin's older brother, joined the company as vice president of finance, with operational and strategic responsibilities as well.

Rapid Growth Ensues

Over the next 11 years, the company's product line evolved to include a widening variety of shirts, shorts, underwear, outerwear, gloves, and other offerings. The strategic intent was to grow the business by replacing products made from cotton and other traditional fabrics with innovatively designed performance products that incorporated a variety of technologically advanced fabrics and specialized manufacturing techniques, all in an attempt to make the wearer feel "drier, lighter, and more comfortable." In 1999 the company began selling its products in Japan through a licensee. On January 1, 2002, prompted by growing operational complexity, increased financial requirements, and plans for further geographic expansion, KP Sports revoked its S corporation status and became a C corporation. The company opened a Canadian sales office in 2003 and began efforts to grow its market presence in Canada. In 2004, KP Sports became the outfitter of the University of Maryland football team and was a supplier to some 400 women's sports teams at NCAA Division I colleges and universities. The company used independent sales agents to begin selling its products in the United Kingdom in 2005. SportsScanINFO estimated that as of 2004, KP Sports had a 73 percent share of the U.S. market for compression tops and bottoms, more than seven times that of its nearest competitor.[6]

Broadening demand for the company's product offerings among professional, collegiate, and Olympic teams and athletes; active outdoor enthusiasts; elite tactical professionals; and consumers with active lifestyles propelled revenue growth from $5.3 million in 2000 to $263.4 million for the 12 months ending September 30, 2005, equal to a compound annual growth rate of 127 percent. Operating income increased from $0.7 million in 2000 to $32.7 million during the same period, a compound annual growth rate of 124 percent. About 90 percent of the company revenues came from sales to some 6,000 retail stores in the United States and 2,000 stores in Canada, Japan, and the United Kingdom. In addition, sales were being made to high-profile athletes and teams, most notably in the NFL, Major League Baseball, the National Hockey League, and major collegiate and Olympic sports. KP Sports had 574 employees at the end of September 2005.

Throughout 2005, KP Sports increased its offerings to include additional men's and women's performance products and, in particular, began entry into such off-field outdoor sports segments as hunting, fishing, running, mountain sports, skiing, and golf. Management expected that its new product offerings in 2006 would include football cleats.

KP Sports Is Renamed Under Armour

In late 2005, the company changed its name to Under Armour and became a public company with an initial public offering of 9.5 million shares of Class A common stock that generated net proceeds of approximately $114.9 million. Simultaneously, existing stockholders sold 2.6 million shares of Class A stock from their personal holdings. The shares were all sold at just above the offer price of $13 per share; on the first day of trading after the IPO, the shares closed at $25.30, after opening at $31 per share. Following these initial sales of Under Armour stock to the general public, Under Armour's outstanding shares of common stock consisted of two classes: Class A common stock and Class B common stock; both classes were identical in all respects except for voting and conversion rights. Holders of Class A common stock were entitled to one vote per share, and holders of Class B common stock were entitled to 10 votes per share on all matters to be voted on by common stockholders. Shares of Class A and Class B common stock voted together as a single class on all matters submitted to a vote of stockholders. All of the Class B common stock was beneficially owned by Kevin Plank, which represented 83 percent of the combined voting power of all of the outstanding common stock. As a result, Plank was able to control the outcome of substantially all matters submitted to a stockholder vote, including the election of directors, amendments to Under Armour's charter, and mergers or other business combinations.

At the time of Under Armour's IPO, Kevin Plank, Kip Fulks, and Ryan Wood were all 33 years old; Scott Plank was 39 years old. After the IPO, Kevin Plank owned 15.2 million shares of Under Armour's Class A shares (and all of the Class B shares); Kip Fulks owned 2.125 million Class A shares, Ryan Wood owned 2.142 million Class A shares, and Scott Plank owned 3.95 million Class A shares. All four had opted to sell a small fraction of their common shares at the time of the IPO—these accounted for a combined 1.83 million of the 2.6 million shares sold from the holdings of various directors, officers, and other entities. Ryan Wood decided to leave his position as senior vice president of sales at Under Armour in 2007 to run a cattle farm. Kip Fulks assumed the position of chief

operating officer at Under Armour in September 2011, after moving up the executive ranks in several capacities, chiefly those related to sourcing, quality assurance, product development, and product innovation. In September 2012, Scott Plank, who was serving as the company's executive vice president of business development after holding several other positions in the company's executive ranks, retired from the company to start a real estate development company and pursue his passion for building sustainable urban environments.

Exhibit 1 summarizes Under Armour's financial performance in five of the seven years following the company's 2005 IPO. Exhibit 2 shows the growth of Under Armour's quarterly revenues for 2010 through mid-2013. The company's stock traded in the $46 to $51 range in the first three months of 2013. Following the announcement of better-than-expected earnings in the first half of 2013 and management forecasts of full-year 2013 revenues of $2.21 billion to $2.23 billion, Under Armour's stock climbed to $57 per share in mid-April 2013.

Under Armour announced sales target was to achieve sales revenues of $2.2 billion in 2013, reaching $4 billion by 2016.[7]

Under Armour's Strategy

Under Armour's mission was "to make all athletes better through passion, design, and the relentless pursuit of innovation." The company's principal business activities in 2012 were the development, marketing, and distribution of branded performance apparel, footwear, and accessories for men, women, and youth. The brand's moisture-wicking fabrications were engineered in many designs and styles for wear in nearly every climate to provide a performance alternative to traditional products. Its products were worn by athletes at all levels, from youth to professional, and by consumers with active lifestyles. Over 90 percent of Under Armour's sales were in North America, but international sales to distributors and

EXHIBIT 1

Selected Financial Data for Under Armour, Inc., 2008–2012 (in 000s, except per share amounts)

	Years Ending December 31				
	2012	2011	2010	2009	2008
Selected Income Statement Data					
Net revenues	$ 1,834,921	$ 1,472,684	$ 1,063,927	$ 856,411	$ 725,244
Cost of goods sold	955,624	759,848	533,420	446,286	372,203
Gross profit	879,297	712,836	530,507	410,125	353,041
Selling, general and administrative expenses	670,602	550,069	418,152	324,852	276,116
Income from operations	208,695	162,767	112,355	85,273	76,925
Interest expense, net	(5,183)	(3,841)	(2,258)	(2,344)	(850)
Other expense, net	(73)	(2,064)	(1,178)	(511)	(6,175)
Income before income taxes	203,439	156,862	108,919	82,418	69,900
Provision for income taxes	74,661	59,943	40,442	35,633	31,671
Net income	$ 128,778	$ 96,919	$ 68,477	$ 46,785	$ 38,229
Net income per common share					
Basic	$1.23	$0.94	$0.67	$0.47	$0.39
Diluted	1.21	0.92	0.67	0.46	0.38
Weighted average common shares outstanding					
Basic	104,343	103,140	101,595	99,696	98,171
Diluted	106,380	105,052	102,563	101,301	100,685
Selected Balance Sheet Data					
Cash and cash equivalents	$ 341,841	$ 175,384	$ 203,870	$ 187,297	$ 102,042
Working capital*	651,370	506,056	406,703	327,838	263,313
Inventories at year-end	319,286	324,409	215,355	148,488	182,232
Total assets	1,157,083	919,210	675,378	545,588	487,555
Total debt and capital lease obligations, including current maturities	61,889	77,724	15,942	20,223	45,591
Total stockholders' equity	816,922	636,432	496,966	399,997	331,097
Selected Cash Flow Data					
Net cash provided by operating activities	$ 199,761	$ 15,218	$ 50,114	$ 119,041	$ 69,516

*Working capital is defined as current assets minus current liabilities.

Source: Company 10-K reports 2012, 2010, and 2008.

retailers outside the North America were growing. Exhibit 3 shows the composition of Under Armour's revenues from 2009 to 2012.

Growth Strategy

Under Armour's announced sales objective was to achieve sales revenues of $4 billion by 2016, up from an estimated $2.2 billion in 2013. The company's growth strategy in 2013 consisted of several strategic initiatives:

• Continuing to broaden the company's product offerings to men, women, and youth for wear in a widening variety of sports and recreational activities.

EXHIBIT 2

Growth in Under Armour's Quarterly Revenues, 2010 through mid-2013 (in 000s)

	Quarter 1 (Jan.–March)		Quarter 2 (April–June)		Quarter 3 (July–Sept.)		Quarter 4 (Oct.–Dec.)	
	Revenues	% Change from Prior Year's Quarter 1	Revenues	% Change from Prior Year's Quarter 2	Revenues	% Change from Prior Year's Quarter 3	Revenues	% Change from Prior Year's Quarter 4
2009	$200,000	—	$164,648	—	$269,546	—	$222,217	—
2010	229,407	14.7%	204,786	24.4%	328,568	21.9%	301,166	35.5%
2011	312,699	36.3%	291,336	42.3%	465,523	41.7%	403,126	33.9%
2012	384,389	23.0%	369,473	26.8%	575,196	23.6%	505,863	25.5%
2013	471,608	22.7%	454,541	23.0%	n.a.	n.a.	n.a.	n.a.

n.a. Not available

Source: Company 10-K reports 2012 and 2010 and company press releases April 24, 2013, and July 25, 2013.

EXHIBIT 3

Composition of Under Armour's Revenues, 2009–2012

A. Net Revenues by Product Category (in thousands of $)

	2012		2011		2010		2009	
	Dollars	Percent	Dollars	Percent	Dollars	Percent	Dollars	Percent
Apparel	$1,385,350	75.5%	$1,122,031	76.2%	$853,493	80.2%	$651,779	76.1%
Footwear	238,955	13.0	181,684	12.3	127,175	12.0	136,224	15.9
Accessories	165,835	9.0	132,400	9.0	43,882	4.1	35,077	4.1
Total net sales	1,790,140	97.6%	1,436,115	97.5%	$1,024,550	96.3%	$823,080	96.1%
License revenues	44,781	2.4	36,569	2.5	39,377	3.7	33,331	3.9
Total net revenues	$1,834,921	100.0%	$1,472,684	100.0%	$1,063,927	100.0%	$856,411	100.0%

B. Net Revenues by Geographic Region (in thousands of $)

	2012		2011		2010		2009	
	Dollars	Percent	Dollars	Percent	Dollars	Percent	Dollars	Percent
North America	$1,726,733	94.1%	$1,383,346	93.9%	$ 997,816	93.7%	$808,020	94.3%
Other foreign countries	108,188	5.9	89,338	6.1	66,111	6.3	48,391	5.7
Total net revenues	$1,834,921	100.0%	$1,472,684	100.0%	$ 1,063,927	100.0%	$856,411	100.0%

Source: Company 10-K reports, 2012 and 2010.

- Targeting additional consumer segments for the company's ever-expanding lineup of performance products.
- Increasing its penetration of the market for athletic footwear (where Nike was the clear-cut global market leader).

- Securing additional distribution of Under Armour products in the retail marketplace in North America via not only store retailers and catalog retailers but also through Under Armour factory outlet and specialty stores and sales at the company's website.

- Expanding the sale of Under Armour products in foreign countries and becoming a global competitor in the world market for sports apparel, athletic footwear, and performance products.

- Growing global awareness of the Under Armour brand name and strengthening the appeal of Under Armour products worldwide.

Product Line Strategy

Under Armour's diverse product offerings in 2013 consisted of apparel, footwear, and accessories for men, women, and youth marketed at multiple price levels in a variety of styles and fits intended to regulate body temperature and enhance comfort, mobility, and performance regardless of weather conditions.

Apparel The company designed and merchandised three lines of apparel gear: Heat-Gear® for hot weather conditions; ColdGear® for cold weather conditions; and AllSeasonGear® for temperature conditions between the extremes.

HeatGear HeatGear was designed to be worn in warm to hot temperatures under equipment or as a single layer. The company's first compression T-shirt was the original HeatGear product and was still one of the company's signature styles in 2013. In sharp contrast to a sweat-soaked cotton T-shirt that could weigh two to three pounds, HeatGear was engineered with a microfiber blend featuring what Under Armour termed a "Moisture Transport System" that ensured the body will stay cool, dry, and light. HeatGear was offered in a variety of tops and bottoms in a broad array of colors and styles for wear in the gym or outside in warm weather.

ColdGear Under Armour high-performance fabrics were appealing to people participating in cold-weather sports and vigorous recreational activities such as snow skiing who needed both warmth and moisture-wicking protection from a sometimes overheated body. ColdGear was designed to wick moisture from the body while circulating body heat from hot spots to maintain core body temperature. All ColdGear apparel provided dryness and warmth in a single light layer that could be worn beneath a jersey, uniform, protective gear or ski vest, or other cold-weather outerwear. ColdGear products generally were sold at higher price levels than other Under Armour gear lines.

AllSeasonGear AllSeasonGear was designed to be worn in changing temperatures and used technical fabrics to keep the wearer cool and dry in warmer temperatures while preventing a chill in cooler temperatures.

Each of the three apparel lines contained three fit types: compression (tight fit), fitted (athletic fit), and loose (relaxed).

As of June 2013, Under Armour was actively pursuing efforts to grow its apparel sales in the men's, women's, and youth segments. The specific sales targets for each segment were:[8]

- Men's apparel: Sales revenues of $960 million in 2013, expanding to $1.5 billion in 2016.

- Women's apparel: Sales revenues of $490 million in 2013, expanding to $960 million in 2016.

- Youth apparel: Sales revenues of $220 million in 2013, expanding to $470 million in 2016.

Under Armour's latest new offerings for women—a studio line that targeted yoga exercisers and a line of Armour Bra products—were said to be selling quite well in the first quarter of 2013.[9]

Footwear Under Armour began marketing footwear products for men, women, and youth in 2006 and had expanded its footwear line every year since. Currently, its offerings included football, baseball, lacrosse, softball, and soccer cleats, slides, performance training footwear, running footwear, basketball footwear, and hunting boots. Under Armour's athletic footwear was light, breathable, and built with performance attributes for athletes. Innovative technologies were used to provide stabilization, directional cushioning, and moisture management, and all models and styles were engineered to maximize the athlete's comfort and control.

As of June 2013, Under Armour had plans in place to grow the company's footwear sales to $290 million in 2013 and to $600 million in 2016.

Accessories   Under Armour's accessory line in 2013 included gloves, socks, headwear, bags, kneepads, custom-molded mouth guards, inflatable basketballs and footballs, and eyewear designed to be used and worn before, during, and after competition. All of these featured performance advantages and functionality similar to other Under Armour products. For instance, the company's baseball batting, football, golf, and running gloves included HeatGear and ColdGear technologies and were designed with advanced fabrications to provide various high-performance attributes that differentiated Under Armour gloves from those of rival brands.

Under Armour had licensing agreements with a number of firms to produce and market its various accessories except for headgear and bags. Under Armour product, marketing, and sales teams were actively involved in all steps of the design process for licensed products in order to maintain brand standards and consistency. Revenues generated from the sale of all licensed accessories are included in the licensing revenue amounts shown in Exhibit 3A.

Marketing, Promotion, and Brand Management Strategies

Under Armour had an in-house marketing and promotions department that designed and produced most of its advertising campaigns to drive consumer demand for its products and build awareness of Under Armour as a leading performance athletic brand. The company's total marketing expenses, including endorsements and advertising, were $205.4 million in 2012, $167.9 million in 2011, $128.2 million in 2010, and $108.9 million in 2009. These totals included the costs of sponsoring events and various sports teams, the costs of athlete endorsements, and advertising expenses.

Sports Marketing   A key element of Under Armour's marketing and promotion strategy was to promote the sales and use of its products to high-performing athletes and teams on the high school, collegiate, and professional levels. This strategy included entering into outfitting agreements with a variety of collegiate and professional sports teams, sponsoring an assortment of collegiate and professional sports events, and selling Under Armour products directly to team equipment managers and to individual athletes.

Management believed that having audiences see Under Armour products (with the interlocking UA logo prominently displayed) being worn by athletes on the playing field helped the company establish on-field authenticity of the Under Armour brand with consumers. Considerable effort went into giving Under Armour products broad exposure at live sporting events, as well as on television, in magazines, and on a wide variety of Internet sites. Exhibit 4 shows the Under Armour logo and examples of its use on Under Armour products.

In 2011–2012, Under Armour was the official outfitter of *all* the athletic teams at Boston College, Texas Tech University, the University of Maryland, the University of South Carolina, Auburn University, and the University of South Florida and *selected* sports teams at the University of Illinois, Northwestern University, the University of Minnesota, the University of Utah, the University of Indiana, the University of Missouri, Georgetown University, the University of Delaware, the University of Hawaii, Southern Illinois University, Temple University, Wichita State University, South Dakota State University, Wagner College, Whittier College, and La Salle University. All told, it was the

EXHIBIT 4

The Under Armour Logo and Its Use on Selected Under Armour Products

official outfitter of over 100 Division I men's and women's collegiate athletic teams, growing numbers of high school athletic teams, and several Olympic sports teams; and it supplied sideline apparel and fan gear for many collegiate teams as well. In addition, Under Armour sold products to high-profile professional athletes and teams, most notably in the NFL, MLB, the National Hockey League, and the NBA. Since 2006, Under Armour had been an official supplier of football cleats to the NFL. Under Armour became the official supplier of gloves to the NFL beginning in 2011, and it began supplying the NFL with training apparel for athletes attending NFL tryout camps beginning in 2012. In 2011 Under Armour became the Official Performance Footwear Supplier of Major League Baseball. Starting with the 2011/2012 season, Under Armour was granted rights by the NBA to show ads and promotional displays of players who were official endorsers of Under Armour products in their NBA game uniforms wearing UA-branded basketball footwear.

Internationally, Under Armour was building its brand image by selling products to European soccer and rugby teams. It was the official supplier of performance apparel to the Hannover 96 and Tottenham Hotspur football clubs and the Welsh Rugby Union, among others. In addition, it was an official supplier of performance apparel to Hockey Canada, had advertising rights at many locations in the Air Canada Center during the Toronto Maple Leafs' home games, and was the Official Performance Product Sponsor of the Toronto Maple Leafs. In 2013, commensurate with its accelerated push to grow international sales, Under Armour was actively pursuing efforts to boost its market profile in foreign countries by signing high-profile foreign sports celebrities to endorsement contracts; top management expected to announce a number of such contracts in the second half of 2013 and the first half of 2014.

Under Armour also had sponsorship agreements with individual athletes. Its strategy was to secure the endorsement of such newly emerging sports stars as Milwaukee Bucks point guard Brandon Jennings, U.S. professional skier and Olympic gold medal winner Lindsey Vonn, professional lacrosse player Paul Rabil, Baltimore Orioles catcher Matthew Wieters, 2012 National League (baseball) Most Valuable Player and World Series Champion Buster Posey, UFC Welterweight Champion Georges St-Pierre, 2012 National League Rookie of the Year Bryce Harper of the Washington Nationals, NBA rookie Kemba Walker, the number two pick in the 2011 NBA draft Derrick Williams, tennis phenom Sloane Stephens, WBC Super-welterweight Boxing Champion Canelo Alvarez, and former world number one amateur golfer Jordan Spieth. In addition, the company's roster of athletes included established stars: NFL football players Tom Brady, Ray Lewis, Brandon Jacobs, Arian Foster, Miles Austin, Julio Jones, Devon Hester, Vernon Davis, Patrick Willis, Santana Moss, and Anquan Boldin; triathlon champion Chris "Macca" McCormack; professional baseball players Ryan Zimmerman, José Reyes, and eight others; U.S. Women's National Soccer Team players Heather Mitts and Lauren Cheney; U.S. Olympic and professional volleyball player Nicole Branagh; Olympic snowboarder Lindsey Jacobellis; U.S. Olympic swimmer Michael Phelps; and professional golfer Hunter Mahan.

During 2010–2012, Under Armour hosted over 100 combines, camps, and clinics for male and female athletes in many sports at various regional sites in the United States. It sponsored American Youth Football (an organization that promoted the development of youth and a variety of camps and clinics), the Under Armour Senior Bowl (a televised annual competition between the top seniors in college football), the Under Armour (Baltimore) Marathon, the Under Armour All-America Lacrosse Classic, and a collection of high-school All-America games in a variety of sports. Under Armour had partnered with Ripken Baseball to outfit some 35,000 Ripken Baseball participants at camps and clinics and to be the title sponsor for all Ripken youth baseball tournaments. It had partnered with the Baseball Factory to outfit top high school baseball athletes from head to toe and serve as the title sponsor for nationally recognized baseball tryouts, training camps, and tournament teams.

Under Armour spent approximately $53.0 million in 2012 for athlete endorsements and various sponsorships, compared to about $43.5 million in 2011 and $29.4 million in 2010. The company was contractually obligated to spend a minimum of $154.5 million for endorsements and sponsorships during 2013–2017.[10] Under Armour did not know precisely what its future sponsorship costs for individual athletes would be because its contractual agreements with these athletes were subject to certain performance-based variables.

Retail Marketing and Product Presentation

The primary thrust of Under Armour's retail marketing strategy was to increase the floor space *exclusively* dedicated to Under Armour products in the stores of its major retail accounts. The key initiative here was to design and fund Under Armour "concept shops"—including flooring, in-store fixtures, product displays, life-size athlete mannequins, and lighting—within the stores of its major retail customers. This shop-in-shop approach was seen as an effective way to gain the placement of Under Armour products in prime floor space, educate consumers about Under Armour products, and create a more engaging and sales-producing way for consumers to shop for Under Armour products.

In stores that did not have Under Armour concept shops, Under Armour worked with retailers to establish optimal placement of its products. In "big box" sporting goods stores, it was important to be sure that the growing variety of Under Armour products were represented in all of the various departments (hunting apparel in the hunting goods department, footwear and socks in the footwear department, and so on). Except for the retail stores with Under Armour concept shops, company personnel worked with retailers to employ in-store fixtures and displays that highlighted the UA logo and conveyed a performance-oriented, athletic look (chiefly through the use of life-size athlete mannequins). The merchandising strategy was not only to enhance the visibility of Under Armour products but also to reinforce the message that the company's brand was distinct from those of competitors.

Media and Promotion Under Armour advertised in national digital, broadcast, and print media outlets, and its advertising campaigns included a variety of lengths and formats. The company's "Protect this House" and "Click-Clack" campaigns featured several NFL players, and its "Protect this House" campaign had been used in several NFL and collegiate stadiums during games as a crowd prompt. Beginning in 2003–2004 and continuing through 2012, Under Armour utilized an ongoing series of TV commercials where the Under Armour brand asked athletes engaged in sporting events at their home field to "Protect this House" and athletes responded to the request with a resounding "I WILL" to familiarize consumers with the Under Armour brand. Top executives believed the long-standing "Protect this House. I WILL" campaign had been instrumental in making the Under Armour brand a widely recognized household name.

In February 2013, Under Armour launched its biggest-ever global marketing campaign featuring Under Armour's now iconic I WILL trademark. The campaign's principal 60-second ads on TV and online depicted four of Under Armour's up-and-coming celebrity endorsers—Canelo Alvarez, Sloane Stephens (the only teenager ranked in the top 20 in the World Tennis Association), Bryce Harper, and Kemba Walker—in their authentic training environments outfitted in the company's most technologically advanced products. The new ad campaign showcased Under Armour's new Spine Venom® and Micro G® Toxic 6 performance footwear collections, the new Cold-Gear infrared insulated apparel collection, and the Armour39® system. The first-of-its-kind

Armour39 system was a digital performance-measuring device that enabled users to track their heart rate, calories burned, and intensity during a workout; the headline attribute of the Armour39 system was a single numerical WILLpower score that reflected an individual's overall effort during a workout session and that served as a gauge of the person's training and athletic potential.

On several occasions, the company had secured the use of Under Armour products in movies, television shows, and video games; management believed the appearance of Under Armour products in these media reinforced authenticity of the brand and provided brand exposure to audiences that may not have seen Under Armour's other advertising campaigns. In 2011–2012, Under Armour significantly grew the company's "fan base" via social sites like Facebook and Twitter; the company's goal in using social media was to engage consumers and promote conversation about the company's products and brand.

Distribution Strategy

Under Armour products were available in more than 25,000 retail stores worldwide at the end of 2011, of which about 18,000 retail stores were in North America. Under Armour also sold its products directly to consumers through its own factory outlet and specialty stores, website, and catalogs.

Wholesale Distribution In 2011–2012, close to 70 percent of Under Armour's net revenues were generated from sales to retailers. The company's two biggest retail accounts were Dick's Sporting Goods and The Sports Authority, which in 2012 accounted for a combined 22 percent of the company's net revenues. Other important retail accounts in the United States included Academy Sports and Outdoors, Hibbett Sporting Goods, Modell's Sporting Goods, Bass Pro Shops, Cabela's, Footlocker, Finish Line, The Army and Air Force Exchange Service, and such well-known department store chains as Macy's, Dillard's, Belk, and Lord &

Taylor. In Canada, the company's biggest customers were SportChek International and Sportman International. Roughly 75 percent of all sales made to retailers were to large-format national and regional retail chains. The remaining 25 percent of wholesale sales were to lesser-sized outdoor and other specialty retailers, institutional athletic departments, leagues, teams, and fitness specialists. Independent and specialty retailers were serviced by a combination of in-house sales personnel and third-party commissioned manufacturer's representatives.

Direct-to-Consumer Sales In 2012, 29 percent of Under Armour's net revenues were generated through direct-to-consumer sales, versus 27 percent in 2011 and 23 percent in 2010; the direct-to-consumer channel included discounted sales at Under Armour's factory outlet stores and full-price sales through its specialty stores, global website (www.ua.com), and catalog. Over the years, Under Armour had opened increasing numbers of Factory House stores, mostly in outlet malls, to help the company sell excess inventory and provide value to customers. Under Armour expanded its factory outlet store base from 80 stores in 34 states at year-end 2011 to 101 stores in 37 states at year-end 2012. The first Factory House store in Canada was opened in 2012. In 2011, Under Armour opened a specialty store in Shanghai, China, to begin learning about Chinese consumers; three additional retail locations in China had been opened as of May 2013.

In late 2007, Under Armour opened its first company-owned retail specialty store location at the Westfield Annapolis mall in Annapolis, Maryland. In May 2008, Under Armour also opened a larger, 6,000-square-foot specialty store at Westfield Fox Valley in Aurora, Illinois (a Chicago suburb). In spring 2013, the company had six Under Armour full-price specialty stores in the United States (three in Maryland and one each in Massachusetts, Illinois, and Colorado); plans had been announced to open several more full-price retail locations in the mid-Atlantic region in 2013–2014. The first

Under Armour specialty store outside of North America was opened in Edinburgh, Scotland—it was owned and operated by First XV, a rugby store that was situated next door.

By the end of 2013 Under Armour expected to have a total of 114 Factory House stores, with an average of 5,800 square feet per location; the goal was to have 141 Factory House locations averaging 7,700 square feet by late 2016.

Under Armour management's website strategy called for e-commerce sales at www.underarmour.com to be a growth vehicle for the company in upcoming years. To help spur website sales, the company was endeavoring to establish a clearer connection between its website offerings and the brand initiatives being undertaken in retail stores. It was also enhancing the merchandising techniques and storytelling regarding the products being marketed at its website. Management estimated that 40 million athletes would shop at the company's website, growing to 90 million athletes worldwide in 2016.

Total direct-to-consumer sales—sales at company stores and www.underarmour.com—were expected to account for 29 percent of the company's estimated 2013 sales of $2.2 billion, increasing to 31 percent of the targeted sales of $4 billion in 2016.[11]

Product Licensing In 2012, 2.4 percent of the company's net revenues came from licensing arrangements to manufacture and distribute Under Armour branded products. Under Armour approved all products manufactured and sold by its licensees, and the company's quality assurance team strived to ensure that licensed products met the same quality and compliance standards as company-sold products. In 2013, Under Armour had relationships with several licensees for team uniforms, eyewear, and custom-molded mouth guards, as well as the distribution of Under Armour products to college bookstores and golf pro shops. In addition, Under Armour had a relationship with a Japanese licensee, Dome Corporation, that had the exclusive rights to distribute Under Armour products in Japan. Dome sold Under

Armour products to professional baseball and soccer teams (including Omiya Ardija, a professional soccer club in Saitama, Japan) and to over 2,000 independent specialty stores and large sporting goods retailers, such as Alpen, Himaraya, The Sports Authority, and Xebio. Under Armour made a minority equity investment in Dome Corporation in January 2011.

Distribution outside North America

Because Under Armour management was convinced that the trend toward using performance products was global, it had begun entering foreign markets as rapidly as was prudent. A European headquarters was opened in 2006 in Amsterdam to conduct and oversee sales, marketing, and logistics activities across Europe. The strategy was to first sell Under Armour products directly to teams and athletes and then leverage visibility in the sports segment to access broader audiences of potential consumers. By 2011, Under Armour had succeeded in selling products to Premier League Football clubs and multiple running, golf, and cricket clubs in the United Kingdom; soccer teams in France, Germany, Greece, Ireland, Italy, Spain, and Sweden; as well as First Division Rugby clubs in France, Ireland, Italy, and the United Kingdom.

Sales to European retailers quickly followed on the heels of gains being made in the sports team segment. In 2012, Under Armour had 4,000 retail customers in Austria, France, Germany, Ireland, and the United Kingdom and was generating revenues from sales to independent distributors that resold Under Armour products to retailers in Italy, Greece, Scandinavia, and Spain. Gradual expansion into other countries in Europe, the Middle East, and Africa was under way in 2013.

In 2010–2011, Under Armour began selling its products in parts of Latin America and Asia. In Latin America, Under Armour sold directly to retailers in some countries and in other countries sold its products to independent distributors that then were responsible for securing sales to retailers. Under Armour was utilizing its four retail locations in China to learn about Chinese consumers and what it would take to succeed in selling Under Armour products in China on a much wider scale. In 2013, distribution to the retail stores in China was handled through a third-party logistics provider based in Hong Kong.

Sales of Under Armour products outside North America accounted for only 5.9 percent of the company's net revenues in 2012, down fractionally from 6.1 percent in 2011 and 6.2 percent in 2010 (see Exhibit 3B). But despite the small percentage declines, dollar sales had risen briskly from $66.1 million in 2010 to $89.3 million in 2011 to $108.2 million in 2012. Top management saw growth in foreign sales as a huge market opportunity for the company in upcoming years, larger than the opportunity to grow sales in North America. But in 2013 the company's strategy for increasing its penetration of foreign markets was fluid and very much in the early stages of being fleshed out. Kevin Plank had opted to be patient in pursuing foreign expansion and take the time to "make the right decisions in Europe, Latin America, and Asia." In the company's 2012 Letter to the Shareholders, he said:[12]

> We are able to take a different, broader approach to how we enter these markets. Our grassroots efforts help us build the Brand by being intensely focused on sport authenticity in local markets. We are able to balance this approach with larger brand-building initiatives . . . in the age where we are all connected like never before through technology, we have the ability to change the traditional approach to reaching consumers in new markets through digital means like Ecommerce and social media.

In June 2013, Under Armour formally announced a new regional organization structure for its Under Armour International division, with targets to boost international sales revenues from 6 percent of total revenues in 2013 to 12 percent of total revenues in 2016. By comparison, in 2012 Nike generated about 59 percent of its revenues outside North America, and adidas, based in Germany, got about 60 percent of its sales outside its home market of Europe—these big international sales percentages for Nike and adidas were a big reason Under Armour executives were confident that growing the company's international sales represented an enormous market opportunity for the company, despite the stiff competition it could expect from these two rivals.

Product Design and Development

Top executives believed that product innovation—as concerns both technical design and aesthetic design—was the key to driving Under Armour's sales growth and building a stronger brand name.

Under Armour products were manufactured with technically advanced specialty fabrics produced by third parties. The company's product development team collaborated closely with fabric suppliers to ensure that the fabrics and materials used had the desired performance and fit attributes. Under Armour regularly upgraded its products as next-generation fabrics with better performance characteristics became available and as the needs of athletes changed. Product development efforts also aimed at broadening the company's product offerings in both new and existing product categories and market segments. An effort was made to design products with "visible technology," utilizing color, texture, and fabrication that would enhance customers' perception and understanding of the use and benefits of Under Armour products.

Under Armour's product development team had significant prior industry experience at leading fabric and other raw material suppliers and branded athletic apparel and footwear companies throughout the world. The team worked closely with Under Armour's sports marketing and sales teams as well as professional and collegiate athletes to identify product trends and determine market needs. Collaboration among the company's product development, sales, and sports marketing team had proved important in identifying the opportunity and market for two product lines launched in 2011:

- Charged Cotton™ products, which were made from natural cotton but performed like the products made from technically advanced synthetic fabrics, drying faster and wicking moisture away from the body.

- Storm Fleece products, which had a unique, water-resistant finish that repelled water without stifling airflow.

Under Armour executives projected that the innovative Charged Cotton and Storm product lines would generate combined revenues of $500 million in 2016.[13] In 2012, in partnership with the Swiss Company Schoeller, Under Armour introduced products with ColdBlack® technology, which repelled heat from the sun and kept the wearer cooler outside.

Sourcing, Manufacturing, and Quality Assurance

The high-tech specialty fabrics and other raw materials used in Under Armour products were all sourced from a limited number of pre-approved specialty fabric manufacturers; no fabrics were manufactured in-house. Under Armour executives believed outsourcing fabric production enabled the company to seek out and utilize whatever fabric suppliers were able to produce the latest and best performance-oriented fabrics to Under Armour's specifications, while also freeing more time for the product development staff to concentrate on upgrading the performance, styling, and overall appeal of existing products and expanding the company's lineup of product offerings.

In 2012, approximately 50 to 55 percent of the fabric used in Under Armour products came from five suppliers, with locations in China, Malaysia, Mexico, Taiwan, and Vietnam. Because a big fraction of the materials used were petroleum-based synthetics, fabric costs were subject to crude oil price fluctuations. The cotton fabrics used in the Charged Cotton products were also subject to price fluctuations and varying availability based on cotton harvests.

In 2012, substantially all Under Armour products were made by 27 primary manufacturers, operating in 14 countries; 10 manufacturers produced approximately 49 percent of Under

Armour's products. Approximately 53 percent were manufactured in Asia, 19 percent in Central and South America, 18 percent in the Middle East, and 8 percent in Mexico. All manufacturers purchased the fabrics they needed from the five fabric suppliers preapproved by Under Armour. All of the makers of Under Armour products were evaluated for quality systems, social compliance, and financial strength by Under Armour's quality assurance team before being selected and also on an ongoing basis. The company strived to qualify multiple manufacturers for particular product types and fabrications and to seek out contractors that could perform multiple manufacturing stages, such as procuring raw materials and providing finished products, which helped Under Armour control its cost of goods sold. All contract manufacturers were required to adhere to a code of conduct regarding quality of manufacturing, working conditions, and other social concerns. However, the company had no long-term agreements requiring it to continue to use the services of any manufacturer, and no manufacturer was obligated to make products for Under Armour on a long-term basis. Under Armour had an office in Hong Kong to support its manufacturing, quality assurance, and sourcing efforts for apparel and offices in Guangzhou, China, to support its manufacturing, quality assurance, and sourcing efforts for footwear and accessories.

Under Armour had a 17,000-square-foot Special Make-Up Shop located at one of its distribution facilities in Maryland where it had the capability to make and ship customized apparel products on tight deadlines for high-profile athletes, leagues, and teams. While these apparel products represented a tiny fraction of Under Armour's revenues, management believed the facility helped provide superior service to select customers.

Distribution Facilities and Inventory Management

Under Armour packaged and shipped the majority of its products for the North American market at two distribution facilities located approximately 15 miles from its Baltimore headquarters. One was a 359,000-square-foot facility built in 2000 and the other was a 308,000-square-foot facility; both were leased. In addition, the company utilized the services of a third-party logistics provider with primary locations in California and in Florida; the company's agreement with this provider continued until May 2023. Distribution to European customers was handled by a third-party logistics provider based in Venlo, The Netherlands; the current agreement with this distribution expired in April 2014. Under Armour had contracted with a third-party logistics provider to handle packing and shipment to customers in Asia. Shipments of apparel, footwear, and accessories to independent distributors in Latin America, Australia, and New Zealand were handled by the company's distribution facilities in the United States. In a few instances, Under Armour arranged to have products shipped from the independent factories that made its products directly to customer-designated facilities. Management expected that the company would add more distribution facilities in the future.

Under Armour based the amount of inventory it needed to have on hand for each item in its product line on existing orders, anticipated sales, and the need to rapidly deliver orders to customers. Its inventory strategy was focused on (1) having sufficient inventory to fill incoming orders promptly and (2) putting strong systems and procedures in place to improve the efficiency with which it managed its inventories of individual products and total inventory. The amounts of seasonal products it ordered from manufacturers were based on current bookings, the need to ship seasonal items at the start of the shipping window in order to maximize the floor space productivity of retail customers, and the need to adequately stock its factory outlet stores. Excess inventories of particular products were either shipped to its factory outlet stores or earmarked for sale to third-party liquidators.

However, the growing number of individual items in the product line and uncertainties surrounding upcoming consumer demand for individual items made it difficult to accurately forecast how many units to order from manufacturers and what the appropriate stocking requirements were for many items. Under Armour's year-end inventories rose from $148.4 million in 2009 to $215.4 million in 2010 to $324.4 million in 2011—percentage increases that exceeded the gains in companywide revenues and that caused days of inventories to climb from 121.4 days in 2009 to 148.4 days in 2010 and to 155.8 days in 2011. The increases were due, in part, to long lead times for design and production of some products and from having to begin manufacturing seasonal products and soon-to-be introduced products before receiving any orders for them. In January 2012, management announced that because inventory growth of 118 percent over the past two years had outstripped revenue growth of 72 percent it was instituting a review of the entire product line with the objectives of reducing production lead times, curtailing the number of distinct individual items included in the company's lineup of product offerings (frequently referred to as SKUs or stock-keeping units), and doing a better job of planning and executing shipments of excess inventory to the company's factory outlet stores. Year-end inventories dropped to $319.3 million in 2012, equal to 120.0 days of inventory. The company's stated target for inventory turns in 2013 was 3.0; the 2016 target was for turns in the 3.0 to 3.3 range.[14]

Competition

The multi-segment global market for sports apparel, athletic footwear, and related accessories was fragmented among some 25 brand-name competitors with diverse product lines and varying geographic coverage and numerous small competitors with specialized-use apparel lines that usually operated within a single country or geographic region. Industry participants included athletic and leisure shoe companies, athletic and leisure apparel companies, sports equipment companies, and large companies having diversified lines of athletic and leisure shoes, apparel, and equipment. In 2012, the global market for athletic footwear was about $75 billion and was forecasted to reach about $85 billion in 2018; growth was expected to be driven by rising population, increasing disposable incomes, rising health awareness and launch of innovative footwear designs and technology.[15] The global market for athletic and fitness apparel was approximately $135 billion in 2012 and was expected to reach $181 billion in 2018. Nike was the clear global market leader, with a global footwear market share of about 17 percent and a sports apparel share of about 4.4 percent. Other prominent competitors besides Under Armour included adidas, Puma, Columbia, Fila, and Polo Ralph Lauren. Exhibit 5 shows a representative sample of the best-known companies and brands.

Competition was intense and revolved around performance and reliability, new-product development, price, product identity through marketing and promotion, and customer support and service. It was common for the leading companies to actively sponsor sporting events and clinics and to contract with prominent and influential athletes, coaches, teams, colleges, and sports leagues to endorse their brands and use their products.

Nike, Inc.

Incorporated in 1968, Nike was engaged in the design, development, and worldwide marketing and selling of footwear, sports apparel, sports equipment, and accessory products. Its principal businesses in 2011–2012 consisted of the businesses in the table on page 264.

Total companywide sales were $20.9 billion in fiscal 2011 and $24.1 billion in 2012. Nike was the world's largest seller of athletic footwear and athletic apparel, with over 40,000 retail accounts, nearly 560 company-owned stores, 19 distribution centers, and selling arrangements with independent distributors and licensees in over 190 countries—see Exhibit 6. About 58 percent of Nike's sales came from

EXHIBIT 5

Major Competitors and Brands in Selected Segments of the Sports Apparel, Athletic Footwear, and Accessory Industry, 2013

Performance Apparel for Sports (Baseball, Football, Basketball, Softball, Volleyball, Hockey, Lacrosse, Soccer, Track & Field, and Other Action Sports)

- Nike
- Under Armour
- Eastbay
- adidas
- Russell

Performance-Driven Athletic Footwear

- Nike
- Reebok
- adidas
- New Balance
- Saucony
- Puma
- Rockport
- Converse
- Ryka
- Asics

Training/Fitness Clothing

- Nike
- Under Armour
- Eastbay
- adidas
- Puma
- Fila
- lululemon athletica
- Champion
- Asics
- SUGOI

Performance Activewear and Sports-Inspired Lifestyle Apparel

- Polo Ralph Lauren
- Lacoste
- Izod
- Cutter & Buck
- Timberland

Performance Skiwear

- Salomon
- North Face
- Descente
- Columbia
- Patagonia
- Marmot
- Helly Hansen
- Bogner
- Spyder
- Many others

Performance Golf Apparel

- Footjoy
- Polo Golf
- Nike
- adidas
- Puma
- Under Armour
- Ashworth
- Cutter & Buck
- Greg Norman
- Many others

outside the United States. Nike's retail account base in the United States included a mix of footwear stores; sporting goods stores; athletic specialty stores; department stores; skate, tennis, and golf shops; and other retail accounts.

During fiscal 2012, Nike's three largest customers accounted for approximately 24 percent of U.S. sales; its three largest customers outside the United States accounted for about 11 percent of total non-U.S. sales. In fiscal 2012, Nike

Businesses	Fiscal 2011 Sales	Fiscal 2012 Sales (in millions)
Nike brand footwear (over 800 models and styles)	$11,518	$13,426
Nike brand apparel	5,513	6,333
Nike brand equipment for a wide variety of sports	1,018	1,202
Converse (a designer and marketer of athletic footwear, apparel, and accessories)	1,131	1,324
Nike Golf (footwear, apparel, golf equipment, accessories)	658	726
Cole Haan (a designer and marketer of dress and casual footwear, apparel, and accessories for men and women)	521	535
Hurley (a designer and marketer of action sports and youth lifestyle footwear and apparel, including shorts, tees, tanks, hoodies, and swimwear)	252	248
Umbro (a prominent British-based global provider of soccer apparel and equipment)	224	262

EXHIBIT 6

Nike's Worldwide Retail and Distribution Network, 2012

United States	Foreign Countries
• About 20,000 retail accounts	• More than 20,000 retail accounts
• 156 Nike factory outlet stores	• 308 Nike factory outlet stores
• 28 Nike and Niketown stores	• 65 Nike and Niketown stores
• 3 Distribution centers	• 16 Distribution centers
• Company website (www.nikestore.com)	• Independent distributors and licensees in over 170 countries
	• Company website (www.nikestore.com)

had sales of $3.5 billion at its company-owned stores and website.

In 2011, Nike established a fiscal 2015 revenue target of $28 billion to $30 billion and reaffirmed its ongoing target of annual earnings per share growth in the 14 to 16 percent range.

Principal Products   Nike's athletic footwear models and styles were designed primarily for specific athletic use, although many were worn for casual or leisure purposes. Running, training, basketball, soccer, sport-inspired casual shoes, and kids' shoes were the company's top-selling footwear categories. It also marketed footwear designed for baseball, cheerleading, football, golf, lacrosse, outdoor activities, skateboarding, tennis, volleyball, walking, and wrestling. The company designed and marketed Nike-branded sports apparel and accessories for most all of these same sports categories, as well as sports-inspired lifestyle apparel, athletic bags, and accessory items. Footwear, apparel, and accessories were often marketed in "collections" of similar design or for specific purposes. It also marketed apparel with licensed college and professional team and league logos. Nike-brand offerings in sport equipment included bags, socks, sport balls, eyewear, timepieces, electronic devices, bats, gloves, protective equipment, and golf clubs.

Exhibit 7 shows a breakdown of Nike's sales of footwear, apparel, and equipment by geographic region for fiscal years 2010–2012.

Marketing, Promotions, and Endorsements

Nike responded to trends and shifts in consumer preferences by (1) adjusting the mix of existing product offerings; (2) developing new products, styles, and categories; and (3) striving to influence sports and fitness preferences through aggressive marketing, promotional activities, sponsorships, and athlete endorsements. Nike spent $2.71 billion in fiscal 2012, $2.45 billion in fiscal 2011, $2.36 billion in fiscal 2010, and $2.35 billion in fiscal 2009 for what it termed "demand creation expenses" that included advertising and promotion expenses and the costs of endorsement contracts. More than 500 professional, collegiate, club, and Olympic sports teams in football, basketball, baseball, ice hockey, soccer, rugby, speed skating, tennis, swimming, and other sports wore Nike uniforms with the Nike swoosh prominently visible. There were over 1,000 prominent professional athletes with Nike endorsement contracts in 2011–2012, including former basketball great Michael Jordan, NFL players Drew Brees, Tim Tebow, Tony Romo, Aaron Rodgers, and Clay Matthews; MLB players Albert Pujols and Alex Rodriguez; NBA players LeBron James and Dwayne Wade; professional golfers Tiger Woods and Michelle Wie; and professional tennis players Victoria Azarenka, Maria Sharapova, Venus and Serena Williams, Roger Federer, and Rafael Nadal. When Tiger Woods turned pro, Nike signed him to a five-year $100 million endorsement contract and made him the centerpiece of its campaign to

EXHIBIT 7

Nike's Sales of Nike Brand Footwear, Apparel, and Equipment, by Geographic Region, Fiscal Years 2010–2012

Sales Revenues and Earnings (In millions)	Fiscal Years Ending May 31		
	2012	2011	2010
North America			
Revenues—Nike Brand footwear	$ 5,887	$ 5,111	$ 4,610
Nike Brand apparel	2,482	2,103	1,740
Nike Brand equipment	470	365	346
Total Nike Brand revenues	$ 8,839	$ 7,579	$ 6,696
Earnings before interest and taxes	$ 2,007	$ 1,736	$ 1,538
Profit margin	22.7%	22.9%	23.0%
Western Europe			
Revenues—Nike Brand footwear	$ 2,526	$ 2,345	$ 2,320
Nike Brand apparel	1,377	1,303	1,325
Nike Brand equipment	241	220	247
Total Nike Brand revenues	$ 4,144	$ 3,868	$ 3,892
Earnings before interest and taxes	$ 597	$ 730	$ 856
Profit margin	14.4%	18.9%	22.0%
Central & Eastern Europe			
Revenues—Nike Brand footwear	$ 671	$ 605	$ 558
Nike Brand apparel	441	359	354
Nike Brand equipment	88	76	81
Total Nike Brand revenues	$ 1,200	$1,040	$ 993
Earnings before interest and taxes	$ 234	$ 244	$ 253
Profit margin	19.5%	23.5%	25.5%
Greater China			
Revenues—Nike Brand footwear	$ 1,518	$ 1,164	$ 953
Nike Brand apparel	896	789	684
Nike Brand equipment	125	107	105
Total Nike Brand revenues	$ 2,539	$ 2,060	$ 1,742
Earnings before interest and taxes	$ 911	$ 777	$ 637
Profit margin	35.9%	37.7%	36.6%
Japan			
Revenues—Nike Brand footwear	$ 438	$ 396	$ 433
Nike Brand apparel	322	302	357
Nike Brand equipment	69	68	92
Total Nike Brand revenues	$ 829	$ 766	$ 882
Earnings before interest and taxes	$ 136	$ 114	$ 180
Profit margin	16.4%	14.9%	20.4%
Emerging Markets			
Revenues—Nike Brand footwear	$ 2,386	$ 1,897	$ 1,458
Nike Brand apparel	815	657	577

	Fiscal Years Ending May 31		
	2012	**2011**	**2010**
Nike Brand equipment	209	182	164
Total Nike Brand revenues	$ 3,410	$ 2,736	$ 2,199
Earnings before interest and taxes	$ 853	$ 688	$ 521
Profit margin	25.0%	25.1%	23.7%
All Regions			
Revenues—Nike Brand footwear	$13,426	$11,518	$10,332
Nike Brand apparel	6,333	5,513	5,037
Nike Brand equipment	1,202	1,018	1,035
Total Nike Brand revenues	$20,961	$18,049	$16,404
Earnings before interest and taxes	$ 4,738	$ 4,289	$ 3,932
Profit margin	22.6%	23.6%	24.0%

Note 1: Nike Brand data do not include Nike Golf and such other Nike-owned businesses as Converse, Cole Haan, and Hurley, all of which are separately organized and do not break their activities down by geographic region for reporting purposes. Nike Golf had revenues of $726 million in fiscal 2012, $658 million in fiscal 2011, $670 million in fiscal 2010, and $648 million in fiscal 2009.
Note 2: The revenue and earnings figures for all geographic regions include the effects of currency exchange fluctuations.

Source: Nike's 10-K Report for Fiscal 2011, pp. 21–24.

make Nike a factor in the golf equipment and golf apparel marketplace. Nike's long-standing endorsement relationship with Michael Jordan led to the introduction of the highly popular line of Air Jordan footwear and, more recently, to the launch of the Jordan brand of athletic shoes, clothing, and gear. In 2003 LeBron James signed an endorsement deal with Nike worth $90 million over seven years. Golfer Rory McIlroy's 2013 deal with Nike was reportedly in the range of $150 million over 10 years. Because soccer was such a popular sport globally, Nike had more endorsement contracts with soccer athletes than with athletes in any other sport; track and field athletes had the second largest number of endorsement contracts.

Research and Development Nike management believed R&D efforts had been and would continue to be a key factor in the company's success. Technical innovation in the design of footwear, apparel, and athletic equipment received ongoing emphasis in an effort to provide products that helped reduce injury, enhance athletic performance, and maximize comfort.

In addition to Nike's own staff of specialists in the areas of biomechanics, chemistry, exercise physiology, engineering, industrial design, and related fields, the company utilized research committees and advisory boards made up of athletes, coaches, trainers, equipment managers, orthopedists, podiatrists, and other experts who reviewed designs, materials, concepts for product improvements, and compliance with product safety regulations around the world. Employee athletes, athletes engaged under sports marketing contracts, and other athletes wear-tested and evaluated products during the design and development process.

Manufacturing In fiscal 2012, about 98 percent of Nike's footwear was produced by contract manufacturers in Vietnam, China, and Indonesia, but the company had manufacturing agreements with independent factories in Argentina, Brazil, India, and Mexico to manufacture footwear for sale primarily within those countries. Nike-branded apparel was manufactured outside of the United States by independent contract manufacturers located in 28 countries; most production occurred in

China, Thailand, Vietnam, Malaysia, Sri Lanka, Indonesia, Turkey, Cambodia, El Salvador, and Mexico.

Divestiture of Cole Haan and Umbro Businesses

At the beginning of fiscal year 2013, Nike announced its intention to sell its Cole Haan footwear and Umbro soccer businesses in order to sharpen its focus on driving growth in its Nike, Jordan, Converse, and Hurley brands. Sale of the Hurley brand to Iconix Brand Group (whose portfolio of brands included Cannon, Joe Boxer, London Fog, Sharper Image, Fieldcrest, Danskin, and 24 others) was announced in October 2012 and completed in December 2012. Sale of the Cole Haan brand to Apax Partners for $570 million was announced in November 2012 and completed in February 2013.

The adidas Group

The mission of The adidas Group was to be the global leader in the sporting goods industry with brands built on a passion for sports and a sporting lifestyle. Headquartered in Germany, its businesses and brands consisted of:

- adidas—a designer and marketer of active sportswear, uniforms, footwear, and sports products in football, basketball, soccer, running, training, outdoor, and six other categories (76.5 percent of The adidas Group sales in 2012).

- Reebok—a well-known global provider of athletic footwear for multiple uses, sports and fitness apparel, and accessories (11.2 percent of Group sales in 2012).

- TaylorMade–adidas Golf—a designer and marketer of TaylorMade golf equipment, adidas golf shoes and golf apparel, and Ashworth golf apparel (9.1 percent of Group sales in 2012).

- Rockport—a designer and marketer of dress, casual, and outdoor footwear that largely targeted metropolitan professional consumers (1.9 percent of Group sales in 2012).

- Reebok CCM Hockey—one of the world's largest designers, makers, and marketers of hockey equipment and apparel under the brand names Reebok Hockey and CCM Hockey (1.6 percent of Group sales in 2011).

Exhibit 8 shows the company's financial highlights for 2008–2012.

The company sold products in nearly every country. In 2012, its extensive product offerings were marketed through thousands of third-party retailers (sporting goods chains, department stores, independent sporting goods retailer buying groups, lifestyle retailing chains, and Internet retailers), 1,353 company-owned and franchised adidas and Reebok branded "concept" stores, 730 company-owned adidas and Reebok factory outlet stores, 279 other adidas and Reebok stores with varying formats, and various company websites (such as www.adidas.com, www.reebok.com, and www.taylormadegolf.com). Wholesale sales to third-party retailers in 2012 were €9.5 billion (64.2 percent of the company's 2012 total net sales of €14.8 billion), while retail sales at the company's various stores and websites were €3.4 billion (25.1 percent of 2012 net sales).

Like Under Armour and Nike, both adidas and Reebok were actively engaged in sponsoring major sporting events, teams, and leagues and in using athlete endorsements to promote their products. Recent high-profile sponsorships and promotional partnerships included Official Sportswear Partner of the 2012 Olympic Games (adidas), outfitting all volunteers, technical staff, and officials as well as all the athletes in Team Great Britain; Official Sponsors and ball supplier of the 2010 FIFA World Cup, the 2011 FIFA Women's World Cup Germany, and numerous other important soccer tournaments held by FIFA and the Union of European Football Associations or UEFA (adidas); Official Outfitters of NHL (Reebok), NFL (Reebok), NBA (adidas), WNBA (adidas), and NBA-Development League (adidas); Official Apparel and Footwear Outfitter for Boston Marathon (adidas); Official Licensee of Major League Baseball fan and lifestyle

EXHIBIT 8

Financial Highlights for The adidas Group, 2008–2012 (in millions of €)

Income Statement Data	2012	2011	2010	2009	2008
Net sales	€14,883	€13,322	€11,990	€10,381	€10,799
Gross profit	7,103	6,329	5,730	4,712	5,256
Gross profit margin	47.7%	47.5%	47.8%	45.4%	48.7%
Operating profit	1,185	953	894	508	1,070
Operating profit margin	6.2%	7.2%	7.5%	4.9%	9.9%
Net income	791	613	567	245	642
Net profit margin	5.3%	4.6%	4.7%	2.4%	5.9%
Balance Sheet Data					
Inventories	€2,486	€2,502	€2,119	€1,471	€1,995
Working capital	2,503	1,990	1,972	1,649	1,290
Net sales by brand					
adidas	€11,344	€9,867	€8,714	€7,520	€7,821
Reebok	1,667	1,940	1,913	1,603	1,717
TaylorMade-adidas Golf	1,344	1,044	909	831	812
Rockport	285	261	252	232	243
Reebok-CCM Hockey	243	210	200	177	188
Net sales by product					
Footwear	€6,992	€6,275	€5,389	€4,642	€4,919
Apparel	6,290	5,734	5,380	4,663	4,775
Equipment	1,691	1,335	1,221	1,076	1,105
Net sales by region					
Western Europe	€4,076	€3,922	€3,543	€3,261	€3,527
European Emerging Markets	1,947	1,596	1,385	1,122	1,179
North America	3,410	3,102	2,805	2,362	2,520
Greater China	1,562	1,229	1,000	967	1,077
Other Asian Markets	2,407	2,125	1,972	1,647	1,585
Latin America	1,481	1,368	1,285	1,006	893

Source: Company annual reports, 2012, 2011, 2010, 2009, and 2008.

apparel (Reebok). Athletes who were under contract to endorse various of the company's brands included NBA players Derrick Rose, Tim Duncan, and John Wall; professional golfers Paula Creamer (LPGA), Jim Furyk, Sergio Garcia, Retief Goosen, Dustin Johnson, Kenny Perry, Justin Rose, and Mike Weir; soccer player David Beckham; and various participants in the 2012 Summer Olympics in London. In 2003, David Beckham, who had been wearing adidas products since the age of 12, signed a $160 million lifetime endorsement deal with adidas that called for an immediate payment of $80 million and subsequent payments said to be worth an average of $2 million annually for the next 40 years.[16] Adidas was anxious to sign Beckham to a lifetime deal not only to prevent Nike from trying to sign him but also because soccer was considered the world's most lucrative sport and adidas management believed that Beckham's endorsement of adidas products resulted in more sales than all of the company's other athlete endorsements combined. In 2011, the company launched its biggest-ever global advertising campaign for adidas-brand products. Companywide expenditures for advertising, event sponsorships, athlete endorsements, and other marketing activities were €1.50 billion in 2012, up from €1.36 billion in 2011 and €1.29 billion in 2010.

Research and development activities commanded considerable emphasis at The adidas Group. Management had long stressed the critical importance of innovation in improving the performance characteristics of its products. New apparel and footwear collections featuring new fabrics, colors, and the latest fashion were introduced on an ongoing basis to heighten consumer interest, as well as to provide performance enhancements—there were 35 "major product launches" in 2009, 39 in 2010, 48 in 2011, and 39 in 2012. About 1,000 people were employed in R&D activities at 10 locations, of which 4 were devoted to adidas products, 3 to Reebok products, and 1 each for TaylorMade-adidas Golf, Rockport, and Reebok-CCM Hockey. In addition to its own internal activities, the company drew upon the services of well-regarded researchers at universities in Canada, the United States, England, and Germany. R&D expenditures in 2012 were €128 million, up from €115 million in 2011, €102 million in 2010, €86 million in 2009, and €81 million in 2008.

Over 95 percent of production was outsourced to 337 independent contract manufacturers located in China and other Asian countries (76 percent), the Americas (16 percent), and Europe (8 percent). The adidas Group operated 10 relatively small production and assembly sites of its own in Germany (1), Sweden (1), Finland (1), the United States (4), and Canada (3). Close to 96 percent of footwear production was performed in Asia; annual volume sourced from footwear suppliers had ranged from a low of 191 million pairs to a high of 245 million pairs during 2007–2012. During the same time frame, apparel production ranged from 239 million to 321 million units and the production of hardware products ranged from 34 million to 51 million units.

Executives at The adidas Group expected that global sales would be about €15.44 in 2013, and would reach €17 billion in 2015. More than half of the sales gains were expected to come from North America, China (where the company was rapidly opening new stores), and the Commonwealth of Independent States (made up of the former Soviet republics).[17]

ENDNOTES

[1] Daniel Roberts, "Under Armour Gets Serious," *Fortune,* November 7, 2011, p. 153; and "What's Driving Big Growth for Under Armour," www.trefis.com, accessed April 24, 2013.

[2] Roberts, "Under Armour Gets Serious," p. 156.

[3] Ibid.

[4] Ibid.

[5] Ibid.

[6] As stated on p. 53 of Under Armour's Prospectus for its Initial Public Offering of common stock, dated November 17, 2005.

[7] As stated in the company's slide presentation for Investors Day 2013, June 5, 2013.

[8] Information contained in management's slide presentation for Investors Day 2013, June 5, 2013.

[9] According to information in John Kell, "Under Armour Arrives on Global Stage," *The Wall Street Journal,* June 3, 2013, p. B2.

[10] Company 10-K reports, 2009, 2010, 2011, and 2012.

[11] According to information in the company's slide presentation for Investors Day 2013, June 5, 2013.

[12] 2012 Annual Report, p. 2.

[13] According to data in the company's slide presentation for Investors Day 2013, June 5, 2013.

[14] As stated in the company's slide presentation for Investors Day 2013, June 5, 2013.

[15] According to a report by Transparency Market Research, "Athletic Footwear Market—Global Industry Size, Market Share, Trends, Analysis and Forecast, 2012—2018," that was summarized in a September 26, 2012, press release by PR Newswire, www.prnewswire.com, accessed May 1, 2013.

[16] Steve Seepersaud, "5 of the Biggest Athlete Endorsement Deals," www.askmen.com, accessed February 5, 2012.

[17] Jonathan Buck, "Adidas Will Outrun the Pack," *Barron's,* April 23, 2013, p. M7.

connect

ARTHUR A. THOMPSON The University of Alabama

In early 2012, investor interest in lululemon athletica—a designer and retailer of high-end, yoga-inspired athletic apparel under the lululemon athletica and ivivva athletica brand names—was surging. Over the past 30 months, growing numbers of female shoppers were patronizing the company's stores to pay premium prices for lululemon-branded items that offered performance, fit, and comfort and were stylish as well. The company's functional and stylish apparel had taken on "must have" status among growing numbers of fitness-conscious women. People were flocking to lululemon stores not only because of the fashionable products but also because of the store ambience and attentive, knowledgeable store personnel. The company had responded by opening additional stores—35 in 2010 and 40 in 2011—and embellishing its product offerings to create a comprehensive line of apparel and accessories designed for athletic pursuits such as yoga, running, and general fitness; technical clothing for active female youths; and athletic products for men.

As lululemon's sales revenues climbed rapidly toward $1 billion annually, the company's stock price had risen from $2.25 per share on March 9, 2009, to close at $64.58 per share on February 3, 2012. Business analysts were speculating how long the lululemon athletica phenomenon would last and whether the company could carve out a sustainable market position for itself in the fitness and athletic apparel industry against such competing names as Nike, Under Armour, adidas, and Reebok.

In 2012, the company's products could be bought at its 174 retail stores in the United States, Canada, Australia, and New Zealand, and at the company's website, **www.lululemon. com**. For the fiscal year ending January 29, 2012, lululemon reported net revenues of $1.0 billion and net earnings of $184.1 million. Retail store sales accounted for 81.7 percent of company revenues, website sales accounted for 10.6 percent, and other (including wholesale sales to franchised stores, showroom sales, and sales at outlet centers) accounted for 7.7 percent.

Company Background

A year after selling his eight-store surf-, skate-, and snowboard-apparel chain called Westbeach Sports, Chip Wilson took the first commercial yoga class offered in Vancouver, British Columbia, and found the result exhilarating. But he found the cotton clothing used for sweaty, stretchy power yoga completely inappropriate. Wilson's passion was technical athletic fabrics and in 1998 he opened a design studio for yoga clothing that also served as a yoga studio at night to help pay the rent. He began offering upscale yoga clothing made of performance fabrics and asked local yoga instructors to wear the products and give him feedback. Gratified by the positive response to yoga apparel, Wilson opened lululemon's first real store in the

Copyright © 2013 by Arthur A. Thompson. All rights reserved.

beach area of Vancouver, called Kitsilano, in November 2000.

While the store featured Wilson-designed yoga clothing, Chip Wilson's vision was for the store to be a community hub where people could learn and discuss the physical aspects of healthy living—from yoga and diet to running and cycling, plus the yoga-related mental aspects of living a powerful life of possibilities. But the store's clothing selections proved so popular that dealing with customers crowded out the community-based discussions and training about the merits of living healthy lifestyles. Nonetheless, Chip Wilson and store personnel were firmly committed to healthy, active lifestyles, and Wilson soon came to the conclusion that for the store to provide staff members with the salaries and opportunities to experience fulfilling lives, the one-store company needed to expand into a multistore enterprise. Wilson believed that the increasing number of women participating in sports, and specifically yoga, provided ample room for expansion, and he saw lululemon athletica's yoga-inspired performance apparel as a way to address a void in the women's athletic apparel market. Wilson also saw the company's mission as one of providing people with the components to live a longer, healthier, and more fun life.

Several new stores were opened in the Vancouver area, with operations conducted through a Canadian operating company, initially named Lululemon Athletica, Inc., and later renamed lululemon canada inc. In 2002, the company expanded into the United States and formed a sibling operating company, Lululemon Athletica USA Inc. (later renamed as lululemon usa, inc.), to conduct its U.S. operations. Both operating companies were wholly owned by affiliates of Chip Wilson. In 2004, the company opened a franchised store in Australia as a means of more quickly disseminating the lululemon athletica brand name, conserving on capital expenditures for store expansion, and boosting revenues and profits. The company wound up its fiscal year ending January 31, 2005, with 14 company-owned stores,

1 franchised store, and net revenues of $40.7 million. A second franchised store was opened in Japan later in 2005. Franchisees paid lululemon a onetime franchise fee and an ongoing royalty based on a specified percentage of net revenues; lululemon supplied franchised stores with garments at a discount to the suggested retail price.

Five years after opening the first retail store, it was apparent that lululemon apparel was fast becoming something of a cult phenomenon and a status symbol among yoga fans in areas where lululemon stores had opened. Avid yoga exercisers were not hesitating to purchase $120 color-coordinated lululemon yoga outfits that felt comfortable and made them look good. Mall developers and mall operators knew what lululemon was and had begun actively recruiting lululemon to locate stores in their malls.

In December 2005, with 27 company-owned stores, 2 franchised stores, and record sales en route to $85 million annually, Chip Wilson sold 48 percent of his interest in the company's capital stock to a group of private equity investors led by Advent International Corporation, which purchased 38.1 percent of the stock, and Highland Capital Partners, which purchased a 9.6 percent ownership interest. In connection with the transaction, the owners formed lululemon athletica inc. to serve as a holding company for all of the company's related entities, including the two operating subsidiaries, lululemon canada inc. and lululemon usa inc. Robert Meers, who had 15 years experience at Reebok and was Reebok's CEO from 1996 to 1999, joined lululemon as CEO in December 2005. Chip Wilson headed the company's design team and played a central role in developing the company's strategy and nurturing the company's distinctive corporate culture; he was also chairman of the company's board of directors, a position he had held since founding the company in 1998. Wilson and Meers assembled a management team with a mix of retail, design, operations, product sourcing, and marketing experience from such leading apparel and retail companies as Abercrombie & Fitch, Limited Brands, Nike, and Reebok.

Brisk expansion ensued. The company ended fiscal 2006 with 41 company-owned stores, 10 franchised stores, net revenues of $149 million, and net income of $7.7 million.

In 2007, the company's owners elected to take the company public. The initial public offering took place on August 2, 2007, with the company selling 2,290,909 shares to the public and various stockholders selling 15,909,091 shares of their personal holdings. Shares began trading on the NASDAQ under the symbol LULU and on the Toronto Exchange under the symbol LLL.

The company's announced growth strategy had five key elements:

1. *Grow the company's store base in North America.* The strategic objective was to add new stores to strengthen the company's presence in locations where it had existing stores and then selectively enter new geographic markets in the United States and Canada. Management believed that the company's strong sales in U.S. stores demonstrated the portability of the lululemon brand and retail concept. Plans were to open 20 to 25 stores in fiscal 2007 and 30 to 35 stores in fiscal 2008 in the United States and Canada.

2. *Increase brand awareness.* This initiative entailed leveraging the publicity surrounding the opening of new stores with grassroots marketing programs that included organizing events and partnering with local fitness practitioners.

3. *Introduce new product technologies.* Management intended to continue to focus on developing and offering products that incorporated technology-enhanced fabrics and performance features that differentiated lululemon apparel and helped broaden the company's customer base.

4. *Broaden the appeal of lululemon products.* This initiative entailed (1) adding a number of apparel items for men, (2) expanding product offerings for women and young females in such categories as athletic bags, undergarments, outerwear, and sandals, and (3) adding products suitable for additional sports and athletic activities.

5. *Expand beyond North America.* In the near term, the company planned to expand its presence in Australia and Japan and then, over time, pursue opportunities in other Asian and European markets that offered similar, attractive demographics.

The company's growth and success over the next five years were impressive by any standard. Exhibit 1 summarizes the company's recent performance. In March 2012, top management projected that lululemon's

EXHIBIT 1

Financial and Operating Highlights, lululemon athletica, Fiscal Years 2007–2012 (in millions of $)

	Fiscal Year Ending Jan. 31, 2012	Fiscal Year Ending Jan. 30, 2011	Fiscal Year Ending Jan. 31, 2010	Fiscal Year Ending Feb. 1, 2009	Fiscal Year Ending Jan. 31, 2007
Selected Income Statement Data					
Net revenues	$1,000.8	$711.7	$452.9	$353.5	$148.0
Cost of goods sold	431.6	316.8	229.8	174.4	72.2
Gross profit	569.3	394.9	223.1	179.1	75.7
Selling, general, and administrative expenses	282.3	212.8	136.2	118.1	51.9
Operating profit	287.0	180.4	86.5	56.6	16.6
Net profit (loss)	185.0	121.8	58.3	39.4	7.7

(*Continued*)

EXHIBIT 1   (*Concluded*)

	Fiscal Year Ending Jan. 31, 2012	Fiscal Year Ending Jan. 30, 2011	Fiscal Year Ending Jan. 31, 2010	Fiscal Year Ending Feb. 1, 2009	Fiscal Year Ending Jan. 31, 2007
Earnings per share					
Basic	$1.29	$0.86	$0.41	$0.29	$0.06
Diluted	1.27	0.85	0.41	0.28	0.06
Balance Sheet Data					
Cash and cash equivalents	$409.4	$316.3	$159.6	$56.8	$15.5
Inventories	104.1	57.5	44.1		26.6
Total assets	734.6	499.3	307.3	211.6	71.3
Stockholders' equity	606.2	394.3	233.1	154.8	37.4
Cash Flow and Other Data					
Net cash provided by operating activities	$203.6	$180.0	$118.0	$45.4	25.4
Capital expenditures	116.9	30.4	15.5	40.5	13.3
Store Data					
Number of corporate-owned stores open at end of period	174	133	110	103	41
Number of franchised stores open at end of period	0	4	14	10	10
Sales per gross square foot at corporate-owned stores open at least one full year	$2,004	$1,726	$1,318	$1,450	$1,411
Average sales at corporate-owned stores open at least one year	$5.33 million	$4.96 million	$3.76 million	$4.06 million	$4.93 million

Source: Company 10-K reports for fiscal years ending January 31, 2007, February 1, 2009, January 30, 2011, and January 31, 2012.

full-year fiscal 2012 net revenues would be in the range of $1.3 billion to $1.325 billion and that diluted earnings per share would be in the range of $1.50 to $1.57. In early May 2012, lululemon's stock traded in the $75 to $80 price range, up from $15 per share at the beginning of 2010.

In January 2008, Christine M. Day joined the company as executive vice president, retail operations. Previously, she had worked at Starbucks, functioning in a variety of capacities and positions, including president, Asia Pacific Group (July 2004 to February 2007), co-president for Starbucks Coffee International (July 2003 to October 2003), senior vice president, North American Finance & Administration; and vice president of sales and operations for Business Alliances. In April 2008, Day was appointed as lululemon's president and chief operating officer, and was named chief executive officer and member of the board of directors in July 2008. She held those positions in early 2012. During her tenure as CEO, Day had expanded and strengthened the company's management team to support its expanding operating activities and geographic scope, favoring the addition of people with relevant backgrounds and experiences at such companies as Nike, Abercrombie & Fitch, The Gap, and Speedo International. She also spent a number of hours each week in the company's stores observing how customers shopped, listening to their comments and complaints, and using the information to tweak product offerings, merchandising, and store operations.

Company founder Chip Wilson stepped down from his executive position as lululemon's chief innovation and branding officer effective January 29, 2012, but continued in his role of chairman of the company's board of directors.

Lululemon's Strategy and Business in 2012

In 2012, lululemon athletica continued to view its core mission as "providing people with the components to live a longer, healthier and more fun life." Its primary target market was:

> a sophisticated and educated woman who understands the importance of an active, healthy lifestyle. She is increasingly tasked with the dual responsibilities of career and family and is constantly challenged to balance her work, life, and health. We believe she pursues exercise to achieve physical fitness and inner peace.

Management believed that other athletic apparel companies were not effectively addressing the unique style, fit, and performance needs of women who were embracing yoga and a variety of other fitness and athletic activities. lululemon sought to address this void in the marketplace by incorporating style, feel-good comfort, and functionality into its apparel products and using its retail store network to market directly to these women. Almost 16 million Americans, of which nearly 73 percent were women, spent an estimated $5.7 billion on yoga classes and products in 2011.[1] However, while the company was founded to address the unique needs and preferences of women, management recognized the merits of broadening the company's market target to include other population segments. Recently, it had begun designing and marketing products for men and athletic female youths who appreciated the technical rigor and premium quality of athletic and fitness apparel. Management also believed that participation in athletic and fitness activities was destined to climb as people over 60 years of age became increasingly focused on living longer, healthier, active lives

in their retirement years and engaged in regular exercise and recreational activities. Another demand-enhancing factor was that consumer decisions to purchase athletic, fitness, and recreational apparel were being driven not only by an actual need for functional products but also by a desire to create a particular lifestyle perception through the apparel they wore. Consequently, senior executives were positioning the company to capitalize on the broadening market potential for lululemon apparel that loomed ahead.

The chief components of the business strategy that top management had launched when lululemon athletica became a public company in mid-2007 remained largely intact in 2012:

- Grow the store base in North America, primarily the United States.

- Open additional stores outside of North America.

- Increase awareness of the lululemon brand and apparel line.

- Incorporate next-generation fabrics and technologies in the company's products to strengthen consumer association of the lululemon brand with technically advanced apparel products and enable lululemon to command higher prices for its apparel products compared to the prices of traditional athletic apparel.

- Broaden the product line by designing lululemon products for a bigger range of athletic activities.

- Provide a distinctive in-store shopping experience, complemented with strong ties to fitness instructors and fitness establishments, local athletes and fitness-conscious people, and various community-based athletic and fitness events.

Perhaps the two biggest strategic adjustments since 2007 had been to discontinue and reverse the use of franchising as a component of the company's retailing and store expansion strategy and to launch a direct-to-consumer strategic initiative whose principal thrust was selling apparel at the company's website, **www. lululemon.com**.

Retail Distribution and Store Expansion Strategy

After several years of experience in establishing and working with franchised stores in the United States, Australia, Japan, and Canada, top management in 2010 determined that having franchised stores was not in the company's best long-term strategic interests. A strategic initiative was begun to either acquire the current stores of franchisees and operate them as company stores or convert the franchised stores to a joint-venture arrangement where by lululemon owned the controlling interest in the store and the former franchisee owned a minority interest. In some cases, contracts with franchisees contained a clause allowing lululemon to acquire a franchised store at a specified percentage of trailing 12-month sales. The three franchised stores in Canada became company-owned in 2009 and 2010. The franchise rights of nine store locations in Australia, in which lululemon already had an ownership interest, were acquired during 2010; five of nine franchised stores in the United States were converted to company-owned in 2010 and 2011. The franchised store established in Japan in 2005 was converted to a company-owned store months after it opened. The last four franchised stores—three in Colorado and one in California—were reacquired in 2011.

As of February 2012, lululemon's retail footprint included:

- 47 stores in Canada scattered across seven provinces, but mainly located in British Columbia, Alberta, and Ontario.
- 108 company-owned stores in the United States (27 states and the District of Columbia).
- 18 stores in Australia.
- 1 store in New Zealand (opened in 2011).

Virtually all stores were branded lululemon athletica, but five company-owned stores were branded ivivva athletica and specialized in dance-inspired apparel for female youths.

Current store expansion efforts were concentrated mainly in the United States. The company's plans for 2012 called for opening 30 new stores in the United States, 2 ivivva athletica–branded stores in Canada, and 5 new stores in Australia and New Zealand. Over time, management expected to expand into additional countries, primarily Asia and Europe, either by opening company-owned stores or by entering into joint ventures with experienced and capable retail partners.

Lululemon management undertook ongoing evaluations of the company's portfolio of company-owned store locations. Underperforming store locations were closed. One California store was closed in 2009. In 2010, one corporate-owned ivivva athletica store in British Columbia and one corporate-owned lululemon athletica store in Australia were closed. No stores were closed in 2011.

In fiscal year 2011 ending January 31, 2012, the company's retail stores that had been open at least one year had average sales of $2,004 per square foot, versus average sales per square foot of $1,726 in fiscal 2010 and $1,318 in fiscal 2009 (Exhibit 1). Management believed its sales-per-square-foot performance had consistently been the best in the retail apparel sector—for example, the stores of specialty fashion retailers like J Crew and Abercrombie & Fitch typically had annual sales averaging $600–$700 per square foot.

Lululemon's Store Showroom Strategy

In 2012 lululemon had "showrooms" in 35 locations in the United States, 4 Australian locations, 2 New Zealand locations, and 1 location in Hong Kong. Showrooms functioned as a means of introducing the lululemon brand and culture to a community, developing relationships with fitness instructors and fitness enthusiasts, and hosting community-related fitness events, all in preparation for the likely opening of a new lululemon athletica retail store in the near future. Showroom personnel worked with local athletes, recruited fitness instructors to be ambassadors for lululemon products and lululemon-sponsored fitness events, hosted get-acquainted parties for fitness instructors and fitness enthusiasts, and acted as local experts on where to find great yoga or Pilates classes, fitness centers, and health and wellness information and events. Showrooms were only open part of the week so that personnel could be out in the community meeting people, participating in local yoga and fitness classes, and promoting attendance at various fitness activities and wellness events. In addition, showroom personnel began the process of recruiting well-regarded local yoga studios, health clubs, and fitness centers to stock and retail a selection of lululemon's products.

Wholesale Sales Strategy

Lululemon marketed its products to select yoga studios, health clubs, and fitness centers as a way to gain the implicit endorsement of local fitness instructors and personnel for lululemon branded apparel, familiarize the customers of these establishments with the lululemon brand, and give them an opportunity to conveniently purchase lululemon apparel. There was no intent to grow wholesale sales to these types of establishments into a significant revenue contributor. Rather, the strategic objective was to build brand awareness, especially in new geographic locales.

Website Sales Strategy

In 2009, lululemon launched its e-commerce website to enable customers to make online purchases and supplement its already-functioning phone sales activities. Management saw online sales as having three strategic benefits: (1) providing added convenience for core customers, (2) making lululemon products available in geographic markets where there were no lululemon stores, and (3) helping build brand awareness, especially in new markets, including those outside of North America. The company's direct-to-consumer channel (online and phone sales) quickly became an increasingly substantial part of the

company's business, accounting for revenues of $57.3 million in fiscal 2010 (8.1 percent of net revenue) and $106.3 million in fiscal 2011 (10.6 percent of net revenue). lululemon provided free shipping on all orders.

In addition to making purchases, website visitors could browse information about what yoga was, what the various types of yoga were, and their benefits; learn about fabrics and technologies used in lululemon's products; read recent posts on lululemon's yoga blog; and stay abreast of lululemon activities in their communities.

Retail Stores

The company's retail stores were located primarily on street locations, in upscale strip shopping centers, in lifestyle centers, and in malls. Typically, stores were leased and were 2,500 to 3,000 square feet in size. Most all stores included space for product display and merchandising, checkout, fitting rooms, a restroom, and an office/storage area. While the leased nature of the store spaces meant that each store had its own customized layout and arrangement of fixtures and displays, each store was carefully decorated and laid out in a manner that projected the ambience and feel of a home-spun local apparel boutique rather than the more impersonal, cookie-cutter atmosphere of many apparel chain stores.

One unique feature of lululemon's retail stores was that the floor space allocated to merchandising displays and customer shopping could be sufficiently cleared to enable the store to hold an in-store yoga class before or after regular shopping hours. Every store hosted a complimentary yoga class each week, complete with yoga mats and a professional yoga instructor; when the class concluded, the attendees were given a 15 percent–off coupon to use in shopping for products in the store. From time to time, yoga ambassadors demonstrated their moves in the store windows and on the sales floor. Exhibit 2 shows the exteriors and interiors of representative lululemon athletica stores.

EXHIBIT 2

Representative Exterior and Interior Scenes at lululemon Stores

Women		Men
• Sports bras	• Skirts and dresses	• Tops
• Tanks	• Socks and underwear	• Jackets and hoodies
• Tops	• Gear bags	• Shorts
• Jackets	• Caps and headbands	• Pants
• Hoodies	• Sweat cuffs and gloves	• Gear bags
• Pants	• Water bottles	• Socks and underwear
• Crops	• Yoga mats and props	• Caps and gloves
• Shorts	• Instructional yoga DVDs	• Yoga mats, props, and instructional DVDs

The company's goal was to sell all of its products at full price.[2] Special colors and seasonal items were in stores for only a limited time—such products were on 3-, 6-, or 12-week life cycles so that frequent shoppers could always find something new. Store inventories of short-cycle products were deliberately limited to help foster a sense of scarcity, condition customers to buy when they saw an item rather than wait, and avoid any need to discount unsold items. In one instance, a hot-pink color that launched in December was supposed to have a two-month shelf life, but supplies sold out in the first week. However, supplies of core products that did not change much from season to season were more ample to minimize the risk of lost sales due to items being out-of-stock. Approximately 95 percent of the merchandise in lululemon stores was sold at full price.[3]

Product Line

In 2012, lululemon offered a diverse and growing selection of premium-priced performance apparel and accessories (see the table above) for women, men, and female youths that were designed for healthy lifestyle activities such as yoga, running, and general fitness. While many of its products were specifically intended for the growing number of people that participated in yoga, the company had for some years been broadening its product range to address the needs of other activities.

Exhibit 3 shows a sampling of lululemon's garment offerings.

Product Design and Development

Lululemon's product design efforts were led by a team of designers based in Vancouver and headed by the company's founder, Chip Wilson. The team collaborated closely with various international designers. The lululemon design team included athletes and users of the company's products who embraced lululemon's design philosophy and dedication to premium quality. Input was also actively sought from the fitness ambassadors recruited by store personnel and store customers—ambassadors had become an integral part of the product design process, testing and evaluating products and providing real-time feedback on performance and functionality. Design team members regularly worked at stores to interact with and receive direct feedback from customers. In addition, the design team used various market intelligence sources to identify and track market trends. Plus, the team hosted meetings each year in several geographic markets to discuss the company's products with local athletes, trainers, yogis, and members of the fitness industry and gather their ideas for product improvements and new products. The design team incorporated all of this input to make fabric selections, develop new products, and make adjustments in the fit, style, and function of existing products.

The design team worked closely with its apparel manufacturers to incorporate innovative fabrics that gave lululemon garments such characteristics as stretch ability, moisture-wicking capability, color fastness, feel-good comfort, and durability. Fabric quality was evaluated via actual wear tests and by a leading testing facility. Before bringing out new products with new fabrics, lululemon used the services of a leading independent inspection, verification, testing, and certification company to conduct a battery of tests on fabrics for such performance characteristics as pilling, shrinkage, abrasion resistance, and colorfastness. Lastly, lululemon design personnel worked with leading fabric suppliers to

EXHIBIT 3

Examples of lululemon Apparel Items

Source: **www.lululemon.com**, accessed February 13, 2012.

identify opportunities to develop fabrics that lululemon could trademark and thereby gain added brand recognition and brand differentiation. Trademarked fabrics currently incorporated in lululemon products included:

- *Luon*—a fabric that was designed to wick away moisture, move with the body, and eliminate irritation (was included in more than half of the company's products).

- *Luxtreme*—a wicking fabric that was silky and lightweight and primarily used in running products.

- *Silverescent*—a fabric that reduced odors as a result of the antibacterial properties of the silver in the fabric.

Where appropriate, product designs incorporated convenience features, such as pockets to hold credit cards, keys, digital audio players, and clips for heart rate monitors, and long sleeves that covered the hands for cold-weather exercising. Product specifications called for the use of advanced sewing techniques, such as flat seaming, that increased comfort and functionality, reduced chafing and skin irritation, and strengthened important seams. All of these design elements and fabric technologies were factors in enabling lululemon to price its high-quality technical athletic apparel at prices above those of traditional athletic apparel.

Typically, it took 8 to 10 months for lululemon products to move from the design stage to availability in its retail stores; however, the company had the capability to bring select new products to market in as little as two months. Management believed its lead times were shorter than those of most apparel brands due to the company's streamlined design and development process, the real-time input received from customers and ambassadors at its store locations, and the short times it took to receive and approve samples from manufacturing suppliers. Short lead times facilitated quick responses to emerging trends or shifting market conditions.

Sourcing and Manufacturing

Production was the only value chain activity that lululemon did not perform internally. lululemon did not own or operate any manufacturing facilities to produce fabrics or make garments. All of its products were sourced from a group of 45 manufacturers, five of which produced approximately 67 percent of the company's products in fiscal 2011. However, the company deliberately refrained from entering into long-term contracts with any of its manufacturing suppliers, preferring instead to transact business on an order-by-order basis and rely on the close working relationships it had developed with its suppliers over the years. The fabrics used in lululemon products were sourced by the manufacturers from a limited number of pre-approved suppliers. During the fiscal year ending January 31, 2012, approximately 49 percent of lululemon's apparel products were produced in China, approximately 41 percent in South/South East Asia, approximately 3 percent in Canada, and the remainder in the United States, Israel, Peru, Egypt, and other countries.

Lululemon took great care to ensure that its manufacturing suppliers shared lululemon's commitment to quality and ethical business conduct. All manufacturers were required to adhere to a code of conduct regarding quality of manufacturing, working conditions, environmental responsibility, fair wage practices, and compliance with child labor laws, among others. lululemon utilized the services of a leading inspection and verification firm to closely monitor each supplier's compliance with applicable law, lululemon's workplace code of conduct, and other business practices that could reflect badly on lululemon's choice of suppliers.

The company's North American manufacturers were the reason lululemon had the capability to speed select products to market and respond quickly to changing trends and unexpectedly high buyer demand for certain products. While management expected to utilize manufacturers outside of North America to supply the bulk of its apparel requirement in the years to come, it intended to maintain production in Canada and the United States whenever possible.

Distribution Facilities

Lululemon shipped products to its stores in North America from a leased 102,000-square-foot facility in Vancouver, British Columbia, and a leased 82,000-square-foot facility in Sumner, Washington. Both were modern and cost-efficient. In 2011, the company began operations at a leased 54,000-square-foot distribution center in Melbourne, Australia, to supply its stores in Australia and New Zealand. Management believed these three facilities would be sufficient to accommodate its expected store growth and expanded product offerings over the next several years. Merchandise was typically shipped to retail stores through third-party delivery services multiple times per week, providing them with a steady flow of new inventory.

Community-Based Marketing

One of lululemon's differentiating characteristics was its community-based approach to building brand awareness and customer loyalty. Local fitness practitioners chosen to be ambassadors introduced their fitness class attendees to the lululemon brand, thereby leading to interest in the brand, store visits, and word-of-mouth marketing. Each yoga-instructor ambassador was also called upon to conduct a complimentary yoga class every four to six weeks at the local lululemon store they were affiliated with. In return for helping drive business to lululemon stores and conducting classes, ambassadors were periodically given bags of free products, and billboard-size portraits of each ambassador wearing lululemon products and engaging in physical activity at a local landmark were posted in their local lululemon store, which helped them expand their clientele.

Every lululemon store had a dedicated community coordinator who developed a customized plan for organizing, sponsoring, and participating in athletic, fitness, and philanthropic events in the local area. In addition, each store had a community events bulletin board for posting announcements of upcoming activities, providing fitness education information and brochures, and promoting the local yoga studios and fitness centers of ambassadors. There was also a chalkboard in each store's fitting room area where customers could scribble comments about lululemon products or their yoga class experiences or store personnel; these comments were relayed to lululemon headquarters every two weeks. Customers could use a lululemon micro website to track their progress regarding fitness or progress toward life goals.

lululemon made little use of traditional print or television advertisements, preferring instead to rely on its various grassroots, community-based marketing efforts.

Store Personnel

As part of the company's commitment to providing customers with an inviting and educational store environment, lululemon's store sales associates, who the company referred to as educators, were coached to personally engage and connect with each guest who entered the store. Educators, many of whom had prior experience as a fitness practitioner or were avid runners or yoga enthusiasts, received approximately 30 hours of in-house training within the first three months of their employment. Training was focused on teaching educators about leading a healthy and balanced life, exercising self-responsibility, and setting lifestyle goals, and preparing them to explain the technical features of all lululemon products and to serve as knowledgeable references for customers seeking information on fitness classes, instructors, and events in the community. New hires that lacked knowledge about the intricacies of yoga were given subsidies to attend yoga classes so they could understand the activity and better explain the benefits of lululemon's yoga apparel.

People who shopped at lululemon stores were called "guests," and store personnel were taught how to "educate" guests about lululemon apparel, not sell to them. To provide a personalized, welcoming, and relaxed experience, store educators referred to their guests on a first-name basis in the fitting and changing area, allowed them to use store restrooms, and offered them complimentary fresh-filtered water. Management believed that such a soft-sell, customer-centric environment encouraged product trial, purchases, and repeat visits.

As of January 29, 2012, lululemon had 5,807 employees, of which 4,872 were employed in the company's retail stores, 157 were employed in distribution, 132 were employed in design, merchandise, and production, and the remaining 646 performed selling, general and administrative tasks, and other functions. None of the company's employees were covered by a collective bargaining agreement and there had been no labor-related work stoppages. Management believed its relations with employees were excellent.

Core Values and Culture

Consistent with the company's mission of "providing people with the components to live a longer, healthier and more fun life," lululemon executives sought to promote and ingrain a set of core values centered on developing the highest-quality products, operating with integrity, leading a healthy balanced life, self-empowerment and self-responsibility, positive inner development, and individual goal-setting. The company sought to provide employees with a supportive and goal-oriented work environment; all employees were encouraged to set goals aimed at reaching their full professional, health, and personal potential. The company offered personal development workshops and goal-coaching to assist employees in achieving their goals. Many lululemon employees had a written set of professional, health, and personal goals. All employees had access to a "learning library" of personal development books that included Stephen Covey's *The Seven Habits of Highly Effective People,* Rhonda Byrne's *The Secret,* and Brian Tracy's *The Psychology of Achievement.* To celebrate their first anniversary as a lululemon employee, staff members and store educators were rewarded with company-paid admission to a three-day weekend Landmark Forum seminar, a transformative workshop intended to help people think and act outside existing limits, act responsibly, and put themselves on a path to realizing their potential. lululemon's CEO, who had attended this Landmark Forum seminar, said, "We feel like Landmark is a tool. It has created a culture of accountability."[4]

All of this culture-related training was a direct result of Chip Wilson's long-term efforts to help employees live healthy, active, and fun lives. From the company's earliest days, Chip Wilson had maintained he didn't start lululemon just to sell premium-priced apparel; he believed an integral part of the company's mission was to give employees and customers a proactive assist on their journey to self-esteem, empowerment, and a fulfilling lifestyle. In the "Chip's Musings" section of the company website, Wilson said, "The law of attraction"—(that visualizing goals is the key to attaining them, a central tenet of *The Secret*)—"is the fundamental law that lululemon was built on from its 1998 inception."[5] He went on to say that "Our vision is 'to elevate the world from mediocrity to greatness,' and we are growing so we can train more people and spread the word of *The Secret*—which to us at lululemon is not so secret."[6] Wilson, who was the chairman of lululemon's board of directors and owned 35 percent of the company's stock in 2012, was the principal architect of the company's culture and core values, and the company's work climate reflected his business and lifestyle philosophy. He had digested much of his philosophy about life in general and personal development into a set of statements and prescriptions that he called "the lululemon manifesto" (see Exhibit 4). The manifesto was a core element of lululemon's culture.

Senior executives believed the company's work climate and core values attracted passionate and motivated employees who were driven to succeed, and they viewed the lululemon workforce as a valuable resource in enabling the company to successfully execute its business strategy, develop brand loyalty, connect with customers, and achieve strong financial performance. Moreover, many customers reacted quite positively to the educational emphasis store personnel placed on health, wellness, and personal development and to what they had seen or heard about lululemon's manifesto, corporate philosophy, and business mission.

Competition

Competition in the athletic apparel industry is principally centered on product quality, performance features, innovation, fit and style,

EXHIBIT 4

The lululemon Manifesto

The lululemon Manifesto

- Drink FRESH water and as much water as you can. Water flushes unwanted toxins from your body and keeps your brain sharp.
- A daily hit of athletic-induced endorphins gives you the power to make better decisions, helps you be at peace with yourself, and offsets stress.
- Do one thing a day that scares you.
- Listen, listen, listen, and then ask strategic questions.
- Write down your short- and long-term GOALS four times a year. Two personal, two business, and two health goals for the next 1, 5, and 10 years. Goal setting triggers your subconscious computer.
- Life is full of setbacks. Success is determined by how you handle setbacks.
- Your outlook on life is a direct reflection of how much you like yourself.
- That which matters the most should never give way to that which matters the least.
- Stress is related to 99 percent of all illness.
- Jealousy works the opposite way you want it to.
- The world is changing at such a rapid rate that waiting to implement changes will leave you two steps behind. DO IT NOW, DO IT NOW, DO IT NOW!
- Friends are more important than money.
- Breathe deeply and appreciate the moment. Living in the moment could be the meaning of life.
- Take various vitamins. You never know what small mineral can eliminate the bottleneck to everlasting health.
- Don't trust that an old age pension will be sufficient.
- Visualize your eventual demise. It can have an amazing effect on how you live for the moment.
- The conscious brain can only hold one thought at a time. Choose a positive thought.
- Live near the ocean and inhale the pure salt air that flows over the water. Vancouver will do nicely.
- Observe a plant before and after watering and relate these benefits to your body and brain.
- Practice yoga so you can remain active in physical sports as you age.
- Dance, sing, floss, and travel.
- Children are the orgasm of life. Just like you did not know what an orgasm was before you had one, nature does not let you know how great children are until you have them.
- Successful people replace the words "wish," "should," and "try," with "I will."
- Creativity is maximized when you're living in the moment.
- Nature wants us to be mediocre because we have a greater chance to survive and reproduce. Mediocre is as close to the bottom as it is to the top, and will give you a lousy life.
- lululemon athletica creates components for people to live longer, healthier, and more fun lives. If we can produce products to keep people active and stress-free, we believe the world will become a much better place.
- Do not use cleaning chemicals on your kitchen counters. Someone will inevitably make a sandwich on your counter.
- SWEAT once a day to regenerate your skin.
- Communication is COMPLICATED. We are all raised in a different family with slightly different definitions of every word. An agreement is an agreement only if each party knows the conditions for satisfaction and a time is set for satisfaction to occur.
- What we do to the earth we do to ourselves.
- The pursuit of happiness is the source of all unhappiness.

Source: www.lululemon.com, accessed February 12, 2012.

distribution capabilities, brand image and recognition, and price. Rivalry among competing brands is vigorous, involving both established companies who were expanding their production and the marketing of performance products and recent entrants attracted by the growth opportunities.

Lululemon competed with wholesalers and direct sellers of technical athletic apparel, most especially Nike, The adidas Group AG (which marketed athletic and sports apparel under its adidas, Reebok, and Ashworth brands), and Under Armour. Nike had a powerful and well-known global brand name, an extensive and diverse line of athletic and sports apparel, 2011 apparel sales of $5.5 billion, and 2011 total revenues (footwear, apparel, and equipment) of $20.9 billion. Nike was the world's largest seller of athletic footwear and athletic apparel, with over 40,000 retail accounts, and over 470 company-owned stores, 19 distribution centers, and selling arrangements with independent distributors and licensees in over 170 countries; its retail account base for sports apparel in the United States included a mix of sporting goods stores, athletic specialty stores, department stores, and skate, tennis, and golf shops.

Adidas and Reebok were both global brands that produced worldwide sports apparel revenues of approximately $7.5 billion in 2011; their product lines consisted of high-tech performance garments for a wide variety of sports and fitness activities, as well as recreational sportswear. The adidas Group sold products in virtually every country of the world. In 2011, its extensive product offerings were marketed through third-party retailers (sporting goods chains, department stores, independent sporting goods retailer buying groups, lifestyle retailing chains, and Internet retailers), 1,355 company-owned and franchised adidas and Reebok "concept" stores, 734 company-owned adidas and Reebok factory outlet stores, 312 other adidas and Reebok stores with varying formats, and various company websites (including **www.adidas.com** and **www.reebok.com**).

Under Armour, an up-and-coming designer and marketer of performance sports apparel, had apparel sales totaling $1.0 billion in 2011; as of early 2012, Under Armour products were available in 25,000 retail stores worldwide, 18,000 of which were in Canada and the United States. Under Armour also sold its products directly to consumers through its own factory outlet and specialty stores, website, and catalogs.

Nike, The adidas Group, and Under Armour all aggressively marketed and promoted their high-performance apparel products and spent heavily to grow consumer awareness of their brands and build brand loyalty. All three sponsored numerous athletic events, provided uniforms and equipment with their logos to collegiate and professional sports teams, and paid millions of dollars annually to numerous high-profile male and female athletes to endorse their products. Like lululemon, they designed their own products but outsourced the production of their garments to contract manufacturers.

Lululemon also competed with specialty department store retailers that carried women's athletic apparel, including:

- **The Gap**—a specialty fashion chain with more than 1,100 stores in North America and a product line that included its Bodyfit collection of performance and lifestyle products.

- **Athleta**—a new 10-store chain and online retailer that specialized in comfortable, fashionable, high-performance women's apparel for workouts, sports, physically active recreational activities, and leisure wear. Athleta was a subsidiary of Gap, Inc., and plans called for more than tripling the number of Athleta store locations in upscale metropolitan shopping areas across the United States over the next several years. In 2012, Athleta initiated its first national advertising campaign, "Power to the She," to promote the Athleta brand.

- **Nordstrom**—a nationally respected retailer that had recently introduced its own Zella line of attire for yoga, other fitness activities, and leisure wear; many of the initial products in the Zella collection were designed by a former member of lululemon's design team. In 2012, Zella-branded items could be purchased online at Nordstrom's website and at some 200 Nordstrom full-line department stores (typically 140,000 to 250,000 square feet in size) and Nordstrom Rack stores (typically 30,000 to 50,000 square feet in size) in 28 states.

- **Lucy**—Lucy was a women's activewear brand designed for style, performance, and fit that was intended for yoga, running, training, and other fitness and active recreational activities; the product offerings included tops, bottoms, skirts, dresses, jackets, hoodies, sports bras, socks, caps, headbands, and bags/totes. Lucy-branded performance apparel was sold at 65 company-owned Lucy stores across the United States and at **www.lucy.com**. Lucy was a wholly owned subsidiary of VF Corp., a designer, marketer, wholesaler, and retailer of 23 brands of apparel and footwear, with 2011 sales of $9 billion.

- **bebe stores**—a 200+ store and online retailer of women's apparel; the company's BEBE SPORT collection was targeted for a variety of fitness and sports activities and included sports bras, tops, pants, shorts, jackets, hoodies, and tennis outfits.

The items in the Gap Bodyfit, Athleta, Zella, Lucy, and BEBE SPORT collections were typically priced 10 percent to 25 percent below similar kinds of lululemon products. Gap's Athleta stores also offered free yoga classes, sold direct to consumers at **www.athleta.com** (with free shipping), and were sponsoring 20 female athletes in 2012 (the group included yoga teachers, a karate instructor, a mountain climber, a skier, runners, and a mountain bike racer). In addition, Athleta had a special social media website, **www.athleta.net/chi**, that connected women with interests in sports and fitness, nutrition and health, tutorials and training plans, and travel and adventure.

ENDNOTES

[1] "Yoga in America," *Yoga Journal,* January 27, 2012, posted at **http://yogawithgaileee.blogspot.com/2010/01/yoga-in-america-study-by-yoga-journal.html**, and accessed February 12, 2012.

[2] Dana Mattioli, "Lululemon's Secret Sauce," *The Wall Street Journal,* March 22, 2012, pp. B1–B2.

[3] Ibid.

[4] As quoted in Danielle Sacks, "Lululemon's Cult of Selling," *Fast Company,* April 1, 2009, posted at **www.fastcompany.com** and accessed on February 12, 2012.

[5] Ibid.

[6] Ibid.

Coach Inc. in 2012: Its Strategy in the "Accessible" Luxury Goods Market

▓ connect®   JOHN E. GAMBLE Texas A&M University — Corpus Christi
RONALD W. EASTBURN University of South Alabama

Coach Inc.'s strategy that created the "accessible" luxury market in ladies handbags made it among the best-known luxury brands in North America and Asia and had allowed its sales to grow at an annual rate of 20 percent between 2000 and 2011, reaching $4.2 billion. During that period, the company's net income increased from $16.7 million to $880 million. In 2012, Coach Inc. designed and marketed women's and men's bags, leather accessories, leather apparel items, business cases, footwear, jewelry, travel bags, watches, and fragrances. All of the company's leather products were manufactured by third-party suppliers in Asia, while Coach-branded footwear, eyewear, watches, and fragrances were made available through licensing agreements.

Coach's strategy, which focused on matching key luxury rivals in quality and styling while beating them on price by 50 percent or more, yielded a competitive advantage in attracting not only middle-income consumers desiring a taste of luxury, but also affluent and wealthy consumers with the means to spend considerably more on a handbag. Another distinctive element of the company's strategy was its multichannel distribution model, which included indirect wholesale sales to third-party retailers but focused primarily on direct-to-consumer sales. In 2012, Coach operated 345 full-price retail stores and 143 factory outlets in North America, 169 stores in Japan, and 66 stores in China, along with Internet and catalog sales. The direct-to-consumer segment accounted for 87 percent of the company's 2011 net sales. Coach's indirect wholesaler segment had 2011 net sales of $540 million, with the U.S. wholesale segment serving about 970 department store locations and the Coach International group supplying 211 department store locations in 20 countries.

The company's two primary strategic priorities in 2012 were to increase global distribution and improve same-store sales productivity. The company's strategy focused on five key initiatives:

- Build market share in North America by opening approximately 15 new full-price retail stores and 25 factory outlets.

- Build market share in Japan through the addition of 15 new locations.

- Raise brand awareness and build share in underpenetrated markets, including Europe and South America and, most notably Asia, with 30 new locations planned in the region.

- Increase sales of products targeted toward men. Specifically, new store openings in North America and Japan would focus on men's products, while the new shops in China would offer dual-gender product lines.

Copyright © 2012 by John E. Gamble and Ronald W. Eastburn. All rights reserved.

- Raise brand awareness and build market share through **coach.com,** global e-commerce sites, and social networking initiatives.

While the company's performance was commendable and its strategy seemed to have merit, the company's profit margins were still below the levels achieved prior to the onset of a slowing economy in 2007. In addition, its share price had experienced a sharp decline during the first six months of 2012. Going into fiscal 2013, it was undecided if the company's recent growth could be sustained and its competitive advantage would hold in the face of new accessible luxury lines launched by such aggressive and successful luxury brands as Michael Kors, Salvatore Ferragamo, Prada, Giorgio Armani, Dolce & Gabbana, and Versace.

Company History

Coach was founded in 1941 when Miles Cahn, a New York City leather artisan, began producing ladies handbags. The handbags crafted by Cahn and his family in their SoHo loft were simple in style and extremely resilient to wear and tear. Coach's classic styling and sturdy construction proved popular with discriminating consumers, and the company's initial line of 12 unlined leather bags soon developed a loyal following. Over the next 40 years, Coach was able to grow at a steady rate by setting prices about 50 percent lower than those of more luxurious brands, adding new models, and establishing accounts with retailers such as Bloomingdale's and Saks Fifth Avenue. The Cahn family also opened company-owned stores that sold Coach handbags and leather accessories. After 44 years of family management, Coach was sold to diversified food and consumer goods producer, Sara Lee.

Sara Lee's 1985 acquisition of Coach left the handbag manufacturer's strategy and approach to operations more-or-less intact. The company continued to build a strong reputation for long-lasting, classic handbags. However,

by the mid-1990s the company's performance began to decline as consumers developed a stronger preference for stylish French and Italian designer brands such as Gucci, Prada, Louis Vuitton, Dolce & Gabbana, and Ferragamo. By 1995, annual sales growth in Coach's best-performing stores declined from 40 percent to 5 percent as the company's traditional leather bags fell out of favor with consumers.

In 1996, Sara Lee made 18-year-Coach-veteran Lew Frankfort head of its languishing handbag division. Frankfort's first move was to hire Reed Krakoff, a top Tommy Hilfiger designer, as Coach's new creative director. Krakoff believed new products should be based upon market research rather than designers' instincts about what would sell. Under Krakoff, Coach conducted extensive consumer surveys and held focus groups to ask customers about styling, comfort, and functionality preferences. The company's research found that consumers were looking for edgier styling, softer leathers, and leather-trimmed fabric handbags. Once prototypes had been developed by a team of designers, merchandisers, and sourcing specialists, hundreds of previous customers were asked to rate prototype designs against existing handbags. The prototypes that made it to production were then tested in selected Coach stores for six months before a launch was announced. The design process developed by Krakoff also allowed Coach to launch new collections every month. Prior to Krakoff's arrival, Coach introduced only two collections per year.

Frankfort's turnaround plan also included a redesign of the company's flagship stores to complement Coach's contemporary new designs. Frankfort abandoned the stores' previous dark, wood-paneled interiors in favor of minimalist architectural features that provided a bright and airy ambience. The company also improved the appearance of its factory stores, which carried test models, discontinued models, and special lines that sold at discounts ranging from 15 percent to 50 percent. Such discounts were made possible by the company's policy of outsourcing production to 40 suppliers in 15 countries. The outsourcing agreements allowed Coach to maintain a sizeable pricing advantage relative to other luxury handbag brands in its full-price stores as well. Handbags sold in Coach full-price stores ranged from $200 to $500, which was well below the $700 to $800 entry-level price charged by other luxury brands.

Coach's attractive pricing enabled it to appeal to consumers who would not normally consider luxury brands, while the quality and styling of its products were sufficient to satisfy traditional luxury consumers. In fact, a *Women's Wear Daily* survey found that Coach's quality, styling, and value mix was so powerful that affluent women in the United States ranked Coach ahead of much more expensive luxury brands like Hermès, Ralph Lauren, Prada, and Fendi.[1]

By 2000, the changes to Coach's strategy and operations allowed the brand to build a sizable lead in the "accessible luxury" segment of the leather handbags and accessories industry and made it a solid performer in Sara Lee's business lineup. With the turnaround successfully executed, Sara Lee management elected to spin off Coach through an IPO in October 2000 as part of a restructuring initiative designed to focus the corporation on food and beverages.

Coach Inc.'s financial results and stock price performance proved to be stellar, as evidenced by its quadrupled growth in annual sales from $555 million in 1999 to more than $4.2 billion in 2012, reflecting its success in identifying and capitalizing quickly on opportunities for growth. This was translated into earnings over the same time frame from $16.7 million to $880 million. Though Coach Inc.'s share price had fallen dramatically at the beginning of the economic slowdown in 2007, it rebounded after its profitability improved in 2010.

Exhibit 1 presents Coach's income statements for fiscal 2007 through fiscal 2011. Exhibit 2 presents the company's balance sheets for fiscal 2010 and fiscal 2011. Exhibit 3 provides a review of Coach's stock price performance since October 2000.

EXHIBIT 1

Coach Inc.'s Consolidated Statements of Income, Fiscal 2007–Fiscal 2011 (in thousands, except share amounts)

	2011	2010	2009	2008	2007
Net sales	$4,158,507	$3,607,636	$3,230,468	$3,180,757	$2,612,456
Cost of goods sold	1,134,966	973,945	907,858	773,654	589,470
Gross profit	3,023,541	2,633,691	2,322,610	2,407,103	2,022,986
Selling, general, and administrative expenses	1,718,617	1,483,520	1,350,697	1,259,974	1,029,589
Operating income	1,304,924	1,150,171	971,913	1,147,129	993,397
Interest income	1,031	7,961	10,779	44,639	41,273
Income tax	425,155	423,192	359,323	408,729	398,141
Net income	$ 880,800	$ 734,940	$ 623,369	$ 783,039	$ 636,529
Dividends declared per common share	$0.68	$0.38	$0.08	$0.00	$0.00
Net income per share					
Basic shares	$2.99	$2.36	$1.93	$2.20	$1.72
Diluted shares	$2.92	$2.33	$1.91	$2.17	$1.69
Shares					
Basic shares outstanding	294,877	311,413	323,714	355,731	369,661
Diluted shares outstanding	301,558	315,848	325,620	360,332	377,356

Source: Coach Inc. 10-Ks, various years.

EXHIBIT 2

Coach Inc.'s Balance Sheets, Fiscal 2010–Fiscal 2011 (in thousands)

	July 2, 2011	July 3, 2010
Assets		
Current assets:		
Cash and cash equivalents	$ 699,782	$ 596,470
Short-term investments	2,256	99,928
Trade accounts receivable (less allowances of $9,544 and $6,374, respectively)	142,898	109,068
Inventories	421,831	363,285
Deferred income taxes	93,902	77,355
Prepaid expenses	38,203	30,375
Other current assets	53,516	26,160
Total current assets	1,452,388	1,302,641
Long-term investments		
Property and equipment, net	582,348	548,474
Goodwill and intangible assets	340,792	315,649
Deferred income taxes	103,657	156,465
Other assets	155,931	143,886
Total assets	$2,635,116	$2,467,115
Liabilities and Stockholders' Equity		
Current liabilities:		
Accounts payable	$ 118,612	$105,569
Accrued liabilities	473,610	422,725
Revolving credit facilities		
Current portion of long-term debt	795	742
Total current liabilities	593,017	529,036
Deferred income taxes		
Long-term debt	23,360	24,159
Other liabilities	406,170	408,627
Total liabilities	1,022,547	961,822
Stockholders' equity:		
Preferred stock: (auth. 25,000,000 shares; $0.01 par value) none issued	—	—
Common stock: (authorized 1,000,000,000 shares; $0.01 par value)	2,886	2,969
Issued and outstanding 288,514,529 and 296,867,247, respectively		
Additional paid-in capital	2,000,426	150,2982
Accumulated deficit	(445,654)	(30,053)
Accumulated other comprehensive income	54,911	29,395
Total stockholders' equity	1,612,569	1,505,293
Total liabilities and stockholders' equity	$2,635,116	$2,467,115

Source: Coach Inc. 2011 10-K, 2010 10-K.

Overview of the Global Luxury Goods Industry in 2012

According to a 2011 Bank of America/Merrill Lynch study, the world's most well-to-do consumers spent more than $224 billion on luxury goods in 2010. The United States represented 30 percent of industry sales, Europe accounted for 30 percent, 20 percent of industry sales were made in China, and Japan was responsible for 11 percent of total industry sales. Italian companies commanded 27 percent of industry sales, while French companies held a 22 percent share, Swiss companies possessed a 19 percent share, and U.S. companies accounted for 14 percent of industry sales. The most valuable

EXHIBIT 3

Performance of Coach Inc.'s Stock Price, October 2000–June 2012

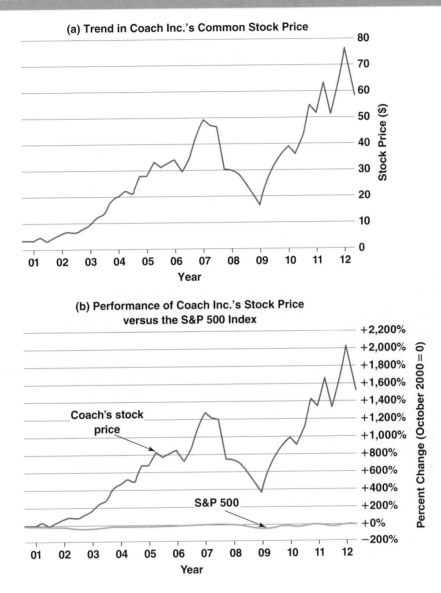

luxury brands in terms of annual revenues in 2011 were Louis Vuitton, Gucci, Hermès, and Cartier. The handbag and leather accessories segment of the industry was estimated at $28 billion in 2010 (see Exhibit 4).

The global luxury goods retail market was significantly affected by the economic slowdown and financial crisis of 2007–2009 as consumers in most income categories cut back on discretionary purchases. The poor general economic conditions created a 0.6 percent annual decline in industry sales between 2006 and 2010. However, while sales declined in the United States, Japan, and Europe, emerging markets, and especially China, became a key growth driver for the industry from 2006 to 2009. Continued growth in China and other emerging markets was expected to allow luxury goods sales to increase by 7.8 percent annually through 2015 to reach a staggering $350 billion.

Luxury brands, in general, relied on creative designs, high quality, and brand reputation to

EXHIBIT 4

The Global Handbag and Accessories Market (dollar amounts in billions)

	U.S.	Japan	China	Asia (including Japan and China)	Other/Europe	Total
Sales	$10.0	$4.4	$3.2	$12.0	$6.0	$28.0
Share of market	36%	16%	11%	43%	21%	100%
			Gender Mix Estimates			
Men's	15%	20%	45%	25%	15%	15%
Women's	85%	80%	55%	75%	85%	85%

Source: J.P. Morgan Analyst Report and Coach reports.

attract customers and build brand loyalty. Price sensitivity for luxury goods was driven by brand exclusivity, customer-centric marketing, and to a large extent some emotional sense of status and value. The market for luxury goods was divided into three main categories: haute couture, traditional luxury, and the growing submarket "accessible luxury." At the apex of the market was haute couture with its very high-end "custom" product offering that catered to the extremely wealthy. Leading brands in the traditional luxury category included such fashion design houses as Prada, Burberry, Hermès, Gucci, Polo Ralph Lauren, Calvin Klein, and Louis Vuitton. Some of these luxury goods makers also broadened their appeal with diffusion lines in the accessible luxury market to compete with Coach, DKNY, and other lesser luxury brands. For example, while Dolce & Gabbana dresses might sell at price points between $1,000 and $1,500, under the D&G affordable luxury brand—dresses of similar appearance were priced at $400 to $600. Giorgio Armani's Emporio Armani line and Gianni Versace's Versus lines typically sold at price points about 50 percent less than similar-looking items carrying the marquee labels. Profit margins on marquee brands approximated 40–50 percent, while most diffusion brands carried profit margins of about 20 percent. Luxury goods manufacturers believed diffusion brands' lower profit margins were offset by the opportunity for increased sales volume and the growing size of the accessible luxury market and protected margins on

such products by sourcing production to low-wage countries.

Industry sales in the United States had become more dependent on the success of diffusion lines in the accessible luxury category. Although primary traditional luxury consumers in the United States comprised the top 1 percent of wage earners with household incomes of $300,000 or better, those consumers who earned substantially less also aspired to own products with higher levels of quality and styling. The growing desire for luxury goods by middle-income consumers was thought to be a result of a wide range of factors, including effective advertising and television programming that promoted conspicuous consumption. The demanding day-to-day rigor of a two-income household was another factor suggested to urge middle-income consumers to reward themselves with luxuries. An additional factor contributing to rising sales of luxury goods in the United States was the "Trade up, trade down"[2] shopping strategy, whereby consumers would balance their spending by offsetting gains made with lower-priced necessities purchased at major retailers (e.g., Walmart and Target) to enable more discretionary spending available for indulgences on high-end product purchases.

The Growing Demand for Luxury Goods in Emerging Markets

Emerging markets, especially China and India, were expected to provide a major boost to the luxury goods market because of rapidly increasing wealth levels and standard of living gains. In 2012, 2.7 million individuals in China had a net worth of more than $1 million, and 63,500 individuals had net worths of more than $15 million. Luxury goods were also highly demanded by China's middle class, which allowed it to become the world's third-largest luxury market in 2010, with sales of luxury goods approaching $32 billion. Luxury goods spending in China was expected to overtake that of Japan and the United States, making China the world's largest market for luxury goods by 2015.

This is a remarkable outcome considering the luxury market has only been in existence there since the 1990s. Prior to this time, market entry by outsiders was restricted by the Chinese government despite the so-called open-door policy and economic reform. However, this all changed around 2000, along with the rapid economic and social developments occurring in China, and a group of luxury brands, such as Chanel, Prada, and Dolce & Gabbana, entered the market. Others, like Coach, entered with local distributors. From 2007 to 2010, the Chinese luxury goods market was one of the key growth drivers to the global luxury goods market, and the competition of luxury brands gradually moved from major cities to smaller-tier ones. In 2012, close to 1,000 store locations operated within the Chinese market under the brands of approximately 25 leading luxury marketers. Leading the charge was Hugo Boss with 114 stores, followed by Armani with 104 stores. Coach was ranked eighth in luxury goods store locations in China with 52 stores.

Luxury goods producers were also opening retail stores in India, which was another rapidly growing market for luxury goods. India's booming economy had created a new class of "business maharajahs"—highly affluent and globalized professionals. To serve this consumer segment, some 60 global luxury fashion and accessories brands had begun selling their products in India, mainly through local franchise partners who manage the brand. However, this opportunity came with some distinct challenges. For example, sales of Western women's clothing had struggled because Indian women still consider elaborate, highly crafted saris and other traditional items the garments of choice for formal occasions. Also, local designers such as Tarun Tahiliani and Satya Paul had more local brand recognition than some European or U.S. fashion houses. Watches, jewelry, and handbags, most of which have immediate brand recognition, fared better and accounted for the largest portion of luxury goods sales in India.

Counterfeiting

It was estimated that between $300 billion and $600 billion worth of counterfeit goods were sold in countries throughout the world. European and American companies that produced highly sought after branded products were most vulnerable to counterfeiting, with fakes plaguing almost every industry. Fake Rolex watches or Ralph Lauren Polo shirts had long been a problem, but by the mid-2000s, counterfeiters were even making knockoffs of branded auto parts and prescription drugs. Counterfeiting had become so prevalent that the Global Congress on Combating Counterfeiting estimated that 9 percent of all goods sold worldwide were not genuine. About two-thirds of all counterfeit goods were produced by manufacturers in China and Asian countries.

Luxury brands have found it financially and operationally beneficial to team up to combat counterfeiters. Luxury brands such as LVMH and Estèe Lauder had collaborated to develop best practices for measuring and implementing international piracy enforcement. LVMH and Apple teamed up and shared enforcement costs once it was discovered that counterfeit iPhone and iPad covers with LV logos were being produced—mutually gaining from their partnership.

Coach's Strategy and Industry Positioning

Coach offered distinctive, easily recognizable luxury products that were extremely well made and provided excellent value. The company's array of products included ladies handbags, leather accessories such as key fobs, belts, electronic accessories, and cosmetics cases, and outerwear such as gloves, hats, and scarves. Also, Coach designed and marketed leather business cases and luggage. It also expanded its accessories product offerings through licensing agreements with the Movado Group for Coach-branded watches in 1998, the Jimlar Corporation for Coach-branded ladies footwear in 1999, and Marchon Eyewear, Inc., for Coach eyewear in 2003. However, Coach entered into a licensing agreement with Luxottica in 2010 that would transition its eyewear products business beginning in the second half of 2012. The new agreement would expand its collection of prescription glasses and sunglasses marketed in Coach retail stores, at coach.com, in department stores, and select sunglass retailers and optical retailers in major markets. In spring 2010, Estèe Lauder agreed to produce a fragrance for Coach that would be distributed through Coach retail stores, coach.com, and about 3,000 U.S. department stores. Coach offered four women's fragrances and one men's fragrance.

Handbags accounted for 63 percent of Coach's 2011 sales of $4.2 billion, while accessories made up 27 percent. All other products accounted for 10 percent of company sales, which reflected a slight product mix change favoring the other product groupings since 2007, where the sales mix was 64 percent, 28 percent, and 8 percent, respectively. Royalties from Coach's licensing agreements with Movado, Jimlar, and Marchon accounted for approximately 1 percent of sales and was not a major contributor to overall earnings.

Coach positioned its brand in the lower part of the accessible or affordable luxury pyramid. This particular market provides a larger opportunity relative to that of more exclusive brands. Coach targeted the top 20 percent of Americans by household income, as opposed to the top 3 to 5 percent targeted by most European luxury brands. Coach had focused on sales in China, Japan, and the United States because these three countries led global luxury goods

spending. The company's sales in Japan had increased from $144 million in 2002 to $748 million in 2011, and its market share in the United States had nearly doubled since 2002.

During 2011, roughly 84 percent of Coach's total net sales (up from 75 percent in 2010) were generated from products introduced within the year. Given that the collections are seasonal and are planned to be sold in stores for short promotional periods of time, production quantities are limited and are designed to minimize risks associated with owning inventory. Sales of Coach's products for men grew from about 2.5 percent to nearly 5 percent of its global business, increasing to more than $200 million by 2011. Over time, Coach expected men's products to account for 15 percent or more of its global sales. The company's emphasis on dual-gender product offerings reflects the uptrend in the men's luxury goods market.

Flexible Sourcing

All of Coach's production was outsourced to contract manufacturers, with vendors in China accounting for 85 percent of its production requirements. Vendors located in Vietnam and India produced the remaining 15 percent of Coach's product requirements. Management controlled quality throughout the process with product development offices in Hong Kong, China, South Korea, India, and Vietnam. This broad-based, global manufacturing strategy was designed to optimize the mix of cost, lead times, and construction capabilities.

Approach to Differentiation

The market research design process developed by Executive Creative Director Reed Krakoff provided the basis of Coach's differentiated product line: Each quarter, major consumer research is undertaken to define product trends, selections, and consumer desires. This, together with the company's procurement process that selected only the highest-quality leathers and its sourcing agreements with quality offshore manufacturers, contributed to the company's reputation for high quality and value. Monthly product launches enhanced the company's voguish image and gave consumers reason to make purchases on a regular basis. The company's market research found its best customers visited a Coach store once every two months and made a purchase every seven months. Research in 2006 suggested the average Coach customer purchased four handbags per year. Lew Frankfort said the increase was attributable to monthly product launches that "increase the frequency of consumer visits" and women's changing style preference of "using bags to complement their wardrobes in the same way they used to use shoes."[3] A retail analyst agreed with Frankfort's assessment of the importance of frequent product introductions, calling it "a huge driver of traffic and sales and has enabled them to capture the . . . customer who wants the newest items and fashions."[4] Seventy percent of Coach's sales came from products introduced within the fiscal year. However, the company's Coach Classics collection, which was made up of lighter-weight, updated versions of iconic Coach handbag designs from the 1970s and 1980s, was among its best-selling lines in 2012.

The aesthetic attractiveness of Coach's full-price stores, which were designed by an in-house architectural group under the direction of Krakoff, further enhanced the company's luxury image. The company's stores significantly enhanced the Coach brand and were consistent with Coach's strategy of raising awareness and aggressively growing market share, For example, a 9,400-square-foot store opened in 2012 featured an impressive four-story glass and stainless steel back-lit facade, as well as the Coach Horse and Carriage logo. Coach sought to make customer service experiences an additional differentiating aspect of the brand. It had agreed since its founding to refurbish or replace damaged handbags, regardless of the age of the bag. The company provided store employees with regular customer service training programs and scheduled additional personnel during peak shopping periods to ensure all customers were attended to satisfactorily. Through the company's Special Request service, customers were allowed to order

merchandise for home delivery if the particular handbag or color wasn't available during a visit to a Coach store.

Coach also saw its communications with its customers as an opportunity for further differentiation. It communicated with customers through a wide range of direct marketing activities that included e-mail contacts, websites, catalogs, and brochures. In fiscal 2011, Coach reported that consumer contacts increased 52 percent to over 625 million and were primarily driven by increased e-mail communications. The company contact list included approximately 19 million active households in North America and 4.2 million active households in Japan. Also in 2011, Coach distributed approximately a million catalogs in its stores in Japan, Hong Kong, Macau, and mainland China.

Retail Distribution

Coach channels of distribution involved direct-to-consumer channels and indirect channels. Direct-to-consumer channels included full-price stores in the United States, factory stores in the United States, Internet sales, catalog sales, and stores in both Japan and China. Indirect sales included wholesale accounts with department stores in the United States and other international markets. Exhibit 5 provides the number of Coach retail stores by geographic region for 2007 through 2011. Exhibit 6 presents

---

EXHIBIT 5

Coach Inc.'s Retail Stores by Geographic Region, 2007–2011

	2007	2008	2009	2010	2011
North American retail stores	259	297	330	342	345
North American factory stores	93	102	111	121	143
Coach Japan locations	137	149	155	161	169
Coach China locations	16	24	28	41	66
Total stores	505	572	624	665	723

Source: Coach Inc., 10-Ks, various years.

EXHIBIT 6

Selected Financial Data for Coach Inc. by Channel of Distribution, Fiscal 2009–Fiscal 2011 (in thousands)

	Direct-to-Consumer	Indirect Corporate	Unallocated	Total
Fiscal 2011				
Net sales	$3,621,886	$536,621		$4,158,507
Operating income (loss)	1,423,191	296,032	$(414,299)	1,304,924
Fiscal 2010				
Net sales	3,155,860	451,776		3,607,636
Operating income (loss)	1,245,400	256,637	(351,866)	1,150,171
Fiscal 2009				
Net sales	2,726,891	503,577		3,230,468
Operating income (loss)	996,285	290,981	(315,353)	971,913

Source: Coach Inc. 2011 10-K.

Coach's net sales and operating income by channel of distribution for 2009 through 2011.

Full-Price Stores In 2011, Coach had 345 full-price retail stores in the United States, which comprised 70 percent of its total U.S. outlets. Full-price stores were divided into three categories—core locations, fashion locations, and flagship stores. Under Coach's tiered merchandising strategy, the company's flagship stores carried the most sophisticated and highest-priced items, while core stores carried widely demanded lines. The company's fashion locations tended to stock a blend of Coach's best-selling lines and chic specialty bags.

Coach's site selection process placed its core and fashion stores in upscale shopping centers and downtown shopping areas, while flagship stores were restricted to high-profile fashion districts in cities such as New York, Chicago, Beverly Hills, and San Francisco. Even though flagship stores were "a beacon for the brand"[5] as Frankfort described them, the company had been very prudent in the number of flagship stores it operated since such stores, by definition, were required to be located on the world's most expensive parcels of real estate.

A further advance launched in 2010 was the Coach brand "Reed Krakoff," created as a stand-alone entity with higher average price points than the Coach brand, with store openings initially planned for North America and Japan to bridge the more traditional luxury market.

Factory Stores Coach had 143 factory stores by 2011. The company had placed an additional emphasis on factory stores since the onset of the economic downturn, with the number of factory stores increasing by about nine annually between 2007 and 2011. Coach's factory stores in the United States were generally located 40 or more miles from its full-price stores. About 75 percent of factory store inventory was produced specifically for Coach's factory stores, while the remaining 25 percent was made up of overstocked items and discontinued models. Coach's 10 to 50 percent discounts offered in factory stores allowed the company to maintain a year round full-price policy in full-price stores. Coach CEO Lew Frankfort believed discounted prices were critical to success in retailing since 80 percent of women's apparel sold in the United States was bought on sale or in a discount store. "Women in the U.S. have been trained to expect to be able to find a bargain if they either go through the hunt . . . or are willing to buy something after the season," said Frankfort.[6]

Therefore, Coach's factory stores target value-oriented customers who might not otherwise buy a Coach product. Both factory store customers and full-price customers were equally brand loyal, but there was a distinct demographic difference between the shopper segments. The company's market research found the typical full-price store shopper was a 35-year-old, college-educated, single or newly married working woman. The typical factory store shopper was a 45-year-old, college-educated, married, professional woman with children. The average annual spending in a Coach store by full-price shoppers was $1,100. Factory store shoppers spent about $770 annually on Coach products, with 80 percent spent in factory stores and 20 percent spent in a full-price store.

The factory store strategy capitalized on the brand's lead luxury image projected at Coach's flagship and retail stores, and ensured it maintained its own individual identity so as not to dilute the foundation of the Coach brand. While the company had accelerated factory store openings, Frankfort did not want factory outlet stores to grow too rapidly since "Our destiny lies in our ability to grow full-price stores."[7] Some analysts were worried that Coach's highly successful factory stores might someday dilute its image. A Luxury Institute analyst described the dilemma faced by Coach and luxury diffusion brands by commenting, "To be unique and exclusive you cannot be ubiquitous."[8]

Coach Japan Coach sold its products in Japan in shop-in-shop department store locations, Coach full-price retail stores, and Coach factory outlets. The company had 169 retail locations in Japan in 2011, which generated $748 million in sales. The company's management believed Japan could support as many as 180 Coach retail outlets. The Japanese luxury goods market has been flat to slightly growing over the last several years, but Coach planned to drive growth in Japan by focusing on the market for men's luxury goods, which represented 25 percent of sales in the market in 2011.

Coach China Coach had 66 stores in China in 2011, up from 41 stores in 2010. The company had targeted 120 cities in China with populations of at least 1 million for future store openings. The majority of Coach's stores in China carried dual-gender product lines since about 45 percent of China's luxury market was men's products. The market for men's luxury goods represented about 15 percent of sales in the United States and 20 percent of sales in Japan.

Rivalry in the luxury goods industry in China was very intense, with 26 luxury goods brands operating 969 retail stores in the market in 2011. Hugo Boss had the largest number of stores in China with 114 stores, followed by Armani with 104 stores. In 2011, Gucci operated 45 stores in China, Prada had 14 stores, and Kate Spade had 5 stores in China. Coach anticipated recording fiscal 2012 revenues in China of approximately $300 million.

U.S. Wholesale Coach's products were sold in approximately 970 wholesale locations in the United States and Canada. The most significant U.S. wholesale customers included Macy's (including Bloomingdale's), Dillard's, Nordstrom, Lord & Taylor, and Saks Fifth Avenue. Wholesale sales of Coach products to U.S. department stores increased by 5 percent per year during 2006 to 2011 to reach approximately $300 million. However, department stores were becoming less relevant in the U.S. retailing industry with the average consumer spending less time in malls and shopping in fewer stores during visits to malls. The share of the U.S. retail market held by department stores declined from about 30 percent in 1990 to less than 20 percent in 2011.

International Wholesale Coach's wholesale distribution in international markets involved department stores, freestanding retail locations, shop-in-shop locations, and specialty retailers in 18 countries. The company's largest international wholesale accounts were the DFS Group, Lotte Group, Shila Group, Tasa Meng Corporation, and Imaginex. The largest

EXHIBIT 7

Breakdown of Coach Inc.'s Selling, General, and Administrative Expenses, Fiscal 2007–Fiscal 2011 (in thousands)

	2011	2010	2009	2008	2007
Selling	$1,180	$1,049	$ 981	$ 865	$ 718
Advertising	224	179	164	148	120
Distribution	58	48	52	48	53
Administration	204	153	130	167	139
Administration adjustment	51	54	24	32	0
Total	1,718	1,483	1,351	1,260	1,030

Source: Coach Inc. 10-Ks, various years.

portion of sales by these companies was to traveling affluent Chinese and Japanese consumers. Coach's largest wholesale country markets were Korea, Hong Kong, Taiwan, Singapore, Japan, Saudi Arabia, Australia, Mexico, Thailand, Malaysia, the Caribbean, China, New Zealand, and France. In 2006, international wholesale accounts amounted to $147 million and have grown some 7.8 percent per year to reach approximately $230 million in 2011. A breakdown of the company's selling, general, and administrative expenses for 2007 through 2011 are presented in Exhibit 7.

Coach's Strategic Options in 2012

In 2012, Coach was evolving into more of a global growth–oriented company. Lew Frankfort's key growth initiatives involved store expansion in the United States, Japan, Hong Kong, and mainland China; increasing sales to existing customers to drive comparable store growth, building market share in the men's market by introducing men's-only stores and building on the dual-gender store concept, and creating alliances to exploit the Coach brand in additional luxury categories. In addition, Coach was also considering opportunities to expand into the European luxury goods market. However, the company faced threats from prestigious European and North American luxury goods brands that had developed diffusion lines that carried price points similar to those offered by Coach. In addition, all of the world's major luxury brands were racing to establish a retail presence and brand loyalty in China, India, and other developing countries that would soon account for a large percentage of industry sales. In addition to market-related threats, Coach management also needed to consider how best to boost its profit margins to levels achieved in previous years and stabilize its stock price, which fell by nearly $20 during the first six months of 2012.

ENDNOTES

[1] "How Coach Got Hot," *Fortune* 146, no. 8 (October 28, 2002).

[2] As quoted in "Stores Dancing Chic to Chic," *Houston Chronicle,* May 6, 2000.

[3] As quoted in "Fashions Keep Retailer Busy," *Investor's Business Daily,* February 10, 2005, p. A04.

[4] Ibid.

[5] As quoted in "Coach's Split Personality," *BusinessWeek,* November 7, 2005.

[6] As quoted in "Coach Sales Strategy Is in the Bag," *Financial Times,* April 18, 2006.

[7] Ibid.

[8] As quoted in "Expansion into U.S.: Extending the Reach of the Exclusive Lifestyle Brands," *Financial Times,* July 8, 2006, p. 17.

Chipotle Mexican Grill in 2013: Can It Hit a Second Home Run?

connect ARTHUR A. THOMPSON The University of Alabama

In early 2012, it was obvious that founder, co-CEO, and Chairman Steve Ells's vision and strategy for Chipotle Mexican Grill had resulted in a home run. His vision for Chipotle (pronounced chi-POAT-lay) was "to change the way people think about and eat fast food." Taking his inspiration from features commonly found in many fine-dining restaurants, Ells's strategy for Chipotle was predicated on five elements:

- Serving a focused menu of burritos, tacos, burrito bowls (a burrito without the tortilla), and salads.

- Using high-quality raw ingredients and classic cooking methods to create great-tasting, reasonably priced dishes that were ready to be served to customers minutes after they were ordered.

- Creating an operationally efficient restaurant with an aesthetically pleasing and distinctive interior setting.

- Having friendly people take care of each customer.

- Doing all of this with increasing awareness and respect for the environment, the use of organically grown fresh produce, and meats raised in a humane manner without hormones and antibiotics.

Since 1993, the company had grown from a 1-unit operation in Denver into a 1,458-unit operation serving more than 900,000 customers a day in 43 states, the District of Columbia, Canada, the United Kingdom, and France as of spring 2013. In 2012, Chipotle reported revenues of $2.7 billion, net income of $278.0 million, and diluted earnings per share of $8.75. When the company went public in January 2006, the stock doubled on its first day of trading, jumping from the initial offering price of $22 per share to close at $44 per share. In April 2012, Chipotle Mexican Grill's stock price reached a record high of $440, then dropped to a 2012 low of $243 in October on fears of slowing growth and increased competition from Taco Bell's recently introduced upscale menu offerings. In the succeeding months, Chipotle's stock price recovered much of its former luster and was trading in the $370 range in May 2013.

But Steve Ells was not content to capitalize on the growing demand for healthier, more wholesome fast foods and continue on a path of opening several hundred new domestic and international Chipotle Mexican Grill locations annually, perhaps eventually mounting a challenge to McDonald's, the solidly entrenched global leader of the fast-food industry and the company that had invented the fast-food concept in the 1950s. McDonald's currently had 34,000 company-owned and franchised restaurant locations serving about 69 million customers in 119 countries daily. In 2011–2013, Ells and other Chipotle executives were busily testing and refining a second restaurant concept, Shophouse Southeast Asian Kitchen, predicated on much the same

Copyright © 2013 by Arthur A. Thompson. All rights reserved.

strategic principles as Chipotle Mexican Grill but with a different menu. Ells believed that "the Chipotle model could work well with a variety of different cuisines." The first Shophouse restaurant in Washington, D.C., opened in the summer of 2011. During 2013, the company expected to open a second Shophouse unit in Washington and a third location in the Los Angeles area. Part of Chipotle's lofty stock price in 2012–2013 was predicated on investors' belief that Chipotle was likely to hit a second home run with Shophouse, a rare and unusual feat for a relatively young company still rounding the bases on its first home run. In February 2012, one Wall Street analyst called Chipotle Mexican Grill "the perfect stock," and another believed that Chipotle could well prove to be the next McDonald's.[1]

Chipotle Mexican Grill's Early Years

Steve Ells graduated from the Culinary Institute of America and then worked for two years at Stars Restaurant in San Francisco. Soon after moving to Denver, he began working on plans to open his own restaurant. Guided by a conviction that food served fast did not have to be low quality and that delicious food did not have to be expensive, he came up with the concept of Chipotle Mexican Grill. When the first Chipotle restaurant opened in Denver in 1993, it became an instant hit. Patrons were attracted by the experience of getting better-quality food served fast and dining in a restaurant setting that was more upscale and appealing than those of traditional fast-food enterprises. Over the next several years, Ells opened new Chipotle restaurants in Denver and other Colorado locations.

In 1998, intrigued by what it saw happening at Chipotle, McDonald's acquired an initial ownership stake in the fledgling company, then acquired a controlling interest in early 2000. But McDonald's recognized the value of Ells's visionary leadership and kept him in the role of Chipotle's chief executive after it gained majority ownership. Drawing upon the investment capital provided by McDonald's and its

decades of expertise in supply chain logistics, expanding a restaurant chain, and operating restaurants efficiently, Chipotle—under Ells's watchful and passionate guidance—embarked on a long-term strategy to open new restaurants and expand its market coverage. By year-end 2005, Chipotle had 489 locations in 24 states. As 2005 drew to a close, in somewhat of a surprise move, McDonald's top management determined that instead of continuing to parent Chipotle's growth, it would take the company public and give Chipotle management a free rein in charting the company's future growth and strategy. An initial public offering of shares was held in January 2006, and Steve Ells was designated as Chipotle's CEO and chairman of the board. During 2006, through the January IPO, a secondary offering in May 2006, and a tax-free exchange offer in October 2006, McDonald's disposed of its entire ownership interest in Chipotle Mexican Grill.

When Chipotle became an independent enterprise, Steve Ells and the company's other top executives kept the company squarely on a path of rapid expansion and continued to employ the same basic strategy elements that were the foundation of the company's success. Ells functioned as the company's principal driving force for ongoing innovation and constant improvement. He pushed especially hard for new ways to boost "throughput"—the number of customers whose orders could be taken, prepared, and served per hour.[2] By 2012, Ells's mantra of "slow food, fast" had resulted in throughputs of 300 customers per hour at Chipotle's best restaurants.

During 2007–2012, Chipotle's revenues grew at a robust compound average rate of 20.3 percent. Net income grew at a compound rate of 31.6 percent, due to gains in operating efficiency that boosted profit margins. Average annual sales for restaurants open at least 12 full months climbed from $1,085,000 in 2007 to $2,113,000 in 2011, owing to increased customer traffic, higher expenditures per customer, and price increases. The average tab per customer ran $8 to $9 in 2011–2013.[3] Exhibit 1 presents recent financial and operating data for Chipotle Mexican Grill.

EXHIBIT 1

Financial and Operating Highlights for Chipotle Mexican Grill, Selected Years, 2007–2012 (in $000s)

Income Statement Data	2012	2011	2010	2009	2007
Total revenue	$2,731,224	$2,269,548	$1,835,922	$1,518,417	$1,085,782
Food, beverage and packaging costs	891,003	738,720	561,107	466,027	346,393
As a % of total revenue	32.6%	32.5%	30.6%	30.7%	31.9%
Labor costs	641,836	543,119	453,573	385,072	289,417
As a % of total revenue	23.5%	23.9%	24.7%	25.4%	26.7%
Occupancy costs	171,435	147,274	128,933	114,218	75,891
As a % of total revenue	6.3%	6.5%	7.0%	7.5%	7.0%
Other operating costs	286,610	251,208	202,904	174,581	131,512
As a % of total revenue	10.5%	11.1%	11.1%	11.5%	12.1%
General and administrative expenses	183,409	149,426	118,590	99,149	75,038
As a % of total revenue	6.7%	6.6%	6.5%	6.5%	6.9%
Depreciation and amortization	84,130	74,938	68,921	61,308	43,595
Pre-opening costs	11,909	8,495	7,767	8,401	9,585
Loss on disposal of assets	5,027	5,806	6,296	5,956	6,168
Total operating expenses	2,275,359	1,918,986	1,548,091	1,314,712	977,599
Operating income	455,865	350,562	287,831	203,705	108,183
Interest and other income (expense) net	1,820	(857)	1,230	520	5,819
Income before income taxes	457,685	349,705	289,061	204,225	114,002
Provision for income taxes	(179,685)	(134,760)	(110,080)	(77,380)	(43,439)
Net income	$ 278,000	$ 214,945	$ 178,981	$ 126,845	$ 70,563
Earnings per share					
Basic	$8.82	$6.89	$5.73	$3.99	$2.16
Diluted	8.75	6.76	5.64	3.95	2.13
Weighted average common shares outstanding					
Basic	31,513	31,217	31,234	31,766	32,672
Diluted	31,783	31,775	31,735	32,102	33,146
Selected Balance Sheet Data					
Total current assets	$ 546,607	$ 501,192	$ 406,221	$297,454	$201,844
Total assets	1,668,667	1,425,308	1,121,605	961,505	722,115
Total current liabilities	186,852	157,453	123,054	102,153	73,301
Total liabilities	422,741	381,082	310,732	258,044	160,005
Total shareholders' equity	1,245,926	1,044,226	810,873	703,461	562,110
Other Financial Data					
Net cash provided by operating activities	$419,963	$411,096	$289,191	$260,673	$146,923
Capital expenditures	197,000	151,100	113,200	117,200	141,000
Restaurant Operations Data					
Restaurants open at year-end	1,410	1,230	1,084	956	704
Average annual sales for restaurants open at least 12 full months (in $000s)	$2,113	$2,013	$1,840	$1,728	$1,085
Comparable restaurant sales increases	7.1%	11.2%	9.4%	2.2%	10.8%
Development and construction costs per newly opened restaurant (in $000s)	$800	$800	$795	$850	$880

Note: Comparable restaurant sales increases represent the change in period-over-period sales for restaurants beginning in their 13th full calendar month of operation.

Source: Company 10-K reports, 2012, 2011 and 2008.

Menu and Food Preparation

The menu at Chipotle Mexican Grill restaurants was unusually limited—burritos, burrito bowls, tacos, and salads, plus soft drinks, fruit drinks, and milk. Except in restaurants where there were restrictions on serving alcoholic beverages, the drink options also included a selection of beers and margaritas. However, customers could customize their burritos, burrito bowls, tacos, and salads to their liking. Options included four meats—marinated and grilled chicken and steak, carnitas (seasoned and braised pork), and barbacoa (spicy shredded beef)—pinto beans, vegetarian black beans, brown or white rice tossed with lime juice and fresh-chopped cilantro, and such extras as sautéed peppers and onions, salsas, guacamole, sour cream, shredded cheese, lettuce, and tortilla chips seasoned with fresh lime and salt. In addition, it was restaurant policy to make special dishes for customers if the requested dish could be made from the ingredients on hand. Exhibit 2 describes the favorite dishes of some of Chipotle's employees. Exhibit 3 shows some of the menu dishes served at Chipotle.

From the outset, Chipotle's menu strategy had been to keep it simple, do a few things exceptionally well, and avoid selections (such as coffee and desserts) that complicated store operations and impaired efficiency. While it was management practice to consider menu additions, the menu offerings had remained fundamentally the same for many years. So far, Steve Ells had rejected the idea of adding a breakfast menu and opening earlier in the day.

EXHIBIT 2

Examples of Favorite Menu Items and Meals of Chipotle Mexican Grill Employees

- Chicken burrito with cilantro lime rice, vegetarian black beans, roasted chili corn salsa, green tomatillo salsa, sour cream, and cheese.
- A pair of soft corn tacos, one chicken or carnitas and one steak, both with green tomatillo salsa, fresh tomato salsa, a little sour cream and lettuce. Some chips and a side of sour cream, corn salsa, and green salsa mixed together.
- Steak fajita burrito with brown rice, red hot tomatillo salsa, sour cream, cheese, guacamole, and lettuce.
- Soft corn barbacoa tacos with cilantro and fresh squeezed lime juice.
- Veggie bowl with brown rice, pinto beans, corn salsa, green tomatillo salsa, red tomatillo salsa, cheese, and guacamole.
- Barbacoa burrito with cilantro lime rice, pinto beans, two scoops of red tomatillo salsa, cheese, and a touch of guacamole.

Source: Information posted in the careers section at www.chipotle.com, accessed February 19, 2012.

However, in February 2013 Chipotle began testing a new vegetarian menu item called "Sofritas" in seven restaurants in the San Francisco Bay Area. The feature ingredient of Sofritas was shredded organic tofu braised with chipotle chilis, roasted poblanos, and a blend of aromatic spices.

The food preparation area of each restaurant was equipped with stoves and grills, pots and pans, and an assortment of cutting knives, wire whisks, and other kitchen utensils. A walk-in

EXHIBIT 3

Representative Dishes Served at Chipotle Mexican Grill Restaurants

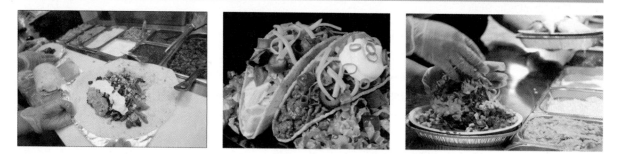

refrigerator was stocked with ingredients, and herbs, spices, and dry goods such as rice were on hand. The work space more closely resembled the layout of the kitchen in a fine dining restaurant than the cooking area of a typical fast-food restaurant that made extensive use of automated cooking equipment and microwaves. All the menu selections and optional extras were prepared from scratch—hours went into preparing food on-site, but some items were prepared from fresh ingredients in nearby commissaries. Kitchen crews used classic cooking methods: They marinated and grilled the chicken and steak, hand-cut produce and herbs, made fresh salsa and guacamole, and cooked rice in small batches throughout the day. While the food preparation methods were labor-intensive, the limited menu created efficiencies that helped keep costs down.

Serving Orders Quickly

One of Chipotle's biggest innovations had been creating the ability to have a customer's order ready quickly. As customers moved along the serving line, customers selected exactly what they wanted and how they wanted it by speaking directly to the employees that prepared the food and were assembling the order behind the counter. Much experimentation and fine-tuning had gone into designing a restaurant layout and serving line that made the food-ordering and dish-creation process intuitive and time-efficient, thereby enabling a high rate of customer throughput. The throughput target was at least 200 and up to 300 customers per hour in order to keep the numbers of customers waiting in line at peak hours to a tolerable minimum. Management was focused on further improving the speed at which customers moved through the service line in all restaurants, so that orders placed by fax, online, or via a smartphone ordering app could be accommodated without slowing service to in-store customers and compromising the interactions between customers and crew members on the service line. The attention to serving orders quickly was motivated by management's belief that while customers returned because of the great-tasting food they also liked their orders served fast without having a "fast-food" experience (even when they were not in a hurry).

The Commitment to "Food with Integrity"

Beginning in 2003–2004, Chipotle began a move to make increasing use of organically grown local produce, organic beans, organic dairy products, and meats from animals that were raised in accordance with animal welfare standards and were never given feeds containing antibiotics and growth hormones to speed weight gain. This shift in ingredient usage was part of a long-term management campaign to use top-quality, nutritious ingredients and improve "the Chipotle experience"—an effort that Chipotle management designated as "Food with Integrity." The company began working with experts in the areas of animal ethics to try to support more humane farming environments, and it started visiting the farms and ranches from which it obtained ingredients. It also began investigating using more produce supplied by farmers who respected the environment, avoided use of chemical fertilizers and pesticides, followed U.S. Department of Agriculture standards for growing organic products, and used agriculturally sustainable methods such as conservation tillage that improved soil conditions and reduced erosion. Simultaneously, efforts were made to source a greater portion of products locally (within 350 miles of the restaurants where they were used) while in season.

The transition to using organically grown local produce and naturally raised meats occurred gradually rather than being an all-at-once switch because it took time for Chipotle to develop sufficient supply sources to accommodate the requirements of all of its restaurants. Supplies of organic products, locally grown produce, and naturally raised meats were constrained because consumers were purchasing growing volumes of these items at their local farmers markets and supermarkets and because the chefs at many fine-dining establishments were making concerted efforts to incorporate organic, locally grown produce and natural meats into their dishes. Organic farmers and the growers of animals that were fed only vegetarian diets containing no antibiotics or hormones and raised these animals in a humane fashion (what Chipotle called naturally raised meats) were having difficulty keeping up with growing market demand for their products. Frequent supply-demand imbalances had resulted in market conditions where certain organic products and natural meats were sometimes either unavailable or prohibitively high-priced.

As of December 31, 2011, all of the sour cream and cheese Chipotle purchased was made from milk that came from cows that were not given rBGH (recombinant bovine growth hormone). The milk used to make much of the purchased cheese and a portion of the purchased sour cream was sourced from dairies that provided pasture access for their cows rather than housing them in confined spaces. A portion of the beans the company used was organically grown and a portion was being grown by farmers who used sustainable agricultural practices. And Chipotle was serving exclusively naturally raised meats in all of its restaurants in the United States, although there were ongoing challenges regarding both price and the availability of adequate meat supplies and organic vegetables. Some Chipotle restaurants were forced to serve conventionally raised chicken or steak for much of 2011. Chipotle restaurants in a few markets reverted to the use of conventionally raised beef in early 2012. But the supply shortages had been largely resolved by early 2013. While adequate supplies of organic produce and organically grown beans were normally available, prices in some instances had crept upward because of cost pressures—organic and sustainable crops often took longer to grow and crop yields could be lower for organically or sustainably grown produce. Rising market prices for organically grown ingredients and naturally raised meats largely accounted for why Chipotle's costs for food, beverages, and packing rose from 30.6

percent of revenues in 2010 to 32.6 percent of revenues in 2012 (see Exhibit 1) and to 33.0 percent in the first quarter of 2013.

Going forward, Chipotle executives were firmly committed to continuing the Food with Integrity initiative, despite the attendant price-cost challenges and supply chain complications. They wanted Chipotle to be at the forefront in responding to mounting consumer concerns about food nutrition, where their food came from, how fruits and vegetables were grown, and how animals used for meat were raised. And they wanted customers to view Chipotle Mexican Grill as a place that used high-quality, "better for you" ingredients in its dishes. Nonetheless, top management expected there would be times when the prices of certain organic products and naturally raised meats would mean that some Chipotle restaurants would temporarily revert to using conventional produce and meats in its dishes in the interest of preserving the company's reputation for providing great food at reasonable prices and protecting profit margins. Over the longer term, top executives anticipated that the price volatility and shortages of organically grown ingredients and natural meats would gradually dissipate as growing demand for such products attracted more small farmers and larger agricultural enterprises to boost supplies. But it was also anticipated that most of these organic and natural meat ingredients would remain more expensive than conventionally raised, commodity-priced equivalents.

Supply Chain Management Practices

Top executives were acutely aware that maintaining high levels of food quality in its restaurants depended in part on acquiring high-quality, fresh ingredients and other necessary supplies that met company specifications. However, Chipotle did not purchase ingredients for its dishes directly from farmers or purchase paper products, plastic ware, and other restaurant supplies directly from manufacturers. Rather, over the years, the company had developed long-term relationships with a number of reputable food industry suppliers that could provide high-quality, fresh ingredients and other products that met Chipotle's specifications. It then worked with these suppliers on an ongoing basis to establish and implement a set of forward, fixed, and formula-pricing protocols for determining the prices that suppliers charged Chipotle for various items. Reliable suppliers that could meet Chipotle's quality specifications and were willing to comply with Chipotle's set of forward, fixed, and formula-pricing protocols and guidelines for certain products were put on Chipotle's list of approved suppliers. The number of approved suppliers was small for such key ingredients as beef, pork, chicken, beans, rice, sour cream, and tortillas. Recently, however, Chipotle had strived to increase the number of approved suppliers for ingredients subject to volatile prices and short supplies.

Instead of making purchases directly from approved suppliers, Chipotle utilized the services of 23 independently owned and operated regional distribution centers to purchase and deliver ingredients and other supplies to Chipotle restaurants. These distribution centers were required to make all purchases from Chipotle's list of approved suppliers in accordance with the agreed-upon pricing guidelines and protocols. As Chipotle continued to expand geographically, Chipotle management planned to add more regional distribution centers.

In addition, Chipotle personnel diligently monitored industry news, trade issues, weather, exchange rates, foreign demand, crises, and other world events so as to better anticipate potential impacts on ingredient prices.

Quality Assurance and Food Safety

Chipotle had a quality assurance department that established and monitored quality and food safety throughout the company's supply chain and all the way through the serving lines at restaurants. There were quality and food safety standards for certain farms that grew ingredients used by company restaurants, approved suppliers, and the regional distribution centers that purchased and delivered products to the restaurants. Chipotle's training and risk management departments developed and implemented operating standards for food quality, preparation, cleanliness, and safety in company restaurants. The food safety programs for suppliers and restaurants were designed to ensure compliance with applicable federal, state, and local food safety regulations.

Restaurant Management and Operations

Each Chipotle Mexican Grill typically had a general manager (a position top management characterized as the most important in the company), an apprentice manager (in about 75 percent of the restaurants), one or two hourly service managers, one or two hourly kitchen managers, and an average of 21 full- and part-time crew members. Busier restaurants had more crew members. Chipotle generally had two shifts at its restaurants, which simplified scheduling and facilitated assigning hourly employees with a regular number of work hours each week. Most employees were cross-trained to work at a variety of stations, both to provide people with a variety of skills and to boost labor efficiency during busy periods. Personnel were empowered to make decisions within their assigned areas of responsibility. Restaurant managers and crew members were expected to welcome and interact with customers throughout the day. The designs of the open kitchen and service line placed crew members up front where they could speak to customers in a personal and hospitable manner, whether preparing food items or customizing the dish ordered by a customer moving along the service line. Crew members were expected to deliver a customer-pleasing experience "one burrito at a time," give each customer individual attention, and make every effort to respond positively to customer requests and suggestions.

The general managers of Chipotle restaurants strived to hire and retain crew members and other employees who had a strong work ethic, took pride in preparing food items correctly, enjoyed interacting with other people, exhibited enthusiasm in serving customers, and were team players in striving to operate the restaurant in accordance with the high standards expected by management. A sizable number of Chipotle's crew members had been attracted to apply for a job at Chipotle because of either encouragement from an acquaintance who worked at Chipotle or their own favorable impressions of the work atmosphere while going through the serving line and dining at a Chipotle Mexican Grill. New crew members received hands-on, shoulder-to-shoulder training. In 2012–2013, full-time crew members had average earnings of nearly $18,250 (regular compensation and bonuses), plus benefits of about $2,830 (clothes, meals, insurance, and 401k contributions).[4] Total earnings and benefits averaged $27,000 for hourly managers, $50,000 for apprentice managers, and $63,000 for general managers. Top-performing employees and crew members could expect to be promoted because of the company's unusually heavy reliance on promotion from within—almost 98 percent of salaried managers and more than 98 percent of hourly managers had been promoted from positions as crew members. In several instances, a newly hired crew member had risen rapidly through the ranks and become the general manager of a restaurant in 9 to 12 months; many more high-performing crew members had been promoted to general managers within two to four years. The long-term career opportunities for Chipotle employees were quite attractive because of the company's rapid growth and the speed with which it was opening stores in both new and existing markets.

Chipotle executives sought to build and nurture a people-oriented, performance-based culture in each Chipotle restaurant, believing that such a culture led to the best possible experience for both customers and employees. The foundation of that culture started with hiring good people to manage and staff the company's restaurants. The general managers of restaurants that were especially successful in developing a high-performing team of hourly managers and crew members were promoted to restaurateur, a position that entailed average total compensation of $99,000 companywide in 2012–2013. The most outstanding restaurateurs were given responsibility for mentoring one or more nearby restaurants, thus providing an opportunity for restaurateurs to develop field leadership roles and also earn up to $129,000 annually. Restaurateurs whose mentoring efforts resulted in high-performing teams at four restaurants and the promotion of at least one of the four restaurant managers to restaurateur could themselves be promoted to the position of apprentice team leader and become a full-time member of the company's field support staff.

The field support staff included apprentice team leaders, team leaders or area managers, team directors, and regional director. The principal task of people in these positions was to foster a culture of high standards, constant improvement, and employee empowerment in each of Chipotle's restaurants. One of Chipotle's field support staff members in 2013 had been hired as a crew member in 2003, promoted to general manager in 12 months, and—eight years after starting with Chipotle—was appointed as a team director (with responsibilities for 57 restaurants and more than 1,400 employees as of 2013).[5]

Marketing

Chipotle's advertising and marketing costs totaled $35.0 million in 2012, versus $31.9 million in 2011, $26.2 million in 2010, and $21.0 million in 2009 (these costs were included in "Other operating costs" in Exhibit 1). Chipotle utilized print, outdoor, transit, theater, radio, and online ads. In February 2012, Chipotle Mexican Grill ran its first-ever national TV commercial during the broadcast of the Grammy Awards. The commercial was actually a short film, "Back to the Start," that Chipotle had shown in 2011 in theaters and online and was an unusually long commercial for a national broadcast. In addition, Chipotle generated considerable media coverage from scores of publications that had largely favorable articles describing Chipotle's food, restaurant concept, and business; the company had also been featured in a number of television programs.

Recently, Chipotle had been testing use of more "owned media," including new video and music programs, and a more visible event strategy that included the launch of the company's first festival of food, music, and ideas, Cultivate Chicago, and participation in community events in markets where the company had restaurants or was opening new restaurants. Management believed these newer programs allowed the company to forge stronger emotional connections with customers and communicate its story better and with more nuance than it could do through traditional advertising. The company was also increasing its use of digital, mobile, and social media in its overall marketing mix because it gave customers greater opportunity to access Chipotle in ways that were convenient for them and broadened Chipotle's ability to engage with its customers individually.

Chipotle executives were of the opinion that the best and most recognizable brands were built through all of the ways people experienced the brand as well as through advertising or promotional campaigns. Marketing personnel paid close attention to presenting the Chipotle brand consistently and keeping advertising and promotional programs, in-store communications, and menus closely aligned with who Chipotle was and what the Chipotle experience was all about.

When Chipotle opened restaurants in new markets, it initiated a range of promotional activities to introduce Chipotle to the local community and to create interest in the restaurant. In markets where there were existing Chipotle restaurants, newly opened restaurants typically attracted customers in volumes at or near market averages without having to initiate special promotions or advertising to support a new opening.

Chipotle's collective marketing efforts, together with the considerable word-of-mouth publicity from customers telling others about their favorable experiences at Chipotle restaurants, had enabled the company to build good brand awareness among consumers with relatively low advertising expenditures—even in the highly competitive fast-food and fast-casual segments of the restaurant industry—and to differentiate Chipotle from its competitors.

Restaurant Site Selection

Chipotle had an internal team of real estate managers that devoted substantial time and effort to evaluating potential locations for new restaurants. The site selection process entailed studying the surrounding trade area, demographic and business information within that area, and available information on competitors. In addition, advice and recommendations were solicited from external real estate brokers with expertise in specific markets. Locations proposed by the internal real estate team were visited by a team of operations and development management as part of a formal site ride; the team toured the surrounding trade area, reviewed demographic and business information on the areas, and evaluated the food establishment operations of competitors. Based on this analysis, along with the results of predictive modeling based on proprietary formulas, the company came up with projected sales and targeted returns on investment for a new location. Chipotle Mexican Grills had proved successful in a number of different types of locations, including in-line or end-cap locations in strip or power centers, regional malls and downtown business districts, freestanding buildings, and even a location at Dulles International Airport outside Washington, D.C. In recent months, the company had begun exploring new restaurant locations in areas where it had little or no prior experience, including smaller or more economically mixed communities, highway sites, outlet centers, and restaurants in airports, food courts, or on military bases.

Development and Construction Costs for New Restaurants

Chipotle opened a net of 146 restaurants in 2011 and 180 restaurants in 2012; plans called for opening between 165 and 180 restaurants in 2013. Roughly 30 percent of the 2012 openings were slightly scaled-back "A Model" restaurants located primarily in secondary trade areas with attractive demographics. The A Model restaurants typically had lower investment and occupancy costs than the restaurants that Chipotle had traditionally opened. To lower the average development costs for new restaurants, Chipotle had recently begun using a new, simpler design for its restaurants that incorporated some A Model design elements. Exhibit 4 shows the interiors and exteriors of several Chipotle Mexican Grills.

The company's average development and construction costs per restaurant decreased from about $850,000 in 2009 to about $800,000 in 2011 and 2012 (see Exhibit 1), chiefly because of cost savings realized from building more lower-cost A Model restaurants and growing use of its new, simpler restaurant design. Chipotle anticipated that average development costs for new restaurants to be opened in 2013 would be similar to those in 2011–2012. In 2013, senior Chipotle executives expected that the company's annual cash flows from operations, together with current cash on hand, would be adequate to meet ongoing capital expenditures, working capital requirements, and other cash needs for the foreseeable future. Capital expenditures in 2013 were expected to be about $210 million, of which about $160 million was for construction of new restaurant locations; capital expenditures in prior years are shown in Exhibit 1.

The ShopHouse Test Concept

The ShopHouse Southeast Asia Kitchen format being tested grew out of Steve Ells's belief that the fundamental principles on which Chipotle Mexican Grill restaurants were based—finding the very best sustainably raised ingredients, prepared and cooked using classical methods in front of the customer, and served in an interactive format by special people dedicated to providing a great dining experience—could be adapted to other cuisines. To test the Chipotle model with different ingredients and a different style of food, the company opened its first ShopHouse Southeast Asian Kitchen on DuPont Circle in Washington, D.C., in September 2011. ShopHouse served a focused menu consisting of rice bowls, noodle bowls, and banh mi sandwiches, made with a choice of grilled steak, grilled chicken satay, pork and chicken meatballs, or organic tofu. In addition to a choice of meats or tofu, the rice and noodle bowls included choices of four fresh vegetables, a sauce (red or green curry or tamarind vinaigrette), and a garnish and topping (including chili-jam marmalade, roast corn with scallions, Chinese broccoli, pickled vegetables, and assorted aromatic herbs). Customers could have their dishes made anywhere from mega-spicy to mild. The flavors were a blend of Thai, Vietnamese, and Malaysian.

As was the case at Chipotle, customers moved along a cafeteria-style line, with servers behind the counter customizing each order; there was room for seating or customers could have orders readied for take-out. The interior of the Dulles Circle ShopHouse resembled Chipotle interiors—sparse and a bit industrial, with an attention to such environmentally green detail as high-efficiency lighting. Much of the dining area was constructed with recycled materials, including dark maple treated to look like teak.

Competition

Chipotle competed with national and regional fast-casual, quick-service, and casual-dining restaurant chains, as well as locally owned restaurants and food-service establishments. The number, size, and strength of competitors varied by region, local market area, and a particular restaurant's location within a given community. Competition among the various types of restaurants and food-service establishments was based on such factors as type of food served, menu selection (including the availability of low-calorie and nutritional items), food quality and taste, speed of service, price and value, dining ambience, name recognition and

EXHIBIT 4

Representative Interiors and Exteriors of Chipotle Mexican Grills

reputation, convenience of location, and customer service.

A myriad of dining establishments specialized in Mexican food. The leading fast-food chain in the Mexican-style food category was Taco Bell. Chipotle's two biggest competitors in the fast-casual segment were Moe's Southwest Grill and Qdoba Mexican Grill. Two smaller chains, Baja Fresh and California Tortilla, were also competitors in a small number of geographic locations

Taco Bell

Since 2005, Taco Bell locations had been struggling to attract customers. Throughout 2005–2011, the total number of Taco Bell restaurants, both domestically and internationally, declined as more underperforming locations were closed than new Taco Bell units were opened.

In 2010, Taco Bell had U.S. sales of $6.9 billion at combined company-owned and franchised Taco Bell locations, compared with $6.8 billion in 2009 and $6.7 billion in 2008. Average sales at Taco Bell restaurants were $1.28 million in 2011, versus averages of $1.29 million in 2010 and $1.26 million in 2009. Sales at company-owned Taco Bell restaurants in the United States open at least 12 or more months declined by 2 percent in 2011.[6] The sluggish sales performance at Taco Bell restaurants, most especially those in the United States, was viewed as mainly attributable to a loss of customers to Chipotle Mexican Grill, Moe's Southwest Grill, and Qdoda Mexican Grill, all of which had more upscale menu selections and used better-quality ingredients. Several fast-food hamburger chains, including McDonald's, had recently introduced upscaled hamburgers to better compete with the quality of the made-to-order burgers available at Five Guys and Smashburger locations, two up-and-coming fast-casual chains. A September 2011 survey by *Nation's Restaurant News* and consultant WD Partners found that Taco Bell scored the lowest in food quality and atmosphere among limited-service Mexican eateries, a group that included Chipotle Mexican Grill and Qdoba Mexican Grill.[7]

In late 2011, Taco Bell's parent company, Yum! Brands, began a multiple-year campaign to reduce company ownership of Taco Bell locations from 23 percent of total locations to about 16 percent; 1,276 company-owned Taco Bell locations were sold to franchisees in 2010–2012. Yum! Brands also owned Pizza Hut and KFC (Kentucky Fried Chicken); the company sold its A&W All American and Long John Silver's brands in December 2011.

To counter stagnant sales and begin a strategy to rejuvenate Taco Bell, during 2010–2011 Taco Bell restaurants began rolling out a new taco with a Doritos-based shell called Doritos Locos Taco, which management termed a

"breakthrough product designed to reinvent the taco." The launch was supported with an aggressive advertising campaign to inform the public about the new Doritos Locos Taco. The effort was considered a solid success, driving record sales of 375 million tacos in one year. In March 2012, Taco Bell began introducing a new Cantina Bell menu, a group of upgraded products conceptualized by celebrity Miami chef Lorena Garcia that included such ingredients and garnishes as black beans, cilantro rice, and corn salsa.[8] The new Cantina Bell menu items had undergone extensive testing in select geographic areas. In addition to the upscaled Cantina Bell selections, Taco Bell also introduced several new breakfast selections. According to Taco Bell President Greg Creed, it was Taco Bell's biggest new-product launch ever. The upscaled menu at Taco Bell was a competitive response to growing consumer preferences for the higher-caliber, made-to-order dishes they could get at fast-casual Mexican-food chains such as Chipotle, Moe's, and Qdoba. Taco Bell's new Cantina Bell items were priced below similar types of Chipotle products—the average ticket price for the new Cantina Bell selections was about $4.50 (compared to averages of $7 to $9 for meals at Chipotle, Moe's, and Qdoba). The rollout of the Cantina Bell menu was supported with a new slogan and brand campaign. Within a few months, it was clear that the new tacos and Cantina Bell menu selections were boosting customer traffic and sales at Taco Bell locations. As of year-end 2012, Taco Bell was the leader in the U.S. Mexican quick-service restaurant segment, with a 49 percent market share, and the outlook for Taco Bell seemed much more promising.[9] Sales growth at Taco Bell restaurants in 2012 was an estimated 6.8 percent.[10]

In 2012–2013 expansion of Taco Bell locations had resumed, with the vast majority of the new additions being franchised. In early 2013, Yum! Brands announced a long-term goal to grow the number of Taco Bell locations worldwide from 5,000 units to 8,000 units. Going into 2013, Taco Bell had 5,695 company-owned and franchised restaurant locations in the United

States, plus another 285 international locations. About 20 percent of the locations in the United States were company-owned and just three of the foreign locations (all in India) were company-owned.

Moe's Southwest Grill

Moe's Southwest Grill was founded in Atlanta, Georgia, in 2000 and acquired in 2007 by Atlanta-based Focus Brands, an affiliate of Roark Capital, a private equity firm. Focus Brands was a global franchisor of over 3,300 Carvel Ice Cream, Cinnabon, Schlotzsky's, Moe's Southwest Grill, and Auntie Anne's locations. In 2013, there were more than 495 fast-casual Moe's Southwest Grill locations in 36 states and the District of Columbia.

The menu at Moe's featured burritos, quesadillas, tacos, nachos, burrito bowls (with meat selections of chicken, pork, or tofu), and salads with a choice of two homemade dressings. Main dishes could be customized with a choice of 20 items that included a choice of protein (sirloin steak, chicken breast, pulled pork, ground beef, or organic tofu); grilled peppers, onions, and mushrooms; black olives; cucumbers; fresh chopped or pickled jalapenos; pico de gallo (handmade fresh daily); lettuce; and six salsas. There was a kids' menu and vegetarian, gluten-free, and low-calorie options, as well as a selection of five side items (including queso and guacamole), two desserts (cookie or brownie), soft drinks, iced tea, and bottled water. All meals were served with chips and salsa. Moe's used high-quality ingredients, including all-natural, cage-free, white breast meat chicken; steroid-free, grain-fed pulled pork; 100 percent sirloin, grass-fed steak; and organic tofu. No dishes included trans fats or MSG (monosodium glutamate—a flavor enhancer), and no use was made of microwaves.

Moe's provided catering; the catering menu included a fajitas bar, a taco bar, a salad bar, mini-burrito appetizers, a burrito box, a selection of dips, cookies, and drinks. At some locations, customer orders could be taken online.

The company and its franchisees emphasized friendly hospitable service. When customers entered a Moe's location, it was the practice for employees to do a "Welcome to Moe's!" shout-out.

Qdoba Mexican Grill

The first Qdoba Mexican Grill opened in Denver in 1995. Rapid growth ensued and the company was acquired by Jack in the Box, Inc., a large operator and franchisor of Jack in the Box quick-service restaurants best known for its hamburgers. Jack in the Box had fiscal year 2012 revenues of $1.5 billion (the company's fiscal year was October 1 through September 30), and its Jack in the Box system included 2,250 company-owned and franchised locations in 21 states. Corporate management at Jack in the Box was executing a long-term campaign to sell company-owned Jack in the Box restaurants to franchisees and to boost the number and percentage of company-owned Qdoba restaurants by acquiring locations from franchisees.

In October 2012, there were more than 630 Qdoba restaurants in 44 states and the District of Columbia, of which 316 were company-operated and 311 were franchise-operated. A net of 58 new Qdoba locations had opened in fiscal year 2012, versus 58 units in fiscal 2011, 15 units in fiscal 2010, and 56 in fiscal 2009. Qdoba was the second-largest fast-casual Mexican brand in the United States as of early 2013, based on number of restaurants. In 2012, sales revenues at all company-operated and franchise-operated Qdoba restaurant locations averaged $966,000, compared to $961,000 in fiscal 2011 and $923,000 in fiscal 2010. Sales at Qdoba restaurants open more than 12 months rose 2.4 percent in fiscal 2012, 5.3 percent in fiscal 2011, and 2.8 percent in fiscal 2010.

Menu Offerings and Food Preparation

Qdoba Mexican Grill billed itself as an "artisanal Mexican kitchen" where dishes were handcrafted with fresh ingredients and innovative flavors by skilled cooks. The menu included burritos, tacos, taco salads, three-cheese nachos, grilled quesadillas, tortilla soup, Mexican gumbo, chips and dips, five meals for kids, and, at select locations, a variety of breakfast burritos and breakfast quesadillas. Burritos and tacos could be customized with choices of five meats or just vegetarian ingredients. Salads were served in a crunchy flour tortilla bowl with a choice of two meats, or vegetarian, and included black bean corn salsa and fat-free picante ranch dressing.

Throughout each day at Qdoba restaurants, guacamole was prepared on site using fresh avocados, black and pinto beans were slow-simmered, shredded beef and pork were slow-roasted, and adobo-marinated chicken and steak were flame-grilled. Orders were prepared in full view, with customers having multiple options to customize meals to their individual taste and nutritional preferences. Qdoba restaurants offered a variety of catering options that could be tailored to feed groups of five to several hundred. Most Qdoba restaurants operated from 10:30 a.m. to 10:00 p.m. and had seating capacity for 60 to 80 persons, including outdoor patio seating at many locations. The average check at company-operated restaurants in fiscal 2012 was $10.28.

Site Selection and New Restaurant Development
Site selections for all new company-operated Qdoba restaurants were made after an economic analysis and a review of demographic data and other information relating to population density, traffic, competition, restaurant visibility and access, available parking, surrounding businesses, and opportunities for market penetration. Restaurants developed by franchisees were built to the parent-company specifications on sites it had reviewed. Most Qdoba restaurants were located in leased spaces in conventional large-scale retail projects and food courts in malls, smaller neighborhood retail strip centers, on or near college campuses, and in airports. Development costs for new Qdoba restaurants typically ranged from $0.6 million to $1.0 million, depending on the geographic region.

Restaurant Management and Operations
At Qdoba's company-owned restaurants, emphasis was placed on attracting, selecting, engaging, and retaining people who were committed to creating long-lasting, positive impacts on operating results. The company's core development tool was a "Career Map" that provided employees with detailed education by position, from entry level to area manager. High-performing general managers and hourly team members were certified to train and develop employees through a series of on-the-job and classroom training programs that focused on knowledge, skills, and behaviors. The Team Member Progression program within the Career Map tool recognized and rewarded three levels of achievement for cooks and line servers who displayed excellence in their positions. Team members had to possess, or acquire, specific technical and behavioral skill sets to reach an achievement level. All restaurant personnel were expected to contribute to delivering a great guest experience in the company's restaurants.

There was a three-tier management structure for company-owned Qdoba restaurants. Division vice presidents supervised regional operations managers, who supervised district managers, who in turn supervised restaurant managers. All three levels were eligible for periodic performance bonuses based on goals related to restaurant sales, profit optimization, guest satisfaction, and other operating performance standards

Beginning in March 2012, Qdoba and 90 percent of its franchisees entered into a five-year contract with an independent distributor to provide purchasing and distribution services for food ingredients and other supplies to Qdoba restaurants.

Advertising and Promotion
The goals of Qdoba's advertising and marketing activities were to build brand awareness and generate customer traffic. Both company-owned and franchised restaurants contributed to a fund primarily used for producing media ads and running regional or local advertising campaigns—so far, Qdoba had not undertaken any national advertising or promotions, although it did have a national presence on several social

media networks. The majority of Qdoba's marketing was done at the local level and entailed engaging and partnering with local schools, sports teams, community organizations, and businesses. There was growing use of digital marketing.

Expansion Plans Top management at Qdoba believed there was significant opportunity for continued long-term growth at Qdoba, with potential for approximately 2,000 Qdoba units across the United States. In fiscal 2013 (October 2012 through September 2013), management planned to open 70 to 85 new company and franchised restaurants.

Restaurant Industry Statistics

Restaurant industry sales were forecast to be a record-high $660 billion in 2013 at some 980,000 food establishments in the United States; this sales projection represented a 3.8 percent increase from 2012. In 2012, there were about 61 billion visits to commercial restaurant establishments across the United States.[11] According to survey data reported in the National Restaurant Association's 2012 *Restaurant Industry Forecast*, nearly 75 percent of consumers said they were more likely to visit a restaurant that offered locally produced food items; a similar percentage said they were trying to eat healthier now at restaurants than they did in 2009–2010. A majority of restaurants surveyed reported that their customers were ordering healthier, more nutritious menu items.

The fast-casual segment represented only about 4 percent of the overall commercial restaurant industry, with total sales estimated to be in the neighborhood of $31 billion in 2012.[12] However, it was a fast-growing category, having boosted its share of all quick-service restaurant sales from 5 percent to 14 percent over the past 10 years.[13] Systemwide sales for the Top 150 fast-casual restaurant chains grew 13.1 percent in 2012 and boosted their number of unit locations by 9.3 percent.[14] In 2012, 8 of the 10 fastest-growing restaurant chains were classified as

fast-casual restaurants—Chipotle Mexican Grill was ranked seventh in the top 10 (Chipotle, Moe's, and Qdoba were classified as fast-casual restaurants; Taco Bell was considered to be in the quick-service restaurant category).[15] Fast-casual was the only restaurant segment that had continued to grow in the United States during the recessionary period of 2008–2009 and sluggish economic recovery in 2010–2011, largely because consumers had responded quite positively to those fast-casual restaurants that used fresh ingredients and offered made-to-order alternatives to traditional fast food.[16] While some fast-casual restaurant concepts had faltered during the tough economic times, the segment as a whole benefited from fast-food consumers trading up and full-service consumers trading down.[17] According to the NPD Group, the unit counts of restaurant locations classified as fast-casual had risen over the past five years:[18]

During the same five-year period, unit counts among quick-service restaurants hovered between 1 percent growth and 2 percent declines. Unit counts at midscale restaurants decreased between 1 and 4 percent during the period; unit counts at casual-dining chains increased 2 percent in 2008, but then dropped by 2 to 3 percent in the three subsequent years. Many fast-casual chains were relatively small—only 35 of the top 100 fast-casual chains had 2012 sales of more than $100 million.

In 2011, the average consumer made nearly 61 visits to restaurants across all categories, of which 4 percent, or about 2.35 billion, were to

	Unit Count	Increase over Prior Year
2007	11,013	11%
2008	12,108	10%
2009	12,801	6%
2010	13,161	4%
2011	13,643	7%
2012*	14,911	9.3%

*Based on estimated unit growth of 9.3 percent, as cited in Naomi Van Til, "How the Fastest of the Fast-Casual Chains Sustain Growth," Technomic blog, http://blogs.Technomic.com, accessed June 12, 2013. Data for 2012 was not publicly available from the NPD Group.

restaurants classified as fast-casual.[19] About 61 percent of the customer traffic went to quick-service restaurants, while midscale restaurants and casual-dining chains received 10 percent and 11 percent, respectively. According to a 2013 Technomic study, 85 percent of consumers surveyed said they ate at fast-casual restaurants at least once a month.[20]

ENDNOTES

[1] See Dan Caplinger, "Has Chipotle Become the Perfect Stock?" www.dailyfinance.com, accessed February 14, 2012; and Tim Begany, "Why This Stock Could Be the Next McDonald's," www.streetauthority.com, accessed February 14, 2012.

[2] David A. Kaplan, "Chipotle's Growth Machine," *Fortune,* September 26, 2011, p. 138.

[3] Ibid; Aimee Picchi, "Chipotle Hints at a Price Increase," *MSN Money,* January 18, 2013, www.money.msn.com, accessed May 13, 2013; and "Chipotle Prices May Rise on Higher Food Costs," *The Huffington Post,* January 17, 2013, www.huffingtonpost.com, accessed May 13, 2013.

[4] According to information posted in the careers section at www.chipotle.com, accessed February 18, 2012, and May 13, 2013.

[5] Ibid.

[6] Company press release, February 6, 2012.

[7] Ibid.

[8] Leslie Patton, "Taco Bell Sees Market Share Recouped with Chipotle Menu," *Bloomberg,* January 11, 2012, www.bloomberg.com, accessed February 20, 2012.

[9] According to The NPD Group, Inc./Crest, year ending December 2012, based on consumer spending; this market share statistic from the NPD Group was cited in Yum! Brands 2012 10-K report, p. 4.

[10] According to information in "Fast Casuals Leading Restaurant Growth," www.fastcasual.com, March 21, 2013, accessed May 14, 2013.

[11] NPD Group press release, January 23, 2013.

[12] According to "2013 Fast Casual Top 100 Movers and Shakers Revealed," www.fastcasual.com, May 21, 2013, accessed June 12, 2013.

[13] "Top 100 Movers and Shakers: Fast Casual Trends," www.fastcasual.com, January 24, 2013, accessed May 14, 2013.

[14] Naomi Van Til, "How the Fastest of the Fast-Casual Chains Sustain Growth," Technomic blog, http://blogs.Technomic.com, accessed June 12, 2013.

[15] According to information posted at www.fast-casual.com, accessed June 12, 2013; the data source was Technomic, a provider of restaurant industry statistics.

[16] Valerie Killifer, "NPD: Fast Casual Only Growth Segment during Down Economy," www.fastcasual.com, accessed February 21, 2012. This article utilized information from a market research report by Bonnie Riggs, "Fast Casual: A Growing Market," NPD Group, which became available in February 2012.

[17] NPD Group, press release, February 8, 2012, www.npd.com, accessed February 21, 2012.

[18] Killifer, "NPD: Fast Casual Only Growth Segment during Down Economy."

[19] Ibid.

[20] Joe Satran, " 'Fast-Casual' Restaurants Are Visited by 85% of Americans at Least Once a Month," *The Huffington Post,* February 13, 2013, www.huffingtonpost.com, accessed May 14, 2013.

Mc Graw Hill Education **connect**   JOHN E. GAMBLE   Texas A&M University – Corpus Christi

Google was the leading Internet search firm in 2013, with nearly a 67 percent market share in search from home and work computers and a 97 percent share of searches performed from mobile devices. Google's business model allowed advertisers to bid on search terms that would describe their product or service on a cost-per-impression (CPI) or cost-per-click (CPC) basis. Google's search-based ads were displayed near Google's search results and generated advertising revenues of more than $43.6 billion in 2012. The company also generated revenues of about $2.4 billion in 2012 from licensing fees charged to businesses that wished to install Google's search appliance on company intranets. In addition, a variety of new ventures contributed to the company's consolidated revenues. The most notable of which was the company's recently acquired Motorola Mobility division that contributed revenues of $4.1 billion in 2012. New ventures such as the acquisition of Motorola's smartphone operations were becoming a growing priority with Google management since the company dominated the market for search-based ads and sought additional opportunities to sustain its extraordinary growth in revenues, earnings, and net cash provided by operations.

Another important initiative under way in 2013 was Google's cloud computing productivity package that was intended to change the market for commonly used business applications such as word processing, spreadsheets, and presentation software by moving them from the desktop to the Internet. Google had also entered into alliances with Intel, Sony, DISH Network, Logitech, and other firms to develop the technology and products required to launch Google TV. Google TV was launched in the United States in 2011 and allowed users to search live network and cable programming, streaming videos from providers such as Netflix, Amazon Video On Demand, and YouTube, and recorded programs on a DVR. The company also launched its Google + social networking site in 2011 to capture additional advertising opportunities. The company's Google Glass wearable interactive computer display was among the company's most publicized new projects and ventures. The eyeglasses containing a camera and computer display were expected to be available to consumers by year-end 2013. The company was also developing an Android-powered wristwatch and a video game console to compete against Microsoft's Xbox One, Sony's PlayStation 4, and Nintendo's Wii.

While Google's growth initiatives seemed to take the company into new industries and thrust it into competition with companies ranging from Facebook to Microsoft to Apple, its CEO, Eric Schmidt, saw the new ventures as natural extensions of the company's mission to "organize the world's information and make it universally accessible and useful."[1] In April 2012, he explained the company's wide-ranging strategic initiatives by commenting, "In some ways we have run the company as to let

Copyright © 2013 by John E. Gamble. All rights reserved.

1,000 flowers bloom, but once they do bloom you want to put together a coherent bouquet."[2]

Company History

The development of Google's search technology began in January 1996 when Stanford University computer science graduate students Larry Page and Sergey Brin collaborated to develop a new search engine. They named the new search engine BackRub because of its ability to rate websites for relevancy by examining the number of back links pointing to the website. The approach for assessing the relevancy of websites to a particular search query used by other websites at the time was based on examining and counting meta tags and keywords included on various websites. By 1997, the search accuracy of BackRub had allowed it to gain a loyal following among Silicon Valley Internet users. Yahoo co-founder David Filo was among the converted, and in 1998 he convinced Brin and Page to leave Stanford to focus on making their search technology the backbone of a new Internet company.

BackRub would be renamed Google, which was a play on the word *googol*—a mathematical term for a number represented by the numeral 1 followed by 100 zeroes. Brin and Page's adoption of the new name reflected their mission to organize a seemingly infinite amount of information on the Internet. In August 1998, a Stanford professor arranged for Brin and Page to meet at his home with a potential angel investor to demonstrate the Google search engine. The investor, who had been a founder of Sun Microsystems, was immediately impressed with Google's search capabilities but was too pressed for time to hear much of Brin and Page's informal presentation. The investor stopped the two during the presentation and suggested, "Instead of us discussing all the details, why don't I just write you a check?"[3] The two partners held the investor's $100,000 check, made payable to Google Inc., for two weeks while they scrambled to set up a corporation named Google Inc. and open a corporate bank account. The two officers of the freshly incorporated company went on to raise a total of $1 million in venture capital from family, friends, and other angel investors by the end of September 1998.

Even with a cash reserve of $1 million, the two partners ran Google on a shoestring budget, with its main servers built by Brin and Page from discounted computer components and its four employees operating out of a garage owned by a friend of the founders. By year-end 1998, Google's beta version was handling 10,000 search queries per day and *PC Magazine* had named the company to its list of "Top 100 Web Sites and Search Engines for 1998."

The new company recorded successes at a lightning-fast pace, with the search kernel answering more than 500,000 queries per day and Red Hat agreeing to become the company's first search customer in early 1999. Google attracted an additional $25 million in funding from two leading Silicon Valley venture capital firms by midyear 1999 to support further growth and enhancements to Google's search technology. The company's innovations in 2000 included wireless search technology, search capabilities in 10 languages, and a Google Toolbar browser plug-in that allowed computer users to search the Internet without first visiting a Google-affiliated web portal or Google's home page. Features added through 2004 included Google News, Google Product Search, Google Scholar, and Google Local. The company also expanded its index of web pages to more than 8 billion and increased its country domains to more than 150 by 2004.

The Initial Public Offering

Google's April 29, 2004, initial public offering (IPO) registration became the most talked-about planned offering involving an Internet company since the dot-com bust of 2000. At the conclusion of the first day of trading, Google's shares had appreciated by 18 percent to make Brin and Page each worth approximately $3.8 billion. Also, an estimated 900 to 1,000 Google employees were worth at least $1 million, with 600 to 700 holding at least $2 million in Google stock. On average, each of Google's 2,292 staff members held approximately $1.7 million in company stock, excluding the holdings of the top five executives. Stanford University also enjoyed a $179.5 million windfall from its stock holdings granted for its early investment in Brin and Page's search engine. Some of Google's early contractors and consultants also profited handsomely from forgoing fees in return for stock options in the company. One such contractor was Abbe Patterson, who took options for 4,000 shares rather than a $5,000 fee for preparing a PowerPoint presentation and speaking notes for one of Brin and Page's first presentations to venture capitalists. After two splits and four days of trading, her 16,000 shares were worth $1.7 million.[4] The company executed a second public offering of 14,159,265 shares of common stock in September 2005. The number of shares issued represented the first eight digits to the right of the decimal point for the value of π (pi). The issue added more than $4 billion to Google's liquid assets.

Exhibit 1 tracks the performance of Google's common shares between August 19, 2004, and June 2013.

Google Feature Additions between 2005 and 2013

Google used its vast cash reserves to make strategic acquisitions that might lead to the development of new Internet applications offering advertising opportunities. Google Earth was launched in 2005 after the company acquired Keyhole, a digital mapping company, in 2004. Google Earth and its companion software Google Maps were enhanced in 2007 with the addition of street-view images taken by traveling Google camera cars. Digital images, webcam feeds, and videos captured by Internet users could be linked to locations displayed by Google Maps. Real estate listings and short personal messages could also be linked to Google Maps locations. In 2010, Google further enhanced Google Maps with the inclusion of an Earth View mode that allowed users to view 3-D images of various locations from the ground level. Other search features added to

Google between 2005 and 2013 that users found particularly useful included Book Search, Music Search, Video Search, Patent Search, and the expansion of Google News to include archived news articles dating to 1900.

Google also expanded its website features beyond search functionality to include its Gmail software, a web-based calendar, web-based document, and spreadsheet applications, its Picasa web photo albums, and a translation feature that accommodated 71 languages. The company also released services for mobile phone uses such as Mobile Web Search, Blogger Mobile, Gmail, Google News, and Maps for Mobile.

Google's Business Model

Google's business model had evolved since the company's inception to include revenue beyond the licensing fees charged to corporations needing search capabilities on company intranets or websites. The 2000 development of keyword-targeted advertising expanded its business model to include revenues from the placement of highly targeted text-only sponsor ads adjacent to its search results. Google was able to target its ads to specific users based on the user's browsing history. The addition of advertising-based revenue allowed Google to increase annual revenues from $220,000 in 1999 to more than $86 million in 2001. A summary of Google's financial performance for selected years between 2001 and 2012 is presented in Exhibit 2. The company's balance sheets for 2011 and 2012 are presented in Exhibit 3.

Google Search Appliance

Google's search technology could be integrated into a third party's website or intranet if search functionality was important to the customer. Google's Site Search allowed enterprises ranging from small businesses to public companies to license Google's search appliance for use on their websites for as little as $100 per year. The Google Search Appliance was designed for use on corporate intranets to allow employees to search company documents and databases. The Search

EXHIBIT 1

Performance of Google's Stock Price, August 19, 2004, to June 2013

(a) Trend in Google Inc.'s Common Stock Price

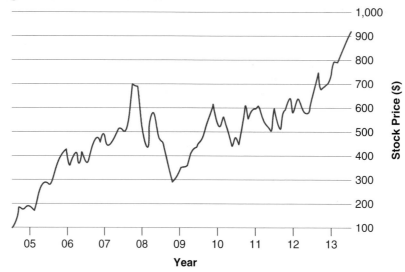

(b) Performance of Google Inc.'s Stock Price versus the S&P 500 Index

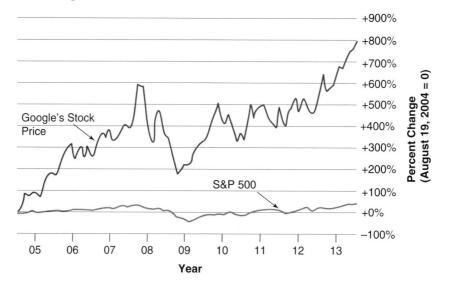

Appliance included a variety of security features to ensure that only employees with proper authority were able to view restricted documents. The Google Mini Search Appliance was designed for small businesses with 50,000 to 300,000 documents stored on local PCs and servers. The Google Mini hardware and software package could be licensed online (at www.google.com/enterprise/mini) at prices ranging from $2,990 to $9,900, depending on document count capability.

Google's more robust search appliance had a document count capability of up to 30 million documents and was designed for midsized to global businesses. Licensing fees for the Google Search Appliance ranged from $30,000 to $600,000, depending on document count capability.

AdWords

Google AdWords allowed advertisers, either independently through Google's automated

EXHIBIT 2

Financial Summary for Google, 2001, 2005, 2008–2012 ($ millions, except per share amounts)

	2012	2011	2010	2009	2008	2005	2001
Revenues:							
Google (advertising and other)	$46,039	$37,905	$29,321	$23,651	$21,796	$6,139	$ 86
Motorola Mobility	4,136	—	—	—	—	—	—
Total revenues:	$50,175	$37,905	$29,321	$23,651	$21,796	$6,139	$ 86
Costs and expenses:							
Cost of revenues—Google	17,176	13,188	10,417	8,844	8,622	2,577	14
Cost of revenues—Motorola Mobile	3,458	—	—	—	—	—	—
Research and development	6,793	5,162	3,762	2,843	2,793	600	17
Sales and marketing	6,143	4,589	2,799	1,984	1,946	468	20
General and administrative	3,845	2,724	1,962	1,667	1,803	387	25
Contribution to Google Foundation	—	—	—	—	—	90,000	—
Total costs and expenses	37,415	26,163	18,940	15,338	15,164	4,121	75
Income (loss) from Operations	12,760	11,742	10,381	8,312	6,632	2,017	11
Impairment of equity investments	—	—	—	—	(1,095)	—	—
Interest income (expense) and other, net	626	584	415	69	316	124	(1)
Income (loss) before income taxes	13,386	12,326	10,796	8,381	5,854	2,142	10
Provision for income taxes	2,598	2,589	2,291	1,861	1,627	676	3
Net income (loss)	$ 10,737	$ 9,737	$ 8,505	$ 6,520	$ 4,227	$ 1,465	$ 7
Net income (loss) per share:							
Basic	$32.81	$30.17	$26.69	$20.62	$13.46	$5.31	$0.07
Diluted	$32.31	$29.76	$26.31	$20.41	$13.31	$5.02	$0.04
Number of shares used in per share calculations:							
Basic	327	323	319	316	314	276	95
Diluted	331	327	323	319	318	292	187
Net cash provided by operating activities	$ 16,619	$14,565	$11,081	$ 9,316	$ 7,853	$ 2,459	n.a.
Cash, cash equivalents, and marketable securities	48,088	44,626	34,975	24,485	15,846	8,034	n.a.
Total assets	93,798	72,574	57,851	40,497	31,768	10,272	n.a.
Total long-term liabilities	7,746	5,516	1,614	1,745	1,227	107	n.a.
Total stockholders' equity	71,715	58,145	46,241	36,004	28,239	9,419	n.a.

Source: Google, Form S-1, filed April 29, 2004; Google 10-K reports, various years.

tools or with the assistance of Google's marketing teams, to create text-based ads that would appear alongside Google search results. AdWords users could evaluate the effectiveness of their advertising expenditures with Google through the use of performance reports that tracked the effectiveness of each ad. Google also offered a keyword targeting program that suggested synonyms for keywords entered by advertisers, a traffic estimator that

helped potential advertisers anticipate charges, and multiple payment options that included charges to credit cards, debit cards, and monthly invoicing.

Larger advertisers were offered additional services to help run large, dynamic advertising campaigns. Such assistance included the availability of specialists with expertise in various industries to offer suggestions for targeting potential customers and identifying relevant

EXHIBIT 3

Google's Balance Sheets, 2011–2012 ($ millions, except per share amounts)

	2012	2011
Assets		
Current assets:		
Cash and cash equivalents	$14,778	$ 9,983
Marketable securities	33,310	34,643
Accounts receivable, net of allowance of $133 and $101	7,885	5,427
Inventories	505	—
Receivable under reverse repurchase agreements	700	745
Deferred income taxes, net	1,144	215
Prepaid revenue share, expenses, and other assets	2,132	1,745
Total current assets	60,454	52,758
Prepaid revenue share, expenses, and other assets, non-current	2,011	499
Non-marketable equity securities	1,469	790
Property and equipment, net	11,854	9,603
Intangible assets, net	7,473	1,578
Goodwill	10,537	7,346
Total assets	$93,798	$72,574
Liabilities and Stockholders' Equity		
Current liabilities:		
Accounts payable	$ 2,012	$ 588
Short-term debt	2,549	1,218
Accrued compensation and benefits	2,239	1,818
Accrued expenses and other current liabilities	3,258	1,370
Accrued revenue share	1,471	1,168
Securities lending payable	1,673	2,007
Deferred revenue	895	547
Income taxes payable, net	240	197
Total current liabilities	14,337	8,913
Long-term debt	2,988	2,986
Deferred revenue, long-term	100	44
Income taxes payable, long-term	2,046	1,693
Deferred income taxes, net, non-current	1,872	287
Other long-term liabilities	740	506
Stockholders' equity:		
Common stock and additional paid-in capital	22,835	20,264
Accumulated other comprehensive income	538	276
Retained earnings	48,342	37,605
Total stockholders' equity	71,715	58,145
Total liabilities and stockholders' equity	$93,798	$72,574

Source: Google 2012 10-K report.

keywords. Google's advertising specialists helped develop ads for customers that would increase click-through rates and purchase rates. Google also offered its large advertising customers bulk posting services that helped launch and manage campaigns including ads using hundreds or thousands of keywords.

Google's search-based ads were priced using an auction system that allowed advertisers to bid on keywords that would describe their product or service. Bids could be made on a cost-per-impression (CPI) or cost-per-click (CPC) basis. Most Google advertisers placed bids based on CPC frequency rather than how many times an ad was displayed by Google. Google's auction pricing model assigned each bidder a quality score, which was determined by the advertiser's past keyword click-through rate and the relevance of the ad text. Advertisers with high quality scores were offered lower minimum bids than advertisers with poor quality scores.

Google allowed users to pay a CPC rate lower than their bid price if their bid was considerably more than the next highest bid. For example, an advertiser who bid $0.75 per click for a particular keyword would be charged only $0.51 per click if the next highest bid was only $0.50. The AdWords discounter ensured that advertisers paid only 1 cent more than the next highest bid, regardless of the actual amount of their bid.

AdSense

Google's AdSense program allowed web publishers to share in the advertising revenues generated by Google's text ads. The AdSense program served content-relevant Google text ads to pages on Google Network websites. For example, an Internet user reading an article about the state of the economy at Reuters.com would see Google text ads by investment magazines and companies specializing in home business opportunities. Google Network members shared in the advertising revenue whenever a site visitor clicked a Google ad

displayed on their sites. The more than 1 million Google Network members did not pay a fee to participate in the program and received about 60 percent of advertising dollars generated from the ads. Google's AdSense program also allowed mobile phone operators to share in Google revenues if text and image ads were displayed on mobile handsets. Owners of dormant domain names, web-based game sites, video sites, and news feed services could also participate in the AdSense program. The breakdown of Google's revenues by source for 2008 through 2012 is presented in Exhibit 4.

Motorola Mobility and Other Revenue Sources

The 2006 acquisition of YouTube allowed Google to receive advertising revenues for ads displayed during Internet videos, while its 2008 $3.1 billion acquisition of DoubleClick allowed the company to generate advertising revenues through banner ads. The company's 2008 launch of Google Checkout generated fees of as much as 2 percent of the transaction amount for purchases made at participating e-retailer sites. Google's business model was further expanded in 2008 to include licensing fees paid by users of its web-based Google Apps document, spreadsheet, and presentation software. While the number of Google Apps users were growing, the cloud-based productivity software package had yet to develop significant revenues

EXHIBIT 4					
Google's Revenues by Source, 2008–2012 ($ millions)					
	2012	**2011**	**2010**	**2009**	**2008**
Advertising revenues:					
Google websites	$31,221	$26,145	$19,444	$15,722	$14,414
Google Network websites	12,465	10,386	8,792	7,167	6,715
Total advertising revenues	43,686	36,531	28,236	22,889	21,129
Licensing and other revenues	2,353	1,374	1,085	762	667
Total Google revenues	46,039	37,905	29,321	23,651	21,796
Total Motorola Mobility revenues	4,136	—	—	—	—
Consolidated revenues	$50,175	$37,905	$29,321	$23,651	$21,796

Source: Google 10-K reports, various years.

through 2012. And, while generating YouTube advertising revenues had proven challenging through 2010, Google's revenues from banner ads displayed on YouTube and other websites were projected to approach $3.7 billion in 2013.

The company's most ambitious new venture was its 2012 acquisition of Motorola Mobility for $12.5 billion, which put it in the hardware segment of the smartphone and tablet computer industries. Analysts following the transaction saw the move to acquire Motorola Mobility as a direct attempt to mimic Apple's strategy used for the iPhone and iPad that tightly integrated hardware and software for its most profitable and fastest growing products. Google had launched its Android operating system for mobile phones in 2008 and allowed wireless phone manufacturers such as Samsung, HTC, and Nokia to produce Internet-enabled phones boasting features similar to those available on Apple's iPhone. By 2012, Android was the leading smartphone platform with a 50.9 percent market share. Google's acquisition of Motorola Mobility boosted 2012 revenues by more than $4 billion from the sale of smartphones, tablet computers, and communication devices for the home.

Google's Strategy and Competitive Position in 2013

Google's Strategies to Dominate Internet Advertising

The majority of Google's acquisitions since its 2004 IPO, and its research and development activities, were directed at increasing the company's dominance in Internet advertising. The addition of Google Maps, local search, airline travel information, weather, Book Search, Gmail, Blogger, and other features increased traffic to Google sites and gave the company more opportunities to serve ads to Internet users. However, not all of Google's innovations became a success in the marketplace. For example, the company abandoned its Knol open-source encyclopedia in 2012, and its Orkut social networking site had proven to be an abject failure.

Google made a second attempt at developing a social networking site in 2011 when it launched Google+ . Like Facebook, users could maintain profiles, post comments, link to content from other Internet sites, and keep online photo albums. Google+ also worked on mobile devices, and allowed users to participate in multiperson video chats. In 2013, Google+ had 100 million users, who were logged on an average of 6.8 minutes per month, compared to Facebook's 850 million users, who spent about 6.7 hours per month updating their pages. The company believed that Google+ would grow to challenge Facebook since Google+ account information could be linked with Google's other products and services. For example, Google+ users who used Google to search for a friend with a common name could pull up information on the exact individual linked to their Google+ account.

Google's strategy to dominate Internet advertising also entailed becoming the number one search engine used not only in the United States but also around the world. In 2013, Google's search-based ads could be delivered to Internet users in 41 languages. More than 50 percent of the company's 2012 revenues and traffic were generated from outside the United States, and the percentage of sales from outside the United States was expected to grow as Google entered emerging markets such as Russia and China. China was a particularly attractive market for Google since it had more Internet users (over 300 million) than any other country in the world. However, Google's 2006 entry into China was accompanied by challenges, including strong competition from local search provider Baidu and requirements by the Chinese government to censor search results that were critical of the government. Google complied with government censorship requirements until early 2010, when it began redirecting users of its censored Google.cn site in China to its uncensored Hong Kong search site, Google.com.hk. After continuing disagreements with the Chinese government, Google agreed in June 2010 to stop the automatic redirects to its Hong Kong site. Instead, it presented

Google.cn users with a link to Google.com.hk. In 2013, 65 percent of Internet searches in China were performed by Baidu, while Google held a 3 percent share of searches in that country.

Google's Emerging Rivalry with Apple in Smartphones and Tablet Computers

In 2012, more than 6.8 billion people worldwide and 234 million Americans ages 13 and older owned and used mobile phones. More than 103 million Americans and about 2 billion mobile phone users worldwide accessed the Internet from smartphones. Apple Inc. built its early reputation in the 1980s and 1990s on its innovative Mac computer lines, but in 2012, only $23.2 billion of its net sales of $156.5 billion came from the sale of computers. In 2013, Apple was the world's largest seller of tablet computers and personal media players with market shares of 40 percent and 73 percent, respectively. The company's iPhone was the second best-selling smartphone with a 17 percent market share in early 2013. The iPhone's market share had declined from 25 percent at year-end 2012, as had its share of the tablet computer market. The iPad's market share had fallen from 85 percent in 2011 and 58 percent in 2012. Nevertheless, Apple's sales of iPads and iPhones had grown dramatically since 2010. The iPhone accounted

for $80.5 billion of Apple's total sales of $156.5 billion in 2012 compared to $25.2 billion of total sales of $65.2 billion in 2010. The iPad contributed revenues of $32.4 billion in 2012 compared to $5 billion in 2010. The iPod and related music products accounted for sales of more than $14.1 billion in 2012. The company's hefty profit margins on its electronic devices allowed it to record a net income of $41.7 billion in 2012.

Apple's revenue growth continued in 2013, with the company setting a revenue record during the second quarter of 2013. The record sales and earnings were driven largely by the iPhone, which grew to a record 37.4 million units during the quarter, compared to 35.1 million in the same quarter during 2012. iPad sales had increased from 11.8 million units in the second quarter of 2012 to 19.5 million units during the second quarter of 2013. The company's strong performance in 2011 allowed its stock price to increase so much that it became the most valuable company in the world, as measured by market capitalization. Even though the company continued to set new revenue records each quarter during 2012 and early 2013, the company's declining market shares in key product categories and declining profit margins had contributed to a drop in its stock price from a high of $702 in September 2012 to a range of $390 to $425 in mid-2013. A summary of Apple's financial performance between 2008 and 2012 is presented in Exhibit 5.

EXHIBIT 5

Financial Summary for Apple Inc., 2008–2012 ($ millions)

	Fiscal Year Ended June 30				
	2012	**2011**	**2010**	**2009**	**2008**
Net sales	$156,508	$108,249	$65,225	$42,905	$37,491
Operating income	55,241	33,790	18,385	11,740	8,327
Net income	41,733	25,922	14,013	8,235	6,119
Cash, cash equivalents, and marketable securities	$121,251	$81,570	$51,011	$33,992	$24,490
Total assets	176,064	116,371	75,183	47,501	36,171
Long-term obligations	16,664	10,100	5,531	3,502	1,745
Stockholders' equity	118,210	76,615	47,791	31,640	22,297

Source: Apple Inc. 10-K reports, various years.

Google's introduction of its Android operating system for smartphones in 2008 allowed it to increase its share of mobile searches from about 60 percent to approximately 97 percent in 2013. Android was not a phone but an operating system that Google made available free to any phone manufacturer wishing to market mobile devices with Internet capability. Android's core applications matched most features of Apple's iPhone. By 2010, all major mobile phone providers had added smartphone models running Android software to its lineup of handsets, and despite Google's late entry into the market, Android's market share had increased from zero in 2008 to more than 52 percent in May 2013 (see Exhibit 6).

Similar to its relationship with mobile phone manufacturers, Google allowed mobile apps developers to use the Android operating system free of licensing fees. The worldwide market for mobile apps was estimated at $17.5 billion by 2012, and in 2013 more than 800,000 free and paid smartphone apps were available at both Apple's App Store and the Google Play Store. Google escalated its growing competitive rivalry with Apple in 2012 with its $12.5 billion acquisition of Motorola Mobility. The acquisition would allow Google to design and market its own line of smartphones and tablet computers and begin earning profits from the sale of hardware. Google launched its first internally developed tablet computer in June 2012. The $199 Nexus 7 included a 7-inch screen and a camera and was designed to display books and other media available through the company's Google Play service. The second-generation Nexus tablets were expected to be launched in July 2013. Also in 2013, Google's Motorola Mobility division offered 22 various smartphone models and a dual-core XOOM tablet computer. Motorola Home division that produced and marketed modems, digital baby monitors, cordless telephones, weather radios, and other home communication devices was divested by Google in December 2012 for $2.35 billion.

Google's Strategic Offensive to Control the Desktop

Google's senior management believed that, in the very near future, most computer software programs used by businesses would move from local hard drives or intranets to the Internet. Many information technology analysts agreed that cloud computing would become a common software platform that was expected to become a $95 billion market by 2013. Moving software applications to the cloud offered many possible benefits to corporate users, including lower software acquisition costs, lower computing support costs, and easier collaboration among employees in different locations. Google Apps was launched in 2008 as a competing product to Microsoft Office and was hosted on computers in Google's data centers and included Gmail, a calendar, instant messaging, word processing, spreadsheets, presentation software, and file storage space. Google Apps could be licensed by corporate customers

---

EXHIBIT 6

U.S. Smartphone Platform Market Share Rankings, Selected Periods, May 2010–May 2013

Smartphone Platform	May 2010	May 2011	May 2012	May 2013
Android	13.0%	38.1%	50.9%	52.4%
Apple	24.4	28.6	31.9	39.2
BlackBerry	41.7	24.7	11.4	4.8
Microsoft	13.2	5.8	4.0	3.2
Others	7.7	2.8	1.8	0.4
Total	100.0%	100.0%	100.0%	100.0%

Source: ComScore.com.

at $50 per user per year. The licensing fee for the Microsoft Office and Outlook package was typically $350 per user per year. Five million businesses had subscribed to Google Apps by year-end 2012, generating an estimated $1 billion in revenue for the year. Microsoft had developed a competing cloud-based Office 365 productivity package that small businesses could subscribe to for $150 per year.

Google's Chrome browser, which was launched in September 2008, and Chrome operating system (OS) launched in July 2009 were developed specifically to accommodate cloud computing applications. The bare-bones Chrome browser was built on a multiprocessor design that would allow users to operate spreadsheets, word processing, video editing, and other applications on separate tabs that could be run simultaneously. The Chrome browser also provided Google with a defense against moves by Microsoft to make it more difficult for Google to deliver relevant search-based ads to Internet users. Microsoft's Internet Explorer 10 allowed users to hide their Internet address and viewing history, which prevented Google from collecting user-specific information needed for ad targeting. Mozilla's Firefox browser employed a similar feature that prevented third parties from tracking a user's viewing habits. Google had entered into agreements with Samsung, Acer, Hewlett-Packard, and Lenovo to begin producing Chromebook portable computers that would use the Chrome OS and Chrome browser to

access the cloud-based Google Apps productivity software. Worldwide market share statistics for the leading browsers for selected periods between June 2010 and June 2013 are presented in Exhibit 7.

Google's Initiatives to Expand Search to Television

In mid-2010, Google entered an alliance with Intel, Sony, Logitech, Best Buy, DISH Network, and Adobe to develop Google TV. Google TV would be built on the Android platform and would run the Chrome browser software to search live network and cable programming; streaming videos from providers such as Netflix, Amazon Video On Demand, and YouTube; and recorded programs on a DVR. Google TV users would also be able to use their televisions to browse the web and run cloud-based applications such as Google Apps. DISH Network satellite service customers could use Google TV's features with the addition of a Logitech set-top box or Sony Internet TV.

Google acquired On2 Technologies, which was the leading developer of video compression technology, in February 2010 in a $124 million stock and cash transaction. The acquisition of On2 was expected to improve the video streaming capabilities of Google TV. Google also lobbied the U.S. Federal Communications Commission for "Net neutrality" rules that would require Internet providers to manage traffic in a manner that would not restrict

EXHIBIT 7

Worldwide Browser Market Share Rankings, Selected Periods, June 2010–June 2013

Browser	June 2010	June 2011	June 2012	June 2013
Chrome	9%	22%	32%	43%
Internet Explorer	53	42	32	25
Firefox	31	28	25	20
Safari	4	5	7	8
Opera	2	2	2	1
Others	1	1	2	3
Total	100%	100%	100%	100%

Source: gs.statcounter.com.

high-bandwidth services such as Internet television. The company was also testing an ultrafast broadband network in several cities across the United States that was as much as 100 times faster than what was offered by competing Internet providers. Google management had stated that the company did not intend to launch a nationwide Internet service, but did want to expose consumers to Internet applications and content that would be possible with greater bandwidth and faster transmission speeds.

Google's Internet Rivals

Google's ability to sustain its competitive advantage among search companies was a function of its ability to maintain strong relationships with Internet users, advertisers, and websites. In 2012, Google was the world's most-visited Internet site, with more than 900 million unique Internet users going to Google sites each month to search for information. A comparison of the percentage of Internet searches among websites offering search capabilities for selected periods between May 2010 and June 2013 is shown in Exhibit 8.

Microsoft Online Services

Microsoft Corporation recorded fiscal 2012 revenues and a net income of approximately $73.7 billion and $17.0 billion, respectively, through the sales of computer software, consulting services, video game hardware, and online services. Windows and Microsoft Office accounted for more than one-half of the company's 2012 revenues and nearly all of its operating profit. The company's online services business recorded sales of nearly $2.9 billion and an operating loss of $8.2 billion during fiscal 2012. The operating loss in 2012 included a onetime goodwill impairment charge of $6.2 billion. Microsoft's online services business generated revenues from banner ads displayed at the company's MSN Web portal and its affiliated websites and search-based ads displayed with Bing results. Microsoft's websites made the company among the most-visited Internet destinations in 2013, with approximately 500 million unique visitors each month. A financial summary for Microsoft Corporation and its Online Services Division is provided in Exhibit 9.

Microsoft's search business was launched in November 2004 as Live Search to compete directly with Google and slow whatever intentions Google might have to threaten Microsoft in its core operating system and productivity software businesses. Microsoft's concern with threats posed by Google arose shortly after Google's IPO, when Bill Gates noticed that many of the Google job postings on its site were nearly identical to Microsoft job specifications. Recognizing that the position announcements had more to do with operating-system design than search, Gates e-mailed key Microsoft executives, warning, "We have to watch these

EXHIBIT 8

U.S. Search Engine Market Share Rankings, Selected Periods, May 2010–June 2013

Search Entity	Percent of Searches			
	May 2010	July 2011	May 2012	June 2013
Google Sites	63.7%	65.1%	66.7%	66.7%
Microsoft Sites	12.1	14.4	15.4	17.9
Yahoo Sites	18.3	16.1	13.4	11.4
Ask.com	3.6	2.9	3.0	2.7
AOL	2.3	1.5	1.5	1.3
Total	100.0%	100.0%	100.0%	100.0%

Source: ComScore.com.

EXHIBIT 9

Financial Summary for Microsoft Corporation and Microsoft's Online Services Business Unit, 2008–2012 ($ millions)

Financial Summary for Microsoft Corporation

	2012	2011	2010	2009	2008
Revenue	$73,723	$69,943	$62,484	$58,437	$60,420
Operating income	21,763	27,161	24,098	20,363	22,492
Net income	16,978	23,150	18,760	14,569	17,681
Cash, cash equivalents, and short-term investments	$63,040	$52,772	$36,788	$31,447	$23,662
Total assets	121,271	108,704	86,113	77,888	72,793
Long-term obligations	22,220	22,847	13,791	11,296	6,621
Stockholders' equity	66,363	57,083	46,175	39,558	36,286

Financial Summary for Microsoft's Online Services Business Unit

	2012	2011	2010	2009	2008
Revenue	$2,867	$2,528	$2,201	$2,121	$3,214
Operating income (loss)	(8,121)	(2,557)	(2,337)	(1,641)	(1,233)

Source: Microsoft 10-K reports, various years.

guys. It looks like they are building something to compete with us."[5] Gates later commented that Google was "more like us than anyone else we have ever competed with."[6]

Gates speculated that Google's long-term strategy involved the development of web-based software applications comparable to Word, Excel, PowerPoint, and other Microsoft products. Microsoft's strategy to compete with Google was keyed to making its search tool more effective than Google at providing highly relevant search results. Microsoft believed that any conversion of Google users to Live Search would reduce the number of PC users who might ultimately adopt Google's web-based word processing, spreadsheet, and presentation software packages. In 2008, Microsoft paid more than $100 million to acquire Powerset, which was the developer of a semantic search engine. Semantic search technology offered the opportunity to surpass the relevancy of Google's search results since semantic search evaluated the meaning of a word or phrase and considered its context when returning search results. Even though semantic search had the capability to answer questions stated in

common language, semantic search processing time took several seconds to return results. The amount of time necessary to conduct a search had caused Microsoft to limit Powerset's search index to only articles listed in Wikipedia. Microsoft's developers were focused on increasing the speed of its semantic search capabilities so that its search index could be expanded to a greater number of Internet pages. The company's developers also incorporated some of Powerset's capabilities into its latest-generation search engine, Bing, which was launched in June 2009. Banner ads comprised the bulk of Microsoft's online advertising revenues, since its Bing search engine accounted for only 17.9 percent of online searches in July 2013.

Microsoft was also moving forward with its own approach to cloud computing. The company's Windows Live service allowed Internet users to store files online at its password-protected SkyDrive site. SkyDrive's online file storage allowed users to access and edit files from multiple locations, share files with co-workers who might need editing privileges, or make files available in a public folder for wide distribution. Office 365 was Microsoft's cloud-based productivity software package and Azure was intended to allow businesses to reduce computing costs by allowing Microsoft to host its operating programs and data files. In addition to reducing capital expenditures for software upgrades and added server capacity, Azure's offsite hosting provided data security in the event of natural disasters such as fires or hurricanes.

Google's Performance in Early 2013

During its first quarter of fiscal 2013, Google had been able to achieve year-over-year revenue growth of 31 percent. The company's advertising revenues increased by 16 percent compared to the same period in 2012, and its operating income and net income recorded year-over-year increases of 25 percent and 24 percent, respectively. Commenting on the company's early 2013 successes, CEO Larry Page said the company was "investing in our products that aim to improve billions of people's lives all around the world."[7]

The company's strategic priorities in 2013 focused on expanding its share of mobile search and smartphone platforms, making Google+ some a strong competitor to Facebook, pushing forward with its plans to become the dominant provider of cloud computing solutions, expanding its broadband television service, increasing search advertising revenues from markets outside the United States, and extending its migration into hardware design, production, and marketing.

Generating an acceptable return on its $12.5 billion Motorola Mobility acquisition was Google's highest priority in its hardware-related ventures. Google was able to offset the cost of the acquisition through the sale of Motorola patents that generated $4 billion and through the sale of the Motorola Home division for $2.35 billion. However, some industry observers were skeptical of the value of the

acquisition at any price given the maturity of the market and Google's lack of experience in hardware design and manufacturing. As of mid-2013, Motorola was not among the leading brands of smartphones, and reviews on the Moto X—the first Google-designed Motorola product—were lackluster. Such reviews were expected by Google executives since the company had been careful not to provide the Motorola division with any technological advantages that might adversely affect its key Android hardware partners such as Samsung, HTC, or LG. Additionally, the market growth for smartphones in most developed countries had slowed considerably since Google announced its intention to acquire Motorola Mobility. The maturing of the smartphone market in developed countries had already given rise to increased price competition in the United States in 2013. Google's Motorola division recorded operating losses of $353 million during the fourth quarter of 2012 and $271 billion during the first quarter of 2013.

The company did expect its acquisition of Motorola Mobility to provide the capabilities needed to expand into a variety of consumer electronics product categories beyond smartphones. In mid-2013, the company had a waiting list for its $1,500 developer model Google Glass models and expected to launch a lower-priced mass market line by year-end 2013. The Glass project was not without challenges as individuals and privacy groups were concerned about the capacity of Google Glass wearers to record the conversations and actions of those near the wearer. Less-controversial new hardware projects under development at Google in 2013 were a wristwatch powered by the Android operating system and a video-game console. The company's ability to sustain its lofty stock price, which had appreciated by approximately 30 percent during the first six months of 2013, would ultimately be determined by the quality of its strategy and execution in all of its business units.

ENDNOTES

[1] Google, www.google.com/corporate, accessed July 13, 2010.

[2] As quoted in Brad Stone, "The Education of Larry Page," *Bloomberg Businessweek,* April 15, 2012, pp. 12–14.

[3] Quoted in Google's Corporate Information, www.google.com/corporate/history.html.

[4] "For Some Who Passed on Google Long Ago, Wistful Thinking," *The Wall Street Journal Online,* August 23, 2004.

[5] Quoted in "Gates vs. Google," *Fortune,* April 18, 2005.

[6] Ibid.

[7] As quoted in "Google Announces First Quarter 2013 Results," Google press r elease, April 18, 2013.

Nucor Corporation in 2012: Using Economic Downturns as an Opportunity to Grow Stronger

ARTHUR A. THOMPSON The University of Alabama

In 2012, Nucor Corp., with a production capacity approaching 27 million tons, was the largest manufacturer of steel and steel products in North America and ranked as the 11th-largest steel company in the world based on tons shipped in 2011. It was regarded as a low-cost producer, and it had a sterling reputation for being a global leader in introducing innovative steelmaking technologies throughout its operations. Nucor began its journey from obscurity to a steel industry leader in the 1960s. Operating under the name of Nuclear Corporation of America in the 1950s and early 1960s, the company was a maker of nuclear instruments and electronics products. After suffering through several money-losing years and facing bankruptcy in 1964, Nuclear Corporation of America's board of directors opted for new leadership and appointed F. Kenneth Iverson as president and CEO. Shortly thereafter, Iverson concluded that the best way to put the company on sound footing was to exit the nuclear instrument and electronics business and rebuild the company around its profitable South Carolina–based Vulcraft subsidiary that was in the steel joist business—Iverson had been the head of Vulcraft prior to being named president. Iverson moved the company's headquarters from Phoenix, Arizona, to Charlotte, North Carolina, in 1966, and proceeded to expand the joist business with new operations in Texas and Alabama. Then, in 1968, top management decided to integrate backward into steelmaking, partly because of the benefits of supplying its own steel requirements for producing steel joists and partly because Iverson saw opportunities to capitalize on newly emerging technologies to produce steel more cheaply. In 1972, the company adopted the name Nucor Corporation, and Iverson initiated a long-term strategy to grow Nucor into a major player in the U.S. steel industry.

By 1985 Nucor had become the seventh-largest steel company in North America, with revenues of $758 million, six joist plants, and four state-of-the-art steel mills that used electric arc furnaces to produce new steel products from recycled scrap steel. Nucor was regarded as an excellently managed company, an accomplished low-cost producer, and one of the most competitively successful manufacturing companies in the country.[1] A series of articles in *The New Yorker* related how Nucor, a relatively small American steel company, had built an enterprise that led the whole world into a new era of making steel with recycled scrap steel. NBC did a business documentary that used Nucor to make the point that American manufacturers could be successful in competing against low-cost foreign manufacturers.

Copyright © 2012 by Arthur A. Thompson. All rights reserved.

During the 1985–2000 period, Nucor continued to construct additional steelmaking capacity, adopt trailblazing production methods, and expand its lineup of steel products. By 2000, Nucor was the second-largest steel producer in the United States and charging to overtake long-time leader United States Steel. Nucor's sales in 2000 exceeded 11 million tons annually and revenues were nearly $4.8 billion. Nucor continued its long-term growth strategy during 2006–2011, constructing additional plants and acquiring other (mostly troubled) steel facilities at bargain basement prices, enabling it to enter new product segments and offer customers a diverse variety of steel shapes and steel products. Heading into 2012, Nucor was solidly entrenched as the largest steel producer in North America (based on production capacity) with 23 plants having the capacity to produce 27 million tons of assorted steel shapes (steel bars, sheet steel, steel plate, and structural steel) and additional steel manufacturing facilities with the capacity to make 4.7 million tons of steel joists, steel decking, cold finish bars, steel buildings, steel mesh, steel grating, steel fasteners, and fabricated steel reinforcing products. The company had 2011 revenues of $20.0 billion and net profits of $778.2 million, well below its prerecession peak in 2008 of $23.7 billion in revenues and $1.8 billion in net profits.

With the exception of three quarters in 2009 and one quarter in 2010 (when the steel industry in the United States was in the midst of a deep economic downturn and the demand for steel was unusually weak), Nucor had earned a profit in every quarter of every year since 1966—a truly remarkable accomplishment in a mature and cyclical business where it was common for industry members to post losses when demand for steel sagged. As of April 2012, Nucor had paid a dividend for 156 consecutive quarters and had raised the base dividend it paid to stockholders every year since 1973 when the company first began paying cash dividends (in years when earnings and cash flows permitted, it was Nucor's practice to pay a supplemental year-end dividend

in addition to the base quarterly dividend). Exhibit 1 provides highlights of Nucor's growth between 1970 and 2011.

Standard & Poor's, in a January 9, 2012 report titled "North American Metals and Mining Companies, Strongest to Weakest," ranked Nucor number one for credit rating and credit outlook among a universe of 68 companies, in large part because of the company's strong competitive position and profit performance relative to peer companies in the steel industry.

Nucor in 2012

Ken Iverson, the architect of Nucor's climb to prominence in the steel industry, was regarded by many as a "model company president." Under Iverson, who served as Nucor's CEO until late 1998, Nucor was known for its aggressive pursuit of innovation and technical excellence, rigorous quality systems, strong emphasis on employee relations and workforce productivity, cost-conscious corporate culture, and its ability to achieve low costs per ton produced. The company had a very streamlined organizational structure, incentive-based compensation systems, and steel mills that were among the most modern and efficient in the United States. Iverson proved himself a master in crafting and executing a low-cost leadership strategy, and he made a point of making sure that he practiced what he preached when it came to holding down costs. The offices of executives and division general managers were simply furnished. There were no company planes and no company cars, and executives were not provided with company-paid country club memberships, reserved parking spaces, executive dining facilities, or other perks. To save money on his own business expenses and set an example for other Nucor managers, Iverson flew coach class and took the subway when he was in New York City.

When Iverson left the company in 1998 following disagreements with the board of directors, he was succeeded briefly by John Correnti and then Dave Aycock, both of whom had worked in various roles under Iverson for a

EXHIBIT 1

EXHIBIT 1

Nucor's Growing Presence in the Market for Steel, 1970–2011

Year	Total Tons Sold to Outside Customers	Average Price per Ton	Net Sales (in millions)	Earnings before Taxes (in millions)	Pretax Earnings per Ton	Net Earnings (in millions)
1970	207,000	$245	$ 50.8	$ 2.2	$ 10	$ 1.1
1975	387,000	314	121.5	11.7	30	7.6
1980	1,159,000	416	482.4	76.1	66	45.1
1985	1,902,000	399	758.5	106.2	56	58.5
1990	3,648,000	406	1,481.6	111.2	35	75.1
1995	7,943,000	436	3,462.0	432.3	62	274.5
2000	11,189,000	425	4,756.5	478.3	48	310.9
2001	12,237,000	354	4,333.7	179.4	16	113.0
2002	13,442,000	357	4,801.7	227.0	19	162.1
2003	17,473,000	359	6,265.8	70.0	4	62.8
2004	19,109,000	595	11,376.8	1,725.9	96	1,121.5
2005	20,465,000	621	12,701.0	2,027.1	104	1,310.3
2006	22,118,000	667	14,751.3	2,692.4	129	1,757.7
2007	22,940,000	723	16,593.0	2,253.3	104	1,471.9
2008	25,187,000	940	23,663.3	2,790.5	116	1,831.0
2009	17,576,000	637	11,190.3	(470.4)	(28)	(293.6)
2010	22,019,000	720	15,844.6	194.9	9	134.1
2011	23,044,000	869	20,023.6	1,169.9	53	778.2

Source: Company records posted at www.nucor.com, accessed April 8, 2012.

number of years. In 2000, Daniel R. DiMicco, who had joined Nucor in 1982 and risen up through the ranks to executive vice president, was named president and CEO. DiMicco was Nucor's chairman and CEO in 2012. Like his predecessors, DiMicco continued to pursue a rapid growth strategy, expanding the company production capabilities via both acquisition and new plant construction and boosting tons sold from 11.2 million in 2000 to 25.2 million in 2008 before the financial crisis in the fourth quarter of 2008 and the subsequent economic fallout caused tons sold in 2009 to plunge to 17.6 million tons and revenues to nosedive from $23.7 billion in 2008 to $11.2 billion in 2009. Nucor's business was still in the recovery stages in 2010–2011 (see Exhibit 2).

In the 12 years of Dan DiMicco's leadership, Nucor was quite opportunistic in initiating

actions to strengthen its competitive position during periods when the demand for steel was weak and then to capitalize on these added strengths in periods of strong market demand for steel products and significantly boost financial performance. According to Dan DiMicco:[2]

> Our objective is to deliver improved returns at every point in the economic cycle. We call it delivering higher highs and higher lows. In the last major economic slump, from 2001 through 2003, Nucor had total net earnings of $339.8 million. During the even deeper slump of 2009 through 2011, Nucor earned $618.7 million, an increase of 82 percent. The most recent peak to peak earnings grew from $310.9 million in 2000 to $1.83 billion in 2008, an increase of 489 percent.

> Nucor uses each economic downturn as an opportunity to grow stronger. We use the good times to prepare for the bad, and we

EXHIBIT 2

Five-Year Financial and Operating Summary, Nucor Corporation, 2007–2011 ($ in millions, except per share data and sales per employee)

For the Year	2011	2010	2009	2008	2007
Net sales	$20,023.6	$15,844.6	$11,190.3	$23,663.3	$16,593.0
Costs, expenses and other:					
Cost of products sold	18,075.0	15,001.0	11,035.9	19,612.3	13,462.9
Marketing, administrative, and other expenses	520.6	391.4	351.3	714.1	553.1
Equity in losses of minority-owned enterprises	10.0	32.1	82.3	36.9	24.6
Impairment of non-current assets				105.2	
Interest expense, net	166.1	153.1	134.7	90.5	5.5
Total	18,771.8	15,577.5	11,604.3	20,559.0	14,046.2
Earnings (loss) before income taxes and non-controlling interests	1,251.8	267.1	(414.0)	3,104.4	2,546.8
Provision for (benefit from) income taxes	390.8	60.8	(176.8)	959.5	781.4
Net earnings (loss)	861.0	206.3	(237.2)	2,144.9	1,765.4
Less earnings attributable to minority ownership in unconsolidated enterprises	82.8	72.2	56.4	13.9	293.5
Net earnings (loss) attributable to Nucor stockholders	$ 778.2	$ 134.1	$ (293.6)	$ 1,831.0	$ 1,471.9
Net earnings (loss) per share:					
Basic	$2.45	$0.42	$ (0.94)	$5.99	$4.96
Diluted	2.45	0.42	(0.94)	5.98	4.94
Dividends declared per share	$1.4525	$1.4425	$1.41	$1.91	$2.44
Percentage of net earnings to net sales	3.9%	0.8%	−2.6%	7.7%	8.9%
Return on average stockholders' equity	10.7%	1.8%	−3.8%	28.1%	29.4%
Capital expenditures	$450.6	$345.3	$ 390.5	$ 1,019.0	$520.3
Acquisitions (net of cash acquired)	4.0	64.8	32.7	1,826.0	1,542.7
Depreciation	522.6	512.1	494.0	479.5	403.2
Sales per employee (000s)	974	777	539	1,155	1,085
At Year End					
Cash, cash equivalents, and short-term investments	$ 2,563.3	$ 2,479.0	$ 2,242.0	$ 2,355.1	$ 1,576.4
Current assets	6,708.1	5,861.2	5,182.2	6,397.5	5,073.2
Current liabilities	2,396.1	1,504.4	1,227.1	1,854.2	1,582.0
Working capital	4,312.0	4,356.8	3,995.1	4,543.3	3,491.2
Cash provided by operating activities	1,032.6	873.4	1,173.2	2,502.1	1,953.3
Current ratio	2.8	3.9	4.2	3.5	3.2
Property, plant, and equipment	$ 3,755.6	$ 3,852.1	$ 4,013.8	$ 4,131.9	$ 3,233.0
Total assets	14,570.4	13,921.9	12,571.9	13,874.4	9,826.1
Long-term debt (including current maturities)	4,280.2	4,280.2	3,086.2	3,266.6	2,250.3
Stockholders' equity	7,474.9	7,120.1	7,390.5	7,929.2	5,112.9
Percentage of long-term debt to total capital*	35.7%	36.9%	28.9%	28.3%	29.4%
Shares outstanding (000s)	316,749	315,791	314,856	313,977	287,993
Employees	20,800	20,500	20,400	21,700	18,000

*Total capital is defined as stockholders' equity plus long-term debt.
Source: Nucor's 2011 Annual Report, p. 39.

use the bad times to prepare for the good. Emerging from downturns stronger than we enter them is how we build long-term value for our stockholders. We get stronger because our team is focused on continual improvement and because our financial strength allows us to invest in attractive growth opportunities throughout the economic cycle.

Nucor's top executives expected the full benefits of the $7 billion in investments made from 2007 through 2011 (plus whatever amounts the company invested in 2012 and 2013) to lead to significantly higher revenues and profits when healthy economic conditions and strong market demand for steel products reappeared.

Nucor's Ever-Growing Product Line, 1967–2012

Over the years, Nucor had expanded progressively into the manufacture of a wider and wider range of steel shapes and steel products, enabling it in 2012 to offer steel users the broadest product lineup of any North American steel producer. Steel shapes and steel products were considered commodities. While some steelmakers had plants where production quality was sometimes inconsistent or on occasions failed to meet customer-specified metallurgical characteristics, most steel plants turned out products of comparable metallurgical quality—one producer's reinforcing bar was essentially the same as another producer's reinforcing bar, a particular type and grade of sheet steel made at one plant was essentially identical to the same type and grade of sheet steel made at another plant. The commodity nature of steel products forced steel producers to be very price competitive, with the market price of each particular steel product being driven by demand-supply conditions for that product.

Steel Products   Nucor's first venture into steel in the late 1960s, via its Vulcraft division, was principally one of fabricating steel joists and joist girders from steel that was purchased from various steelmakers. Vulcraft expanded into the fabrication of steel decking in 1977.

The division expanded its operations over the years and, as of 2012, Nucor's Vulcraft division was the largest producer and leading innovator of open-web steel joists, joist girders, and steel deck in the United States. It had seven plants with an annual capacity of 715,000 tons that made steel joists and joist girders and six plants with 530,000 tons of capacity that made steel deck; in 2010–2011 about 90 percent of the steel needed to make these products was supplied by various Nucor steelmaking plants. Vulcraft's joist, girder, and decking products were used mainly for roof and floor support systems in retail stores, shopping centers, warehouses, manufacturing facilities, schools, churches, hospitals, and, to a lesser extent, multistory buildings and apartments. Customers for these products were principally nonresidential construction contractors.

In 1979, Nucor began fabricating cold finished steel products. These consisted mainly of cold drawn and turned, ground, and polished steel bars or rods of various shapes—rounds, hexagons, flats, channels, and squares—made from carbon, alloy, and leaded steels based on customer specifications or end-use requirements. Cold finished steel products were used in tens of thousands of products, including anchor bolts, hydraulic cylinders, farm machinery, air conditioner compressors, electric motors, motor vehicles, appliances, and lawn mowers. Nucor sold cold finish steel directly to large-quantity users in the automotive, farm machinery, hydraulic, appliance, and electric motor industries and to steel service centers that in turn supplied manufacturers needing only relatively small quantities. In 2011, Nucor Cold Finish was the largest producer of cold finished bar products in North America and had facilities in Missouri, Nebraska, South Carolina, Utah, Wisconsin, and Ontario, Canada. It obtained most of its steel from Nucor's mills that made steel bar. This factor, along with the fact that all of Nucor's cold finished facilities employed the latest technology and were among the most modern in the world, resulted in Nucor Cold Finish having a highly competitive cost structure. It maintained sufficient inventories of cold finish products to fulfill anticipated orders.

Nucor produced metal buildings and components throughout the United States under several brands: Nucor Building Systems, American Buildings Company, Kirby Building Systems, Gulf States Manufacturers, and CBC Steel Buildings. In 2012, the Nucor Buildings Group had 11 metal buildings plants with an annual capacity of approximately 465,000 tons. Sales were 232,000 tons in 2011, a decrease of 3 percent from 239,000 tons in 2010. Nucor's Buildings Group began operations in 1987 and currently had the capability to supply customers with buildings ranging from less than 1,000 square feet to more than 1,000,000 square feet. Complete metal building packages could be customized and combined with other materials such as glass, wood, and masonry to produce a cost-effective, aesthetically pleasing building built to a customer's particular requirements. The buildings were sold primarily through an independent builder distribution network. The primary markets served were commercial, industrial, and institutional buildings, including distribution centers, automobile dealerships, retail centers, schools, warehouses, and manufacturing facilities. Nucor's Buildings Group obtained a significant portion of its steel requirements from the Nucor bar and sheet mills.

Another Nucor division produced steel mesh, grates, and fasteners. Various steel mesh products were made at three facilities in the United States and one in Canada that had combined annual production capacity of about 248,000 tons. Steel and aluminum bar grating, safety grating, and expanded metal products were produced at several North American locations that had combined annual production capacity of 103,000 tons. Nucor Fastener, located in Indiana, began operations in 1986 with the construction of a $25 million plant. At the time, imported steel fasteners accounted for 90 percent of the U.S. market because U.S. manufacturers were not competitive on cost and price. Iverson said, "We're going to bring that business back; we can make bolts as cheaply

as foreign producers." Nucor built a second fastener plant in 1995, giving it the capacity to supply about 20 percent of the U.S. market for steel fasteners. Currently, these two facilities had annual capacity of over 75,000 tons and produced carbon and alloy steel hex head cap screws, hex bolts, structural bolts, nuts and washers, finished hex nuts, and custom-engineered fasteners that were used for automotive, machine tool, farm implement, construction, military, and various other applications. Nucor Fastener obtained much of the steel for making these products from Nucor mills that made steel bars and maintained sufficient inventories of its various products to meet anticipated demand from customers in the United States and Canada.

Beginning in 2007, Nucor—through its newly acquired Harris Steel subsidiary—began fabricating, installing, and distributing steel reinforcing bars (rebar) for highways, bridges, schools, hospitals, airports, stadiums, office buildings, high-rise residential complexes, and other structures where steel reinforcing was essential to concrete construction. Harris Steel had over 70 fabrication facilities in the United States and Canada, with each facility serving the surrounding local market. Since acquiring Harris Steel, Nucor had more than doubled its rebar fabrication capacity to 1,695,000 tons annually. Two new rebar facilities had been added in 2011, and total fabricated rebar sales in 2011 were 1,074,000 tons, up 9 percent over the 981,000 tons sold in 2010. Much of the steel used in making fabricated rebar products was obtained from Nucor steel plants that made steel bar. Fabricated reinforcing products were sold only on a contract bid basis.

Steelmaking   In 1968, Nucor got into basic steelmaking, building a mill in Darlington, South Carolina, to manufacture steel bars. The Darlington mill was one of the first plants of major size in the United States to use electric arc furnace technology to melt scrap steel and cast molten metal into various shapes. Electric arc furnace technology was particularly appealing because the labor and capital requirements to melt steel scrap and produce crude steel were far lower than those at conventional integrated steel mills where raw steel was produced using coke ovens, basic oxygen blast furnaces, ingot casters, and multiple types of finishing facilities to make crude steel from iron ore, coke, limestone, oxygen, scrap steel, and other ingredients. By 1981, Nucor had four steel mills making carbon and alloy steels in bars, angles, and light structural shapes. Since then, Nucor had undertaken extensive capital projects to keep these facilities modernized and globally competitive. In 2000–2011, Nucor aggressively expanded its market presence in steel bars and by 2012 had 13 bar mills located across the United States that produced concrete reinforcing bars, hot-rolled bars, rods, light shapes, structural angles, channels and guard rails in carbon and alloy steels. These 13 plants had total annual capacity of approximately 9.1 million tons. Four of the 13 mills made hot-rolled special-quality bars manufactured to exacting specifications. Nucor had plans to invest an additional $290 million in three of the special bar quality mills that would add the capability to produce 1 million additional tons annually by early 2014. The products of the 13 bar mills had wide usage and were sold primarily to customers in the agricultural, automotive, construction, energy, furniture, machinery, metal building, railroad, recreational equipment, shipbuilding, heavy truck, and trailer industries. In addition, the company's newly renovated wire rod and bar mill in Kingman, Arizona, had the ability to increase its production from 200,000 tons annually to 500,000 tons annually with very little additional investment, thus putting the company in a strong position to serve wire rod and rebar customers in the southwestern U.S. market. Nucor executives expected that the added capacity at the three special bar quality mills and at the Kingman plant would be an important source of growth in upcoming years.

In the late 1980s, Nucor entered into the production of sheet steel at a newly constructed plant in Crawfordsville, Indiana. Flat-rolled sheet steel was used in the production of motor vehicles, appliances, steel pipe and tubes, and other durable goods. The Crawfordsville plant was the first in the world to employ a revolutionary thin slab casting process that substantially reduced the capital investment and costs to produce flat-rolled sheet steel. Thin-slab casting machines had a funnel-shaped mold to squeeze molten steel down to a thickness of 1.5–2.0 inches, compared to the typically 8- to 10-inch-thick slabs produced by conventional casters. It was much cheaper to then build and operate facilities to roll thin-gauge sheet steel from 1.5- to 2-inch-thick slabs than from 8- to 10-inch-thick slabs. When the Crawfordsville plant opened in 1989, it was said to have costs $50 to $75 per ton below the costs of traditional sheet steel plants, a highly significant cost advantage in a commodity market where the going price at the time was $400 per ton. *Forbes* magazine described Nucor's pioneering use of thin slab casting as the most substantial, technological, industrial innovation in the past 50 years.[3] By 1996, two additional sheet steel mills that employed thin slab casting technology were constructed, and a fourth mill was acquired in 2002, giving Nucor the capacity to produce 11.3 million tons of sheet-steel products annually as of 2012. Nucor also operated two Castrip sheet production facilities, one built in 2002 at the Crawfordsville plant and a second built in Arkansas in 2009. These facilities used the breakthrough strip casting technology that involved the direct casting of molten steel into a final shape and thickness without further hot or cold rolling. The process allowed for lower capital investment, reduced energy consumption, smaller scale plants, and improved environmental impact (because of significantly lower emissions).

Also in the late 1980s, Nucor added wide-flange steel beams, pilings, and heavy structural steel products to its lineup of product offerings. Structural steel products were used in buildings, bridges, overpasses, and similar such projects where strong weight-bearing support was needed. Customers included construction companies, steel fabricators, manufacturers, and steel service centers. To gain entry to the structural steel segment, in 1988 Nucor entered into a joint venture with Yamato-Kogyo, one of Japan's major producers of wide-flange beams, to build a new structural steel mill in Arkansas; a second mill was built on the same site in the 1990s that made the Nucor-Yamato venture in Arkansas the largest structural beam facility in the Western Hemisphere. In 1999, Nucor started operations at a third structural steel mill in South Carolina. The mills in Arkansas and South Carolina both used a special continuous casting method that was quite cost-effective. Going into 2012, Nucor had the capacity to make 3.7 million tons of structural steel products annually.

Starting in 2000, Nucor began producing steel plate of various thicknesses and lengths that was sold to manufacturers of heavy equipment, ships, barges, bridges, rail cars, refinery tanks, pressure vessels, pipe and tube, wind towers, and similar products. Steel plate was made at two mills in Alabama and North Carolina that had combined capacity of about 2.9 million tons. In early 2011, Nucor started operations at a newly constructed 125,000-ton heat-treating facility at the plate mill in North Carolina. Heat-treated steel plate was used in applications requiring higher strength, abrasion resistance, and toughness.

All of Nucor's steel mills used electric arc furnaces, whereby scrap steel and other metals were melted and the molten metal then poured into continuous casting systems. Sophisticated rolling mills converted the billets, blooms, and slabs produced by various casting equipment into rebar, angles, rounds, channels, flats, sheet, beams, plate, and other finished steel products. Nucor's steel mill operations were highly automated, typically requiring fewer operating employees per ton produced than the mills of rival companies. High worker productivity at all Nucor steel mills resulted in labor costs roughly 50 percent lower than the labor costs at the integrated mills of companies using union labor and conventional blast furnace technology. Nucor's value chain (anchored in using electric arc furnace technology to recycle scrap steel) involved far fewer production steps, far

less capital investment, and considerably less labor than the value chains of companies with integrated steel mills that made crude steel from iron ore.

Exhibit 3 shows Nucor's sales by product category for 1990–2011. The breadth of Nucor's product line made it the most diversified steel producer in North America, and all of its steel mills were among the most modern and efficient mills in the United States. The company had market leadership in several product categories—it was the largest U.S. producer of steel bars, structural steel, steel reinforcing bars, steel joists and girders, steel deck, and cold-finished steel products bars. And Nucor was among the leading producers of sheet steel, steel plate, steel fasteners, metal building systems, light gauge steel framing, and rebar fabrication.

The average capacity utilization rates at Nucor's steel mills were 70 percent in 2010 and 74 percent in 2011; the average capacity utilization rates at Nucor's steel products facilities were 54 percent in 2010 and 57 percent in 2011.

Pricing and Sales In 2011, approximately 86 percent of the production by Nucor's steel mills segment was sold to external customers. The balance of the company's steel mill production went to supply the steel needs of the company's joist, deck, rebar fabrication, fastener, metal buildings, and cold finish operations.

The commodity nature of steel products meant that the prices a company could command were driven by prevailing market demand-supply conditions which changed more or less continually. The big majority of Nucor's steel sales were to customers who placed orders monthly based on their immediate upcoming needs; sales were made at the prevailing spot market price, as determined by current market demand-supply conditions. As a consequence, Nucor's average sales prices per ton varied considerably from quarter to quarter (see Exhibit 4). Nucor's strategy was to quote the same payment terms to all customers and for customers to pay all shipping charges.

Nucor marketed the output of its steel mills and steel products facilities mainly through an

EXHIBIT 3

Nucor's Sales of Steel and Steel Products, by Product Category, 1990–2011

Tons Sold to Outside Customers (in thousands)

	Steel Mill Products					Finished Steel Products				
Year	Sheet Steel (2011 capacity of ~11.3 million tons)	Steel Bars (2011 capacity of ~9.1 million tons)	Structural Steel (2011 capacity of ~3.7 million tons)	Steel Plate (2011 capacity of ~2.9 million tons)	Total (2011 capacity of ~27 million tons)	Steel Joists (2011 capacity of ~715,000 tons)	Steel Deck (2011 capacity of ~530,000 tons)	Cold Finished Steel (2011 capacity of ~860,000 tons)	Rebar Fabrication and Other Products*	Total Tons
2011	7,500	4,680	2,338	2,278	16,796	288	312	494	5,154	23,044
2010	7,434	4,019	2,139	2,229	15,821	276	306	462	5,154	22,019
2009	5,212	3,629	1,626	1,608	12,075	264	310	330	4,596	17,576
2008	7,505	5,266	2,934	2,480	18,185	485	498	485	4,534	25,187
2007	8,266	6,287	3,154	2,528	20,235	542	478	449	1,236	22,940
2006	8,495	6,513	3,209	2,432	20,649	570	398	327	174	22,118
2005	8,026	5,983	2,866	2,145	19,020	554	380	342	169	20,465
2004	8,078	5,244	2,760	1,705	17,787	522	364	271	165	19,109
2003	6,954	5,530	2,780	999	16,263	503	353	237	117	17,473
2002	5,806	2,947	2,689	872	12,314	462	330	226	110	13,442
2001	5,074	2,687	2,749	522	11,032	532	344	203	126	12,237
2000	4,456	2,209	3,094	20	9,779	613	353	250	194	11,189
1995	2,994	1,799	1,952	—	6,745	552	234	234	178	7,943
1990	420	1,382	1,002	—	2,804	443	134	163	104	3,648

*Includes steel fasteners (steel screws, nuts, bolts, washers, and bolt assemblies), steel mesh, steel grates, metal building systems, light gauge steel framing, and scrap metal.

Source: Company records posted at www.nucor.com, accessed April 9, 2012.

EXHIBIT 4

Nucor's Average Quarterly Sales Prices for Steel Products, by Product Category, 2011–2012

Period	Sheet Steel	Steel Bars	Structural Steel	Steel Plate	Average of All Steel Mill Products	Average of All Steel Products*
2011						
Qtr 1	$755	$779	$831	$ 880	$789	$1,274
Qtr 2	894	803	923	1,029	891	1,361
Qtr 3	800	811	901	1,021	847	1,381
Qtr 4	744	796	891	946	806	1,395
2012						
Qtr 1	780	823	866	929	824	1,413
Qtr 2	770	795	905	922	812	1,416

*An average of the steel prices for steel deck, steel joists and girders, steel buildings, cold finished steel products, steel mesh, fasteners, fabricated rebar, and other steel products.

Source: Company records posted at www.nucor.com, accessed April 23, 2012.

in-house sales force; there were salespeople located at most every Nucor production facility. In 2011, approximately 50 percent of Nucor's sheet steel sales were to contract customers (versus 40 percent in 2010 and 30 percent in 2009). These contracts for sheet steel were usually for periods of 6 to 12 months and permitted price adjustments to reflect changes in prevailing raw material costs. The other 50 percent of Nucor's sheet steel production and virtually all of the company's plate, structural, and bar steel was sold to customers who typically placed orders monthly based on their immediate upcoming needs; sales were made at the prevailing spot market price, as determined by current market demand-supply conditions. Nucor's steel mills maintained inventory levels deemed adequate to fill the expected incoming orders from customers.

Nucor sold steel joists and joist girders, and steel deck on the basis of firm, fixed-price contracts that, in most cases, were won in competitive bidding against rival suppliers. Longer-term supply contracts for these items that were sometimes negotiated with customers contained clauses permitting price adjustments to reflect changes in prevailing raw materials costs. Steel joists, girders, and deck were manufactured to customers' specifications and

shipped immediately; Nucor's plants did not maintain inventories of steel joists, girders, or steel deck. Nucor also sold fabricated reinforcing products only on a construction contract bid basis. However, cold finished steel, steel fasteners, steel grating, wire, and wire mesh were all manufactured in standard sizes, with each facility maintaining sufficient inventories of its products to fill anticipated orders; most all sales of these items were made at the prevailing spot price.

Strategy

Starting in 2000, Nucor embarked on a five-part growth strategy that involved new acquisitions, new plant construction, continued plant upgrades and cost reduction efforts, international growth through joint ventures, and greater control over raw materials costs.

Strategic Acquisitions Beginning in the late 1990s, Nucor management concluded that growth-minded companies like Nucor might well be better off purchasing existing plant capacity rather than building new capacity, provided the acquired plants could be bought at bargain prices, economically retrofitted with new equipment if need be, and then operated at costs comparable to (or even below) those of newly constructed state-of-the-art plants. At the time, the steel industry worldwide had far more production capacity than was needed to meet market demand, forcing many companies to operate in the red. Nucor had not made any acquisitions since about 1990, and a team of five people was assembled in 1998 to explore acquisition possibilities that would strengthen Nucor's customer base, geographic coverage, and lineup of product offerings.

For almost three years, no acquisitions were made. But then the economic recession that hit Asia and Europe in the late 1990s reached the United States in full force in 2000–2001. The September 11, 2001, terrorist attacks further weakened steel purchases by such major steel-consuming industries as construction, automobiles, and farm equipment. Many steel companies in the United States and other parts of the world were operating in the red. Market conditions in the United States were particularly grim. Between October 2000 and October 2001, 29 steel companies in the United States, including Bethlehem Steel Corp. and LTV Corp., the nation's third- and fourth-largest steel producers, respectively, filed for bankruptcy protection. Bankrupt steel companies accounted for about 25 percent of U.S. capacity. *The Economist* noted that of the 14 steel companies tracked by Standard & Poor's, only Nucor was indisputably healthy. Some experts believed that close to half of the U.S. steel industry's production capacity might be forced to close before conditions improved; about 47,000 jobs in the U.S. steel industry had vanished since 1997.

One of the principal reasons for the distressed market conditions in the United States was a surge in imports of low-priced steel from foreign countries. Outside the United States, weak demand and a glut of capacity had driven commodity steel prices to 20-year lows in 1998. Globally, the industry had about 1 billion tons of annual capacity, but puny demand had kept production levels in the 750 to 800 million tons per year range during 1998–2000. A number of foreign steel producers, anxious to keep their mills running and finding few good market opportunities elsewhere, began selling steel in

the U.S. market at cut-rate prices in 1997–1999. Nucor and other U.S. companies reduced prices to better compete and several filed unfair trade complaints against foreign steelmakers. The U.S. Department of Commerce concluded in March 1999 that steel companies in six countries (Canada, South Korea, Taiwan, Italy, Belgium, and South Africa) had illegally dumped stainless steel in the United States, and the governments of Belgium, Italy, and South Africa further facilitated the dumping by giving their steel producers unfair subsidies that at least partially made up for the revenue losses of selling at below-market prices. Congress and the Clinton administration opted to not impose tariffs or quotas on imported steel, which helped precipitate the number of bankruptcy filings. However, the Bush administration was more receptive to protecting the U.S. steel industry from the dumping practices of foreign steel companies. In October 2001, the U.S. International Trade Commission (ITC) ruled that increased steel imports of semi-finished steel, plate, hot-rolled sheet, strip and coils, cold-rolled sheet and strip, and corrosion-resistant and coated sheet and strip were a substantial cause of serious injury, or threat of serious injury, to the U.S. industry. In March 2002, the Bush administration imposed tariffs of up to 30 percent on imports of selected steel products to help provide relief from Asian and European companies dumping steel in the United States at ultra-low prices.

Even though market conditions were tough for Nucor, management concluded that oversupplied steel industry conditions and the number of beleaguered U.S. companies made it attractive to expand Nucor's production capacity via acquisition. Starting in 2001, the company proceeded to make a series of acquisitions:

- In 2001, Nucor paid $115 million to acquire substantially all of the assets of Auburn Steel Company's 400,000-ton steel bar facility in Auburn, New York. This acquisition gave Nucor expanded market presence in the Northeast and was seen as a good source of supply for a new Vulcraft joist plant being constructed in Chemung, New York.

- In November 2001, Nucor announced the acquisition of ITEC Steel Inc. for a purchase price of $9 million. ITEC Steel had annual revenues of $10 million and produced load-bearing light gauge steel framing for the residential and commercial market at facilities in Texas and Georgia. Nucor was impressed with ITEC's dedication to continuous improvement and intended to grow ITEC's business via geographic and product line expansion. ITEC Steel's name was changed to Nucon Steel Commercial Corporation in 2002.

- In July 2002, Nucor paid $120 million to purchase Trico Steel Company, which had a 2.2-million-ton sheet steel mill in Decatur, Alabama. Trico Steel was a joint venture of LTV (which owned a 50 percent interest), and two leading international steel companies—Sumitomo Metal Industries and British Steel. The joint-venture partners had built the mill in 1997 at a cost of $465 million, but Trico was in Chapter 11 bankruptcy proceedings at the time of the acquisition and the mill was shut down. The Trico mill's capability to make thin sheet steel with a superior surface quality added competitive strength to Nucor's strategy to gain sales and market share in the flat-rolled sheet segment. By October 2002, two months ahead of schedule, Nucor had restarted operations at the Decatur mill and was shipping products to customers.

- In December 2002, Nucor paid $615 million to purchase substantially all of the assets of Birmingham Steel Corporation, which included four bar mills in Alabama, Illinois, Washington, and Mississippi. The four plants had a capacity of approximately 2 million tons annually. The purchase price also included approximately $120 million in inventory and receivables, the assets of Port Everglade Steel Corp., the assets of Klean Steel, Birmingham Steel's ownership interest in Richmond Steel Recycling, and

a mill in Memphis, Tennessee, that was not currently in operation. Top executives believed the Birmingham Steel acquisition would broaden Nucor's customer base and build profitable market share in bar steel products.

- In August 2004, Nucor acquired a cold rolling mill in Decatur, Alabama, from Worthington Industries for $80 million. This 1-million-ton mill, which opened in 1998, was located adjacent to the previously acquired Trico mill and gave Nucor added ability to service the needs of sheet steel buyers located in the southeastern United States.

- In June 2004, Nucor paid a cash price of $80 million to acquire a plate mill owned by Britain-based Corus Steel that was located in Tuscaloosa, Alabama. The Tuscaloosa mill, which currently had a capacity of 700,000 tons that Nucor management believed was expandable to 1 million tons, was the first U.S. mill to employ a special technology that enabled high-quality wide steel plate to be produced from coiled steel plate. The mill produced coiled steel plate and plate products that were cut to customer-specified lengths. Nucor intended to offer these niche products to its commodity plate and coiled sheet customers.

- In February 2005, Nucor completed the purchase of Fort Howard Steel's operations in Oak Creek, Wisconsin; the Oak Creek facility produced cold finished bars in size ranges up to 6-inch rounds and had approximately 140,000 tons of annual capacity.

- In June 2005, Nucor purchased Marion Steel Company located in Marion, Ohio, for a cash price of $110 million. Marion operated a bar mill with annual capacity of about 400,000 tons; the Marion location was within close proximity to 60 percent of the steel consumption in the United States.

- In May 2006, Nucor acquired Connecticut Steel Corporation for $43 million in cash. Connecticut Steel's bar products mill in

Wallingford had annual capacity to make 300,000 tons of wire rod and rebar and approximately 85,000 tons of wire mesh fabrication and structural mesh fabrication, products that complemented Nucor's present lineup of steel bar products provided to construction customers.

- In late 2006, Nucor purchased Verco Manufacturing Co. for approximately $180 million; Verco produced steel floor and roof decking at one location in Arizona and two locations in California. The Verco acquisition further solidified Vulcraft's market leading position in steel decking, giving it total annual capacity of over 500,000 tons.

- In January 2007, Nucor acquired Canada-based Harris Steel for about $1.07 billion. Harris Steel had 2005 sales of Cdn$1.0 billion and earnings of Cdn $64 million. The company's operations consisted of (1) Harris Rebar, which was involved in the fabrication and placing of concrete reinforcing steel and the design and installation of concrete post-tensioning systems; (2) Laurel Steel, which manufactured and distributed wire and wire products, welded wire mesh, and cold finished bar; and (3) Fisher & Ludlow, which manufactured and distributed heavy industrial steel grating, aluminum grating, and expanded metal. In Canada, Harris Steel had 24 reinforcing steel fabricating plants, two steel grating distribution centers, and one cold finished bar and wire processing plant; in the United States, it had 10 reinforcing steel fabricating plants, two steel grating manufacturing plants, and three steel grating manufacturing plants. Harris had customers throughout Canada and the United States and employed about 3,000 people. For the past three years, Harris had purchased a big percentage of its steel requirements from Nucor. Nucor management opted to operate Harris Steel as an independent subsidiary.

- Over several months in 2007 following the Harris Steel acquisition, Nucor through its new Harris Steel subsidiary acquired rebar fabricator South Pacific Steel Corporation, Consolidated Rebar, Inc., a 90 percent equity interest in rebar fabricator Barker Steel Company, and several smaller transactions—all aimed at growing its presence in the rebar fabrication marketplace.

- In August 2007, Nucor acquired LMP Steel & Wire Company for a cash purchase price of approximately $27.2 million, adding 100,000 tons of cold drawn steel capacity.

- In October 2007, Nucor completed the acquisition of Nelson Steel, Inc., for a cash purchase price of approximately $53.2 million, adding 120,000 tons of steel mesh capacity.

- In the third quarter of 2007, Nucor completed the acquisition of Magnatrax Corporation, a leading provider of custom-engineered metal buildings, for a cash purchase price of approximately $275.2 million. The Magnatrax acquisition enabled Nucor's Building System Group to become the second-largest metal building producer in the United States.

- In August 2008, Nucor's Harris Steel subsidiary acquired Ambassador Steel Corporation for a cash purchase price of about $185.1 million. Ambassador Steel was a one of the largest independent fabricators and distributors of concrete reinforcing steel—in 2007, Ambassador shipped 422,000 tons of fabricated rebar and distributed another 228,000 tons of reinforcing steel. Its business complemented that of Harris Steel and represented another in a series of moves to greatly strengthen Nucor's competitive position in the rebar fabrication marketplace.

- Another small rebar fabrication company, Free State Steel, was acquired in late 2009, adding to Nucor's footprint in rebar fabrication.

By 2005–2006, steel industry conditions worldwide had improved markedly. Prices in the United States were about 50 percent higher than in 2000 and Nucor's sales and earnings were robust in 2005–2008 (see Exhibit 1). But Nucor's performance slumped badly when the sudden financial crisis and economic downturn that hit in the fourth quarter of 2008 spilled over into 2009 and caused the demand for steel to plummet—Nucor's utilization of its steel mill capacity fell to 54 percent in 2009 from 91 percent in the first three quarters of 2008. Operating rates at Nucor's steel mills recovered modestly to 70 percent in 2010 and 74 percent in 2011. Market conditions in the steel industry remained challenging in 2012 in light of the slow economic recovery, making the 2009–2012 period one of the longest and deepest economic slumps in several decades.

The Commercialization of New Technologies and New Plant Construction

The second element of Nucor's growth strategy was to continue to be a technology leader and to be opportunistic in constructing new plant capacity that would enable the company to expand its presence in attractive new or existing market segments. From its earliest days, Nucor had been an early and aggressive investor in two types of steelmaking breakthroughs:

- *Disruptive technological innovations*—production processes and equipment that would give Nucor a commanding market advantage and thus be disruptive to the efforts of competitors in matching Nucor's cost competitiveness and/or product quality.

- *Leapfrog technological innovations*—production processes and equipment that would enable Nucor to overtake competitors in terms of product quality, cost per ton, or market share.

One of Nucor's biggest and most recent successes in pioneering new technology had been at its Crawfordsville facilities, where Nucor had the world's first installation of direct strip casting of carbon sheet steel—a process called Castrip®. After several years of testing and process refinement at Crawfordsville, Nucor announced in 2005 that the Castrip process was ready for commercialization; Nucor had

exclusive rights to Castrip technology in the United States and Brazil. The process, which had proven to be quite difficult to bring to commercial reality, was a major technological breakthrough for producing flat-rolled, carbon, and stainless steels in very thin gauges; it involved far fewer process steps to cast metal at or very near customer-desired thicknesses and shapes. The Castrip process drastically reduced capital outlays for equipment and produced savings on operating expenses as well—major expense savings included being able to use lower-quality scrap metal and 90 percent less energy to process liquid metal into hot-rolled steel sheets. A big environmental benefit of the Castrip process was cutting greenhouse gas emissions by up to 80 percent. Nucor's Castrip facility at Crawfordsville had the capacity to produce 500,000 tons annually. In 2006, Nucor built a second Castrip facility on the site of its structural steel mill in Arkansas.

Nucor's growth strategy also included investing in the construction of new plant capacity whenever management spotted opportunities to strengthen its market presence:

- In 2006, Nucor announced that it would construct a new $27 million facility to produce metal buildings systems in Brigham City, Utah. The new plant, Nucor's fourth building systems plant, had capacity of 45,000 tons and gave Nucor national market reach in building systems products.

- In 2006, Nucor initiated construction of a $230 million state-of-the-art steel mill in Memphis, Tennessee, with annual capacity to produce 850,000 tons of special-quality steel bars. Management believed this mill, together with the company's other special bar quality mills in Nebraska and South Carolina, would give Nucor the broadest, highest-quality, and lowest-cost SBQ product offering in North America.

- In 2009, Nucor opened an idle and newly renovated $50 million wire rod and bar mill in Kingman, Arizona, that had been acquired in 2003. Production of straight-length rebar, coiled rebar, and wire rod began in mid-2010; the plant had initial capacity of 100,000 tons, with the ability to increase annual production to 500,000 tons.

- A new $150 million galvanizing facility located at the company's sheet steel mill in Decatur, Alabama, began operations in mid-2009. This facility gave Nucor the ability to make 500,000 tons of 72-inch-wide galvanized sheet steel, a product used by motor vehicle and appliance producers and in various steel frame and steel stud buildings. The galvanizing process entailed dipping steel in melted zinc at extremely high temperatures; the zinc coating protected the steel surface from corrosion.

- Construction and installation of new vacuum degassers at Nucor's Hickman, Arkansas, sheet mill and Hertford County, North Carolina, plate mill were expected to begin operating in 2012, enabling these mills to produce increased volumes of higher-grade sheet steel.

- Construction of a heat-treating facility at the company's recently opened steel plate mill in Hertford County, North Carolina, began in 2011. The heat-treat line had estimated annual capacity of 125,000 tons and the ability to produce heat-treated plate from 3/16 of an inch through 2 inches thick.

- In January 2012, Nucor announced that it would invest $290 million for projects to be completed at the company's special bar quality mills in Memphis, Tennessee; Norfolk, Nebraska; and Darlington, South Carolina—steel mills that would expand its production capacities by a combined million tons. The planned capital expenditures included putting in place state-of-the-art quality inspection capabilities that would enable these plants to produce bar and wire rod for the most demanding engineered bar applications. Nucor expected to complete these projects by year-end 2013.

The Drive for Plant Efficiency and Low-Cost Production

A key part of Nucor's strategy was to make ongoing capital investments to improve efficiency and production costs at each and every facility it operated. From its earliest days in the steel business, Nucor had built state-of-the-art facilities in the most economical fashion possible and then made it standard company practice to invest in plant modernization and efficiency improvements as technology advanced and new cost-saving opportunities emerged. Nucor management made a point of staying on top of the latest advances in steelmaking around the world, diligently searching for emerging cost-effective technologies it could adopt or adapt in its facilities. Executives at Nucor had a longstanding commitment to provide the company's workforce with the best technology available to get the job done safely and in an environmentally responsible manner. When Nucor acquired plants, it immediately began getting them up to Nucor standards—a process it called "Nucorizing." This included increasing operational efficiency by reducing the amount of time, space, energy, and manpower it took to produce steel or steel products and paying close attention to worker safety and environmental protection practices.

Nucor management also stressed continual improvement in product quality and cost at each one of its production facilities. Most all of Nucor's production locations were ISO 9000 and ISO 14000 certified. The company had a "BESTmarking" program aimed at being the industry-wide best performer on a variety of production and efficiency measures. Managers at all Nucor plants were accountable for demonstrating that their operations were competitive on both product quality and cost vis-à-vis the plants of rival companies. One trait of Nucor's corporate culture was the expectation that plant-level managers would be persistent in implementing methods to improve product quality and keep costs per ton low relative to rival plants.

Examples of Nucor's latest efforts to upgrade and fully modernize the operations of its production facilities included a three-year bar mill modernization program and adding vacuum degassers to its four sheet steel mills. The addition of the vacuum degassers not only improved Nucor's ability to produce some of the highest-quality sheet steel available but also resulted in expanded capacity at low incremental cost. Nucor's capital expenditures for new technology, plant improvements, and equipment upgrades in 2000–2011 are shown in Exhibit 5; capital expenditures in 2012–2013 were expected to be close to $1 billion.

Nucor management viewed the task of optimizing its manufacturing operations as a continuous process. According to CEO Dan DiMicco:[4]

> We talk about "climbing a mountain without a peak" to describe our constant improvements. We can take pride in what we have accomplished, but we are never satisfied.

Global Growth via Joint Ventures In 2007, Nucor management decided it was time to begin building an international growth platform. The company's strategy to grow its international revenues had two elements:

- Establishing foreign sales offices and exporting U.S-made steel products to foreign markets. Because about 60 percent of Nucor's steelmaking capacity was located on rivers with deep water transportation access, management believed that the company could be competitive in shipping U.S.-made steel products to customers in a substantial number of foreign markets.

- Entering into joint ventures with foreign partners to invest in steelmaking projects outside North America. Nucor executives believed that the success of this strategy element was finding the right partners to grow with internationally.

Nucor opened a trading office in Switzerland and proceeded to establish international sales offices in Mexico, Brazil, Colombia, the Middle East, and Asia. The company's trading office bought and sold steel and steel products that Nucor and other steel producers had manufactured. In 2010, approximately 11 percent of the shipments from Nucor's steel mills were exported. Customers in South and Central America presented the most consistent opportunities for export sales, but there was growing interest from customers in Europe and other locations.

In January 2008, Nucor entered into a 50/50 joint venture with the European-based Duferco Group to establish the production of beams and other long products in Italy, with distribution in Europe and North Africa. A few months later, Nucor acquired 50 percent of the stock of Duferdofin-Nucor S.r.l. for approximately $667 million (Duferdofin was Duferco's Italy-based steelmaking subsidiary). Duferdofin-Nucor operated a steel melt shop and bloom/billet caster in San Zeno, Italy, with an annual capacity of 1.1 million tons and three rolling mills in Pallanzeno in the Piedmont region and Giammoro, Sicily, with combined capacity of 1.1 million tons. Total production in the joint venture's fiscal year ended September 30, 2008, was approximately 1,080,000 tons. A new merchant bar mill with annual capacity of

---

EXHIBIT 5

Nucor's Capital Expenditures for New Technology, Plant Improvements, and Equipment Upgrades, 2000–2011

Year	Capital Expenditures (in millions)	Year	Capital Expenditures (in millions)
2000	$ 415.0	2006	$ 338.4
2001	261.0	2007	520.4
2002	244.0	2008	1,019.0
2003	215.4	2009	390.5
2004	285.9	2010	345.3
2005	331.5	2011	440.5

495,000 tons was in the final stages of construction at the Giammoro plant and began production in 2009. Duferdofin-Nucor also operated a 60,000-ton trackshoes/cutting edges mill. The customers for the products produced by Duferdofin-Nucor were primarily steel service centers and distributors located both in Italy and throughout Europe. So far, the joint-venture project had not lived up to the partners' financial expectations because all of the plants made construction-related products. The European construction industry had been hard hit by the economic events of 2008–2009, and the construction-related demand for steel products in Europe was very slowly creeping back toward pre-crisis levels. The two joint-venture partners had agreed to consider investing in additional projects in future years.

In early 2010, Nucor invested $221.3 million to become a 50/50 joint venture partner with Mitsui USA to form NuMit LLC—Mitsui USA was the largest wholly owned subsidiary of Mitsui & Co., Ltd., a diversified global trading, investment, and service enterprise headquartered in Tokyo, Japan. NuMit LLC owned 100 percent of the equity interest in Steel Technologies LLC, an operator of 25 sheet steel processing facilities throughout the United States, Canada, and Mexico. The NuMit partners agreed that Nucor's previously announced plans to construct a greenfield flat-rolled processing center in Monterrey, Mexico, would be implemented by Steel Technologies.

Raw Materials Strategy   Scrap metal and scrap substitutes were Nucor's single biggest cost—all of Nucor's steel mills used electric arc furnaces to make steel products from recycled scrap steel, scrap iron, pig iron, hot briquetted iron (HBI), and direct reduced iron (DRI). On average, it took approximately 1.1 tons of scrap and scrap substitutes to produce a ton of steel—the proportions averaged about 70 percent scrap steel and 30 percent scrap substitutes. Nucor was the biggest user of scrap metal in North America, and it also purchased millions of tons of pig iron, HBI, DRI, and other iron products annually—top-quality scrap substitutes were especially critical in making premium grades of sheet steel, steel plate, and special bar quality steel at various Nucor mills. Scrap prices were driven by market demand-supply conditions and could fluctuate significantly (see Exhibit 6). Rising

EXHIBIT 6

Nucor's Costs for Scrap Steel and Scrap Substitute, 2000–2011

Period	Average Cost of Scrap and Scrap Substitute per Ton Used	Period	Average Cost of Scrap and Scrap Substitute per Ton Used
2000	$120	**2010** Quarter 1	$318
2001	101	Quarter 2	373
2002	110	Quarter 3	354
2003	137	Quarter 4	359
2004	238	**Full-Year Average**	351
2005	244		
2006	246	**2011** Quarter 1	424
2007	278	Quarter 2	444
2008	438	Quarter 3	449
2009	303	Quarter 4	441
		Full-Year Average	439

Source: Nucor's annual reports for 2011, 2009, 2007, and information posted in the investor relations section at www.nucor.com, accessed October 25, 2006, and April 12, 2012.

scrap prices adversely impacted the company's costs and ability to compete against steelmakers that made steel from scratch using iron ore, coke, and traditional blast furnace technology.

Nucor's raw materials strategy was aimed at achieving greater control over the costs of all types of metallic inputs (both scrap metal and iron-related substitutes) used at its steel plants. A key element of this strategy was to backward-integrate into the production of 6,000,000 to 7,000,000 tons per year of high-quality scrap substitutes (chiefly pig iron and direct reduced iron) either at its own wholly owned and operated plants or at plants jointly owned by Nucor and other partners—integrating backward into supplying a big fraction of its own iron requirements held the promise of raw material savings and less reliance on outside iron suppliers. The costs of producing pig iron and direct reduced iron (DRI) were not as subject to steep swings as was the price of scrap steel.

Nucor's first move to execute its long-term raw materials strategy came in 2002 when it partnered with The Rio Tinto Group, Mitsubishi Corporation, and Chinese steelmaker Shougang Corporation to pioneer Rio Tinto's HIsmelt® technology at a new plant to be constructed in Kwinana, Western Australia. The HIsmelt technology entailed converting iron ore to liquid metal or pig iron and was both a replacement for traditional blast furnace technology and a hot metal source for electric arc furnaces. Rio Tinto had been developing the HIsmelt technology for 10 years and believed the technology had the potential to revolutionize iron-making and provide low-cost, high-quality iron for making steel. Nucor had a 25 percent ownership in the venture and had a joint global marketing agreement with Rio Tinto to license the technology to other interested steel companies. The Australian plant represented the world's first commercial application of the HIsmelt technology; it had a capacity of over 880,000 tons and was expandable to 1.65 million tons at an attractive capital cost per incremental ton. Production started in January 2006. However, the joint-venture partners opted to permanently close the HIsmelt

plant in December 2010 because the project, while technologically acclaimed, proved to be financially unviable. Nucor's loss in the joint-venture partnership amounted to $94.8 million.

In April 2003, Nucor entered a joint venture with Companhia Vale do Rio Doce (CVRD) to construct and operate an environmentally friendly $80 million pig iron project in northern Brazil. The project, named Ferro Gusa Carajás, utilized two conventional mini-blast furnaces to produce about 418,000 tons of pig iron per year, using iron ore from CVRD's Carajás mine in northern Brazil. The charcoal fuel for the plant came exclusively from fast-growing eucalyptus trees in a cultivated forest in northern Brazil owned by a CVRD subsidiary. The cultivated forest removed more carbon dioxide from the atmosphere than the blast furnace emitted, thus counteracting global warming—an outcome that appealed to Nucor management. Nucor invested $10 million in the project and was a 22 percent owner. Production of pig iron began in the fourth quarter of 2005; the joint-venture agreement called for Nucor to purchase all of the plant's production.

Nucor's third raw-material sourcing initiative came in 2004 when it acquired an idled direct reduced iron (DRI) plant in Louisiana, relocated all of the plant assets to Trinidad (an island off the coast of South America near Venezuela), and expanded the project to a capacity of nearly 2 million tons. The plant used a proven technology that converted iron ore pellets into direct reduced iron. The Trinidad site was chosen because it had a long-term and very cost-attractive supply of natural gas (large volumes of natural gas were consumed in the plant's production process), along with favorable logistics for receiving iron ore and shipping direct reduced iron to Nucor's steel mills in the United States. Nucor entered into contracts with natural gas suppliers to purchase natural gas in amounts needed to operate the Trinidad through 2028. Production began in January 2007. Nucor personnel at the Trinidad plant had recently achieved world-class product quality levels in making DRI; this achievement allowed Nucor to use an even larger percentage of DRI in producing the most demanding steel products. In 2011, construction was underway to increase the Trinidad DRI plant's annual capacity to approximately 2,200,000 tons.

In September 2010, Nucor announced plans to build a $750 million DRI facility with an annual capacity of 2.5 million tons on a 4,000-acre site in St. James Parish, Louisiana. This investment moved Nucor two-thirds of the way toward its long-term objective of being able to supply 6 to 7 million tons of its requirements for high-quality scrap substitutes. However, the new DRI facility was the first phase of a multiphase plan that included a second 2.5-million-ton DRI facility, a coke plant, a blast furnace, an iron ore pellet plant, and a steel mill. Permits for both DRI plants were received from the Louisiana Department of Environmental Quality in January 2011. Construction of the first DRI unit at the St. James site began in 2011, and production startup was scheduled for mid-2013. Because producing DRI was a natural gas–intensive process, Nucor had entered into a long-term, onshore natural gas working interest drilling program with one of North America's largest producers of natural gas to help offset the company's exposure to future increases in the price of natural gas consumed by the DRI facility in St. James Parish. All natural gas from Nucor's working interest drilling program was being sold to outside parties.

In February 2008, Nucor acquired The David J. Joseph Company (DJJ) and related affiliates for a cash purchase price of approximately $1.44 billion, the largest acquisition in Nucor's history. DJJ was one of the leading scrap metal companies in the United States, with 2007 revenues of $6.4 billion. It processed about 3.5 million tons of scrap iron and scrap steel annually at some 35 scrap yards and brokered over 20 million tons of iron and steel scrap and over 500 million pounds of nonferrous materials in 2007. The DJJ Mill and Industrial Services business provided logistics and metallurgical blending operations and offered onsite handling and trading of industrial scrap. The DJJ Rail Services business owned over 2,000 railcars dedicated to the movement of scrap metals and offered complete railcar fleet management and leasing services. All of these businesses had strategic value to Nucor in helping gain control over its scrap metal costs. Nucor was familiar with DJJ and its various operations because it had obtained scrap from DJJ since 1969. Within months of completing the DJJ acquisition (which was operated as a separate subsidiary), the DJJ management team acquired four other scrap processing companies. A fifth scrap processor was acquired in 2010. Since becoming a Nucor subsidiary, DJJ had added approximately 1.1 million tons of scrap processing capacity and 27 locations through five acquisitions and the opening of three new scrapyards. This gave Nucor total annual scrap processing capacity of almost 5 million tons and, because of DJJ's railcar fleet, the ability to improve the cost and speed with which scrap could be delivered to its steel mills. DJJ obtained scrap from industrial plants, the manufacturers of products that contained steel, independent scrap dealers, peddlers, auto junkyards, demolition firms, and other sources. In 2011, approximately 12 percent of the ferrous and nonferrous metals and scrap substitute tons processed and sold by DJJ were sold to external customers, and the remainder was delivered to various Nucor steel mills.

Nucor's Newest Strategic Initiative: Shifting Production from Lower-End Steel Products to Value-Added Products

In 2010–2012, Nucor shifted a growing percentage of the production tonnage at its steel mills and steel products facilities to "value-added products" that could command higher prices and yield better profit margins than could be had by producing lower-end or commodity steel products. Examples included:

- The new galvanizing capability at the Decatur, Alabama, mill that enabled Nucor to sell 500,000 tons of corrosion-resistant, galvanized sheet steel for high-end applications.

- The ability to supply customers with an additional 200,000 tons per year of cut-to-length and tempered steel plate due to expanding the cut-to-length capabilities at the Tuscaloosa, Alabama, mill.

- Shipping 250,000 tons of new steel plate and structural steel products in 2010 that were not offered in 2009, and further increasing shipments of these same new products to 500,000 tons in 2011.

- Being able to supply customers with 125,000 tons of new products annually because of the new heat-treat facility at the Hertford plate mill in North Carolina.

- Being able to upgrade the caliber of sheet steel and steel plate produced at the Hickman and Hertford mills because of the investments made in vacuum degassers.

Similar product offering upgrades were underway at Nucor's special bar quality, cold-finished, and fastener facilities.

In 2010–2011, approximately 55 percent of Nucor's steel mill shipments were to customers who bought multiple types of products from the company.

Nucor's Commitment to Being a Global Leader in Environmental Performance

Every Nucor facility was evaluated for actions that could be taken to promote greater environmental sustainability. Measurable objectives and targets relating to such outcomes as the reduced use of oil and grease, more efficient use of electricity, and site-wide recycling were in place at each plant. Computerized controls on large electric motors and pumps and energy-recovery equipment to capture and reuse energy that otherwise would be wasted had been installed throughout Nucor's facilities to lower energy usage—Nucor considered itself to be among the most energy-efficient steel companies in the world. All of Nucor's facilities had water-recycling systems. Nucor even recycled the dust from its electric arc furnaces because scrap metal contained enough zinc, lead, chrome, and other valuable metals to recycle into usable products; the dust was captured in each plant's state-of-the-art bag house

air pollution control devices and then sent to a recycler that converted the dust into zinc oxide, steel slag, and pig iron. All of Nucor's steelmaking operations had ISO 14001 certified Environmental Management Systems in place in 2011.

Nucor's sheet mill in Decatur, Alabama, used a measuring device called an opacity monitor, which gave precise, minute-by-minute readings of the air quality that passed through the bag house and out of the mill's exhaust system. While rival steel producers had resisted using opacity monitors (because they documented any time a mill's exhaust was out of compliance with its environmental permits, even momentarily), Nucor's personnel at the Decatur mill viewed the opacity monitor as a tool for improving environmental performance. They developed the expertise to read the monitor so well that they could pinpoint in just a few minutes the first signs of a problem in any of the nearly 7,000 bags in the bag house—before those problems resulted in increased emissions. Their early-warning system worked so well that the division had applied for a patent on the process, with an eye toward licensing it to other companies.

Organization and Management Philosophy

Nucor had a simple streamlined organizational structure to allow employees to innovate and make quick decisions. The company was highly decentralized, with most day-to-day operating decisions made by group or plant-level general managers and their staff. Each group or plant operated independently as a profit center and was headed by a general manager, who in most cases also had the title of vice president. The group manager or plant general manager had control of the day-to-day decisions that affected the group or plant's profitability.

The organizational structure at a typical plant had three management layers:

- General manager
- Department manager
- Supervisor/professional
- Hourly employee

Group managers and plant managers reported to one of five executive vice presidents at corporate headquarters. Nucor's corporate staff was exceptionally small, consisting of only 100 people in 2011, the philosophy being that corporate headquarters should consist of a small cadre of executives who would guide a decentralized operation where liberal authority was delegated to managers in the field. Each plant had a sales manager who was responsible for selling the products made at that particular plant; such staff functions as engineering, accounting, and personnel management were performed at the group/plant level. There was a minimum of paperwork and bureaucratic systems. Each group/plant was expected to earn about a 25 percent return on total assets before corporate expenses, taxes, interest, or profit-sharing. As long as plant managers met their profit targets, they were allowed to operate with minimal restrictions and interference from corporate headquarters. There was a very friendly spirit of competition from one plant to the next to see which facility could be the best performer, but since all of the vice presidents and general managers shared the same bonus systems, they functioned pretty much as a team despite operating their facilities individually. Top executives did not hesitate to replace group or plant managers who consistently struggled to achieve profitability and operating targets.

Workforce Compensation Practices

Nucor was a largely nonunion "pay for performance" company with an incentive compensation system that rewarded goal-oriented individuals and did not put a maximum on what they could earn. All employees, except those in the recently acquired Harris Steel and DJJ subsidiaries that operated independently from the rest of Nucor, worked under one of four basic compensation plans, each featuring incentives related to meeting specific goals and targets:

1. *Production Incentive Plan*—Production line jobs were rated on degree of responsibility required and assigned a base wage comparable to the wages paid by other manufacturing plants in the area where a Nucor plant was located. But in addition to their base wage, operating and maintenance employees were paid weekly bonuses based on the number of tons by which the output of their production team or work group exceeded the "standard" number of tons. All operating and maintenance employees were members of a production team that included the team's production supervisor, and the tonnage produced by each work team was measured for each work shift and then totaled for all shifts during a given week. If a production team's weekly output beat the weekly standard, team members (including the team's production supervisor) earned a specified percentage bonus for each ton produced above the standard—production bonuses were paid weekly (rather than quarterly or annually) so that workers and supervisors would be rewarded immediately for their efforts. The standard rate was calculated based on the capabilities of the equipment employed (typically at the time plant operations began), and no bonus was paid if the equipment was not operating (which gave maintenance workers a big incentive to keep a plant's equipment in good working condition)—Nucor's philosophy was that when equipment was not operating, everybody suffered and the bonus for downtime ought to be zero. Production standards at Nucor plants were seldom raised unless a plant underwent significant modernization or important new pieces of equipment were installed that greatly boosted labor productivity. It was common for production incentive bonuses to run from 50 to 150 percent of an employee's base pay, thereby pushing compensation levels up well above those at other nearby manufacturing plants. Worker efforts to exceed the standard and get a bonus did not so much involve working harder as it involved good teamwork and close collaboration in resolving problems

and figuring out how best to exceed the production standards.

2. *Department Manager Incentive Plan*—Department managers earned annual incentive bonuses based primarily on the percentage of net income to dollars of assets employed for their division. These bonuses could be as much as 80 percent of a department manager's base pay.

3. *Professional and Clerical Bonus Plan*—A bonus based on a division's net income return on assets was paid to employees who were not on the production worker or department manager plan.

4. *Senior Officers Incentive Plan*—Nucor's senior officers did not have employment contracts and did not participate in any pension or retirement plans. Their base salaries were set at approximately 90 percent of the median base salary for comparable positions in other manufacturing companies with comparable assets, sales, and capital. The remainder of their compensation was based on Nucor's annual overall percentage of net income to stockholder's equity (ROE) and was paid out in cash and stock. Once Nucor's ROE reached a threshold of not less than 3 percent or more than 7 percent (as determined annually by the compensation committee of the board of directors), senior officers earned a bonus equal to 20 percent of their base salary. If Nucor's annual ROE was 20 percent or higher, senior officers earned a bonus equal to 225 percent of their base salary. Officers could earn an additional bonus up to 75 percent of their base salary based on a comparison of Nucor's net sales growth with the net sales growth of members of a steel industry peer group. There was also a long-term incentive plan that provided for stock awards and stock options. The structure of these officer incentives was such that bonus compensation for Nucor officers fluctuated widely—from close to zero (in years like 2003 when industry conditions were bad and Nucor's performance was sub-par) to

400 percent (or more) of their base salary (when Nucor's performance was excellent, as had been the case in 2004–2008).

Nucor management had designed the company's incentive plans for employees so that bonus calculations involved no discretion on the part of a plant/division manager or top executives. This was done to eliminate any concerns on the part of workers that managers or executives might show favoritism or otherwise be unfair in calculating or awarding incentive awards.

There were two other types of extra compensation:

- *Profit Sharing*—Each year, Nucor allocated 10 percent of its operating profits to profit-sharing bonuses for all employees (except senior officers). Depending on company performance, the bonuses could run anywhere from 1 percent to over 20 percent of pay. Twenty percent of the bonus amount was paid to employees in the following March as a cash bonus and the remaining 80 percent was put into a trust for each employee, with each employee's share being proportional to their earnings as a percent of total earnings by all workers covered by the plan. An employee's share of profit-sharing became vested after one full year of employment. Employees received a quarterly statement of their balance in profit sharing.

- *401(k) Plan*—Both officers and employees participated in a 401(k) plan where by the company matched from 5 percent to 25 percent of each employee's first 7 percent of contributions; the amount of the match was based on how well the company was doing.

In 2012, an entry-level worker at a Nucor plant could expect to earn about $47,000 to $50,000 annually (including bonuses). Total compensation for Nucor's plant employees in 2011 was in the range of $70,000 to $100,000 annually. It was common for worker compensation at Nucor plants to be double or more the average earned by workers at other manufacturing companies in the states where Nucor's plants were located. At Nucor's new $450 million plant in Hertford County, North Carolina, where jobs were scarce and poverty was common, Nucor employees earned three times the local average manufacturing wage. Nucor management philosophy was that workers ought to be excellently compensated because the production jobs were strenuous and the work environment in a steel mill was relatively dangerous.

Employee turnover in Nucor mills was extremely low; absenteeism and tardiness were minimal. Each employee was allowed four days of absences and could also miss work for jury duty, military leave, or the death of close relatives. After this, a day's absence cost a worker their entire performance bonus pay for that week, and being more than a half-hour late to work on a given day resulted in no bonus payment for the day. When job vacancies did occur, Nucor was flooded with applications from people wanting to get a job at Nucor; plant personnel screened job candidates very carefully, seeking people with initiative and a strong work ethic.

Employee Relations and Human Resources

Employee relations at Nucor were based on four clear-cut principles:

1. Management is obligated to manage Nucor in such a way that employees will have the opportunity to earn according to their productivity.

2. Employees should feel confident that if they do their jobs properly, they will have a job tomorrow.

3. Employees have the right to be treated fairly and must believe that they will be.

4. Employees must have an avenue of appeal when they believe they are being treated unfairly.

The hallmarks of Nucor's human resources strategy were its incentive pay plan for production exceeding the standard and the job security provided to production workers—despite being in an industry with strong downcycles, Nucor had made it a practice not to lay off workers. Instead, when market conditions were tough and production had to be cut back, workers were assigned to plant maintenance projects, cross-training programs, and other activities calculated to boost the plant's performance when market conditions improved.

Nucor took an egalitarian approach to providing fringe benefits to its employees; employees had the same insurance programs, vacation schedules, and holidays as upper-level management. However, certain benefits were not available to Nucor's officers. The fringe benefit package at Nucor included:

- *Medical and Dental Plans*—The company had a flexible and comprehensive health benefit program for officers and employees that included wellness and health care spending accounts.

- *Tuition Reimbursement*—Nucor reimbursed up to $3,000 of an employee's approved educational expenses each year and up to $1,500 of a spouse's educational expenses for two years.

- *Service Awards*—After each five years of service with the company, Nucor employees received a service award consisting of five shares of Nucor stock.

- *Scholarships and Educational Disbursements*—Nucor provided the children of every employee (except senior officers) with college funding of $3,000 per year for four years to be used at accredited academic institutions. As of 2011, Nucor had paid out over $61 million.

- *Other benefits*—Long-term disability, life insurance, vacation.

Most of the changes Nucor made in work procedures and in equipment came from employees. The prevailing view at Nucor was that the employees knew the problems of their jobs better than anyone else and were thus in the best position to identify ways to improve how things were done. Most plant-level managers spent considerable time in the plant, talking and meeting with frontline employees and listening carefully to suggestions. Promising ideas and suggestions were typically acted upon quickly and implemented—management was willing to take risks to try worker suggestions for doing things better and to accept the occasional failure when the results were disappointing. Teamwork, a vibrant team spirit, and a close worker–management partnership were much in evidence at Nucor plants.

Nucor plants did not utilize job descriptions. Management believed job descriptions caused more problems than they solved, given the teamwork atmosphere and the close collaboration among work group members. The company saw formal performance appraisal systems as a waste of time and added paperwork. If a Nucor employee was not performing well, the problem was dealt with directly by supervisory personnel and the peer pressure of work group members (whose bonuses were adversely affected).

Employees were kept informed about company and division performance. Charts showing the division's results in return-on-assets and bonus payoff were posted in prominent places in the plant. Most all employees were quite aware of the level of profits in their plant or division. Nucor had a formal grievance procedure, but grievances were few and far between. The corporate office sent all news releases to each division where they were posted on bulletin boards. Each employee received a copy of Nucor's annual report; it was company practice for the cover of the annual report to consist of the names of all Nucor employees.

All of these practices had created an egalitarian culture and a highly motivated workforce that grew out of former CEO Ken Iverson's radical insight: that employees, even hourly clock punchers, would put forth extraordinary effort and be exceptionally productive if they were richly rewarded, treated with respect, and given real power to do their jobs as best they saw fit.[5] There were countless stories of occasions when managers and workers had gone beyond the call of duty to expedite equipment repairs (in many instances even using their weekends to go help personnel at other Nucor plants solve a crisis); the company's workforce was known for displaying unusual passion and company loyalty even when no personal financial stake was involved. As one Nucor worker put it, "At Nucor, we're not 'you guys' and 'us guys.' It's all of us guys. Wherever the bottleneck is, we go there, and everyone works on it."[6]

It was standard procedure for a team of Nucor veterans, including people who worked on the plant floor, to visit with their counterparts as part of the process of screening candidates for acquisition.[7] One of the purposes of such visits was to explain the Nucor compensation system and culture face-to-face, gauge reactions, and judge whether the plant would fit into "the Nucor way of doing things" if it was acquired. Shortly after making an acquisition, Nucor management moved swiftly to institute its pay-for-performance incentive system and to begin instilling the egalitarian Nucor culture and idea-sharing. Top priority was given to looking for ways to boost plant production using fewer people and without making substantial capital investments; the take-home pay of workers at newly acquired plants typically went up rather dramatically. At the Auburn Steel plant, acquired in 2001, it took Nucor about six months to convince workers that they would be better off under Nucor's pay system; during that time Nucor paid people under the old Auburn Steel system but posted what they would have earned under Nucor's system. Pretty soon, workers were convinced to make the changeover—one worker saw his pay climb from $53,000 in the year prior to the acquisition to $67,000 in 2001 and to $92,000 in 2005.[8]

New Employees   Each plant/division had a "consul" responsible for providing new employees with general advice about becoming a Nucor teammate and serving as a resource for inquiries about how things were done at Nucor, how to navigate the division and company, and how to resolve issues that might come up.

Nucor provided new employees with a personalized plan that set forth who would give them feedback about how well they were doing and when and how this feedback would be given; from time to time, new employees met with the plant manager for feedback and coaching. In addition, there was a new employee orientation session that provided a hands-on look at the plant/division operations; new employees also participated in product group meetings to provide exposure to broader business and technical issues. Each year, Nucor brought all recent college hires to the Charlotte headquarters for a forum intended to give the new hires a chance to network and provide senior management with guidance on how best to leverage their talent.

The World Steel Industry

Both 2010 and 2011 were record years for global production of crude steel, with worldwide production reaching 1,559 million tons in 2010 and 1,680 million tons in 2011 (see Exhibit 7). Steelmaking capacity worldwide was approximately 2,090 million tons in 2011, resulting in a 2011 capacity utilization rate of 80 percent versus just over 75 percent in 2010. Worldwide demand for steel mill products had grown about 5.5 percent annually since 2000 (well above the 1.1 percent growth rate from 1975 to 2000), but there had been periods of both strong and weak demand during the 2000–2011 time frame (see Exhibit 7). The six biggest steel-producing countries in 2011 are shown in the table immediately following Exhibit 7.

EXHIBIT 7

Worldwide Production of Crude Steel, with Compound Average Growth Rates, 1975–2011

Year	World Crude Steel Production (millions of tons)	Compound Average Growth Rates in World Crude Steel Production	
		Period	Percentage Rate
1975	707	1975–1980	2.2%
1980	788	1980–1985	0.1
1985	791	1985–1990	1.4
1990	847	1990–1995	−0.5
1995	827	1995–2000	2.4
2000	933	2000–2005	6.2
2001	936	2005–2010	4.4
2002	995	2010–2011	4.4
2003	1,067		
2004	1,178		
2005	1,258		
2006	1,372		
2007	1,481		
2008	1,462		
2009	1,356		
2010	1,559		
2011	1,680		

Source: World Steel Association, *Steel Statistical Yearbook, various years,* accessed at www.worldsteel.org on April 23, 2012.

Country	Total Production of Crude Steel	Percent of Worldwide Production
China	752 million tons	45.9%
Japan	118 million tons	7.2%
United States	95 million tons	5.8%
India	79 million tons	4.8%
Russia	76 million tons	4.6%
South Korea	75 million tons	4.6%

Exhibit 8 shows the world's 15 largest producers of steel in 2010.

Steelmaking Technologies

Steel was produced by either integrated steel facilities or "mini-mills" that employed electric arc furnaces. Integrated mills used blast furnaces to produce hot metal typically from iron ore pellets, limestone, scrap steel, oxygen, assorted other metals, and coke (coke was produced by firing coal in large coke ovens and was the major fuel used in blast furnaces to produce molten iron). Melted iron from the blast furnace process was then run through the basic oxygen process to produce liquid steel. To make flat rolled steel products, liquid steel either was fed into a continuous caster machine and cast into slabs or was cooled in slab form for later processing. Slabs were further shaped or rolled at a plate mill or hot strip mill. In making certain sheet steel products, the hot strip mill process was followed by various finishing processes, including pickling, cold-rolling, annealing, tempering, galvanizing, or other coating procedures. These various processes for converting raw steel into finished steel products were often distinct steps undertaken at different times and in different onsite or offsite facilities rather than

EXHIBIT 8

Top 15 Steel Companies Worldwide, Based on Crude Steel Production, 2010

		Crude Steel Production (in millions of tons)	
2010 Rank	Company (Headquarters)	2005	2010
1.	ArcelorMittal (Luxembourg)	120.9	98.2
2.	Baosteel (China)	25.0	37.0
3.	POSCO (South Korea)	33.6	35.4
4.	Nippon Steel (Japan)	35.3	35.0
5.	JFE (Japan)	32.9	31.1
6.	Jiangsu Shagang (China)	n.a.	23.2
7.	Tata Steel (India)	n.a.	23.2
8.	United States Steel (USA)	21.3	22.3
9.	Ansteel (China)	13.1	22.1
10.	Gerdau (Brazil)	15.1	18.7
11.	Nucor (USA)	20.3	18.3
12.	Severstal (Russia)	15.0	18.2
13.	Wuhan (China)	14.3	16.6
14.	ThyssenKrupp (Germany)	18.2	16.4
15.	Evraz (Russia)	15.3	16.3
14.	Gerdau (Brazil)	15.1	16.1
15.	Severstal (Russia)	15.0	14.1

n.a. Not available

Source: World Steel Association, www.worldsteel.org, accessed on November 6, 2006 and April 25, 2012.

being done in a continuous process in a single plant facility—an integrated mill was thus one that had multiple facilities at a single plant site and could therefore not only produce crude (or raw) steel but also run the crude steel through various facilities and finishing processes to make hot-rolled and cold-rolled sheet steel products, steel bars and beams, stainless steel, steel wire and nails, steel pipes and tubes, and other finished steel products. The steel produced by integrated mills tended to be purer than steel produced by electric arc furnaces since less scrap was used in the production process (scrap steel often contained nonferrous elements that could adversely affect metallurgical properties). Some steel customers required purer steel products for their applications.

Mini-mills used an electric arc furnace to melt steel scrap or scrap substitutes into molten metal that was then cast into crude steel slabs, billets, or blooms in a continuous casting process. As was the case at integrated mills, the crude steel was then run through various facilities and finishing processes to make hot-rolled and cold-rolled sheet steel products, steel bars and beams, stainless steel, steel wire and nails, steel pipes and tubes, and other finished steel products. Mini-mills could accommodate short production runs and had relatively fast product changeover times. The electric arc technology employed by mini-mills offered two primary competitive advantages: capital investment requirements that were 75 percent lower than those of integrated mills and a smaller workforce (which translated into lower labor costs per ton shipped).

Initially, companies that used electric arc furnace technology were able to only make low-end steel products (such as reinforcing rods and steel bars). But when thin-slab casting technology came on the scene in the 1980s, mini-mills were able to compete in the market for flat-rolled carbon sheet and strip products; these products sold at substantially higher prices per ton and thus were attractive market segments for mini-mill companies. Carbon sheet and strip steel products accounted for about 50 to 60 percent of total steel production and represented the last big market category controlled by the producers employing basic oxygen furnace and blast furnace technologies. Thin-slab casting technology, which had been developed by SMS Schloemann-Siemag AG of Germany, was pioneered in the United States by Nucor at its plants in Indiana and elsewhere. Other mini-mill companies in the United States and across the world were quick to adopt thin-slab casting technology because the low capital costs of thin-slab casting facilities, often coupled with lower labor costs per ton, gave mini-mill companies a cost and pricing advantage over integrated steel producers, enabling them to grab a growing share of the global market for flat-rolled sheet steel and other carbon steel products. Many integrated producers also switched to thin-slab casting as a defensive measure to protect their profit margins and market shares.

In 2011–2012, about 70 percent of the world's steel mill production was made at large integrated mills and about 29 percent was made at mills that used electric arc furnaces. In the United States, however, roughly 60 percent of the steel was produced at mills employing electric arc furnaces and 40 percent at mills using blast furnaces and basic oxygen processes. Large integrated steel mills using blast furnaces, basic oxygen furnaces, and assorted casting and rolling equipment typically had the ability to manufacture a wide variety of steel mill products but faced significantly higher energy costs and were often burdened with higher capital and fixed operating costs. Electric-arc furnace mill producers were challenged by increases in scrap prices but tended to have lower capital and fixed operating costs compared to the integrated steel producers.

The global marketplace for steel was considered to be relatively mature and highly cyclical as a result of ongoing ups and downs in the world economy or the economies of particular countries. However, in 2010–2012, the world steel market was divided into "two separate worlds." In those places like Europe, the United States, and Japan where recovery from the 2008–2009 financial crisis and economic recession was slow, the demand for steel was weak and there was abundant excess steelmaking capacity. In fast-developing areas of the world—like Asia (especially China and India) and many countries in Latin America and the Middle East—the demand for steel was strong and often exceeded the capacity of local steelmakers, many of which were adding new capacity.

In general, competition within the global steel industry was intense and expected to remain so. Companies with excess production capacity were active in seeking to increase their exports of steel to foreign markets. During the 2005–2011 period, the biggest steel-exporting countries were China, Japan, South Korea, Russia, the Ukraine, and Germany; the biggest steel-importing countries during this same time were France, Germany, Italy, the United States, China, and South Korea. China, Germany, and South Korea were both big exporters and big importers because they had more capacity to make certain types and grades of steel than was needed inside their borders (and thus local steelmakers sought to export supplies to other countries) but lacked sufficient internal capacity to supply local steel users with other types and grades of steel.

Industry Consolidation   In both the United States and across the world, industry downturns had resulted in numerous mergers and acquisitions. Some of the mergers/acquisitions were the result of a financially and managerially strong company seeking to acquire a high-cost or struggling steel company at a bargain price and then pursue cost reduction initiatives to make newly acquired steel mill operations more cost competitive. Other mergers/acquisitions reflected the strategies of growth-minded steel companies looking to expand both their production capacity and geographic market presence.

Nucor and Competition in the Market for Steel in the United States

Nucor competed in the markets for a wide variety of finished steel products and unfinished steel products, plus the markets for scrap steel and scrap substitutes. Nucor executives considered all these markets to be highly competitive and populated with many domestic and foreign firms. Competition for steel mill products and finished steel products (like steel joists, steel deck, steel mesh, fasteners, cold-finished items, and fabricated rebar) was centered on price and the ability to meet customer delivery requirements.

Most recently, Nucor had experienced mounting competitive pressures in the market for sheet steel in the United States, largely because of significant increases in rivals' production capacity. Since the beginning of 2010, domestic sheet capacity had increased by approximately 5,000,000 tons as a result of the opening of a very large sheet facility in Alabama owned by ThyssenKrupp, capacity additions at several existing sheet mills, and the reopening of a previously shuttered sheet mill in Maryland.

However, Nucor considered that one of its most formidable competitive threats in the U.S. market came from foreign steelmakers who were intent on exporting some of their production to the United States. Many foreign steel producers had costs on a par with or even below those of Nucor, although their competitiveness in the U.S. market varied significantly according to the prevailing strength of their local currencies versus the U.S. dollar. But the unique challenge that Nucor faced from foreign steelmakers was that many were often able to undercut the prices of domestic steel producers because they received various types of subsidies from their own governments, either directly or indirectly through government-owned enterprises or government-owned or controlled financial institutions in their countries. Many Chinese steelmakers were government-owned in whole or in part, and, in the opinion of Nucor executives, benefited from their government's manipulation of foreign currency exchange rates as well as from the receipt of government subsidies. According to Dan DiMicco, who was a frequent spokesman for the domestic steel industry in voicing complaints against the below-market prices of foreign steel producers and calling upon government policymakers to enforce global trade agreements and address the jobs crisis in the United States:[9]

Artificially cheap exports by some of our major foreign competitors to the United States and elsewhere reduce our net sales and adversely impact our financial results. Direct steel imports in 2010 accounted for a 21 percent share of the U.S. market despite significant unused domestic steelmaking capacity. Aggressive enforcement of trade rules by the World Trade Organization (WTO) to limit unfairly traded imports remains uncertain, although it is critical to our ability to remain competitive. We have been encouraged by recent actions the United States government has taken before the WTO to challenge some of China's trade practices as violating world trade rules, and we continue to believe that assertive enforcement of world trade rules must be one of the highest priorities of the United States government.

In Nucor's 2011 10-K report, management said:[10]

China's unfair trade practices seriously undermine the ability of the Company and other domestic producers to compete on price when left unchallenged. That country's artificially lowered production costs have significantly contributed to the exodus of manufacturing jobs from the United States. When such a flight occurs, Nucor's customer base is diminished, thereby providing us with fewer opportunities to supply steel to those shuttered businesses. Rigorous trade law enforcement is critical to our ability to maintain our competitive position against foreign producers that engage in unlawful trade practices.

Foreign imports accounted for approximately 22 percent of the U.S. steel market in 2011. In 2011 and the first three months of 2012, foreign steel producers were selling an average of 2.2 million tons of steel products per month to customers in the United States. Nearly 100,000 tons per month of these imported steel products were coming from steelmakers in China. In the first three months of 2012, steel imports from Turkey jumped to an average of 178,000 tons per month, up sharply from an average of about 58,000 tons per month in 2011. A big fraction of the remaining import tonnage came from steelmakers in Europe, Asia, and Brazil.

Exhibit 9 shows shipments, exports, and imports of steel mill products in the United States for 2000–2011 (not included are statistics relating to the shipments, exports, and imports of such finished steel products as steel joists, steel deck, cold finished items, fabrication rebar, and steel fasteners). The average capacity

---

EXHIBIT 9

Apparent Consumption of Steel Mill Products in the United States, 2000–2010 (in millions of tons)

Year	U.S. Shipments of Steel Mill Products	U.S. Exports of Steel Mill Products	U.S. Imports of Steel Mill Products	Apparent U.S. Consumption of Steel Mill Products*
2000	109.1	6.5	38.0	140.6
2001	99.1	6.4	30.8	123.5
2002	100.7	6.2	33.3	127.8
2003	103.0	8.5	23.8	118.3
2004	109.6	8.6	36.0	137.0
2005	104.4	10.4	33.2	127.2
2006	108.4	10.5	46.4	144.3
2007	107.9	10.8	30.5	127.6
2008	100.5	13.2	27.1	114.4
2009	64.0	10.2	16.9	70.7
2010	88.5	13.0	24.8	100.3

*Apparent U.S. consumption equals total shipments minus exports plus imports.

Source: World Steel Association, *Steel Statistical Yearbook,* 2011. Accessed at www.worldsteel.org, April 24, 2012.

utilization rate of U.S. steel mills was at a historically unprecedented low of 52 percent in 2009. Since then, the average capacity utilization rate had improved to 70 percent in 2010 and 75 percent in 2011. These rates, though improved, still compared unfavorably to the capacity utilization rates of 87 percent in 2007 and 81 percent in 2008. Domestic demand for steel and steel products was expected to improve slowly in 2012, making it unlikely that 2012 capacity utilization rates would increase significantly.

Nucor's Two Largest Domestic Competitors

Consolidation of the industry into a smaller number of larger and more efficient steel producers had heightened competitive pressures for Nucor and most other steelmakers. Nucor had two major rivals in the United States—the USA division of ArcelorMittal and United States Steel. ArcelorMittal USA competed chiefly in carbon steel product categories, with much of its production going to customers in the automotive, trucking, off-highway, agricultural equipment, and railway industries. It also was a supplier to companies in the appliance, office furniture, electrical motor, packaging, and industrial machinery sectors, as well as to steel service centers. In 2011, ArcelorMittal USA operated about 20 facilities, including large integrated steel mills, plants that used electric arc furnaces, and rolling and finishing plants. Its facilities were considered to be modern and efficient. The company's shipments of steel products in North America (the United States and Canada) totaled 21.7 million tons in 2011 and 19.5 million tons in 2010. ArcelorMittal's earnings before interest, taxes, depreciation, amortization (EBITDA) in North America were $1.7 billion in 2011 and $754 million in 2010. ArcelorMittal's worldwide operations had sales revenues of $94.0 billion and net earnings of $2.3 billion in 2011 and sales revenues of $78.0 billion and net earnings of $2.9 billion in 2010.[11]

U.S. Steel had net sales of $19.9 billion in 2011 and $17.4 billion in 2010, down from a peak of $23.8 billion in 2008; the company reported net losses of $53 million in 2011 and $482 million in 2010, far below its peak earnings of $2.1 billion in 2008. Its steel shipments from mills in North America were 17.3 million tons in 2011 and 16.8 million tons in 2010 (the company's integrated steel mills in Slovakia and Serbia shipped 4.9 million tons in 2011 and 5.5 million tons in 2010—however, all of the company's operations in Serbia were sold to the Republic of Serbia for $1 on January 31, 2012, resulting in a loss of approximately $400 million). At year-end 2011, U.S. Steel had approximately 24,000 employees in North America and 19,000 employees in Europe. In North America, the company operated 23 steelmaking facilities in the United States, 4 in Canada, and 2 in Mexico that produced sheet steel, steel pipe and other tubular products, steel plate, and tin mill products. Principal customers included steel service centers and companies in the transportation (including automotive), construction, container, appliance, electrical equipment, oil, gas, and petrochemical sectors, as well as manufacturers that bought steel mill products for conversion into a variety of finished steel products. U.S. Steel exported 736,000 tons of its steel mill products in 2011, 746,000 tons in 2010, and 390,000 tons in 2009. U.S. Steel had a labor cost disadvantage versus Nucor and ArcelorMittal USA, partly due to the lower productivity of its unionized workforce and partly due to its retiree pension costs.

ENDNOTES

[1] Tom Peters and Nancy Austin, *A Passion for Excellence: The Leadership Difference* (New York: Random House, 1985); and "Other Low-Cost Champions," *Fortune,* June 24, 1985.

[2] Nucor's 2011 Annual Report, p. 4.

[3] According to information posted at www.nucor.com, accessed October 11, 2006.

[4] Nucor's 2008 Annual Report, p. 5.

[5] Nanette Byrnes, "The Art of Motivation," *BusinessWeek,* May 1, 2006, p. 57.

[6] Ibid., p. 60.

[7] Ibid.

[8] Ibid.

[9] Nucor's 2010 Annual Report, p. 22.

[10] Company 10-K report, 2011, p. 6.

[11] Company annual report, 2011.

Tata Motors: Can It Become a Global Contender in the Automobile Industry?

connect

DAVID L. TURNIPSEED University of South Alabama

JOHN E. GAMBLE Texas A&M University – Corpus Christi

Tata Motors, Ltd., was India's leading automobile company by revenue and was the number one commercial vehicle manufacturer and the number three passenger vehicle manufacturer in India in 2012. It was also the world's fourth-largest medium- and large-sized bus manufacturer, and the fourth-largest truck manufacturer in the world. Tata's passenger car portfolio ranged from the world's least expensive four-wheel automobile, the Nano, to luxury automobile brands Jaguar and Land Rover. The company manufactured vehicles in India, the United Kingdom, Thailand, South Africa, Morocco, South Korea, and Spain. As of 2012, Tata employed over 1,400 engineers and scientists in six research and development centers in India, Italy, the UK, and South Korea.

Although Tata Motors was a very successful competitor in India and many international markets, poor macroeconomic conditions, increasing competition, and a variety of other strategic issues had created challenges that would need to be addressed by the division's top management. The possible elimination of diesel subsidies by the Indian government might possibly affect the demand for its diesel-powered vehicles sold in India. Also, the company's managers needed to consider how to

expand the market for its low-priced Nano, which had required substantial investment during its development. In addition, the company needed to capture the benefits of its recent acquisitions of Jaguar and Land Rover and expand the market for its commercial vehicles outside of India.

The History of Tata Motors

Tata Motors was a division of the Tata Group, which was India's largest corporation, owning more than 90 companies spanning seven business sectors (chemicals, information technology and communications, consumer products, engineering, materials, services, and energy). In 2012, the corporation had operations in over 80 countries and had gross revenues of $83.5 billion in 2011. Nearly 60 percent of the Tata Group's revenues were generated from outside of India. The Tata Group was a powerful symbol of India's emergence as a world economic power and was India's largest private-sector employer with over 425,000 employees. A financial summary for the Tata Group for fiscal 2010 and fiscal 2011 is presented in Exhibit 1.

Copyright © 2012 by David L. Turnipseed. All rights reserved.

EXHIBIT 1

Financial Summary for the Tata Group, Fiscal 2010–Fiscal 2011* (in billions of U.S. dollars)

	Fiscal 2011	Fiscal 2010	% Change
Total revenue	$ 83.3	$ 67.4	23.6%
Sales	82.2	65.6	25.3
International revenues	48.3	38.4	25.8
Profit after tax	5.8	1.74	233.3
Total assets	68.9	52.8	30.5

*Fiscal period April–March.

Exchange rate: 1 USD = Rs45.57 for 2011 and 1 USD = Rs47.41 for 2010.

Source: www.tata.com.

Tata Motors' history began in 1945 when Tata Engineering and Locomotive Company began manufacturing locomotives and engineering products. In 1948, Tata began production of steam road rollers, in collaboration with UK manufacturer Marshall Sons. In 1954, the company entered into a 15-year collaborative agreement with Daimler Benz AG, Germany, to manufacture medium-sized commercial vehicles. The company began producing hydraulic excavators in collaboration with Japan's Hitachi in 1985. The first independently designed light commercial vehicle, the Tata 407 "pickup," was produced in 1986, followed by the Tata 608 light truck. Tata Engineering began manufacturing passenger cars in 1991 and entered into a joint agreement with Cummins Engine Co. in 1993 to manufacture high horsepower and low-emission diesel engines for cars and trucks.

In 1994, the company began a joint venture with Daimler–Benz/Mercedes-Benz to manufacture Mercedes-Benz passenger cars in India. Also that year, Tata signed a joint-venture agreement with Tata Holset Ltd., UK, to manufacture turbochargers for the Cummins engines. India's first sports utility vehicle, the Tata Safari, was launched in 1998 and its independently designed Indica V2 became the number one car in its segment in India in 2001. Also during 2001, Tata exited its joint venture with Daimler Chrysler and entered

into a product agreement with UK-based MG Rover in 2002.

Tata Engineering changed its name to Tata Motors Limited in 2003 and in that year the company produced its three millionth vehicle. The next year, Tata Motors and South Korea's Daewoo Commercial Vehicle Co. Ltd. entered into a joint venture that produced and marketed heavy-duty commercial trucks in South Korea. Tata Motors acquired 21 percent interest in Spanish bus manufacturer Hipo Carrocera SA in 2005 and began production of several new vehicles, including small trucks and SUVs.

Tata Motors produced its four millionth vehicle in 2006, and in that year began a joint venture with Brazil's Marcopolo to manufacture buses for India and foreign markets, expanded Tata Daewoo's product line to include LNG-powered tractor-trailer trucks, and established three joint ventures with Fiat. The company formed a joint venture with Thonburi Automotive Assembly Plant Co. in Thailand to manufacture, assemble, and market pickup trucks. In 2007, Tata sold all its interest in Tata-Holset to Cummins, Inc.

In 2008, Tata purchased the iconic British brands Land Rover and Jaguar and began selling passenger cars and pickup trucks in the D.R. Congo and announced its "People's Car," named the Nano. The Nano hit the market in 2009 at a base price of about $2,250, and won India's Car of the Year award. Tata began exporting the Nano to South Africa, Kenya, and developing countries in Asia and Africa. In that year, Tata purchased the remaining 79 percent of Hipo Carrocera and purchased a 50.3 percent interest in Miljø Grenland/Innovasjon, a Norwegian firm specializing in electric vehicle technology. Also, Tata entered into an agreement with Motor Development International (MDI) from Luxembourg to develop an air-powered car. In 2010, the Tata Nano Europa was set up for sale in developed economies, especially country markets in Europe.

Tata celebrated its 50th year in international business in 2011. During that year, the company announced the opening of a commercial vehicle assembly plant in South Africa and a Land Rover assembly plant in India. Two long-distance buses, the Tata Divo Luxury Coach and the Tata Starbus Ultra, were introduced, and two new SUVs—the Tata Sumo Gold and the Range Rover Evoque—went on the market. Also in 2011, upscale Tata Manza and the Prima heavy truck were launched in South Africa.

During 2011, Tata won two prestigious awards, helping bring the company to global prominence. The Jaguar c-x75 won the Louis Vuitton award in Paris, and the Range Rover Evoque won Car Design of the Year. The new Pixel, Tata's city car concept for Europe, was displayed at the 81st Geneva Motor Show and its Tata 407 light truck celebrated its silver anniversary in 2011, selling 7 out of every 10 vehicles in the light commercial vehicle (LCV) category. The company began exporting the Nano to Sri Lanka, and launched the Tata Magic IRIS, a four-to-five seater four-wheel passenger carrier (top speed of 34 MPH) for public transportation. Also in that year, the Tata Ace Zip, a small "micro truck" for deep-penetration goods transport on the poor roads of rural India, and the new Tata Indica eV2, the most fuel-efficient car in India, were introduced.

Continuing its innovative operations, Tata signed an agreement of cooperation in 2012 with Malaysia's DRB-HICOM's Defense Technologies'

Tata also introduced its Anti-Terrorist Indoor Combat Vehicle concept at DEFEXPO-India. The company brought out three new vehicles at the 2012 Auto Expo: Tata Safari Storme, a large SUV; Tata Ultra, a light commercial vehicle (truck); and the Tata LPT 3723, a medium-duty truck and India's first five-axle rigid truck. The air-powered car developed with MDI from Luxembourg is showing promise and could serve a large market niche that wants ultra-economical transportation.

Tata Motors' joint ventures, subsidiaries, and associated companies are presented in Exhibit 2. Consolidated summarized income statements and balance sheets for Tata Motors are presented in Exhibits 3 and 4, respectively.

Macroeconomic Conditions in India in 2012

As of 2012, India was the seventh-largest nation in area, with about one-third the land size of the United States. It was the second most populous

---

EXHIBIT 2

Tata Motors Joint Ventures, Subsidiaries, and Associate Companies in 2012

Subsidiaries, JVS, and Associates

Jaguar Land Rover
Tata Daewoo Commercial Vehicle Company Ltd. (TDCV)
Tata Marcopolo Motors Ltd. (TMML)
Tata Hispano Motors Carrocera S. A.
Tata Motors (Thailand) Ltd. (TMTL)
Tata Motors (SA) Proprietary Ltd. (TMSA)
TML Drivelines Ltd.
Telco Construction Equipment Co. Ltd. (Telcon)
TAL Manufacturing Solutions Ltd. (TAL)
Tata Motors European Technical Centre plc. (TMETC)
Tata Technologies Ltd. (TTL) and its subsidiaries
TML Distribution Company Ltd. (TDCL)
Concorde Motors (India) Ltd. (Concorde)
Tata Motors Finance Limited
Tata Motors Insurance Broking & Advisory Services Ltd. (TMIBASL)
TML Holdings Pte. Ltd. (TML)
Sheba Properties Ltd. (Sheba)

Source: Tata Motors Annual Report, 2012.

EXHIBIT 3

Tata Motors' Consolidated Summarized Income Statements, Fiscal 2011–Fiscal 2012*
(in crore rupees or 10 million rupees)

	Year Ending March 31, 2012	Year Ending March 31, 2011
Income		
Revenue from operations	170,677.58	126,414.24
Less: Excise duty	5,023.09	4,286.32
	165,654.49	122,127.92
Other income	661.77	429.46
	166,316.26	122,557.38
Expenditures		
Cost of material consumed	100,797.44	70,453.73
Purchase of products for sale	11,205.86	10,390.84
Changes in inventories of furnished goods, work-in-progress, and products for sale	(2,535.72)	(1,836.19)
Employee cost/benefits expense	12,298.45	9,342.67
Finance cost	2,982.22	2,385.27
Depreciation and amortization expense	5,625.38	4,655.51
Product development expense / engineering expenses	1,389.23	997.55
Other expenses	28,453.97	21,703.09
Expenditure transferred to capital and other accounts	(8,265.98)	(5,741.25)
Total expenses	151,950.85	112,351.22
Profit/(loss) before tax	14,365.41	10,206.16
Exchange loss/(gain) (net) including on revaluation of foreign currency borrowings, deposits and loan	654.11	(231.01)
Goodwill impairment and other costs	177.43	—
Profit before tax	13,533.87	10,437.17
Tax expense/(credit)	(40.04)	1,261.38
Profit after tax from continuing operations (3–4)	13,573.91	9,220.79
Share of profit from associates (net)	24.92	101.35
Minority interest	(82.33)	(48.52)
Profit for the year	13,516.50	9,273.62

*Fiscal period April–March.

Source: Tata Motors Annual Report, 2012.

country on earth with 1.2 billion people (versus the United States with 313 million). The average age in India was 26.2 years (36.9 in the United States), and the population growth was 1.3 percent per year (0.89 percent in the United States); however, 25 percent were below the poverty line in 2011. The Indian GDP (purchasing power parity) in 2011 ranked fourth in the world, at about $4.5 trillion. Indian per capita GDP was about $3,700 in 2011 (versus $48,000 in the United States) and was growing at about 7.2 percent per year (the 26th highest growth rate in the world).

India's economy recovered well from the global recession, primarily because of strong domestic demand, with economic growth over 8 percent. However, in 2011, this growth slowed due to the lack of progress on economic reforms, high interest rates, and continuing high inflation. The Indian government subsidized several fuels (including diesel, which is a component in its inflation index), and as crude prices remained high, the fuel subsidy expenditures caused an increasing fiscal deficit and current account deficit. In 2010, 2011, and continuing into 2012, India suffered from

EXHIBIT 4

Tata Motors' Consolidated Summarized Balance Sheets, Fiscal 2011–Fiscal 2012*
(in crore rupees or 10 million rupees)

	Year Ending March 31, 2012	Year Ending March 31, 2011
Assets		
Fixed assets	56,212.50	43,221.05
Goodwill	4,093.74	3,584.79
Noncurrent investments	1,391.54	1,336.79
Deferred tax assets (net)	4,539.33	632.34
Long-term loans and advances	13,657.95	9,818.30
Other noncurrent assets	574.68	332.27
Foreign currency monetary item translation difference account (net)	451.43	—
Current assets	64,461.47	42,088.82
Total assets	145,382.64	101,014.18
Liabilities		
Long-term borrowings	27,962.48	17,256.00
Other long-term liabilities	2,458.58	2,292.72
Long-term provisions	6,071.38	4,825.64
Net worth		
Share capital	634.75	637.71
Reserves and surplus	32,515.18	18,533.76
Minority interest	307.13	246.60
Deferred tax liabilities (net)	2,165.07	2,096.13
Current liabilities	73,268.07	55,125.62
Total liabilities	145,382.64	101,014.18

*Fiscal period April–March.

Source: Tata Motors Annual Report, 2012.

numerous serious corruption scandals that sidetracked legislative work, and little economic reform occurred as a result.

Despite the scandals, poor infrastructure, a lack of nonagricultural employment, limited access to education, and the rapid migration of the population to unprepared urban centers, growth over the next three to five years is projected to approach 7 percent. This growth would result from India's young population (average age 26.5 years), which has a low dependency ratio and high savings (household savings were about 30 percent of annual income) and investment rates. The Reserve Bank of India suggested that inflation, which had been between 7 and 10 percent since 2009, peaked and then dropped to 6.6 percent in early 2012. The inflationary situation was not likely to show further improvement in 2013 because of increases in energy prices. There was the very real probability of spikes in crude oil processes resulting from the unstable political situation in the Middle East. Between 2011 and 2012, the rupee became cheaper by about 12 percent, relative to the U.S. dollar, giving Indian exporters a competitive advantage.

Education was highly valued in India and the Indian workforce was well-educated, which allowed India to become a major provider of engineering, design, and information technology services. Despite pressing problems such as significant overpopulation, environmental degradation, extensive poverty, and widespread corruption, rapid economic development was fueling India's rise on the world stage.

The Indian Automotive Industry

The Indian automobile industry was dominated by Maruti (an Indian subsidiary of Suzuki), Hyundai, and Tata. Mahindra was a distant fourth in the industry. The Indian automobile industry was rapidly growing in 2012 and benefited from four significant factors: urbanization, growth in road infrastructure, increasing disposable income (resulting from an increase in the income level and a decrease in income tax), and a rapidly growing population.

India had 10 of the 30 fastest-growing urban areas in the world. By 2050, over 700 million people were forecasted to move to India's urban centers. The country had the third-highest amount of road miles in the world, and an estimated 5.2 billion rupees would be spent on national highways, as well as state and rural roads, between 2010 and 2014.

Commercial vehicle sales in India grew at the fastest rate of all countries, including China, in 2011. India was the world's fastest-growing truck and bus market for the second consecutive year. Sales of commercial vehicles, primarily trucks, buses, and light cargo vehicles, grew by 22 percent between 2010 and 2011. Exhibit 5 presents sales of commercial vehicles for the five largest country markets in 2010 and 2011.

The Indian automobile industry had evolved during three relatively unique periods: protectionism (until the early 1990s), economic liberalism (early 1990s–2007), and then a period of globalization. The protectionist years were characterized by a closed economy with high duties and sales taxes. The automobile industry at that time was a seller's market with long waits for automobiles.

The period of economic liberalism that began in the early 1990s included the deregulation of industries, the privatization of state-owned businesses, and reduced controls on foreign trade and investment, which increased the entry of foreign businesses. This period triggered economic growth that averaged over 7 percent annually between 1997 and 2011. During the economic liberalization period, automobile financing greatly expanded and the automobile market became more competitive.

Indian auto sales reached record levels in the first quarter of 2012, as consumers increased their purchasing—primarily of diesel vehicles—due to concerns that the government would raise taxes on diesel vehicles in the next fiscal year. Increased loan rates and higher fuel prices in 2011 reduced the demand for cars; however, the boom in diesel sales lifted overall sales to a new high of 211,402 autos in April 2012. The demand for diesel vehicles grew to 45 percent of total demand, up from 30 percent in 2010. Diesel was more fuel-efficient than gas, and the Indian government instituted controls on the price of diesel because of its impact on inflation. In the first quarter of 2012, diesel was 40 percent cheaper than gasoline.

Several trends impacted the Indian passenger car industry: household income level, especially in the middle income segment, which accounted for the largest number of auto sales,

EXHIBIT 5

Sales of Commercial Vehicles in Selected Country Markets, 2010 and 2011

Country	2011	2010	Growth (%)
India	882,557	725,531	+22
China	3,933,550	4,367,678	−10
USA	5,687,427	5,031,439	+13
Japan	1,240,129	1,318,558	−6
Canada	1,144,410	1,101,112	+4

Source: "India Tops Commercial Vehicles Sales Chart," *Economic Times,* March 30, 2012.

was expected to have significant growth. This was predicted to increase the demand for passenger cars. Exhibit 6 presents the actual and projected disposable income in India from 1985 to 2025.

Ongoing national urban and rural highway projects through 2014 would increase national and state highways by 110,000 kilometers (68,350 miles) and rural roads by 411,000 kilometers (255,000 miles). This large increase in roads was also expected to increase the demand for cars, especially the more affordable models targeting rural customers. The almost certainty of increasing fuel prices would force successful automakers to focus on increasing fuel efficiency and to search for alternative fuels, which was one of Tata's competencies. Exhibit 7 presents domestic unit sales for various types of vehicles in India for fiscal 2005 through fiscal 2011.

EXHIBIT 6

Average Household Disposable Income in India, 1985–2005 (Actual) and 2005–2025 (Forecasted) (in thousands of Indian rupees)

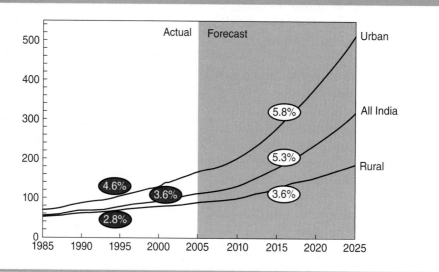

*Circled figures represent compound annual growth rates.

Source: McKinsey Global Institute.

EXHIBIT 7

Domestic Vehicle Unit Sales in India, Fiscal 2005–Fiscal 2011 (in thousands)

Category	2005	2006	2007	2008	2009	2010	2011
Passenger Vehicles	1,061	1,143	1,379	1,549	1,552	1,951	2,520
Commercial Vehicles	318	351	467	490	384	532	676
Three Wheelers	307	359	403	364	349	440	526
Two Wheelers	6,209	7,052	7,872	7,249	7,437	9,370	11,790
Total	7,897	8,906	10,123	9,654	9,724	12,295	15,513

Source: Society of Indian Automobile Manufacturers, 2012.

Tata Motors' Business Strategy in 2012

Tata Motors' Strategy in Passenger Cars

Tata Motors' strategy for its passenger car division was keyed to leveraging its broad product line and concentrating on all-around value, including fuel efficiency. The company offered compact-sized Indica and midsized Indigo passenger cars for sales primarily in India, although the company exported passenger cars to parts of Europe and Africa. The company's passenger cars were powered by 1.2-to-1.4-liter gasoline and diesel engines, and the lineup also included the electric-powered Indica Vista. The division also produced the widely publicized Nano micro-sized car.

The passenger vehicle strategy also focused on aggressive growth of new vehicle sales, service locations, and growth in the used-car business through *Tata Assured.* Tata management believed that a better sales and service network would enhance customer care and increase sales. The Jaguar and Land Rover brands were targeted for international growth in the key markets of China, Russia, and Brazil. Tata Motors' passenger vehicle strategy included exporting the Nano to markets throughout the developing world, where there was a sizable number of lower- and middle-income consumers needing basic transportation.

The "People's Car"—Tata Nano

In 2009, even though India's population was the second-largest on earth and its economy was rapidly growing, there were only 12 cars per thousand people (compared to 56 per thousand in China, 178 per thousand in Brazil, and 439 per thousand in the United States). In contrast, there were over 7 million scooters and motorcycles sold in India that year. The two-wheeled vehicle sales were the result of India's large population, high urban density, and low income level. Tata Motors recognized the huge market for very-low-cost motorized transportation that was being filled by scooters and motorcycles.

The middle-class household income in India started at about $4,500 in 2007. Tata believed that a car costing about $2,500 would be able to take advantage of the very large market that was being served only by two-wheel vehicles. In 2007, about 7.75 million Indians owned automobiles; however, more than 17 million others had the financial ability to purchase an automobile. Tata Motors' management believed that the potential market for automobiles priced under $3,000 could grow to about 30 million consumers in India. Tata Motors created the Tata Nano to capture such demand for low-cost automobiles and switch a large portion of the demand for two-wheeled vehicles to the Nano.

Ratan Tata, the chairman of Tata Motors' board, viewed the Nano as the "People's car." Mr. Tata once remarked about the many families riding on scooters: The father would drive with a child standing in front of him; the mother seated behind him and holding a baby. The Nano was intended to be the means to keep Indian middle-class families from transporting the entire family on one scooter. The Nano was widely anticipated in India, and it was anticipated that the Nano might have an effect on the used-car market because of its low price.

Tata Motors began the Nano design with a comprehensive study of potential customers, their needs, wants, and purchasing ability. In a unique pricing approach, the company set the base price at $2,500, which was the price Tata thought its customers could pay, and worked backward into the design. The base price at introduction was about $2,000 U.S.; however, it quickly went up to $2,300, and by 2012, the price was about $2,600. A typical 2012 Nano model is presented in Exhibit 8.

The base Nano model had a 625cc two-cylinder engine, which produced a top speed of 65 miles per hour and offered gas mileage of nearly 50 miles per gallon. The small engine was well-matched to the driving conditions in urban markets in India, which were

EXHIBIT 8

The 2012 Tata Nano

Source: NationalTurk.com, 2012.

characterized by crowded streets with an average speed of less than 20 miles per hour. The base Nano model did not include air conditioning, nor a radio or CD player, and access to the trunk was through the interior—there was no trunk door on the outside of the vehicle. Every possible cost saving was implemented: There were only three lug nuts on the wheels, no airbags, one windshield wiper, and the speedometer was in the middle of the dash rather than behind the steering wheel, which saved on parts and reduced cost. A supplier of suspension parts used a hollow steel tube to replace the solid steel tube normally used so as to save on steel costs.

The Nano was manufactured using a module design, which allowed components to be built separately and shipped to a location where they could be assembled. Tata Motors created a geographically dispersed network of Nano dealers in developing countries such as Brazil, China, Malaysia, Nepal, Bangladesh, Nigeria, Myanmar, and Indonesia. Tata Motors' distribution network also included dealers in the Middle East, South Africa, and the African continent.

Despite very high expectations, Nano sales were less than expected after its introduction. Sales for calendar year 2010 were 59,576. For fiscal year 2011, sales rose to 70,432. Sales then rose by 6 percent in 2012 to 74,527. Analysts estimated that approximately 200,000 to 250,000 Nanos per year would need to be sold for Tata Motors to achieve an acceptable return on its $400 million investment in the Nano's development.

The potential of a low-price car in the global automobile marketplace was widely recognized, and there were several potential competitors with plans to enter the market. There were rumors in the industry that GM was working with Wuling Automotive in China to design and produce a car that would directly compete with the Nano. Ford opened its second plant in India in 2011, and had invested over $2 billion in its manufacturing facilities in India. Ford's new Figo offered features close to those of American cars at a price of slightly over $7,000 for the base model. Volkswagen also opened a manufacturing plant in India and was selling its base VW Polo for $8,495, which was well-equipped compared to the Nano and the Ford's Figo. France's Renault also offered an economical car, the Pulse, which was very well-equipped, for about $7,850. In turn, Nissan sold its Micra for about $7,650, Maruti offered the Ritz for $7,500, and Chevrolet put out the Beat, which is priced at $8,030.

Commercial Vehicles

Tata's commercial vehicle strategy focused on providing a wide range of products that offered the lowest cost of ownership for truck users in developing countries. Tata's strategy was to continuously evaluate the entire commercial product range with the intent of offering a very strong combination of existing products and new commercial platforms and products. Tata Motors offered small commercial vehicles that could be used for local deliveries, light pickup trucks, and light commercial vehicles capable of carrying larger payloads. The company also produced a full line of large buses and coaches, as well as medium and heavy commercial vehicles suitable for long-haul trucking.

Growth in international markets was a strategic priority, which Tata planned to address by combining the efforts of Tata Motors Limited, Hispano (Spain), Tata Motors Thailand, and Tata Daewoo Commercial Vehicles, and expanding its international manufacturing (Tata opened an assembly plant in South Africa in 2011). Tata's commercial vehicle strategy also included plans to refurbish commercial vehicles, sell annual maintenance contracts, and provide parts and services to the defense department in India.

Tata's strategy included a commitment to quality and the lowest total cost of ownership. This was to be achieved by the company's in-depth knowledge of the Indian market and leveraging development and design capabilities. The company planned an increased customer-centric operation, which was to be accomplished by a focus on customer services throughout the entire product life cycle, the use of Customer Relationship Technology, and an increase in the availability of customer financing.

Jaguar and Land Rover

The Jaguar and Land Rover (JLR) brands were in a separate division within Tata Motors and had a significantly different target market than Tata-branded passenger cars. Tata Motors' strategy for JLR was to capitalize on growth opportunities in the premium market segments with the two globally recognized brands. The strategy included achieving additional synergy and benefits with the support of Tata Motors. There were plans for substantial investment in new JLR technologies and products, more competitive powertrain combinations, and new body styles. Revenues for the JLR division had increased from 36,245 crore rupees in fiscal 2009 to 103,635 crore rupees in fiscal 2012. The division's EBITDA had improved from a loss of 63 crore rupees in fiscal 2009 to a profit of 17,035 crore rupees in fiscal 2012. The division's rise in sales and profitability was largely a result of the growing popularity of its Land Rover brand, which included the Defender, LR2, LR4, Range Rover Evoque, Range Rover Sport, and Range Rover models. Land Rover sales accounted for 82.8 percent of the luxury division's unit sales in 2012. Exhibit 9 presents total unit sales and the change in geographic distribution of JLR sales by brand in 2011, along with the first nine months of 2012.

EXHIBIT 9

Total Unit Sales by Brand and Geographic Region for Tata Motors' Jaguar/Land Rover Division

Sales by Region	Fiscal 2011	First Nine Months of Fiscal 2012
United Kingdom	24.0%	19.1%
North America	21.6	19.4
China	11.0	16.3
Europe	22.4	22.4
Russia	4.8	5.2
Rest of the world	16.2	17.6
Total	100.0%	100.0%
Sales by brand		
Jaguar	52,993	39,921
Land Rover	190,628	176,491
Total	243,621	216,412

Source: Tata Motors Ltd., Road Show Presentation, 2012.

Tata Motors' Situation Going into 2013

Tata Motors Group had a successful fiscal 2012, with net revenues increasing by 36 percent and profits after tax increasing by 46 percent. Tata Motors' domestic commercial vehicle segment experienced a 19 percent increase in sales with light commercial vehicles achieving a market share in its segment of 59.6 percent and medium-heavy commercial vehicles obtaining a market share in its segment of the Indian market of 62.2 percent.

Tata's domestic passenger car grew about 4 percent in 2012—which was the same rate as industry growth. The company increased prices for its passenger cars by an average of about 3.3 percent. The customers' preference for diesel over gas engines helped Tata because of its large line of diesel passenger cars. During 2012, passenger car exports continued to grow with Bangladesh and Sri Lanka becoming Tata Motors' largest export markets. Exports to countries in Africa also grew at a healthy pace.

The Jaguar/Land Rover segment of Tata continued its very strong growth. Sales for the Jaguar/Land Rover division increased by 29.1 percent in 2012, being bolstered by the new Range Rover Evoque, which was launched in September 2011. The Evoque had won over 100 international awards for styling, quality, and performance. The Jaguar XF included an optional 2.2 diesel engine, which made it the most fuel-efficient Jaguar. Tata signed a joint-venture agreement with Chery Automotive Co., Ltd., a Chinese automobile manufacturer, to design, manufacture, and sell Jaguars in the Chinese market, pending Chinese regulatory approval. Also, the company had begun purchasing selected subassemblies such as automatic transmissions from suppliers in China and planned to construct a new engine plant in Wolverhampton, UK, that would manufacture low-emission engines.

The Tata Group believed that future growth for its subsidiaries would come from both investments in the growing Indian economy and opportunities in international markets. Tata Motors' management believed that the Indian passenger car industry would experience strong growth over the next 10 years, growing faster than the top five markets (United States, China, Japan, Germany, and Brazil) and become the third-largest passenger car market (after the United States and China) by 2021. The company believed that the introduction of a national goods and services tax to replace the present VAT administered by the separate states would be favorable for the automobile industry. Also, Tata Motors' management expected that the increase in CNG fueling centers and increasing GDP growth would further improve growth in the market. There was a question about how the U.S. market might fit into the company's plans. Jaguar and Land Rover were popular brands in the United States, but the majority of American consumers had never heard of Tata, and was unaware that Jaguar and Land Rover were owned by an Indian company. There were no other Tata Motors vehicles sold in the United States. Although, Tata Motors had showcased the Nano to the American market at the 2010 Detroit auto show, it would need significant upgrades to meet U.S. safety requirements. Adapting the Nano to meet these safety requirements would add over $2,500 to the cost of the car, bringing the base model price up over $5,000.

In addition to the safety and cost issues, the Nano might not match the needs and wants of American auto consumers. The Nano was a very basic car, and the cars sold in the United States competed vigorously with numerous convenience and comfort features. However, some analysts believed the Nano would be a good alternative to used cars for consumers seeking basic transportation. The Nano might also be attractive to consumers living in large, congested cities.

Of course, rising interest rates, significant increases in oil prices, or a slowdown in GDP would hurt passenger car sales. Also, if the Indian government accelerated the implementation of domestic emission standards equal to those of the United States, the domestic passenger car industry in India would likely suffer. Many opportunities existed in the industry, but the costs of mistakes could be very high in the global automobile industry. Tata Motors' managers would be required to carefully evaluate the domestic and global opportunities and the emerging opportunities and determine the best course for the company.

The Walt Disney Company: Its Diversification Strategy in 2012

JOHN E. GAMBLE Texas A&M University – Corpus Christi

The Walt Disney Company was a broadly diversified media and entertainment company with a business lineup that included theme parks and resorts, motion picture production and distribution, cable television networks, the ABC broadcast television network, eight local television stations, and a variety of other businesses that exploited the company's intellectual property. The company's revenues increased from $35.5 billion in fiscal 2007 to $40.9 billion in fiscal 2011, and its share price had consistently outperformed the S&P 500 since 2003. While struggling somewhat in the mid-1980s, the company's performance had been commendable in almost every year since Walt Disney created Mickey Mouse in 1928. Disney CEO Robert Iger commented on the company's performance since becoming its chief manager in 2005, as well as on its situation in 2012 during an investor's conference in May 2012.[1]

I inherited a great company seven years ago, obviously a strong brand in Disney and a strong business in ESPN. As I look back on the seven years, what I think I'm most proud of is that I made a strong company stronger with the acquisition of some very, very valuable and important brands for the company—notably, Pixar and Marvel. And the company today is extremely brand-focused. It's where we invest most of our capital. And those brands are not only

stronger in the United States than they were before, but they are stronger globally.

With that in mind, the company is also more diversified in terms of the territories that it does business in. So, while we are still predominantly a U.S.-based company, meaning well more than 50 percent of our bottom-line profits are generated from the U.S., we're far more global than we ever have been. And we've planted some pretty important seeds to make the international side of our business even bigger in the years ahead—notably, in some of the big emerging markets but also in some of the more developed markets outside the U.S.

We also adopted, I think, just at the right time, seven years ago, a technology-friendly approach, believing that nothing the company was going to do was going to stand in the way of technology and its developments. And, rather than watch technology throw threat after threat at us and disrupt our very valuable business models, we decided to embrace it and use it to not only enhance the quality of our product and the connection we have to our customers and make the company more efficient but, ultimately, to reach more people in more ways. And I'm pleased to say that that has definitely worked.

The other thing that I think is very notable about the company is that, as many businesses as we are in, and as many territories as we operate in, the company is managed in a very cohesive fashion. The credit really belongs

Copyright © 2012 by John E. Gamble. All rights reserved.

to a senior management team that knows where the value is created at the company, is invested in The Walt Disney Company and not in [their] individual business, and [strives for] coordination between the businesses . . . is a real distinguishing factor or attribute of our company. And it sets us apart from many companies in the world, and it certainly sets us apart from all media companies.[2]

As the company entered its fourth quarter of 2012, it was coming off of a record-setting third quarter, but faced several strategic issues. The company had invested nearly $15 billion in capital in its businesses during the past five years, including a 43 percent investment in a $4.5 billion theme park in China, the construction of two new 340-meter ships for its Disney Cruise Line, and the acquisitions of Pixar and Marvel. The company had also funded an aggressive share buyback plan that had placed demands on its cash reserves. In addition, not all of the company's business units were providing sufficient returns on invested capital and some business units competed in challenging industry environments. Going into 2013, Iger and Disney's management team planned to evaluate the corporation's diversification strategy.

Company History

Walt Disney's venture into animation began in 1919 when he returned to the United States from France, where he had volunteered to be an ambulance driver for the American Red Cross during World War I. Disney volunteered for the American Red Cross only after being told he was too young to enlist for the United States Army. Upon returning after the war, Disney settled in Kansas City, Missouri, and found work as an animator for Pesman Art Studio. Disney, and fellow Pesman animator, Ub Iwerks, soon left the company to found Iwerks-Disney Commercial Artists in 1920. The company lasted only briefly, but Iwerks and Disney were both able to find employment with a Kansas City company that produced short animated advertisements for local movie theaters. Disney left his job again in 1922 to found Laugh-O-Grams, where he employed Iwerks and three

other animators to produce short animated cartoons. Laugh-O-Grams was able to sell its short cartoons to local Kansas City movie theaters, but its costs far exceeded its revenues—forcing Disney to declare bankruptcy in 1923. Having exhausted his savings, Disney had only enough cash to purchase a one-way train ticket to Hollywood, California, where his brother, Roy, had offered a temporary room. Once in California, Walt Disney began to look for buyers for a finished animated-live action film he retained from Laugh-O-Grams. The film was never distributed, but New York distributors Margaret Winkler and Charles Mintz were impressed enough with the short film that they granted Disney a contract in October 1923 to produce a series of short films that blended cartoon animation with live action motion picture photography. Disney brought Ub Iwerks from Kansas City to Hollywood to work with Disney Brothers Studio (later to be named Walt Disney Productions) to produce the Alice Comedies series that would number 50-plus films by the series end in 1927. Disney followed the Alice Comedies series with a new animated cartoon for Universal Studios. After Disney's *Oswald the Lucky Rabbit* cartoons quickly became a hit, Universal terminated Disney Brothers Studio and hired most of Disney's animators to continue producing the cartoon.

In 1928, Disney and Iwerks created Mickey Mouse to replace Oswald as the feature character in Walt Disney Studios cartoons. Unlike with Oswald, Disney retained all rights over Mickey Mouse and all subsequent Disney characters. Mickey Mouse and his girlfriend, Minnie Mouse, made their cartoon debuts later in 1928 in the cartoons *Plane Crazy, The Gallopin' Gaucho*, and *Steamboat Willie. Steamboat Willie* was the first cartoon with synchronized sound and became one of the most famous short films of all time. The animated film's historical importance was recognized in 1998 when it was added to the National Film Registry by the United States Library of Congress. Mickey Mouse's popularity exploded over the next few decades with a Mickey Mouse Club being created in 1929, new accompanying characters such as Pluto, Goofy, Donald Duck, and Daisy Duck being added to Mickey Mouse cartoon storylines, and Mickey Mouse appearing in Walt Disney's 1940 feature length film, *Fantasia*. Mickey Mouse's universal appeal reversed Walt Disney's series of failures in the animated film industry and became known as the mascot of Disney Studios, Walt Disney Productions, and The Walt Disney Company.

The success of The Walt Disney Company was sparked by Mickey Mouse, but Disney Studios also produced several other highly successful animated feature films including *Snow White and the Seven Dwarfs* in 1937, *Pinocchio* in 1940, *Dumbo* in 1941, *Bambi* in 1942, *Song of the South* in 1946, *Cinderella* in 1950, *Treasure Island* in 1950, *Peter Pan* in 1953, *Sleeping Beauty* in 1959, and *One Hundred and One Dalmatians* in 1961. What would prove to be Disney's greatest achievement began to emerge in 1954 when construction began on his Disneyland Park in Anaheim, California. Walt Disney's Disneyland resulted from an idea that Disney had many years earlier while sitting on an amusement park bench watching his young daughters play. Walt Disney thought that there should be a clean and safe park that had attractions that both parents and children alike would find entertaining. Walt Disney spent years planning the park and announced the construction of the new park to America on his *Disneyland* television show that was launched to promote the new $17 million park. The park was an instant success when it opened in 1955 and recorded revenues of more than $10 million during its first year of operation. After the success of Disneyland, Walt Disney began looking for a site in the eastern United States for a second Disney park. He settled on an area near Orlando, Florida, in 1963 and acquired more than 27,000 acres for the new park by 1965.

Walt Disney died of lung cancer in 1966, but upon his death, Roy O. Disney postponed retirement to become president and CEO of Walt Disney Productions and oversee the development of Walt Disney World Resort. Walt Disney World Resort opened in October 1971—only two months before Roy O. Disney's death in December 1971. The company was led by Donn Tatum from 1971 to 1976. Tatum had been with Walt Disney Productions since 1956 and led the further development of Walt Disney World Resort and began the planning of EPCOT in Orlando and Tokyo

Disneyland. Those two parks were opened during the tenure of Esmond Cardon Walker, who had been an executive at the company since 1956 and chief operating officer since Walt Disney's death in 1966. Walker also launched The Disney Channel before his retirement in 1983. Walt Disney Productions was briefly led by Ronald Miller, who was the son-in-law of Walt Disney. Miller was ineffective as Disney chief executive officer and was replaced by Michael Eisner in 1984.

Eisner formulated and oversaw the implementation of a bold strategy for Walt Disney Studios, which included the acquisitions of ABC, ESPN, Miramax Films, and the Anaheim Angels, and the Fox Family Channel, the development of Disneyland Paris, Disney-MGM Studios in Orlando, Disney California Adventure Park, Walt Disney Studios theme park in France, and Hong Kong Disneyland, and the launch of the Disney Cruise Line, the Disney Interactive game division, and the Disney Store retail chain. Eisner also restored the company's reputation for blockbuster animated feature films with the creation of *The Little Mermaid* in 1989, *Beauty and the Beast* in 1991, *Aladdin* in 1992, and *The Lion King* in 1994. Despite Eisner's successes, his tendencies toward micromanagement and skirting board approval for many of his initiatives and his involvement in a long-running derivatives suit led to his removal as chairman in 2004 and his resignation in 2005.

The Walt Disney Company's CEO in 2012, Robert (Bob) Iger, became a Disney employee in 1996 when the company acquired ABC. Iger was president and CEO of ABC at the time of its acquisition by The Walt Disney Company and remained in that position until made president of Walt Disney International by Alan Eisner in 1999. Bob Iger was promoted to president and chief operating officer of The Walt Disney Company in 2000 and was named as Eisner's replacement as CEO in 2005. Iger's first strategic moves in 2006 included the $7.4 billion acquisition of Pixar animation studios and the purchase of the rights to Disney's first cartoon character, Oswald the Lucky Rabbit, from NBCUniversal. In 2007, Robert Iger commissioned two new 340-meter ships for the Disney Cruise Lines that would double its fleet size from two ships to four. The new ships ordered by Iger were 40 percent larger than Disney's two older vessels and entered service in 2011 and 2012. Iger also engineered the acquisition of Marvel Entertainment in 2009, which would enable the Disney production motion pictures featuring Marvel comic book characters such as Iron Man, the Incredible Hulk, Thor, Spider-Man, and Captain America. All of the movies produced by Disney's Marvel unit had performed exceptionally well at the box office, with *The Avengers*, which was released in May 2012, recording worldwide box office receipts of more than $1 billion. Disney's Miramax film production company and Dimension film assets were divested by Iger in 2010 for $663 million. A financial summary for The Walt Disney Company for 2007 through 2011 is provided in Exhibit 1. Exhibit 2 tracks the performance of The Walt Disney Company's common shares between August 2002 and August 2012.

EXHIBIT 1

Financial Summary for The Walt Disney Company, Fiscal 2007–Fiscal 2011 (in millions)

	2011[1]	2010[2]	2009[3]	2008[4]	2007[5][6]
Revenues	$40,893	$38,063	$36,149	$37,843	$35,510
Income from continuing operations	5,258	4,313	3,609	4,729	4,851
Income from continuing operations attributable to Disney	4,807	3,963	3,307	4,427	4,674
Per common share					
Earnings from continuing operations attributable to Disney					
Diluted	$2.52	$2.03	$1.76	$2.28	$2.24
Basic	2.56	2.07	1.78	2.34	2.33
Dividends	0.40	0.35	0.35	0.35	0.31
Balance sheets					
Total assets	$72,124	$69,206	$63,117	$62,497	$60,928
Long-term obligations	17,717	16,234	16,939	14,889	14,916
Disney shareholders' equity	37,385	37,519	33,734	32,323	30,753
Statements of cash flows					
Cash provided by operations	$6,994	$6,578	$5,319	$5,685	$5,519
Investing activities					
Investments in parks, resorts, and other property	(3,559)	(2,110)	(1,753)	(1,578)	(1,566)
Proceeds from dispositions	564	170	185	14	1,530
Acquisitions	(184)	(2,493)	(176)	(660)	(608)
Financing activities					
Dividends	(756)	(653)	(648)	(664)	(637)
Repurchases of common stock	(4,993)	(2,669)	(138)	(4,453)	(6,923)
Supplemental cash flow information					
Interest paid	377	393	485	555	551
Income taxes paid	2,341	2,170	1,609	2,768	2,796

[1] The fiscal 2011 results include restructuring and impairment charges that rounded to $0.00 per diluted share and gains on the sales of Miramax and BASS ($0.02 per diluted share), which collectively resulted in a net adverse impact of $0.02 per diluted share. See the discussion of the per share impacts in Item 7.

[2] During fiscal 2010, the Company completed a cash and stock acquisition for the outstanding capital stock of Marvel for $4.2 billion (see Note 4 to the Consolidated Financial Statements for further discussion). In addition, results include restructuring and impairment charges ($0.09 per diluted share), gains on the sales of investments in two television services in Europe ($0.02 per diluted share), a gain on the sale of the *Power Rangers* property ($0.01 per diluted share), and an accounting gain related to the acquisition of The Disney Store Japan ($0.01 per diluted share). Including the impact of rounding, these items collectively resulted in a net adverse impact of $0.04 per diluted share.

[3] The fiscal 2009 results include restructuring and impairment charges ($0.17 per diluted share), a non-cash gain in connection with the AETN/Lifetime merger ($0.08 per diluted share) and a gain on the sale of their investment in two pay television services in Latin America ($0.04 per diluted share). Including the impact of rounding, these items collectively resulted in a net adverse impact of $0.06 per diluted share.

[4] The fiscal 2008 results include an accounting gain related to the acquisition of the Disney Stores North America and a gain on the sale of movies.com (together $0.01 per diluted share), the favorable resolution of certain income tax matters ($0.03 per diluted share), a bad debt charge for a receivable from Lehman Brothers ($0.03 per diluted share) and an impairment charge ($0.01 per diluted share). These items collectively had no net impact on earnings per share.

[5] During fiscal 2007, the Company concluded the spin-off of the ABC Radio business and thus reports ABC Radio as discontinued operations for all periods presented.

[6] The fiscal 2007 results include gains from the sales of E! Entertainment and Us Weekly (together $0.31 per diluted share), the favorable resolution of certain income tax matters ($0.03 per diluted share), an equity-based compensation plan modification charge ($0.01 per diluted share), and an impairment charge ($0.01 per diluted share). These items collectively resulted in a net benefit of $0.32 per diluted share.

Source: The Walt Disney Company 2008 and 2011 10-Ks.

EXHIBIT 2

Performance of The Walt Disney Company's Stock Price, August 2002 to August 2012

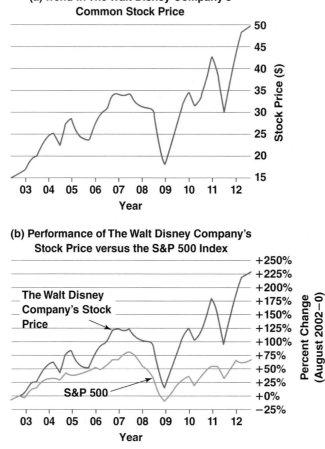

(a) Trend in The Walt Disney Company's Common Stock Price

(b) Performance of The Walt Disney Company's Stock Price versus the S&P 500 Index

The Walt Disney Company's Corporate Strategy and Business Operations in 2012

In 2012, The Walt Disney Company was broadly diversified into theme parks, hotels and resorts, cruise ships, cable networks, broadcast television networks, television production, television station operations, live action and animated motion picture production and distribution, music publishing, live theatrical productions, children's book publishing, interactive media, and consumer products retailing. The company's corporate strategy was centered on (1) creating high-quality family content, (2) exploiting technological innovations to make entertainment experiences more memorable, and (3) international expansion. The company's 2006 acquisition of Pixar and 2009 acquisition of Marvel were executed to enhance the resources and capabilities of its core animation business with the addition of new animation skills and characters. The company's 2010 acquisition of Playdom gave the company new online gaming capabilities, and its 2011 acquisition of UTV was engineered to facilitate its international expansion efforts. When asked about the company's recent acquisitions during a media, cable, and telecommunications conference in May 2012, Disney Chief Financial Officer Jay Rasulo made the following comments:[3]

Our acquisition strategy is pretty clear. Either we are buying IP that is under-exploited, underused by the owners . . . or we're buying capabilities to reach consumers in new places or in new ways.

Marvel, like Pixar, was primarily an IP acquisition. We knew there was buried treasure there. The company was doing well to exploit it, but it was doing it largely through third parties.

We decided to make our big play on *Avengers*. . . . It's done $1.3 billion as of today in the worldwide box office. Hasn't even opened in Japan yet. So it's definitely still got some running room. And in addition to the box office, it's hitting in consumer products. There's a social game. It's just exactly what we envisioned when we purchased [Marvel].

If you look at the other end of the spectrum . . . Playdom did not own a lot of IP but had a capability in social gaming that we simply did not have. Certainly we could have built it, but it would have taken a long time. Social gaming, as you all know, was taking off and continues to rise like a rocket. And we wanted to jumpstart ourselves into that space, so we bought that company with the idea of using both IP we had and the creation of new IP to get into the social space.

UTV . . . is sort of a geographic. We want to grow in India. We want to grow in China. We want to grow in Russia and in Turkey, the big four and the ten after. But you need an entry strategy. And with UTV, we became the largest studio, an owner of nine television networks, and a bigger and more grounded distribution network for the Disney IP than we have in that market. Our ambition in India is clear. We want to be the family brand of India.

Disney's corporate strategy also called for sufficient capital to be allocated to its core theme parks and resorts business to sustain its advantage in the industry. The company expanded the range of attractions at its Disney California Adventure park with the addition of the $75 million World of Color water and light show in 2010 and the $200 million Radiator Springs outdoor race track in Cars Land in 2012. Bob Iger, Disney's chairman and CEO, discussed the company's approach to allocating financial resources during an investors' conference in May 2012:[4]

Well, first of all, it begins with an overall evaluation of how we deploy capital across the company. So, if the theme park group comes to us with a proposal to renovate Fantasyland in Florida, we obviously look at it in a very discrete fashion, meaning what are the likely returns on that specific capital investment. But we look at it against the whole capital expenditure needs of the company over a given year, or over a given period of time.

So, if you look back in the seven years since I've been CEO, we've actually deployed capital in multiple ways. We've just increased our dividend. We've purchased a fair amount of our stock. We have now 103 Disney Channels worldwide, which took capital to do that. And, of course, we've invested more in our parks and resorts, which includes our theme parks.

Once we decide what kind of capital we believe we might be willing to invest over a period of time as a company, we take a very, very hard look at the specific opportunity or the specific request.

The Walt Disney Company's corporate strategy also attempted to capture synergies existing between its business units. Two of the company's highest grossing films, *Pirates of the Caribbean: On Stranger Tides* and *Cars 2*, were also featured at the company's Florida and California theme parks. Disney had also made much of its content available digitally, including its WatchESPN services for Internet, smartphone, and table computer users, its growing list of Disney Publishing e-book offerings, and family content available through its Disney.com/YouTube partnership.

Disney's international expansion efforts were largely directed at exploiting opportunities in emerging markets. In 2012, the Disney Channel reached 75 percent of viewers in China and Russia and was available in more than 100 countries, compared to 19 countries in 2002. Disney opened a Toy Story Land attraction at Hong Kong Disneyland in 2011 and had two more lands planned for the Hong Kong resort. The company was also developing the Shanghai Disney Resort that would include two themed hotels, attractions, and the largest interactive Magic Kingdom–style castle built at any Disney park. Bob Iger also made the following comments about the company's international strategy during the May 2012 investors' conference:[5]

> When we talk about growing internationally for instance, we know that we've had opportunities to invest in that business to, essentially, increase our footprint internationally. So the opening of Hong Kong Disneyland in 2005 and the expansion of Hong Kong Disneyland that's already underway—in fact, we're opening three new lands. One's already open, one is opening this summer, and then there's a third to come later in the year.
>
> And then, of course, Shanghai Disneyland—and that's one where I think is probably the best opportunity the company's had since Walt Disney bought land in central Florida in the 1960s. This is a 7.5-square-kilometer piece of land sitting in Pudong, right in the heart of Shanghai. 330 million live within three hours commuting distance to this park. We stood on a tower overlooking a cleared piece of property recently. I couldn't believe its size. But I'm certain that it will fulfill its potential in what is the world's most populous country.

In 2012, the company's business units were organized into five divisions: media networks, parks and resorts, studio entertainment, consumer products, and interactive media.

Media Networks

The Walt Disney Company's media networks business unit included its domestic and international cable networks, the ABC television network, television production, and U.S. domestic television stations. The company's television production was limited to television programming for ABC and its eight local television stations were all ABC affiliates. Six of Disney's eight domestic television stations were located in the 10 largest U.S. television markets. In all, ABC had 238 affiliates in the United States. When asked about Disney's ABC-related businesses, Bob Iger suggested that the businesses made positive contributions to the company's overall performance.[6]

The television studio, ABC, the network, and the eight stations that we own are a nicely profitable business for us and should continue to be nicely profitable. One of the reasons they're profitable is that, by using the studio and the network to support the creation of pretty high-quality, intellectual property or filmed entertainment, we've taken advantage of what has been a real growth market globally in the consumption of American-based filmed entertainment.

We think we have distinctive, local news brands. Our stations tend to be—most of them are number one in the market. If they're not number one, they're number two. And they tend to rely on a very strong local news brand.

Exhibit 3 provides the market ranking for Disney's local stations and its number of subscribers and ownership percentage of its cable networks. The exhibit also provides a brief description of its ABC broadcasting and television production operations. The division also included Radio Disney, which aired family-oriented radio programming on 34 terrestrial radio stations (31 of which were owned by Disney) in the United States. Radio Disney was also available on SiriusXM satellite radio, iTunes Radio Tuner and Music Store, XM/DIRECTV, and on mobile phones. Radio Disney was also broadcast throughout most of South America on Spanish-language terrestrial radio stations. The company's 2011 acquisition of UTV would expand the division's television broadcasting and production capabilities to India.

Among the most significant challenges to Disney's media networks division was the competition for viewers, which impacted advertising rates and revenues. Not only did the company compete against other broadcasters and cable networks for viewers, it also competed against other types of entertainment that consumers might enjoy. For example, consumers might prefer to watch a DVD, play video games, or browse the Internet rather than watch television. The effect of the Internet on broadcast news had been significant and the growth of streaming services had the potential to affect the advertising revenue potential of all of Disney's media businesses. However,

EXHIBIT 3

The Walt Disney Company's Media Networks, 2011

Cable Networks	Estimated Subscribers (in millions)[1]	Ownership %
ESPN[2]		
ESPN	99	80.0
ESPN2	99	80.0
ESPNEWS	73	80.0
ESPN Classic	33	80.0
ESPNU	72	80.0
Disney Channels Worldwide		
Disney Channel–Domestic	99	100.0
Disney Channels–International[3]	141	100.0
Disney Junior[3]	58	100.0
Disney XD – Domestic	78	100.0
Disney XD – International[3]	91	100.0
ABC Family	98	100.0
SOAPnet	74	100.0
A&E/Lifetime		
A&E[2]	99	42.1
Lifetime Television	99	42.1
HISTORY	99	42.1
Lifetime Movie Network	82	42.1
The Biography Channel	65	42.1
History International	64	42.1
Lifetime Real Women[3]	18	42.1

Broadcasting
ABC Television Network (238 local affiliates reaching 99% of U.S. television households)

Television Production
ABC Studios and ABC Media Productions (daytime, primetime, late night, and news television programming)

Domestic Television Stations

Market	TV Station	Television Market Ranking[4]
New York, NY	WABC-TV	1
Los Angeles, CA	KABC-TV	2
Chicago, IL	WLS-TV	3
Philadelphia, PA	WPVI-TV	4
San Francisco, CA	KGO-TV	6
Houston, TX	KTRK-TV	10
Raleigh-Durham, NC	WTVD-TV	24
Fresno, CA	KFSN-TV	55

[1]Estimated U.S. subscriber counts according to Nielsen Media Research as of September 2011, except as noted below.

[2]ESPN and A&E programming is distributed internationally through other networks discussed below.

[3]Subscriber counts are not rated by Nielsen and are based on internal management report.

[4]Based on Nielsen Media Research, U.S. Television Household Estimates, January 1, 2011.

Source: The Walt Disney Company 2011 10-K.

Bob Iger believed that technology provided great opportunities for Disney.[7]

It's no longer just a television market . . . it's a media world. And it's rich. And it's no longer just in the home; it's everywhere. It's in school, in your car, walking down the street. You name it, you can consume media. And it's not just filmed entertainment, it's casual games and surfing websites and social networking.

We're launching a TV everywhere app for the Disney Channel. This is like the WatchESPN app that we launched a while back, an app that will enable kids or anyone, for that matter, to watch the Disney Channel and its programs on a mobile device using our app, provided they are subscribers of a multichannel service. . . . And I know that the adoption rate for the ESPN app has been great. It's a fantastic product. And, we're going to launch . . . ABC, ABC Family, and so on.

In summarizing his thoughts about the opportunities for Disney's media programming, Iger concluded,[8]

We believe that high-quality, branded entertainment is going to continue to deliver real value to our shareholders, not just the value that we've delivered in the past but growth in a world that enables more and more distribution of that product and more consumption of it. Every one of our brands is in high demand by any new platform. You can't launch a platform today without some good content on it, and we're very well-positioned, probably better than anybody in the business, in that regard.

Operating results for Disney's media networks division for fiscal 2009 through fiscal 2011 is presented in Exhibit 4.

Parks and Resorts

The Walt Disney Company's parks and resorts division included the Walt Disney World Resort in Orlando, the Disneyland Resort in California, the Aulani Disney Resort and Spa in Hawaii, the Disney Vacation Club, and the Disney Cruise Line. The company also owned a 51 percent interest in Disneyland Paris, a 47 percent interest in Hong Kong Disneyland Resort, and a 43 percent interest in Shanghai Disney Resort. Disney also licensed the operation of Tokyo Disney Resort in Japan. Revenue for the division was primarily generated through park admission fees, hotel room charges, merchandise sales, food and beverage sales, sales and rentals of vacation club properties, and fees charged for cruise vacations.

Revenues from hotel lodgings and food and beverage sales were a sizable portion of the division's revenues. For example, at the 25,000-acre Walt Disney World Resort alone, the company operated 17 resort hotels with approximately 22,000 rooms. An 18th hotel with 2,000 rooms would be added at the Walt Disney World Resort in 2012. Walt Disney World Resort also included the 120-acre Downtown Disney retail, dining, and entertainment

EXHIBIT 4

Operating Results for Walt Disney's Media Networks Business Unit, Fiscal 2009–Fiscal 2011 (in millions)

	2011	2010	2009
Revenues			
Affiliate fees	$8,790	$8,082	$7,407
Advertising	7,598	7,028	6,566
Other	2,326	2,052	2,236
Total revenues	18,714	17,162	16,209
Operating expenses	10,376	9,888	9,464
Selling, general, administrative, and other	2,539	2,358	2,341
Depreciation and amortization	237	222	206
Equity in the income of investees	(584)	(438)	(567)
Operating Income	$6,146	$5,132	$4,765

Source: The Walt Disney Company 2011 10-K.

complex where visitors could dine and shop during or after park hours. Walt Disney World Resort in Orlando also included four championship golf courses, full-service spas, tennis courts, sailing facilities, water skiing, two water parks, and a 220-acre sports complex that was host to over 200 amateur and professional events each year.

Walt Disney's 461-acre resort in California included two theme parks—Disneyland and Disney California Adventure—along with three hotels and its Downtown Disney retail, dining, and entertainment complex. Disney California Adventure was opened in 2001 adjacent to the Disneyland property and included four lands—Golden State, Hollywood Pictures Backlot, Paradise Pier, and Bug's Land. The park was initially built to alleviate overcrowding at Disneyland and was expanded with the addition of World of Color in 2010 and Cars Land in 2012 to strengthen its appeal with guests. Rasulo discussed the history and shortcomings of Disney California Adventure in 2012:[9]

> We were starting to see rejection from Disneyland because it was simply too crowded every day. And we built [Disney California Adventure] both to expand the resort in terms of its offering, but also to pull people away from Disneyland.
>
> Well, the concept wasn't strong enough. It didn't have a great nighttime appeal, so the stays over there were very short, and the people would come back to Disneyland in the evening and accentuate the problem. Now you will see a totally renewed park with a real strong concept called Cars Land, built around the movie *Cars*. It's 12 acres. It's compelling. It's one of the biggest attractions we've ever done with a land around it. And we've already seen World of Color increase attendance at the resort.

Disney held a 51 percent ownership stake in Disneyland Paris and its seven hotels, convention center, shopping, dining, and entertainment complex, and 27-hole golf facility. The company had a 47 percent ownership interest in Hong Kong Disneyland Resort, which included two hotels. A staged expansion of Hong Kong Disneyland, that included three new lands—Toy Story Land, Grizzly Gulch, and Mystic Point—was expected to be completed by 2013. Disney received royalties from the operation of Tokyo Disney Resort, which was owned and operated by Oriental Land Company, a Japanese corporation in which Disney had no ownership interest. Disney would have a 43 percent ownership interest in Shanghai Disney Resort, which would be a $4.5 billion project including Shanghai Disneyland, two themed hotels, a retail, dining, and entertainment complex, and an outdoor recreational area. The resort in China was expected to open in 2016.

The company also offered time-share sales and rentals in 11 resort facilities through its Disney Vacation Club. The Disney Cruise Line operated ships out of Port Canaveral, Florida, and Los Angeles. Disney's cruise activities were developed to appeal to the interests of children and families. Its Port Canaveral cruises included a visit to Disney's Castaway Cay, a 1,000-acre private island in the Bahamas. The popularity of Disney's cruise vacations allowed its original two-ship fleet to be booked to full capacity year-round. Bob Iger commented on the business's strong performance while addressing investors in May 2012:[10]

> The cruise ships [were] a solid business in that we had mid-teen returns on invested capital in two legacy ships that had been built in the 1990s. We believe that we had a quality product, that there was definitely room for us to add capacity, and that the market was there for us to expand in it. And we built two ships, the *Dream*, which launched in early 2011, and the *Fantasy*, which launched a couple of months ago. Again, a very specific look at return on invested capital for the two new ships. Interestingly enough, our four ships are about 90 percent booked for the year. The *Dream*, which we sailed, as I mentioned, [in] early 2011, was accretive, bottom line, the first full quarter of operation. The same thing will be true for the *Fantasy*. And it's just an incredible, high-quality product.

The division's operating results for fiscal 2009 through fiscal 2011 are presented in Exhibit 5.

EXHIBIT 5

Operating Results for Walt Disney's Parks and Resorts Business Unit, Fiscal 2009–Fiscal 2011 (in millions)

	2011	2010	2009
Revenues			
Domestic	$ 9,302	$ 8,404	$ 8,442
International	2,495	2,357	2,225
Total revenues	11,797	10,761	10,667
Operating expenses	7,383	6,787	6,634
Selling, general, administrative, and other	1,696	1,517	1,467
Depreciation and amortization	1,165	1,139	1,148
Operating Income	$ 1,553	$ 1,318	$ 1,418

Source: The Walt Disney Company 2011 10-K.

Studio Entertainment

The Walt Disney Company's studio entertainment division produced live-action and animated motion pictures, pay-per-view and DVD home entertainment, musical recordings, and *Disney on Ice* and *Disney Live!* live performances. The division's motion pictures were produced and distributed under the Walt Disney Pictures, Pixar, and Marvel banners. The division also distributed motion pictures under the Touchstone Pictures banner. Bob Iger summarized the division's strategy with the following comments.[11]

> The strategy for our motion picture group, or our studio, is very clear. We are likely to make two animated films a year, a Pixar and a Disney. There will be some times over the next five years that you could see two Pixar films in one year and a Disney. But, basically, you're looking at two a year. We intend to make, probably, two Marvel films a year going forward, and that slate is pretty defined over the next three to four years. And then, somewhere in the neighborhood of six to eight, probably closer to six, Disney-branded live action films. . . . We're not in the business of making 20 films a year or more than that. We are only in the business of making those branded films—Disney, Pixar, and Marvel. We believe that our returns on investment in those branded movies are likely to be better than the overall industry. And, when we have success with a Disney, Pixar, or a Marvel film, we can leverage it

much more broadly and deeply and for a longer period of time than we can in any other film that we might make.

Most motion pictures typically incurred losses during the theatrical distribution of the film because of production costs and the cost of extensive advertising campaigns accompanying the launch of the film. Profits for many films did not occur until the movie became available on DVD or Blu-ray disks for home entertainment, which usually began three to six months after the film's theatrical release. Revenue was also generated when a movie moved to pay-per-view (PPV)/video-on-demand (VOD) two months after the release of the DVD and when the motion picture became available on subscription premium cable channels such as HBO about 16 months after PPV/VOD availability. Broadcast networks such as ABC could purchase telecast rights to movies later as could basic cable channels such as Lifetime, Hallmark Channel, and ABC Family. Premium cable channels such as Showtime and Starz might also purchase telecast rights to movies long after their theatrical release. Telecast right fees decreased as the length of time from initial release increased. Also, the decline in DVD sales and rentals had affected industry revenues as motion pictures moved to lower-revenue-generating telecasts more quickly. The operating results for The Walt Disney Company's

Studio Entertainment division for fiscal 2009 through fiscal 2011 is presented in Exhibit 6.

Consumer Products

The company's consumer products division included the company's Disney Store retail chain and businesses specializing in merchandise licensing and children's book and magazine publishing. In 2011, the company owned and operated 208 Disney Stores in North America, 103 stores in Europe, and 46 stores in Japan. Its publishing business included comic books, various children's book and magazine titles available in print and e-book format, and smartphone and tablet computer apps designed for children. The company's best-selling apps in 2011 were Disney Princess Dress-Up and Cars 2. Licensing revenues were generated from the use of Disney's portfolio of characters by manufacturers of toys, apparel, home décor, stationery, footwear, and consumer electronics. In 2011, Disney was the largest licensor of character-based merchandise in the world. The division's sales were primarily affected by seasonal shopping trends and changes in consumer disposable income. An overview of the division's operating results for fiscal 2009 through fiscal 2011 is presented in Exhibit 7.

EXHIBIT 6

Operating Results for Walt Disney's Studio Entertainment Business Unit, Fiscal 2009–Fiscal 2011 (in millions)

	2011	2010	2009
Revenues			
Theatrical distribution	$1,733	$2,050	$1,325
Home entertainment	2,435	2,666	2,762
Television distribution and other	2,183	1,985	2,049
Total revenues	6,351	6,701	6,136
Operating expenses	3,136	3,469	3,210
Selling, general, administrative, and other	2,465	2,450	2,687
Depreciation and amortization	132	89	60
Equity in the income of investees	—	—	(4)
Operating Income	$ 618	$ 693	$ 175

Source: The Walt Disney Company 2011 10-K.

EXHIBIT 7

Operating Results for Walt Disney's Consumer Products Business Unit, Fiscal 2009–Fiscal 2011 (in millions)

	2011	2010	2009
Revenues			
Licensing and publishing	$1,933	$1,725	$1,584
Retail and other	1,116	953	841
Total revenues	3,049	2,678	2,425
Operating expenses	1,334	1,236	1,182
Selling, general, administrative, and other	794	687	597
Depreciation and amortization	105	78	39
Equity in the income of investees	—	—	2
Operating Income	$ 816	$ 677	$ 609

Source: The Walt Disney Company 2011 10-K.

Interactive Media

Disney's interactive media business unit produced video games for handheld game devices, game consoles, and smartphone platforms. The division also developed games and other content for **Disney.com** and Disney's websites for its parks and resorts and studio entertainment division. The interactive media division had found it difficult to compete in the highly seasonal video game industry and had suffered losses each year between fiscal 2009 and fiscal 2011. In addition, the division's sales were affected dramatically by the timing of new console releases and the popularity of its game titles. In 2010, the company acquired Playdom, Inc., a company that developed online games for social networking sites to help speed the company's product development capabilities in that area. In summing up the division's performance and future prospects, CEO Iger stated:[12]

We have an interactive division that includes games and a number of our Disney-branded websites. We've lost money in that space. The division overall is small when you compare it with the other big divisions of the company and it will continue to be relatively small. We've said that we're targeting 2013 as a year of profitability. It's about time, because we've invested a fair amount. . . . Our goal now and our strategy is to diversify our gaming efforts. Some modest investment on the console front, very Disney-branded and Marvel-branded, some investment on the mobile front, and investment on the social games front.

Operating results for Disney's Interactive Media division for fiscal 2009 through fiscal 2011 are presented in Exhibit 8. The Walt Disney Company's consolidated statements of income for fiscal 2009 through fiscal 2011 are presented in Exhibit 9. The company's consolidated balance sheets for fiscal 2010 and fiscal 2011 are presented in Exhibit 10.

EXHIBIT 8

Operating Results for Walt Disney's Interactive Media Business Unit, Fiscal 2009–Fiscal 2011 (in millions)

	2011	2010	2009
Revenues			
Game sales and subscriptions	$ 768	$ 563	$ 565
Advertising and other	214	198	147
Total revenues	982	761	712
Operating expenses	732	581	623
Selling, general, administrative, and other	504	371	336
Depreciation and amortization	54	43	50
Equity in the income of investees	—	—	2
Operating Loss	$(308)	$(234)	$(295)

Source: The Walt Disney Company 2011 10-K.

EXHIBIT 9

Consolidated Statements of Income for The Walt Disney Company, Fiscal 2009–Fiscal 2011 (in millions, except per share data)

	2011	2010	2009
Revenues	$40,893	$38,063	$36,149
Costs and expenses	33,112	31,337	30,452
Restructuring and impairment charges	55	270	492
Add: Other income	75	140	342

	2011	2010	2009
Net interest expense	343	409	466
Add: Equity in the income of investees	585	440	577
Income before income taxes	8,043	6,627	5,658
Income taxes	2,785	2,314	2,049
Net Income	5,258	4,313	3,609
Less: Net Income attributable to noncontrolling interests	451	350	302
Net Income attributable to The Walt Disney Company (Disney)	$ 4,807	$ 3,963	$ 3,307
Earnings per share attributable to Disney:			
Diluted	$2.52	$2.03	$1.76
Basic	$2.56	$2.07	$1.78
Weighted average number of common and common equivalent shares outstanding:			
Diluted	1,909	1,948	1,875
Basic	1,878	1,915	1,856

Source: The Walt Disney Company 2011 10-K.

EXHIBIT 10

Consolidated Balance Sheets for The Walt Disney Company, Fiscal 2010–Fiscal 2011 (in millions, except per share data)

	October 1, 2011	October 2, 2010
Assets		
Current assets		
Cash and cash equivalents	$ 3,185	$ 2,722
Receivables	6,182	5,784
Inventories	1,595	1,442
Television costs	674	678
Deferred income taxes	1,487	1,018
Other current assets	634	581
Total current assets	13,757	12,225
Film and television costs	4,357	4,773
Investments	2,435	2,513
Parks, resorts, and other property, at cost		
Attractions, buildings, and equipment	35,515	32,875
Accumulated depreciation	(19,572)	(18,373)
	15,943	14,502
Projects in progress	2,625	2,180
Land	1,127	1,124
	19,695	17,806
Intangible assets, net	5,121	5,081
Goodwill	24,145	24,100
Other assets	2,614	2,708
Total assets	$72,124	$69,206
Liabilities and Equity		
Current liabilities		
Accounts payable and other accrued liabilities	$ 6,362	$ 6,109
Current portion of borrowings	3,055	2,350
Unearned royalties and other advances	2,671	2,541
Total current liabilities	12,088	11,000

Continued

EXHIBIT 10

Consolidated Balance Sheets for The Walt Disney Company, Fiscal 2010–Fiscal 2011 (in millions, except per share data) *(Continued)*

	October 1, 2011	October 2, 2010
Borrowings	10,922	10,130
Deferred income taxes	2,866	2,630
Other long-term liabilities	6,795	6,104
Commitments and contingencies		
Equity		
Preferred stock, $.01 par value		
Authorized—100 million shares, Issued—none	—	—
Common stock, $.01 par value		
Authorized—4.6 billion shares, Issued—2.7 billion shares	30,296	28,736
Retained earnings	38,375	34,327
Accumulated other comprehensive loss	(2,630)	(1,881)
	66,041	61,182
Treasury stock, at cost, 937.8 million shares at October 1, 2011 and 803.1 million shares at October 2, 2010	(28,656)	(23,663)
Total Disney Shareholder's equity	37,385	37,519
Noncontrolling interests	2,068	1,823
Total Equity	39,453	39,342
Total liabilities and equity	$72,124	$69,206

Source: The Walt Disney Company 2011 10-K.

The Walt Disney Company's Third Quarter 2012 Performance and Its Future ProspectS

The Walt Disney Company recorded record earnings per share during its first nine months of fiscal 2012 with its media networks division achieving an 8 percent period-over-period increase in operating profit, its parks and resorts division seeing a 24 percent increase in operating profits, its studio entertainment division operating profit increasing by 28 percent, and its consumer electronics operating profit increasing by 10 percent between the first nine months of 2011 and the same period in 2012. The operating loss for Disney's interactive division decreased from $214 million for the nine

months ending July 2, 2011 to $140 million for the nine months ending June 30, 2012. Disney CEO Bob Iger summarized the company's position at mid-2012:[13]

I can say I look back at the last year and breaking ground in Shanghai, launching two new cruise ships, opening up *Cars Land* in a couple of weeks, buying a media company in India, buying a network in Russia to brand the Disney Channel, all big—and buying our stock back and increasing our dividend and, I think, proving to the world that the Marvel acquisition was a strong acquisition. So it's been, I'll call it a rich and aggressive time, one that we feel good about in terms of the impact on our bottom line, both current and future. And we'll continue to look opportunistically. We obviously have demonstrated that we're not averse to allocating capital in multiple directions.

ENDNOTES

[1] As quoted by Bob Iger, Chairman and Chief Executive Officer of The Walt Disney Company, during the Sanford C. Bernstein Strategic Decisions Conference, May 30, 2012.

[2] Ibid.

[3] As quoted by Jay Rasulo, Senior Executive Vice President and Chief Financial Officer of The Walt Disney Company, during the Nomura U.S. Media, Cable, and Telecom Summit, May 30, 2012.

[4] As quoted by Bob Iger, Chairman and Chief Executive Officer of The Walt Disney Company, during the Sanford C. Bernstein Strategic Decisions Conference, May 30, 2012.

[5] Ibid.

[6] Ibid.

[7] Ibid.

[8] Ibid.

[9] As quoted by Jay Rasulo, Senior Executive Vice President and Chief Financial Officer of The Walt Disney Company, during the Nomura U.S. Media, Cable, and Telecom Summit, May 30, 2012.

[10] As quoted by Bob Iger, Chairman and Chief Executive Officer of The Walt Disney Company, during the Sanford C. Bernstein Strategic Decisions Conference, May 30, 2012.

[11] Ibid.

[12] Ibid.

[13] Ibid.

Mc Graw Hill Education **connect**

JOSEPH LAMPEL   City University London

It was in the spring of the second year of his insurrection against the High Sheriff of Nottingham that Robin Hood took a walk in Sherwood Forest. As he walked he pondered the progress of the campaign, the disposition of his forces, the Sheriff's recent moves, and the options that confronted him.

The revolt against the Sheriff had begun as a personal crusade. It erupted out of Robin's conflict with the Sheriff and his administration. However, alone Robin Hood could do little. He therefore sought allies, men with grievances and a deep sense of justice. Later he welcomed all who came, asking few questions and demanding only a willingness to serve. Strength, he believed, lay in numbers.

He spent the first year forging the group into a disciplined band, united in enmity against the Sheriff and willing to live outside the law. The band's organization was simple. Robin ruled supreme, making all important decisions. He delegated specific tasks to his lieutenants. Will Scarlett was in charge of intelligence and scouting. His main job was to shadow the Sheriff and his men, always alert to their next move. He also collected information on the travel plans of rich merchants and tax collectors. Little John kept discipline among the men and saw to it that their archery was at the high peak that their profession demanded. Scarlock took care of the finances, converting loot to cash, paying shares of the take, and finding suitable hiding places for the surplus. Finally, Much the Miller's son had the difficult task of provisioning the ever-increasing band of Merry Men.

The increasing size of the band was a source of satisfaction for Robin, but also a source of concern. The fame of his Merry Men was spreading, and new recruits were pouring in from every corner of England. As the band grew larger, their small bivouac became a major encampment. Between raids the men milled about, talking and playing games. Vigilance was in decline, and discipline was becoming harder to enforce. "Why," Robin reflected, "I don't know half the men I run into these days."

The growing band was also beginning to exceed the food capacity of the forest. Game was becoming scarce, and supplies had to be obtained from outlying villages. The cost of buying food was beginning to drain the band's financial reserves at the very moment when revenues were in decline. Travelers, especially those with the most to lose, were now giving the forest a wide berth. This was costly and inconvenient to them, but it was preferable to having all their goods confiscated.

Robin believed that the time had come for the Merry Men to change their policy of outright confiscation of goods to one of a fixed transit tax. His lieutenants strongly resisted this idea. They were proud of the Merry Men's famous motto: "Rob the rich and give to the poor." "The farmers and the townspeople," they argued, "are our most important allies. How can we tax them, and still hope for their help in our fight against the Sheriff?"

Copyright © 1991 by Joseph Lampel. All rights reserved.

Robin wondered how long the Merry Men could keep to the ways and methods of their early days. The Sheriff was growing stronger and becoming better organized. He now had the money and the men and was beginning to harass the band, probing for its weaknesses. The tide of events was beginning to turn against the Merry Men. Robin felt that the campaign must be decisively concluded before the Sheriff had a chance to deliver a mortal blow. "But how," he wondered, "could this be done?"

Robin had often entertained the possibility of killing the Sheriff, but the chances for this seemed increasingly remote. Besides, killing the Sheriff might satisfy his personal thirst for revenge, but it would not improve the situation. Robin had hoped that the perpetual state of unrest and the Sheriff's failure to collect taxes would lead to his removal from office. Instead, the Sheriff used his political connections to obtain reinforcement. He had powerful friends at court and was well regarded by the regent, Prince John.

Prince John was vicious and volatile. He was consumed by his unpopularity among the people, who wanted the imprisoned King Richard back. He also lived in constant fear of the barons, who had first given him the regency but were now beginning to dispute his claim to the throne. Several of these barons had set out to collect the ransom that would release King Richard the Lionheart from his jail in Austria. Robin was invited to join the conspiracy in return for future amnesty. It was a dangerous proposition. Provincial banditry was one thing, court intrigue another. Prince John had spies everywhere, and he was known for his vindictiveness. If the conspirators' plan failed, the pursuit would be relentless and retributions swift.

The sound of the supper horn startled Robin from his thoughts. There was the smell of roasting venison in the air. Nothing was resolved or settled. Robin headed for camp promising himself that he would give these problems his utmost attention after tomorrow's raid.

Herman Miller Inc.: Unrelenting Pursuit of Reinvention and Renewal[1]

Mc Graw Hill Education connect

FRANK SHIPPER Salisbury University
KAREN MANZ Author and Researcher
STEVEN B. ADAMS Salisbury University
CHARLES C. MANZ University of Massachusetts

Herman Miller was widely recognized as the leader in the office furniture industry and had built a reputation for innovation in products and processes since D. J. De Pree became president over 90 years ago. Herman Miller was one of only four companies and the only non-high-technology enterprise named to *Fortune*'s "Most Admired Companies" and "The 100 Best Companies to Work For" lists and also to *Fast Company*'s "Most Innovative Companies" list in both 2008 and 2010. The three high-technology organizations selected for these lists were Microsoft, Cisco, and Google. Unlike most firms, especially those in mature industries and most of its office furniture rivals, Herman Miller had pursued a path distinctively marked by reinvention and renewal.

This path had served it well over the decades. It survived the Great Depression early in its history and multiple recessions in the 20th century. In the early part of the 21st century, it recovered from the dot-com bust. Next, sales dropped approximately 34 percent between 2008 and 2010 due to the Great Recession. As Herman Miller entered 2013, sales were on the rebound. Would its propensity for using innovation to reinvent and renew its business once again allow the company to flourish and grow? How far and how fast might the company be able to push its annual revenues above the 2012 level of $1.72 billion?

Company Background

Herman Miller's roots go back to 1905 and the Star Furniture Company, a manufacturer of traditional-style bedroom suites in Zeeland, Michigan. In 1909, it was renamed Michigan Star Furniture Company and hired Dirk Jan De Pree as a clerk. De Pree became president in 1919 and four years later convinced his father-in-law, Herman Miller, to purchase the majority of shares; De Pree renamed the company Herman Miller Furniture Company in recognition of Miller's support.

In 1927, De Pree committed himself to treating "all workers as individuals with special talents and potential." This occurred after he visited the family of a millwright who had died unexpectedly. During the visit, the widow read some poetry. Upon asking the widow who the poet was, De Pree was surprised to learn it was the millwright. This led him to wonder whether the millwright was a worker who wrote poetry or a poet who worked as a millwright. This story was part of Herman Miller's corporate culture, which continued to generate respect for all employees and fueled the quest to tap the diversity of gifts and skills held by all.

Copyright © 2013 by Frank Shipper, Karen Manz, Steven Adams, and Charles Manz. All rights reserved.

In 1930, the United States was in the Great Depression and Herman Miller was in financial trouble. As De Pree was looking for a way to save the company, Gilbert Rhode, a designer from New York, approached him and told him about his design philosophy. Rhode then asked for an opportunity to design a bedroom suite for a fee of $1,000. When De Pree reacted negatively to such a fee, Rhode suggested an alternative payment plan—a 3 percent royalty on the furniture sold—to which De Pree agreed, figuring that there was nothing to lose.

A few weeks later, De Pree received the first designs from Rhode. Again, he reacted negatively. In response, Rhode wrote De Pree a letter explaining his design philosophy: "[First,] utter simplicity: no surface enrichment, no carvings, no moldings, [and second,] furniture should be anonymous. People are important, not furniture. Furniture should be useful." Rhode's designs were antithetical to traditional designs, but De Pree saw merit in them and set Herman Miller on a course of designing and selling furniture that reflected a way of life.

In 1942, Herman Miller produced its first office furniture—a Gilbert Rhode design referred to as the Executive Office Group. Rhode died two years later, and De Pree began a search for a new design leader. After reading an article in *Life* magazine about designer George Nelson, De Pree hired Nelson as Herman Miller's first design director.

In 1946, De Pree hired Charles and Ray Eames, a husband-and-wife design team based in Los Angeles. In the same year, Charles Eames's designs were featured in the first one-man furniture exhibit at New York's Museum of Modern Art. Some of his designs became part of the museum's permanent collection.

In 1950, Herman Miller, under the guidance of Dr. Carl Frost, a professor at Michigan State University, became the first company in the state of Michigan to implement a Scanlon Plan, a productivity incentive program devised by labor expert Joseph N. Scanlon. Underlying the Scanlon Plan were the "principles of equity and justice for everyone in the company." Two major functional elements of Scanlon Plans were the use of committees for sharing ideas on improvements and a structure for sharing increased profitability. The relationship between Frost and Herman Miller continued for at least four decades.

During the 1950s, Herman Miller introduced a number of new furniture designs, including those by Alexander Girard, Charles and Ray Eames, and George Nelson. Specifically, the company introduced the first molded fiberglass chairs and the Eames lounge chair and ottoman (see Exhibit 1). The Eames designs were introduced on NBC's *Home Show* with Arlene Francis, a precursor to the *Today* show. Also in the 1950s, Herman Miller began its first overseas foray, selling its products in the European market. In 1962, D. J. De Pree became chairman of the board and his son, Hugh De Pree, became president and chief executive officer. D. J. De Pree had served for more than 40 years as the president of Herman Miller.

During the 1960s, Herman Miller introduced many new designs for both home and office. The most notable design was the Action Office System, the world's first open-plan modular office arrangement of movable panels and attachments. By the end of the 1960s, Herman Miller had formed a subsidiary in England with sales and marketing responsibility throughout England and the Scandinavian countries. The company also established dealers in South and Central America, Australia, Canada, Europe, Africa, the Near East, and Japan.

In 1970, Herman Miller went public and made its first stock offering. The stock certificate was designed by the Eames office staff. The company entered the health/science market in 1971 and introduced the Ergon chair, its first design based on scientific observation and ergonomic principles, in 1976. In 1979, in conjunction with the University of Michigan, Herman Miller established the Facility Management Institute, which pioneered the profession of facility management. The company continued to expand overseas and introduce new designs throughout the 1970s.

By 1977, more than half of Herman Miller's 2,500 employees worked outside the production

EXHIBIT 1

Eames Lounge Chair and Ottoman

area. The Scanlon Plan therefore needed to be overhauled, since it had been designed originally for a production workforce. In addition, employees worked at multiple U.S. and overseas locations. In 1978, an ad hoc committee of 54 people from nearly every segment of the company was elected to examine the need for changes and to make recommendations. By January 1979, the committee had developed a final draft. The plan established a new organization structure based on work teams, caucuses, and councils. All employees were given an opportunity to discuss the new plan in small group settings. On January 26, 1979, 96 percent of the employees voted to accept the new plan.

After 18 years as president and CEO, Hugh De Pree stepped down; his younger brother, Max De Pree, became chairman and chief executive officer in 1980. In 1981, Herman Miller took a major initiative to become more efficient and environmentally friendly. Its Energy Center generated both electrical and steam power to run its 1-million-square-foot facility by burning waste.

In 1983, Herman Miller established a plan whereby all employees became shareholders. This initiative occurred approximately 10 years before congressional incentives fueled employee stock ownership plan (ESOP) growth.

In 1984, Herman Miller introduced the Equa chair, a second chair based on ergonomic principles; many other designs followed in the 1980s. In 1987, the first non–De Pree family member, Dick Ruch, became chief executive officer.

By the end of the decade, *Time* magazine had recognized the Equa chair as a Design of the Decade. Also, in 1989, Herman Miller established its Environmental Quality Action Team, whose purpose was to "coordinate environmental programs worldwide and involve as many employees as possible."

In 1990, Herman Miller became a founding member of the Tropical Forest Foundation and was the only furniture manufacturer to belong. That same year, it discontinued using endangered rosewood in its award-winning Eames lounge chair and ottoman, and substituted cherry and walnut from sustainable sources. It also became a founding member of the U.S. Green Building Council in 1994. Some of the buildings at Herman Miller were used to establish Leadership in Energy and Environmental Design (LEED) standards. Because

EXHIBIT 2

The Herman Miller Aeron Chair

of its environmental efforts, Herman Miller received awards from *Fortune* magazine and the National Wildlife Federation in the 1990s.

Also in the 1990s, Herman Miller again introduced some groundbreaking designs. In 1994, it introduced the Aeron chair (see Exhibit 2), which almost immediately was added to the New York Museum of Modern Art's permanent design collection. In 1999, the Aeron chair won the Design of the Decade Award from *Business-Week* and the Industrial Designers Society of America.

In 1992, J. Kermit Campbell became Herman Miller's fifth CEO and president. He was the first person from outside the company to hold either position. In 1995, Campbell resigned and

Mike Volkema was promoted to CEO. Volkema, just 39 years old, had been with a company called Meridian for seven years before Herman Miller acquired it in 1990, so when he became CEO he had been with either Herman Miller or its subsidiary for 12 years. At the time, the industry was in a slump and Herman Miller was being restructured. Sales were approximately $1 billion annually.

In 1994, the company launched a product line called Herman Miller for the Home to focus on the residential market. It reintroduced some of its modern classic designs from the 1940s, 1950s, and 1960s as well as new designs. In 1998, it set up a specific website (www. hmhome.com) to tap into this market.

The company took additional marketing initiatives to focus on small and midsize businesses. It established a network of 180 retailers to focus on small businesses and made a 3-D design computer program available to midsize customers. In addition, its order entries were digitally linked among the company and its suppliers, distributors, and customers to expedite orders and improve their accuracy.

The First Decade of the 21st Century

The first decade of the 21st century started off spectacularly for Herman Miller, with record profits and sales in 2000 and 2001. The company offered an employee stock option plan (ESOP) in July 2000, and *Time* magazine selected the Eames molded plywood chair a Design of the Century. Sales had more than doubled in the six years that Mike Volkema had been CEO.

Then the dot-com bubble burst and the terrorist attacks of September 11, 2001, shook the U.S. economy. Herman Miller's sales dropped by 34 percent, from more than $2.2 billion in 2001 to less than $1.5 billion in 2002. In the same two years, the company saw a decline in profits from a positive $144 million to a negative $56 million. In an interview for *Fast Company* magazine in 2007, Volkema said, "One night I went to bed a genius and woke up the town idiot."

Although sales continued to drop in 2003, Herman Miller returned to profitability in that year. To do so, Herman Miller had to drop its long-held tradition of lifelong employment; approximately 38 percent of the workforce was laid off, and an entire plant in Georgia was closed. Mike Volkema and Brian Walker, then president of Herman Miller North America, met with all the workers to tell them what was happening and why it had to be done. One of the workers being laid off was so moved by Volkema and Walker's presentation that she told them she felt sorry for them having to personally lay off workers.

To replace the tradition of lifelong employment, Volkema, with input from many others, developed what the company referred to as "the new social contract." He explained it as follows:

> We are a commercial enterprise, and the customer has to be on center stage, so we have to first figure out whether your gifts and talents have a match with the needs and wants of this commercial enterprise. If they don't, then we want to wish you the best, but we do need to tell you that I don't have a job for you right now.

As part of the implementation of the social contract, the company redesigned benefit plans such as educational reimbursement and 401(k) plans to be more portable. This was done to decrease the cost of changing jobs for employees whose gifts and talents no longer matched customer needs.

Herman Miller's sales and profits began to climb from 2003 to 2008. In 2008, even though sales were not at an all-time high, the company's profits had reached a record level. Walker became president in 2003 and CEO in 2004. Volkema became chairman of the board in 2004.

Then Herman Miller was hit by the recession of 2009. Sales dropped by 19 percent, from approximately $2.0 billion in 2008 to approximately $1.6 billion in 2009. In the same years, profits dropped from $152 million to $68 million. In March 2009, Mark Schurman, director of external communications at Herman Miller, predicted that the changes made to recover from the 2001–2003 recession would help the company weather the recession that began in late 2007.

In 2010, Herman Miller introduced the SAYL line of chairs. The big selling point for the line was its affordability while offering a full-featured, ergonomically sound chair for which Herman Miller was famous. Although it was approximately half as expensive as the Aeron chair, it continued Herman Miller's tradition of design excellence. It won Product Design of the Year from the 2010 International Design Awards (IDA) jury, a Silver 2011 International Design Excellence Award (IDEA) award in the category of "Office & Productivity," and a 2011

Core77 Design Award in the "Furniture and Lighting—Professional Designer" category.

Herman Miller in 2013

Herman Miller had codified its long-practiced organizational values and published them on its website on a page titled "What We Believe." Those beliefs, listed as follows, were intended as a basis for uniting all employees, building relationships, and contributing to communities:

- **Curiosity & Exploration:** These are two of our greatest strengths. They lie behind our heritage of research-driven design. How do we keep our curiosity? By respecting and encouraging risk, and by practicing forgiveness. You can't be curious and infallible. In one sense, if you never make a mistake, you're not exploring new ideas often enough. Everybody makes mistakes: We ought to celebrate honest mistakes, learn from them, and move on.

- **Engagement:** For us, it is about being owners—actively committed to the life of this community called Herman Miller, sharing in its success and risk. Stock ownership is an important ingredient, but it's not enough. The strength and the payoff really come when engaged people own problems, solutions, and behavior. Acknowledge responsibility, choose to step forward and be counted. Care about this community and make a difference in it.

- **Performance:** Performance is required for leadership. We want to be leaders, so we are committed to performing at the highest level possible. Performance isn't a choice. It's up to everybody at Herman Miller to perform at his or her best. Our own high performance—however we measure it—enriches our lives as employees, delights our customers, and creates real value for our shareholders

- **Inclusiveness:** To succeed as a company, we must include all the expressions of human talent and potential that society

offers. We value the whole person and everything each of us has to offer, obvious or not so obvious. We believe that every person should have the chance to realize his or her potential regardless of color, gender, age, sexual orientation, educational background, weight, height, family status, skill level—the list goes on and on. When we are truly inclusive, we go beyond toleration to understanding all the qualities that make people who they are, that make us unique, and most important, that unite us.

- **Design:** Design for us is a way of looking at the world and how it works—or doesn't. It is a method for getting something done, for solving a problem. To design a solution, rather than simply devising one, requires research, thought, sometimes starting over, listening, and humility. Sometimes design results in memorable occasions, timeless chairs, or really fun parties. Design isn't just the way something looks; it isn't just the way something works, either.

- **Foundations:** The past can be a tricky thing—an anchor or a sail, a tether or a launching pad. We value and respect our past without being ruled by it. The stories, people, and experiences in Herman Miller's past form a unique foundation. Our past teaches us about design, human compassion, leadership, risk taking, seeking out change, and working together. From that foundation, we can move forward together with a common language, a set of owned beliefs and understandings. We value our rich legacy more for what it shows us we might become than as a picture of what we've been.

- **A Better World:** This is at the heart of Herman Miller and the real reason why many of us come to work every day. We contribute to a better world by pursuing sustainability and environmental wisdom. Environmental advocacy is part of our heritage and a responsibility we gladly bear for future generations. We reach for a better world by giving time and money to our communities and causes outside the company; through becoming a good corporate citizen worldwide; and even in the (not so) simple act of adding beauty to the world. By participating in the effort, we lift our spirits and the spirits of those around us.

- **Transparency:** Transparency begins with letting people see how decisions are made and owning the decisions we make. So when you make a decision, own it. Confidentiality has a place at Herman Miller, but if you can't tell anybody about a decision you've made, you've probably made a poor choice. Without transparency, it's impossible to have trust and integrity. Without trust and integrity, it's impossible to be transparent.

All employees were expected to live these values.

Herman Miller's Living Office

As 2013 began, Herman Miller introduced Living Office (Exhibit 3). The Living Office was an open office, but unlike any prior open offices. It could also be viewed as the antithesis of the cubicle office about which Scott Adams, the creator of Dilbert, lampoons frequently in his comic strip. The Living Office was featured on *CBS Sunday Morning* and was described as having design elements akin to a living room or Starbucks coffee shop. Robert Propst, the designer of the Action Office in the 1960s for Herman Miller, was quoted on the show saying, "Not all organizations are as intelligent and progressive, they make little bitty cubicles and stuff people in them, barren rat hole places."[2] In contrast, the Living Office is designed to foster camaraderie, connection, spontaneous interaction, and group expression—attributes that Herman Miller believes were essential "to attract, nurture, enable, and retain the talent to drive innovation and execution, and bring an organization's strategy to life. Also, featured on the CBS show was Brian Walker's new wall-less Living Office. It was introduced to the industry

at the NeoCon trade show in June 2013 to critical acclaim.

Management

Mike Volkema remained chairman of the board in 2012, and Brian Walker was president and CEO. Walker's compensation was listed by *Bloomberg Businessweek* as $693,969 in 2011. The magazine listed compensation for CEOs at four competitors as ranging from $778,000 to $973,000. Walker and four other top executives at Herman Miller took a 10 percent pay cut in January 2009 and, along with all salaried workers, another 10 percent cut in March 2009. The production workers were placed on a work schedule that consisted of nine days in two weeks, effectively cutting their pay by 10 percent as well. That the executives would take a pay cut before salaried workers, and one twice as much as that required by workers, was just one way human compassion was practiced at Herman Miller. However, most employees' pay cuts and furloughs were ended in June 2010 when the company's financial performance began to improve.

By U.S. Securities and Exchange Commission (SEC) regulations, a publicly traded company had to have a board of directors. By Herman Miller's corporate policy, the majority of the 14 members of the board had to be independent. To be judged independent, the individual as a minimum had to meet the NASDAQ National Market requirements for independent directors (NASDAQ Stock Market Rule 4200). In addition, the individual could not have any "other material relationship with the company or its affiliates or with any executive officer of the company or his or her affiliates." Moreover, according to company documents, any "transaction between the Company and any executive officer or director of the Company (including that person's spouse, children, stepchildren, parents, stepparents, siblings, parents-in-law, children-in-law, siblings-in-law, and persons sharing the same residence) must be disclosed to the Board of Directors and is subject to the approval of the Board of Directors or the Nominating and Governance Committee unless the proposed transaction is part of a general

EXHIBIT 3

Scenes from a Living Office

program available to all directors or employees equally under an existing policy or is a purchase of Company products consistent with the price and terms of other transactions of similar size with other purchasers." Furthermore, "It is the policy of the Board that all directors, consistent with their responsibilities to the stockholders of the company as a whole, hold an equity interest in the company. Toward this end, the Board requires that each director will have an equity interest after one year on the Board, and within five years the Board encourages the directors to have shares of common stock of the company with a value of at least three times the amount of the annual retainer paid to each director." In other words, board members were held to standards consistent with Herman Miller's corporate beliefs and its ESOP program.

Although Herman Miller had departments, the most frequently referenced work unit was the team. Paul Murray, director of environmental health and safety, explained the relationship between the team and the department as follows:

> At Herman Miller, *team* has just been the term that has been used since the Scanlon Plan and the De Prees brought that into Herman Miller. And so I think that's why we use that almost exclusively. The department—as a department, we help facilitate the other teams. And so they aren't just department driven.

Teams were often cross-functional. Membership on a team was based on the employee's ability to contribute to that team. As Gabe Wing, lead chemical engineer for the company's Design for the Environment division, described it,

> You grab the appropriate representative who can best help your team achieve its goal. It doesn't seem to be driven based on title. It's based on who has the ability to help us drive our initiatives towards our goal.

Teams were often based on product development. When the product had been developed, the members of that team were redistributed to new projects. New projects could come from any level in the organization. One way in which leadership was shared at Herman Miller was through the concept of "talking up and down the ladder." Workers at all levels were encouraged to put forth new ideas. Herman Miller environmental specialist Rudy Bartels said,

> If they try something . . . they have folks there that will help them and be there for

them. . . . That requires a presence of one of us or an e-mail or just to say, "Yeah, I think that's a great idea." That's how a lot . . . in the organization works.

Because Herman Miller workers felt empowered, a new manager could run into some startling behavior. Paul Murray recalled,

> I can remember my first day on the job. I took my safety glasses off . . . and an employee stepped forward and said, "Get your safety glasses back on." At [Company X, Company Y],[3] there was no way they would have ever talked to a supervisor like that, much less their supervisor's manager. It's been a fun journey when the workforce is that empowered.

The company's beliefs were also reinforced through the Employee Gifts Committee and the Environmental Quality Action Team. True to Herman Miller's practice of shared leadership, the Employee Gifts Committee distributed funds and other resources based on employee involvement. Jay Link, manager of corporate giving, explained the program as follows:

> Our first priority is to honor organizations where our employees are involved. We believe that it's important that we engender kind of a giving spirit in our employees, so if we know they're involved in organizations, which is going to be where we have a manufacturing presence, then our giving kind of comes alongside organizations that they're involved with. So that's our first priority.

In addition, all Herman Miller employees could work 16 paid hours a year with a charitable organization of their choice. The company set goals for the number of employee volunteer hours contributed annually to its communities. Progress toward meeting those goals was reported to the CEO.

The Environmental Affairs Team, formed in 1988 with the authorization of Max De Pree, had responsibility for such activities as recycling solid waste and designing products from sustainable resources. One of the team's successes was in the reduction of solid waste taken to landfills. In 1991, Herman Miller was sending 41 million pounds of solid waste to landfills. That figure was down to 24 million pounds by 1994 and to 3.6 million pounds by 2008. Such improvements were both environmentally friendly and cost-effective.

Herman Miller's beliefs carried over to the family and the community. Gabe Wing related, "I've got the worst lawn in my neighborhood. That's because I don't spread pesticides on it, and I don't put fertilizer down." He went on to say that he and his wife had to make a difficult decision in the summer of 2009 because Herman Miller had a policy "to avoid PVC [polyvinyl chloride] wherever possible." In restoring their home, they chose fiber cement board over PVC siding even though the fiber cement board was considerably more costly. Wing said, "Seven years ago, I didn't really think about it."

Rudy Bartels was involved in a youth soccer association that raised money to buy uniforms by collecting newspapers and aluminum cans. Bartels said, "When I'll speak they'll say, 'Yeah, that's Rudy. He's Herman Miller. You should—you know we're gonna have to do this.'"

The company's beliefs carried over to all functional areas of the business. Some of them were obviously beneficial, and some were simply the way Herman Miller chose to conduct its business.

Marketing

Herman Miller products were sold internationally through wholly owned subsidiaries in countries including Canada, France, Germany, Italy, Japan, Mexico, Australia, Singapore, China, India, and the Netherlands. Its products were offered through independent dealerships. The customer base was spread over 100 countries.

Herman Miller used so-called green marketing to sell its products. For example, the Mirra chair—introduced in 2003 with PostureFit Technology (see Exhibit 4)—was developed from its inception to be environmentally friendly. The Mirra was made of 45 percent recycled materials, and 96 percent of its materials were, in turn, recyclable. In addition, assembly of the chairs used 100 percent renewable energy. In 2003, *Architectural Record* and *Environmental Building News* named the Mirra chair among its lists of "Top 10 Green Products." Builders who used Herman Miller products in their buildings could earn points toward Leadership in Energy and Environmental Design (LEED) certification.

In addition, Herman Miller engaged in cooperative advertising with strategic partners. For example, at Hilton Garden Inns, some rooms were equipped with Herman Miller's Mirra chairs. On the desk in the room was a card that explained how to adjust the chair for comfort and listed a Hilton Garden Inn website where the chair could be purchased.

Herman Miller segmented its markets into work, home, health care education, and government. Many products were marketed across segments. To enhance its marketing analysis and promotions, Herman Miller also segmented its markets geographically. The North American, Asian, European, and Latin American markets were all tracked independently.

Production/Operations

Herman Miller was globally positioned in terms of manufacturing operations. In the United States, its manufacturing operations were located in Michigan, Georgia, and Wisconsin. In Europe, it had considerable manufacturing presence in the United Kingdom, its largest market outside the United States. In Asia, it had manufacturing operations in Ningbo, China.

Herman Miller used a system of lean manufacturing techniques collectively referred to as the Herman Miller Production System (HMPS)—see Exhibit 5. The HMPS strove to maintain efficiencies and cost savings by minimizing the amount of inventory on hand through a just-in-time process. Some suppliers delivered parts to Herman Miller production facilities five or six times per day.

Production was order-driven, with direct materials and components purchased as needed to meet demand. The standard lead time for the

EXHIBIT 4

An Example of Cooperative Advertising

In-Room Comfort Guide

Everything. Right where you need it.®

The ergonomic Mirra® chair by Herman Miller.

Sitting down to work should never be a pain in the neck. Or in the back, for that matter. With the Mirra chair at your desk, you'll stay comfortable and alert while working in the privacy of your guestroom.

How to adjust the Mirra chair for your comfort

Arm Angle
Front of each armpad

Arm Width
Button on inside of each armpad

Arm Height
Tab on outside lower base of each arm

Seat Height
Tab on lower right

⊕HermanMiller

To purchase a Mirra chair for your home, please visit **HGI.com/chair**
User Name: **hilton@ezconnect.com** Password: **hilton1**

EXHIBIT 5

The Herman Miller Production System

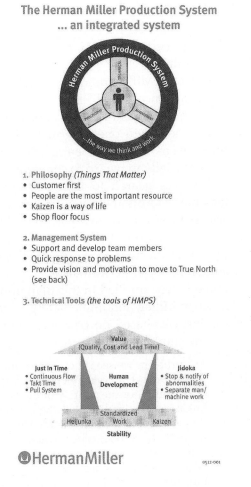

The Herman Miller Production System ... an integrated system

1. Philosophy (*Things That Matter*)
- Customer first
- People are the most important resource
- Kaizen is a way of life
- Shop floor focus

2. Management System
- Support and develop team members
- Quick response to problems
- Provide vision and motivation to move to True North (see back)

3. Technical Tools (*the tools of HMPS*)

Value
(Quality, Cost and Lead Time)

Just In Time
- Continuous Flow
- Takt Time
- Pull System

Human Development

Jidoka
- Stop & notify of abnormalities
- Separate man/machine work

Standardized Work
Heijunka   Kaizen

Stability

HermanMiller   0512-001

True North (*perfection is the goal*)

Customer Satisfaction	Human Development
• Zero defects	• Physical and mental safety
• 100% value added	• Security
• 1x1 in sequence on demand	• Professional challenge

Definitions

JIT (Just-In-Time)	Production and conveyance of only what is needed, when it is needed, in the amount needed, meeting the exact demand of the customer.
Continuous Flow	Eliminating the stagnation of work between processes by producing one piece at a time.
Takt Time	Is the time which should be taken to produce a product based on customer demand.
	$$\text{Takt Time} = \frac{\text{Total Daily Operating Time}}{\text{Total Daily Customer Requirement}}$$
Pull System	A production system where processes withdraw from proceeding processes the parts they need, when they need them, in the exact needed amount.
Jidoka	The ability of production lines to be stopped in the event of a problem such as equipment malfunctions or quality problems.
Heijunka	The leveling of the production schedule by volume and variety over a given time period.
Kaizen	The process of people making improvements to eliminate waste and improve their work.
Standardized Work	The most efficient workflow considering safety, quality, quantity and cost with the main consideration on human movement.
Stability	The dependability of 4Ms: man, machine, material, and method in daily production.
Kanban	A visual signal that is the key control tool for JIT production.
7 Forms of Waste	• Over Production • Inventory • Waiting • Motion • Conveyance • Correction • Process

majority of the company's products was 10 to 20 days. As a result, the rate of inventory turnover was high. These combined factors could cause inventory levels to appear relatively low in relation to sales volume. A key element of Herman Miller's manufacturing strategy was to limit fixed production costs by outsourcing component parts from strategic suppliers. This strategy had allowed the company to increase the variable nature of its cost structure while retaining proprietary control over those production processes that it believed provided a competitive advantage. Because of this strategy, manufacturing operations were largely assembly-based.

The success of the HMPS was the result of much hard work. For example, in 1996, business at the Herman Miller subsidiary Integrated Metals Technology (IMT), which supplied the parent company with pedestals, was not going well. IMT's prices were high, its lead time was long, and its quality was in the 70 percent range. Leaders at IMT decided to hire the Toyota Supplier Support Center, the consulting arm of automaker Toyota. By inquiring, analyzing, and "enlisting help and ideas of everyone," IMT made significant improvements. For example, quality defects in parts per million decreased from approximately 9,000 in 2000 to 1,500 in 2006. Concurrently, on-time shipments improved from 80 percent to 100 percent, and safety incidents per 100 employees dropped from 10 to 3 per year.

Herman Miller's organizational values were incorporated into the environmentally friendly design of the Greenhouse, Herman Miller's main production facility in Michigan. For example, the Greenhouse took advantage of natural light and landscaping to grow native plants without the use of fertilizers, pesticides, or irrigation. After the facility was opened, aggressive paper wasps found the design to their liking. Employees and guests were stung, frequently. Rather than using pesticides to kill the wasps, the company sought a solution that would be in keeping with its beliefs. Through research, it learned that honeybees and paper wasps were incompatible. Therefore, the company located 600,000 honeybees in 12 hives on the property. In addition to driving away the wasps, the introduction of the honeybees resulted (via pollination) in a profusion of wildflowers around the facility and, subsequently, the production of a large amount of honey. Guests to the home office were given a four-ounce bottle of the honey, symbolizing Herman Miller's corporate beliefs.

Human Resource Management

Human resource management was considered a strength for Herman Miller. It was routinely listed on *Fortune*'s "100 Best Companies to Work For" list, including in 2010, and it had approximately 278 applicants for every job opening. In 2009, during the ongoing economic downturn, Herman Miller cut its workforce by more than 15 percent, reduced the pay of the remaining workforce by at least 10 percent, and suspended 401(k) contributions. According to the February 8, 2010, issue of *Fortune*, employees praised management for

"handling the downturn with class and doing what is best for the collective whole." *Fortune* also estimated voluntary turnover at Herman Miller to be less than 2 percent. On June 1, 2010, the 10 percent time and pay cuts that the company began in the spring of 2009 were discontinued due to Herman Miller's quick turnaround.

Herman Miller practiced what Hugh De Pree had once called "Business as Unusual." That policy appeared to pay off in both good times and tough ones. Herman Miller shared the gains as well as the pains with its employees, especially in regard to compensation.

Pay was geared to firm performance and took many forms at Herman Miller. All employees received a base pay and, in addition, participated in a profit-sharing program whereby they received stock according to the company's annual financial performance. Employees were immediately enrolled in this plan upon joining Herman Miller, and immediately vested. Profit sharing was based on corporate performance. As one employee explained:

> The problem we see is you get to situations where project X corporately had a greater opportunity for the entirety of the business, but it was difficult to tell these folks that they needed to sacrifice in order to support the entirety of the business when they were being compensated specifically on their portion of the business. So you would get into some turf situations. So we ended up moving to a broader corporate EVA [economic value added] compensation to prevent those types of turf battles.

The company offered an employee stock purchase plan (ESPP) through payroll deductions at a 15 percent discount from the market price. Also, all employees were offered a 401(k) plan; until it was suspended in 2009 due to the recession, the company had offered a matching plan in which employees received a 50 percent match for the first 6 percent of their salaries they contributed to the 401(k). Through the profit-sharing plan and the ESPP, the employees owned approximately 8 percent of the outstanding stock.

Furthermore, all employees were offered a retirement income plan whereby the company deposited into an account 4 percent of compensation, on which interest was paid quarterly. Employees were immediately eligible to participate in this plan upon joining Herman Miller, but were required to participate for five years before being vested. Additionally, a length-of-service bonus was paid after five years of employment. Finally, the company paid a universal annual bonus to all employees based on the company's performance against economic value added (EVA) objectives. EVA was a calculation of the company's net operating profits, after tax, minus a charge for the cost of shareholder capital. The annual EVA bonus came in addition to the other compensation programs, including profit sharing, with the same calculation used to determine both employee and executive bonus potential.

Thus, most forms of compensation at Herman Miller were at least partially, if not wholly, contingent on corporate performance. One employee summed up pay as follows, "You can dip into Herman Miller's pocket several times based on the performance of the company."

Brightscope, a financial information company that focused primarily on retirement plans and wealth management, rated Herman Miller's profit sharing and 401(k) plan as having the lowest fees in the industry while being above average in company generosity, participation rate, and account balances. The average Herman Miller employee balance in the profit sharing and 401(k) plan was approximately $79,000 as of year-end 2011.

Other benefits also took many forms at Herman Miller. As in many other organizations, employees were given a range of benefits. Standard benefits included health insurance, dental insurance, vision care plans, prescription plans, flexible spending accounts, short- and long-term disability plan, life insurance, accidental death and disability insurance, and critical illness / personal accident / long-term care. The company also offered extensive wellness benefits, including fitness facilities or subsidized gym memberships, health services, employee assistance programs, wellness programs/classes, and health risk assessments. Some benefits, however, were quite different from those found in other organizations. For example, the company offered a $100 rebate on a bike purchase, which it justified as "part of our comprehensive program designed for a better world around you." Other benefits included the following:

- 100 percent tuition reimbursement.
- Employee product purchase discounts.
- Flexible schedules, including job-sharing, compressed workweek, and telecommuting options.
- Concierge services, including directions to travel locations, dry cleaning, greeting cards, and take-home meals.
- On-site services, including massage therapy, cafeterias, banking, health services, fitness centers, fitness classes, and personal trainers.

All benefits were available also to domestic partners.

When appropriate, Herman Miller promoted people within the organization. Education and training were seen as key to preparing employees to take on new responsibilities. For example, environmental specialist Rudy Bartels, as well as multiple vice presidents, began their careers at Herman Miller on the production floor.

Three other benefits were unique to Herman Miller. First, every family that gave birth to or adopted a child received a Herman Miller rocking chair. Second, every employee who retired after 25 years with the company and was 55 or older received an Eames lounge chair. Third, Herman Miller had no executive retreat, but it did have an employee retreat, the Marigold Lodge, on Lake Michigan. This retreat was available to employees for corporate-related events, such as retirement parties and other celebrations, and some of those events included invited family and guests.

Finance

During normal economic times, financial management at Herman Miller would have been considered conservative. Through 2006, the company's leverage ratio was below the industry average and its times-interest-earned ratio was over twice the industry average. Due to the drop-off in business during the recession, the debt-to-equity ratio rose precipitously, from 1.18 in 2006 to 47.66 in 2008. To improve this ratio, the company sold more than 3 million shares of stock in fiscal 2009.[4] In the four previous fiscal years, Herman Miller had been repurchasing shares. The debt-to-equity ratio was reduced to 3.81 by the end of 2009. To improve short-term assets, dividends per share were cut by approximately 70 percent and capital expenditures were reduced to zero in 2009. Exhibits 6 and 7 show the company's financial statements for fiscal years 2007–2012.

For fiscal 2008, 15 percent of Herman Miller's revenues and 10 percent of its profits were from non–North American countries. In 2007, non–North American countries accounted for 16.5 percent of revenues and approximately 20 percent of Herman Miller's profits.

Financially, Herman Miller held true to its beliefs. Even in downturns, it invested in research and development (R&D). In the dot-com downturn, it invested tens of millions of dollars in R&D. Inside Herman Miller, this investment project was code-named Purple.

In the December 19, 2007, issue of *Fast Company* magazine, Clayton Christensen, Harvard Business School professor and author of *The Innovator's Dilemma,* commented on the Purple project, saying, "Barely one out of 1,000 companies would do what [Herman Miller] did. It was a daring bet in terms of increasing spending for the sake of tomorrow while cutting back to survive today."

The Accessories Team

Herman Miller's Accessories Team was an outgrowth of project Purple. One of the goals of this project was to stretch beyond the normal business boundaries. Office accessories was one area in which Herman Miller had not been historically involved, even though office accessories were a big part of what independent dealers sold. According to Mark Schurman, director of external communications at Herman Miller, once the company identified accessories as a potential growth area, "Robyn Hofmeyer was tapped to put together a team to really explore this as a product segment that we could get more involved with."

In 2006, Hofmeyer established the Accessories Team by recruiting Larry Kallio to be the head engineer and Wayne Baxter to lead sales and marketing. Together, they assembled a flexible team to launch a new product in 16 months. They recruited people with different disciplines needed to support that goal. Over the next two years, they remained a group of six. Some people started with the team to develop a particular product and, as it got through that piece of work, then went on to different roles within the company. During its first eight months, the Accessories Team met twice a week for half a day. Twenty months out, it met only once a week.

The group acted with a fair amount of autonomy, but it did not want complete autonomy. "We don't want to be out there completely on our own because we have such awesome resources here at Herman Miller," Robyn Hofmeyer explained. When different disciplines were needed for a particular product, the group reached out to other areas in the company and found people who could allocate some of their time to support that product.

Wayne Baxter described what happened on the team as follows:

> We all seem to have a very strong voice regarding almost any topic; it's actually quite fun and quite dynamic. We all have kind of our roles on the team, but I think other than maybe true engineering, we've all kind of tapped into other roles and still filled in to help each other as much as we could.

Another member of the Accessories Team described the group's decision making as follows:

EXHIBIT 6

Herman Miller's Consolidated Balance Sheets, Fiscal Years 2007–2012 ($ millions, except share and pershare data)

	June 2, 2012	May 28, 2011	May 29, 2010	May 30, 2009	May 31, 2008	June 2, 2007
ASSETS						
Current Assets						
Cash and cash equivalents	$ 172.2	$ 142.2	$ 134.8	$ 192.9	$ 155.4	$ 76.4
Short-term investments	—	—	—	—	15.7	15.9
Marketable securities	9.6	11.0	12.1	11.3	—	—
Accounts receivable	159.7	193.1	144.7	148.9	209.0	188.1
Less allowances in each year	—	—	4.4	7.3	5.6	4.9
Inventories, net	59.3	66.2	57.9	37.3	55.1	56.0
Deferred income taxes	20.4	21.2				
Prepaid expenses and other taxes	17.6	25.4	45.2	60.5	58.0	48.3
Other	16.5	12.6	—	—	—	—
Total Current Assets	455.3	478.1	394.7	450.9	493.2	384.7
Property and Equipment						
Land and improvements	19.2	19.9	19.4	18.8	19.0	18.9
Buildings and improvements	146.0	149.5	147.6	137.4	139.4	137.2
Machinery and equipment	533.7	531.0	546.4	552.0	547.4	543.3
Construction in progress	12.6	13.0	10.7	9.8	17.4	17.6
Gross Property & Equipment	711.5	713.4	724.1	718.0	723.2	717,0
Less: accumulated depreciation	(555.5)	(544.3)	(548.9)	(538.8)	(526.9)	(520.4)
Net Property and Equipment	156.0	169.1	175.2	179.2	196.3	196.6
Goodwill	144.7	110.4	132.6	72.7	40.2	39.1
Indefinite-lived intangibles	39.3	23.2	—	—	—	—
Other amortizable intangibles, net	31.1	24.3	25.0	11.3	—	—
Other assets	11.0	9.3	43.1	53.2	53.5	45.8
Total Assets	$ 837.4	$ 808.0	$ 770.6	$ 767.3	$ 783.2	$ 666.2
LIABILITIES AND SHAREHOLDERS' EQUITY						
Current Liabilities						
Unfunded checks	—	$6.4	4.3	3.9	8.5	7.4
Current maturities of long-term debt	—	—	100.0	75.0	—	3.0
Accounts payable	$115.8	112.7	96.3	79.1	117.9	110.5
Accrued liabilities	136.2	153.1	112.4	124.2	184.1	163.6
Total Current Liabilities	252.0	272.2	313.0	282.2	310.5	284.5
Long-term debt, less current maturities	250.0	250.0	201.2	302.4	375.5	173.2
Pension and post-retirement benefits	37.9	51.6	—	—	—	—
Deferred Compensation	12.1	11.0	—	—	—	—
Other liabilities	37.1	24.6	176.3	174.7	73.8	52.9
Total Liabilities	589.1	603.0	690.5	759.3	759.8	510.6
Minority Interest	—	—	—	—	—	.3
Shareholders' Equity						
Preferred stock, no par value (10,000,000 shares authorized, none issued)	—	—	—	—	—	—
Common stock, $0.20 par value (240,000,000 shares authorized, 58,375,931, 55,048,858, 57,002,733 and 53,826,061 shares issued and outstanding in 2012, 2011, 2010 and 2009, respectively)	11.7	11.6	11.4	10.8	11.1	12.6
Additional paid-in capital	90.9	82.0	55.9	5.9	—	—
Retained earnings	288.2	218.2	152.4	129.2	76.7	197.8

Continued

EXHIBIT 6

Herman Miller's Consolidated Balance Sheets, Fiscal Years 2007–2012 ($ millions, except share and pershare data) *(Continued)*

	June 2, 2012	May 28, 2011	May 29, 2010	May 30, 2009	May 31, 2008	June 2, 2007
Accumulated other comprehensive loss	(140.6)	(104.2)	(136.2)	(134.1)	(60.1)	(51.6)
Key executive deferred compensation	(1.9)	(2.6)	(3.4)	(3.8)	(4.3)	(3.5)
Total Shareholders' Equity	248.3	205.0	80.1	8.0	23.4	155.3
Total Liabilities and Shareholders' Equity	$837.4	$814.4	$770.6	$767.3	$783.2	$666.2

Source: Herman Miller 10-K reports, various years.

EXHIBIT 7

Herman Miller's Consolidated Statements of Operations, Fiscal Years 2007–2012 ($ millions, except pershare data)

	June 2, 2012	May 28, 2011	May 29, 2010	May 30, 2009	May 31, 2008	June 2, 2007
Net sales	$1,724.1	$1,649.2	$1,318.8	$1,630.0	$2,012.1	$1,918.9
Cost of sales	1,133.5	1,111.1	890.3	1,102.3	1,313.4	1,273.0
Gross margin	590.6	538.1	428.5	527.7	698.7	645.9
Operating Expenses:						
Selling, general, and administrative	394.9	366.0	317.7	330.8	395.8	395.8
Restructuring expenses	5.4	3.0	16.7	28.4	5.1	—
Design and research	52.7	45.8	40.5	45.7	51.2	52.0
Total operating expenses	453.0	414.8	374.9	404.9	452.1	447.8
Operating earnings	137.6	123.3	53.6	122.8	246.6	198.1
Other Expenses (Income):						
Interest expense	17.5	19.9	21.7	25.6	18.8	13.7
Interest and other investment income	(1.0)	(1.5)	(4.6)	(2.6)	(3.8)	(4.1)
Other, net	1.6	2.4	1.7	.9	1.2	1.5
Net other expenses	18.1	20.8	18.8	23.9	16.2	1
Earnings before income taxes and minority interest	119.5	102.5	34.8	98.9	230.4	187.0
Income tax expense	44.3	31.7	6.5	31.0	78.2	57.9
Minority interest, net of income tax	—	—	—	(.1)	(0.1)	—
Net Earnings	$75.2	$70.8	$28.3	$68.0	$152.3	$129.1
Earnings per share – basic	$1.29	$1.24	$.51	$1.26	$2.58	$2.01
Earnings per share – diluted	$1.29	$1.06	$.43	$1.25	$2.56	$1.98

Source: Herman Miller 10-K reports, various years.

If we wanted to debate and research and get very scientific, we would not be sitting here talking about the things that we've done, we'd still be researching them. In a sense, we rely upon our gut a lot, which I think is, at the end of the day, just fine because we have enough experience. We're not experts, but we're also willing to take risks and we're also willing to evolve.

Thus, leadership and decision making was shared both within the Accessories Team and across the organization. Ideas and other contributions to the success of the team were accepted from all sources.

Out of this process grew Herman Miller's Thrive Collection. The name was chosen to indicate the focus on the individual and the idea of personal comfort, control, and ergonomic health. Thrive Collection products included the Ardea Personal Light, the Leaf Personal Light, the Flo Monitor Arm, and C2 Climate Control. All of these were designed for improving the individual's working environment. Continuing Herman Miller's tradition of innovative design, the Ardea Personal Light earned both Gold and Silver honors from the International Design Excellence Awards (IDEA) in June 2010.

The Industry

Office equipment (classified by Standard & Poor's Research Insight as Office Services & Supplies) was an economically volatile industry. The office furniture segment of the industry was hit hard by the recession. Industry sales decreased by approximately 26.5 percent from 2008 to 2009. Herman Miller's sales dropped 19 percent during that period. Herman Miller's stock market value of more than $1 billion at the end of 2009 represented 7.3 percent of the total stock market value of the industry. The value of Herman Miller's shares had increased to more than $1.4 billion by 2011—representing 10.8 percent of the industry's total stock market value. According to Hoover's, Herman Miller's top three competitors were Haworth, Steelcase, and HNI Corporation.

The industry had been impacted by a couple of trends. First, telecommuting had decreased the need of large companies to have office equipment for all employees. At some companies, such as Oracle, a substantial percentage of employees telecommuted—for example, the majority of JetBlue reservation clerks telecommuted. Second, more employees were spending more hours in front of computer screens than ever before. Due to this trend, the need for ergonomically correct office furniture had increased. Such furniture helped decrease fatigue and injuries like carpal tunnel syndrome. Finally, as with most industries, the cost of raw materials and competition from overseas had had an impact on office furniture. These trends tended to impact low-cost office furniture producers more than they impacted the high-quality producers.

The Future

In a June 24, 2010, press release, Herman Miller's CEO, Brian Walker, stated:

> One of the hallmarks of our company's history has been the ability to emerge from challenging periods with transformational products and processes. I believe our commitment to new products and market development over the past two years has put us in a position to do this once again. Throughout this period, we remained focused on maintaining near-term profitability while at the same time investing for the future. The award-winning new products we introduced last week at the NeoCon trade show are a testament to that focus, and I am incredibly proud of the collective spirit it has taken at Herman Miller to make this happen.

At the 2013 NeoCon trade show, Herman Miller continued to be recognized for its design excellence as the newly introduced Living Office swept the Best of NeoCon showroom design awards, and five of its new designs

EXHIBIT 8

Herman Miller's Fiscal Year 2013 Results (unaudited), Nine Months Ending March 2, 2013

Consolidated Statements of Operations
($ millions, except per share amounts)

| | Nine Months Ended | | | |
	March 3, 2012 (40 wks)	% of Sales	March 2, 2013 (39 wks)	% of Sales
Net Sales	$1,303.5	100.0%	$1,315.0	100.0%
Cost of Sales	862.9	66.2%	872.4	66.3%
Gross Margin	440.6	33.8%	442.6	33.7%
Operating Expenses	332.8	25.5%	362.2	27.5%
Restructuring Expenses	—	—	1.2	0.1%
Operating Earnings	107.8	8.3%	79.2	6.0%
Other Expense, net	14.0	1.1%	13.0	1.0%
Earnings Before Income Taxes	93.8	7.2%	66.2	5.0%
Income Tax Expense	30.6	2.3%	21.4	1.6%
Net Earnings	$ 63.2	4.8%	$ 44.8	3.4%
Earnings Per Share – Basic	$1.09		$0.77	
Weighted Average Basic Common Shares	58,144,031		58,380,853	
Earnings Per Share – Diluted	$1.08		$0.76	
Weighted Average Diluted Common Shares	58,414,707		58,749,485	

Consolidated Statements of Cash Flows
($ millions)

	March 2, 2013 (39 wks)	March 3, 2012 (40 wks)	Percentage Change
Net Earnings	$ 44.8	$ 63.2	−29%
Cash Flows provided by Operating Activities	77.3	82.4	−6%
Cash Flows used for Investing Activities	(40.9)	(6.2)	560%
Cash Flows used for Financing Activities	(9.8)	(0.6)	1533%
Effect of Exchange Rates	(0.7)	—	
Net Increase in Cash	25.9	75.6	−66%
Cash, Beginning of Period	$ 172.2	$ 142.2	21%
Cash, End of Period	$ 198.1	$ 217.8	−9%

Consolidated Balance Sheets
($ millions)

	March 2, 2013	June 2, 2012	Percentage Change
Assets			
Current Assets			
Cash and Cash Equivalents	$ 198.1	$ 172.2	15%
Marketable Securities	10.2	9.6	6%

Continued

EXHIBIT 9

Herman Miller's Fiscal Year 2013 Results, Nine Months Ending March 2, 2013 *(Continued)*

Consolidated Balance Sheets
($ millions)

	March 2, 2013	June 2, 2012	Percentage Change
Accounts Receivable, net	154.6	159.7	–3%
Inventories, net	66.4	59.3	12%
Prepaid Expenses and Other	48.9	54.5	–10%
Total Current Assets	478.2	455.3	5%
Net Property and Equipment	167.8	156.0	8%
Other Assets	230.2	227.8	1%
Total Assets	$ 876.2	$ 839.1	4%
Liabilities and Shareholders' Equity			
Current Liabilities			
Accounts Payable	$ 103.8	$ 115.8	–10%
Accrued Liabilities	146.2	137.9	6%
Total Current Liabilities	250.0	253.7	–1%
Long-term Debt	250.0	250.0	0%
Other Liabilities	83.9	87.1	–4%
Total Liabilities	583.9	590.8	–1%
Shareholders' Equity Totals	292.3	248.3	18%
Total Liabilities and Shareholders' Equity	$ 876.2	$ 839.1	4%

Data Source: Herman Miller Reports Adjusted Earnings Growth of 23% in the Third Quarter of FY2013, press release, March 20, 2013.

received Best of NeoCon recognition. The financial results in 2013 appeared to indicate that this strategy is working. In a press release accompanying the third quarter results for 2013 (see Exhibit 8), Mr. Walker stated,

> Our sales growth this quarter, combined with strong gross margins, helped drive a solid improvement in adjusted earnings from a year ago. While we are pleased with the overall results, net sales and orders fell short of our expectations. The shortfall was primarily driven by the difficult environment in key economies outside the U.S. and declines in business with the U.S. federal government, including within the health care sector. We did, however, offset these negative factors with year-over-year growth in the balance of our North American business. . . .

> This improvement was complemented by double-digit sales growth within our specialty and consumer segment and growth in emerging markets driven by the acquisition of POSH. We are encouraged by the relative strength in the commercial sector of our North American business and in the overall progress we're making in emerging markets and our Specialty and Consumer segment.

While the company's performance had steadily improved through year-end 2012, executives at Herman Miller faced two particular questions: (1) Will the strategies that have made Herman Miller an outstanding and award-winning company continue to provide it with the ability to reinvent and renew itself? and (2) Will disruptive global, economic, and competitive forces compel it to change its business model?

ENDNOTES

1 Many sources were helpful in providing material for this case, most particularly employees at Herman Miller who generously shared their time and viewpoints about the company to help ensure that the case accurately reflected the company's practices and culture. They provided many resources, including internal documents and stories of their personal experiences.

2 "Herman Miller Introduces Living Office™: the Holistic Solution for the New Landscapes of Work," Herman Miller press release, June 10, 2013.

3 The names of the two Fortune 500 companies were deleted by the authors.

4 Herman Miller's fiscal year ends on May 30 of the following calendar year.

■ **connect**   ARMAND GILINSKY Sonoma State University

> There's an old saying in the wine industry that goes, "In order to make a small fortune you need to start out with a *large* one." Unfortunately, I'd never heard of that "rule" before I started out. I came here to the Napa Valley 27 years ago with $40 in my pocket, sold my motorcycle for $5,000 to start a winery, and now I owe $22 million to the bank. And I still haven't been able to buy back my motorcycle, because the current loan covenants with the bank do not permit me to ride, so I'm not sure that I am a success story, really.
>
> —John Williams, founder and CEO, Frog's Leap Winery[1]

From the autumn of 1999 to late spring 2011, most Napa Valley premium wineries were embracing modernity—launching websites, using viral marketing, developing wine clubs, and shifting distribution channels from on-premises accounts to direct sales. John Williams, the co-founder, owner, and CEO/winemaker of Frog's Leap Winery in Rutherford, California, had followed suit by making modest investments in these marketing programs. Williams nevertheless remained skeptical that these changes would dictate *his* winery's future. In May 2011, Williams reflected upon his heritage as the son of upstate New York dairy farmers and his 35 years' working in the wine industry since graduation from Cornell University. Williams not only displayed his normally irreverent humor, but also acknowledged that he had quietly developed the industry's most sophisticated environmental management system.[2] Environmental management systems (EMS) had risen in importance for wine businesses, as they confronted survival threats from the natural world, such as rising energy prices, water scarcity, mounting concerns about chemical exposure, and climate change.[3] Yet Williams wondered aloud: "How could Frog's Leap, which has grabbed the 'low-hanging fruit' of environmental management, become even more sustainable?" See Exhibit 1 for a timeline of events in Frog's Leap's evolution.

Napa Valley and the Premium Wine Industry

Napa Valley was a prominent American Viticultural Area (AVA) in California's North Coast wine-producing region, which encompassed Lake, Napa, Mendocino, and Sonoma counties. [See "Glossary of Common Wine Industry Terminology" at the end of this case.] Since 1999, the number of premium wineries in the North Coast had grown from 329 to 1,250.[4] Of that number, nearly 92 percent could be classified as small or "boutique" wineries—that is, those producing fewer than 50,000 cases per year. The number of boutique wineries increased dramatically during the 12-year period, from 249 to 1,133. By contrast, midsized wineries

Copyright © 2012 by Armand Gilinsky. All rights reserved.

EXHIBIT 1

Evolution of Frog's Leap Winery

Year	Major Events
1884	Welcoming building built as the Adamson Winery
1972	As undergraduate at Cornell, John Williams obtains internship at Taylor Wine Company, falls in love with wine as a result
1975	While touring Napa Valley with a friend, John meets Larry Turley at Larry's newly bought farmstead; returns in summer to begin graduate work in enology at UC Davis; starts working part-time at Stag's Leap Wine Cellars (under Warren Winiarski); makes (and consumes) with Turley the first unofficial Frog's Leap vintage, a fizzy Chardonnay
1980	John returns to Napa Valley to become head winemaker at Spring Mountain, marries Julie Johnson; first Frog's Leap vintage, a Cabernet Sauvignon, is (somewhat unofficially) crushed
1981	John Williams forms Frog's Leap Winery in Napa with Larry Turley; winery is bonded; winery makes its first Sauvignon Blanc and Zinfandel
1984	Julie Williams becomes Frog's Leap's first employee
1985	John leaves Spring Mountain to work full-time at Frog's Leap
1989	Frog's Leap certifies its first organic vineyard
1992	First Frog's Leap Merlot (1990) is released
1993	Larry and John agree to create separate wineries; John and Julie buy Frog's Leap from Larry and begin to look for new home for winery; Larry starts Turley Wine Cellars on original Frog's Leap site (the Frog Farm)
1994–1995	John and Julie purchase defunct Adamson Winery from Freemark Abbey and restart Frog's Leap at the "Red Barn" ranch in Rutherford
1999	First appearance of winery's Rutherford label (1996 vintage); underground barrel *chai* (barrel hall) next to the Red Barn completed; John and Julie are divorced; Julie starts her own winery, Trés Sabores
2002	At urging of John, Rutherford Dust Society begins Napa River Restoration project; debut of winery's Syrah and La Grenouille Rouganté, a dry rosé
2005	Photovoltaic system goes live after installation of 1,020 panels at the Red Barn vineyard; original green mailbox at winery entrance is removed and road signage to winery added
2006	Frog's Leap completes 10-year plan for winery and opens new LEED certified hospitality and administrative offices; Red Barn rebuilt
2009	Frog's Leap creates wine club, "Fellowship of the Frog" and begins developing "wine by the glass program" by packaging wines for delivery to restaurants in half kegs

Sources: Casewriters' research; J. Beer, *Organically Sublime, Sustainably Ridiculous: The First Quarter Century of Frog's Leap* (Kennett Square, PA: Union Street Press, 2007).

(those producing between 50,000–499,999 cases per year) and large wineries (those producing more than 499,999 cases per year) grew more modestly in number during the same period, from 80 to 117.

In the year following the height of the global economic downturn of 2008 and 2009, the premium wine industry witnessed a small but significant rebound in growth. Mid-priced and high-priced wines led that growth. See Exhibit 2 for data comprising the U.S. premium wine industry's percent sales growth, margins, and pretax profits from 2002 to 2010. Exhibit 3

presents volume and value changes for various price points of wines during 2010.

Consumer Segments for Premium Wines

The United States surpassed both France and Italy in 2008 as the world's largest consumer of wine by dollar value. In 2010, U.S. wine consumption in terms of volume reached an all-time peak of 2.54 gallons per resident over 21. In that same year, 25- to 44-year-olds emerged

EXHIBIT 2

EXHIBIT 2

U.S. Premium Wine Industry—Key Financial Data, 2002–2010

	2002	2003	2004	2005	2006	2007	2008	2009	2010
Annual Sales Growth	5.2%	17.6%	25.5%	19.4%	21.2%	22.3%	2.0%	−3.8%	10.8%
Gross Margin	51.5%	50.2%	51.5%	52.8%	54.5%	57.1%	55.3%	52.4%	53.7%
Pretax Profit	3.2%	6.3%	7.6%	12.6%	11.3%	16.3%	9.5%	2.2%	6.7%

Source: Silicon Valley Bank, *2011–12 State of the Wine Industry,* April 2011, p. 11.

EXHIBIT 3

U.S. Wine Industry—Price Segment Data, December 31, 2009–December 31, 2010

Price Segment	Last 52 Wks $ Share	Value % Change		Volume % Change	
		Last 52 Wks	Last 26 Wks	Last 52 Wks	Last 26 Wks
Total table wine		+4.5%	+4.8%	+3.2%	+3.5%
$ 0–$ 2.99	8.4	−1.3	−2.5	−2.4	−2.6
$ 3–$ 5.99	29.3	+4.4	+4.2	+4.8	+4.9
$ 6–$ 8.99	20.2	−3.4	−3.3	−1.0	−0.9
$ 9–$11.99	20.8	+10.0	+10.5	+12.4	+12.5
$12–$14.99	10.0	+7.8	+8.1	+10.3	+10.2
$15–$19.99	6.2	+7.0	+9.4	+7.7	+10.3
>$ 20	5.0	+11.4	+11.8	+9.2	+11.0
	100.0%				

Source: The Nielsen Companies, in Silicon Valley Bank, *2011–12 State of the Wine Industry,* April 2011, p. 4.

as the largest segment of wine consumers, supplanting the baby boom generation that had led much of the industry's growth during the prior 30 years. Consumer demographics of the U.S. wine industry in 2010 is shown in Exhibit 4.

Trends in consumer health awareness also had a considerable impact on U.S. wine consumption. The baby boomers increasingly desired to stave off aging and infirmity by incorporating better nutrition and wellness into their lives. The postulated positive health aspects of drinking red wine in moderation contributed to increasing wine sales across all age groups.

So-called "green" consumers comprised an emerging demographic segment called LOHAS (Lifestyles of Health and Sustainability). This segment sought a better world for themselves and their children. LOHAS consumers were savvy, sophisticated, ecologically and economically aware and believed that society

had reached a watershed moment in history because of increasing public scrutiny of corporations' environmental and ethical practices.[5] The LOHAS consumer focused on health and fitness, the environment, personal development, sustainable living, and social justice. The segment was estimated at about 38 million people, or 17 percent of the U.S. adult population, with a spending power of $209 billion annually.[6] Among all ages of consumers, younger consumers, aged 14–24, were reported to be the most concerned about issues such as climate change and environmental protection, and were the major drivers of growth in the LOHAS segment. See Exhibit 5 for demographic data on "green" consumers versus all consumers.

Yet considerable confusion remained among wine consumers of all ages regarding organic wine versus wine made from organically grown grapes. Organic wine was fermented and aged without sulfites, regardless of how the grapes

EXHIBIT 4

Consumer Demographics Data for the U.S. Wine Industry in 2010

	Unemployment Rate	% of Population	% of Wine-Drinking Population
Race/Ethnicity			
White	8.5%	68.9%	78.5%
Hispanic	13.0%	13.4%	8.9%
African-American	15.8%	10.8%	7.3%
Age			
21–24	15.3%	7.4%	4.0%
25–34	10.1%	18.7%	13.6%
35–44	7.8%	19.6%	16.3%
45–54	7.5%	20.6%	22.0%
55+	6.9%	33.7%	44.1%
Education			
High school diploma	15.3%	19.2%	10.2%
Some college	10.6%	28.4%	20.2%
College grad	4.9%	24.3%	39.9%

Source: The Nielsen Companies, in Silicon Valley Bank, *2011–12 State of the Wine Industry,* April 2011, p. 13.

EXHIBIT 5

Profile of the "Green" Consumer

	All Consumers	"Green" Consumers
Average age	44	40
Gender		
Female	51%	54%
Male	49%	46%
Ethnicity		
Caucasian/other	75%	62%
Hispanic	13%	21%
African-American	11%	16%
College educated	25%	31%
Median household income	$58,700	$65,700

Source: S. Brooks, "The Green Consumer," *Restaurant Business,* September 2009, pp. 20–21.

were grown. Wine made from organically grown grapes might or might not have sulfites added to preserve shelf life. The two products were considerably different in origin, composition, and potential shelf lives.[7] Furthermore, wines labeled as organic or biodynamic were typically placed in a separate section away from other mainstream brands in supermarkets and specialist shops. Nevertheless, U.S. sales of certified organic wine and those made with organic grapes reached $80 million in

2006, and rose to nearly $130 million in 2008, an increase of 28 percent over 2004, according to the Organic Trade Association.[8]

Sustaining the California Wine Industry

After a period of unprecedented and sustained growth from 2002 to 2007, wine producers sought an edge to differentiate their brands and also to reduce costs during the 2008–2009 industry downturn. Many wineries faced financial difficulties due to market saturation. Almost all 6,785 wineries across the United States (of which 3,306 were in California) faced downward pressure on prices and margins. Some industry observers opined that wine producers faced a newly "hyper-competitive" trading environment: the rate of new brand introductions slowed in 2009 and 2010, in a period when wholesalers and distributors of wine were struggling to sell off a backlog of wine inventory and thus were less receptive to taking on new wines to sell.[9]

Barbara Banke was co-proprietor of Jackson Family Wines in Santa Rosa, California (Sonoma County), a wine business known for its Kendall-Jackson, Hartford Family, Matanzas Creek, and Cardinale brands. Banke listed sustainability as one of the greatest challenges the wine industry faced in 2011:

> We've had a reduction in the workforce last year, and we focused on controlling our costs and not investing so much capital. We have a constant battle to get the recognition we deserve with all the work we've done on sustainability. The industry is very green—and yet that's something that's not widely known. The California wine industry should work on enhancing its reputation for sustainability.[10]

To many in the wine industry, sustainability was defined as the "triple bottom line," meaning that producers needed to measure the impacts of their activities upon "people, planet, and profit"—that is, how it created social, environmental, and economic value. That the wine industry was greening was borne out by a report issued by the California Sustainable Winegrowing Alliance in 2009.[11] Some 1,237 California vineyard and 329 winery owners voluntarily participated in the Sustainable Winegrowing Program (SWP), despite widespread perceptions that sustainable farming practices increased the cost of production and lowered crop yields. Information about the SWP is shown in Exhibit 6. According to the Napa Valley Vintners Association, Napa Valley boasted 404 premium wineries, of which

60 were classified as "Green" or "Sustainable" in some fashion. See Exhibit 7 for more information on the 60 "Green" wineries in Napa in 2011.

Frog's Leap had hosted a Sustainable Wine Growers conference each year since 2006. The purpose of these conferences was to share information and best practices. Attendance had grown from 10 to over 250 California wineries (out of 329 members of the California Sustainable Winegrowing Alliance) in just five years. At the 2010 conference, Ted Hall, owner of Long Meadow Ranch, an organic Napa vineyard located in the Mayacamas Mountains above the valley, said:

> There is only one reason we farm organically, and that's because it results in higher quality and lower costs. Organic growing could double the life of a vineyard, perhaps to 40 years. That should be considered in calculating its costs. The fundamental objective of organic farming is to create a healthy plant. We're trying to create a plant that is balanced and appropriate for its site, slope and conditions. A healthy plant can produce fantastic flavors at full physiological ripeness without practices like water stress and long hang-time that can weaken the plant. You have to take a systems approach to organic growing. You can't just substitute organic pesticides or fertilizers for conventional chemicals. As much as we like to believe when we tell the rest of the world about the value of the Napa Valley appellation, not every piece of [Napa vineyard] property is suitable for growing quality grapes [organically] at a reasonable cost.[12]

A 2011 survey of 98 U.S. wine producers found that wineries appeared highly aware of sustainability issues and recognized the importance of caring for the environment.[13] Notably, about one-third of the respondents had increased investment in EMS during the recent recession. However, although many reportedly had adopted some sustainable practices such as organic and biodynamic cultivation, energy-efficient production, and dry farming, the *perceived* benefits of going beyond those practices to the adoption of a

EXHIBIT 6

Overview of the California Sustainable Winegrowing Program

Wine Institute and the California Association of Wine Growers (CAWG) partnered to design and launch the Sustainable Winegrowing Program (SWP) in 2002. The California Sustainable Winegrowing Alliance (CSWA) was incorporated a year later to continue implementing this program.

Mission

The long-term mission for the SWP includes:

- Establishing voluntary high standards of sustainable practices to be followed and maintained by the entire California wine community;

- Enhancing grower-to-grower and vintner-to-vintner education on the importance of sustainable practices and how self-governance improves the economic viability and future of the wine community; and

- Demonstrating how working closely with neighbors, communities, and other stakeholders to maintain an open dialogue addresses concerns, enhances mutual respect, and accelerates positive results.

Vision

The vision of the SWP is the sustainability of the California wine community for future generations. In the context of winegrowing, the program defines sustainability as wine grape growing and winemaking practices that are sensitive to the environment (Environmentally Sound), responsive to the needs and interest of society at-large (Socially Equitable), and economically feasible to implement and maintain (Economically Feasible). The combination of these three principles is often referred to as the three E's of sustainability. These important principles are translated into information and education about specific practices that are documented in the program's comprehensive Code workbook and are conveyed during the program's targeted education events that are aimed to encourage the adoption of improvements over time.

SWP Voluntary Participation Data, 2004 and 2009

VINEYARD DATA COMPARISON	2004	2009	
Number of Distinct Vineyard Organizations	813	1,237	
Total Vineyard Acres Farmed by the 1,237 Organizations	223,971	358,121	*(68.1% of 526,000 total statewide acres)*
Number of Vineyard Acres Assessed by the 1,237 Organizations	137,859	241,325	*(45.9% of 526,000 total statewide acres)*
Number of Vineyard Organizations that Submitted Assessment Results	614	868	*(70.2% of 1,237 total organizations)*
Total Vineyard Acres from 868 Organizations Assessed and Submitted	124,576	206,899	*(39.3% of 526,000 total statewide acres)*
WINERY DATA COMPARISON	**2004**	**2009**	
Number of Distinct Winery Organizations	128	329	
Total Winery Cases Produced by 329 Organizations	145.6M	150M	*(62.5% of 240 million total statewide cases)*
Number of Winery Cases Assessed by 329 Organizations	126.6M	141.5M	*(59% of 240 million total statewide cases)*
Number of Winery Organizations that Submitted Assessment Results	86	173	*(52.6% of 329 total organizations)*
Total Winery Cases from 173 Organizations Assessed and Submitted	96.8M	134.6M	*(56.1% of 240 million total statewide cases)*

Sources: California Wine Community, Sustainability Report 2009, pp. 6–7; S. Brodt and A. Thrupp, "Understanding Adoption and Impacts of Sustainable Practices in California Vineyards," California Sustainable Winegrowing Alliance, July 2009, pp. 5–8, www.sustainablewinegrowing.org.

formal EMS program remained unclear. There was a perception of a cost advantage benefit to a formal EMS program, but not necessarily a differentiation benefit, with the possible exception of an increased ability to enter new market segments.

Frog's Leap in 2011

Frog's Leap commenced production with 653 cases of Sauvignon Blanc in 1981. By 2010, the winery produced 62,000 cases of predominantly red wines. Varietal brands included white

EXHIBIT 7

"Green" Wineries in Napa Valley in 2011

	Winery Name	Annual Case Production (est.)	Certified Napa Green *Land*[1]	Certified Napa Green *Winery*[2]	Sustainable Practices[3]
1	Araujo Estate Wines	5,000–49,999	X	X	X
2	Artesa	50,000–499,999	X		X
3	Beaulieu Vineyard	500,000+	X		X
4	Beringer Vineyards	500,000+	X	X	X
5	Boeschen Vineyards	<1,000		X	X
6	Bouchaine Vineyards	5,000–49,999	X		X
7	CADE Winery	5,000–49,999		X	X
8	Cain Vineyard & Winery	5,000–49,999	X		X
9	Cakebread Cellars	50,000–499,999	X	X	X
10	Chateau Boswell Winery	1,000–4,999	X	X	X
11	Chateau Montelena	5,000–49,999		X	X
12	Clark-Claudon Vineyards	1,000–4,999	X		X
13	Clos Du Val	50,000–499,999	X	X	X
14	Clos Pegase	5,000–49,999	X		X
15	CONSTANT	1,000–4,999		X	X
16	Cuvaison Estate Wines	50,000–499,999	X	X	X
17	Duckhorn Vineyards	50,000–499,999	X		X
18	Etude	5,000–49,999	X	X	X
19	Franciscan Estate	50,000–499,999	X	X	
20	Frog's Leap	50,000–499,999	X	X	X
21	Gargiulo Vineyards	1,000–4,999	X		
22	HALL	5,000–49,999	X		X
23	HdV Wines – Hyde de Villaine	1,000–4,999	X		X
24	Heitz Wine Cellars	5,000–49,999	X		X
25	Hess Collection Winery, The	500,000 +	X	X	X
26	Honig Vineyard & Winery	5,000–49,999	X		X
27	Jericho Canyon Vineyard	1,000–4,999	X	X	X
28	Joseph Phelps Vineyards	50,000–499,999	X		X
29	Judd's Hill	1,000–4,999		X	X
30	Krupp Brothers	5,000–49,999	X		X
31	Ladera Vineyards	5,000–49,999	X		X
32	Larkmead Vineyards	5,000–49,999		X	X
33	Long Meadow Ranch Winery	5,000–49,999	X		X
34	Markham Vineyards	50,000–499,999	X		
35	Merryvale Vineyards	50,000–499,999	X	X	X
36	Mumm Napa	50,000–499,999		X	X
37	Opus One	5,000–49,999	X	X	X
38	Ovid Napa Valley	<1,000		X	X
39	Parry Cellars	5,000–49,999	X		X
40	Peju	<1,000	X		X
41	Quintessa	5,000–49,999	X		X
42	Robert Craig Winery	5,000–49,999		X	X

	Winery Name	Annual Case Production (est.)	Certified Napa Green Land[1]	Certified Napa Green Winery[2]	Sustainable Practices[3]
43	Robert Mondavi Winery	50,000–499,999	X		X
44	Saintsbury	50,000–499,999	X		X
45	Salvestrin	1,000–4,999	X		X
46	Schramsberg Vineyards	50,000–499,999	X	X	
47	Silver Oak Cellars	5,000–49,999	X		
48	Silverado Vineyards	50,000–499,999	X		X
49	Spottswoode Estate Vineyard & Winery	1,000–4,999	X	X	X
50	St. Supéry Estate	50,000–499,999	X		X
51	Stag's Leap Wine Cellars[4]	50,000–499,999	X	X	X
52	Stags' Leap Winery[5]	50,000–499,999	X		
53	Sterling Vineyards	50,000–499,999	X	X	X
54	Stony Hill Vineyard	5,000–49,999	X		X
55	Trefethen Family Vineyards	50,000–499,999	X	X	X
56	Trinchero Napa Valley	500,000+	X		X
57	V. Sattui Winery	50,000–499,999	X		X
58	Volker Eisele Family Estate	50,000–499,999	X		
59	White Rock Vineyards	1,000–4,999	X		X
60	William Hill Estate Winery	50,000–499,999	X		X

Notes:

[1]The **Certified Napa Green Land** program was a third-party certified, voluntary program for Napa vintners and grape growers. The program sought to restore, protect, and enhance the regional watershed and included restoration of wildlife habitat, healthy riparian environments, and sustainable agricultural practices. As of 2011, approximately 45,000 acres were enrolled in this program and more than 19,000 acres were certified.

[2]Founded in 2007, the **Certified Napa Green Winery** designation was developed by the Napa Valley Vintners Association in coordination with the County's Department of Environmental Management (DEM), and was based on the Association of Bay Area Government's (ABAG) Green Business Program. ABAG's winery-specific checklist included water conservation, energy conservation, pollution prevention, and solid waste reduction.

[3]The Napa Valley Vintners Association defined **Sustainable practices** as environmentally sound, economically viable, and socially responsible winegrowing methods. Examples of sustainable practices that pertained to resource conservation and/or effective vineyard management included:

- Cover crops
- Reduced tillage
- Reduced risk pesticides
- Use only organic inputs
- Erosion control measures
- Hedgerows/habitat management
- Installing bird boxes
- Integrated pest management (monitoring of pests and beneficial plants, reduced-risk materials, leaf-pulling)
- Energy conservation
- Weather station
- Renewable energy (solar, biofuels)
- Creek and river restoration

[4]Founder Warren Winiarski sold Stag's Leap Winery in 2007 to a joint venture between Chateau Ste. Michelle (Washington state) and Marchesi Antinori (Italy). Notably, Stag's Leap's Cabernet Sauvignon won a gold medal in the famous Paris wine tasting in 1978, an event that suddenly put Napa on the map as a global wine producer. Warren Winiarski was John Williams's first employer in the Napa wine industry.

[5]Often misspelled and confused with Stag's Leap Winery, Stags' Leap was purchased by Beringer Wine Estates in 1999, and is currently owned by Treasury Wine Estates, a recent spinoff of Foster's Group (Australia).

Sources: Napa Valley Vintners Association Green Wineries Program, http://www.napavintners.com/wineries/napa_green_wineries.asp, accessed May 23, 2011, company websites, *Wines and Vines.*

wines made from Sauvignon Blanc ($18 retail) and Chardonnay grapes ($26), and red wines from Zinfandel ($27), Merlot ($34), two wines made from Cabernet Sauvignon ($42 and $70), and Petite Sirah ($35). Frog's Leap also sold the amusingly named Frogenbeerenauslese ($25), a 100 percent Riesling, and La Grenouille Rougante ($14), a rosé blend made from Gamay and a touch of Riesling. In addition, the winery produced its own olive oil and honey.[14]

Staff headcount at Frog's Leap grew 100 percent over 12 years, from 25 to 50 personnel. Most of the new hires were fieldworkers. Other employees included those in its tasting room, such as Shannon Oren, tasting room assistant. In 2011, three managers reported to John Williams. Paula Moschetti, after five years' service as enologist for the firm, was promoted to assistant winemaker. Jonah Beer, former director of sales for Stag's Leap Wine Cellars, was hired as director of sales, marketing, and public relations in August 2003, and soon after became the winery's first general manager. Upon the retirement of Gary Gates, Frog's Leap's longtime financial consultant, the firm hired Doug DeMerritt as its chief financial officer. DeMerritt had served in a similar capacity at another Napa winery, Duckhorn Vineyards, from 2002 until that company's acquisition by a private equity firm in August 2007.

From 1999 to 2010, Frog's Leap purchased 100 acres of vineyards in the surrounding Rutherford area in Napa Valley, effectively doubling its acreage under production in an area where land for vineyards was valuable and seldom available for purchase. Wine case production grew comparatively more modestly, from 59,000 cases to 62,000 cases. Williams commented,

> The true growth of Frog's Leap over the last 10 years has been the acquisition and planting of vineyards, which has reduced our income, increased our debt, and added significantly to our operating costs in the short term BUT has guaranteed a high-quality source of grapes for the future—a future which seems to be heading in the direction of grape supply shortage and rising prices.

Company net sales grew from $7 million in 1999 to $12 million in 2010. Frog's Leap's portfolio of premium wines was sold primarily via what was called the "Three-tier distribution" chain in the alcoholic beverages industry. Resellers included wine specialists and selected supermarkets (off-premises accounts) or restaurants and hotels (on-premises accounts). Approximately 80 percent of 2010 company net sales in the United States were to resellers. Exports, primarily to Japan, accounted for about 7 to 8 percent of company net sales. The remainder was sold to consumers from Frog's Leap's tasting room and hospitality center, opened in 2006, and its "Fellowship of the Frog" wine club, created in 2009. Direct sales to consumers, where permitted by state laws regarding the sale of alcohol, had become increasingly important to wineries during the 2008–2010 recession to reduce backlogged inventories of wine. Direct sales to consumers also generated higher gross profit margins for wineries than sales to resellers, as wineries could charge consumers full retail prices (or provide a slight discount for wine club members), whereas wines to resellers typically sold at 50 percent off the retail price, in order to provide markup incentives for moving products along the chain.

Although Frog's Leap's reputation in the wine industry had begun with a 1982 review by Terry Robards in *The New York Times* ("Frog's Leap: A Prince of a Wine"), Williams subsequently paid little attention to ratings of his wines by popular wine critics. While many winemakers and winery owners depended on high ratings by wine critics to drive consumer demand, Williams commented on the fact that only two of his wines had ever been reviewed:

> . . . we built our brand on Frog's Leap and fun. We started developing a loyal following that reduced our reliance on establishing our brand through traditional channels. I've made wine for 27 years, and I think [that] only two of our wines have ever been reviewed by Robert Parker [editor of *Wine Advocate*]. That's just fine with me. I don't have to worry about reviews that fail to recognize the brilliance of our wines, because our customers will go out and buy the wine because they love it no matter what other people say. The love of our brand evolved

out of our approach, and it has allowed me to be freer as a winemaker, and more edgy in my winemaking.[15]

A Philosophy of Sustainability

Frog's Leap adhered to pre-1970s Napa Valley winemaking traditions, such as dry farming. Dry farming involved growing grape vines without using drip irrigation systems. Growing grapes without drip irrigation resulted in minimal water use and a more European style and wine flavor profile, with far lower alcohol content and fruitiness than the wines that had been produced by other Napa Valley wineries since 1970.

Other EMS practices adopted by Frog's Leap over the years included organic and biodynamic growing techniques. According to Williams, both techniques primarily involved building soil health through the use of cover crops and compost. Healthy, living soils produced healthy, living plants that naturally resisted disease. Natural-based soil fertility worked to regulate the vigor of the grapevine and naturally conferred its health and balance to the fruit, and thus to the fermenting wine, thereby avoiding many of the problems he would otherwise have had to confront in the wine cellar at a later stage of the production process.

Creating its own source of compost was another money saver for Frog's Leap. Field workers gathered the major byproducts of winemaking (like stems and pomace, or grape skins), added in all the coffee grounds, garden waste, and vegetable or fruit scraps from the kitchen, covered the pile, and let it turn into compost. Temperature readings indicated when and how often the compost pile needed to be turned. Frog's Leap saved money by not paying someone to haul the waste away, which was in keeping with the tenets of sustainable farming.

Why did Frog's Leap convert its grape production to organic and biodynamic and develop an EMS? According to Paula Moschetti, assistant winemaker,

It's what we believe. We know that it not only produces better quality wine, but it just makes sense for the quality of life for the employees; it makes sense for giving back to society; it makes sense for the environment. Like everybody says, "Respect where the grapes are grown." We try to optimize that, but also to not take wine too seriously. We want to make great, world-class wine, but with a sense of humor, a tongue-in-cheek attitude. And I think people really respond to that.[16]

Meanwhile, Frog's Leap moved toward energy self-sufficiency via investments in geothermal and solar power. Williams would not disclose the cost of the geothermal system, but it was known to be one of the relatively few such systems in California. Cost of the solar power system, installed in February 2005, was $1.2 million, offset by a $600,000 cash rebate from the local power utility company. That system generated sufficient electricity to power 150 homes, and any excess power generated was sold back to the public utility. Jonah Beer, general manager, described some of the cost advantages provided by Frog's Leap's energy systems:

There is virtually no cost to operate the geothermal heating and cooling system . . . and the cost payback is only about six years. It comes with a 30-year warranty for the pumps, and the wells have a lifetime warranty. The exchanger itself is 70 percent more efficient at its job because it only has to do one thing. Plus, our pumps use the electricity from our own solar power. The savings from solar is very obvious; what's amazing is that everyone *isn't* doing it. While the upfront cost estimate was $1.2 million, Pacific Gas & Electric (PG&E) gave [us] a $600,000 cash rebate upfront, and [our] bank gave [us] a loan on the rest. As far as payback goes, we're actually paying less on the loan per month than we were paying on our electric bill. We're cash flow positive, and we'll be paid back in seven years. The system has a 25-year warranty. So we get 18 years of free electricity. Even if you don't care about green at all, it's kind of silly not to do it. [Our] system produces 450,000 KW-hours of electricity, which will save CO_2 emissions equal to not driving four million miles.[17]

In 2006, Frog's Leap opened the industry's first LEED-certified wine tasting and office facility, primarily from recycled building materials. LEED was an acronym for *Leadership in Energy and Environmental Design*. Buildings attained LEED certification from the U.S. Green Business Council. Lower operation costs were typically associated with a LEED building: approximately 30 to 40 percent less energy use and 40 percent less water. Application for LEED certification of an existing property could cost upward of $10,000, depending upon the size of the building, the number of rooms, and the level of certification sought.[18]

Frog's Leap provided full-time, year-round employment and benefits for winery personnel, who were mostly immigrant laborers. According to Williams:

> The Mexican workforce has been wonderful for us, and we try to return that favor. The workers don't have to be laid off after pruning in January until tying canes in May, or from leafing until harvest. In between, our workers can prune trees, turn compost, bottle Sauvignon Blanc, harvest broccoli, rack and wash barrels, thin pears and apples, bottle Merlot, etc. They work full time—and get paid, three-week vacations, 401(k) plans and health benefits. We also have fewer safety issues, because they're well-trained and experienced. They're an engaged and highly motivated workforce. Are there higher overall labor costs? How can you really measure your labor costs? The workers get stable wages, they don't have to worry about housing and health care and where their kids go to school. They're a community of workers. There are fewer problems with documentation, better health, less crime and use of the community's safety net.[19]

While other winery operators remained dubious about the cost/benefit trade-off of investing in EMS and providing full-time employment to immigrant workers, Frog's Leap remained mostly profitable during the 2009–10 recession.[20] To generate incremental cash flows, Frog's Leap augmented its sales via conventional distribution channels by an innovative "wine-by-the-glass" program using kegs (instead of bottles) of wine, and by initiating direct-to-consumer programs, including a tasting room, and the "Fellowship of the Frog" wine club. Exhibit 8 presents Frog's Leap's income statements for 2000–01 and 2009–10. The company's balance sheets for 2000–01 and 2009–10 are presented in Exhibit 9. Williams commented:

> Over the long term, we have seen that our methods are viable. This is not just an

EXHIBIT 8

Frog's Leap Winery Statements of Income, 2000–2001 and 2009–2010 (dollar amounts in thousands)

	2000	% of Sales	2001	% of Sales	2009	% of Sales	2010	% of Sales
Cases sold	61,000		54,000		53,000		62,000	
Sales	$9,638	100%	$9,180	100%	$10,017	100%	$12,152	100%
Cost of goods sold	4,514	46.8%	4,050	44.1%	4,346	43.4%	4,960	40.8%
Gross profit	5,124	53.2%	5,130	55.9%	5,671	56.6%	7,192	59.2%
Operating expenses:								
Sales & marketing	1,580	16.4%	1,615	17.6%	2,853	28.5%	3,337	27.5%
General & administrative	1,200	12.5%	1,300	14.2%	1,678	16.8%	1,483	12.2%
Depreciation & amortization	675	7.0%	900	9.8%	1,250	12.5%	1,100	9.1%
Total operating expenses	2,780	28.8%	2,915	31.8%	4,531	45.2%	4,820	39.7%
Operating income	2,344	24.3%	2,215	24.1%	1,140	11.4%	2,372	19.5%
Interest expense	450	4.7%	875	9.5%	1,420	14.2%	1,420	11.7%
Earnings before taxes	$1,894	19.7%	$1,340	14.6%	$ (280)	−2.8%	$ 952	7.8%

Source: Frog's Leap Winery. Some data have been disguised by the company, but the relationships are accurate.

EXHIBIT 9

Frog's Leap Winery Balance Sheets, 2000–2001 and 2009–2010 (dollar amounts in thousands)

	2000	% of Total Assets	2001	% of Total Assets	2009	% of Total Assets	2010	% of Total Assets
ASSETS								
Current assets								
Cash	$ 130	0.7%	$ 80	0.4%	$ 10	0.0%	$ 20	0.1%
Accounts receivable	400	2.1%	550	2.6%	1,650	4.1%	1,950	5.0%
Inventory	6,500	33.5%	7,560	35.5%	12,010	30.1%	11,550	29.5%
Prepaid and other expenses	125	0.6%	250	1.2%	320	0.8%	325	0.8%
Total current assets	7,155	36.9%	8,440	39.6%	13,990	35.0%	13,845	35.4%
Property, plant and equipment	15,250	78.6%	16,150	75.8%	36,750	92.1%	37,100	94.9%
Less: Accumulated depreciation & amort.	3,150	16.2%	3,450	16.2%	10,925	27.4%	11,950	30.6%
net property, plant and equipment	12,100	62.4%	12,700	59.6%	25,825	64.7%	25,150	64.3%
Other assets	150	0.8%	175	0.8%	100	0.3%	110	0.3%
Total assets	$19,405	100.0%	$21,315	100.0%	$39,915	100.0%	$39,105	100.0%
LIABILITIES & CAPITAL								
Current liabilities								
Notes payable	$ 3,150	16.2%	$ 4,370	20.5%	$ 2,450	6.1%	$ 2,425	6.2%
Accounts payable and accruals	2,610	13.5%	1,470	6.9%	2,325	5.8%	2,150	5.5%
Current portion of LTD	540	2.8%	960	4.5%	890	2.2%	950	2.4%
Total current liabilities	6,300	32.5%	6,800	31.9%	5,665	14.2%	5,525	14.1%
Long-term debt	5,030	25.9%	7,040	33.0%	20,400	51.1%	19,500	49.9%
Total liabilities	11,330	58.4%	13,840	64.9%	26,065	65.3%	25,025	64.0%
Shareholder equity	8,075	41.6%	7,475	35.1%	13,850	34.7%	14,080	36.0%
Total liabilities and equity	$19,405	100.0%	$21,315	100.0%	$39,915	100.0%	$39,105	100.0%

Source: Frog's Leap Winery. Some data have been disguised by the company, but the relationships are accurate.

experiment. [From a cash flow perspective] we are a thriving business with above average margins and below average operating expenses. Our cost here for making a bottle of wine is equal to or less than the industry average.[21]

For purposes of comparison, Exhibit 10 provides financial ratios and benchmarks compiled by Silicon Valley Bank based on actual data from several anonymous wineries similar in size to Frog's Leap during the 2000–2001 and 2009–2010 time periods.

A reporter for the *San Francisco Chronicle* opined, "Frog's Leap could be the poster child for a new generation of Napa wineries: beautifully appointed, genteel, terroir-oriented and dedicated to a green agenda."[22]

Open Other End

Early in Frog's Leap's history, John Williams had managed to persuade the U.S. Alcohol Tobacco Tax and Trade Bureau (known in the industry as

EXHIBIT 10

Financial Ratios and Benchmarks for Frog's Leap Peer Wineries, 2000–2001 and 2009–2010

	2000	2001	2009	2010
Year-Over Year Growth Rate, Cased Goods Revenue	—	−14.1%	—	+2.9%
Current Ratio (x)	2.11x	1.76x	1.91x	2.29x
Quick Ratio (x)	0.49x	0.30x	0.22x	0.08x
Working Capital ($000)	$ 4,203	$ 3,941	$ 6,063	$ 8,518
Cased Goods Revenues/Net Working Capital (x)	1.67x	1.53x	1.84x	1.35x
Account Receivable Days (365)	95.3	91.1	39.8	14.8
Inventory Days	575	805	1,118	1,533
Tangible Net Worth (TNW, $000)	$ 4,499	$ 4,361	$ 12,863	$ 13,597
Total Liabilities to TNW (x)	0.9x	1.3x	1.6x	1.7x
Senior Liabilities/TNW + Subordinate Debt (x)	0.9x	1.3x	1.4x	1.4x
Gross Profit Margin (%)	45.70%	45.30%	67.20%	70.00%
Sales & Marketing Expenses/Sales (% of sales)	9.50%	12.20%	10.90%	9.80%
Net Margin (Return on sales, %)	14.70%	5.70%	9.10%	9.70%
EBITDA ($000)	$ 1,528	$ 799	$ 3,964	$ 4,269
EBITDA, Less Distributions or Dividends ($000)	$ 218	$ 325	$ 3,502	$ 4,062
Debt Service Coverage (x)	6.4x	3.9x	2.0x	2.4x
Total Interest / Total Senior Debt (%)	7.50%	4.90%	6.80%	6.00%
Conventional ROE (%)	22.70%	7.80%	7.90%	8.20%
Operating Return on Assets (%)	11.90%	3.50%	3.00%	3.10%

Source: Casewriter's research, based on data provided by Silicon Valley Bank that were compiled from anonymous wineries similar in size to Frog's Leap. For more highly aggregated financial data, see D.J. Jordan, D. Aguilar, and A. Gilinsky, "Benchmarking Northern California Wineries," *Wine Business Monthly,* October 2010, pp. 60–67.

the TTB), which has to approve all bottle labeling, that it was not frivolous to mark the bottom of his wine bottles with a sage precaution: "Open Other End." The word "Ribbit" was printed on the cork of every bottle of Frog's Leap wine.

Humorous presentations aside, Williams remained serious about sustaining growth of his business while remaining at the same level of production output. "How can we continue to grow sales and profits while remaining a small winery production-wise? I know that some business people are trained to think outside of the box, but first I want to know *where* the box is and what is *in* the box before I think about what's outside," he quipped in May 2011.

One option for sustaining Frog's Leap's growth was to pursue other EMS projects. Williams maintained that Frog's Leap still had a long way to go to become a truly sustainable winery:

> We're not 100 percent there. We're not even close. But we've done a lot of interesting

things, and a lot of the big projects are behind us. Now we're into some of the more fun and challenging ideas that will help us take our philosophy further: Healthier field workers; healthier, longer living vineyards; enriched soil fertility; less erosion; lessened environmental contamination; greater trust with our consumers; and even considerably higher wine quality, converting farm equipment to biodiesel and reducing employee car use by commuting. Startups are going to be more expensive. There's no getting around it. However, if you take the long view of it, once you get past 10 years, the costs are less, and you've got a vineyard that will outlast everyone else's.[23]

> Over time, it has developed that every decision at Frog's Leap is weighed at least in some measure by its social and ecological costs and benefits. We believe that these are the kinds of questions all businesses will have to ask and answer if we wish [to have] a sustainable future. . .[24]

Williams felt that pursuing any new sustainability projects in the near-to-medium term would have highly uncertain associated costs and benefits. Building out the direct-to-consumer sales channels (tasting room and wine club) was another option under consideration, but might come at the expense of taking attention away from distributors. A longer-term question about sustainability was also nagging at him: Frog's Leap's debt load. Williams and his former wife, Julie (who now owned another winery, Trés Sabores), had three sons who would presumably take over the business someday:

> Right now my kids think my legacy is $22 million of debt (laughs). You know I don't really think about my legacy too often. I'm happy about growing grapes and making wine and having fun doing it. But I believe our winery has changed the dialogue about the healthy growing of grapes, conservation of soil, and natural resources. I hope to be remembered for that.[25]

Williams's eldest son was working for another winery, his middle child was starting business school in fall 2011, and his youngest was preparing to start law school. Now entering his mid-50s, Williams wondered aloud how to "position the business to be successful for the next 10–20 years, after which time the transition to that next generation would *inevitably* begin."

Glossary of Common Wine Industry Terminology

American Viticultural Area (AVA)—A designated "viticultural area" (e.g., Napa Valley, Sonoma, Central Coast) that must produce 85 percent of the grapes processed for bottling and sale. For a specified vineyard name, a particular vineyard must grow 95 percent of the grapes, and all grapes used must be from the AVA.

Appellation—Similar to an AVA, the term appellation is used by other wine-producing nations to demarcate a legally defined and specific region where wine grapes are grown. A wine claiming to be sourced from a named

boundary (e.g., Côtes du Rhône in France, Chianti in Italy, or Rioja in Spain) must be comprised of at least 75 percent of the grapes grown within that boundary.

Biodynamics—Biodynamics, a growing agricultural movement both in the United States and internationally, is based on a series of lectures given in the 1920s by Austrian philosopher Rudolf Steiner. The movement views the vineyard (or farm) as an ecological whole—not just the vines, but also the soil, insects, and other local flora and fauna. Like organic farmers, biodynamic growers are interested in naturally healthy plants, and in enriching their soil without artificial fertilizers or pesticides. Where biodynamics differs from classic organics, however, is in the belief that agriculture can be aligned to the spiritual forces of the cosmos. This may mean harvesting grapes when the moon is passing in front of a certain constellation, or sometimes by creating a homeopathic mixture that, when sprayed on the vines, will—in theory—help the grapes ripen and improve their flavors.

Brand—The name of the product. This can be a made-up name, the name of the actual producer, a virtual winery, or it could be a restaurant or grocery store chain that contracts with a winery for a "special label" purchase.

Chai—A barrel *chai* is a wine shed, or other *storage* place above ground, used for storing *casks;* common in Bordeaux. Usually different types of wine are kept in separate sheds. The New World counterpart to the *chai* may be called the barrel hall. In Bordeaux, the person in charge of vinification and ageing of all wine made at an estate, or the *chais* of a *négociant,* is titled a *Maître de Chai.*

Dry farming—For most of the history of agriculture, grape growers dry-farmed their lands, and they still do in many wineries in Europe. Then, in the 1970s, drip irrigation conquered the world. A farming practice as old as agriculture itself fell to the wayside as wells were drilled, streams tapped, and pipes and hoses were run through thousands of acres of vineyards and orchards. By no coincidence, water supplies have now entered an era of decline in California, where land is subsiding in many regions as the aquifers below are emptied. Above ground, many small streams have drained into the earth; they may still flow—just underground. Dry-farmed wines, many sources say, are better, as grapevines, working under stressed conditions, produce smaller grapes than watered vines. The result is a greater quantity of tannin-rich skins and seeds to volume of juice, which can render denser, richer wines. For a dry farmer, the challenge is to lock the winter and spring rainfall in the soil for the duration of the dry season.

Economy wine—Regardless of where they are produced, table wines that retail for less than $3.00 per 750ml bottle are deemed to be in the generic, economy, or "jug" wine category.

Organic grapes—Organically grown grapes follow a broad definition of organic farming issued by the U.S. Department of Agriculture: "Organic farming is a production system which avoids or largely excludes the use of synthetically compounded fertilizers, pesticides, growth regulators, and livestock feed additives. To the maximum extent feasible, organic farming systems rely on crop rotations, crop residues, animal manures, legumes, green manures, off farm organic wastes and aspects of biological pest control to maintain soil productivity and tilth, to supply plant nutrients and to control insects, weeds and other pests. . . . The concept of soil as a 'living system' is central to this definition." Wines made from organically grown grapes must be referred to as "wines made from organic grapes" (or organically grown grapes), as they are allowed to contain up to 100 ppm of added sulfites.

Organic wine—Organic wine is defined by the U.S. Department of Agriculture as "a wine made from organically grown grapes *and* without any added sulfites."

Premium wine—Wines selling for more than $3.00 per bottle are considered to be in the premium wine category. Most bottled wines in the premium category show a vintage date on their labels—that is, the product is made with at least 95 percent of grapes harvested, crushed, and fermented in the calendar year shown on the label and also uses grapes from an appellation of origin (i.e., Napa Valley, Central Coast, Willamette Valley). Several market segments within the premium category are based on retail price points, typically double the wholesale value of a bottle or case of wine. *Impact Databank, Review & Forecast of the Wine Industry,* classifies wines "Sub-Premium" as those that retail for $3.00 to $6.00 per bottle; the "Premium" category retail for $7.00 to $9.99; the "Super-Premium" category retail for $10.00 to $13.99 per bottle, while the "Deluxe" segment are wines commanding a retail price above $14.00. Motto Kryla Fisher, a Napa Valley wine consulting firm, further refines the "Deluxe" segment into sub-segments: "Ultra Premium" wines, priced from $14.00 to $29.99, and "Luxury" wines, that retail in excess of $30.00 per bottle.

Three-tier distribution—Myriad state laws and regulations restricting the sale of alcoholic beverages generally require wineries to use a "three-tier" distribution system (winery to distributor to retailer to consumer). However, distributor consolidation (through termination or acquisition) increased substantially since the May 16, 2005, *Granholm v. Heald* U.S. Supreme Court decision, prohibiting discrimination between in-state products and products from out of state, and that subsequently served to increase liberalization of shipping wine across some state lines, direct from producers to consumers.

Varietal—A type of grape (i.e., Merlot, Cabernet Sauvignon, Zinfandel, Chardonnay, etc.). To declare a "varietal" on the label, at least 75 percent of the wine must consist of that variety of grape. Some wineries use almost 100 percent of the same varietal. Some blend a principal varietal (the one named on the label) with wines made from other varieties of the same color for better flavor balance. Others blend in "filler" varieties, which usually go unlisted, to get the most out of their supply of then-popular varieties, which are the ones touted on the label. If the label mentions a varietal, it will always be in conjunction with an appellation to inform consumers of the source of the varietal grape.

Vintage—The year in which the harvest of the wine grapes occurs. By law, grapes grown in a declared vintage year (harvest year) must account for 95 percent of the wine if the label declares a vintage year.

Source: Casewriters' research; MDM Distribution.

ENDNOTES

[1] Originally quoted in P. Rainsford, "Frog's Leap Winery" (video case presented to the North American Case Research Association conference in Santa Rosa, California, 1999). Williams updated this quotation during interviews at Frog's Leap Winery in May and September 2011; Jonah Beer, Doug DeMerritt, and Shannon Oren also agreed to be interviewed on camera for the video case.

[2] J. Intardonato, "Frog's Leap Pursues Their Green Vision," *Wine Business Monthly* online, June 15, 2007, http://www.winebusiness.com/wbm/?go 5 getArticle&dataId 5 48589, accessed April 10, 2011.

[3] M. Hertsgaard, "Grapes of Wrath," *Mother Jones,* July/August 2010, pp. 37–39.

[4] Wines and Vines (1999, 2004, 2009), *Wines and Vines Annual Directory,* San Francisco.

[5] P. Ekberg, "The Keyword Is LOHAS," *Japan Spotlight,* Japan Economic Foundation (JEF), March 1, 2006, p. 146.

[6] As cited by S. Brooks, "The Green Consumer," *Restaurant Business,* September 2009, pp. 20–21.

[7] M. A. Delmas and L.E. Grant, "Eco-labeling Strategies: The Eco-Premium Puzzle in the Wine Industry," AAWE working paper no. 13, March 2008; G. T. Guthey and G. Whiteman, "Social and Ecological Transitions: Winemaking in California," *E:CO* 11, no. 3 (2009), pp. 37–48.

[8] Delmas and Grant, "Eco-labeling Strategies."

[9] C. Penn, "Review of the Industry: Outlook and Trends," *Wine Business Monthly,* February 15, 2011, p. 70.

[10] Ibid.

[11] S. Brodt and A. Thrupp, "Understanding Adoption and Impacts of Sustainable Practices in California Vineyards," California Sustainable Winegrowing Alliance, July 2009, www.sustainablewinegrowing.org, accessed April 12, 2011.

[12] P. Franson, "Organic Grapegrowing for Less," *Wines & Vines,* July 28, 2010, http://www.winesandvines.com/template.cfm?section 5 news&content 5 76728, accessed April 10, 2011.

[13] T. Atkin, A. Gilinsky, and S. K. Newton, "Sustainability in the Wine Industry: Altering the Competitive Landscape?" paper presented to the

6th Academy of Wine Business Research Conference, June 9–11, 2011, Bordeaux, France.

[14] K. Saekel, "Napa Frog's Leap Comes with a Bit of Whimsy," *San Francisco Chronicle,* May 13, 2009, http://www.seattlepi.com/default/article/Napa-winery-Frog-s-Leapcomes-with-a-bit-of-whimsy-1303945.php, accessed April 10, 2011.

[15] As quoted in L. Cutler, "Industry Roundtable: Humor in the Wine Trade," *Wine Business Monthly* online, February 15, 2008, http://www.winebusiness.com/wbm/?go 5 ge tArticle&dataId 5 54456, accessed April 10, 2011.

[16] D. Brenner, "Paula Moschetti," *Women of the Vine* (Hoboken, NJ: John Wiley & Sons, 2006), p. 168.

[17] J. Intardonato, "Frog's Leap Pursues Their Green Vision."

[18] For more on LEED-certified buildings in Northern California, see: http://www.mlandman.com/gbuildinginfo/leedbuildings.shtml (updated every eight weeks, accessed May 25, 2011).

[19] P. Franson, "Winegrowers Cash in on Other Crops," *Wines & Vines,* May 25, 2010, http://www.winesandvines.com/template.cfm?section 5 news&content 5 74538&htitle 5 Winegr owers%20Cash%20in%20on%20 Other%20 Crops, accessed April 10, 2011.

[20] Hertsgaard, "Grapes of Wrath"; Guthey and Whiteman, "Social and Ecological and Transitions."

[21] Intardonato, "Frog's Leap Pursues Their Green Vision."

[22] Saekel, "Napa Frog's Leap Comes with a Bit of Whimsy."

[23] Ibid.

[24] As quoted by L. Daniel, "Grapegrower Interview: John Williams: Winegrowing from the Roots Up," November 1, 2011, http://www.allbusiness.com/agriculture-forestry/agriculture-animal-farming/16738095-1.html#ixzz1kPJtKSHF, accessed January 26, 2012.

[25] C. Walters, "How Organic and Biodynamic Viticulture Will Change the Way You Think: An Interview with Frog's Leap Owner and Winemaker John Williams," *Indigo Wine Blog,* May 3, 2010, http://indigowinepress.com/2010/05/how-organic-and-biodynamicviticulture-will-change-the-way-you-thinkan-interview-with-frogs-leap-owner-andwinemaker-john-williams, accessed January 29, 2011.

PHOTO CREDITS

CASE 2

Page 256(all photos): Courtesy of Under Armour.

CASE 3

Page 278(clockwise from top right): © Adrian Brown/Sipa/Newscom; © Benjamin Norman/Bloomberg via Getty Images; © B Christopher/Alamy; © Jeff Greenberg "0 people images"/Alamy; © Colin McConnell/Toronto Star via Getty Images; © Wolffy/Alamy; © Kimberly White/Reuters/Corbis; © Benjamin Norman/Bloomberg via Getty Images; p. 280(clockwise from top right): © Benjamin Norman/Bloomberg via Getty Images; © Kevork Djansezian/Getty Images News/Getty Images; © Adrian Brown/Sipa/Newscom; © Adrian Brown/Sipa /Newscom; © Ross Hailey/Fort Worth Star-Telegram/MCT via Getty Images; © Benjamin Norman/Bloomberg via Getty Images.

CASE 5

Page 302(left): © ZUMA Press, Inc./Alamy; p. 302(center): © Mitch Hrdlicka/Getty Images RF; p. 302(right): © Michael Tercha/MCT/Newscom; p. 309(clockwise from top right): © Craig F. Walker/The Denver Post via Getty Images; © Jeff Kowalsky/Bloomberg via Getty Images; © Katie Orlinsky/Sipa Press/Newscom; © Gus Ruelas/Reuters/Corbis; © Patrick T. Fallon/Bloomberg via Getty Images; © Katie Orlinsky/Sipa Press/Newscom.

CASE 8

Page 368: © Indranil Mukherjee/AFP/Getty Images.

INDEXES

Organization

a

A&W, 143, 153, 310
ABC, 372, 374, 378
Abercrombie & Fitch, 276
Acer, 325
Adelphia, 229
adidas, 73, 248, 268–270, 284, 285
Adobe, 325
Advent International Corporation, 272
Alcohol Tobacco Tax and Trade Bureau, U.S. (TTB), 422
Amazon, 73, 77, 100, 120, 233
Ambassador Steel Corporation, 342
American Apparel, 130
American Express, 120
American Youth Football, 257
Anaheim Angels, 374
Ann Taylor Stores, 128
Apax Partners, 268
Apple, Inc., 5, 72, 100, 121, 128, 131, 165, 194, 293, 315, 322–324
Aral, 148
Aravind Eye Care System, 107
ArcelorMittal USA, 359
Architectural Record and *Environmental Building News*, 399
Arco, 148
Armani, 293
Ashworth, 284
Athleta, 285, 286
Auburn Steel Company, 340, 353
Audi, 111
Aulani Disney Resort, 380
Auntie Anne's, 311
Avon Products, 62

b

BackRub, 316
Baidu, 323
Baja Fresh, 309
Bank of America, 126
Bank of America/Merrill Lynch, 290
Barker Steel Company, 342
Barnes & Noble, 73
Baseball Factory, 257
BASF, 97
bebe stores, 286
Ben & Jerry's, 202

Bentley, 103
Best Buy, 325
Bethlehem Steel Corp., 340
Birmingham Steel Corp., 341
Bloomingdale's, 297
BMW, 100, 111
Body Shop, 202
Bosch, 100
Boston Beer Company, 127
BP, 147–148
Bridgestone/Firestone, 43–44
Brightscope, 403
Bristol-Myers Squibb, 126
British Petroleum (BP), 222
British Steel, 341
BTR, 178
Burt's Bees, 199, 205
BusinessWeek, 393
BYD, 132

c

Cadillac, 111
California Sustainable Winegrowing Alliance (CSWA), 415, 416
California Tortilla, 309
Campbell, 100
Canon, 212
Carmelite Order, 243–247
Cartier, 103, 291
Carvel Ice Cream, 311
Caterpillar, 100
Catholic Church, 243, 246
CBS, 77, 396
CGA, Inc., 106
Chanel, 100
Chaps menswear, 123
Charles Schwab, 100
Chery Automotive Co., Ltd., 370
Chevrolet, 368
Chipotle Mexican Grill, 299–314
Chrysler, 117
Ciba Vision, 221
Cinnabon, 311
Cirque du Soleil, 119
Cisco, 74, 125, 131, 390
Citigroup, 178
The Clorox Company, 199
Club Monaco, 123
CNN, 121
Coach Inc., 287–298

Coca-Cola, 19, 52, 100, 124
Cole Haan, 268
Colgate-Palmolive, 130
Comedy Central, 106
Community Coffee, 106
Companhia Vale do Rio Doce (CVRD), 347
Connecticut Steel Corporation, 341–342
Consolidated Rebar, Inc., 342
Continental, 43–44
Continental Airlines. *See* United–Continental
Converse, 268
Corus Steel, 341
Costco Wholesale, 109
Countrywide Financial, 126, 229
Cummins, Inc., 361
Cummins Engine Co., 361

d

Daewoo Commercial Vehicle Co. Ltd., 361
Daimler AG, 132
Daimler Benz AG, 361
Daimler–Benz/Mercedes-Benz, 361
Daimler Chrysler, 361
The David J. Joseph Company (DJJ), 348, 350
Dell Computer, 83, 103, 154, 191
Department of Agriculture, U.S., 303, 425
Department of Commerce, U.S., 340
DFS Group, 297
DHL, 222
Dick's Sporting Goods, 250, 258
Diebold, Inc., 191
Dillard's, 297
Discovery Channel, 106
DISH Network, 315, 325
Disney Brothers Studio, 373
Disney California Adventure Park, 374
Disney Channel, 380
Disney Cruise Line, 373, 374, 380, 381
Disney Interactive, 374
Disneyland Paris, 374, 380
Disneyland Park, 374
Disneyland Resort, 380–381
Disney-MGM Studios, 374
Disney's Castaway Cay, 381
Disney Store, 374
Disney Studios, 374
DJJ Mill and Industrial Services, 348
DJJ Rail Services, 348